Business Accounting 1

Frank Wood Bsc (Econ), FCA

Fifth Edition

Pitman

PITMAN PUBLISHING
128 Long Acre, London, WC2E 9AN

A Division of Longman Group UK Limited

© Frank Wood 1967
© Longman Group UK Limited 1972, 1979, 1984, 1989

Fifth edition first published in Great Britain 1989

British Library Cataloguing in Publication Data

Wood, Frank
  Business accounting – 5th ed.
  1. Accounting
  I. Title
  657

ISBN 0 273 02973 8
ISBN 0 273 03119 8 ISE edition

Typesetting by P4 Graphics, London, England
Printed in Great Britain by
Richard Clay Ltd, Bungay, Suffolk

Contents

Preface to the fifth edition

This textbook has been written so that a very thorough introduction to Accounting is covered in two volumes. The fact that this task has been split between two volumes is a recognition of the fact that many students will find all that they require contained in Volume 1. Volume 2 will then carry the studies of the remainder of the readers to a more advanced stage.

Volume 1 fully covers the requirements of the following syllabuses at the time of writing:

- Association of Accounting Technicians: Preliminary and Intermediate
- Chartered Association of Certified Accountants: Paper 1.1 Accounting
- Chartered Institute of Management Accountants: Stage I (Financial Accounting content only)

- General Certificate of Secondary Education
- London Chamber of Commerce: Level 1
- Royal Society of Arts: Stage I

In addition it provides the basic groundwork needed for all other examinations in financial accounting, including General Certificate of Education 'A' level and Institute of Chartered Secretaries and Administrators.

The questions set at the end of the relevant chapters are either from past examination papers or have been specially devised by me. All questions set can be answered by students who have worked through the text up to the chapter concerned.

The fifth edition varies from the fourth edition in various ways. These can be listed as follows:

1   The chapter on Stock Valuation has been transferred from Volume 2 to Volume 1.

2   A chapter on Accounting Theory has been included in this volume.

3   The chapters on Funds Flow Statements, Limited Company Accounts and Analysis and Interpretation of Accounting Statements have been substantially altered.

4   Many of the questions devised by the author have been replaced by questions from past examination papers.

5   The answers at the back of the book are now shown fully displayed instead of being in an abbreviated form.

Anyone who has studied book-keeping or accounting previously may well question the validity of having assets on the left-hand side of the balance sheet and capital and liabilities on the right-hand side, as previously they used to be the opposite to that. However, the Companies Act lays it down that in two-sided balance sheets assets must be shown on the left-hand side of the balance sheet and capital and liabilities on the right-hand side. In the interest of standardisation, and to avoid confusion, the balance sheets for sole traders and partnerships will also be drawn up in the same way.

In fact the new method makes book-keeping and accounting easier to learn than previously. It is however a point to bear in mind when looking at other textbooks which have not been updated.

Generally, the figures used for exhibits and for exercises have been kept down to relatively small amounts. This has been done deliberately to make the work of the user of this book that much easier. Constantly handling large figures does not add anything to the study of the principles of accounting, instead it simply wastes a lot of the student's time, and he/she will probably make far more errors if larger figures are used. It could lead to the author being accused of not being 'realistic' with the figures given, but I believe that it is far more important to make learning easier for the student.

I would like to thank all those lecturers and teachers who gave me their advice as to the changes they would like to see incorporated in this edition. Most of their suggestions have borne fruit. Joe Townsley, B Com, FCA, who has been associated with me in authorship for over twenty years, has provided his usual encouragement and advice.

I also wish to acknowledge the permission to use past examination papers granted by the University of London, the Associated Examining Board, the London Chamber of Commerce, the Joint Matriculation Board, the Chartered Association of Certified Accountants, the Chartered Institute of Management Accountants, the Association of Accounting Technicians and the Institute of Chartered Secretaries and Administrators.

Frank Wood

Matrix of subjects covered and examining bodies

CHAPTERS	ATT PRELIM & INTER	ACCA 1.1	CIMA STAGE I	ICAEW	LCC LEVEL 1 & 2	RSA I & II	GCSE	CISA PART 2	GCE 'A' LEVEL
1-23 Basic accounting	X	X	X	X	X	X	X	X	X
24 Capital & revenue	X	X	X	X	X	X	X	X	X
25 Bank reconciliation	X	X	X	X	X	X	X	X	X
26 Petty cash	X	X	X	X	X	X	X	X	X
27/28 Errors	X	X	X	X	X	X	X	X	X
29 Control accounts	X	X	X	X	X	X	X	X	X
30 Accounting ratios	X	X	X	X	X	X	X	X	X
31 Incomplete records	X	X	X	X	X	X	X	X	X
32 Income and expenditure	X	X	X	X	X	X	X	X	X
33 Manufacturing accounts	X	O	X	X	X	X	X	X	X
34 Departmental accounts	O	X	X	X	X	O	O	X	X
35 Columnar day books	X	X	X	X	X	X	O	O	X
36 Partnership accounts	X	X	O	X	X	X	X	X	X
37 Goodwill	X	X	X	X	X	O	O	X	X
38 Partnership: revaluation	X	X	O	X	X	O	O	X	X
39 Limited companies	X	X	X	X	X	X	X	X	X
40 Purchase of businesses	O	X	X	X	X	O	O	X	X
41 Funds flow	X	X	X	X	X	X	X	X	X
42 Wages & salaries	X	X	X	X	O	X	O	O	X
43 Stock valuation	X	O	X	X	X	X	X	X	X
44 Analysis & interpretation	X	X	X	X	X	X	X	X	X
45 Accounting theory	O	X	X	X	O	O	O	X	X

Key:

X = included in syllabus
O = not in syllabus

1

The accounting equation and the balance sheet

Accounting is often said to be the language of business. It is used in the business world to describe the transactions entered into by all kinds of organisations. Accounting terms and ideas are therefore used by people associated with business, whether they are managers, owners, investors, bankers, lawyers, or accountants. As it is the language of business there are words and terms that mean one thing in accounting, but whose meaning is completely different in ordinary language usage. Fluency comes, as with other languages, after a certain amount of practice. When fluency has been achieved, that person will be able to survey the transactions of businesses, and will gain a greater insight into the way that business is transacted and the methods by which business decisions are taken.

The actual record-making phase of accounting is usually called **book-keeping**. However, accounting extends far beyond the actual making of records. Accounting is concerned with the use to which these records are put, their analysis and interpretation. An accountant should be concerned with more than the record- making phase. In particular he should be interested in the relationship between the financial results and the events which have created them. He should be studying the various alternatives open to the business, and be using his accounting experience in order to aid the management to select the best plan of action for the business. The owners and managers of a business will need some accounting knowledge in order that they may understand what the accountant is telling them. Investors and others will need accounting knowledge in order that they may read and understand the financial statements issued by the business, and adjust their relationships with the business accordingly.

Probably there are two main questions that the managers or owners of a business want to know: first, whether or not the business is operating at a profit; second, they will want to know whether or not the business will be able to meet its commitments as they fall due, and so not have to close down owing to lack of funds. Both of these questions should be answered by the use of the accounting data of the firm.

The accounting equation

The whole of financial accounting is based on the accounting equation. This can be stated to be that for a firm to operate it needs resources, and that these resources have had to be supplied to the firm by someone. The resources possessed by the firm are known as **Assets**, and obviously some of these resources will have been supplied by the owner of the business. The total amount supplied by him is known as **Capital**. If in fact he was the only one who had supplied the assets then the following equation would hold true:

$$\text{Assets} = \text{Capital}$$

On the other hand, some of the assets will normally have been provided by someone other than the owner. The indebtedness of the firm for these resources is known as **Liabilities**. The equation can now be expressed as:

$$\text{Assets} = \text{Capital} + \text{Liabilities}$$

It can be seen that the two sides of the equation will have the same totals. This is because we are dealing with the same thing from two different points of view. It is:

Resources: What they are = Resources: Who supplied them
(Assets)   (Capital + Liabilities)

It is a fact that the totals of each side will always equal one another, and that this will always be true no matter how many transactions are entered into. The actual assets, capital and liabilities may change, but the equality of assets with that of the total of capital and liabilities will always hold true.

Assets consist of property of all kinds, such as buildings, machinery, stocks of goods and motor vehicles, also benefits such as debts owing by customers and the amount of money in the bank account.

Liabilities consist of money owing for goods supplied to the firm, and for expenses, also for loans made to the firm.

Capital is often called the owner's equity or net worth.

The balance sheet and the effects of business transactions

The accounting equation is expressed in a financial position statement called the **Balance Sheet**. It is not the first accounting record to be made, but it is a convenient place to start to consider accounting.

The introduction of capital

On 1 May 19-7 B Blake started in business and deposited £5,000 into a bank account opened specially for the business. The balance sheet would appear:

B Blake
Balance Sheet as at 1 May 19-7

Assets	£		£
Cash at bank	5,000	Capital	5,000
	5,000		5,000

The purchase of an asset by cheque

On 3 May 19-7 Blake buys a building for £3,000. The effect of this transaction is that the cash at the bank is decreased and a new asset, i.e. buildings, appears.

B Blake
Balance Sheet as at 3 May 19-7

Assets	£		£
Buildings	3,000	Capital	5,000
Cash at bank	2,000		
	5,000		5,000

The purchase of an asset and the incurring of a liability

On 6 May 19-7 Blake buys some goods for £500 from D Smith, and agrees to pay for them some time within the next two weeks. The effect of this is that a new asset, stock of goods, is acquired, and a liability for the goods is created. A person to whom money is owed for goods is known in accounting language as a **creditor**.

B Blake

Balance Sheet as at 6 May 19-7

Assets	£	Capital and Liabilities	£
Buildings	3,000	Capital	5,000
Stock of goods	500	Creditor	500
Cash at bank	2,000		
	5,500		5,500

Sale of an asset on credit

On 10 May 19-7 goods which had cost £100 were sold to J Brown for the same amount, the money to be paid later. The effect is a reduction in the stock of goods and the creation of a new asset. A person who owes the firm money is known in accounting language as a **debtor**. The balance sheet now appears:

B Blake

Balance Sheet as at 10 May 19-7

Assets	£	Capital and Liabilities	£
Buildings	3,000	Capital	5,000
Stock of goods	400	Creditor	500
Debtor	100		
Cash at bank	2,000		
	5,500		5,500

Sale of an asset for immediate payment

On 13 May 19-7 goods which had cost £50 were sold to D Daley for the same amount, Daley paying for them immediately by cheque. Here one asset, stock of goods, is reduced, while another asset, bank, is increased. The balance sheet now appears:

B Blake

Balance Sheet as at 13 May 19-7

Assets	£	Capital and Liabilities	£
Buildings	3,000	Capital	5,000
Stock of goods	350	Creditor	500
Debtor	100		
Cash at bank	2,050		
	5,500		5,500

The payment of a liability

On 15 May 19-7 Blake pays a cheque for £200 to D Smith in part payment of the amount owing. The asset of bank is therefore reduced, and the liability of the creditor is also reduced. The balance sheet now appears:

B Blake

Balance Sheet as at 15 May 19-7

Assets	£	Capital and Liabilities	£
Buildings	3,000	Capital	5,000
Stock of goods	350	Creditor	300
Debtor	100		
Cash at bank	1,850		
	5,300		5,300

Collection of an asset

J Brown, who owed Blake £100, makes a part payment of £75 by cheque on 31 May 19-7. The effect is to reduce one asset, debtor, and to increase another asset, bank. This results in a balance sheet as follows:

B Blake

Balance Sheet as at 31 May 19-7

Assets	£	Capital and Liabilities	£
Buildings	3,000	Capital	5,000
Stock of goods	350	Creditor	300
Debtor	25		
Cash at bank	1,925		
	5,300		5,300

It can be seen that every transaction has affected two items. Sometimes it has changed two assets by reducing one and increasing the other. Other times it has reacted differently. A summary of the effect of transactions upon assets, liabilities and capital is shown below.

Example of transaction

1	Buy goods on credit.	Increase Asset (Stock of Goods)	Increase Liability (Creditors)
2	Buy goods by cheque.	Increase Asset (Stock of Goods)	Decrease Asset (Bank)
3	Pay creditor by cheque.	Decrease Asset (Bank)	Decrease Liability (Creditors)
4	Owner pays more capital into the bank.	Increase Asset (Bank)	Increase Capital
5	Owner takes money out of the business bank for his own use.	Decrease Asset (Bank)	Decrease Capital
6	Owner pays creditor from private money outside the firm.	Decrease Liability (Creditors)	Increase Capital

Each transaction has therefore maintained the equality of the total of assets with that of capital and liabilities. This can be shown:

Number of transaction as above	Assets	Liabilities and Capital	Effect on balance sheet totals
1	+	+	Each side added to equally.
2	+		A plus and a minus both on the assets side cancelling out each other.
3	−	−	Each side has equal deductions.
4	+	+	Each side has equal additions.
5	−	−	Each side has equal deductions.
6		−	A plus and a minus both on the liabilities
		+	and capital side cancelling out each other.

Notes:

(*a*) Anyone who has studied book-keeping or accounting previously may well question the validity of having assets on the left-hand side of the balance sheet and capital and liabilities on the right-hand side, as previously they used to be the opposite to that. However, the Companies Act 1985 lays it down that in two-sided balance sheets assets must be shown on the left-hand side of the balance sheet and capital and liabilities on the right-hand side. In the interest of standardisation, and to avoid confusion, the balance sheets for sole traders and partnerships will also be drawn up in the same way.

In fact the new method does make book-keeping and accounting much easier to learn than previously. It is however a point to bear in mind when looking at other textbooks which have not been updated.

(*b*) Generally, the figures used for exhibits and for exercises have been kept down to relatively small amounts. This has been done deliberately to make the work of the user of this book that much easier. Constantly handling large figures does not add anything to the study of the principles of accounting, instead it simply wastes a lot of the student's time, and he/she will probably make far more errors if larger figures are used.

It could lead to the author being accused of not being 'realistic' with the figures given, but I believe that it is far more important to make learning easier for the student.

Review questions

Note: Questions with the letter A shown after the question number do not have answers shown at the back of the book. Answers to the others are shown on page 502 onwards.

There is a bank of multiple-choice questions on page 489. These are to be attempted later in the course.

1.1 You are to complete the gaps in the following table:

	Assets	Liabilities	Capital
	£	£	£
(*a*)	12,500	1,800	?
(*b*)	28,000	4,900	?
(*c*)	16,800	?	12,500
(*d*)	19,600	?	16,450
(*e*)	?	6,300	19,200
(*f*)	?	11,650	39,750

1.2A You are to complete the gaps in the following table:

	Assets	Liabilities	Capital
	£	£	£
(a)	55,000	16,900	?
(b)	?	17,200	34,400
(c)	36,100	?	28,500
(d)	119,500	15,400	?
(e)	88,000	?	62,000
(f)	?	49,000	110,000

1.3 Distinguish from the following list the items that are liabilities from those that are assets:

(a) Office machinery
(b) Loan from C Shirley
(c) Fixtures and fittings
(d) Motor vehicles
(e) We owe for goods
(f) Bank balance

1.4A Classify the following items into liabilities and assets:

(a) Motor vehicles
(b) Premises
(c) Creditors for goods
(d) Stock of goods
(e) Debtors
(f) Owing to bank
(g) Cash in hand
(h) Loan from D Jones
(i) Machinery

1.5 State which of the following are shown under the wrong classification for J White's business:

Assets	Liabilities
Loan from C Smith	Stock of goods
Cash in hand	Debtors
Machinery	Money owing to bank
Creditors	
Premises	
Motor Vehicles	

1.6A Which of the following are shown under the wrong headings:

Assets	Liabilities
Cash at bank	Loan from J Graham
Fixtures	Machinery
Creditors	Motor vehicles
Building	
Stock of goods	
Debtors	
Capital	

1.7 A Smart sets up a new business. Before he actually sells anything, he has bought Motor Vehicles £2,000, Premises £5,000, Stock of goods £1,000. He did not pay in full for his stock of goods and still owes £400 in respect of them. He had borrowed £3,000 from D Bevan. After the events just described, and before trading starts, he has £100 cash in hand and £700 cash at bank. You are required to calculate the amount of his capital.

1.8A T Charles starts a business. Before he actually starts to sell anything, he has bought Fixtures £2,000, Motor Vehicles £5,000 and a stock of goods £3,500. Although he has paid in full for the fixtures and the motor vehicle, he still owes £1,400 for some of the goods. J Preston had lent him £3,000. Charles, after the above, has £2,800 in the business bank account and £100 cash in hand. You are required to calculate his capital.

1.9 Draw up A Foster's balance sheet from the following as at 31 December 19-4.

	£
Capital	23,750
Debtors	4,950
Motor vehicles	5,700
Creditors	2,450
Fixtures	5,500
Stock of goods	8,800
Cash at bank	1,250

1.10A Draw up Kelly's balance sheet as at 30 June 19-2 from the following items:

	£
Capital	13,000
Office machinery	9,000
Creditors	900
Stock of goods	1,550
Debtors	275
Cash at bank	5,075
Loan from C Smith	2,000

1.11 Complete the columns to show the effects of the following transactions:

	Effect upon		
	Assets	*Liabilities*	*Capital*

(*a*)   We pay a creditor £70 in cash.
(*b*)   Bought fixtures £200 paying by cheque.
(*c*)   Bought goods on credit £275.
(*d*)   The proprietor introduces another £500.
cash into the firm.
(*e*)   J Walker lends the firm £200 in cash
(*f*)   A debtor pays us £50 by cheque.
(*g*)   We return goods costing £60 to a supplier
whose bill we had not paid.
(*h*)   Bought additional shop premises paying £5,000 by cheque.

1.12A Complete the columns to show the effects of the following transactions:

	Effect upon		
	Assets	*Liabilities*	*Capital*

(*a*)   Bought a motor van on credit £500.
(*b*)   Repaid by cash a loan owed to P Smith £1,000.
(*c*)   Bought goods for £150 paying by cheque.
(*d*)   The owner puts a further £5,000 cash into the business.
(*e*)   A debtor returns to us £80 goods. We agree to make an
allowance for them.
(*f*)   Bought goods on credit £220.
(*g*)   The owner takes out £100 cash for his personal use
(*h*)   We pay a creditor £190 by cheque.

1.13 C Sangster has the following items in his balance sheet as on 30 April 19-4.

Capital £18,900; Loan from T Sharples £2,000; Creditors £1,600; Fixtures £3,500; Motor Vehicle £4,200; Stock of Goods £4,950; Debtors £3,280; Cash at Bank £6,450; Cash in Hand £120.

During the first week of May 19-4 Sangster:

(*a*) Bought extra stock of goods £770 on credit.
(*b*) One of the debtors paid us £280 in cash.
(*c*) Bought extra fixtures by cheque £1,000.

You are to draw up a balance sheet as on 7 May 19-4 after the above transactions have been completed.

1.14A F Dale has the following assets and liabilities as on 30 November 19-1:

Creditors £3,950; Equipment £11,500; Motor Vehicle £6,290; Stock of Goods £6,150; Debtors £5,770; Cash at Bank £7,280; Cash in Hand £40.

  The Capital at that date is to be deduced by you.

  During the first week of December 19-1, Dale:

(*a*) Bought extra equipment on credit for £1,380.
(*b*) Bought extra stock by cheque £570.
(*c*) Paid creditors by cheque £790.
(*d*) Debtors paid us £840 by cheque and £60 by cash.
(*e*) D Terry lent Dale £250 cash.

You are to draw up a balance sheet as on 7 December 19-1 after the above transactions have been completed.

2

The double-entry system for assets and liabilities

It has been seen that each transaction affects two items. To show the full effect of each transaction, accounting must therefore show its effect on each of the two items, be they assets capital or liabilities. From this need arose the double-entry system where to show this twofold effect each transaction is entered twice, one to show the effect upon one item, and a second entry to show the effect upon the other item.

It may be thought that drawing up a new balance sheet after each transaction would provide all the information required. However, a balance sheet does not give enough information about the business. It does not, for instance, tell who the debtors are and how much each one of them owes the firm, nor who the creditors are and the details of money owing to each of them. Also, the task of drawing up a new balance sheet after each transaction becomes an impossibility when there are many hundreds of transactions each day, as this would mean drawing up hundreds of balance sheets daily. Because of the work involved, balance sheets are in fact only drawn up periodically, at least annually, but sometimes half-yearly, quarterly, or monthly.

The double-entry system has an account (meaning details of transactions in that item) for every asset, every liability and for capital. Thus, there will be a Shop Premises Account (for transactions in shop premises), a Motor Vans Accounts (for transactions in Motor Vans), and so on for every asset, liability and for capital.

Each account should be shown on a separate page. The double-entry system divides each page into two halves. The left-hand side of each page is called the **debit side**, while the right-hand side is called the **credit side**. The title of each account is written across the top of the account at the centre,

It must not be thought that the words 'debit' and 'credit' in book-keeping mean the same as the words 'debit' or 'credit' in normal language usage. Anyone who does will become very confused.

This is a page of an accounts book:

Title of account written here	
Left-hand side of the page. This is the 'debit' side.	Right-hand side of the page. This is the 'credit' side.

If you have to make an entry of £10 on the debit side of the account, the instructions could say 'debit the account with £10' or 'the account needs debiting with £10'.

In Chapter 1 transactions were to increase or decrease assets, liabilities or capital. Double-entry rules for accounts are:

Accounts	To record	Entry in the account
Assets	an increase	Debit
	a decrease	Credit
Liabilities	an increase	Credit
	a decrease	Debit
Capital	an increase	Credit
	a decrease	Debit

Once again look at the accounting equation.

	Assets	=	Liabilities	and	Capital
To increase each item	Debit		Credit		Credit
To decrease each item	Credit		Debit		Debit

The double-entry rules for liabilities and capital are the same, but they are exactly the opposite as those for assets. This is because assets are on the opposite side of the equation and therefore follow opposite rules.

Looking at the accounts the rule will appear as:

Any asset account		Any liability account		Capital account	
Increases	Decreases	Decreases	Increases	Decreases	Increases
+	−	−	+	−	+

There is not enough space in this book to put each account on a separate page, so we will have to list the accounts under each other. In a real firm at least one full page would be taken for each account.

The entry of a few transactions can now be attempted:

1 The proprietor starts the firm with £1,000 in cash on 1 August 19-6.

Effect	Action
(a) Increases the asset of cash in the firm	Debit the cash account
(b) Increases the capital	Credit the capital account

These are entered:

Cash

19-6	£
Aug 1	1,000

Capital

		19-6	£
		Aug 1	1,000

The date of the transaction has already been entered. Now there remains the description which is to be entered alongside the amount. This is completed by a cross reference to the title of the other account in which double entry is completed. The double entry to the item in the cash account is completed by an entry in the capital account, therefore the word 'Capital' will appear in the cash account. Similarly, the double entry to the item in the capital account is completed by an entry in the cash account, therefore the word 'Cash' will appear in the capital account.

It always used to be the custom to prefix the description on the debit side of the books with the word 'To', and to prefix the description on the credit side of the books with the word 'By'. These have now fallen into disuse in modern firms, and as they serve no useful purpose they will not be used in this book.

The finally completed accounts are therefore:

Cash

19-6	£		
Aug 1 Capital	1,000		

Capital

		19-6	£
		Aug 1 Cash	1,000

2   A motor van is bought for £275 cash on 2 August 19-6

Effect	*Action*
(*a*) Decrease the asset of cash	Credit the cash account
(*b*) Increases the asset of motor van	Debit the motor van account

Cash

		19-6	£
		Aug 2 Motor van	275

Motor Van

19-6	£		
Aug 2 Cash	275		

3   Fixtures bought on credit from Shop Fitters £115 on 3 August 19-6.

Effect	*Action*
(*a*) Increase in the asset of fixtures	Debit fixtures account
(*b*) Increases in the liability of the firm to Shop Fitters	Credit Shop Fitters account

Fixtures

19-6	£		
Aug 3 Shop Fitters	115		

Shop Fitters

		19-6	£
		Aug 3 Fixtures	115

4   Paid the amount owing in cash to Shop Fitters on 17 August 19-6.

Effect	*Action*
(*a*) Decrease in the asset of cash	Credit the cash account
(*b*) Decrease in the liability of the firm to Shop Fitters	Debit Shop Fitters account

Cash

		£
	19-6	
	Aug 17 Shop Fitters	115

Shop Fitters

19-6	£
Aug 17 Cash	115

Transactions to date

Taking the transactions numbered 1 to 4 above, the records will now appear:

Cash

19-6		£	19-6		£
Aug 1	Capital	1,000	Aug 2 Motor van		275
			,, 17 Shop Fitters		115

Motor Van

19-6		£
Aug 2	Cash	275

Shop Fitters

19-6	£	19-6		£
Aug 17 Cash	115	Aug 3	Fixtures	115

Fixtures

19-6		£
Aug 3	Shop Fitters	115

Capital

		£
19-6		
Aug 1	Cash	1,000

A further worked example

Now you have actually made some entries in accounts you are to go carefully through the following example. Make certain you can understand every entry.

Transactions	Effect	Action
19-4		
May 1 Started an engineering business putting £1,000 into a business bank account.	Increases asset of bank. Increases capital of proprietor.	Debit bank account. Credit capital account.
,, 3 Bought works machinery on credit from Unique Machines £275.	Increases asset of machinery. Increases liability to Unique Machines.	Debit machinery account Credit Unique Machines account.
,, 4 Withdrew £200 cash from the bank and placed it in the cash till.	Decreases asset of bank. Increases asset of cash.	Credit bank account Debit cash account
,, 7 Bought motor van paying in cash £180.	Decreases asset of cash. Increases asset of Motor van.	Credit cash account. Debit motor van account.
,, 10 Sold some of machinery for £15 on credit to B Barnes.	Decreases asset of machinery. Increases asset of money owing from B Barnes.	Credit machinery account. Debit B Barnes account.
,, 21 Returned some of machinery value £27 to Unique Machines.	Decreases asset of machinery. Decreases liability to Unique Machines.	Credit Machinery account. Debit Unique Machines.
,, 28 B Barnes pays the firm the amount owing, £15, by cheque.	Increases asset of bank. Decreases asset of money owing to B Barnes.	Debit bank account. Credit B Barnes account.
,, 30 Bought another motor van paying by cheque £420.	Decreases asset of bank. Increases asset of motor vans.	Credit bank account. Debit motor van account.
,, 31 Paid the amount of £248 to Unique Machines by cheque	Decreases asset of bank. Decreases liability to Unique Machines.	Credit bank account. Debit Unique Machines.

In account form this is shown:

Bank

	£			£
May 1 Capital	1,000	May 4 Cash		200
,, 28 B Barnes	15	,, 30 Motor van		420
		,, 31 Unique Machines		248

Cash

	£		£
May 4 Bank	200	May 7 Motor van	180

Capital

		£
	May 1 Bank	1,000

Machinery

	£		£
May 3 Unique Machines	275	May 10 B Barnes	15
		,, 21 Unique Machines	27

Motor van

	£
May 7 Cash	180
,, 30 Bank	420

Unique Machines

	£		£
May 21 Machines	27	May 3 Machinery	275
,, 31 Bank	248		

B Barnes

	£		£
May 10 Machinery	15	May 28 Bank	15

Abbreviation of 'Limited'

In this book when we come across our transactions with limited companies the use of letters 'Ltd' is used as the abbreviation for 'Limited Company'. Thus we will know that if we see the name of a firm as F Wood Ltd, then that the firm will be a limited company. In our books the transactions with F Wood Ltd will be entered the same as for any other customer or supplier. It will be seen later that some limited companies use plc instead of Ltd.

Review questions

Note: Questions with the letter A shown after the question number do not have answers shown at the back of the book. Answers to the others are shown on page 502 onwards.

2.1 Complete the following table:

	Account to be debited	Account to be credited
(a) Bought office machinery on credit from D Isaacs Ltd.		
(b) The proprietor paid a creditor, C Jones, from his private monies outside the firm.		
(c) A debtor, N Fox, paid us in cash.		
(d) Repaid part of loan from P Exeter by cheque.		
(e) Returned some of office machinery to D Isaacs Ltd.		
(f) A debtor, N Lyn, pays us by cheque.		
(g) Bought motor van by cash.		

2.2A Complete the following table showing which accounts are to be debited and which to be credited:

		Account to be debited	Account to be credited
(a)	Bought motor lorry for cash.		
(b)	Paid creditor, T Lake, by cheque.		
(c)	Repaid P Logan's loan by cash.		
(d)	Sold motor lorry for cash.		
(e)	Bought office machinery on credit from Ultra Ltd.		
(f)	A debtor, A Hill, pays us by cash.		
(g)	A debtor, J Cross, pays us by cheque.		
(h)	Proprietor puts a further amount into the business by cheque.		
(i)	A loan of £200 in cash is received from L Lowe.		
(j)	Paid a creditor, D Lord, by cash.		

2.3 Write up the asset and liability and capital accounts to record the following transactions in the records of G Powell.

19-3
July   1   Started business with £2,500 in the bank.
  ,,   2   Bought office furniture by cheque £150.
  ,,   3   Bought machinery £750 on credit from Planers Ltd.
  ,,   5   Bought a motor van paying by cheque £600.
  ,,   8   Sold some of the office furniture – not suitable for the firm – for £60 on credit to J Walker & Sons.
  ,,   15   Paid the amount owing to Planers Ltd £750 by cheque.
  ,,   23   Received the amount due from J Walker £60 in cash.
  ,,   31   Bought more machinery by cheque £280.

2.4 You are required to open the asset and liability and capital accounts and record the following transactions for June 19-4 in the records of C Williams.

19-4
June   1   Started business with £2,000 in cash.
  ,,   2   Paid £1,800 of the opening cash into a bank account for the business.
  ,,   5   Bought office furniture on credit from Betta-Built Ltd for £120.
  ,,   8   Bought a motor van paying by cheque £950.
  ,,   12   Bought works machinery from Evans & Sons on credit £560.
  ,,   18   Returned faulty office furniture costing £62 to Betta-Built Ltd.
  ,,   25   Sold some of the works machinery for £75 cash.
  ,,   26   Paid amount owing to Betta-Built Ltd £58 by cheque.
  ,,   28   Took £100 out of the bank and put it in the cash till.
  ,,   30   J Smith lent us £500 – giving us the money by cheque.

2.5A Write up the asset, capital and liability accounts in the books of C Walsh to record the following transactions:

19-5

June 1   Started business with £5,000 in the bank.

,,   2   Bought motor van paying by cheque £1,200.

,,   5   Bought office fixtures £400 on credit from Young Ltd.

,,   8   Bought motor van on credit from Super Motors £800.

,,   12   Took £100 out of the bank and put it into the cash till.

,,   15   Bought office fixtures paying by cash £60.

,,   19   Paid Super Motors a cheque for £800.

,,   21   A loan of £1,000 cash is received from J Jarvis.

,,   25   Paid £800 of the cash in hand into the bank account.

,,   30   Bought more office fixtures paying by cheque £300.

2.6A Write up the accounts to record the following transactions:

19-3

March 1   Started with £1,000 cash.

,,   2   Received a loan of £5,000 from M Chow by cheque, a bank account being opened and the cheque paid into it.

,,   3   Bought machinery for cash £60.

,,   5   Bought display equipment on credit from Better-View Machines £550.

,,   8   Took £300 out of the bank and put it into the cash till.

,,   15   Repaid part of Chow's loan by cheque £800.

,,   17   Paid amount owing to Better-View Machines £550 by cheque.

,,   24   Repaid part of Chow's loan by cash £100.

,,   31   Bought additional machinery, this time on credit from D Smith for £500.

3

The asset of stock

Goods are sometimes sold at the same price at which they are bought, but this is not usually the case. Normally they are sold above cost price, the difference being **profit**; sometimes however they are sold at less than cost price, the difference being **loss**.

If all sales were at cost price, it would be possible to have a stock account, the goods sold being shown as a decrease of an asset, i.e. on the credit side. The purchase of stock could be shown on the debit side as it would be an increase of an asset. The difference between the two sides would then represent the cost of the goods unsold at that date, if wastages and losses of stock are ignored. However, most sales are not at cost price, and therefore the sales figures include elements of profit or loss. Because of this, the difference between the two sides would not represent the stock of goods. Such a stock account would therefore serve no useful purpose.

The **Stock Account** is accordingly divided into several accounts, each one showing a movement of stock. These can be said to be:

1   *Increases in the stock.* This can be due to one of two causes.

(*a*) By the purchase of additional goods.

(*b*) By the return in to the firm of goods previously sold. The reasons for this are numerous. The goods may have been the wrong type, they may have been surplus to requirements, have been faulty and so on.

To distinguish the two aspects of the increase of stocks of goods two accounts are opened. These are:

(i)   **Purchases Account** – in which purchases of goods are entered.

(ii) **Returns Inwards Account** – in which goods being returned in to the firm are entered. The alternative name for this account is the **Sales Returns Account**.

2   *Decreases in the stock of goods.* This can be due to one of two causes if wastages and losses of stock are ignored.

(*a*) By the sale of goods.

(*b*) Goods previously bought by the firm now being returned out of the firm to the supplier.

To distinguish the two aspects of the decrease of stocks of goods two accounts are opened. These are:

(i)   **Sales Account** – in which sales of goods are entered.

(ii) **Returns Outwards Account** – in which goods being returned out to a supplier are entered. The alternative name for this is the **Purchases Returns Account**.

Some illustrations can now be shown.

Purchase of stock on credit

1 August. Goods costing £165 are bought on credit from D Henry.

First, the twofold effect of the transactions must be considered in order that the book-keeping entries can be worked out.

1 The asset of stock is increased. An increase in an asset needs a debit entry in an account. Here the account concerned is a stock account showing the particular movement of stock, in this case it is the 'Purchases' movement so that the account concerned must be the purchases account.

2 An increase in a liability. This is the liability of the firm to D Henry in respect of the goods bought which have not yet been paid for. An increase in a liability needs a credit entry, so that to enter this aspect of the transaction a credit entry is made in D Henry's account.

Purchases

	£
Aug 1 D Henry	165

D Henry

	£
Aug 1 Purchases	165

Purchases of stock for cash

2 August. Goods costing £22 are bought, cash being paid for them immediately.

1 The asset of stock is increased, so that a debit entry will be needed. The movement of stock is that of a purchase, so that it is the purchases account which needs debiting.

2 The asset of cash is decreased. To reduce an asset a credit entry is called for, and the asset is that of cash so that the cash account needs crediting.

Cash

	£
Aug 2 Purchases	22

Purchases

	£
Aug 2 Cash	22

Sales of stock on credit

3 August. Sold goods on credit for £250 to J Lee.

1 The asset of stock is decreased. For this a credit entry to reduce an asset is needed. The movement of stock is that of a 'Sale' so the account credited is the sales account.

2 An asset account is increased. This is the account showing that J Lee is a debtor for the goods. The increase in the asset of debtors requires a debit and the debtor is J Lee, so that the account concerned is that of J Lee.

Sales

	£
Aug 3 J Lee	250

J Lee

	£
Aug 3 Sales	250

Sales of stock for cash

4 August. Goods are sold for £55, cash being received immediately upon sale.

1   The asset of cash is increased. This needs a debit in the cash account to show this.

2   The asset of stock is reduced. The reduction of an asset requires a credit and the movement of stock is represented by 'Sales'. Thus the entry needed is a credit in the sales account.

Sales

		£
	Aug 4 Cash	55

Cash

	£
Aug 4 Sales	55

Returns inwards

5 August. Goods which had been previously sold to F Lowe for £29 are now returned by him.

1   The asset of stock is increased by the goods returned. Thus a debit representing an increase of an asset is needed, and this time the movement of stock is that of **Returns Inwards**. The entry therefore required is a debit in the returns inwards account.

2   A decrease in an asset. The debt of F Lowe to the firm is now reduced, and to record this a credit is needed in F Lowe's account.

Returns Inwards

	£
Aug 5 F Lowe	29

F Lowe

		£
	Aug 5 Returns Inwards	29

An alternative name for a Returns Inwards Account would be a **Sales Returns Account**.

Returns outwards

6 August. Goods previously bought for £96 are returned by the firm to K Howe.

1   The asset of stock is decreased by the goods sent out. Thus a credit representing a reduction in an asset is needed, and the movement of stock is that of **Returns Outwards** so that the entry will be a credit in the returns outwards account.

2   The liability of the firm to K Howe is decreased by the value of the goods returned to him. The decrease in a liability needs a debit, this time in K Howe's account.

Returns Outwards

		£
	Aug 6 K Howe	96

K Howe

	£
Aug 6 Returns outwards	96

An alternative name for a Returns Outwards Account would be a **Purchases Returns Account**.

A worked example

May   1 Bought goods on credit £68 from D Small
,,   2 Bought goods on credit £77 from A Lyon & Son
,,   5 Sold goods on credit to D Hughes for £60
,,   6 Sold goods on credit to M Spencer for £45
,,   10 Returned goods £15 to D Small
,,   12 Goods bought for cash £100.
,,   19 M Spencer returned £16 goods to us
,,   21 Goods sold for cash £150
,,   22 Paid cash to D Small £53
,,   30 D Hughes paid the amount owing by him £60 in cash
,,   31 Bought goods on credit £64 from A Lyon & Son.

Purchases

19-5	£
May 1 D Small	68
,, 2 A Lyon & Son	77
,, 12 Cash	100
,, 31 A Lyon & Son	64

Sales

19-5	£
May 5 D Hughes	60
,, 6 M Spencer	45
,, 21 Cash	150

Returns Outwards

19-5	£
May 10 D Small	15

Returns Inwards

19-5	£
May 19 M Spencer	16

D Small

19-5	£	19-5	£
May 10 Returns outwards	15	May 1 Purchases	68
,, 22 Cash	53		

A Lyon & Son

19-5	£	19-5	£
		May 2 Purchases	77
		,, 31 Purchases	64

D Hughes

19-5	£	19-5	£
May 5 Sales	60	May 30 Cash	60

M Spencer

19-5	£	19-5	£
May 6 Sales	45	May 19 Returns inwards	16

19-5		£	19-5		£
May 21 Sales		150	May 12 Purchases		100
,, 30 D Hughes		60	,, 22 D Small		53

Special meaning of 'Sales' and 'Purchases'

It must be emphasised that 'Sales' and 'Purchases' have a special meaning in accounting when compared to ordinary language usage.

'**Purchases**' in accounting means the purchase of those goods which the firm buys with the prime intention of selling. Obviously, sometimes the goods are altered, added to, or used in the manufacture of something else, but it is the element of resale that is important. To a firm that deals in typewriters for instance, typewriters constitute purchases. If something else is bought, such as a motor van, such an item cannot be called purchases, even though in ordinary language it may be said that a motor van has been purchased. The prime intention of buying the motor van is for usage and not for resale.

Similarly, '**Sales**' means the sale of those goods in which the firm normally deals and were bought with the prime intention of resale. The word 'Sales' must never be given to the disposal of other items.

Failure to keep to these meanings would result in the different forms of stock account containing something other than goods sold or for resale.

Comparison of cash and credit transactions for purchases and sales

The difference between the records needed for cash and credit transactions can now be seen.

The complete set of entries for purchases of goods where they are paid for immediately needs entries:
1 Credit the cash account.
2 Debit the purchases account.

On the other hand the complete set of entries for the purchase of goods on credit can be broken down into two stages. First, the purchase of the goods and second, the payment for them.

The first part is:
1 Debit the purchases account.
2 Credit the supplier's account.

While the second part is:
1 Credit the cash account.
2 Debit the supplier's account.

The difference can now be seen in that with the cash purchase no record is kept of the supplier's account. This is because cash passes immediately and therefore there is no need to keep a check of indebtedness to a supplier. On the other hand, in the credit purchase the records should reveal the identity of the supplier to whom the firm is indebted until payment is made.

A study of cash sales and credit sales will reveal a similar difference.

Cash Sales
Complete entry:
   Debit cash account
   Credit sales account

Credit Sales
First part:
   Debit customer's account
   Credit sales account
Second part:
   Debit cash account
   Credit customer's account

Review questions

Note: Questions with the letter A shown after the question number do not have answers shown at the back of the book. Answers to the other questions are shown on page 502 onwards.

3.1 Complete the following table showing which accounts are to be credited and which are to be debited:

	Account to be debited	Account to be credited
(a) Goods bought on credit from J Reid.		
(b) Goods sold on credit to B Perkins.		
(c) Motor vans bought on credit from H Thomas.		
(d) Goods sold, a cheque being received immediately.		
(e) Goods sold for cash.		
(f) Goods we returned to H Hardy.		
(g) Machinery sold for cash.		
(h) Goods returned to us by J Nelson.		
(i) Goods bought on credit from D Simpson.		
(j) Goods we returned to H Forbes.		

3.2A Complete the following table:

	Account to be debited	Account to be credited
(a) Goods bought on credit from T Morgan.		
(b) Goods returned to us by J Thomas.		
(c) Machinery returned to L Jones Ltd.		
(d) Goods bought for cash.		
(e) Motor van bought on credit from D Davies Ltd.		
(f) Goods returned by us to I Prince.		
(g) D Picton paid us his account by cheque.		
(h) Goods bought by cheque.		
(i) We paid creditor, B Henry, by cheque.		
(j) Goods sold on credit to J Mullings.		

3.3 You are to write up the following in the books:

19-4
July	1	Start business with £500 cash
,,	3	Bought goods for cash £85
,,	7	Bought goods on credit £116 from E Morgan
,,	10	Sold goods for cash £42
,,	14	Returned goods to E Morgan £28
,,	18	Bought goods on credit £98 from A Moses
,,	21	Returned goods to A Moses £19
,,	24	Sold goods to A Knight £55 on credit
,,	25	Paid E Morgan's account by cash £88
,,	31	A Knight paid us his account in cash £55.

3.4 You are to enter the following in the accounts needed:

19-6

Aug 1 Started business with £1,000 cash
,, 2 Paid £900 of the opening cash into the bank
,, 4 Bought goods on credit £78 from S Holmes
,, 5 Bought a motor van by cheque £500
,, 7 Bought goods for cash £55
,, 10 Sold goods on credit £98 to D Moore
,, 12 Returned goods to S Holmes £18
,, 19 Sold goods for cash £28
,, 22 Bought fixtures on credit from Kingston Equipment Co £150.
,, 24 D Watson lent us £100 paying us the money by cheque
,, 29 We paid S Holmes his account by cheque £60
,, 31 We paid Kingston Equipment Co by cheque £150.

3.5 Enter up the following transactions in the records of E Sangster:

19-7

July 1 Started business with £10,000 in the bank
,, 2 T Cooper lent us £400 in cash
,, 3 Bought goods on credit from F Jones £840 and S Charles £3,600
,, 4 Sold goods for cash £200
,, 6 Took £250 of the cash and paid it into the bank
,, 8 Sold goods on credit to C Moody £180
,, 10 Sold goods on credit to J Newman £220
,, 11 Bought goods on credit from F Jones £370
,, 12 C Moody returned goods to us £40
,, 14 Sold goods on credit to H Morgan £190 and J Peat £320
,, 15 We returned goods to F Jones £140
,, 17 Bought motor van on credit from Manchester Motors £2,600
,, 18 Bought office furniture on credit from Faster Supplies Ltd £600
,, 19 We returned goods to S Charles £110
,, 20 Bought goods for cash £220
,, 24 Goods sold for cash £70
,, 25 Paid money owing to F Jones by cheque £1,070
,, 26 Goods returned to us by H Morgan £30
,, 27 Returned some of office furniture costing £160 to Faster Supplies Ltd
,, 28 E Sangster put a further £500 into the business in the form of cash
,, 29 Paid Manchester Motors £2,600 by cheque
,, 31 Bought office furniture for cash £100.

3.6A Enter up the following transactions in the records:

19-5

May	1	Started business with £2,000 in the bank
,,	2	Bought goods on credit from C Shaw £900
,,	3	Bought goods on credit from F Hughes £250
,,	5	Sold goods for cash £180
,,	6	We returned goods to C Shaw £40
,,	8	Bought goods on credit from F Hughes £190
,,	10	Sold goods on credit to G Wood 390
,,	12	Sold goods for cash £210
,,	18	Took £300 of the cash and paid it into the bank
,,	21	Bought machinery by cheque £550
,,	22	Sold goods on credit to L Moore £220
,,	23	G Wood returned goods to us £140
,,	25	L Moore returned goods to us £10
,,	28	We returned goods to F Hughes £30
,,	29	We paid Shaw by cheque £860
,,	31	Bought machinery on credit from D Lee £270.

3.7A You are to enter the following in the accounts needed:

July	1	Started business with £1,000 cash
,,	2	Paid £800 of the opening cash into a bank account for the firm
,,	3	Bought goods on credit from H Grant £330
,,	4	Bought goods on credit from D Clark £140
,,	8	Sold goods on credit to B Miller £90
,,	8	Bought office furniture on credit from Barrett's Ltd £400
,,	10	Sold goods for cash £120
,,	13	Bought goods for credit from H Grant £200
,,	14	Bought goods for cash £60
,,	15	Sold goods on credit to H Sharples £180
,,	16	We returned goods £50 to H Grant
,,	17	We returned some of the office furniture £30 to Barrett's Ltd
,,	18	Sold goods on credit to B Miller £400
,,	21	Paid H Grant's account by cheque £480
,,	23	B Miller paid us the amount owing in cash £490
,,	24	Sharples returned to us £50 goods
,,	25	Goods sold for cash £150
,,	28	Bought goods for cash £370
,,	30	Bought motor van on credit from J Kelly £600.

4

The double-entry system for expenses and revenues. The effect of profit or loss on capital

Up to now this book has been concerned with the accounting need to record changes in assets and liabilities. There is, however, one item that we have not recorded. This is the change in the capital caused by the profit earned in the business. By profit is meant the excess of revenues over expenses for a particular period. Revenues consist of the monetary value of goods and services that have been delivered to customers. Expenses consist of the monetary value of the assets used up in obtaining these revenues. Particularly in American accounting language the word 'income' is used instead of 'profit'.

It is possible to see the effect of profit upon capital by means of an example:

On 1 January the assets and liabilities of a firm are:

Assets: Motor van £500, Fixtures £200, Stock £700, Debtors £300, Cash in Bank £200.

Liabilities: Creditors £600.

The capital is therefore found by the formula

Assets − Liabilities = Capital.

£500 + £200 + £700 + £300 + £200 − £600 = £1,300.

During January the whole of the £700 stock is sold for £1,100 cash, so that a £400 profit has been made. On 31 January the assets and liabilities have become:

Assets: Motor van £500, Fixtures £200, Stock − , Debtors £300, Cash in Bank £1,300.

Liabilities: Creditors £600.

Assets − Liabilities = Capital

£500 + £200 + £300 + £1,300 − £600 = £1,700.

Profit therefore affects the capital thus:

Old capital + Profit = New Capital

£1,300 + £400 = £1,700

On the other hand a loss would have reduced the capital so that it would become:

Old Capital − Loss = New Capital.

To alter the capital account it will therefore have to be possible to calculate profits and losses. They are, however, calculated only at intervals, usually annually but sometimes more often. This means that accounts will be needed to collect together the expenses and revenues pending the periodical calculation of profits. All the expenses could be charged to an omnibus **Expenses Account**, but obviously it is far more informative if full details of different expenses are shown in **Profit** and **Loss Calculations**. The same applies to revenues. Therefore, a separate account is opened for every type of expense and revenue. For instance there may be accounts as follows:

Rent Account	Postages Account
Wages Account	Stationery Account
Salaries Account	Insurance Account
Telephone Account	Motor Expenses Account
Rent Receivable Account	General Expenses Account

It is purely a matter of choice in a firm as to the title of each expense or revenue account. For example, an account for postage stamps could be called 'Postage Stamps Account', 'Postages Account', 'Communication Expenses Account', and so on. Also different firms amalgamate expenses, some having a 'Rent and Telephone Account', others a 'Rent, Telephone and Insurance Account', etc. Infrequent or small items of expense are usually put into a 'Sundry Expenses Account' or a 'General Expenses Account'.

Debit or credit

It must now be decided as to which side of the records revenues and expenses are to be recorded. Assets involve expenditure by the firm and are shown as debit entries. Expenses also involve expenditure by the firm and are therefore also recorded on the debit side of the books. In fact assets may be seen to be expenditure of money for which something still remains, while expenses involve expenditure of money which has been used up in the running of the business and for which there is no benefit remaining at the date of the balance sheet.

Revenue is the opposite of expenses and therefore appears on the opposite side to expenses, that is revenue accounts appear on the credit side of the books. Revenue also increases profit, which in turn increases capital. Pending the periodical calculation of profit therefore, revenue is collected together in appropriately named accounts, and until it is transferred to the profit calculations it will therefore need to be shown as a credit.

An alternative explanation may also be used for expenses. Every expense results in a decrease in an asset or an increase in a liability, and because of the accounting equation this means that the capital is reduced by each expense. The decrease of capital needs a debit entry and therefore expense accounts contain debit entries for expenses.

Consider too that expenditure of money pays for expenses, which are used up in the short term, or assets, which are used up in the long term, both for the purpose of winning revenue. Both of these are shown on the debit side of the pages, while the revenue which has been won is shown on the credit side of the pages.

Effect of transactions

A few illustrations will demonstrate the double entry required.

1   The rent of £20 is paid in cash.

Here the twofold effect is:

(a)   The asset of cash is decreased. This means crediting the cash account to show the decrease of the asset.

(b)   The total of the expenses of rent is increased. As expense entries are shown as debits, and the expense is rent, so the action required is the debiting of the rent account.

Summary: Credit the cash account with £20.

Debit the rent account with £20.

2   Motor expenses are paid by cheque £55.

The twofold effect is:

(*a*)   The asset of money in the bank is decreased. This means crediting the bank account to show the decrease of the asset.

(*b*)   The total of the motor expenses paid is increased. To increase an expenses account needs a debit, so the action required is to debit the motor expenses account.

Summary: Credit the bank account with £55.

Debit the motor expenses account with £55.

3   £60 cash is received for commission earned by the firm.

(*a*)   The asset of cash is increased. This needs a debit in the cash account to increase the asset.

(*b*)   The revenue of commissions received is increased. Revenue is shown by a credit entry, therefore to increase the revenue account in question the Commissions Received Account is credited.

Summary: Debit the cash account.

Credit the commissions received account.

It is now possible to study the effects of some more transactions showing the results in the form of a table:

			Increase	Action	Decrease	Action
June	1	Paid for postage stamps by cash £5	Expenses of postages	Debit postages account	Asset of cash	Credit cash account
,,	2	Paid for electricity by cheque £29	Expense of electricity	Debit electricity account	Asset of bank	Credit bank account
,,	3	Received rent in cash £38	Asset of cash Revenue of rent	Debit cash account Credit rent received account		
,,	4	Paid insurance by cheque £42	Expense of insurance	Debit insurance account	Asset of bank	Credit bank account

The above four examples can now be shown in account form:

Cash

	£		£
June 3 Rent received	38	June 1 Postages	5

Bank

			£
		June 2 Electricity	29
		,, 4 Insurance	42

Electricity

	£
June 2 Bank	29

Insurance

	£
June 4 Bank	42

	£
June 1 Cash	5

Rent Received

	£
June 3 Cash	38

It is clear from time to time the proprietor will want to take cash out of the business for his private use. In fact he will sometimes take goods. This will be dealt with later. However, whether the withdrawals are cash or goods they are known as **Drawings**. Drawings in fact decrease the claim of the proprietor against the resources of the business, in other words they reduce the amount of capital. According to the way in which the accounting formula is represented by debits and credits the decrease of capital needs a debit entry in the capital account. However, the accounting custom has grown up of debiting a **Drawings Account** as an interim measure.

An example will demonstrate the twofold effect of cash withdrawals from the business.

Example: 25 August. Proprietor takes £50 cash out of the business for his own use.

Effect	*Action*
1 Capital is decreased by £50	Debit the drawings account £50
2 Cash is decreased by £50	Credit the cash account £50

Cash

	£
Aug 25 Drawings	50

Drawings

	£
Aug 25 Cash	50

Review questions

4.1 From the following statements which give the cumulative effects of individual transactions, you are required to state as fully as possible what transaction has taken place in each case. There is no need to copy out the table.

Transaction:		A	B	C	D	E	F	G	H	I
Assets	£000	£000	£000	£000	£000	£000	£000	£000	£000	£000
Land and Buildings	450	450	450	450	575	575	275	275	275	275
Motor vehicles	95	100	100	100	100	100	100	100	100	100
Office equipment	48	48	48	48	48	48	48	48	48	48
Stock	110	110	110	110	110	110	110	110	110	93
Debtors	188	188	188	188	188	108	108	108	108	120
Bank	27	22	22	172	47	127	427	77	77	77
Cash	15	15	11	11	11	11	11	11	3	3
	933	933	929	1,079	1,079	1,079	1,079	729	721	716

Liabilities										
Capital	621	621	621	621	621	621	621	621	621	616
Loan from Lee	200	200	200	350	350	350	350	–	–	–
Creditors	112	112	108	108	108	108	108	108	100	100
	933	933	929	1,079	1,079	1,079	1,079	729	721	716

Note: the sign £000 means that all the figures shown underneath it are in thousands of pounds, e.g. Office Equipment book value is £48,000. It saves constantly writing out 000 after each figure, and is done to save time and make comparison easier.

4.2A The following table shows the cumulative effects of a succession of separate transactions on the assets and liabilities of a business.

Transaction:		A	B	C	D	E	F	G	H	I
Assets	£000	£000	£000	£000	£000	£000	£000	£000	£000	£000
Land and Buildings	500	500	535	535	535	535	535	535	535	535
Equipment	230	230	230	230	230	230	230	200	200	200
Stocks	113	140	140	120	120	120	120	120	119	119
Trade debtors	143	143	143	173	160	158	158	158	158	158
Prepaid expenses	27	27	27	27	27	27	27	27	27	27
Cash at bank	37	37	37	37	50	50	42	63	63	63
Cash on hand	9	9	9	9	9	9	9	9	9	3
	1,059	1,086	1,121	1,131	1,131	1,129	1,121	1,112	1,111	1,105

Liabilities										
Capital	730	730	730	740	740	738	733	724	723	717
Loan	120	120	155	155	155	155	155	155	155	155
Trade creditors	168	195	195	195	195	195	195	195	195	195
Accrued expenses	41	41	41	41	41	41	38	38	38	38
	1,059	1,086	1,121	1,131	1,131	1,129	1,121	1,112	1,111	1,105

Required: Identify clearly and as fully as you can what transaction has taken place in each case. Give two possible explanations for transaction 1. Do not copy out the table but use the reference letter for each transaction.

(Association of Accounting Technicians)

Note by author: We have not yet come across the term 'accrued expenses'. It means the same as expenses owing, so in F obviously £3,000 was paid off expenses owing as well as another £5,000 being used for something else.

4.3 Complete the following table, showing the accounts to be debited and those to be credited:

		Account to be debited	Account to be credited
(a)	Paid insurance by cheque.		
(b)	Paid motor expenses by cash.		
(c)	Rent received in cash.		
(d)	Paid rates by cheque.		
(e)	Received refund of rates by cheque.		
(f)	Paid for stationery expenses by cash.		
(g)	Paid wages by cash.		
(h)	Sold surplus stationery receiving proceeds by cheque.		
(i)	Received sales commission by cheque.		
(j)	Bought motor van by cheque.		

4.4 You are to enter the following transactions, completing double-entry in the books for the month of May 19-7.

19-7

May	1	Started business with £2,000 in the bank
,,	2	Purchased goods £175 on credit from M Mills
,,	3	Bought fixtures and fittings £150 paying by cheque
,,	5	Sold goods for cash £275
,,	6	Bought goods on credit £114 from S Waites
,,	10	Paid rent by cash £15
,,	12	Bought stationery £27, paying in cash
,,	18	Goods returned to M Mills £23
,,	21	Let off part of the premises receiving rent by cheque £5
,,	23	Sold goods on credit to U Henry for £77
,,	24	Bought a motor van paying by cheque £300
,,	30	Paid the month's wages by cash £117
,,	31	The proprietor took cash for himself £44

4.5 Write up the following transactions in the books of L Thompson:

19-8

March	1	Started business with cash £1,500
,,	2	Bought goods on credit from A Hanson £296
,,	3	Paid rent by cash £28
,,	4	Paid £1,000 of the cash of the firm into a bank account
,,	5	Sold goods on credit to E Linton £54
,,	7	Bought stationery £15 paying by cheque
,,	11	Cash Sales £49
,,	14	Goods returned by us to A Hanson £17
,,	17	Sold goods on credit to S Morgan £29
,,	20	Paid for repairs to the building by cash £18
,,	22	E Linton returned goods to us £14
,,	27	Paid Hanson by cheque £279
,,	28	Cash purchases £125
,,	29	Bought a motor van paying by cheque £395
,,	30	Paid motor expenses in cash £15
,,	31	Bought fixtures £120 on credit from A Webster

4.6A Enter the following transactions in double entry:

July 1 Started business with £8,000 in the bank
,, 2 Bought stationery by cheque £30
,, 3 Bought goods on credit from I Walsh £900
,, 4 Sold goods for cash £180
,, 5 Paid insurance by cash £40
,, 7 Bought machinery on credit from H Morgan £500
,, 8 Paid for machinery expenses by cheque £50
,, 10 Sold goods on credit to D Small £320
,, 11 Returned goods to I Walsh £70
,, 14 Paid wages by cash £70
,, 17 Paid rent by cheque £100
,, 20 Received cheque £200 from D Small
,, 21 Paid H Morgan by cheque £500
,, 23 Bought stationery on credit from Express Ltd £80
,, 25 Sold goods on credit to N Thomas £230
,, 28 Received rent £20 in cash for part of premises sub-let
,, 31 Paid Express Ltd by cheque £80

4.7A Write up the following transactions in the records of D DaSilva:

Feb 1 Started business with £3,000 in the bank and £500 cash
,, 2 Bought goods on credit: T Small £250; C Todd £190; V Ryan £180
,, 3 Bought goods for cash £230.
Feb 4 Paid rent in cash £10
,, 5 Bought stationery paying by cheque £49
,, 6 Sold goods on credit: C Crooks £140; R Rogers £100; B Grant £240
,, 7 Paid wages in cash £80
,, 10 We returned goods to C Todd £60.
Feb 11 Paid rent in cash £10
,, 13 R Rogers returns goods to us £20
,, 15 Sold goods on credit to: J Burns £90; J Smart £130; N Thorn £170
,, 16 Paid rates by cheque £130.
Feb 18 Paid insurance in cash £40
,, 19 Paid rent by cheque £10
,, 20 Bought motor van on credit from C White £600
,, 21 Paid motor expenses in cash £6.
Feb 23 Paid wages in cash £90
,, 24 Received part of amount owing from B Grant by cheque £200
,, 28 Received refund of rates £10 by cheque
,, 28 Paid by cheque: T Small £250; C Todd £130; C White £600

5

Balancing off accounts

What you have been reading about so far is the recording of transactions in the books by means of debit and credit entries. Every so often we will have to look at each account to see what is revealed by the entries.

Probably the most obvious reason for this is to find out how much our customers owe us in respect of goods we have sold to them. In most firms the custom is that this should be done at the end of each month.

Let us look at the account of one of our customers, K Tanner, in respect of transactions in August 19-6:

K Tanner

19-6	£	19-6	£
Aug 1 Sales	144	Aug 22 Bank	144
Aug 19 Sales	300	Aug 28 Bank	300

This shows that during the month we sold a total of £444 goods to Tanner and been paid a total of £444 by him. At the close of business at the end of August he therefore owes us nothing. His account can accordingly be closed off on 31 August 19-6 by simply inserting the totals on each side, as follows:

K Tanner

19-6	£	19-6	£
Aug 1 Sales	144	Aug 22 Bank	144
Aug 19 Sales	300	Aug 28 Bank	300
	444		444

Notice that totals in accounting are shown with a single line above them, and a double line underneath.

Totals on accounts at the end of a period are always shown on a level with one another, as shown in the following completed account for C Lester.

C Lester

19-6	£	19-6	£
Aug 11 Sales	177	Aug 30 Bank	480
Aug 19 Sales	203		
Aug 22 Sales	100		
	480		480

32

In this case, C Lester also owed us nothing at the end of August 19-6, as he had paid us for all sales to him.

On the other hand, a considerable number of our customers will still owe us something at the end of the month. In these cases the totals of each side would not equal one another. Let us look at the account of D Knight for August 19-6:

D Knight

19-6		£	19-6		£
Aug 1 Sales		158	Aug 28 Bank		158
Aug 15 Sales		206			
Aug 30 Sales		118			

If you add up the figures, you will see that the debit side adds up to £482 and the credit side adds up to £158. You should be able to deduce what the difference of £324 (i.e. £482 − £158) represents. It consists of sales of £206 and £118 not paid for and therefore owing to us on 31 August 19-6.

In double entry we only enter figures as totals if the totals on both sides of the account agree. We do, however, want to close off the account for August, but showing that Knight owed us £324. It follows that if he owed £324 at close of business on 31 August 19-6 then he will still owe us that same figure when the business first opens on 1 September 19-6.

To show that the amount is owing at the start of the new period, 1 September 19-6, the figure of £324 is entered on the credit side of the account so that now both sides of the account add up to £482. The totals of £482 can now be entered on both sides of the account. As £324 has been entered on the credit side, double entry demands an entry of £324 on the debit side. This is shown as the first item under the total of the debit side and dated as 1 September 19-6.

The difference of £324 between the two original totals is known in accounting as **balance**. The balance on 31 August is described as **balance carried down** and the balance on 1 September is described as **balance brought down**.

Knight's account when 'balanced off' will appear as follows:

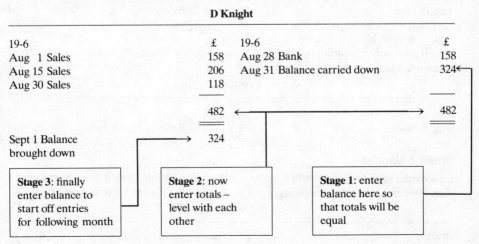

D Knight

19-6		£	19-6		£
Aug 1 Sales		158	Aug 28 Bank		158
Aug 15 Sales		206	Aug 31 Balance carried down		324
Aug 30 Sales		118			
		482			482
Sept 1 Balance brought down		324			

Stage 3: finally enter balance to start off entries for following month

Stage 2: now enter totals – level with each other

Stage 1: enter balance here so that totals will be equal

We can now look at another account prior to balancing:

H Henry

19-6		£	19-6		£
Aug 5 Sales		300	Aug 24 Returns Inwards		50
Aug 28 Sales		540	Aug 29 Bank		250

This time, and we will always do this in future, for it will save us unnecessary writing, we will abbreviate 'carried down' to 'c/d' and 'brought down' to 'b/d'.

H Henry

19-6		£	19-6		£
Aug 5 Sales		300	Aug 24 Returns Inwards		50
Aug 28 Sales		540	Aug 29 Bank		250
			Aug 31 Balance c/d		540
		840			840
Sept 1 Balance b/d		540			

Notes:

1   The date given to balance c/d is the last day of the period which is finishing, and balance b/d is given the opening date of the next period.

2   As the total of the debit side originally exceeded the total of the credit side, the balance is said to be a debit balance. This being a personal account (for a person), the person concerned is said to be a debtor – the accounting term for anyone who owes money to the firm. The use of the term debtor for a person whose account has a debit balance can again thus be seen.

If accounts contain only one entry it is unnecessary to enter the total. A double line ruled under the entry will mean that the entry is its own total. For example:

B Walters

19-6		£	19-6		£
Aug 18 Sales		51	Aug 31 Balance c/d		51
Sept 1 Balance b/d		51			

If an account contains only one entry on each side which are equal to one another, totals are again unnecessary. For example:

D Hylton

19-6		£	19-6		£
Aug 6 Sales		214	Aug 12 Bank		214

Credit balances

Exactly the same principles will apply when the balances are carried down to the credit side. We can look at two accounts of our suppliers which are to be balanced off.

E Williams

19-6		£	19-6		£
Aug 21 Bank		100	Aug 2 Purchases		248
			,, 18 ,,		116

K Patterson

19-6		£	19-6		£
Aug 14	Returns Outwards	20	Aug 8	Purchases	620
,, 28	Bank	600	,, 15	Purchases	200

When balanced these will appear as:

E Williams

19-6		£	19-6		£
Aug 21	Bank	100	Aug 2	Purchases	248
,, 31	Balance c/d	264	,, 18	,,	116
		364			364
			Sept 1	Balance b/d	264

Stage 1: enter balance here so that totals will be equal

Stage 2: now enter totals – level with each other

Stage 3: finally enter balance to start off entries for following month

K Patterson

19-6		£	19-6		£
Aug 14	Returns Outwards	20	Aug 8	Purchases	620
,, 28	Bank	600	,, 15	Purchases	200
,, 31	Balance c/d	200			
		820			820
			Sept 1	Balance b/d	200

Before you read further attempt Review Questions 5.1 and 5.2.

Computers and book-keeping equipment

Throughout the main part of this book the type of account used shows the left-hand side of the account as the debit side, and the right-hand side is shown as the credit side. However, when most computers or book-keeping equipment is used the style of the ledger account is different. It appears as three columns of figures, being one column for debit entries, another column for credit entries, and the last column for the balance. If you have a current account at a bank your bank statements will normally be shown using this method.

The accounts used in this chapter will now be redrafted to show the ledger accounts drawn up in this way.

K Tanner

			Debit	Credit	Balance (and whether debit or credit)
19-6			£	£	£
Aug	1	Sales	144		144 Dr
,,	19	Sales	300		444 Dr
,,	22	Bank		144	300 Dr
,,	28	Bank		300	0

C Lester

			Debit	Credit	Balance
19-6			£	£	£
Aug	11	Sales	177		177 Dr
,,	19	Sales	203		380 Dr
,,	22	Sales	100		480 Dr
,,	30	Bank		480	0

D Knight

			Debit	Credit	Balance
19-6			£	£	£
Aug	1	Sales	158		158 Dr
,,	15	,,	206		364 Dr
,,	28	Bank		158	206 Dr
,,	30	Sales	118		324 Dr

H Henry

			Debit	Credit	Balance
19-6			£	£	£
Aug	5	Sales	300		300 Dr
,,	24	Returns		50	250 Dr
,,	28	Sales	540		790 Dr
,,	29	Bank		250	540 Dr

B Walters

			Debit	Credit	Balance
19-6			£	£	£
Aug	18	Sales	51		51 Dr

D Hylton

			Debit	Credit	Balance
19-6			£	£	£
Aug	6	Sales	214		214 Dr
,,	12	Bank		214	0

E Williams

19-6		Debit	Credit	Balance
		£	£	£
Aug 2	Purchases		248	248 Cr
,, 18	,,		116	364 Cr
,, 21	Bank	100		264 Cr

K Patterson

19-6		Debit	Credit	Balance
		£	£	£
Aug 8	Purchases		620	620 Cr
,, 14	Returns	20		600 Cr
,, 15	Purchases		200	800 Cr
,, 28	Bank	600		200 Cr

It will be noticed that the balance is calculated afresh after every entry. This can be done quite simply when using book-keeping machinery or a computer because it is the machine which automatically calculates the new balance. However, when manual methods are in use it is often too laborious to have to calculate a new balance after each entry, and it also means that the greater the number of calculations the greater the possible number of errors. For these reasons it is usual for students to use two-sided accounts. However, it is important to note that there is no difference in principle, the final balances are the same using either method.

Review questions

5.1 Enter the following items in the necessary debtors acounts only, do *not* write up other accounts. Then balance down each personal account at the end of the month. (Keep your answer, it will be used as a basis for question 5.3).

19-6
May 1 Sales on credit to H Harvey £690, N Morgan £153, J Lindo £420
  ,,   4 Sales on credit to L Masters £418, H Harvey £66
  ,, 10 Returns inwards from H Harvey £40, J Lindo £20
  ,, 18 N Morgan paid us by cheque £153
  ,, 20 J Lindo paid us £400 by cheque
  ,, 24 H Harvey paid us £300 by cash
  ,, 31 Sales on credit to L Masters £203.

5.2 Enter the following in the personal accounts only. Do *not* write up the other accounts. Then balance down each personal account at the end of the month. (Keep your answer, it will be used as the basis for question 5.4)

19-8
June 1 Purchases on credit from J Young £458, L Williams £120, G Norman £708
  ,,   3 Purchases on credit from L Williams £77, T Harris £880
  ,, 10 We returned goods to G Norman £22, J Young £55
  ,, 15 Purchases on credit from J Young £80
  ,, 19 We paid T Harris by cheque £880
  ,, 28 We paid J Young by cash £250
  ,, 30 We returned goods to L Williams £17.

5.3 Redraft each of the accounts given in your answer to 5.1 in three-column ledger style accounts.

5.4 Redraft each of the accounts given in your answer to 5.2 in three-column ledger style accounts.

5.5 Enter the following in the personal accounts only, do *not* write up the other accounts. Balance down each personal account at the end of the month. After completing this state which of the balances represent debtors and those which are creditors.

19-4

Sept	1	Sales on credit to D Williams £458, J Moore £235, G Grant £98
,,	2	Purchases on credit A White £77, H Samuels £231, P Owen £65
,,	8	Sales on credit to J Moore £444, F Franklin £249
,,	10	Purchases on credit from H Samuels £12, O Oliver £222
,,	12	Returns Inwards from G Grant £9, J Moore £26
,,	17	We returned goods to H Samuels £24, O Oliver £12
,,	20	We paid A White by cheque £77
,,	24	D Williams paid us by cheque £300
,,	26	We paid O Oliver by cash £210
,,	28	D Williams paid us by cash £100
,,	30	F Franklin pays us by cheque £249

5.6A Enter the following, personal accounts only. Bring down balances at end of the month. After completing this state which of the balances represent debtors and those which are creditors.

19-7

May	1	Credit sales B Flynn £241, R Kelly £29, J Long £887, T Fryer £124
,,	2	Credit purchases from S Wood £148, T DuQuesnay £27, R Johnson £77, G Henriques £108
,,	8	Credit sales to R Kelly £74, J Long £132
,,	9	Credit purchases from T DuQuesnay £142, G Henriques £44
,,	10	Goods returned to us by J Long £17, T Fryer £44
,,	12	Cash paid to us by T Fryer £80
,,	15	We returned good to S Wood £8, G Henriques £18
,,	19	We received cheques from J Long £500, B Flynn £241
,,	21	We sold goods on credit to B Flynn £44, R Kelly £280
,,	28	We paid by cheque the following: S Wood £140; G Henriques £50; R Johnson £60
,,	31	We returned good to G Henriques £4.

5.7A Redraft each of the accounts given in your answer to 5.6A in three-column style accounts.

5.8A On 2 November 19-7 Fred Bilding set up in business on his own account as an Estate Agent. The following transactions occurred during the month of November:

Nov	2	Fred Bilding paid £10,000 into a bank account for the business and immediately withdrew £200 in cash.
Nov	3	An office was rented for the business and the rent of £750 for November was paid by cheque.
Nov	4	Office furniture costing £2,400 was purchased from Grumwicks plc under their 'interest-free' credit scheme. A down payment of £600 was paid immediately by cheque. The balance is to be paid in three equal monthly instalments.
Nov	5	A wordprocessor costing £525 was purchased for the office and paid for by cheque.
Nov	6	Office supplies of £155 were purchased and paid for by cheque.
Nov	13	Fred Bilding received a cheque for £600 as commission in respect of the sale of a client's home.

Nov 19 The home of another client, Jacob Podmore, was sold. The commission on this sale was £875 but it will not be received in cash until later in December.

Nov 25 Advertising bills totalling £410 were paid by cheque of which £110 was incurred advertising the home of Jacob Podmore. This amount is recoverable from the client.

Nov 26 Further office supplies costing £97 were purchased and paid for in cash.

Nov 28 Fred Bilding transferred £604 from his business bank account to his private bank account, £84 of which was to reimburse himself for motor expenses incurred on business use. The remaining £520 was withdrawn for private purposes.

Required:

(a) Show by means of ledger accounts how the above transactions would be recorded in the books of Fred Bilding, and

(b) Balance off those ledger accounts containing more than one entry as at 30 November 19-7 entering the correct balances in the accounts.

(*Association of Accounting Technicians*)

6

The trial balance

You have already seen that the method of book-keeping in use is that of the double-entry method. This means:
1 For each debit entry there is a corresponding credit entry.
2 For every credit entry there is a corresponding debit entry.

All the items recorded in all the accounts on the debit side should equal in *total* all the items recorded on the credit side of the books. To see if the two totals are equal, or in accounting terminology to see if the two sides of the books 'balance', a **Trial Balance** may be drawn up periodically.

A form of a trial balance could be drawn up by listing all the accounts and adding together all the debit entries, at the same time adding together all the credit entries. Using the worked exercise on pp 20-21 such a trial balance would appear as follows, bearing in mind that it could not be drawn up until after all the entries had been made, and will therefore be dated as on 31 May 19-6.

Trial Balance as at 31 December 19-6

	Dr	Cr
	£	£
Purchases	309	
Sales		255
Returns outwards		15
Returns inwards	16	
D Small	68	68
A Lyon & Son		141
D Hughes	60	60
M Spencer	45	16
Cash	210	153
	708	708

However, this is not the normal method of drawing up a trial balance, but it is the easiest to understand in the first instance. Usually, a trial balance is a list of balances only, arranged as to whether they are debit balances or credit balances. If the above trial balance had been drawn up using the conventional balances method it would have appeared as follows:

Trial Balance as on 31 May 19-6

	Dr	Cr
	£	£
Purchases	309	
Sales		255
Returns outwards		15
Returns inwards	16	
A Lyon & Son		141
M Spencer	29	
Cash	57	
	411	411

Here the two sides also 'balance'. The sums of £68 in D Small's account, £60 in D Hughes' account, £16 in M Spencer's account and £153 in the cash account have however been cancelled out from each side of these accounts by virtue of taking only the balances instead of totals. As equal amounts have been cancelled from each side, £297 in all, the new totals should still equal one another, as in fact they do at £411.

This latter form of trial balance is the easiest to extract when there are more than a few transactions during the period, also the balances are either used later when the profits are being calculated, or else appear in a balance sheet, so that it is not just for ascertaining whether or not errors have been made that trial balances are extracted.

Trial balances and errors

It may at first sight appear that the balancing of a trial balance proves that the books are correct. This however is quite wrong. It means that certain types of errors have not been made, but there are several types of errors that will not affect the balancing of a trial balance. Examples of the errors which would be revealed, provided there are no compensating errors which cancel them out, are errors in additions, using one figure for the debit entry and another figure for the credit entry, entering only one aspect of a transaction and so on. We shall consider these in greater detail in later chapters.

Multiple-choice self-test questions

A growing practice of examining boards is to set multiple-choice questions in Accounting.

Multiple-choice questions certainly give an examiner the opportunity to cover large parts of the syllabus briefly but in detail. Students who omit to study areas of the syllabus will be caught out by an examiner's judicious use of multiple-choice questions. No longer will it be possible to say that it is highly probable a certain topic will not be tested – the examiner can easily cover it with a multiple-choice question.

We have deliberately set blocks of multiple-choice questions at given places in this textbook, rather than a few at the end of each chapter. Such questions are relatively easy to answer a few minutes after reading the chapter. By asking the questions later your powers of recall and understanding are far better tested. It also gives you practice at answering a few questions in one block, as in an examination.

Each multiple-choice question has a 'stem', this is a part which poses the problem, a 'key' which is the one correct answer, and a number of 'distractors', i.e. incorrect answers. The key plus the distractors are known as the 'options'.

If you do not know the answer you should guess. You may be right by chance, or you may remember something subconsciously. In any event, unless the examiner warns otherwise, he will expect you to guess if you don't know the answer.

You should now attempt Set No 1, which contains 20 multiple choice questions, on page 488.

Review questions

6.1 You are to enter up the necessary amounts for the month of May from the following details, and then balance off the accounts and extract a trial balance as at 31 May 19-6.

19-6

May	1	Started firm with capital in cash of £250
,,	2	Bought goods on credit from the following persons: D Ellis £54; C Mendez £87; K Gibson £25; D Booth £76; L Lowe £64
,,	4	Sold goods on credit to: C Bailey £43; B Hughes £62; H Spencer £176
,,	6	Paid rent by cash £12
,,	9	Bailey paid us his account by cheque £43
,,	10	H Spencer paid us £150 by cheque
,,	12	We paid the following by cheque: K Gibson £25; D Ellis £54
,,	15	Paid carriage by cash £23
,,	18	Bought goods on credit from C Mendez £43; D Booth £110
,,	21	Sold goods on credit to B Hughes £67
,,	31	Paid rent by cheque £18.

6.2 Enter up the books from the following details for the month of March, and extract a trial balance as at 31 March 19-6.

19-6

March	1	Started business with £800 in the bank
,,	2	Bought goods on credit from the following persons: K Henriques £76; M Hyatt £27; T Braham £56
,,	5	Cash sales £87
,,	6	Paid wages in cash £14
,,	7	Sold goods on credit to: H Elliott £35; L Lane £42; J Carlton £72
,,	9	Bought goods for cash £46
,,	10	Bought goods on credit from: M Hyatt £57; T Braham £98
,,	12	Paid wages in cash £14
,,	13	Sold goods on credit to: L Lane £32; J Carlton £23
,,	15	Bought shop fixtures on credit from Betta Ltd £50
,,	17	Paid M Hyatt by cheque £84
,,	18	We returned goods to T Braham £20
,,	21	Paid Betta Ltd a cheque for £50
,,	24	J Carlton paid us his account by cheque £95
,,	27	We returned goods to K Henriques £24
,,	30	J King lent us £60 by cash
,,	31	Bought a motor van paying by cheque £400

6.3A Record the following details for the month of November 19-3 and extract a trial balance as at 30 November:

19-3

Nov	1	Started with £5,000 in the bank
,,	3	Bought goods on credit from: T Henriques £160; J Smith £230; W Rogers £400; P Boone £310
,,	5	Cash sales £240

,,	6	Paid rent by cheque £20
,,	7	Paid rates by cheque £190
,,	11	Sold goods on credit to: L Matthews £48; K Allen £32; R Hall £1,170
,,	17	Paid wages by cash £40
,,	18	We returned goods to: T Henriques £14; P Boone £20
,,	19	Bought goods on credit from: P Boone £80; W Rogers £270; D Diaz £130
,,	20	Goods were returned to us by K Alberga £2; L Matthews £4
,,	21	Bought motor van on credit from U Z Motors £500
,,	23	We paid the following by cheque: T Henriques £146; J Smith £230; W Rogers £300
,,	25	Bought another motor van, paying by cheque immediately £700
,,	26	Received a loan of £400 cash from A Williams
,,	28	Received cheques from: L Matthews £44; K Allen £30
,,	30	Proprietor brings a further £300 into the business, by a payment into the business bank account.

6.4A Record the following for the month of January, balance off all the accounts, and then extract a trial balance as at 31 January 19-4:

19-4

Jan	1	Started business with £3,500 cash
,,	2	Put £2,800 of the cash into a bank account
,,	3	Bought goods for cash £150
,,	4	Bought goods on credit from L Coke £360; M Burton £490; T Hill £110; C Small £340
,,	5	Bought stationery on credit from Swift Ltd £170
,,	6	Sold goods on credit to: S Walters £90; T Binns £150; C Howard £190; P Peart £160
,,	8	Paid rent by cheque £55
,,	10	Bought fixtures on credit from Matalon Ltd £480
,,	11	Paid salaries in cash £120
,,	14	Returned goods to M Burton £40; T Hill £60
,,	15	Bought motor van by cheque £700
,,	16	Received loan from J Henry by cheque £600
,,	18	Goods returned to us by: S Walters £20; C Howard £40
,,	21	Cash sales £90
,,	24	Sold goods on credit to: T Binns £100; P Peart £340; J Smart £115
,,	26	We paid the following by cheque: M Burton £450; T Hill £50
,,	29	Received cheques from: J Smart £115; T Binns £250
,,	30	Received a further loan from J Henry by cash £200
,,	30	Received £500 cash from P Peart.

7

Trading and profit and loss accounts: an introduction

Probably the main objective of the accounting function is the calculation of the profits earned by a business or the losses incurred by it. The earning of profit is after all usually the main reason why the business was set up in the first place, and the proprietor will want to know for various reasons how much profit has been made. First he will want to know how the actual profits compare with the profits he had hoped to make. He may also want to know his profits for such diverse reasons as: to assist him to plan ahead, to help him to obtain a loan from a bank or from a private individual, to show to a prospective partner or to a person to whom he hopes to sell the business, or maybe he will need to know his profits for income tax purposes.

Chapter 4 dealt with the grouping of revenue and expenses prior to bringing them together to compute profit. In the case of a trader, meaning by this someone who is mainly concerned with buying and selling, the profits are calculated by drawing up a special account called a **Trading and Profit and Loss Account**. For a manufacturer it is also useful to prepare **Manufacturing Accounts** as well, but this will be dealt with in a later chapter.

Undoubtedly one of the most important uses of the trading and profit and loss account is comparing the results obtained with the results expected. Many businesses attach a great deal of importance to their gross profit percentage. This is the amount of **Profit** made, before deducting expenses, for every £100 of sales. In order that this may easily be deduced from the profit calculations, the account in which profit is computed is split into two sections – one in which the **Gross Profit** is found, and the next section in which the **Net Profit** is calculated.

Gross Profit (calculated in the Trading Account)	This is the excess of sales over the cost of goods sold in the period.
Net Profit (calculated in the Profit and Loss Account)	What remains after all other costs used up in the period have been deducted from the gross profit.

The gross profit, found by the use of the **Trading Account**, is the excess of sales over the cost of goods sold. The net profit, found when the **Profit and Loss Account** is prepared, consists of the gross profit plus any revenue other than that from sales, such as discounts received or commissions earned, less the total costs used up during the period. Where the cost of goods sold is greater than the sales the result would be a **Gross Loss**, but this is a relatively rare occurrence. Where the costs used up exceed the gross profit plus other revenue then the result is said to be a **Net Loss**. By taking the figure of sales less the cost of goods sold, it can be seen that the accounting custom is to calculate a trader's profits only when the goods have been disposed of and not before.

As was seen in Chapter 4, profit increases the capital of the proprietor, profit in this context meaning the net profit. The fact that an interim figure of profit, known as the gross profit is calculated, is due to the two figures of profit being more useful for purposes of comparison with both these profits of previous periods, than by just comparing net profits only. Were it not for this accounting custom it would not be necessary to calculate gross profit at all.

The trial balance of B Swift, Exhibit 7.1 drawn up as on 31 December 19-5 after the completion of his first year in business can now be looked at.

Exhibit 7.1

B Swift
Trial Balance as on 31 December 19-5

	Dr	Cr
	£	£
Sales		3,850
Purchases	2,900	
Rent	240	
Lighting expenses	150	
General expenses	60	
Fixtures and fittings	500	
Debtors	680	
Creditors		910
Bank	1,510	
Cash	20	
Drawings	700	
Capital		2,000
	6,760	6,760

The first task is to draw up the trading account using the above information. Immediately there is a problem. Sales less the cost of goods sold is the definition of gross profit, but purchases will only equal cost of goods sold if in fact all the goods purchased had been sold leaving no stock of goods on 31 December 19-5. It would be normal to find that a trader always keeps a stock of goods for resale, as the stock of goods is constantly being replenished. However, there is no record in the books of the value of the stock of unsold goods, and the only way that Swift can find this out is by stock-taking on 31 December 19-5 after the business of that day. By stock-taking is meant that he would make a list of all the unsold goods and then find out their value. The value he would normally place on them would be the cost price of the goods. Assume that this was £300. Then the cost of purchases less the cost of unsold goods would equal the cost of goods sold, ignoring losses by theft or wastage. This figure would then be deducted from the figure of sales to find the gross profit.

Swift could perform this calculation arithmetically:

Sales – Cost of goods sold = Gross Profit
  (Purchases – unsold stock)
£3,850 – (£2,900 – £300) = £1,250

This however is not performing the task by using double entry accounts. In double entry the balance of the sales account is transferred to the trading account by debiting the sales account (thus closing it) and crediting the trading account. The balance of the purchases account would then be transferred by crediting the purchases account (thus losing it) and debiting the trading account. Now the accounts connected with stock movements have been closed, and accounts are being drawn up to a point in time, in this case 31 December 19-5. At this point of time Swift has an asset, namely stock (of unsold goods), for which no account exists. This must be rectified by opening a stock account and debiting the amount of the asset to it. Now as already stated, the closing stock needs to be brought into the calculation of the gross profit, and the calculation of the gross profit is effected in the trading account. Therefore the credit for the closing stock should be in the trading account thus completing the double entry.

It is now usual for the trading and profit and loss accounts to be shown under one combined heading, the trading account being the top section and the profit and loss account being the lower section of this combined account.

B Swift

Trading and Profit and Loss Account for the year ended 31 December 19-5

	£		£
Purchases	2,900	Sales	3,850
Gross profit c/d	1,250	Closing stock	300
	4,150		4,150
		Gross profit b/d	1,250

The balance shown on the trading account is shown as gross profit rather than being described as a balance. When found the gross profit is carried down to the profit and loss section of the account.

The accounts so far used appear as follows:

Sales

19-5	£	19-5	£
Dec 31 Trading	3,850	Dec 31 Balance b/d	3,850

Purchases

19-5	£	19-5	£
Dec 31 Balance b/d	2,900	Dec 31 Trading	2,900

Stock

19-5	£
Dec 31 Trading	300

The entry of the Closing Stock on the credit side of the trading and profit and loss account is in effect a deduction from the puchases on the debit side. In present-day accounting it is usual to find the closing stock actually shown as a deduction from the puchases on the debit side, and the figure then disclosed being described as 'cost of goods sold'. This is illustrated in Exhibit 7.2

The profit and loss account can now be drawn up. Any revenue accounts, other than sales which have already been dealt with, would be transferred to the credit of the profit and loss account. Typical examples are commissions received and rent received. In the case of B Swift there are no such revenue accounts.

The costs used up in the year, in other words the expenses of the year, are transferred to the debit of the profit and loss account. It may also be thought, quite rightly so, that as the fixtures and fittings have been used during the year with the subsequent deterioration of the asset, that something should be charged for this use. The methods for doing this are left until Chapter 20.

The revised trading account with the addition of the profit and loss account will now appear as follows:

Exhibit 7.2

B Swift

Trading and Profit and Loss Account for the year ended 31 December 19-5

	£		£
Purchases	2,900	Sales	3,850
Less Closing stock	300		
	———		
Cost of goods sold	2,600		
Gross Profit	c/d 1,250		
	———		———
	3,850		3,850
	=====		=====
Rent	240	Gross Profit b/d	1,250
Lighting expenses	150		
General expenses	60		
Net Profit	800		
	———		———
	1,250		1,250
	=====		=====

The expense accounts closed off will now appear as:

Rent

19-5	£	19-5	£
Dec 31 Balance b/d	240	Dec 31 Profit and Loss	240
	=====		=====

Lighting Expenses

19-5	£	19-5	£
Dec 31 Balance b/d	150	Dec 31 Profit and Loss	150
	=====		=====

General Expenses

19-5	£	19-5	£
Dec 31 Balance b/d	60	Dec 31 Profit and Loss	60
	=====		=====

Net profit increases the capital of the proprietor. The credit entry for the net profit is therefore in the capital account. The trading and profit and loss accounts, and indeed all the revenue and expense accounts can thus be seen to be devices whereby the capital account is saved from being concerned with unnecessary detail. Every sale of a good at a profit increases the capital of the proprietor as does each item of revenue such as rent received. On the other hand each sale of a good at a loss, or each item of expense decreases the capital of the proprietor. Instead of altering the capital afresh after each transaction the respective items of profit and loss and of revenue and expense are collected together using suitably described accounts. Then the whole of the details are brought together in one set of accounts, the trading and profit and loss account and the increase to the capital, i.e. the net profit is determined. Alternatively, the decrease in the capital as represented by the Net Loss is ascertained.

The fact that a separate drawings account has been in use can now also be seen to have been in keeping with the policy of avoiding unnecessary detail in the capital account. There will thus be one figure for drawings which will be the total of the drawings for the whole of the period, and will be transferred to the debit of the capital account.

The capital account, showing these transfers, and the drawings account now closed is as follows:

Capital

19-5		£	19-5			£
Dec 31	Drawings	700	Jan 1	Cash		2,000
,, 31	Balance c/d	2,100	Dec 31	Net Profit from Profit and Loss		800
		2,800				2,800
			19-6			
			Jan 1	Balance b/d		2,100

Drawings

19-5		£	19-5		£
Dec 31	Balance b/d	700	Dec 31 Capital		700

It should be noticed that not all the items in the trial balance have been used in the Trading and Profit and Loss Account. The remaining balances are assets or liabilities or capital, they are not expenses or sales. These will be used up later when a balance sheet is drawn up, for as has been shown in Chapter 1, assets, liabilities and capital are shown in balance sheets.

In Exhibit 7.3, although it is not necessary to redraft the trial balance after the trading and profit and loss accounts have been prepared, it will be useful to do so in order to establish which balances still remain in the books. The first thing to notice is that the stock account, not originally in the trial balance, is in the redrafted trial balance, as the item was not created as a balance in the books until the trading account was prepared. These balances will be used by us when we start to look at the balance sheets.

Exhibit 7.3

B Swift

Trial Balance as on 31 December 19-5
(after Trading and Profit and Loss Accounts completed)

	Dr	Cr
	£	£
Fixtures and fittings	500	
Debtors	680	
Creditors		910
Stock	300	
Bank	1,510	
Cash	20	
Capital		2,100
	3,010	3,010

Review questions

7.1 From the following trial balance of B Webb, extracted after one year's trading, prepare a trading and profit and loss account for the year ended 31 December 19-6. A balance sheet is not required.

Trial Balance as on 31 December 19-6

	Dr	Cr
	£	£
Sales		18,462
Purchases	14,629	
Salaries	2,150	
Motor expensess	520	
Rent	670	
Insurance	111	
General expenses	105	
Premises	1,500	
Motor vehicles	1,200	
Debtors	1,950	
Creditors		1,538
Cash at bank	1,654	
Cash in hand	40	
Drawings	895	
Capital		5,424
	25,424	25,424

Stock at 31 December 19-6 was £2,548.

(Keep your answer, it will be used later in question 8.1)

7.2 From the following trial balance of C Worth after his first year's trading, you are required to draw up a trading and profit and loss account for the year ended 30 June 19-4. A balance sheet is not required.

Trial Balance as on 30 June 19-4

	Dr	Cr
	£	£
Sales		28,794
Purchases	23,803	
Rent	854	
Lighting and heating expenses	422	
Salaries and wages	3,164	
Insurance	105	
Buildings	50,000	
Fixtures	1,000	
Debtors	3,166	
Sundry expenses	506	
Creditors		1,206
Cash at bank	3,847	
Drawings	2,400	
Motor vans	5,500	
Motor running expenses	1,133	
Capital		65,900
	95,900	95,900

Stock at 30 June 19-4 was £4,166.

(Keep your answer, it will be used later in question 8.2)

7.3A From the following trial balance of F Chaplin drawn up on conclusion of his first year in business, draw up a trading and profit and loss account for the year ended 31 December 19-8. A balance sheet is not required.

Trial Balance as on 31 December 19-8

	Dr	Cr
	£	£
General expenses	210	
Rent	400	
Motor expenses	735	
Salaries	3,560	
Insurance	392	
Purchases	18,385	
Sales		26,815
Motor vehicle	2,800	
Creditors		5,160
Debtors	4,090	
Premises	20,000	
Cash at bank	1,375	
Cash in hand	25	
Capital		24,347
Drawings	4,350	
	56,322	56,322

Stock at 31 December 19-8 was £4,960.

(Keep your answer, it will be used later in question 8.3A)

7.4A Extract a trading and profit and loss account for the year ended 30 June 19-4 for F Kidd. The trial balance as at 30 June 19-4 after his first year of trading, was as follows:

	Dr	Cr
	£	£
Rent	1,560	
Insurance	305	
Lighting and heating expenses	516	
Motor expenses	1,960	
Salaries and wages	4,850	
Sales		35,600
Purchases	30,970	
Sundry expenses	806	
Motor vans	3,500	
Creditors		3,250
Debtors	6,810	
Fixtures	3,960	
Buildings	28,000	
Cash at bank	1,134	
Drawings	6,278	
Capital		51,799
	90,649	90,649

Stock at 30 June 19-4 was £9,960.

(Keep your answer, it will be used later in question 8.4A)

8
Balance sheets

After the trading and profit and loss accounts have been completed, a statement is drawn up in which the remaining balances in the books are arranged according to whether they are asset balances or liability or capital balances. This statement is called a balance sheet (*see* Chapter 1). The assets are shown on the left-hand side and the liabilities on the right-hand side.

It is very important to know that the balance sheet is not part of the double- entry system. This contrasts with the trading and profit and loss account which is part of double-entry. The use of the word 'account' indicates that it is part of double-entry.

It was seen in the last chapter that when sales, purchases and the various expenses were taken into the profit calculations an entry was actually made in each account showing that the item had been transferred to the trading account or the profit and loss account. The balance sheet however is not part of double-entry, it is simply a list of the balances remaining after the trading and profit and loss accounts have been prepared. Therefore items are *not* transferred from accounts to the balance sheet, and accordingly entries are *not* made in the various accounts when a balance sheet is drawn up.

In Exhibit 8.1 the trial balance is shown again of B Swift as on 31 December 19-5 *after* the Trading and Profit and Loss Account had been prepared.

Exhibit 8.1

B Swift
Trial Balance as at 31 December 19-5
(after Trading and Profit and Loss Accounts completed)

	Dr	Cr
	£	£
Fixtures and fittings	500	
Debtors	680	
Creditors		910
Stock	300	
Bank	1,510	
Cash	20	
Capital		2,100
	3,010	3,010

A balance sheet, Exhibit 8.2, can now be drawn up as at 31 December 19-5. At this point we will not worry whether or not the balance sheet is set out in good style.

Exhibit 8.2

B Swift
Balance Sheet as at 31 December 19-5

Assets	£	Capital and liabilities	£
Fixtures and fittings	500	Capital	2,100
Stock	300	Creditors	910
Debtors	680		
Bank	1,510		
Cash	20		
	3,010		3,010

Remember, all of the balances per Exhibit 8.1 still remain in the accounts, *no* entries were made in the accounts for the purpose of drawing up the balance sheet. As has been stated already, this is in direct contrast to the trading and profit and loss accounts. The word 'account' means in fact that it is part of the double entry system, so that anything which is not an account is outside the double entry system.

Balance sheet layout

You would not expect to go into a first-class store and see the goods for sale all mixed up and not laid out properly. You would expect that the goods would be so displayed so that you could easily find them. Similarly in balance sheets we do not want all the items shown in any order. We would really want them displayed so that desirable information could easily be seen.

For people such as bank managers, accountants and investors who look at a lot of different balance sheets, we would want to keep to a set pattern so as to enable comparison of balance sheets to be made easier. What you are about to look at is a suggested method for displaying items in balance sheets.

Let us look at the assets side first. We are going to show the assets under two headings, **Fixed Assets** and **Current Assets**.

Assets are called Fixed Assets when they are of long life, are to be used in the business and were *not* bought with the main purpose of resale. Examples are buildings, machinery, motor vehicles and fixtures and fittings.

On the other hand, assets are called Current Assets when they represent cash or are primarily for conversion into cash or have a short life. An example of a short-lived asset is that of the stock of oil held to power the boilers in a factory, as this will be used up in the near future. Other examples of current assets are cash itself, stocks of goods, debtors and bank balances.

There is a choice of two methods of listing the assets under their respective headings. The first, being the most preferable since it helps standardise the form of sole traders' accounts with those of limited companies, is that the assets are listed starting with the most permanent asset, or to put it another way, the most difficult to turn into cash, progressing to the asset which is least permanent or easiest to turn into cash. The fixed assets will thus appear under that heading followed by the current assets under their heading. The other method, used by banks but fast falling into disuse in most other kinds of organisations, is the complete opposite. In this method it is the least permanent asset that appears first and the most permanent asset which appears last.

Using the first method an illustration may now be seen of the order in which assets are displayed:

Fixed Assets
Land and buildings
Fixtures and fittings
Machinery
Motor Vehicles
Current Assets
Stock
Debtors
Bank
Cash

The order with which most students would disagree is that stock has appeared before debtors. On first sight stock would appear to be more easily realisable than debtors. In fact, however, debtors could normally be more quickly turned into cash by factorising them, i.e. selling the rights to the amounts owing to a finance company for an agreed amount. On the other hand, to dispose of all the stock of a business is often a long and difficult task. Another advantage is that the method follows the order in which full realisation of the assets takes place. First, before any sale takes place there must be a stock of goods, which when sold on credit turns into debtors, and when payment is made by the debtors it turns into cash.

The order of the other side of the balance sheet is preferably that of starting with capital, progressing via **long-term liabilities** such as loans not requiring repayment within the near future, and finishing with **current liabilities**, being liabilities such as debts for goods which will have to be discharged in the near future. This then would be the order in which the claims against the assets would be met. The other method of listing the liabilities is the complete opposite of this, starting with current liabilities and finishing at the bottom with capital. This method conflicts with company accounts and is best avoided if the benefits of standardisation are to be attained.

Exhibit 8.3 shows Exhibit 8.2 drawn up in better style. Also read the notes following the exhibit.

Exhibit 8.3

B Swift
Balance Sheet as at 31 December 19-5

	£	£		£	£
Fixed Assets			*Capital*		
Furniture and fittings		500	Cash introduced	2,000	
			Add Net profit		
Current Assets			for the year	800	
Stock	300				
Debtors	680			2,800	
Bank	1,510		*Less* Drawings	700	
Cash	20				2,100
		2,510	*Current Liabilities*		
			Creditors		910
		3,010			3,010

Notes to Exhibit 8.3

1   A total for capital and for each class of assets and liabilities should be shown, e.g. the £2,510 total of current assets. For this purpose the individual figures of current assets are inset and the resultant total extended into the end column.

2   It is not necessary to write the word 'account' after each item.

3   The proprietor will obviously be most interested in his capital. To have merely shown the balance of £2,100 would invariably invite his request to show how the final balance of the capital account had been arrived at. To overcome this, accounting custom always shows the full details of the capital account. Compare this with the other items above where only the closing balance is shown.

4   Compare the date on the balance sheet with that on the trading and profit and loss account. You can see from these that the essential natures of these two statements are revealed. A trading and profit and loss account is a period statement, because it covers a specified period of time, in this case the whole of 19-5. On the other hand a balance sheet is a position statement; it is drawn up at a particular point in time, in this case at the precise end of 19-5.

The next step

Before attempting any of the review questions which follow, you should read Appendix I on page 481.

The reason for this instruction should be obvious to you after reading the Appendix. If effort is needed to bring work to the required standard, it is more likely that the effort will be made if you can understand why the author should make such a request.

Review questions

8.1   Complete question 7.1 by drawing up a balance sheet as at 31 December 19-6.

8.2   Complete question 7.2 by drawing up a balance sheet as at 30 June 19-4.

8.3A   Complete question 7.3A by drawing up a balance sheet as at 31 December 19-8.

8.4A   Complete question 7.4A by drawing up a balance sheet as at 30 June 19-4.

9

Trading and profit and loss accounts and balance sheets: further considerations

Returns inwards and returns outwards

In Chapter 3 the idea of different accounts for different movements of stock was introduced. There were accordingly sales, purchases, returns inwards and returns outwards accounts. In our first look at the preparation of a trading account in Chapter 7, returns inwards and returns outwards were omitted. This was done deliberately so that the first sight of trading and profit and loss accounts would not be a difficult one.

However, a large number of firms will return goods to their suppliers (returns outwards), and will have goods returned to them by their customers (returns inwards). When the gross profit is calculated these returns will have to come into the calculations. Suppose that in Exhibit 7.1, the trial balance of B Swift, the balances showing stock movements had instead been as follows:

Trial Balance as at 31 December 19-5

	Dr	Cr
	£	£
Sales		4,000
Purchases	3,120	
Returns inwards	150	
Returns outwards		220

Looking at Exhibit 7.1 it can be seen that originally the example used was of Sales £3,850 and Purchases £2,900. If it had been as now shown instead, the Trading Account can be shown as it would have been for the year, and what gross profit would have been.

Comparing the two instances, they do in fact amount to the same things as far as gross profit is concerned. Sales were £3,850 in the original example. In the new example returns inwards should be deducted to get the correct figure for goods sold to customers and *kept* by them, i.e. £4,000 − £150 = £3,850. Purchases were £2,900; in the new example returns outwards should be deducted to get the correct figure of purchases *kept* by Swift. The gross profit will remain at £1,250 as per Exhibit 7.1

The trading account will appear as in Exhibit 9.1.

Exhibit 9.1

Trading and Profit and Loss Account for the year ended 31 December 19-5

	£	£		£	£
Purchases	3,120		Sales	4,000	
Less Returns outwards	220	2,900	*Less* Returns inwards	150	3,850
Less Closing stock		300			
Cost of goods sold		2,600			
Gross profit c/d		1,250			
		3,850			3,850

The term used for Sales less Returns Inwards is often called 'Turnover'. In the illustration in Exhibit 9.1 it is £3,850.

Carriage

Carriage (cost of transport of goods) into a firm is called **carriage inwards**. Carriage of goods out of a firm to its customers is called **carriage outwards**.

When goods are bought the cost of carriage inwards may either be included as part of the price, or else the firm may have to pay separately for it. Suppose the firm was buying exactly the same goods. One supplier might sell them for £100, and he would deliver the goods and not send you a bill for carriage. Another supplier might sell the goods for £95, but you would have to pay £5 to a haulage firm for carriage inwards, i.e. a total cost of £100.

To keep cost of buying goods being shown on the same basis, carriage inwards is always added to the purchases in the trading account.

Carriage outwards to customers is not part of our firm's expenses in buying goods, and is always entered in the profit and loss account.

Suppose that in the illustration shown in this chapter, the goods had been bought for the same total figure of £3,120, but in fact £2,920 was the figure for purchases and £200 for carriage inwards. The trial balance and trading account appear as Exhibit 9.2.

Exhibit 9.2

Trial Balance as at 31 December 19-5

	Dr	Cr
	£	£
Sales		4,000
Purchases	2,920	
Returns inwards	150	
Returns outwards		220
Carriage inwards	200	

Trading and Profit and Loss Account for the year ended 31 December 19-5

	£	£		£	£
Purchases	2,920		Sales	4,000	
Less Returns outwards	220	2,700	*Less* Returns inwards	150	3,850
Carriage inwards		200			
		2,900			
Less Closing stock		300			
Cost of goods sold		2,600			
Gross profit c/d		1,250			
		3,850			3,850
			Gross profit b/d		1,250

It can be seen that Exhibits 7.1, 9.1 and 9.2 have been concerned with the same overall amount of goods bought and sold by the firm, at the same overall prices. Therefore, as shown, in each case the same gross profit of £1,250 is shown.

Before you proceed further you are to attempt Exercises 9.1 and 9.2A.

Swift's second year

At the end of his second year of trading, on 31 December 19-6, B Swift extracts another trial balance.

Exhibit 9.3

B Swift
Trial Balance as at 31 December 19-6

	Dr	Cr
	£	£
Sales		6,700
Purchases	4,260	
Lighting and Heating expenses	190	
Rent	240	
Wages: shop assistant	520	
General expenses	70	
Carriage outwards	110	
Buildings	2,000	
Fixtures and fittings	750	
Debtors	1,200	
Creditors		900
Bank	120	
Cash	40	
Loan from J Marsh		1,000
Drawings	900	
Capital		2,100
Stock (at 31 December 19-5)	300	
	10,700	10,700

The stock shown in the trial balance is that brought forward from the previous year on 31 December 19-5; it is therefore the opening stock of 19-6. The closing stock at 31 December 19-6 can only be found by stocktaking. Assume it amounts at cost to be £550.

First of all calculate the cost of goods sold, showing the calculation in a normal arithmetical fashion.

	£
Stock of goods at start of year	300
add purchases	4,260
Total goods available for sale	4,560
less what remains at the end of the year:	
i.e stock of goods at close	550
Therefore cost of goods that have been sold	4,010

Now look at the diagram to illustrate this in Exhibit 9.4.

Exhibit 9.4

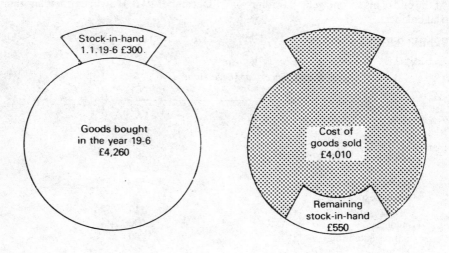

The sales were £6,700, so Sales £6,700 − Cost of Goods Sold £4,010 = Gross Profit £2,690.

Now the trading and profit and loss accounts can be drawn up using double-entry. *See* Exhibit 9.5.

Exhibit 9.5

B Swift

Trading and Profit and Loss Account for the year ended 31 December 19-6

	£		£
Opening stock	300	Sales	6,700
add Purchases	4,260		
	4,560		
less Closing stock	550		
Cost of goods sold	4,010		
Gross profit c/d	2,690		
	6,700		6,700
Wages	520	Gross profit b/d	2,690
Lighting and heating expenses	190		
Rent	240		
General expenses	70		
Carriage outwards	110		
Net profit	1,560		
	2,690		2,690

The balances now remaining in the books, including the new balance on the stock account, are now drawn up in the form of a balance sheet. *See* Exhibit 9.6.

Exhibit 9.6

B Swift

Balance Sheet as at 31 December 19-6

Fixed Assets	£	£	*Capital*	£	£
Buildings		2,000	Balance 1 Jan 19-6	2,100	
Fixtures and fittings		750	Add Net Profit for year	1,560	
		2,750		3,660	
			less Drawings	900	
Current Assets					2,760
Stock	550		*Long-term Liability*		
Debtors	1,200		Loan from J Marsh		1,000
Bank	120		*Current Liabilities*		
Cash	40		Creditors		900
		1,910			
		4,660			4,660

61

Stock account

It is perhaps helpful if the stock account covering both years can now be seen:

Stock

19-5		£	19-6		£
Dec 31 Trading A/c		300	Jan 1 Trading A/c		300
19-6					
Dec 31 Trading A/c		550			

Final accounts

The term **Final Accounts** is often used to mean collectively the trading and profit and loss account and the balance sheet. The term can be misleading as the balance sheet is not an account.

Other expenses in the trading account

The cost of putting goods into a saleable condition should be charged in the Trading Account. In the case of a trader these are relatively few. An instance could be a trader who sells clocks packed in boxes. If he bought the clocks from one source, and the boxes from another source, both of these items would be charged in the Trading Account as Purchases. In addition, if a man's wages are paid to pack the clocks, then such wages would be charged in the Trading Account. The wages of shop assistants who sold the clocks would be charged in the Profit and Loss Account. The wages of the man packing the clocks would be the only wages in this instance concerned with 'putting the goods into a saleable condition'.

Review questions

9.1 From the following details draw up the Trading Account of T Clarke for the year ended 31 December 19-3, which was his first year in business:

	£
Carriage inwards	670
Returns outwards	495
Returns inwards	890
Sales	38,742
Purchases	33,333
Stocks of goods: 31 December 19-3	7,489

9.2A The following details for the year ended 31 March 19-8 are available. Draw up the Trading Account of K Taylor for that year.

	£
Stocks: 31 March 19-8	18,504
Returns inwards	1,372
Returns outwards	2,896
Purchases	53,397
Carriage inwards	1,122
Sales	54,600

9.3 From the following trial balance of R Graham draw up a trading and profit and loss account for the year ended 30 September 19-6, and a balance sheet as at that date.

	Dr	Cr
	£	£
Stock 1 October 19-5	2,368	
Carriage outwards	200	
Carriage inwards	310	
Returns inwards	205	
Returns outwards		322
Purchases	11,874	
Sales		18,600
Salaries and wages	3,862	
Rent	304	
Insurance	78	
Motor expenses	664	
Office expenses	216	
Lighting and heating expenses	166	
General expenses	314	
Premises	5,000	
Motor vehicles	1,800	
Fixtures and fittings	350	
Debtors	3,896	
Creditors		1,731
Cash at bank	482	
Drawings	1,200	
Capital		12,636
	33,289	33,289

Stock at 30 September 19-6 was £2,946.

9.4 The following trial balance was extracted from the books of B Jackson on 30 April 19-7. From it, and the notes, prepare his Trading and Profit and Loss Account for the year ended 30 April 19-7, and a balance sheet as at that date.

	Dr	Cr
	£	£
Sales		18,600
Purchases	11,556	
Stock 1 May 19-6	3,776	
Carriage outwards	326	
Carriage inwards	234	
Returns inwards	440	
Returns outwards		355
Salaries and wages	2,447	
Motor expenses	664	
Rent	576	
Sundry expenses	1,202	
Motor vehicles	2,400	
Fixtures and fittings	600	
Debtors	4,577	
Creditors		3,045
Cash at bank	3,876	
Cash in hand	120	
Drawings	2,050	
Capital		12,844
	34,844	34,844

Stock at 30 April 19-7 was £4,998.

9.5A The following is the trial balance of J Smailes as at 31 March 19-6. Draw up a set of final accounts for the year ended 31 March 19-6.

	Dr	Cr
	£	£
Stock 1 April 19-5	18,160	
Sales		92,340
Purchases	69,185	
Carriage inwards	420	
Carriage outwards	1,570	
Returns outwards		640
Wages and salaries	10,240	
Rent and rates	3,015	
Communication expenses	624	
Commissions payable	216	
Insurance	405	
Sundry expenses	318	
Buildings	20,000	
Debtors	14,320	
Creditors		8,160
Fixtures	2,850	
Cash at bank	2,970	
Cash in hand	115	
Loan from K Ball		10,000
Drawings	7,620	
Capital		40,888
	152,028	152,028

Stock at 31 March 19-6 was £22,390.

9.6A L Stokes drew up the following trial balance as at 30 September 19-8. You are to draft the Trading and Profit and Loss Account for the year to 30 September 19-8 and a balance sheet as at that date.

	Dr	Cr
	£	£
Loan from P Owens		5,000
Capital		25,955
Drawings	8,420	
Cash at bank	3,115	
Cash in hand	295	
Debtors	12,300	
Creditors		9,370
Stock 30 September 19-7	23,910	
Motor van	4,100	
Office equipment	6,250	
Sales		130,900
Purchases	92,100	
Returns inwards	550	
Carriage inwards	215	
Returns outwards		307
Carriage outwards	309	
Motor expenses	1,630	
Rent	2,970	
Telephone charges	405	
Wages and salaries	12,810	
Insurance	492	
Office expenses	1,377	
Sundry expenses	284	
	171,532	171,532

Stock at 30 September 19-8 was £27,475.

10

Accounting concepts and Statements of Standard Accounting Practice

This book so far has been concerned with the recording of transactions in the books. Much of the rest of the book is about the classifying, summarising and interpreting of the records that have been made. Before this second stage is reached it would be beneficial for the reader to examine the concepts of accounting, and the **Statements of Standard Accounting Practice** (from now on this will be abbreviated as SSAP).

The work that you have done in this subject so far has been based on various assumptions. These assumptions have deliberately not been discussed in much detail, they are much easier to understand after basic double entry has been dealt with. These assumptions are known as the 'concepts' of accounting.

The trading and profit and loss account and balance sheets shown in the previous chapter were drawn up so as to be of benefit to the owner of the business. Of course, as is shown later in the book, businesses are often owned by more than just one person and these accounting statements are for the benefit of them all. Now in the case of a sole trader he may well also use copies of the Final Accounts for the purpose of showing them as evidence when he wants to obtain a loan from a bank or from some other person. He may well also show a copy to someone who is interested in buying his business from him, or if he wants to have extended credit for a large amount from a supplier, as proof of his financial stability. In the case of partners and shareholders for businesses owned by more than one person the final accounts will be used for similar purposes.

Now of course if it had always been the custom to draft different kinds of final accounts for different purposes, so that one type was given to a banker, another type to someone wishing to buy the business, etc., then Accounting would be different than it is today. However, as yet it is deemed appropriate to give copies of the same set of final accounts to all the various parties, so that the banker, the prospective buyer of the business, the owner and the other people involved see the same Trading and Profit and Loss Account and Balance Sheet. This is not really an ideal situation as the interests of each party are different and really demand different kinds of information from that possessed by the others. For instance the bank manager would really like to know how much the assets would fetch if the firm ceased trading, so that he could judge in that case what the possibility would be of the bank obtaining repayment of its loan. Other parties would also like to see the information expressed in terms of values which were relevant to them. Yet in fact normally only one sort of final accounts is available for these different parties.

This means that Trading and Profit and Loss Accounts are multi-purpose documents, and to be of any use the various parties have to agree to the way in which they are drawn up. Assume that you are in a class of students and that you are faced with the problem of valuing your assets, which consists of ten textbooks. The first value you decide to assess is that of how much you could sell them for. Your own assessment is £30, but the other members of the class may give figures ranging from, say, £15 to £50. Suppose that you now decide to put a value on their use to you. You may well think that the use of these books will enable you to pass your examinations and so you will get a good job. Another person may well have completely the opposite idea concerning the use of the books to him. The use values placed on the book by individuals will therefore tend to vary widely. Finally you decide to value them by reference to cost. You take out of your pocket the bills for the books which show that you paid a total of £60 for the books. Assuming that the rest of the class do not think that you have altered the bills in any way, then they also can all agree that the value expressed as cost is £60. As this is the only value that you can all agree to then each of you decides to use the idea of showing the value of his asset of books at the cost price.

The use of a measure which gains consensus of opinion, rather than to use one's own measure which might conflict with other people's, is said to be objective. Thus the use of cost for asset valuation is an attempt to be objective. On the other hand the use of your own measure irrespective of whether people agree with it or not is said to be subjective. The desire to provide the same set of accounts for many different parties, and thus to provide a measure that gains their consensus of opinion, means that objectivity is sought for in financial accounting. If you are able to understand this desire for objectivity, then many of the apparent contradictions can be understood because it is often at the heart of the financial accounting methods in use at the present time.

Financial accounting seeks objectivity, and of course it must have rules which lay down the way in which the activities of the business are recorded. These rules are known as concepts.

Basic concepts

The cost concept

The need for this has already been described. It means that assets are normally shown at cost price, and that this is the basis for assessing the future usage of the asset.

The money measurement concept

Accounting is only concerned with those facts that can be measured in monetary terms with a fair degree of objectivity. This means that accounting can never show the whole of the information needed to give you a full picture of the state of the business or how well it is being conducted. Accounting does not record that the firm has a good, or a bad, management team. It does not show that the poor morale prevalent among the staff is about to lead to a serious strike, or that various managers will not co-operate with one another. Nor would it reveal that a rival product is about to take over a larger part of the market occupied at present by the firm's own goods.

This means quite simply that just looking at a set of accounting figures does not tell you all that you would like to know about a business. Some people imagine that accounting gives you a full picture, but from what has been said they are quite obviously deluding themselves. Others would maintain that really accounting ought to put monetary values on these other factors as yet ignored in accounting. Those who object to this state that this would mean a considerable loss of objectivity. Imagine trying to place a value of the future services to be given to the firm by one of its managers. Different people would tend to give different figures, and so, at present, as the final accounts are of a multi-purpose nature, which figures would be acceptable to the many parties who use the accounts? As the answer is that no one set of acceptable figures could be agreed in this case by all parties, then in accounting as it stands the task is just not undertaken at all. It would seem likely that, eventually the vital factor of placing a value on labour and management, usually known as **human asset** accounting, will play a full part in the construction of balance sheets.

The going concern concept

Unless the opposite is known accounting always assumes that the business will continue to operate for an indefinitely long period of time. Only if the business was going to be sold or closed down would it be necessary to show how much the assets would fetch. In the accounting records normally this is assumed to be of no interest to the firm. This is obviously connected with the cost concept, as if firms were not assumed to be going concerns the cost concept could not really be used, e.g. if firms were always to be treated as though they were going to be sold immediately after the accounting records were drafted, then the saleable value of the assets would be more relevant than cost.

The business entity concept

The transactions recorded in a firm's books are the transactions that affect the firm. The only attempt to show how the transactions affect the owners of a business is limited to showing how their capital in the firm is affected. For instance, a proprietor puts £1,000 more cash into the firm as capital. The books will then show that the firm has £1,000 more cash and that its capital has increased by £1,000. They do not show that he has £1,000 less cash in his private resources. The accounting records are therefore limited to the firm and do not extend to the personal resources of the proprietors.

The realisation concept

In accounting, profit is normally regarded as being earned at the time when the goods or services are passed to the customer and he incurs liability for them, i.e. this is the point at which the profit is treated as being realised. Note that it is not when the order is received, nor the contract signed, neither is it dependent on waiting until the customer pays for the goods or services. It can mean that profit is brought into account in one period, and it is found to have been incorrectly taken as such when the goods are returned in a later period because of some deficiency. Also the services can turn out to be subject to an allowance being given in a later period owing to poor performance. If the allowances or returns can be reasonably estimated an adjustment may be made to the calculated profit in the period when they passed to the customer.

The dual aspect concept

This states that there are two aspects of accounting, one represented by the assets of the business and the other by the claims against them. The concept states that these two aspects are always equal to each other. In other words:

Assets = Liabilities + Capital.

Double entry is the name given to the method of recording the transactions so that the dual aspect concept is upheld.

The accruals concept

The fact that net profit is said to be the difference between revenues and expenses rather than between cash receipts and expenditures is known as the **accruals concept**. A great deal of attention is therefore paid to this which, when the mechanics needed to bring about the accruals concept are being performed, is known as 'matching' expenses against revenues.

This concept is particularly misunderstood by people not well versed in accounting. To many of them, actual payment of an item in a period is taken as being matched agains the revenue of the period when the net profit is calculated. The fact that expenses consist of the assets used up in a particular period in obtaining the revenues of that period, and that cash paid in a period and expenses of a period are usually different as you will see later, comes as a surprise to a great number of them.

Further over-riding concepts

The concepts of accounting already discussed have become accepted in the business world, their assimilation having taken place over many years. These concepts, however, are capable of being interpreted in many ways. What has therefore grown up in accounting are generally accepted approaches to the application of the earlier concepts. The main ones in these further concepts may be said to be: materiality, prudence and consistency.

Materiality

Accounting does not serve a useful purpose if the effort of recording a transaction in a certain way is not worthwhile. Thus, if a box of paper-clips was bought it would be used up over a period of time, and this cost is used up every time someone uses a paper-clip. It is possible to record this as an expense every time it happens, but obviously the price of a box of paper-clips is so little that it is not worth recording it in this fashion. The box of paper-clips is not a material item, and therefore would be charged as an expense in the period it was bought, irrespective of the fact that it could last for more than one accounting period. **In other words do not waste your time in the elaborate recording of trivial items.**

Similarly, the purchase of a cheap metal ashtray would also be charged as an expense in the period it was bought because it is not a material item, even though it may in fact last for twenty years. A motor lorry would however be deemed to be a material item, and so, as will be seen in Chapter 20 on depreciation, an attempt is made to charge each period with the cost consumed in each period of its use.

Firms fix all sorts of arbitrary rules to determine what is material and what is not. There is no law that lays down what these should be, the decision as to what is material and what is not is dependent upon judgment. A firm may well decide that all items under £100 should be treated as expenses in the period which they were bought even though they may well be in use in the firm for the following ten years. Another firm, especially a large one, may fix the limit of £1,000. Different limits may be set for different types of item.

It can be seen that the size and the type of firm will affect the decisions as to which items are material. With individuals, an amount of £1,000 may well be more than you, as a student, possess. For a multi-millionaire as to what is a material item and what is not will almost certainly not be comparable. Just as individuals vary then so do firms. Some firms have a great deal of machinery and may well treat all items of machinery costing less than £1,000 as not being material, whereas another firm which makes about the same amount of profits, but has very little machinery, may well treat a £600 machine as being a material item as they have fixed their limit at £250.

Prudence

Very often an accountant has to make a choice as to which figure he will take for a given item. The prudence concept means that normally he will take the figure which will understate rather than overstate the profit. Alternatively, this could be expressed as choosing the figure which will cause the capital of the firm to be shown at a lower amount rather than at a higher one. This could also be said to be to make sure that all losses are recorded in the books, but that profits should not be anticipated by recording them prematurely.

It was probably this concept that led to accountants being portrayed as being rather miserable by nature; they were used to favouring looking on the black side of things and ignoring the bright side. However, the concept has seen considerable changes in the last few decades, and there has been a shift along the scale away from the gloomy view and more towards the desire to paint a brighter picture when it is warranted.

The use of the term 'prudence' for this concept started in the 1970s. Prior to that it had always been known as 'conservatism', and this latter term will still be found in quite a lot of literature concerning accounting.

Consistency

The concepts already listed are so broad that in fact there are many different ways in which items may be recorded in the accounts. Each firm should, within these limits, select the methods which give the most equitable picture of the activities of the business. However, this cannot be done if one method is used in one year and another method in the next year and so on. Constantly changing the methods would lead to a distortion of the profits calculated from the accounting records. Therefore the concept of consistency comes into play. This concept is that when a firm has once fixed a method of the accounting treatment of an item it will enter all similar items that follow in exactly the same way.

However, it does not bind the firm to following the method until the firm closes down. A firm can change the method used, but such a change is not affected without the deepest consideration. When such a change occurs and the profits calculated in that year are affected by a material amount, then either in the profit and loss account itself or in one of the reports accompanying it, the effect of the change should be stated.

The assumption of the stability of currency

One does not have to be very old to remember that a few years ago many goods could be bought with less money than today. If one listens to one's parents or grandparents then many stories will be heard of how little this item or the other could be bought for x years ago. The currencies of the countries of the world are not stable in terms of what each unit of currency can buy over the years.

Accounting, however, uses the cost concept, this stating that the asset is normally shown at its cost price. This means that accounting statements will be distorted because assets will be bought at different points in time at the price then ruling, and the figures totalled up to show the value of the assets in cost terms. For instance, suppose that you had bought a building 20 years ago for £20,000. You now decide to buy an identical additional building, but the price has now risen to £40,000. You buy it, and the buildings account now shows buildings at a figure of £60,000. One building is measured cost-wise in terms of the currency of 20 years ago, while the other is taken at today's currency value. The figure of a total of £60,000 is historically correct, but, other than that, the total figure cannot be said to be particularly valid for any other use.

This means that to make a correct assessment of accounting statements one must bear in mind the distorting effects of changing price levels upon the accounting entries as recorded. There are techniques of adjusting accounts so as to try and eliminate these distortions. These are dealt with in Chapter 45.

Statements of Standard Accounting Practice (SSAPs)

Despite the use of the concepts there will still be differences of opinion between accountants when profits are being calculated. In the late 1960s a number of cases led to a general outcry against the lack of uniformity in accounting. One concerned the takeover of AEI (Associated Electrical Industries) by GEC (General Electric Company). AEI had resisted the takeover, and had produced a profit forecast, in the tenth month of their financial year, that profit before tax for the year would be £10 million. After the takeover, the accounts for AEI for that year showed a loss of £4½ million. Of this difference of £14½ million, £5 million was said to be matters of fact, while the remaining £9½ million was attributed to adjustments which remain matters substantially of judgment arising from variations in accounting policies.

To reduce the possibility of such large variations in reported profits, the accountancy bodies have responded by issuing SSAPs, these are Statements of Standard Accounting Practice. Twenty-four SSAPs had been issued to the date of writing this impression of the book. Accountants and auditors are expected to comply with the SSAPs, if they are not complied with then the audit report should give the reasons why the SSAP has been ignored.

The advent of the SSAPs does not mean that two identical businesses will show exactly the same profits year by year. They have, however, considerably reduced the possibilities of very large variations in such profit reporting.

In this volume of the book the SSAPs will only be mentioned when it is essential. Volume Two will examine the SSAPs in greater detail.

Statements of Recommended Practice (SORPs)

These do not have the status of SSAPs as they do not have to be complied with. They are really statements recording the best practice in specific cases, and are often of a specialised nature.

SSAP 2

It is rather unfortunate that this SSAP mentions 'four fundamental concepts', and to a student it could be misunderstood to mean that there are *only* four concepts. In fact it has simply limited its investigations to the ones it considered most important, i.e. accruals, consistency, going concern and prudence. The academic world does not limit its concern with concepts to these four concepts only.

Concepts in action

This is too early a stage in your studies to be able to appreciate more fully how the concepts work in practice. It is far better left towards the end of this book, and therefore we consider it on page 445.

11
The basic structure of accounting records

With the very smallest type of organisation, it would possibly be sufficient to have the book-keeping records written in just one book. This we would call the **ledger**. As the organisation grew the amount of book-keeping entries needed would outgrow the limitations of the use of one ledger only.

This problem could be solved in several ways. One method would be to have more than one ledger, but the accounts contained in each ledger would be chosen simply by chance. There would be no set method for deciding which account should go into which ledger. This would not be very efficient, as it would be difficult to remember which accounts were in each ledger.

Another method would be to divide the ledger up into different books and each book would be for a specific purpose or function. The functions could be:

(*a*) One book just for customers' personal accounts. We could call this the **Sales Ledger**.

(*b*) Another book just for suppliers' personal accounts. We could call this the **Purchases Ledger** or **Bought Ledger**.

(*c*) A book concerned with the receiving and paying out of money both by cash and cheque. This would be a **Cash Book**.

(*d*) The remaining accounts would be contained in a ledger which we could call a **General Ledger**, an alternative name being a **Nominal Ledger**.

These ledgers all contain accounts and are part of double entry.

If more than one person becomes involved in book-keeping, the fact that the ledger has been divided into different books would make their job easier. The book-keeping to be done would be split between the people concerned, each book-keeper having charge of one or more books.

The General Ledger would be used quite a lot, because it would contain the sales account, purchases accounts, returns inwards and returns outwards accounts, as well as all the other accounts for assets, expenses, income, etc.

When the General Ledger becomes overloaded, we could deal with this problem by taking a lot of the detailed work out of it. Most entries in it would have been credit sales, credit purchases and returns inwards and returns outwards. We can therefore start four new books, for credit transactions only. One book will be for credit sales (the **Sales Journal**), one for credit purchases (the **Purchases Journal**) and one each for Returns Inwards (the **Returns Inwards Journal**) and Returns Outwards (**the Returns Outwards Journal**).

When a credit sale is made it will be entered in the customer's personal account in the Sales Ledger exactly the same way as before. However, instead of entering the sale in the sales account in the General Ledger, we would enter it in the Sales Journal. At regular intervals, usually once a month, the total of the Sales Journal would be transferred to the credit of the Sales Account in the General Ledger.

What this means is that even if there were 1,000 credit sales in the month, only one entry, the total of the Sales Journal, would need entering in the General Ledger. This saves the General Ledger from being overloaded with detail.

Similarly credit purchases are entered in the suppliers' account and listed in a Purchases Journal. The total is then entered, at regular intervals, in the debit side of the Purchases Account.

Returns inwards are entered in the customer's personal accounts, and are listed in the Returns Inwards Journal. The total is then transferred to the debit of the Returns Inwards Account.

Returns outwards are entered in the suppliers' personal accounts, and are listed in the Returns Outwards Journal. The total is then transferred to the credit of the Returns Outwards Account.

Sales Ledger
Purchases Ledger   All contain accounts and are therefore part of
Cash Book   the double-entry system
General Ledger

Sales Journal
Purchases Journal   Mere listing devices to save the accounts in the
Returns Inwards Journal   General Ledger from unnecessary detail.
Returns Outwards Journal

These will be described in full detail in the following chapters.

Computers and accounting

At this point it might be thought that the author had never heard of computers, as the text has been discussing 'books' of various sorts, and it is well-known that computers do not use bound books.

In fact the term 'book' or 'journal' is simply a convenient way of describing what is in effect a 'collection point' for a particular type of information. The principles of accounting can therefore be more easily discussed if the author keeps to standard terms. The principles remain exactly the same no matter whether manual, computerised or other methods are in use.

Classifications of accounts

Some people describe all accounts either as **Personal Accounts** or as **Impersonal Accounts**. Personal accounts are those of debtors and creditors. Impersonal accounts are then divided up further into **Real** accounts and **Nominal** accounts. Real accounts refer to accounts in which property is recorded, such as building, machinery, or stock. Nominal accounts are those which are concerned with revenue and expenses.

The accountant as a communicator

Quite often the impression is given that all that the accountant does is to produce figures, arranged in various ways. Naturally, such forms of computation do take up quite a lot of the accountant's time, but what then takes up the rest of his time is exactly how he communicates these figures to other people.

First of all, he can obviously arrange the figures in such a way as to present the information in as meaningful a way as possible. Suppose for instance that the figures he has produced are to be given to several people all of whom are very knowledgeable about accounting. He could, in such an instance, present the figures in a normal accounting way, knowing full well that the recipients of the information will understand it.

On the other hand, the accounting figures may well be needed by people who have absolutely no knowledge at all of accounting. In such a case a normal accounting statement would be no use to them at all, they would not understand it. In this case he might set out the figures in a completely different way to try to make it easy for them to grasp. For instance, instead of preparing a normal Trading and Profit and Loss Account he might show it as follows:

		£
In the year ended 31 December 19-6 you sold goods for		50,000
Now how much had those goods cost you to buy?		
At the start of the year you had stock costing	6,000	
+ You bought some more goods in the year costing	28,000	
So altogether you had goods available to sell of	34,000	
− At the end of the year you had stock of goods		
unsold of	3,000	
So the goods you had sold in the year had cost you	31,000	
Let us deduct this from what you had sold the goods for		31,000
This means that you had made a profit on buying and selling		
goods, before any other expenses had been paid, amounting to		19,000
(We call this sort of profit the Gross Profit)		
But you suffered other expenses such as wages, rent, lighting and so		
on, and during the year the amount of these expenses, not		
including anything taken for yourself, amounted to		9,000
So, if this year your sales value exceeded all the cost involved in		
running the business, so that the sales could be made, by		£10,000
(We call this sort of profit the Net Profit)		

If an accountant cannot arrange the figures to make them meaningful to the recipient then he is failing in his task. His job is not just to produce figures for himself to look at, his job is to communicate these results to other people.

Very often the accountant will have to talk to people to explain the figures, or send a letter or write a report concerning them. He will also have to talk or write to people to find out exactly what sort of accounting information is needed by them or explain to them what sort of information he could provide. This means that if accounting examinations consist simply of computational type questions then they will not test the ability of the candidate to communicate in any other way than by writing down accounting figures. In recent years more attention has been paid by examining boards to these aspects of an accountant's work.

12
The banking system

Bank accounts

Banks operate two main types of account, a current account and a deposit or savings account.

Current accounts

These are the accounts used for the regular banking and withdrawal of money. With this type of account a cheque book will be given by the bank to the customer for him to make payments to people to whom he owes money. He will also be given a paying-in book for him to pay money into the account.

Deposit accounts

This kind of account is one which will be concerned normally with putting money into the bank and not withdrawing it for some time. The usual object of having a deposit account is that interest is given on the balance held in the account, while interest is not usually given on balances in current accounts.

The remainder of this chapter will be concerned with current accounts.

Cheques

When the bank has agreed to let you open a current account it will ask you for a specimen signature. This enables them to ensure that your cheques are in fact signed by you, and have not been forged. You will then be issued with a cheque book.

We can then use the cheques to make payments out of the account. Normally we must ensure that we have banked more in the account than the amount paid out. If we wish to pay out more money then we have banked, we will have to see the bank manager. We will then discuss the reasons for this with him, and if he agrees he will give his permission for us to 'overdraw' our account. This is known as a **bank overdraft**.

The person filling in the cheque and using it for payment, is known as the **drawer**.

The person to whom the cheque is paid is known as the **payee**.

We can now look at Exhibit 12.1, which is a blank cheque form before it is filled in.

Exhibit 12.1

On the face of the cheque are various sets of numbers. These are:

914234   Every cheque printed for the Cheshire Bank will be given a different number, so that individual items can be traced.

09-07-99   Each branch of each bank in the United Kingdom has a different number given to it. Thus this branch has a **code number** 09-07-99.

058899   Each account with the bank is given a different number. This particular number is kept only for the account of J Woodstock at the Stockport branch.

When we fill in the cheque we copy the details on the counterfoil which we then detach and keep for our records.

We can now look at the completion of a cheque. Let us assume that we are paying seventy-two pounds and eighty-five pence to K Marsh on 22 May 19-5. Exhibit 12.2 shows the completed cheque.

Exhibit 12.2

In Exhibit 12.2:

The drawer is: J Woodstock

The payee is: K Marsh

The two parallel lines across the face of the cheque are drawn as a safeguard. If we had not done this the cheque would have been an **uncrossed cheque**. If someone had stolen a signed uncrossed cheque he could have gone to the Stockport branch of the Cheshire Bank and obtained cash in exchange for the cheque. When the cheque is crossed it *must* be paid into a bank account, Post Office Giro bank or Saving Bank.

Cheques can be further safeguarded by using specific crossings, i.e. writing a form of instruction within the crossing on the cheques as shown in Exhibit 12.3.

Exhibit 12.3

These are specific instructions to the banks about the use of the cheque. The use of **Account Payee only** means the cheques should be paid only into the account of the payee named. If cheques are lost or stolen the drawer must advise his bank immediately and confirm by letter. These cheques will be 'stopped', i.e. payment will not be made on these cheques, provided you act swiftly. The safest crossing is that of **A/c Payee only, Not Negotiable**. If the cheque is lost or stolen it will be of no use to the thief or finder. This is because it is impossible for this cheque to be paid into any bank account other than that of the named payee.

Paying-in slips

When we want to pay money into our current accounts, either cash or cheques, or both, we use a paying-in slip. One of these is shown as Exhibit 12.4.

J Woodstock has banked the following items:

Four	£5 notes	
Three	£1 coins	
One	50p coin	
Other silver	30p	
Bronze coins	12p	
Cheques received from:		Code numbers:
E Kane & Son	£184.15	02-58-76
J Gale	£ 65.44	05-77-85

Exhibit 12.4

Face of paying in-slip

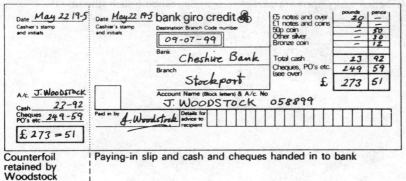

Counterfoil retained by Woodstock | Paying-in slip and cash and cheques handed in to bank

Reverse side of paying-in slip

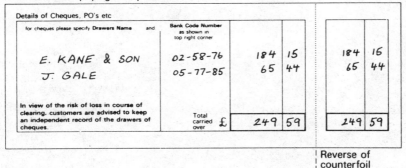

| | | | | |
Reverse of counterfoil

Cheque clearings

We will now look at how cheques paid from one person's bank account pass into another person's bank account.

Let us look at the progress of the cheque in Exhibit 12.2. We will assume that the Post Office is being every efficient and delivering all letters the following day after being posted.

19-5

May 22 Woodstock, in Stockport, sends the cheque to K Marsh, who lives in Leeds. Woodstock enters the payment in his cash book.

May 23 Cheque received by Marsh. He banks it the same day in his bank account at Barclays Bank in Leeds. Marsh shows the cheque in his cash book as being received and banked on 23 May.

May 24 Barclays in London receive it. They exchange it with the Head Office of the Cheshire Bank in London.
The Cheshire bank send the cheque to their Stockport branch.

May 25 The Stockport branch of the Cheshire bank examine the cheque. If there is nothing wrong with it, the cheque can now be debited by the bank to J Woodstock's account.

In Chapter 22 we will be examining bank reconciliation statements. What we have looked at –

19-5

May 22 This is the day on which Woodstock has made the entry in his cash book.

May 25 This is the day when the bank makes an entry in Woodstock's account in respect of the cheque.

– will become an important part of your understanding such statements.

13

Two-column cash books

The cash book is merely the cash account and the bank account brought together in one book. Previously we would have shown these two accounts on two separate pages of the ledger. Now it is more convenient to place the account columns together so that the recording of all money received and of all money paid out on a particular date can be found on the same page. The cash book is ruled so that the debit column of the cash account is placed alongside the debit column of the bank account, and the credit columns of the cash and the bank accounts are also placed alongside each other.

We can now look at a cash account and a bank account in Exhibit 13.1 as they would have been if they had been kept separately, and then in Exhibit 13.2 as they would be shown if the transactions had instead been kept in a cash book.

The bank column contains details of the payments made by cheques and of the money received and paid into the bank account. The bank which is handling the firm's money will of course have a copy of the account in its own books. The bank will periodically send a copy of the account in the bank's books to the firm, this copy usually being known as the **bank statement**. When the firm receives the bank statement it will check it against the bank column in its own cash book to ensure that there are no discrepancies.

Exhibit 13.1

Cash

19-5		£	19-5		£
Aug 1	Balance b/d	33	Aug 8	Rent	20
,, 5	G Bernard	25	,, 12	M Prince	19
,, 15	B Hussey	37	,, 28	Wages	25
,, 30	H Howe	18	,, 31	Balance c/d	49
		113			113
Sept 1	Balance b/d	49			

Bank

19-5		£	19-5		£
Aug 1	Balance b/d	949	Aug 7	Rates	105
,, 3	I Powell Ltd	295	,, 12	D Squire Ltd	95
,, 16	G Potter	408	,, 26	N Foster	268
,, 30	B Smith	20	,, 31	Balance c/d	1,204
		1,672			1,672
Sept 1	Balance b/d	1,204			

Exhibit 13.2

Cash Book

19-5		Cash £	Bank £	19-5		Cash £	Bank £
Aug	1 Balances b/d	33	949	Aug	7 Rates		105
,,	3 I Powell Ltd		295	,,	8 Rent	20	
,,	5 G Bernard	25		,,	12 M Prince	19	
,,	15 B Hussey	37		,,	,, D Squire Ltd		95
,,	16 G Potter		408	,,	26 N Foster		268
,,	30 B Smith		20	,,	28 Wages	25	
,,	,, H Howe	18		,,	31 Balance c/d	49	1,204
		113	1,672			113	1,672
Sept	1 Balances b/d	49	1,204				

Cash paid into the bank

In Exhibit 13.2, the payments into the bank have consisted of cheques received by the firm which have been banked immediately. There is, however, the case to be considered of cash being paid into the bank.

Now let us look at the position when a customer pays his account in cash, and later a part of this cash is paid into the bank. The receipt of the cash is debited to the cash column on the date received, the credit entry being in the customer's personal account. The cash banked has the following effect needing action as shown:

Effect	Action
1 Asset of cash is decreased	Credit the asset account, i.e the cash account which is represented by the cash column in the cash book.
2 Asset of bank is increased	Debit the asset account, i.e. the bank account which is represented by the bank column in the cash book.

A cash receipt of £100 from J Davies on 1 August 19-5, later followed by the banking on 3 August of £80 of this amount would appear in the cash book as follows:

19-5		Cash £	Bank £	19-5		Cash £	Bank £
Aug	1 J Davies	100		Aug	3 Bank	80	
,,	3 Cash		80				

The details column shows entries against each item stating the name of the account in which the completion of double entry had taken place. Against the cash payment of £80 appears the word 'bank', meaning that the debit £80 is to be found in the bank column, and the opposite applies.

Where the whole of the cash received is banked immediately the receipt can be treated in exactly the same manner as a cheque received, i.e. it can be entered directly in the bank column.

Sometimes, when the firm requires cash for future payments and it has not got a sufficient amount of cash in hand for the purpose, it may withdraw cash from the bank. This is done by making out a cheque to pay itself a certain amount of cash. The proprietor, or an authorised person, visits the bank where he is given cash in exchange for the cheque. This is sometimes known as 'cashing' a cheque for business use.

The twofold effect and the action required may be summarised as follows:

Effect	Action
1 Asset of bank is decreased	Credit the asset account, i.e the bank column in the cash book.
2 Asset of cash is increased	Debit the asset account, i.e. the cash column in the cash book.

A withdrawal of £75 cash on 1 June 19-5 from the bank would appear in the cash book thus:

	Cash	Bank		Cash	Bank
19-5	£	£	19-5	£	£
June 1 Bank		75	June 1 Cash		75

Where an item does not need entering in another book as double entry has already taken place within the cash book, then this item is known as a **contra** being the Latin work for against. Thus cash paid into the bank and cash withdrawn from the bank are both contra items. As there is a debit item and a credit item for the same amount double entry has already been completed, so that no account exists elsewhere for contra items in the cash book.

The use of folio columns

As you have already seen, the details column in an account contains the name of the other account in which double entry has been completed. Anyone looking through the books for any purpose would therefore be helped to find where the other half of the double entry was situated. However, with the growth in the number of books in use the mere mention of the name of the other account would not be sufficient to give quick reference to the other account. An extra aid is therefore needed and this is brought about by the use of a **folio** column. In each account and in each book in use an extra column is added, this always being shown on the immediate left of the money columns. In this column the name of the other book, in abbreviated form, and the number of the page in the other book where double entry is completed is stated against each and every entry in the books.

Thus an entry of receipt of cash from C Koote whose account was on page 45 of the sales ledger, and the cash recorded on page 37 of the cash book, would use the folio column thus:

In the cash book: In the folio column alongside the entry of the amount would appear SL 45.

In the sales ledger: In the folio column alongside the entry of the amount would appear CB 37.

By this means full cross reference would be given. Each of the contra items, being shown of the same page of the cash book, would use the letter 'C' in the folio column.

The folio column is only filled in when double entry for the item has been completed. The act of using one book as a means for entering the items to the other account so as to complete double entry is known as 'posting' the items. Where the folio column has not been filled it will be seen at a glance that double entry has not been completed, thus the error made when only one-half of the double entry is completed is made less often and can often be detected easily.

A worked example

The following transactions are written up in the form of a cash book. The folio columns are also filled in as though double entry has been completed to the other ledgers.

19-5		£
Sept 1	Balances brought forward from last month:	
	Cash	20
	Bank	940
,, 2	Received cheque from M Black	115
,, 4	Cash Sales	82
,, 6	Paid rent by cash	35
,, 7	Banked £50 of the cash held by the firm	50
,, 15	Cash sales paid direct into the bank	40
,, 23	Paid cheque to M Brown	277
,, 29	Withdrew cash from bank	120
,, 30	Paid wages in cash	118

Cash Book

	Folio	Cash	Bank		Folio	Cash	Bank
19-5		£	£	19-5		£	£
Sept 1 Balances	b/d	20	940	Sept 6 Rent	GL65	35	
,, 2 M Black	SL98		115	,, 7 Bank	C	50	
,, 4 Sales	GL87	82		,, 23 M Brown	PL23		277
,, 7 Cash	C		50	,, 29 Cash	C		120
,, 15 Sales	GL87		40	,, 30 Wages	GL39	118	
,, 29 Bank	C	120		,, 30 Balances	c/d	19	748
		222	1,145			222	1,145
Oct 1 Balances	b/d	19	748				

Now attempt set no 2 of multiple choice questions, see page 491.

Review questions

13.1 Write up a two-column cash book from the following details, and balance off as at the end of the month:

19-5
May 1 Started business with capital in cash £100
,, 2 Paid rent by cash £10
,, 3 F Lake lent us £500, paid by cheque
,, 4 We paid B McKenzie by cheque £65
,, 5 Cash sales £98
,, 7 N Miller paid us by cheque £62
,, 9 We paid B Burton in cash £22
,, 11 Cash sales paid direct into the bank £53
,, 15 G Moores paid us in cash £65
,, 16 We took £50 out of the cash till and paid it into the bank account
,, 19 We repaid F Lake £100 by cheque
,, 22 Cash sales paid direct into the bank £66
,, 26 Paid motor expenses by cheque £12
,, 30 Withdrew £100 cash from the bank for business use
,, 31 Paid wages in cash £97.

13.2 Write up a two-column cash book from the following details, and balance off as at the end of the month:

19-6

Mar 1 Balances brought down from last month:
Cash in hand £56: Cash in Bank £2,356

,, 2 Paid rates by cheque £156

,, 3 Paid for postage stamps in cash £5

,, 5 Cash sales £74

,, 7 Cash paid into bank £60

,, 8 We paid T Lee by cheque £75: We paid C Brooks in cash £2

,, 12 J Moores pays us £150, £50 being in cash and £100 by cheque

,, 17 Cash drawings by proprietor £20

,, 20 P Jones pays us by cheque £79

,, 22 Withdrew £200 from the bank for business use

,, 24 Bought a new motor van for £195 cash

,, 28 Paid rent by cheque £40

,, 31 Cash sales paid direct into the bank £105.

13.3A Write up a two-column cash book from the following:

19-6

Nov 1 Balance brought forward from last month: Cash £105: Bank £2,164

,, 2 Cash Sales £605

,, 3 Took £500 out of the cash till and paid it into the bank

,, 4 J Matthews paid us by cheque £217

,, 5 We paid for postage stamps in cash £60

,, 6 Bought office equipment by cheque £189

,, 7 We paid J Lucas by cheque £50

,, 9 Received rates refund by cheque £72

,, 11 Withdrew £250 from the bank for business use

,, 12 Paid wages in cash £239

,, 14 Paid motor expenses by cheque £57

,, 16 L Levy lent us £200 in cash

,, 20 R Norman paid us by cheque £112

,, 28 We paid general expenses in cash £22

,, 30 Paid insurance by cheque £74.

14

Cash discounts and the three-column cash book

Cash discounts

To encourage customers to pay their accounts promptly a firm may offer to accept a lesser sum in full settlement providing payment is made within a specified period of time. The amount of the reduction of the sum to be paid is known as a **cash discount**. The term cash discount thus refers to the allowance given for speedy payment, it is still called cash discount even if the account is paid by cheque

The rate of cash discount is usually quoted as a percentage, and full details of the percentage allowed and the period within which payment is to be made are quoted on all sale documents by the selling company. A typical period during which discount may be allowed is one month from the date of the original transaction.

A firm will meet with cash discounts in two different ways. First, it may allow cash discounts to firms to whom it sells goods, and second it may receive cash discounts from firms from whom it buys goods. To be able to distinguish easily between the two, the first kind are known as **discounts allowed**, the second kind are known as **discounts received**.

We can now see the effect of discounts by looking at two examples.

Example 1

W Clarke owed us £100. He pays on 2 September 19-5 by cash within the time limit laid down, and the firm allows him 5 per cent cash discount. Thus he will pay £100 − £5 = £95 in full settlement of his account.

Effect	Action
1 Of cash: Cash is increased by £95.	Debit cash account, i.e. enter £95 in debit column of cash book.
Asset of debtors is decreased by £95	Credit W Clarke £95.
2 Of discounts: Asset of debtors is decreased by £5. (After the cash was paid the balance still appeared of £5. As the account is deemed to be settled this asset must now be cancelled.)	Credit W Clarke £5.
Expenses of discounts allowed increased by £5.	Debit discounts allowed account £5.

Example 2

The firm owed W Small £400. It pays him on 3 September 19-5 by cheque within the time limit laid down by him and he allows 2½ per cent cash discount. Thus the firm will pay £400−£10 = £390 in full settlement of the account.

Effect	Action
1 Of cheque:	
Asset of bank is reduced by £390.	Credit bank, i.e. enter in credit bank column, £390.
Liability of creditors is reduced by £390.	Debit W Small's account £390.
2 Of discounts:	
Liability of creditors is reduced by £10. (After the cheque was paid the balance of £10 remained. As the account is deemed to be settled the liability must now be cancelled.)	Debit W Small's account £10.
Revenue of discounts received increased by £10.	Credit discounts received account £10.

The accounts in the firm's books would appear:

Cash Book (Page 32)

		Cash	Bank			Cash	Bank
19-5		£	£	19-5		£	£
Sept 2 W Clarke	SL12	95		Sept 3 W Small	PL75		390

Discounts Received (General Ledger page 18)

				19-5		£
				Sept 2 W Small	PL75	10

Discounts Allowed (General Ledger page 17)

19-5		£
Sept 2 W Clarke	SL12	5

W Clarke (Sales Ledger page 12)

19-5		£	19-5		£
Sept 1 Balance b/d		100	Sept 2 Cash	CB32	95
			,, 2 Discount	GL17	5
		100			100

W Small (Purchases Ledger page 75)

19-5		£	19-5		£
Sept 3 Bank	CB32	390	Sept 1 Balance b/d		400
,, 3 Discount	GL18	10			
		400			400

It is the accounting custom merely to enter the word 'Discount' in the personal account, not stating whether it is a discount received or a discount allowed. This is obviously to save time as the full description against each discount would be unnecessary. After all, the sales ledger accounts will only contain discounts allowed, and the purchases ledger accounts will only contain discounts received.

The discounts allowed account and the discounts received account are contained in the general ledger along with all the other revenue and expense accounts. It has already been stated that every effort should be made to avoid constant reference to the general ledger. In the case of discounts this is achieved quite simply by adding an extra column on each side of the cash book in which the amounts of discounts are entered. Discounts received are entered in the discounts column on the credit side of the cash book, and discounts allowed in the discounts column on the debit side of the cash book.

The cash book, if completed for the two examples so far dealt with, would appear:

			Cash Book					
	Discount	Cash	Bank			Discount	Cash	Bank
19-5		£	£	£	19-5		£	£	£
Sept 2 W Clarke	SL12	5	95		Sept 3 W Small	PL75	10		390

There is no alteration to the method of showing discounts in the personal accounts.

The discounts columns in the cash book are not however part of the double entry system. They are merely lists of discounts. Half of the double entry has already been made in the personal accounts. What is now required is the entry in the discounts accounts. The way it is done in this case is by transferring the total of the discounts received column to the credit of a discounts received account, and the total of the discounts allowed account is transferred to the debit of a discounts allowed account.

This at first sight appears to be incorrect. How can a debit total be transferred to the debit of an account? Here one must look at the entries for discounts in the personal accounts. Discounts allowed have been entered on the credit sides of the individual personal accounts. The entry of the total in the expense account of discount allowed must therefore be on the debit side to preserve double entry balancing. The opposite sides apply to discounts received.

The following is a worked example of a three-column cash book for the whole of a month, showing the ultimate transfer of the totals of the discount columns to the discount accounts.

				£
19-5				
May	1	Balances brought down from April:		
		Cash Balance		29
		Bank Balance		654
		Debtors accounts:		
		B King		120
		N Campbell		280
		D Shand		40
		Creditors accounts:		
		U Barrow		60
		A Allen		440
		R Long		100
,,	2	B King pays us by cheque, having deducted 2½ per cent cash discount £3		117
,,	8	We pay R Long his account by cheque, deducting 5 per cent cash discount £5		95
,,	11	We withdrew £100 cash from the bank for business use		100
,,	16	N Campbell pays us his account by cheque, deducting 2½ per cent discount £7		273
,,	25	We paid wages in cash		92
,,	28	D Shand pays us in cash after having deducted 2½ per cent cash discount		38
,,	29	We pay U Barrow by cheque less 5 per cent cash discount £3		57
,,	30	We pay A Allen by cheque less 2½ per cent cash discount £11		429

Cash Book

	Folio	Discount	Cash	Bank		Folio	Discount	Cash	Bank
19-5		£	£	£	19-5		£	£	
May 1 Balances	b/d		29	654	May 8 R Long	PL58	5		95
May 2 B King	SL13	3		117	May 11 Cash	C			100
May 11 Bank	C		100		May 25 Wages	GL77		92	
May 16 N Campbell	SL84	7		273	May 29 U Barrow	PL15	3		57
May 28 D Shand	SL91	2	38		May 30 A Allen	PL98	11		429
					May 31 Balances	c/d		75	363
		12	167	1,044			19	167	1,044
Jun 1 Balances	b/d		75	363					

Sales Ledger
B King
Page 13

19-5			£	19-5			£
May	1 Balance b/d		120	May	2 Bank	CB64	117
				,,	2 Discount	CB64	3
			120				120

N Campbell
Page 84

19-5			£	19-5			£
May	1 Balance b/d		280	May	16 Bank	CB64	273
				,,	16 Discount	CB64	7
			280				280

19-5			£	19-5			£
May 1 Balance b/d			40	May 28 Cash	CB64		38
				,, 28 Discount	CB64		2
			40				40

Purchases Ledger
U Barrow   Page 15

19-5			£			£
May 29 Bank	CB64		57	May 1 Balance b/d		60
,, 29 Discount	CB64		3			
			60			60

R Long   Page 58

19-5			£	19-5		£
May 8 Bank	CB64		95	May 1 Balance b/d		100
,, 8 Discount	CB64		5			
			100			100

A Allen   Page 98

19-5			£	19-5		£
May 30 Bank	CB64		429	May 1 Balance b/d		440
,, 30 Discount	CB64		11			
			440			440

General Ledger
Wages   Page 77

19-5			£
May 25 Cash	CB64		92

Discounts Received   Page 88

	19-5			£
	May 31 Total for the month	CB64		19

Discounts Allowed

19-5			£
May 31 Total for the month	CB64		12

As you can check, the discounts received entered in all of the purchases ledger accounts are £3 + £5 + £11 = £19 on the debit side; the total entered in the discounts received account on the credit side amounts also to £19. Thus double-entry principles are upheld. A check on the discounts allowed will reveal a debit of £12 in the discounts allowed account and a total of £3 + £7 + £2 = £12 on the credit side of the accounts in the sales ledger.

Bank overdrafts

A firm may borrow money from a bank by means of a **bank overdraft**. This means that the firm is allowed to pay more out of the bank account, by paying out cheques, for a total amount greater than that which it has placed in the account.

Up to this point the bank balances have all represented money at the bank, thus they have all been assets, i.e. debit balances. When the account is overdrawn the firm owes money to the bank, the account is a liability and the balance becomes a credit one.

Taking the cash book last illustrated, suppose that the amount payable to A Allen was £1,429 instead of £429. Thus the amount placed in the account, £1,044, is exceeded by the amount withdrawn. The Cash book would appear as follows:

Cash Book

	Discount	Cash	Bank		Discount	Cash	Bank
19-5	£	£	£	19-5	£	£	£
May 1 Balances b/d		29	654	May 8 R Long	5		95
„ 2 B King	3		117	„ 11 Cash			100
„ 11 Bank		100		„ 25 Wages		92	
„ 16 N Campbell	7		273	„ 29 U Barrow	3		57
„ 28 D Shand	2	38		„ 30 A Allen	11		1,429
„ 31 Balance c/d			637	„ 31 Balance c/d		75	
	12	167	1,681		19	167	1,681
Jun 1 Balance c/d			75	Jun 1 Balance b/d			637

On a balance sheet a bank overdraft will be shown as an item included under the heading Current Liabilities.

Bank cash books

In the United Kingdom, except for very small organisations, three-column cash books will not often be found. All receipts, whether of cash or cheques, will be banked daily. A **petty cash book** will be used for payments of cash. This means that there will not be a need for cash columns in the cash book itself. This is described on page 208.

This would certainly not be true in many other countries in the world, especially where banking systems are not as developed or as efficient as in the UK. Three-column cash books will be much more widely used in these countries.

Review questions

14.1 Enter up a three-column cash book from the details following. Balance off at the end of the month, and show the relevant discount accounts as they would appear in the general ledger.

19-7

May	1	Started business with £6,000 in the bank
,,	1	Bought fixtures paying by cheque £950
,,	2	Bought goods paying by cheque £1,240
,,	3	Cash Sales £407
,,	4	Paid rent in cash £200
,,	5	N Morgan paid us his account of £220 by a cheque for £210, we allowed him £10 discount
,,	7	Paid S Thompson & Co £80 owing to them by means of a cheque £76, they allowed us £4 discount
,,	9	We received a cheque for £380 from S Cooper, discount having been allowed £20
,,	12	Paid rates by cheque £410
,,	14	L Curtis pays us a cheque for £115
,,	16	Paid M Monroe his account of £210 by cash £114, have deducted £6 cash discount
,,	20	P Exeter pays us a cheque for £78, having deducted £2 cash discount
,,	31	Cash Sales paid direct into the bank £88.

14.2 A three-column cash book is to be written up from the following details, balanced off and the relevant discount accounts in the general ledger shown.

19-5

Mar	1	Balances brought forward: Cash £230; Bank £4,756
,,	2	The following paid their accounts by cheque, in each case deducting 5 per cent cash discounts; Accounts: R Burton £140; E Taylor £220; R Harris £300
,,	4	Paid rent by cheque £120
,,	6	J Cotton lent us £1,000 paying by cheque
,,	8	We paid the following accounts by cheque in each case deducting a 2½ per cent cash discount; N Black £360; P Towers £480: C Rowse £800.
,,	10	Paid motor expenses in cash £44
,,	12	H Hankins pays his account of £77 by cheque £74, deducting £3 cash discount
,,	15	Paid wages in cash £160
,,	18	The following paid their accounts by cheque, in each case deducting 5 per cent cash discount: Accounts: C Winston £260; R Wilson & Son £340; H Winter £460
,,	21	Cash withdrawn from the bank £350 for business use
,,	24	Cash Drawings £120
,,	25	Paid T Briers his account of £140, by cash £133, having deducted £7 cash discount
,,	29	Bought fixtures paying by cheque £650
,,	31	Received commission by cheque £88.

14.3A Enter the following in a three-column cash book. Balance off the cash book at the end of the month and show the discount accounts in the general ledger.

19-8

June 1   Balances brought forward: Cash £97; Bank £2,186.

,,   2   The following paid us by cheque in each case deducting a 5 per cent cash discount; R Harris £1,000; C White £280; P Peers £180; O Hardy £600

,,   3   Cash Sales paid direct into the bank £134

,,   5   Paid rent by cash £88

,,   6   We paid the following accounts by cheque, in each case deducting 2½ per cent cash discount J Charlton £400; H Sobers £640; D Shallcross £200

,,   8   Withdrew cash from the bank for business use £250

,,   10   Cash Sales £206

,,   12   D Deeds paid us their account of £89 by cheque less £2 cash discount

,,   14   Paid wages by cash £250

,,   16   We paid the following accounts by cheque: L Lucas £117 less cash discount £6; D Fisher £206 less cash discount £8

,,   20   Bought fixtures by cheque £8,000

,,   24   Bought motor lorry paying by cheque £7,166

,,   29   Received £169 cheque from D Steel

,,   30   Cash Sales £116

,,   30   Bought stationery paying by cash £60.

15

The sales journal

You have read in Chapter 11 that the recording of transactions has been divided up into the various functions of the business. Mention has been made on page 73 of the fact that, in order to keep the general ledger free from unnecessary detail, separate journals are kept for credit transactions concerning sales and purchases. The **Sales Journal** can now be examined in detail.

There will be many businesses, such as a lot of small retail shops, where all the sales will be cash sales. On the other hand, in many businesses a considerable proportion of sales will be made on credit rather than for immediate cash. In fact, the sales of many businesses will consist entirely of credit sales. For each credit sale the selling firm will send a document to the buyer showing full details of the goods sold and the prices of the goods. This document is known as an **invoice**, and to the seller it is known as a **sales invoice**. The seller will keep one or more copies of each sales invoice for his own use. Exhibit 15.1 is an example of an invoice.

Exhibit 15.1

Your Purchase Order 10/A/980		J. Blake 7 Over Warehouse Leicester LR1 2AP 1 September 19-5
INVOICE No. 16554		
To: D. Prendergast 45 Charles Street, Manchester M1 5ZN		
	Per Unit	Total
	£	£
21 cases McBrand Pears	20	420
5 cartons Kay's flour	4	20
6 cases Joy's Vinegar	20	120
		560
Terms: 1¼% cash discount if paid within one month		

You must not think that all invoices will look exactly like the one chosen as Exhibit 15.1. Each business will have its own design. All invoices will be numbered, and they will contain the names and addresses both of the supplier and of the customer. In this case the supplier is J Blake and the customer is D Prendergast.

As soon as the sales invoices for the goods being sent have been made out, whether they are typed, handwritten, or produced by a computer, they are then despatched to the customer. The firm will keep copies of all these sales invoices. These copies will have been automatically produced at the same time as the original, usually by using some form of carbon paper or special copying paper.

It is from the copy sales invoices that the seller enters up his sales journal. This book is merely a list, in date order, of each sales invoice, showing the date, the name of the firm to whom the goods have been sold, the number of the invoice for reference purposes, and the net amount of the invoice. There is no need to show in the sales journal a description of the goods sold, as this information can be found by referring to the copy of the sales invoice which will have been filed after recording it in the sales journal. The practice of copying all the details of the goods sold in the sales journal finished many years ago.

We can now look at Exhibit 15.2, which is a sales journal, starting with the record of the sales invoice already shown in Exhibit 15.1

Exhibit 15.2

Sales Journal

	Invoice No	Folio	Page 26
19-5			£
Sept 1 D Prendergast	16554	SL 12	560
,, 8 T Cockburn	16555	SL 39	1,640
,, 28 C Carter	16556	SL 125	220
,, 30 D Stevens & Co	16557	SL 249	1,100
Transferred to Sales Account		GL 44	3,520

The entry of these credit sales in the customer's accounts in the sales ledger keeps to the same principles of personal accounts as described in earlier chapters. Apart from the fact that the customers' accounts are now contained in a separate book known as the sales ledger, and that the reference numbers in the folio columns will be different, each individual personal account is the same as previous. The act of using the sales journal entries as the basis for entering up the customers' accounts is known as 'posting' the sales journal.

Sales Ledger

		D Prendergast	Page 12
19-5		£	
Sept 1 Sales	SJ 26	560	

		T Cockburn	Page 39
19-5		£	
Sept 8 Sales	SJ 26	1,640	

		C Carter	Page 125
19-5		£	
Sept 28 Sales	SJ 26	220	

19-5		£
Sept 30 Sales	SJ 26	1,100

You can see that the customers' personal accounts have been debited with a total of £3,520 for these sales. However, as yet no credit entry has been made for these items. The sales journal is simply a list, it is not an account and is therefore not a part of the double-entry system. We must complete double entry however, and this is done by taking the total of the sales journal for the period and entering it on the credit side of the sales account in the general ledger.

General Ledger

Sales   Page 44

	19-5	£
	Sept 30 Credit Sales for	
	the month SJ 26	3,520

If you now compare this with entries that would have been made when all the accounts were kept in one ledger, the overall picture should become clearer. The eventual answer is the same, personal accounts would have been debited with credit sales amounting in total to £3,520 and the sales account would have been credited with sales amounting in total to £3,520. The differences are now that first the personal accounts are contained in a separate sales ledger, and second, the individual items of credit sales have been listed in the sales journal, merely the total being credited to the sales account. The different books in use also mean a change in the reference numbers in the folio columns.

Alternative names for the Sales Journal are **Sales Book** and **Sales Day Book**.

Before you proceed further you are to attempt Question 15.1.

Trade discounts

Suppose you are the proprietor of a business. You are selling to three different kinds of customers:

(*a*) Traders who buy a lot of goods from you.

(*b*) Traders who buy only a few items from you.

(*c*) Direct to the general public.

The traders themselves have to sell the goods to the general public in their own areas. They have to make a profit to help finance their businesses, so they will want to pay you less than retail price.

The traders (*a*) who buy in large quantities will not want to pay as much as traders (*b*) who buy in small quantities. You want to attract such large customers, and so you are happy to sell to traders (*a*) at a lower price.

All of this means that your selling prices are at three levels: (*a*) to traders buying large quantities, (*b*) to traders buying small quantities, and (*c*) to the general public.

To save your staff from dealing with three different price lists, (*a*), (*b*) and (*c*), all goods are shown at the same price. However, a reduction (discount), called a **trade discount**, is given to traders (*a*) and (*b*).

Example

You are selling a make of food mixing machine. The basic price is £200. Traders (*a*) are given 25 per cent trade discount, traders (*b*) 20 per cent, the general public get no trade discount. The prices paid by each type of customer would be:

	Trader (a) £		Trader (b) £		General Public (c) £
Basic price		200		200	200
less Trade discount	(25%)	50	(20%)	40	nil
Price to be paid by customer		150		160	200

Exhibit 15.3 is an invoice for goods sold to D Prendergast. It is for the same items as were shown in Exhibit 15.1, but this time the seller is R Grant and he uses trade discounts to get to the price paid by his customers.

Exhibit 15.3

Your Purchase Order 11/A/G80		R. Grant Higher Side Preston PR1 2NL 2 September 19-5
INVOICE No. 30756		
To: D. Prendergast 45 Charles Street, Manchester M1 5ZN		

	Per Unit	Total
	£	£
21 cases McBrand Pears	25	525
5 cartons Kay's flour	5	25
6 cases Joy's Vinegar	25	150
		700
less 20% Trade discount		140
		560

By comparing Exhibits 15.1 and 15.3 you can see that the prices paid by D Prendergast were the same. It is simply the method of calculating the price that is different.

As trade discount is simply a way of calculating sales prices, no entry for trade discount should be made in the double-entry records nor in the sales journal. The record of this item in R Grant's sales journal and Prendergast's personal account will appear:

Sales Journal

Page 87		Invoice No	Folio	
				£
19-5				
Sept 2 D Prendergast		30756	SL 32	560

Sales Ledger
(page 32)

D Prendergast

			£	
19-5				
Sept 2 Sales	SJ 87		560	

This is in complete contrast to **cash discounts** which are shown in the double-entry accounts.

There are in fact several other reasons for using trade discounts to the one described in this chapter. However, the calculation of the trade discount and its display on the invoice will remain the same as that described in this book.

Review questions

15.1 You are to enter up the sales journal from the following details. Post the items to the relevant accounts in the sales ledger and then show the transfer to the sales account in the general ledger.

19-6

Mar	1	Credit sales to K Gordon	£187
,,	3	Credit sales to G Abrahams	£166
,,	6	Credit sales to V White	£12
,,	10	Credit sales to J Gordon	£55
,,	17	Credit sales to F Williams	£289
,,	19	Credit sales to U Richards	£66
,,	27	Credit sales to V Wood	£28
,,	31	Credit sales to L Simes	£78

15.2A Enter up the sales journal from the following, then post the items to the relevant accounts in the sales ledger. Then show the transfer to the sales account in the general ledger.

19-8

Mar	1	Credit sales to J Johnson	£305
,,	3	Credit sales to T Royes	£164
,,	5	Credit sales to B Howe	£45
,,	7	Credit sales to M Lee	£100
,,	16	Credit sales to J Jakes	£308
,,	23	Credit sales to A Vinden	£212
,,	30	Credit sales to J Samuels	£1,296

15.3 F Benjamin of 10 Lower Street, Plymouth, is selling the following items, the recommended retail prices as shown: white tape £10 per roll, green baize at £4 per metre, blue cotton at £6 per sheet, black silk at £20 per dress length. He makes the following sales:

19-7

May	1	To F Gray, 3 Keswick Road, Portsmouth: 3 rolls white tape, 5 sheets blue cotton, 1 dress length black silk. Less 25 per cent trade discount.
,,	4	To A Gray, 1, Shilton Road, Preston: 6 rolls white tape, 30 metres green baize. less 33⅓ per cent trade discount.
,,	8	To E Hines, 1 High Road, Malton: 1 dress length black silk. No trade discount
,,	20	To M Allen, 1 Knott Road, Southport: 10 rolls white tape, 6 sheets blue cotton, 3 dress lengths black silk, 11 metres green baize. Less 25 per cent trade discount.
,,	31	To B Cooper, 1 Tops Lane, St Andrews: 12 rolls white tape, 14 sheets blue cotton, 9 metres green baise. Less 33⅓ per cent trade discount

You are to (*a*) draw up a sales invoice for each of the above sales, (*b*) enter them up in the Sales Journal, post to the personal accounts, (*c*) transfer the total to the Sales Account in the General Ledger.

15.4A J Fisher, White House, Bolton, is selling the following items, the retail prices as shown: plastic tubing at £1 per metre, polythene sheeting at £2 per length, vinyl padding at £5 per box, foam rubber at £3 per sheet. He makes the following sales:

19-5

June 1 To A Portsmouth, 5 Rockley Road, Worthing: 22 metres plastic tubing, 6 sheets foam rubber, 4 boxes vinyl padding. Less 25 per cent trade discount.

,, 5 To B Butler, 1 Wembley Road, Colwyn Bay: 50 lengths polythene sheeting, 8 boxes vinyl padding, 20 sheets foam rubber. Less 20 per cent trade discount.

,, 11 To A Gate, 1 Bristol Road, Hastings: 4 metres plastic tubing, 33 lengths of polythene sheeting, 30 sheets foam rubber. Less 25 per cent trade discount.

,, 21 To L Mackeson, 5 Maine Road, Bath: 29 metres plastic tubing. No trade discount is given.

,, 30 To M Alison, Daley Road, Box Hill: 32 metres plastic tubing, 24 lengths polythene sheeting, 20 boxes vinyl padding. Less 33⅓ per cent trade discount.

Required:

(*a*) Draw up a sales invoice for each of the above sales, (*b*) then enter up in the Sales Journal and post to the personal accounts, (*c*) transfer the total to the Sales Account in the general ledger.

16

The purchases journal

When a firm buys goods on credit it will receive an invoice from the seller for those goods. In the last chapter, Exhibit 15.1, J Blake sold goods to D Prendergast and sent an invoice with those goods.

To the seller, J Blake, that invoice is a sales invoice. To the buyer, D Prendergast, that same invoice is regarded as a purchases invoice. This often confuses students. What we have to do to identify whether or not an invoice is a sales invoice or a purchases invoice is to think about it from the point of view as to which firm's books we are entering up. If the firm is the buyer of the goods then the invoice is a purchases invoice.

The net amount of the invoice, i.e. after deduction of trade discount, is listed in the purchases journal and the items are then posted to the credit of the personal accounts in the purchases ledger. The invoice is then filed away for future reference. At the end of the period the total of the purchases journal is transferred to the debit of the purchases account in the general ledger. An example of a purchase journal and the posting of the entries to the purchases ledger and the total to the purchases account is now shown:

Purchases Journal

			Invoice No	Folio	Page 49
19-5					£
Sept	2	R Simpson	9/101	PL 16	670
,,	8	B Hamilton	9/102	PL 29	1,380
,,	19	C Brown	9/103	PL 55	120
,,	30	K Gabriel	9/104	PL 89	510
		Transferred to Purchases Account		GL 63	2,680

Purchases Ledger
R Simpson   Page 16

19-5			£
Sept 2 Purchases		PJ 49	670

B Hamilton   Page 29

19-5			£
Sept 8 Purchases		PJ 49	1,380

C Brown   Page 55

19-5			£
Sept 19 Purchases		PJ 49	120

	19-5		£
	Sept 30 Purchases	PJ 49	510

General Ledger
Purchases   Page 63

19-5		£
Sept 30 Credit purchases for	PJ 49	2,680
the month		

The purchases journal is often known also as the **purchases book** or as the **purchases day book**.

Review questions

16.1 B Mann has the following purchases for the month of May 19-4:

19-4

May 1 From K King: 4 radios at £30 each, 3 music centres at £160 each. Less 25 per cent trade discount.

,, 3 From A Bell: 2 washing machines at £200 each, 5 vacuum cleaners at £60 each, 2 dish dryers at £150 each. Less 20 per cent trade discount.

,, 15 From J Kelly: 1 music centre at £300 each, 2 washing machines at £250 each. Less 25 per cent trade discount.

,, 20 From B Powell: 6 radios at £70 each. Less 33⅓ per cent discount.

,, 30 From B Lewis: 4 dish dryers at £200 each. Less 20 per cent trade discount.

Required:
(*a*) Enter up the Purchases Journal for the month.
(*b*) Post the transactions to the supplier's accounts.
(*c*) Transfer the total to the Purchases Account.

16.2A A Rowland has the following purchases for the month of June 19-9:

19-9

June 2 From C Lee: 2 sets golf clubs at £250 each. 5 footballs at £20 each. Less 25 per cent trade discount.

,, 11 From M Elliott: 6 cricket bats at £20 each, 6 ice skates at £30 each, 4 rugby balls at £25 each. Less 25 per cent trade discount.

,, 18 From B Wood: 6 sets golf trophies at £100 each, 4 sets golf clubs at £300. Less 33⅓ per cent trade discount.

,, 25 From B Parkinson: 5 cricket bats at £40 each. Less 25 per cent trade discount.

,, 30 From N Francis: 8 goal posts at £70 each. Less 25 per cent trade discount.

Required:
(*a*) Enter up the Purchases Journal for the month.
(*b*) Post the items to the supplier's accounts.
(*c*) Transfer the total to the Purchases Account.

16.3 C Phillips, a sole trader, has the following purchases and sales for March 19-5:

Mar 1 Bought from Smith Stores: silk £40, cotton £80. All less 25 per cent trade discount

,, 8 Sold to Grantley: linen goods £28, wollen items £44. No trade discount

,, 15 Sold to A Henry: silk £36, linen £144, cotton goods £120. All less 20 per cent trade discount

,, 23 Bought from C Kelly: cotton £88, Linen £52. All less 25 per cent trade discount

,, 24 Sold to D Sangster: linen goods £42, cotton £48. Less 10 per cent trade discount

,, 31 Bought from J Hamilton: Linen goods £270. Less 33⅓ per cent trade discount.

Required:
    (*a*)   Prepare the Purchases and Sales Journals of C Phillips from the above.
    (*b*)   Post the items to the personal accounts.
    (*c*)   Post the totals to the journals to the Sales and Purchases Accounts.

16.4A A Henriques has the following purchases and sales for May 19-6:
19-6

May 1   Sold to M Marshall: brass goods £24, bronze items £36. Less 25 per cent trade discount
 ,,   7   Sold to R Richards: tin goods £70, lead items £230. Less 33⅓ per cent trade discount
 ,,   9   Bought from C Clarke: tin goods £400. Less 40 per cent trade discount
 ,, 16   Bought from A Charles: copper goods £320. Less 50 per cent trade discount
 ,, 23   Sold to T Young: tin goods £50, brass items £70, lead figures £80. All less 20 per cent trade discount
 ,, 31   Bought from M Nelson: brass figures £100. Less 50 per cent trade discount.

Required:
    (*a*)   Write up Sales and Purchases Journals.
    (*b*)   Post the items to the personal accounts.
    (*c*)   Post the totals of the journals to the Sales and Purchases Accounts.

17
The returns journals

The returns inwards journal

Sometimes we will agree to customers returning goods to us. It may be that they had been sent goods of the wrong colour, the wrong type etc., or simply that the customer had found that he had bought more than he needed. At other times goods will have been supplied and there will be something wrong with them. The customer may agree to keep the goods if an allowance is given so as to reduce their price.

In each of the cases a document known as a **credit note** will be sent to the customer, showing the amount of the allowance given by us in respect of the returns or of the faulty goods. The term 'credit note' takes its name from the fact that the customer's account will be credited with the amount of the allowance, so as to show the reduction in the amount owing by him.

Exhibit 17.1

		R. Grant, Higher Side, Preston PR1 2NL 8 September 19-5
To: D. Prendergast 45 Charles Street, Manchester M1 5ZN		
CREDIT NOTE No. 9/37		
	Per Unit	Total
	£	£
2 cases McBrand Pears	25	50
Less 20% Trade Discount		10
		40

Very often credit notes are printed in red so that they are easily distinguishable from invoices.

Imagine that the firm of D Prendergast to whom goods were sold on 1 September 19-5 as per Exhibit 15.3 returned some of the goods on 8 September 19-5. The credit note might appear as shown in Exhibit 17.1.

The credit notes are listed in a Returns Inwards Journal which is then used to post the items to the credit of the personal accounts in the sales ledger. To complete the double entry the total of the returns inwards book for the period is transferred to the debit of the Returns Inwards Account in the general ledger.

An example of a returns inwards book showing the items posted to the sales ledger and the general ledger is now shown:

Returns Inwards Journal

	Note No	Folio	Page 10
19-5			£
Sept 8 D Prendergast	9/37	SL 12	40
,, 17 A Brewster	9/38	SL 58	120
,, 19 C Vickers	9/39	SL 99	290
,, 29 M Nelson	9/40	SL 112	160
Transferred to Returns Inwards Account		GL 114	610

Sales Ledger
D Prendergast — Page 12

19-5		£
Sept 8 Returns Inwards	RI 10	40

A Brewster — Page 58

19-5		£
Sept 17 Returns Inwards	RI 10	120

C Vickers — Page 99

19-5		£
Sept 19 Returns Inwards	RI 10	290

M Nelson — Page 112

19-5		£
Sept 29 Returns Inwards	RI 10	160

General Ledger
Returns Inwards — Page 114

19-5		£
Sept 30 Returns for the month	RI 10	610

Alternative names in use for the returns inwards journal are **Returns Inwards Book** or **Sales Returns Book**, the latter name arising from the fact that it is the sales which are returned at a later date.

The returns outwards journal

The exact opposite to returns inwards is when goods are returned to a supplier. A document called a **debit note** is sent to the supplier stating the amount of allowance to which the firm returning the goods is entitled. The debit note could also cover allowances due because the goods bought were deficient in some way. The term 'debit note' stems from the fact that as the liability to the supplier is accordingly reduced his personal account must be debited to record this. The debit note is the evidence that this has been done.

The debit notes are listed in a Returns Outwards Journal and the items then posted to the debit of the personal accounts in the purchases ledger. To complete double entry the total of the returns outwards journal for the period is transferred to the credit of the Returns Outwards Account in the general ledger. An example of a returns outwards journal followed by the subsequent posting to the purchases ledger and the general ledger is now shown:

Returns Outwards Journal

	Note No	Folio	Page 7
19-5			£
Sept 11 B Hamilton	9/34	PL 29	180
,, 16 B Rose	9/35	PL 46	100
,, 28 C Blake	9/36	PL 55	30
,, 30 S Saunders	9/37	PL 87	360
Transferred to Returns Outwards Account		GL 116	670

Purchases Ledger
B Hamilton
Page 29

19-5		£
Sept 11 Returns Outwards	RO 7	180

B Rose
Page 46

19-5		£
Sept 16 Returns Outwards	RO 7	100

C Blake
Page 55

19-5		£
Sept 28 Returns Outwards	RO 7	30

S Saunders
Page 87

19-5		£
Sept 30 Returns Outwards	RO 7	360

General Ledger
Returns Outwards
Page 116

		19-5		£
		Sept 30 Returns for the month	RO 7	670

Alternative names in use for the returns outwards journal are **Returns Outwards Book** or **Purchases Returns Book**, the latter name arising from the fact that it consists of the purchases which are returned to the supplier at a later date.

Internal check

When sales invoices are being made out they should be scrutinised very carefully. A system is usually set up so that each stage of the preparation of the invoice is checked by someone other than the person whose job it is to send out the invoice. If this was not done then it would be possible for someone inside a firm to send out an invoice, as an instance, at a price less than the true price. Any difference could then be split between that person and the outside firm. If an invoice should have been sent to Ivor Twister & Co for £2,000, but the invoice clerk made it out deliberately for £200, then, if there was no cross-check, the difference of £1,800 could be split between the invoice clerk and Ivor Twister & Co.

Similarly outside firms could send invoices for goods which were never received by the firm. This might be in collaboration with an employee within the firm, but there are firms sending false invoices which rely on the firms receiving them being inefficient and paying for items never received. There have been firms sending invoices for such items as advertisements which have never been published. The cashier of the firm receiving the invoice, if the firm is an inefficient one, might possibly think that someone in the firm had authorised the advertisements and would pay the bill.

Besides these there are of course genuine errors, and these should also be detected. A system is therefore set up whereby the invoices have to be subject to scrutiny, at each stage, by someone other than the person who sends out the invoices or is responsible for paying them. Incoming invoices will be stamped with a rubber stamp with spaces for each stage of the check. For instance, one person will have authority to certify that the goods were properly ordered, another that the goods were delivered in good order, another that the prices are correct, that the calculations are correct, and so on. Naturally in a small firm, simply because the office staff might be quite small, this cross-check may be in the hands of only one person other than the person who will pay it. A similar sort of check will be made in respect of sales invoices being sent out.

Statements

At the end of each month a statement should be sent to each debtor who owes money on the last day of the month. The statement is really a copy of the account for the last month, showing the amount owing at the start of the month, then the totals of each of the sales invoices sent to him in that month, the credit notes sent to him in the month for the goods returned, the cash and cheques received from the debtor, and finally the amount owing at the end of the month.

The debtor will use this to see if the account in his accounting records agree with his account in our records. Put simply, if in our books he is shown as owing £798 then, depending on items in transit betwen us, his books should show us as a creditor for £798. The statement also acts as a reminder to the debtor that he owes us money and will show the date by which he should make payment.

Credit control

Any organisation which sells goods on credit should ensure that a tight control is kept on the amount owing from individual debtors. Failure to do so could mean that the amount of debtors increases past the point which the organisation can afford to finance, also there is a much higher possibility of bad debts occurring if close control is not kept.

For each debtor a credit limit should be set. This will depend partly on the past record of dealings with the debtor, whether or not the relationship has been a good one with the debtor always paying his account on time or not. The size of the debtor firm and the nature of its financial backing will also help determine what would be a safe credit limit to set. For instance, you might set a credit limit of only £250 for a fairly new and untried customer, but this could be as much as, say, £20,000 for a large well-known international firm with large financial resources. In the business world most business people are optimistic by nature, and they usually feel that they can manage to pay off debts much easier than is the case. Therefore it is a wise policy to err on the side of caution. On the other hand this should be tempered down by the fact that if you are too cautious you will probably not do much businesss, so a sensible middle course is the answer.

Therefore the debtor should know the length of the term of credit, i.e. how many days or weeks or months he has in which to pay the bill. He should also know that you will not supply goods to him if the amount that he owes you exceeds a stated amount.

Factoring

One of the problems that face many businesses is the time taken by debtors to pay their accounts. Few businesses have so much cash available to them that they do not mind how long the debtor takes to pay. It is a rather surprising fact that a lot of businesses which become bankrupt do so, not because the business is not making profits, but instead because the business has run out of cash funds. Once that happens, the confidence factor in business evaporates, and the business then finds that very few people will supply it with goods, and it also cannot pay its employees. Closure of the firm then happens fairly quickly in many cases.

In the case of debtors, the cash problem may be alleviated by using the services of a financial intermediary called a **factor**.

Factoring is a financial service designed to improve the cash flow of healthy, growing companies, enabling them to make better use of management time and the money tied up in trade credit to customers.

In essence, factors provide their clients with three closely integrated services covering sales accounting and collection, credit management which can include protection against bad debts, and the availability of finance against sales invoices.

Factors assume total responsibility for these functions, including assessing the creditworthiness of customers, the maintenance of a sales ledger, the dispatch of statements and the collection of money owed.

Factors provide clients with a predictable cash flow by paying them against sales factored either as each individual invoice is settled or on an agreed future date which represents the average time taken by the clients' customers to pay.

In addition, a factor will, if required, make payments against its clients' sales invoices: up to 80 per cent being available immediately with the balance paid when the customers pay the factor or after an agreed period.

In the case of non-recourse factoring, the factor gives 100 per cent protection against bad debts on all approved sales.

The benefits of factoring include savings in administration costs and management time, the elimination of bad debts, a guaranteed cash flow and the availability of funds which would otherwise be financing debtors. Factoring, therefore, provides a logical way for companies to develop, with their cash position always under control and the availability of finance linked to actual sales performance.

Sales and purchases via credit cards

Various banks, building societies and other financial organisations issue credit cards to their customers. Examples are Visa, Access, and American Express. The holder of the credit card purchases items or services without giving cash or cheques, but simply signs a special voucher used by the store or selling organisation. Later on, usually several weeks later, the credit card holder pays the organisation for which he holds the card, e.g. Visa, for all of his previous month's outgoings.

The sellers of the goods or services then present the vouchers to the credit card company and the total of the vouchers less commission is paid to them by that credit card company.

In effect the sales are 'cash sales' for as far as the purchaser is concerned he has seen goods (or obtained services) and has received them, and in his eyes he has paid for them by using his credit card. Such sales are very rarely sales to anyone other than the general public, as compared with professionals in a specific trade.

Once the customer has departed with his goods, or had the necessary services he does not become a debtor needing an entry for him in a sales ledger. All the selling company is then interested in, from a recording point of view, is collecting the money from the credit card company.

The double entry needed is:

Sale of items via credit cards:	Dr: credit card company
	Cr: cash sales
Receipt of money from credit card company:	Dr: Bank
	Cr: Credit card company
Commission charged by credit card company:	Dr: Selling expenses
	Cr: Credit card company

Review questions

17.1 You are to enter up the purchases journal and the returns outwards journal from the following details, then to post the items to the relevant accounts in the purchases ledger and to show the transfers to the general ledger at the end of the month.

19-7

May	1	Credit purchase from H Lloyd £119
,,	4	Credit purchases from the following: D Scott £98; A Simpson £114; A Williams £25; S Wood £56
,,	7	Goods returned by us to the following: H Lloyd £16; D Scott £14
,,	10	Credit purchase from A Simpson £59
,,	18	Credit purchases from the following: M White £89; J Wong £67; H Miller £196; H Lewis £119
,,	25	Goods returned by us to the following: J Wong £5; A Simpson £11
,,	31	Credit purchases from: A Williams £56; C Cooper £98.

17.2A Enter up the sales journal and the returns inwards journal from the following details. Then post to the customer's accounts and show the transfers to the general ledger.

19-4

June	1	Credit sales to: A Simes £188; P Tulloch £60; J Flynn £77; B Lopez £88
,,	6	Credit sales to: M Howells £114; S Thompson £118; J Flynn £66
,,	10	Goods returned to us by: A Simes £12; B Lopez £17
,,	20	Credit sales to M Barrow £970
,,	24	Goods returned to us by S Thompson £5
,,	30	Credit sales to M Parkin £91.

17.3 You are to enter up the sales, purchases and the returns inwards and returns outwards journals from the following details, then to post the items to the relevant accounts in the sales and purchase ledgers. The total of the journals are then to be transferred to the accounts in the general ledger.

19-6

May	1	Credit sales: T Thompson £56; L Rodriguez £148; K Barton £145
,,	3	Credit purchases: P Potter £144; H Harris £25; B Spencer £76
,,	7	Credit sales: K Kelly £89; N Mendes £78; N Lee £257
,,	9	Credit purchases: B Perkins £24; H Harris £58; H Miles £123
,,	11	Goods returned by us to: P Potter £12; B Spencer £22
,,	14	Goods returned to us by: T Thompson £5; K Barton £11; K Kelly £14
,,	17	Credit purchases: H Harris £54; B Perkins £65; L Nixon £75
,,	20	Goods returned by us to B Spencer £14
,,	24	Credit sales: K Mohammed £57; K Kelly £65; O Green £112
,,	28	Goods returned to us by N Mendes £24
,,	31	Credit sales: N Lee £55.

17.4A You are to enter the following items in the books, post to personal accounts, and show transfers to the general ledger.

19-5

July	1	Credit purchases from: K Hill £380; M Norman £500; N Senior £106
,,	3	Credit sales to: E Rigby £510; E Phillips £246; F Thompson £356
,,	5	Credit purchases from: R Morton £200; J Cook £180; D Edwards £410; C Davies £66
,,	8	Credit sales to: A Green £307; H George £250; J Ferguson £185
,,	12	Returns outwards to: M Norman £30; N Senior £16
,,	14	Returns inwards from: E Phillips £18; F Thompson £22
,,	20	Credit sales to: E Phillips £188; F Powell £310; E Lee £420
,,	24	Credit purchases from: C Ferguson £550; K Ennevor £900
,,	31	Returns inwards from: E Phillips £27; E Rigby £30
,,	31	Returns outwards to: J Cook £13; C Davies £11.

18

The journal

Previously it has been shown that the work of recording transactions is divided up into its different functions, there being a separate book (or some other sort of collection point for data) for each major function. The books in which entries are made prior to their posting to the ledgers are known as subsidiary books or as **books of prime entry**. Thus the sales, purchases, returns inwards and returns outwards books are all books of prime entry. The cash book is also regarded as a book of prime entry, although many would regard it as a ledger, for as it has been seen it originated from the cash and bank accounts being detached from the ledger. However, it is the book in which cash and bank entries are first made and from this point of view it may be taken as a book of prime entry.

It is to the firm's advantage if all transactions which do not pass through a book of prime entry are entered in a book called **the journal**. The journal is a form of diary for such transactions. It shows:

1   The date.

2   The name of the account(s) to be debited and the amount(s).

3   The name of the account(s) to be credited and the amount(s).

4   A description of the transaction (this is called a 'narrative').

One would also expect to find a reference number for the documents supporting the transaction.

The advantages to be gained from using a journal may be summarised:

1   It eliminates the need for a reliance on the memory of the book-keeper. Some transactions are of a complicated nature, and without the journal the entries may be difficult, if not impossible, to understand. One must also bear in mind that if the book-keeper left the firm the absence of a journal could leave many unexplained items in the books.

2   Errors, irregularities and fraud are more easily effected when entries are made direct into the ledgers without any explanations being given. The journal acts as an explanation of the entries and details the necessary supporting evidence.

3   The risk of omitting the transaction altogether, or of making one entry only is reduced.

Despite these advantages there are many firms which do not have such a book.

Typical uses of the journal

Some of the main uses of the journal are listed below. It must not be thought that this list is exhaustive.

1   The purchase and sale of fixed assets on credit.

2   The correction of errors.

3   Opening entries. These are the entries needed to open a new set of books.

4   Other transfers.

The layout of the journal can now be shown:

The Journal

Date		Folio	Dr	Cr

The name of the account to be debited.
   The name of the account to be credited.
The Narrative.

To standardise matters the name of the account to be debited should always be shown first. It also helps with the reading of the journal if the name of the account to be credited is written not directly under the name of the account to be debited, but is inset to the right-hand side.

It must be remembered that the journal is not an integral part of the double- entry book-keeping system. It is purely a form of diary, and entering an item in the journal is not the same as recording an item in an account. Once the journal entry is made the necessary entry in the double-entry accounts can then be effected.

Examples of the uses of the journal are now given.

Purchase and sale on credit of fixed assets.

(*a*) A machine is bought on credit from Toolmakers Co for £550 on 1 July.

	Dr	Cr
	£	£
July 1 Machinery	550	
Toolmakers Co		550
Purchase of milling machine on credit, Capital		
Purchases invoice No 7/159		

(*b*) Sale of a Motor Vehicle for £400 on credit to A Barnes on 2 July.

	Dr	Cr
	£	£
July 2 A Barnes	300	
Motor vehicles		300
Sales of Motor vehicles per Capital		
Sales invoice No 7/43		

Correction of errors

These are dealt with in detail in Chapters 27 and 28.

Opening entries

J Brew, after being in business for some years without keeping proper records, now decides to keep a double-entry set of books. On 1 July he establishes that his assets and liabilities are as follows:

Assets: Motor Van £840, Fixtures £700, Stock £390, Debtors — B Young £95, D Blake £45, Bank £80, Cash £20.

Liabilities: Creditors — M Quinn £129, C Walters £41.

The Assets therefore total £840 + £700 + £390 + £95 + £45 + £80 + £20 = £2,170; and the Liabilities total £129 + £41 + = £170.

The Capital consists of Assets − Liabilities, £2,170 − £170 = £2,000.

To start the books off on 1 July showing the existing state of the assets and liabilities and capital, these amounts therefore need entering in the relevant asset, liability and capital accounts. The asset accounts will be opened with debit balances and the liability and capital accounts will be opened with credit balances. The journal therefore shows the accounts which are to be debited and those which are to be credited and this is shown in Exhibit 18.1.

Exhibit 18.1

	The Journal	Folio	Dr	Page 5 Cr
			£	£
July 1	Motor Van	GL 1	840	
	Fixtures	GL 2	700	
	Stock	GL 3	390	
	Debtors—B Young	SL 1	95	
	D Blake	SL 2	45	
	Bank	CB 1	80	
	Cash	CB 1	20	
	Creditors—M Quinn	PL 81		129
	C Walters	PL 2		41
	Capital	GL 4		2,000
	Assets and liabilities at this date entered to open the books			
			2,170	2,170

Now that the journal has been written up, the accounts can be opened as follows:

General Ledger
Motor Van   Page 1

		£
July 1 Balance	J 5	840

Fixtures   Page 2

		£
July 1 Balance	J 5	700

Stock   Page 3

		£
July 1 Balance	J 5	390

Capital   Page 4

			£
July 1 Balance	J 5	2,000

Sales Ledger
B Young   Page 1

		£
July 1 Balance	J 5	95

			£
July	1 Balance	J 5	45

Purchases Ledger

M Quinn   Page 1

				£
July	1 Balance		J 5	129

C Walters   Page 2

				£
July	1 Balance		J 5	41

Cash Book   Page 1

Cash Bank

			£	£
July	1 Balances	J 5	20	80

Once these opening balances have been recorded in the books the day-to-day transactions can be entered in the normal manner. The need for opening entries will not occur very often. They will not be needed each year as the balances from last year will have been brought forward. At the elementary level of examinations in book-keeping, questions are often asked which entail opening a set of books and recording the day-by-day entries for the ensuing period.

Other transfers

These can be of many kinds and it is impossible to construct a complete list. However, two examples can be shown.

(*a*) S Bennett, a debtor, owed £200 on 1 July. He was unable to pay his account in cash, but offers a motor car in full settlement of the debt. The offer is accepted on 5 July.

The personal account is therefore discharged and needs crediting. On the other hand the firm now has an extra asset, a motor car, therefore the motor car account needs to be debited.

The Journal

		Dr	Cr
		£	£
July	5 Motor Car	200	
	S Bennett		200

Accepted motor car in full settlement of debt per letter dated 5/7/- 5

(*b*) G Ames is a creditor. On 10 July his business is taken over by A Iddon to whom the debt now is to be paid.

Here it is just the identity of one creditor being exchanged for another one. The action needed is to cancel the amount owing to G Ames by debiting his account, and to show it owing to Iddon by opening an account for Iddon and crediting it.

	Dr	Cr
	£	£

July 10 G Ames   150

       A Iddon   150

       Transfer of indebtedness as per letter from Ames ref
       A/1335

Review questions

18.1 You are to open the books of K Mullings, a trader, via the journal to record the assets and liabilities, and are then to record the daily transactions for the month of May. A trial balance is to be extracted as on 31 May 19-6.

19-6

May 1   *Assets:* Premises £2,000; Motor Van £450; Fixtures £600; Stock £1,289. Debtors: N Hardy £40; M Nelson £180;. Cash at bank £1,254; Cash in hand £45. *Liabilities:* Creditors; B Blake £60; V Reagan £200.

May 1   Paid rent by cheque £15.

,,   2   Goods bought on credit from B Blake £20; C Harris £56; H Gordon £38; N Lee £69

,,   3   Goods sold on credit to: K O'Connor £56; M Benjamin £78; L Staines £98; N Duffy £48; B Green £118; M Nelson £40

,,   4   Paid for motor expenses in cash £13

,,   7   Cash drawings by proprietor £20

,,   9   Goods sold on credit to: M Benjamin £22; L Pearson £67

,, 11   Goods returned to Mullings by: K O'Connor £16; L Staines £18

,, 14   Bought another motor van on credit from Better Motors Ltd £300

,, 16   The following paid Mullings their accounts by cheque less 5 per cent cash discount: N Hardy; M Nelson: K O'Connor; L Staines

,, 19   Goods returned by Mullings to N Lee £9

,, 22   Goods bought on credit from: J Johnson £89; T Best £72

,, 24   The following accounts were settled by Mullings by cheque less 5 per cent cash discount: B Blake; V Reagan; N Lee

,, 27   Salaries paid by cheque £56

,, 30   Paid rates by cheque £66

,, 31   Paid Better Motors Ltd a cheque for £300

18.2A You are to show the journal entries necessary to record the following items:

(*a*) 19-5 May 1 Bought a motor vehicle on credit from Kingston Garage for £6,790

(*b*) 19-5 May 3 A debt of £34 owing from H Newman was written off as a bad debt

(*c*) 19-5 May 8 Office furniture bought by us for £490 was returned to the supplier Unique Offices, as it was unsuitable. Full allowance will be given us

(*d*) 19-5 May 12 We are owed £150 by W Charles. He is declared bankrupt and we received £39 in full settlement of the debt

(*e*) 19-5 May 14 We take £45 goods out of the business stock without paying for them

(*f*) 19-5 May 28 Some time ago we paid an insurance bill thinking that it was all in respect of the business. We now discover that £76 of the amount paid was in fact insurance of our private house

(*g*) 19-5 May 28 Bought machinery £980 on credit from Systems Accelerated.

18.3A Show the journal entries necessary to record the following items:

19-7

Apr 1   Bought fixtures on credit from J Harper £1,809

,,   4   We take £500 goods out of the business stock without paying for them

,,   9   £28 of the goods taken by us on 4 April is not returned back into stock by us. We do not take any money for the return of the goods

,,   12   K Lamb owes us £500. He is unable to pay his debt. We agree to take some office equipment from him at the value and so cancel the debt.

,,   18   Some of the fixtures bought from J Harper, £65 worth, are found to be unsuitable and are returned to him for full allowance

,,   24   A debt owing to us by J Brown of £68 is written off as a bad debt

,,   30   Office equipment bought on credit from Super Offices for £2,190.

19
Value Added Tax

Value Added Tax, which will be shown hereafter in its abbreviated form as VAT, is charged in the United Kingdom on both the supply of goods and of services by persons and firms who are taxable. Some goods and services are not liable to VAT. Examples of this are food and postal charges. The rates at which VAT is levied have changed from time to time. Some goods have also attracted a different rate of VAT from the normal rate. Instances of this in the past have been motor cars and electrical goods which have varied from the rates levied on most other goods. In this book the examples shown will all be at a VAT rate of 10 per cent. This does not mean that this is the rate applicable at the time when you are reading this book. It is, however, an easy figure to work out in an examination room, and most examining bodies have set questions assuming that the VAT rate was 10 per cent.

The Government department which deals with VAT in the United Kingdom is the Customs and Excise department.

Taxable firms

Imagine that firm A takes raw materials that it has grown and processes them and then wants to sell them. If VAT did not exist it would sell them for £100, but VAT of 10 per cent must be added, so it sells them to firm B for £100 + VAT £10 = £110. Firm A must now pay the figure of £10 VAT to the tax authorities. Firm B having bought for £110 alters the product slightly and then resells to firm C for £140 + 10 per cent VAT £14 = £154. Firm B now give the tax authorities a cheque for the amount added less the amount it had paid to firm A for VAT £10, so that the cheque payable to the tax authorities by firm B is £4. Firm C is a retailer who then sells the goods for £200 to which he must add VAT 10 per cent £20 = £220 selling price to the customer. Firm C then remits £20 − £14 = £6 to the tax authorities.

It can be seen that the full amount of VAT tax has fallen on the ultimate customer who bought the goods from the retail shop, and that he suffered a tax of £20. The machinery of collection was however geared to the value added at each stage of the progress of the goods from manufacture to retailing, i.e. firm A handed over £10, firm B £4 and firm C £6, making £20 in all.

Exempted firms

If a firm is exempted then this means that it does not have to add the VAT tax on to the price at which it sells its products or services. On the other hand it will not get a refund of the amount it has paid itself on the goods and services which it has bought and on which it has paid VAT tax. Thus such a firm may buy goods for £100 + VAT tax £10 = £110. When it sells them it may sell at £130, there being no need to add VAT tax at all. It will not however get a refund of the £10 VAT tax it had itself paid on those goods.

Instances of firms being exempted are insurance companies, which do not charge VAT on the amount of insurance premiums payable by its customers, and banks, which do not add VAT on to their bank charges. Small firms with a turnover of less than a certain amount (the limit is changed upwards from time to time and so is not given here) do not have to register for VAT if they don't want to, and they would not therefore charge VAT on their goods and services. On the other hand many of these small firms could register if they wished, but they would then have to keep full VAT records in addition to charging out VAT. It is simply an attempt by the UK Government to avoid crippling very small businesses with unnecessary record-keeping that gives most small businesses this right to opt out of charging VAT.

Zero rated firms

These do not add VAT tax to the final selling price of their product or services. They do however obtain a refund of all VAT tax paid by them on goods and services. This means that if one of the firms buys goods for £200 + VAT tax £20 = £220, and later sells them for £300 it will not have to add VAT on to the selling price of £300. It will however be able to claim a refund of the £20 VAT tax paid when the goods were purchased. It is this latter element that distinguishes it from an exempted firm. A zero rated firm is therefore in a better position than an exempted firm. Illustrations of these firms are food, publishing and the new construction of buildings.

Partly exempt traders

Some traders will find that they are selling some goods which are exempt and some which are zero rated and others which are standard rated. These traders will have to apportion their turnover accordingly, and follow the rules already described for each separate part of their turnover.

Accounting for VAT

It can be seen that, except for firms that are exempted from VAT, firms do not suffer VAT as one expense. They either get a refund of whatever VAT they have paid, in the case of zero-rated business, or else additionally collect VAT from their customers and merely therefore act as tax collectors in the case of taxable firms. Only the exempted firms actually suffer VAT as they pay it and are not allowed a refund and cannot specifically pass it on to their customers. The following discussion will therefore be split between those two sorts of firms who do not suffer VAT expense, compared with the exempted firms who do suffer VAT.

Firms which can recover VAT paid

Taxable firms

Value Added Tax on sales invoices

A taxable firm will have to add VAT to the value of the sales invoices. It must be pointed out that this is based on the amount of the invoice *after* any trade discount has been deducted.

Exhibit 19.1 is an invoice drawn up from the following details:

On 2 March 19-2, W Frank & Co, Hayburn Road, Stockport, sold the following goods to R Bainbridge Ltd, 267 Star Road, Colchester: Bainbridge's order No was A/4/559, for the following items:

200 Rolls T56 Black Tape at £6 per 10 rolls

600 Sheets R64 Polythene at £10 per 100 sheets
7,000 Blank Perspex B49 Markers at £20 per 1,000

All of these goods are subject to VAT at the rate of 10 per cent. A trade discount of 25 per cent is given by Frank & Co. The sales invoice is numbered 8851.

Exhibit 19.1

	W Frank & Co.	
	Hayburn Road,	
	Stockport SK2 5DB	
	INVOICE No. 8851	Date: 2 March 19-2
To: R Bainbridge Ltd		Your order no A/4/559
267 Star Road		
Colchester CO1 1BT		

	£
200 Rolls T56 Black Tape @ £6 per 10 rolls	120
600 Sheets R64 Polythene @ £10 per 100 sheets	60
7,000 Blank Perspex B49 Markers @ £20 per 1,000	140
	320
less Trade Discount 25%	80
	240
add VAT 10%	24
	264

Where a cash discount is offered for speedy payment, VAT is calculated on an amount represented by the value of the invoice less such a discount. Even if the cash discount is lost because of late payments, the VAT will not change.

The Sales Book will normally have an extra column for the VAT content of the Sales Invoices. This is needed to facilitate accounting for VAT. The entry of several sales invoices in the Sales Book and in the ledger accounts can now be examined:

W Frank & Co sold the following goods during the month of March 19-2:

		Total of invoice, after trade discount deducted but before VAT added	VAT 10%
19-2		£	£
March	2 R Bainbridge Ltd (*see* Exhibit 19.1)	240	24
,,	10 S Lange & Son	300	30
,,	17 K Bishop	160	16
,,	31 R Andrews & Associates	100	10

	Invoice No	Folio	Net	VAT
19-2			£	£
March 2 R Bainbridge Ltd	8851	SL 77	240	24
,, 10 S Lange & Son	8852	SL 119	300	30
,, 17 K Bishop	8853	SL 185	160	16
,, 31 R Andrews & Associates	8854	SL 221	100	10
Transferred to General Ledger		GL 76	800	GL 90 80

The Sales Book having been written up, the first task is then to enter the invoices in the individual customer's accounts in the Sales Ledger. The customer's accounts are simply charged with the full amounts of the invoices including VAT. For instance, K Bishop will owe £176 which he will have to pay to W Frank & Co. He does not remit the VAT £16 to the Customs and Excise, instead he is going to pay the £16 to W Frank & Co who will thereafter ensure that the £16 is included in the total cheque payable to the Customs and Excise.

Sales Ledger
R Bainbridge Ltd   Page 77

19-2			£
March 2 Sales	SB 58		264

S Lange & Son   Page 119

19-2			£
March 10 Sales	SB 58		330

K Bishop   Page 185

19-2			£
March 17 Sales	SB 58		176

R Andrews & Associates   Page 221

19-2			£
March 31 Sales	SB 58		110

In total therefore the personal accounts have been debited with £880, this being the total of the amounts which the customers will have to pay. The actual sales of the firm are not £880, the amount which is actually sales is £800, the other £80 being simply the VAT that W Frank & Co are collecting on behalf of the Government. The credit transfer to the Sales Account in the General Ledger is restricted to the Sales content, i.e. £800. The other £80, being VAT, is transferred to a VAT account.

General Ledger
Sales   Page 76

			£
19-2			
March 31 Credit Sales for the	SB 58		
month			800

	19-2			£
March	31 Sales Book: VAT	SB 58		
	content			80

Value Added Tax and purchases

In the case of a taxable firm, the firm will have to add VAT to its sales invoices, but it will also be able to claim a refund of the VAT which it pays on its purchases. What will happen is that the total of the amount of VAT paid on Purchases will be deducted from the total of the VAT collected by the additions to the Sales Invoices. Normally the VAT on Sales will be greater than that on Purchases, and therefore periodically the net difference will be paid to the Customs & Excise. It can happen sometimes that more VAT has been suffered on Purchases than has been charged on Sales, and in this case it would be the Customs and Excise which would refund the difference to the firm. These payments or receipts via the Customs and Excise will be either monthly or quarterly depending on the arrangement which the particular firm has made.

The recording of Purchases in the Purchases Book and Purchases Ledger is similar to that of Sales, naturally with items being shown in a reverse fashion. These can now be illustrated by continuing the month of March 19-2 in the books of the firm already considered, W Frank & Co, this time for Purchases.

W Frank & Co made the following purchases during the month of March 19-2:

	Total of invoice, after trade discount deducted but before VAT added	*VAT 10%*
19-2	£	£
March 1 E Lyal Ltd (*see* Exhibit 19.2)	180	18
,, 11 P Portsmouth & Co	120	12
,, 24 J Davidson	40	4
,, 29 B Cofie & Son Ltd	70	7

Before looking at the recording of the Purchases Records, compare the first entry for E Lyal Ltd with Exhibit 19.2, to ensure that the correct amounts have been shown.

It can be seen that the purchases invoice from E Lyal Ltd differs slightly in its layout to that of W Frank & Co per Exhibit 19.3. This is to illustrate that in fact each firm designs its own invoices, and there will be wide variations. The basic information shown will be similar, but they may have such information displayed in quite different ways.

Purchases Book   Page 38

	Folio	*Net*		*VAT*	
19-2		£		£	
March 1 E Lyal Ltd	PL 15	180		18	
,, 11 P Portsmouth & Co	PL 70	120		12	
,, 24 J Davidson	PL 114	40		4	
,, 29 B Cofie & Son Ltd	PL 166	70		7	
Transferred to General Ledger	GL 54	410	GL 90	41	

Exhibit 19.2

E Lyal Ltd
College Avenue
St Albans
Hertfordshire ST2 4JA

INVOICE NO K453/A

Date: 1/3/19-2
Your order No BB/667

To: W Frank & Co   Terms: Strictly net 30 days
    Hayburn Road
    Stockport

	£
50 metres of BYC plastic 1 metre wide × £3 per metre	150
1,200 metal tags 500 mm × 10p each	120
	270
less Trade Discount at 33⅓%	90
	180
add VAT 10%	18
	198

These are entered in the Purchases Ledger. Once again there is no need for the VAT to be shown as separate amounts in the accounts of the suppliers.

Purchases Ledger
E Lyal Ltd   Page 15

19-2				£
March	1	Purchases	PB 38	198

P Portsmouth & Co   Page 70

19-2				£
March	11	Purchases	PB 38	132

J Davidson   Page 114

19-2				£
March	24	Purchases	PB 38	44

S Cofie & Son Ltd   Page 166

19-2				£
March	29	Purchases	PB 38	77

The personal accounts have accordingly been credited with a total of £451, this being the total of the amounts which Frank & Co will have to pay to them. The actual purchases are not however, £451; the correct amount is £410 and the other £41 is the VAT which the various firms are collecting for the Customs and Excise, and which amount is reclaimable from the Customs and Excise by Frank & Co. The debit transfer to the Purchases Account is therefore restricted to the figure of £410, for this is the true amount that the goods are costing the firm. The other £41 is transferred to the debit of the VAT account. It will be noticed that in this account there is already a credit of £80 in respect of VAT on Sales for the month.

General Ledger
Purchases   Page 54

19-2		£			
March	31 Credit Purchases for the month	410			

Value Added Tax   Page 90

19-2		£	19-2		£
March	31 Purchase Book: VAT content PB 38	41	March	31 Sales Book: VAT content SB 58	80
,,	31 Balance c/d	39			
		80			80
			April	1 Balance b/d	39

Assuming that a Trading and Profit and Loss Account was being drawn up for the month, the Trading Account would be debited with £410 as a transfer from the Purchases Account, while the £800 in the Sales Account would be transferred to the credit side of the Trading Account. The Value Added Tax would simply appear as a creditor of £39 in the Balance Sheet as at 31 March 19-2.

Zero rated firms

It has been already stated that these firms do not have to add VAT on to their sales invoices, as their rate of VAT is zero or nil. On the other hand any VAT that they pay on Purchases can be reclaimed from the Customs and Excise. Such firms, which include publishers, are therefore in a rather fortunate position. There will accordingly be no need at all to enter VAT in the Sales Book as VAT simply does not apply to Sales in such a firm. The Purchases Book and the Purchases Ledger will appear exactly as has been seen in the case of W Frank & Co. The VAT account will only have debits in it, representing the VAT on Purchases. This balance will be shown on the Balance Sheet as a debtor until it is settled by the Customs and Excise.

Firms which cannot recover VAT paid

These firms do not have to add VAT on to the value of their Sales Invoices. On the other hand they do not get a refund of VAT paid on Purchases. All that happens in this type of firm is that there is no Value Added Tax Account, the VAT paid is simply included as part of the cost of the goods. If therefore a firm receives an invoice from a supplier for Purchases of £80, with VAT added of £8, then £88 will have to be paid for these goods and the firm will not receive a refund from the Customs and Excise. In the Purchases Book the item of Purchases will be shown as £88, and the supplier's account will be credited with £88. As VAT is not added to Sales Invoices then there cannot be any entries for VAT in the Sales Book.

Perhaps a comparison of two firms with identical Purchases from the same supplier, one a zero rated firm, and one a firm which cannot recover VAT paid, would not come amiss here. On the assumption that for each firm the only item of Purchases for the month was that of goods £120 plus VAT £12 from D Oswald Ltd, the entries for the month of May 19-4 would be as follows:

(*a*) Firm which cannot recover VAT:

Purchases Book

		£
19-4		
May 16 D Oswald Ltd		132

Purchases Ledger
D Oswald Ltd

		£
	19-4	
	May 16 D Oswald Ltd	132

General Ledger
Purchases

19-4	£	19-4	£
May 31 Credit Purchases for the month	132	May 31 Transfer to Trading Account	132

Trading Account for the month ended 31 May 19-4 (extract)

	£
Purchases	132

(*b*) Firm which can recover VAT (e.g. zero rated firm):

Purchases Book

	Net	VAT
	£	£
19-4		
May 16 D Oswald Ltd	120	12

Purchases Ledger
D Oswald Ltd

	£
19-4	
May 16 Purchases	132

19-4		£	19-4		£
May	31 Credit Purchases for the month	120	May	31 Transfer to Trading Account	120

Value Added Tax

19-4		£
May	31 Purchases Book	12

Trading Account for the month ended 31 May 19-4 (extract)

	£
Purchases	120

Balance Sheet as at 31 May 19-4 (extract)

	£
Debtor	12

VAT included in gross amount

You will often know only the gross amount of an item, this figure will in fact be made up of the net amount plus VAT. To find the amount of VAT which has been added to the net amount, a formula capable of being used with any rate of VAT can be used. It is:

$$\frac{\% \text{ rate of VAT}}{100 + \% \text{ Rate of VAT}} \times \text{Gross Amount} = \text{VAT in } £$$

Suppose that the gross amount of sales was £1,650 and the rate of VAT was 10%. Find the amount of VAT and the net amount before VAT was added.

Using the formula:

$$\frac{10}{100 + 10} \times £1,650 = \frac{10}{110} \times £1,650 = £150.$$

Therefore the net amount was £1,500, which with VAT £150 added, becomes £1,650 gross.

Given a rate of VAT of 15% (the UK rate prevailing when this edition was written) and that the gross amount of sales was £2,300, the amount of VAT and the net amount before VAT can be calculated using the formula:

$$\frac{15}{100 + 15} \times £2,300 = \frac{15}{115} \times £2,300 = £300 \text{ VAT.}$$

The net amount was therefore £2,000, which with £300 VAT becomes £2,300 gross.

Review questions 19.3, 19.4, 19.5 and 19.6 use a VAT percentage rate of 15 per cent.

VAT on items other than sales and purchases

Value Added Tax is not just paid on purchases, it is also payable on many items of expense and on the purchase of fixed assets. In fact it would not be possible for this to be otherwise, as an item which is a Purchase for one firm would be a Fixed Asset in another. For instance, if a firm which dealt in shop fittings buys a display counter as a fixed asset, the firm which sells the goods on which VAT is added does not concern itself whether or not the firm buying it is doing so for resale, or whether it is for use. The VAT will therefore be added to all of its Sales Invoices. The treatment of VAT in the accounts of the firm buying the item will depend on whether or not that firm can reclaim VAT paid or not. The general rule is that if the VAT can be reclaimed then the item should be shown net, i.e. VAT should be excluded from the expense or fixed asset account. When VAT cannot be reclaimed then VAT should be included in the expense or fixed asset account as part of the cost of the item. For example, two businesses buying similar items, would treat the following items as shown:

	Firm which can reclaim VAT		*Firm which cannot reclaim VAT*	
Buys Machinery	Debit Machinery	£200	Debit Machinery	£220
£200 + VAT £20	Debit VAT Account	£20		
Buys Stationery	Debit Stationery	£150	Debit Stationery	£165
£150 + VAT £15	Debit VAT Account	£15		

VAT owing

VAT owing by or to the firm can be included with debtors or creditors, as the case may be. There is no need to show the amount(s) owing as separate items.

Columnar day books and VAT

The use of columns for VAT in both Sales and Purchases Analysis Books is shown on page 312.

Review questions

19.1 On 1 May 19-7, D Wilson Ltd, 1 Hawk Green Road, Stockport, sold the following goods on credit to G Christie & Son, The Golf Shop, Hole-in-One Lane, Marple, Cheshire:

Order No A/496

3 sets 'Boy Michael' golf clubs at £270 per set.

150 Watson golf balls at £8 per 10 balls.

4 Faldo golf bags at £30 per bag.

Trade discount is given at the rate of 33⅓%.

All goods are subject to VAT at 10%.

(*a*) Prepare the Sales Invoice to be sent to G Christie & Son. The invoice number will be 10586.

(*b*) Show the entries in the Personal Ledgers of D Wilson Ltd and G Christie & Son.

19.2 The following sales and purchases were made by R Colman Ltd during the month of May 19-6.

		Net	VAT added
		£	£
19-6			
May	1 Sold goods on credit to B Davies & Co	150	15
,,	4 Sold goods on credit to C Grant Ltd	220	22
,,	10 Bought goods on credit from:		
	G Cooper & Son	400	40
	J Wayne Ltd	190	19
,,	14 Bought goods on credit from B Lugosi	50	5
,,	16 Sold goods on credit to C Grant Ltd	140	14
,,	23 Bought goods on credit from S Hayward	60	6
,,	31 Sold goods on credit to B Karloff	80	8

Enter up the Sales and Purchases Books, Sales and Purchases Ledgers and the General Ledger for the month of May 19-6. Carry the balance down on the VAT account.

19.3 Mudgee Ltd issued the following invoices to customers in respect of credit sales made during the last week of May 19-7. The amounts stated are all net of Value Added Tax. All sales made by Mudgee Ltd are subject to VAT at 15%.

Invoice No	Date	Customer	Amount £
3045	25 May	Laira Brand	1,060.00
3046	27 May	Brown Bros	2,200.00
3047	28 May	Penfold's	170.00
3048	29 May	T Tyrrell	460.00
3049	30 May	Laira Brand	1,450.00
			£5,340.00

On 29 May Laira Brand returned half the goods (in value) purchased on 25 May. An allowance was made the same day to this customer for the appropriate amount.

On 1 May 19-7 Laira Brand owed Mudgee Ltd £2,100.47. Other than the purchases detailed above Laira Brand made credit purchases of £680.23 from Mudgee Ltd on 15 May. On 21 May Mudgee Ltd received a cheque for £2,500 from Laira Brand.

Required

(*a*) Show how the above transactions would be recorded in Mudgee Ltd's Sales Book for the week ended 30 May 19-7.

(*b*) Describe how the information in the Sales Book would be incorporated into Mudgee Ltd's double-entry system.

(*c*) Reconstruct the personal account of Laira Brand as it would appear in Mudgee Ltd's ledger for May 19-7.

(*Association of Accounting Technicians*)

19.4A Kwella Ltd received the following invoices from suppliers during the week commencing 23 November 19-7. All purchases made by Kwella Ltd are subject to Value Added Tax at 15%. The following list gives the *gross* value of each invoice received.

Date Received	Invoice No	Date of Invoice	Supplier	Gross amount £
23 Nov	GL 788	19 Nov	Glixit plc	506.00
24 Nov	899330	19 Nov	Moblin Ltd	115.00
25 Nov	G 1101	17 Nov	S & G Gates	724.50
26 Nov	AX 1256	23 Nov	Goldrins Glues	1,115.50
27 Nov	CS 772	25 Nov	Wixit Wires Ltd	1,794.00

On 25 November Kwella Ltd rejected all the goods invoiced on 24 November by Moblin Ltd (Invoice No 899330) because they were not what had been ordered. The goods were returned to Moblin Ltd along with Kwella Ltd's debit note (D 56) for the full invoice amount.

On 26 November Kwella Ltd had to return some of the goods purchased on 17 November from S & G Gates (Invoice No G 1101) because they were sub-standard. A debit note (D 57) for a gross value of £241.50 was returned with the goods.

Required:

(*a*) Write up Kwella Ltd's Purchases Book and Purchases Returns Book for the week commencing 23 November 19-7 totalling the columns off as at 28 November 19-7.

(*b*) Describe how the information in the Purchases Book and Purchases Returns Book would be incorporated into Kwella Ltd's ledger.

(*c*) The balance brought forward on S & G Gates' account at 1 November 19- 7 was £920.00 which Kwella Ltd settled in full by cheque on 13 November after deducting 5% discount. There were no other transactions with S & G Gates during the month of November other than those detailed above.

Reconstruct Kwella Ltd's ledger account for S & G Gates for the month of November 19-7 balancing off the account as at the 30 November 19-7.

(*Association of Accounting Technicians*)

19.5A Harold Peacock, a retailer, is registered for VAT purposes.

During September 19-6, the following transactions took place in Harold Peacock's business:

18 September Goods bought, on credit, from T King and Sons Limited, list price £640.00 subject to trade discount of 10% and also a cash discount of 2½% for payment within 30 days.

22 September New car, for use in the business, bought from XL Garages Limited at an agreed price of £8,000.00; payment to be effected on delivery.

25 September Goods sold, on credit, to G Siddle Limited, list price £1,200.00 subject to trade discount of 15% and cash discount of 2% for payment within 30 days.

All the above transactions are subject to VAT at 15%.

Required

Record the above transactions in the ledger accounts of Harold Peacock.

Note: Harold Peacock does not maintain total or control accounts for debtors or creditors (*see* below).

(*Association of Accounting Technicians*)

This note can be ignored at this stage in your studies (author).

19.6A Gala Traders Ltd had £57 cash on hand and a favourable balance of £216 in its business bank account as at the start of business on 2 May 19-8. The following is a list of cash and bank transactions for the week ending 7 May 19-8.

May 2   Paid an insurance premium of £130 by cheque.

May 3   Made a cash sales of £276 inclusive of Value Added Tax.

May 3   Paid travelling expenses in cash £17.

May 3   Paid an invoice for £110 from Supplies Ltd in full after deducting 10% for prompt settlement.

May 4   Received a cheque for £114 from Fred Croxter, a credit customer. Mr Croxter was settling an invoice for £120 and had been entitled to £6 discount.

May 5   Made cash sales of £414 inclusive of Value Added Tax.

May 6   Made cash purchases of £161 including Value Added Tax.

May 6   Paid the week's wages to employees partly by cheque for £107 and partly in cash £75.

May 6   Paid £420 from the safe into the business bank account.

The rate of Value Added Tax is 15%.

Required:

(*a*) Write up Gala Traders Ltd's Cash Book for the week commencing 2 May 19-8 with separate columns for discount, VAT, bank and cash. Balance the Cash Book as at 7 May 19-8.

(*b*) Describe how the totals for the Discount and VAT columns will be entered into the ledger.

(*Association of Accounting Technicians*)

20
Depreciation of fixed assets: nature and calculations

Fixed assets have already been stated to be those assets of material value that are of long-life, are held to be used in the business, and are not primarily for resale or for conversion into cash.

Usually, with the exception of land, fixed assets have a limited number of years of useful life. Motor vans, machines, buildings and fixtures, for instance, do not last for ever. Even land itself may have all or part of its usefulness exhausted after a few years. Some types of land used for quarries, mines, or land of another sort of wasting nature would be examples. When a fixed asset is bought, then later put out of use by the firm, that part of the cost that is not recovered on disposal is called depreciation.

It is obvious that the only time that depreciation can be calculated accurately is when the fixed asset is disposed of, and the difference between the cost to its owner and the amount received on disposal is then ascertained. If a motor van was bought for £1,000 and sold five years later for £20, then the amount of depreciation is £1,000 − £20 = £980.

Depreciation is thus the part of the cost of the fixed asset consumed during its period of use by the firm. Therefore, it has been a cost for services consumed in the same way as costs for such items as wages, rent, lighting etc. Depreciation is, therefore, an expense and will need charging to the profit and loss account before ascertaining net profit or loss. Provision for depreciation suffered will therefore have to be made in the books in order that the net profits may be profits remaining after charging all the expenses of the period.

In fact SSAP 12 defines depreciation as 'the measure of the wearing out, consumption or other loss of **value** of fixed asset whether arising from use, effluxion of time or obsolescence through technology and market changes.' This definition refers to loss of value rather than cost. This has been done deliberately so that it also covers depreciation in any form of inflation accounting system, such systems being outside the scope of this book.

Causes of depreciation

These may be divided into the main classes of physical deterioration, economic factors, the time factor, and depletion.

Physical deterioration is caused mainly from wear and tear when the asset is in use, but also from erosion, rust, rot, and decay from being exposed to wind, rain, sun and other elements of nature.

Economic factors may be said to be those that cause the asset to be put out of use even though it is in good physical condition. These are largely obsolescence and inadequacy.

Obsolescence means the process of becoming obsolete or out of date. An example of this were the steam locomotives, some of them in good physical condition, which were rendered obsolete by the introduction of diesel and electric locomotives. The steam locomotives were put out of use by British Rail when they still had many more miles of potential use, because the newer locomotives were more efficient and economical to run.

Inadequacy refers to the termination of the use of an asset because of the growth and changes in the size of a firm. For instance, a small ferry boat that is operated by a firm at a seaside resort is entirely inadequate when the resort becomes more popular. It is found that it would be more efficient and economical to operate a larger ferry boat, and so the smaller boat is put out of use by the firm.

Both obsolescence and inadequacy do not necessarily mean that the asset is scrapped. It is merely put out of use by the firm. Another firm will often buy it. For example, many of the aeroplanes put out of use by large airlines are bought by smaller firms.

The **time factor** is obviously associated with all the causes mentioned already. However, there are fixed assets to which the time factor is connected in another way. These are assets with a fixed period of legal life such as leases, patents and copyrights. For instance a lease can be entered into for any period, while a patent's legal life is sixteen years, but there are certain grounds on which this can be extended. Provision for the consumption of these assets is called **amortisation** rather than depreciation.

Other assets are of a wasting character, perhaps due to the extraction of raw materials from them. These materials are then either used by the firm to make something else, or are sold in their raw state to other firms. Natural resources such as mines, quarries and oil wells come under this heading. To provide for the consumption of an asset of a wasting character is called **provision for depletion**.

Land and buildings

Prior to SSAP 12, which applied after 1977, freehold and long leasehold properties were very rarely subject to a charge for depreciation. It was contended that, as property values tended to rise instead of falling, it was inappropriate to charge depreciation.

However, SSAP 12 requires that depreciation be written off over the property's useful life, with the exception that freehold land will not normally require a provision for depreciation. This is because land does not normally depreciate. Buildings do however eventually fall into disrepair or become obsolete, and must be subject to a charge for depreciation each year. When a revaluation of property takes place the depreciation charge must be on the revalued figure.

An exception to all this are **investment properties**. These are properties owned not for use, but simply for investment. In this case investment properties will be shown in the balance sheet at their open market value.

Appreciation

At this stage of the chapter the reader may well begin to ask himself about the assets that increase (appreciate) in value. The answer to this is that normal accounting procedure would be to ignore any such appreciation, as to bring appreciation into account would be to contravene both the cost concept and the prudence concept as discussed in Chapter 10. Nevertheless, in certain circumstances appreciation is taken into account in partnership and limited company accounts, but this is left until partnerships and limited companies are considered.

Provision for depreciation as allocation of cost

Depreciation in total over the life of an asset can be calculated quite simply as cost less amount receivable when the asset is put out of use by the firm. If the item is bought and sold within the one accounting period then the depreciation for that period is charged as a revenue expense in arriving at that period's Net Profit. The difficulties start when the asset is used for more than one accounting period, and an attempt has to be made to charge each period with the depreciation for that period.

Even though depreciation provisions are now regarded as allocating cost to each accounting period (except for accounting for inflation), it does not follow that there is any 'true' method of performing even this task. All that can be said is that the cost should be allocated over the life of the asset in such a way as to charge it as equitably as possible to the periods in which the asset is used. The difficulties involved are considerable and some of them are now listed.

1 Apart from a few assets, such as a lease, how accurately can a firm assess an asset's useful life? Even a lease may be put out of use if the premises leased have become inadequate.

2 How does one measure use? A car owned by a firm for two years may have been driven one year by a very careful driver and another year by a reckless driver. The standard of driving will affect the motor car and also the amount of cash receivable on its disposal. How should such a firm apportion the car's depreciation costs?

3 There are other expenses besides depreciation such as repairs and maintenance of the fixed asset. As both of these affect the rate and amount of depreciation should they not also affect the depreciation provision calculations?

4 How can a firm possibly know the amount receivable in x years time when the asset is put out of use?

These are only some of the difficulties. Therefore, the methods of calculating provisions for depreciation are mainly accounting customs.

The main methods of calculating provisions for depreciation

The two main methods in use are the **Straight-Line Method** and the **Reducing Balance Method.** In fact it has now become regarded that though other methods may be more applicable in certain cases, the straight-line method is the one that is generally most suitable.

Straight-line method

This allows an equal amount to be charged as depreciation for each year of expected use of the asset.

The basic formula is:

$$\frac{\text{Cost} - \text{Estimated Residual Value}}{\text{Number of years of expected use}} = \text{Depreciation provision per annum}$$

The reason for this method being called the straight-line method is that if the charge for depreciation was plotted annually on a graph and the points joined together, then the graph would reveal a straight line.

For example, a machine costs £10,000, it has an expected life of four years, and has an estimated residual value of £256. The depreciation provision per annum will be

$$\frac{£10,000 - £256}{4} = £2,436.$$

In practice, the residual value is often ignored where it would be a relatively small amount.

Reducing balancing method

To calculate the depreciation provision annually, a fixed percentage is applied to the balance of costs not yet allocated as an expense at the end of the previous accounting period. The balance of unallocated costs will therefore decrease each year, and as a fixed percentage is being used the depreciation provision will therefore be less with each passing year. Theoretically, the balance of unallocated costs at the end of the expected life should equal the estimated residual value.

The basic formula used to find the requisite percentage to apply with this method is:

$$r = 1 - \sqrt[n]{\frac{s}{c}}$$

where n = the number of years
       s = the net residual value (this must be a significant amount or the answers will be absurd, since the depreciation rate would amount to nearly one)
       c = the cost of the asset
       r = the rate of depreciation to be applied.

Using, as an example, the figures used for the machine for which depreciation provisions were calculated on the straight-line method, the calculations would appear as:

$$r = 1 - \sqrt[4]{\frac{£256}{£10,000}} = 1 - \frac{4}{10} = 0.6 \text{ or } 60 \text{ per cent}$$

The depreciation calculation applied to each of the four years of use would be:

	£
Cost	10,000
Year 1: Depreciation provision 60 per cent of £10,000	6,000
Cost not yet apportioned, end of Year 1.	4,000
Year 2: Depreciation provision 60 per cent of £4,000	2,400
Cost not yet apportioned, end of Year 2.	1,600
Year 3: Depreciation provision 60 per cent of £1,600	960
Cost not yet apportioned, end of Year 3.	640
Year 4: Depreciation provision 60 per cent of £640	384
Cost not yet apportioned, end of Year 4.	256

In this case the percentage to be applied worked out conveniently to a round figure. However, the answer will often come out to several places of decimals. In this case it would be usual to take the nearest whole figure as a percentage to be applied.

The percentage to be applied, assuming a significant amount for residual value, is usually between two to three times greater for the reducing balance method than for the straight-line method.

The advocates of this method usually argue that it helps to even out the total charged as expenses for the use of the asset each year. They state that provisions for depreciation are not the only costs charged, there are the running costs in addition and that the repairs and maintenance element of running costs usually increase with age. Therefore, to equate total usage costs for each year of use the depreciation provisions should fall as the repairs and maintenance element increases. However, as can be seen from the figures of the example already given, the repairs and maintenance element would have to be comparitively large to bring about an equal total charge for each year of use.

To summarise, the people who favour this method say that:

In the early years		*In the later years*
A higher charge for depreciation	will tend to be fairly equal to	A lower charge for depreciation
+		+
A lower charge for repairs and upkeep		A higher charge for repairs and upkeep

Choice of method

The purpose of depreciation is to spread the total cost of the asset over the periods in which it is available to be used. The method chosen should be that which allocates cost to each period in accordance with the amount of benefit gained from the use of the asset in the period.

If, therefore, the main value is to be obtained from the asset in its earliest years, it may be appropriate to use the reducing balance which charges more in the early years. If, on the other hand, the benefits are to be gained evenly over the years then the straight-line method would be more appropriate.

The repairs and maintenance factor also has to be taken into account. One argument has already been mentioned in the last section.

Exhibit 20.1 gives a comparison of the calculations using the two methods, if the same cost is given for the two methods.

Exhibit 20.1

A firm has just bought a machine for £8,000. It will be kept in use for four years, when it will be disposed of for an estimated amount of £500. They ask for a comparison of the amounts charged as depreciation using both methods.

For the straight-line method a figure of $(£8,000 - £500) \div 4 = £7,500 \div 4 = £1,875$ per annum is to be used. For the reducing balance method a percentage figure of 50 per cent will be used.

	Method 1 (Straight Line)		Method 2 (Reducing Balance)
	£		£
Cost	8,000		8,000
Depreciation: Year 1	1,875	(50% of £8,000)	4,000
	6,125		4,000
Depreciation: Year 2	1,875	(50% of £4,000)	2,000
	4,250		2,000
Depreciation: Year 3	1,875	(50% of £2,000)	1,000
	2,375		1,000
Depreciation: Year 4	1,875	(50% of £1,000)	500
Disposal value	500		500

This illustrates the fact that using the reducing balance method has a much higher charge for depreciation in the early years, and lower charges in the later years.

Another name for the reducing balance method is the *diminishing balance method*.

Depreciation provisions and assets bought or sold

There are two main methods of calculating depreciation provisions for assets bought or sold during an accounting period.

1 To ignore the dates during the year that the assets were bought or sold, merely calculating a full period's depreciation on the assets in use at the end of the period. Thus, assets sold during the accounting period will have had no provision for depreciation made for that last period irrespective of how many months they were in use. Conversely, assets bought during the period will have a full period of depreciation provision calculated even though they may not have been owned throughout the whole of the period.

2 Provision for depreciation made on the basis of one month's ownership, one month's provision for depreciation. Fractions of months are usually ignored. This is obviously a more scientific method than that already described.

For examination purposes, where the date on which assets are bought and sold are shown then Method 2 is the method expected by the examiner. If no such dates are given then obviously Method 1 will have to be used.

Other methods of calculating depreciation

There are many more methods of calculating depreciation but they are outside the scope of this chapter. These are fully considered in Chapter 33. You will find the revaluation method, depletion unit method, machine hour method and the sum of the year's digits in that chapter.

Review questions

20.1 D Sankey, a manufacturer, purchases a lathe for the sum of £4,000. It has an estimated life of 5 years and a scrap value of £500.

Sankey is not certain whether he should use the staight-line or the reducing balance basis for the purpose of calculating depreciation on the machine.

You are required to calculate the depreciation on the lathe using both methods, showing clearly the balance remaining in the lathe account at the end of each of the five years for each method. (Assume that 40 per cent per annum is to be used for the reducing balance method.)

20.2 A machine costs £12,500. It will be kept for 4 years, and then sold for an estimated figure of £5,120. Show the calculations of the figures for depreciation (to nearest £) for each of the four years using (*a*) the straight-line method, (*b*) the reducing balance method, for this method using a depreciation rate of 20 per cent.

20.3 A motor vehicle costs £6,400. It will be kept for 5 years, and then sold for scrap £200. Calculate the depreciation for each year using (*a*) the reducing balance method, using a depreciation rate of 50 per cent, (*b*) the straight-line method.

20.4A A machine costs £5,120. It will be kept for 5 years, and then sold at an estimated figure of £1,215. Show the calculations of the figures for depreciation for each year using (*a*) the straight-line method, (*b*) the reducing balance method, for this method using a depreciation rate of 25 per cent.

20.5A A bulldozer costs £12,150. It will be kept for 5 years. At the end of that time agreement has already been made that it will be sold for £1,600. Show your calculations of the amount of depreciation each year if (*a*) the reducing balance method at a rate of 33⅓ per cent was used, (*b*) the straight-line method was used.

20.6A A motor tractor is bought for £6,000. It will be used for 3 years, and then sold back to the supplier for £3,072. Show the depreciation calculations for each year using (*a*) the reducing balance method with a rate of 20 per cent, (*b*) the straight-line method.

20.7 A company, which makes up its accounts annually to 31 December, provides for depreciation of its machinery at the rate of 10 per cent per annum on the diminishing balance system.

On 31 December 19-6, the machinery consisted of three items purchased as under:

	£
On 1 January 19-4 Machine A	Cost 3,000
On 1 April 19-5 Machine B	Cost 2,000
On 1 July 19-6 Machine C	Cost 1,000

Required:
Your calculations showing the depreciation provision for the year 19-6.

21

Double-entry records for depreciation

Looking back quite a few years, the charge for depreciation always used to be shown in the fixed asset accounts themselves. This method has now fallen into disuse.

The method now used is where the fixed assets accounts are always kept for showing the assets at cost price. The depreciation is shown accumulating in a separate 'provision for depreciation' account. This is the method used throughout this book. An illustration can now be looked at.

In a business with financial years ended 31 December a machine is bought for £2,000 on 1 January 19-5. It is to be depreciated at the rate of 20 per cent using the reducing balance method. The records for the first three years are now shown:

No entry is made in the asset account for depreciation. Instead, the depreciation is shown accumulating in a separate account.

The double entry is:

Debit the profit and loss account

Credit the provision for depreciation account

Machinery

19-5		£
Jan 1 Cash		2,000

Provision for Depreciation - Machinery

19-5		£	19-5		£
Dec 31 Balance c/d		400	Dec 31 Profit and Loss		400
19-6			19-6		
Dec 31 Balance c/d		720	Jan 1 Balance b/d		400
			Dec 31 Profit and Loss		320
		720			720
19-7			19-7		
Dec 31 Balance c/d		976	Jan 1 Balance b/d		720
			Dec 31 Profit and Loss		256
		976			976
			19-8		
			Jan 1 Balance b/d		976

19-5	Depreciation	400

19-6	Depreciation	320

19-7	Depreciation	256

Now the balance on the Machinery Account is shown on the balance sheet at the end of each year less the balance on the Provision for Depreciation Account.

Balance Sheets

	£	£
As at 31 December 19-5		
Machinery at cost	2,000	
less Depreciation to date	400	
		1,600
As at 31 December 19-6		
Machinery at cost	2,000	
less Depreciation to date	720	
		1,280
As at 31 December 19-7		
Machinery at cost	2,000	
less Depreciation to date	976	
		1,024

The disposal of an asset

When we charge depreciation on a fixed asset we are having to make guesses. We cannot be absolutely certain how long we will keep the asset in use, nor can we be certain at the date of purchase how much cash will be received for the asset then we dispose of it. To get our guesses absolutely correct would be quite rare. This means that when we dispose of an asset, the cash received for it is usually different from our original guess.

This can be shown by looking back at the illustration already shown in this chapter. At the end of 19-7 the value of the machinery on the balance sheet is shown as £1,024. We can now see the entries needed if (*a*) the machinery was sold on 2 January 19-8 for £1,070 and then (*b*) if instead it had been sold for £950.

(*a*)	Transfer the cost price of the asset sold to an Asset Disposal Account (in this case a Machinery Disposals Account).	(*Dr*) Machinery Disposals Account (*Cr*) Machinery Account
(*b*)	Transfer the depreciation already charged to the Asset Disposal Account.	(*Dr*) Provisions for Depreciation - Machinery (*Cr*) Machinery Disposals Account
(*c*)	For remittance received on disposal.	(*Dr*) Cash Book (*Cr*) Machinery Disposals Account
(*d*)	Transfer balance (difference) on Machinery Disposals Account to the Profit and Loss Account. If the difference is on the debit side of the disposal account, it is a profit on sale. If the difference is on the credit side of the disposal account, it is a loss on sales.	 (*Dr*) Machinery Disposals Account (*Cr*) Profit and Loss account (*Dr*) Profit and Loss Account (*Cr*) Machinery Disposals Account

Asset sold at a profit

Machinery

19-5	£	19-8	£
Jan 1 Cash	2,000	Jan 2 Machinery Disposals	(a) 2,000

Provision for Depreciation: Machinery

19-8	£	19-8	£
Jan 2 Machinery Disposals	(b) 976	Jan 1 Balance b/d	976

Machinery Disposals

19-8	£	19-8	£
Jan 2 Machinery	(a) 2,000	Jan 2 Cash	(c) 1,070
Dec 31 Profit and Loss	(d) 46	Jan 2 Provision for Depreciation	(b) 976
	2,046		2,046

Profit and Loss Account for the year ended 31 December 19-8

		£
Profit on sale of machinery	(d)	46

Asset sold at a loss

Machinery

19-5	£	19-8	£
Jan 1 Cash	2,000	Jan 2 Machinery Disposals	(a) 2,000

Provision for Depreciation: Machinery

19-8	£	19-8	£
Jan 2 Machinery Disposals	(b) 976	Jan 1 Balance b/d	976

Machinery Disposals

19-8	£	19-8	£
Jan 2 Machinery	(a) 2,000	Jan 2 Cash	(c) 950
		Jan 2 Provision for Depreciation	(b) 976
		Dec 31 Profit and Loss	(d) 74
	2,000		2,000

Profit and Loss Account for the year ended 31 December 19-8

		£
Loss on sale of machinery	(d)	74

In many cases the disposal of an asset will mean that we have sold it. This will not always be the case. A car may be put in exchange against the purchase of a new car. Here the disposal value is the exchange value. If a new car costing £10,000 was to be paid for by £6,000 in cash and £4,000 for the old car put in exchange, then the disposal value of the old car is £4,000

Similarly a car may have been in an accident and is now worthless. If insured the disposal value will be the amount received from the insurance company. If an asset is scrapped the disposal value is that received from the sale of the scrap, which may be nil.

Change of depreciation method

It is possible to make a change in the method of calculating depreciation. This should not be done frequently, and it should only be undertaken after a thorough review. Where a change is made the effect, if material (*see* Chapter 10 on materiality) should be shown as a note to the final accounts in the year of change.

Further examples

So far the examples shown have deliberately been kept simple. Only one item of an asset has been shown in each case. Exhibits 21.1 and 21.2 give examples of more complicated cases.

Exhibit 21.1

A Machine is bought on 1 January 19-5 for £1,000 and another one on 1 October 19-6 for £1,200. The first machine is sold on 30 June 19-7 for £720. The firm's financial year ends on 31 December. The machinery is to be depreciated at ten per cent, using the straight line method and based on assets in existence at the end of each year ignoring items sold during the year.

19-5		£			£
Jan 1 Cash		1,000			
19-6			19-6		
Oct 1 Cash		1,200	Dec 31 Balance c/d		2,200
		2,200			2,200
19-7			19-7		
Jan 1 Balance b/d		2,200	Jun 30 Disposals		1,000
			Dec 31 Balance c/d		1,200
		2,200			2,200
19-8					
Jan 1 Balance b/d		1,200			

Provision for Depreciation - Machinery

	£	19-5		£
		Dec 31 Profit and Loss		100
19-6		19-6		
Dec 31 Balance c/d	320	Dec 31 Profit and Loss		220
	320			320
19-7	£	19-7		£
Jun 30 Disposals		Jan 1 Balance b/d		320
(2 years × 10 per cent		Dec 31 Profit and Loss		120
×£1,000)	200			
Dec 31 Balance c/d	240			
	440			440
		19-8		
		Jan 1 Balance b/d		240

Disposals of Machinery

19-7		£	19-7		£
Jun 30 Machinery		1,000	Jun 30 Cash		720
			Jun 30 Provision for		
			Depreciation		200
			Dec 31 Profit and Loss		80
		1,000			1,000

Profit and Loss Account for the year ended 31 December

19-5 Provision for Depreciation	100
19-6 Provision for Depreciation	220
19-7 Provision for Depreciation	120
Loss on machinery sold	80

	£	£
19-5 Machinery at cost price	1,000	
less Depreciation to date	100	
		900
19-6 Machinery at cost	2,200	
less Depreciation to date	320	
		1,880
19-7 Machinery at cost	1,200	
less Depreciation to date	240	
		960

Another example can now be given. This is somewhat more complicated owing first to a greater number of items, and secondly because the depreciation provisions are calculated on a proportionate basis, i.e. one month's depreciation for every one month's ownership.

Exhibit 21.2

A business with its financial year end being 31 December buys two motor vans, No 1 for £800 and No 2 for £500, both on 1 January 19-1. It also buys another motor van, No 3, on 1 July 19-3 for £900 and another, No 4, on 1 October 19-3 for £720. The first two motor vans are sold, No 1 for £229 on 30 September 19-4, and the other No 2, was sold for scrap £5 on 30 June 19-5.

Depreciation is on the straight-line basis, 20 per cent per annum, ignoring scrap value in this particular case when calculating depreciation per annum. Show the extracts from the assets account, provision for depreciation account, disposal account, profit and loss account for the years ended 31 December 19-1, 19-2, 19-3, 19-4, and 19-5, and the balance sheets as at those dates.

Motor Vans

19-1		£			£
Jan	1 Cash	1,300			
19-3					
July	1 Cash	900	19-3		
Oct	1 Cash	720	Dec 31 Balance c/d		2,920
		2,920			2,920
19-4			19-4		
Jan	1 Balance b/d	2,920	Sept 30 Disposals		800
			Dec 31 Balance c/d		2,120
		2,920			2,920
19-5			19-5		
Jan	1 Balance b/d	2,120	June 30 Disposals		500
			Dec 31 Balance c/d		1,620
		2,120			2,120
19-6					
Jan	1 Balance b/d	1,620			

		£			£
			91-1		
			Dec 31 Profit and Loss		260
19-2			19-2		
Dec 31 Balance c/d		520	Dec 31 Profit and Loss		260
		520			520
19-3			19-3		
			Jan 1 Balance b/d		520
Dec 31 Balance c/d		906	Dec 31 Profit and Loss		386
		906			906
19-4			19-4		
Sept 30 Disposals		600	Jan 1 Balance b/d		906
Dec 31 Balance c/d		850	Dec 31 Profit and Loss		544
		1,450			1,450
19-5			19-5		
June 30 Disposals		450	Jan 1 Balance b/d		850
Dec 31 Balance c/d		774	Dec 31 Profit and Loss		374
		1,224			1,224
			19-6		
			Jan 1 Balance b/d		774

Workings – depreciation provisions

		£	£
19-1	20% of £1,300		260
19-2	20% of £1,300		260
19-3	20% of £1,300×12 months	260	
	20% of £900×6 months	90	
	20% of £720×3 months	36	
			386
19-4	20% of £2,120×12 months	424	
	20% of £800×9 months	120	
			544
19-5	20% of £1,620×12 months	324	
	20% of £500×6 months	50	
			374

Workings – transfers of depreciation provisions to disposal accounts

Van 1 Bought Jan 1 19-1 Cost £800
      Sold Sept 30 19-4
      Period of ownership 3¾ years
      Depreciation provisions 3¾×20% ×£800=£600
Van 2 Bought Jan 1 19-1 Cost £500
      Sold June 30 19-5
      Period of ownership 4½ years
      Depreciation provisions 4½×20% ×£500=£450

19-4		£	19-4		£
Sept 30	Motor Van	800	Sept 30	Provision for depreciation	600
Dec 31	Profit and Loss	29	,, ,,	Cash	229
		829			829
19-5			19-5		
Jun 30	Motor Van	500	Jun 30	Provision for Depreciation	450
			,, ,,	Cash	5
			Dec 31	Profit and Loss	45
		500			500

Profit and Loss Account for the year ended 31 December (extracts)

		£			
19-1	Provision for Depreciation	260			
19-2	Provision for Depreciation	260			
19-3	Provision for Depreciation	386			
19-4	Provision for Depreciation	544	19-4	Profit on motor van sold	29
19-5	Provision for Depreciation	374			
	Loss on motor van sold	45			

Balance Sheets (extracts) as at 31 December

		£	£
19-1	Motor Vans at cost	1,300	
	less Depreciation to date	260	
			1,040
19-2	Motor Vans at cost	1,300	
	less Depreciation to date	520	
			780
19-3	Motor Vans at cost	2,920	
	less Depreciation to date	906	
			2,014
19-4	Motor Vans at cost	2,120	
	less Depreciation to date	850	
			1,270
19-5	Motor Vans at cost	1,620	
	less Depreciation to date	774	
			846

This chapter has covered all the principles involved. Obviously an examiner can present his questions in his own way, frequently devised by him to test your understanding by presenting them in different ways. Practice at the questions in this book and comparing them with the answers shown in full will demonstrate the truth of this statement.

Depreciation provisions and the replacement of assets

The purpose of making provision for depreciation is to ensure that the cost of an asset is charged as an expense in a equitable fashion over its useful life in the firm. Parts of the cost are allocated to different years until the whole of the asset's cost has been expensed. This does not mean that depreciation provisions of the type described already provide funds with which to replace the asset when it is put out of use. Such provisions might affect the owner's actions so that funds were available to pay for the replacement of the asset, but this is not necessarily true in all cases.

Imagine a case when a machine is bought for £1,000 and it is expected to last for 5 years, at the end of which time it will be put out of use and will not fetch any money from its being scrapped. If the machine has provisions for depreciation calculated on the straight-line basis then £200 per year will be charged as an expense for 5 years. This means that the recorded net profit will be decreased £200 for each of the 5 years because of the depreciation provisions. Now the owner may well, as a consequence, because his profits are £200 less also reduce his drawings by £200 per annum. If the action of charging £200 each year for depreciation also does reduce his annual drawings by £200, then the amount will increase his bank balance (or reduce his bank overdraft), so that at the end of 5 years he may have the cash available to buy a new machine for £1,000 to replace the one that has been put out of use. In fact this is not necessarily true at all, the owner may still take the same amount of drawings for each of the 5 years whether or not a provision for depreciation is charged. In this case nothing has been deliberately held back to provide the cash with which to buy the replacement machine.

There is nothing by law that says that if your recorded profits are £x then the drawings must not exceed £y. For instance a man may make £5,000 profit for his first year in business while his drawings were £1,000 in that year, while in the second year his profit might be £2,000 and his drawings are £4,000. In the long run an owner may go out of business if his drawings are too high, but in the short term his drawings may well bear no relationship to profits whatsoever. This means that the amounts charged for depreciation provisions thus affecting the profits recorded may not affect the drawings at all in the short term.

Review questions

21.1 A company starts in business on 1 January 19-1. You are to write up the motor vans account and the provision for depreciation account for the year ended 31 December 19-1 from the information given below. Depreciation is at the rate of 20 per cent per annum, using the basis of 1 month's ownership needs one month's depreciation.

19-1　　Bought two motor vans for £1,200 each on 1 January
　　　　Bought one motor van for £1,400 on 1 July

21.2 A company starts in business on 1 January 19-3, the financial year end being 31 December. You are to show:

(a) The machinery account
(b) The provision for depreciation account
(c) The balance sheet extracts for each of the years 19-3, 19-4, 19-5, 19-6.

The machinery bought was:

19-3   1 January   1 machine costing £800
19-4   1 July   2 machines costing £500 each
       1 October   1 machine costing £600
19-6   1 April   1 machine costing £200

Depreciation is at the rate of 10 per cent per annum, using the straight-line method, machines being depreciated for each proportion of a year.

21.3 A company depreciates its plant at the rate of 20 per cent per annum, straight-line method, for each month of ownership. From the following details draw up the Plant Account and the provisions for depreciation account for each of the years 19-4, 19-5, 19-6, and 19-7.

19-4   Bought plant costing £900 on 1 January
       Bought plant costing £600 on 1 October
19-6   Bought plant costing £550 on 1 October
19-7   Sold plant which had been bought on 1 January 19-4 for £900 for the sum of £275 on 30 September 19-7.

You are also required to draw up the plant disposal account and the extracts from the balance sheet as at the end of each year.

21.4 Mavron plc owned the following motor vehicles as at 1 April 19- 6:

Motor Vehicle	Date Acquired	Cost £	Estimated Residual Value £	Estimated Life (years)
AAT 101	1 October 19-3	8,500	2,500	5
DJH 202	1 April 19-4	12,000	2,000	8

Mavron plc's policy is to provide at the end of each financial year depreciation using the straight-line method applied on a month-by-month basis on all motor vehicles used during the year.

During the financial year ended 31 March 19-7 the following occurred:

(*a*) On 30 June 19-6 AAT101 was traded in and replaced KGC303. The trade-in allowance was £5,000. KGC303 cost £15,000 and the balance due (after deducting the trade-in allowance) was paid partly in cash and partly by a loan of £6,000 from Pinot Finance. KGC303 is expected to have a residual value of £4,000 after an estimated economic life of 5 years.

(*b*) The estimated remaining economic life of DJH202 was reduced from 6 years to 4 years with no change in the estimated residual value.

Required

(*a*) Show any Journal entries necessary to give effect to the above.

(*b*) Show the Journal entry necessary to record depreciation on Motor Vehicles for the year ended 31 March 19-7.

(*c*) Reconstruct the Motor Vehicles Account and the Provision for Depreciation Account for the year ended 31 March 19-7.

Show the necessary calculations clearly.

(Association of Accounting Technicians).

21.5A

(a) Identify the four factors which cause fixed assets to depreciate.

(b) Which one of these factors is the most important for each of the following assets?

    (i)   a gold mine.

    (ii) a motor lorry.

    (iii) a 50 year lease on a building.

    (iv) land.

    (v) a ship used to ferry passengers and vehicles across a river following the building of a bridge across the river.

    (vi) a franchise to market a new computer software package in a certain country.

(c) The financial year of Ochre Ltd will end on 31 December 19-6. At 1 January 19-6 the company had in use equipment with a total accumulated cost of £135,620 which had been depreciated by a total of £81,374. During the year ended 31 December 19-6 Ochre Ltd purchased new equipment costing £47,800 and sold off equipment which had originally cost £36,000 and which had been depreciated by £28,224 for £5,700. No further purchases or sales of equipment are planned for December. The policy of the company is to depreciate equipment at 40% using the diminishing balance method. A full year's depreciation is provided for on all equipment in use by the company at the end of each year.

Required

Show the following ledger accounts for the year ended 31 December 19-6:

    (i) the Equipment Account.

    (ii) the Provision for Depreciation Equipment Account.

    (iii) the Assets Disposals Account.

(Association of Accounting Technicians)

21.6A The following information has been extracted from the motor-lorry records of Express Transport Ltd:

Express Transport Limited

Lorry	Date bought	Cost £	Method of payment
B393KPQ	1 October 19-3	22,000	Cash transaction.
B219BXY	1 January 19-4	25,000	Cash transaction.
C198TKL	1 October 19-5	34,000	Cash transaction.
C437FGA	1 April 19-6	28,000	B393KPQ given in part exchange plus cheque for £18,000.

Express Transport Limited, which was incorporated in 19-3, has only owned the vehicles mentioned above during its existence.

Up to 30 September 19-5, the company used the reducing balance method for depreciating its motor lorries: the rate of depreciation being 25% per annum.

However, as from 1 October 19-5 it has been decided to change to the straight-line method for depreciating the motor lorries: the rate of depreciation to be used is 20% per annum and it is assumed that all vehicles will have a nil residual value. As a result of this decision, it will be necessary for appropriate adjustments to be made in the company's accounts so that the balance of the motor lorries provision for depreciation account at 1 October 19-5 will be on the basis of the straight-line method.

Required

(*a*) Prepare the journal entry (or entries) necessitated by the change of depreciation policy on 1 October 19-5 from the reducing balance method to the straightline method. *Note*: Journal entries should include narratives.

(*b*) Prepare the following accounts for the year ended 30 September 19-6 in the books of Express Transport Limited:
Motor Lorries at cost;
Motor Lorries provision for depreciation;
Motor Lorry B393KPQ disposal.

(Association of Accounting Technicians).

21.7 A firm buys a fixed asset for £10,000. The firm estimates that the asset will be used for 5 years, and will have a scrap value of about £100, less removal expenses. After exactly 2½ years, however, the asset is suddenly sold for £5,000. The firm always provides a full year's depreciation in the year of purchase and no depreciation in the year of disposal.

Required

(*a*) Write up the relevant accounts (including disposal account but not profit and loss account) for each of Years 1, 2 and 3:
(*i*) Using the straight-line depreciation method (assume 20% pa);
(*ii*) Using the reducing balance depreciation method (assume 40% pa).
(*b*) (i) What is the purpose of depreciation? In what circumstances would each of the two methods you have used be preferable?
(ii) What is the meaning of the net figure for the fixed asset in the balance sheet at the end of Year 2?
(*c*) If the asset was bought at the beginning of Year 1, but was not used at all until Year 2 (and it is confidently anticipated to last until Year 6), state under each method the appropriate depreciation charge in Year 1, and briefly justify your answer.

(Chartered Association of Certified Accountants)

21.8 You have been given the task, by one of the partners of the firm of accountants for which you work, of assisting in the preparation of a trend statement for a client.

The client's business has been in existence for four years. Figures for the three previous years are known but those for the fourth year need to be calculated. Unfortunately, the supporting workings for the previous years' figures cannot be found and the client's own ledger accounts and workings are not available.

One item in particular, Plant, is causing difficulty and the following figures have been given to you.

	12 months ended 31 March			
	19-4	19-5	19-6	19-7
	£	£	£	£
(*a*) Plant at cost	80,000	80,000	90,000	?
(*b*) Accumulated depreciation	(16,000)	(28,800)	(36,720)	?
(*c*) Net (written down value)	64,000	51,200	53,280	?

The only other information available is that disposals have taken place at the beginning of the financial years concerned.

	Date of Disposal 12 months ended 31 March	Original acquisition	Original cost £	Sales Proceeds £
First disposal	19-6	19-4	15,000	8,000
Second disposal	19-7	19-4	30,000	21,000

Plant sold was replaced on the same day by new plant. The cost of the plant which replaced the first disposal is not known but the replacement for the second disposal is known to have cost £50,000.

Required

(a) Identify the method of providing the depreciation on plant employed by the client, stating how you have arrived at your conclusion;

(b) Reconstruct a working schedule to support the figures shown at line (b) for each of the years ended 31 March 19-4, 19-5 and 19-6. Extend your workings to cover year ended 31 March 1987;

(c) Produce the figures that should be included in the blank spaces on the trend statement at lines (a), (b) and (c) for the year ended 31 March 19-7; and

(d) Calculate the profit or loss arising on each of the two disposals.

(Chartered Association of Certified Accountants)

21.9A A client of the firm of accountants by which you are employed is interested in buying a road transport business from the widow of its deceased owner.

The senior partner of the practice is investigating various aspects of the business and has delegated to you the task of discovering the amount of investment in vehicles at the end of each of the financial years ended 30 September 19-3 to 19-6 inclusive. The business has commenced operations on 1 October 19-2.

The only information available to you is the fact that the owner calculated depreciation at a rate of 20% per annum, using the Reducing Balance method, based on the balance at 30 September each year, and copies of certain ledger accounts which are reproduced below:

Provisions for depreciation of vehicles

		£			£
			19-3		
			1 Oct Balance b/d		32,000
19-4			19-4		
30 Sept	Balance c/d	57,600	30 Sept Profit and loss		25,600
		£57,600			£57,600
		£			£
			1 Oct Balance b/d		57,600
19-5			19-5		
30 Sept	Disposals	10,800	30 Sept Profit and loss (includes £10,000 depreciation on 19-2 acquisitions)		26,640
	Balance c/d	73,440			
		£84,240			£84,240
		£			£
			1 Oct Balance b/d		73,440
19-6			19-6		
30 Sept	Disposals	29,280	30 Sept Profit and loss (includes £20,000 depreciation on 19-3 acquisitions)		35,168
	Balance	79,328			
		£108,608			£108,608
			1 Oct Balance b/d		79,328

		£				£
19-5			19-5			
30 Sept	Vehicles (vehicles originally acquired on 1 October 19-2)	30,000	30 Sept	Provn. for depreciation		10,800
				Bank		16,000
				Profit and loss		3,200
		£30,000				£30,000

		£				£
19-6			19-6			
30 Sept	Vehicles (vehicles originally acquired on 1 October 19-2)	60,000	30 Sept	Provn. for depreciation		29,280
	Profit and loss	11,280		Bank		42,000
		£71,280				£71,280

Required

(*a*) Calculate the cost of the asset, vehicles, held by the business at 30 September in each of the years 19-3 to 19-6 inclusive.

(*b*) Show the detailed composition of the charge for depreciation of the vehicles to profit and loss account at 30 September 19-4, 19-5 and 19-6.

All workings must be shown.

(Chartered Association of Certified Accountants)

22

Bad debts, provisions for bad debts, provisions for discounts on debtors

With many businesses a large proportion, if not all, of the sales are on a credit basis. The business is therefore taking the risk that some of the customers may never pay for the goods sold to them on credit. This is a normal business risk and therefore **bad debts** as they are called are a normal business expense, and must be charged as such when calculating the profit or loss for the period.

When a debt is found to be bad, the asset as shown by the debtor's account is worthless, and must accordingly be eliminated as an asset account. This is done by crediting the debtor's account to cancel the asset and increasing the expenses account of bad debts by debiting it there. Sometimes the debtor will have paid part of the debt, leaving the remainder to be written off as a bad debt. The total of the bad debts account is later transferred to the profit and loss account.

An example of debts being written off as bad can now be shown:

Exhibit 22.1

C Bloom

19-5		£	19-5		£
Jan	8 Sales	50	Dec	31 Bad Debts	50

R Shaw

19-5		£	19-5		£
Feb	16 Sales	240	Aug	17 Cash	200
			Dec	31 Bad Debts	40
		240			240

Bad Debts

19-5		£	19-5		£
Dec	31 C Bloom	50	Dec	31 Profit and Loss	90
,,	,, R Shaw	40			
		90			90

Profit and Loss Account for the year ended 31 December 19-5

	£
Bad Debts	90

151

Provisions for bad debts

The ideal situation from the accounting point of view of measuring net income, i.e. calculating net profit, is for the expenses of the period to be matched against the revenue of that period which the expenses have helped to create. Where an expense such as bad debt is matched in the same period with the revenue from the sale, then all is in order for the purposes of net profit calculation. However, it is very often the case that it is not until a period later than that in which the sale took place that it is realised that the debt is a bad debt.

Therefore, to try to bring into the period in which the sale was made a charge for the bad debts resulting from such sales, the accountant brings in the concept of an estimated expense. Such an item of expense for an expense that had taken place, but which cannot be calculated with substantial accuracy is known as a **provision**. The item of estimated expense for bad debts is therefore known as a **provision for bad debts**.

Thus, in addition to writing off debts that are irrecoverable, i.e. bad, it is necessary as a matter of business prudence, to charge the Profit and Loss Account with the amount of the provision for any debt the recovery of which is in doubt.

The estimate is arrived at on the basis of experience, a knowledge of the customers and of the state of the country's economy at that point in time with its likely effect on customers' debt paying capacity. Sometimes the schedules of debtors are scrutinised and a list of the doubtful debts made. Other firms work on an overall percentage basis to cover possible doubtful debts. Sometimes a provision is based on specified debtors. Another method is that of preparing an ageing schedule and taking different percentages for debts owing for different lengths of time. This is somewhat more scientific than the overall percentage basis, as in most trades and industries the longer a debt is owed the more chance there is of it turning out to be a bad debt. The schedule might appear as in Exhibit 22.2

Exhibit 22.2

Ageing Schedule for Doubtful Debts

Period debt owing	Amount	Estimated percentage doubtful	Provision for bad debts
	£		£
Less than one month	5,000	1	50
1 month to 2 months	3,000	3	90
2 months to 3 months	800	4	32
3 months to 1 year	200	5	10
Over 1 year	160	20	32
	9,160		214

Accounting entries for provisions for bad debts

When the decision has been taken as to the amount of the provision to be made, then the accounting entries needed for the provision are:

Year in which *provision first made*:
   Dr Profit and Loss Account with amount of provision
   Cr Provision for Bad Debts Account

In subsequent years a review has to be made as to whether the provision should then be increased or reduced. The accounting entries, when changes are made are:

To increase the provision:
  Dr Profit and Loss Account with the increase
  Cr Provision for Bad Debts Account

To reduce the provision:
  Dr Provision for Bad Debts Account
  Cr Profit and Loss Account with the reduction

Exhibit 22.3

Year 1

A business started on 1 January 19-4. During its first year £205 of debts were written off as bad, being £50 written off A Jack's account on 9 June 19-4 and £155 written off B Smith on 10 November 19-4.

At the end of the year debtors amounted to £8,000 (this does *not* include the £205 already written off). Considering all factors it was decided that of the £8,000 debts approximately £300 could well turn out eventually to be bad debts, and provision should be made.

The accounting entries are:

Bad Debts

		£			£
19-4			19-4		
Jun 9 A Jack		50	Dec 31 Profit and Loss		205
Nov 10 B Smith		155			
		205			205

Provision for Bad Debts

		£
19-4		
Dec 31 Profit and Loss		300

Profit and Loss Account for the year ended 31 December 19-4

Bad Debts	205
Provision for Bad Debts	300

In the balance sheet the figure of the provision £300 should be deducted from debtors £8,000.

Balance Sheet as at 31 December 19-4

	£	£
Debtors	8,000	
less Provision for bad debts	300	7,700

Year 2

During the year to 31 December 19-5 the following debts were written off as bad debts: C Madden £196 on May 31, R Clarke £280 on October 15 and T Taylor £70 on December 16. At 31 December 19-5 the remaining debts were £11,000 of which £480 might possibly eventually turn out to be bad debts.

The accounting entries will be:

Bad Debts

19-5		£	19-5		£
May	31 C Madden	196	Dec 31 Profit and Loss		546
Oct	15 R Clarke	280			
Dec	16 T Taylor	70			
		546			546

Provision for Bad Debts

19-5		£	19-5		£
Dec 31 Balance c/d		480	Jan 1 Balance b/d		300
			Dec 31 Profit and Loss		180
		480			480
			19-6		
			Jan 1 Balance b/d		480

Profit and Loss Account for the year ended 31 December 19-5

Bad Debts	546
Provision for Bad Debts	180

Note that the entry for the second year in the Profit and Loss Account in respect of the provisions is for the *increase only*.

Balance Sheet as at 31 December 19-5

	£	£
Debtors	11,000	
less Provision for Bad Debts	480	10,520

Year 3

During the year to 31 December 19-6 the following debts were written off as bad debts: M Worth £215 on March 16, P Richards £196 on July 31, L Moore £390 on November 11. At 31 December 19-5 the remaining debts were £10,200 of which £410 might possibly eventually turn out to be bad debts.

Accounting entries needed:

Bad Debts

19-6		£	19-6		£
Mar	16 M Worth	215	Dec 31 Profit and Loss		801
Jul	31 P Richards	196			
Nov	11 L Moore	390			
		801			801

Provision for Bad Debts

19-6			19-6		
Dec 31 Profit and Loss		70	Jan 1 Balance b/d		480
Dec 31 Balance c/d		410			
		480			480
			19-7		
			Jan 1 Balance b/d		410

Profit and Loss Account for the year ended 31 December 19-6

	£		£
Bad Debts	801	Reduction in Provision for Bad Debts	70

Note that the entry for the third year in the Profit and Loss Account in respect of the provision is for the *reduction only*.

Balance Sheet as at 31 December 19-6

	£	£
Debtors	10,200	
less Provision for Bad Debts	410	9,790

(It should be noted that provisions for bad debts are frequently called **provisions for doubtful debts**).

Now work your way through Exhibit 22.4.

Exhibit 22.4

A business starts on 1 January 19-2 and its financial year end is 31 December annually. A table of the debtors, the bad debts written off and the estimated doubtful debts at the end of each year is now given.

Year to 31 December	Debtors at end of year (after bad debts written off)	Bad debts written off during year	Debts thought at end of year to be doubtful to collect
	£	£	£
19-2	6,000	423	120
19-3	7,000	510	140
19-4	8,000	604	155
19-5	6,400	610	130

The accounts for bad debts, provision for bad debts and profit and loss extracts for each of the years 19-2 to 19-5 are now given, as well as balance sheet extracts as at the end of each year.

Bad Debts

19-2		£	19-2		£
Dec 31 Sundries		423	Dec 31 Profit and Loss		423
		═══			═══
19-3			19-3		
Dec 31 Sundries		510	Dec 31 Profit and Loss		510
		═══			═══
19-4			19-4		
Dec 31 Sundries		604	Dec 31 Profit and Loss		604
		═══			═══
19-5			19-5		
Dec 31 Sundries		610	Dec 31 Profit and Loss		610
		═══			═══

Provision for Bad Debts

	£	19-2		£
		Dec 31 Profit and Loss		120
19-3		19-3		
Dec 31 Balance c/d	140	Dec 31 Profit and Loss		20
	───			───
	140			140
	═══			═══
		19-4		
19-4		Jan 1 Balance b/d		140
Dec 31 Balance c/d	155	Dec 31 Profit and Loss		15
	───			───
	155			155
	═══			═══
19-5		19-5		
Dec 31 Profit and Loss	25	Jan 1 Balance b/d		155
,, ,, Balance c/d	130			
	───			───
	155			155
	═══			═══
		19-6		
		Jan 1 Balance b/d		130

Profit and Loss Accounts for the year ended 31 December (extracts)

	£			£
19-2 Bad Debts	423			
Provision for Bad Debts	120			
19-3 Bad Debts	510			
Increase in provision for Bad Debts	20			
19-4 Bad Debts	604			
Increase for provision for Bad Debts	15			
19-5 Bad Debts	610	19-5	Reduction in provision for Bad Debts	25

	£	£
19-2 Debtors	6,000	
less Provision for Bad Debts	120	
		5,880
19-3 Debtors	7,000	
less Provision for Bad Debts	140	
		6,860
19-4 Debtors	8,000	
less Provision for Bad Debts	155	
		7,845
19-5 Debtors	6,400	
less Provision for Bad Debts	130	
		6,270

Bad debts recovered

It is not uncommon for a debt written off in previous years to be recovered in later years. When this occurs, the book-keeping procedures are as follows:

First, re-instate the debt by making the following entries:

Dr Debtors Account

Cr Bad Debts Recovered Account.

The reason for re-instating the debt in the ledger account of the debtor is to have a detailed history of his/her account as a guide for granting credit in future. By the time a debt is written off as bad, it will be recorded in the debtor's ledger account. It is prudent therefore that when such debt is recovered, it also must be reflected in the debtor's ledger account.

When cash/cheque is subsequently received from the debtor in settlement of the account or part thereof,

Dr Cash/Bank

Cr Debtor's Account

with the amount received.

At the end of the financial year, the credit balance in the Bad Debts Recovered Account will be transferred to either Bad Debts Account or direct to the credit side of the Profit and Loss Account. The effect is the same since the Bad Debts Account will in itself be transferred to the Profit and Loss Account at the end of the financial year.

Provisions for discounts on debtors

Some firms create provisions for discounts to be allowed on the debtors outstanding at the balance sheet date. This, they maintain, is quite legitimate, as the amount of debtors less any doubtful debt provision is not the best estimate of collectable debts, owing to cash discounts which will be given to debtors if they pay within a given time. The cost of discounts, it is argued, should be charged in the period when the sales were made.

To do this the procedure is similar to the doubtful debts provision. It must be borne in mind that the estimate of discounts to be allowed should be based on the net figure of debtors less bad debts provision, as it is obvious that discounts are not allowed on bad debts!

Example

Year ended 31 December	Debtors	Provision for Bad Debts	Provision for discounts allowed
	£	£	%
19-3	4,000	200	2
19-4	5,000	350	2
19-5	4,750	250	2

Profit and Loss Account for the year ended 31 December (extracts)

	£		£
19-3 Provision for discounts on debtors (2 per cent of £3,800)	76		
19-4 Increase in provision for discounts on debtors (to 2 per cent of £4,650)	17		
		19-5 Reduction in provision for discounts on debtors (to 2 per cent of £4,500)	3

Provision for Discounts on Debtors

		£			£
				Dec 31 Profit and Loss	76
19-4			19-4		
Dec 31 Balance c/d		93	Dec 31 Profit and Loss		17
		93			93
19-5			19-5		
Dec 31 Profit and Loss		3	Jan 1 Balance b/d		93
,, ,, Balance c/d		90			
		93			93
			19-6		
			Jan 1 Balance b/d		90

Balance Sheets as at 31 December (extracts)

	£	£	£
19-3 Debtors		4,000	
less Provision for Bad Debts	200		
,, Provision for discounts on debtors	76		
		276	
			3,724
19-4 Debtors		5,000	
less Provision for Bad Debts	350		
,, Provision for discounts on debtors	93		
		443	
			4,557
19-5 Debtors		4,750	
less Provision for Bad Debts	250		
,, Provision for discounts on debtors	90		
		340	
			4,410

An alternative method

In accounting there are many ways to the same end result. It would have been possible to join together the Bad Debts Account and the Provision for Bad Debts Account. Question 22.4 illustrates such a point. Attempt it and then compare it with the answer.

If this volume showed you all the possible ways of effecting accounting entries it would be over 1,000 pages long. You are shown the basic methods normally used by accountants.

Multiple-choice questions

Now attempt Set 3 consisting of 20 questions, shown on page 494.

Review questions

22.1 In a new business during the year ended 31 December 19-4 the following debts are found to be bad, and are written off on the dates shown:

30 April	H Gordon	£110
31 August	D Bellamy Ltd	£64
31 October	J Alderton	£12

On 31 December 19-4 the schedule of remaining debtors, amounting in total to £6,850, is examined, and it is decided to make a provision for doubtful debts of £220.

You are required to show:

(a) The Bad Debts Account, and the provision for Bad Debts Account.

(b) The charge to the Profit and Loss Account.

(c) The relevant extracts from the Balance Sheet as at 31 December 19- 4.

22.2 A business started trading on 1 January 19-6. During the two years ended 31 December 19-6 and 19-7 the following debts were written off to bad debts account on the dates stated:

31 August 19-6	W Best	£85
30 September 19-6	S Avon	£140
28 February 19-7	L J Friend	£180
31 August 19-7	N Kelly	£60
30 November 19-7	A Oliver	£250

On 31 December 19-6 there had been a total of debtors remaining of £40,500. It was decided to make a provision for doubtful debts of £550.

On 31 December 19-7 there had been a total of debtors remaining of £47,300. It was decided to make a provision for doubtful debts of £600.

You are required to show:

(i) The Bad Debts Account and the Provision for Bad Debts Account for each of the two years.

(ii) The charges to the Profit and Loss Account for each of the two years.

(iii) The relevant extracts from the Balance Sheets as at 31 December 19- 6 and 19-7.

22.3A A business, which started trading on 1 January 19-5, adjusted its bad debt provisions at the end of each year on a percentage basis, but each year the percentage rate is adjusted in accordance with the current 'economic climate'. The following details are available for the three years ended 31 December 19-5, 19-6 and 19-7.

Bad Debts written off year to 31 December	Debtors at 31 December	Per cent provision for Bad Debts
	£	£	
19-5	656	22,000	5
19-6	1,805	40,000	7
19-7	3,847	60,000	6

You are required to show:

(*i*) Bad Debts Accounts and Provision for Bad Debts accounts for each of the three years.

(*ii*) Balance Sheet extracts as at 31 December 19-5, 19-6 and 19-7.

22.4 The balance sheet as at 31 December 19-5 of Zoom Products Limited included:

Trade debtors   £85,360.

The account for the year ended 31 December 19-5 included a provision for doubtful debts at 31 December 19-5 of 3% of the balance outstanding from debtors. During 19-6, the company's sales totalled £568,000 of which 90%, in value, were on credit and £510,150 was received from credit customers in settlement of debts totalling £515,000. In addition, £3,000 was received from K Dodds in settlement of a debt which had been written off as bad in 19-5; this receipt has been credited to K Dodd's account in the debtors' ledger.

On 30 December 19-6, the following outstanding debts were written off as bad:

J Sinder   £600
K Lambert   £2,000

Entries relating to bad debts are passed through the provision for doubtful debts account whose balance at 31 December 19-6 is to be 3% of the amount due to the company from debtors at that date.

*Required**

(*a*) Write up the provision for doubtful debts accounts for the year ended 31 December 19-6 bringing down the balance at 1 January 19-7.

(*b*) Prepare a computation of the amount to be shown as Trade Debtors in the company's balance sheet at 31 December 19-6.

(Association of Accounting Technicians)

* *See* 'An Alternative Method' on page 159

22.5A The balance sheet as at 31 May 19-7 of Forest Traders Limited included a provision for doubtful debts of £2,300.

The company's accounts for the year ended 31 May 19-8 are now being prepared.

The company's policy now is to relate the provision for doubtful debts to the age of debts outstanding. The debts outstanding at 31 May 19-8 and the required provisions for doubtful debts are as follows:

Debts outstanding	Amount	Provision for doubtful debts
	£	%
Up to 1 month	24,000	1
More than 1 month and up to 2 months	10,000	2
More than 2 months and up to 3 months	8,000	4
More than 3 months	3,000	5

Customers are allowed a cash discount of 2½% for settlement of debts within one month. It is now proposed to make a provision for discounts to be allowed in the company's accounts for the year ended 31 May 19-8

Required:

Prepare the following accounts for the year ended 31 May 19-8 in the books of Forest Traders Limited to record the above transactions:

(*a*) Provision for doubtful debts;

(*b*) Provision for discounts to be allowed on debtors.

(Association of Accounting Technicians)

23

Other adjustments for final accounts: accruals, prepayments, etc.

The trading and profit and loss accounts looked at so far have taken the sales for a period and all the expenses for that period have been deducted, the result being a net profit (or a net loss).

Up to this part of the book it has always been assumed that the expenses belonged exactly to the period of the trading and profit and loss account. If the trading and profit and loss account for the year ended 31 December 19-5 was being drawn up, then the rent paid as shown in the trial balance was exactly for 19-5. There was no rent owing at the beginning of 19-5 nor any owing at the end of 19-5, nor had any rent been paid in advance.

However, where on the other hand the costs used up and the amount paid are not equal to one another, then an adjustment will be required in respect of the overpayment or underpayment of the costs used up during the period.

In all of the following examples the trading and profit and loss accounts being drawn up are for the year ended 31 December 19-5.

Accrued expenses

Consider the case of rent being charged at the rate of £1,000 per year. It is payable at the end of each quarter of the year for the three months' tenancy that has just expired. It can be assumed that the tenancy commenced on 1 January 19-5. The rent was paid for 19-5 on 31 March, 2 July and 4 October and on 5 January 19-6.

During the year ended 31 December 19-5 the rent account will appear:

Rent

19-5		£
Mar 31 Cash		250
Jul 2 ,,		250
Oct 4 ,,		250

The rent paid 5 January 19-6 will appear in the books of the year 19-6 as part of the double-entry.

The costs used up during 19-5 are obviously £1,000, as that is the year's rent, as this is the amount needed to be transferred to the profit and loss account. But if £1,000 was put on the credit side of the rent account (the debit being in the profit and loss account) the account would not balance. There would be £1,000 on the credit side of the account and only £750 on the debit side. To make the account balance the £250 rent owing for 19-5, but paid in 19-6, must be carried down to 19-6 as a credit balance because it is a liability on 31 December 19-5. Instead of Rent Owing it could be called Rent Accrued or just simply as an accrual. The completed account can now be shown.

Rent

19-5		£	19-5		£
Mar 31	Cash	250	Dec 31	Profit and Loss A/c	1,000
Jul 2	,,	250			
Oct 4	,,	250			
Dec 31	Owing c/d	250			
		1,000			1,000
			19-6		
			Jan 1	Owing b/d	250

Expenses prepaid

Insurance premiums have been paid as follows:

Feb 28 19-5 £210 for period of three months to 31 March 19-5.
Aug 31 19-5 £420 for period of six months to 30 September 19-5.
Nov 18 £420 for period of six months to 31 March 19-6.

The insurance account will be shown in the books:

Insurance

19-6		£
Feb 28	Cash	210
Aug 31	,,	420
Nov 18	,,	420

Now the last payment of £420 is not just for 19-5, it can be split as to £210 for the three months to 31 December 19-5 and £210 for the three months ended 31 March 19-6. For a period of 12 months the cost of insurance is £840 and this is therefore the figure to be transferred to the profit and loss account. The amount needed to balance the account will therefore be £210 and at 31 December 19-5 this is a benefit paid for but not used up; it is an asset and needs carrying forward as such to 19-6, i.e. as a debit balance.

The account can now be completed.

Insurance

19-5		£	19-5		£
Feb 28	Cash	210	Dec 31	Profit and Loss A/c	840
Aug 31	,,	420	,, ,,	Prepaid c/d	210
Nov 18	,,	420			
		1,050			1,050
19-6					
Jan 1	Prepaid b/d	210			

Prepayment will also happen when items other than purchases are bought for use in the business, and they are not fully used up in the period.

For instance, packing materials are normally not entirely used up during the period in which they are bought, there being a stock of packing materials in hand at the end of the period. This stock is therefore a form of prepayment and needs carrying down to the following period in which it will be used.

This can be seen in the following example:

Year ended 31 December 19-5
Packing materials bought in the year £2,200
Stock of packing materials in hand as at 31 December 19-5 £400

Looking at the example, it can be seen that in 19-5 the packing materials used up will have been £2,200−£400=£1,800 and there will still be a stock of £400 packing materials at 31 December 19-5 to be carried forward to 19-6. The £400 stock of packing materials will accordingly be carried forward as an asset balance (debit balance) to 19-6.

Packing Materials

19-5		£	19-5		£
Dec 31 Cash		2,200	Dec 31 Profit and Loss A/c		1,800
			,, ,, Stock c/d		400
		2,200			2,200
19-6		£			
Jan 1 Stock b/d		400			

The stock of packing materials is not added to the stock of unsold goods in hand in the balance sheet, but is added to the other prepayments of expenses.

Outstanding revenue other than sales

Sales revenue outstanding is already shown in the books as debit balances on the customers' personal accounts, i.e. debtors. It is the other kinds of revenue such as rent receivable, commissions receivable, etc. which need to be considered. Such revenue to be brought into the profit and loss account is that which has been earned during the period. Should all the revenue earned actually be received during the period, then revenue received and revenue earned will be the same amount and no adjustment would be needed in the revenue account. Where the revenue has been earned, but the full amount has not been received, the revenue due to the business must be brought into the accounts; the amount receivable is after all the revenue used when calculating profit.

Example

The warehouse is larger than is needed. Part of it is rented to another firm for £800 per annum. For the year ended 31 December 19-5 the following cheques were received.

19-5		
Apr 4	For three months to 31 March 19-5	£200
Jul 6	For three months to 30 June 19-5	£200
Oct 9	For three months to 30 September 19-5	£200

The £200 for the three months to 31 December 19-5 was received 7 January 19-6.

The account for 19-5 appeared:

Rent Receivable

		£
19-5		
Apr	4 Bank	200
Jul	6 Bank	200
Oct	9 Bank	200

Any rent paid by the firm would be charged as a debit to the profit and loss account. Any rent received, being the opposite, is accordingly eventually transferred to the credit of the profit and loss account. The amount to be transferred for 19-5 is that earned for the twelve months, i.e. £800. The rent received account is completed by carrying down the balance owing as a debit balance to 19-6. The £200 owing is, after all, an asset on 31 December 19-5.

The Rent Receivable Account can now be completed:

Rent Receivable

19-5		£	19-5		£
Dec 31 Profit and Loss		800	Apr	4 Bank	200
			Jul	6 Bank	200
			Oct	9 Bank	200
			Dec 31 Accrued c/d		200
		800			800
19-6					
Jan 1 Accrued b/d		200			

Expenses and revenue account balances and the balance sheet

In all the cases listed dealing with adjustments in the final accounts, there will still be a balance on each account after the preparation of the trading and profit and loss accounts. All such balances remaining should appear in the balance sheet. The only question left is to where and how they shall be shown.

The amounts owing for expenses are usually added together and shown as one figure. These could be called **expense creditors**, **expenses owing**, or **accrued expenses**. The item would appear under current liabilities as they are expenses which have to be discharged in the near future.

The items prepaid are also added together and are called **prepayments**, **prepaid expenses**, or **payments in advance**. Often they are added to the debtors in the balance sheet, otherwise they are shown next under the debtors.

Amounts owing for rents receivable or other revenue owing are usually added to debtors.

The balance sheet in respect of the accounts so far seen in this chapter would appear:

Balance Sheet as at 31 December 19-5

Current assets	£	Current Liabilities	£
Stock		Trade creditors	
Debtors	200	Accrued Expenses	250
Prepayments	610		
Bank			
Cash			

165

Students are often confused when asked to draw up an expense or revenue account for a full year, and there are amounts owing or prepaid at *both* the beginning and end of the year. We can now see how this is done.

Question A

On 31 December 19-5 3 months rent was owing of £3,000. The rent chargeable per year was £12,000. The following payments were made in the year 19-6:

January 6 £3,000; April 4 £3,000; July 7 £3,000; October 18 £3,000. (Obviously on 31 December 19-6 this means that the final quarter's rent for 19-6 is still owing).

Answer A

The rent account for 19-6 will appear as:

Rent

19-6	£	19-6	£
Jan 6 Bank	3,000	Jan 1 Owing b/f	3,000
Apl 4 Bank	3,000	Dec 31 Profit and Loss	12,000
Jul 7 Bank	3,000		
Oct 18 Bank	3,000		
Dec 31 Owing c/d	3,000		
	15,000		15,000
		19-7	
		Jan 1 Owing b/d	3,000

Question B

On 31 December 19-5 packing materials in hand amounted to £1,850. During the year ended 31 December 19-6 various bank payments were made for packing materials amounting to £27,480 in total. On 31 December 19-6 all stocks of packing materials had been used up, and we still owed £2,750 for packing materials already received and used up.

Answer B

The packing materials account will appear as:

Packing Materials

19-6	£	19-6	£
Jan 1 Stocks b/f	1,850	Dec 31 Profit and Loss	32,080
Dec 31 Bank (various)	27,480		
Dec 31 Owing c/d	2,750		
	32,080		32,080
		19-7	
		Jan 1 Owing b/d	2,750

Question C

Where expenses are combined in one account it can get even more confusing.

Rent is payable of £6,000 per annum. Rates of £4,000 per annum are payable by instalments. The following information is available for the year ended 31 December 19-8.

At 1 January 19-8 Rent had been prepaid £1,000, whereas Rates were owed £400. During 19-5 the following sums were paid: Rent £4,500 and Rates £5,000. At 31 December 19-8 Rent was owed £500 and Rates had been prepaid £600.

A combined Rent and Rates account is to be drawn up for the year 19-8, showing transfer to the Profit and Loss Account, and balances are to be carried down to 19- 9.

Answer C

Rent and Rates

19-8		£	19-8		£
Jan 1 Rent prepaid b/f		1,000	Jan 1 Rates owing b/f		400
Dec 31 Bank: Rent		4,500	Dec 31 Profit and Loss		10,000
,, 31 Rates		5,000			
Dec 31 Rent owing c/d		500	Dec 31 Rates prepaid c/d		600
		11,000			11,000
19-9			19-9		
Jan 1 Rates prepaid b/d		600	Jan 1 Rent owing b/d		500

Goods for own use

A trader will often take items out of his business stocks for his own use, without paying for them. There is certainly nothing wrong about this, but an entry should be made to record the event. This is effected by:

Credit Purchases Account
Debit Drawings Account.

Adjustments may also be needed for other private items. For instance, if a trader's private insurance had been incorrectly charged to the Insurance Account, then the correction would be:

Credit Insurance Account
Debit Drawings Account.

Final accounts for non-traders

If the final accounts are for someone who is not trading in goods as such, for instance accountants, insurance agents, lawyers and the like, there will be no need for a Trading Account. All of the revenue and expense items will be shown in a Profit and Loss Account, disclosing a net profit (or net loss). Balance sheets for such providers of services (i.e. not goods) will be the same as for traders.

Vertical form of accounts

Throughout this book to this point the two-sided presentation of Trading and Profit and Loss Accounts and Balance Sheets is used. For many reasons this is easier to use from a teaching point of view. However, in practice you would not necessarily have to show the final accounts drawn up in that fashion. It would be completely up to the owner(s) of a business to decide on the method of presentation. What really matters is whether or not the presentation still results in the correct answer being shown.

Final accounts are more normally shown in a vertical fashion. This is also referred to as narrative style, or columnar presentation. When this is done the chance is usually taken of displaying 'working capital' as a separate figure. **Working capital** is the term for the excess of the current assets over the current liabilities of a business.

Nearly all examiners will look with favour on final accounts drawn up in a vertical fashion. Often they will insist that the question should be answered in this way. Therefore if you want to gain extra marks ensure that you master this next section.

The translation of a Trading and Profit and Loss Account from a horizontal format to a vertical format can be shown by means of diagram Exhibit 23.2.

Exhibit 23.2

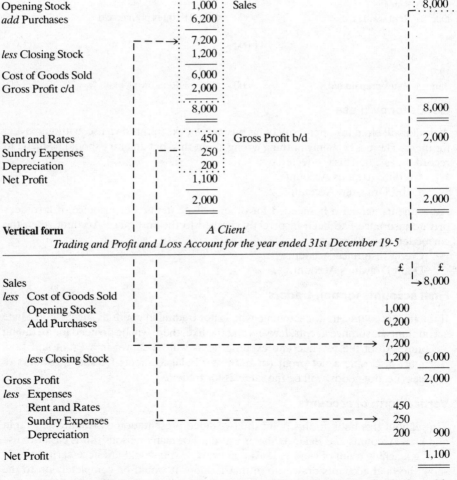

Horizontal form

A Client

Trading and Profit and Loss Account for the year ended 31 December 19-5

	£		£
Opening Stock	1,000	Sales	8,000
add Purchases	6,200		
	7,200		
less Closing Stock	1,200		
Cost of Goods Sold	6,000		
Gross Profit c/d	2,000		
	8,000		8,000
Rent and Rates	450	Gross Profit b/d	2,000
Sundry Expenses	250		
Depreciation	200		
Net Profit	1,100		
	2,000		2,000

Vertical form

A Client

Trading and Profit and Loss Account for the year ended 31st December 19-5

	£	£
Sales		8,000
less Cost of Goods Sold		
Opening Stock	1,000	
Add Purchases	6,200	
	7,200	
less Closing Stock	1,200	6,000
Gross Profit		2,000
less Expenses		
Rent and Rates	450	
Sundry Expenses	250	
Depreciation	200	900
Net Profit		1,100

If there had been any revenue such as commissions or rent received, then this would have followed the figure of gross profit as an addition.

Exhibit 23.3 shows the translation of a balance sheet from the horizontal form to a vertical form.

Exhibit 23.3

Horizontal form

A Client
Balance Sheet as at 31 December 19-5

	£	£		£	£
Fixed Assets			*Capital*		
Fixtures at cost	2,600		Balance as at 1.1.19-5		5,000
less Depreciation to date	200		*add* Net Profit		1,300
		2,400			6,300
			less Drawings		1,100
Current Assets					5,200
Stock	1,200				
Debtors	2,900		*Current Liabilities*		
Cash at Bank	700	4,800	Trade Creditors	1,850	
			Accrued Expenses	150	2,000
		7,200			7,200

Vertical form

A Client
Balance Sheet as at 31 December 19-5

			£	£	£
Fixed Assets					
Fixtures at cost				2,600	
less Depreciation to date				200	2,400
Current Assets					
Stock				1,200	
Debtors				2,900	
Cash at Bank				700	
				4,800	
less Current Liabilities					
Trade Creditors			1,850		
Accrued Expenses			150	2,000	
Working Capital					2,800
					5,200
Financed by:					
Capital					
Balance as at 1.1.19-5					5,000
Add Net Profit					1,300
					6,300
less Drawings					1,100
					5,200

You should note that there is not just one way of presenting final accounts in a vertical fashion, but the ones shown are in a good style.

From this point most of the final accounts are shown in vertical style, as it accords with normal practice in business and would be preferred by examiners. However, on occasion, because of display reasons in fitting a lot of information on a page the horizontal style will be used.

Distinctions between various kinds of capital

The capital account represents the claim of the proprietor against the assets of the business at a point in time. The work **Capital** is, however, often used in a specific sense. The main meanings are listed below.

Capital invested

This means the actual amount of money, or money's worth, brought into the business by the proprietor from his outside interests. The amount of capital invested is not disturbed by the amount of profits made by the business or losses incurred.

Capital employed

Candidates at an early stage in their studies are often asked to define this term. In fact, for those who progress to a more advanced stage, it will be seen in Volume 2 that it could have several meanings as the term is often used quite loosely. At an elementary level it is taken to mean the effective amount of money that is being used in the business. Thus, if all the assets were added together and the liabilities of the business deducted the answer would be that the difference is the amount of money employed in the business. You will by now realise that this is the same as the closing balance of the capital account. It is also sometimes called **Net Assets**.

Working capital

This is a term for the excess of the current assets over the current liabilities of a business.

Final accounts in the services sector

So far we have looked at accounts for people who traded in some sort of goods. Because we wanted to be able to see what the gross profit on goods was for each firm we drew up a Trading Account for that purpose.

There are, however, many firms which do not deal in 'goods' but instead supply 'services'. This will include professional firms such as accountants, solicitors, doctors, estate agents, and the like, also firms with services such as television maintenance, window-cleaning, gardeners, hairdressers, piano-tuning. As 'goods' are not dealt in there is no need for Trading Accounts to be drawn up. Instead a Profit and Loss Account plus a Balance Sheet will be drafted.

The firm item in the Profit and Loss Account will be the revenue which might be called 'work done', 'fees', 'charges', 'accounts rendered', 'takings', etc, depending on the nature of the organisation. Any other items of income will be added, e.g. rent receivable, and then the expenses will be listed and deducted to arrive at a net profit or net loss.

An example of the Profit and Loss Account of a solicitor might be as per Exhibit 23.4.

Exhibit 23.4

J Plunkett, Solicitor
Profit and Loss Account for the year ended 31 December 19-3

	£	£
Revenue:		
Fees Charged		87,500
Insurance Commissions		1,300
		88,800
less Expenses:		
Wages and Salaries	29,470	
Rent and Rates	11,290	
Office Expenses	3,140	
Motor Expenses	2,115	
General Expenses	1,975	
Depreciation	2,720	50,710
Net Profit		38,090

Worksheets

Instead of drawing up a set of final accounts in the way already shown in this textbook, a worksheet could be drawn up instead. It may provide a useful aid where a large number of adjustments are needed.

Worksheets are usually drawn up on specially preprinted types of stationery with suitable columns printed on them. To provide such special stationery in an examination is difficult, also for students to draw up such a worksheet from scratch would be very time-consuming, therefore very few examinations will ask for worksheet operation. However, the examiner may ask you something about worksheets, if this is contained in the syllabus.

In Exhibit 23.5 is shown the worksheet that would have been drawn up as an answer to question 23.8 of the book. Compare your answer to 23.8 drawn up in the usual way with the worksheet. The gross profits and new profits are the same, it is simply the display that is different.

If you were an accountant working for John Brown the final account given to him and to anyone else who was an interested party, such as the Inspector of Taxes or the bank, would be the same as the conventional type. They would not be given the worksheets.

Exhibit 23.5

JOHN BROWN
WORKSHEET
See exercise 23.8

Account	Trial Balance 1 Dr	Trial Balance 2 Cr	Adjustments 3 Dr	Adjustments 4 Cr	Trading Account 5 Dr	Trading Account 6 Cr	Profit & Loss Account 7 Dr	Profit & Loss Account 8 Cr	Balance Sheet 9 Dr	Balance Sheet 10 Cr
Sales		400,000				400,000				
Purchases	350,000				350,000					
Sales Returns	5,000				5,000					
Purchases Returns		6,200				6,200				
Stock 1.1.19-7	100,000				100,000					
Provision for Bad Debt		800		180 (iv)						980
Wages & Salaries	30,000		5,000 (ii)				35,000			
Rates	6,000			500 (iii)			5,500			
Telephone	1,000		220 (v)				1,220			
Shop Fittings	40,000			4,000 (vi)					36,000	
Van	30,000			6,000 (vi)					24,000	
Debtors	9,800								9,800	
Creditors		7,000								7,000
Bad Debts	200						200			
Capital		179,000								179,000
Bank	3,000								3,000	
Drawings	18,000								18,000	
	593,000	593,000								
Stock 31.12.19-7 – Asset			120,000 (i)			120,000			120,000	
Stock 31.12.19-7 – Cost of Goods Sold				120,000 (i)	120,000					
Accrued Expenses				5,000 (ii) / 220 (v)						5,000 / 220
Provision for Bad Debts			180 (iv)				180			
Prepaid Expenses			500 (iii)						500	
Depreciation Shop Fittings			4,000 (vi)				4,000			
Depreciation Van			6,000 (vi)				6,000			
			135,900	135,900						
Gross Profit (balancing figure)					71,200			71,200		
					526,200	526,200				
Net Profit (balancing figure)							19,100			19,100
							71,200	71,200	211,300	211,300
							71,200	71,200		19,100
									211,300	211,300

The basic structure

Now that we have covered all aspects of book-keeping a final accounts, it is, appropriate to show it as a diagram.

Exhibit 23.6

The basic structure of double-entry book-keeping

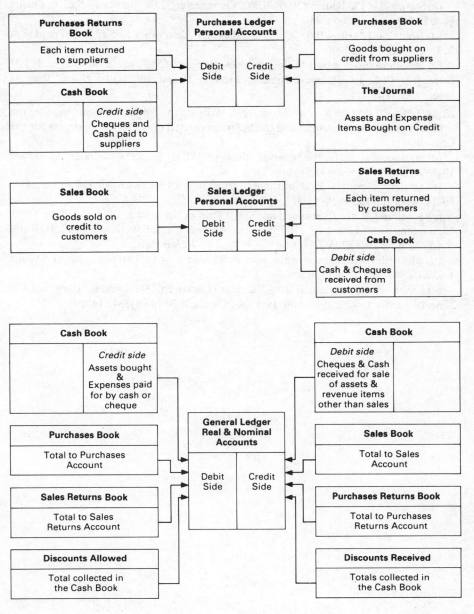

Review questions

23.1 The financial year of H Saunders ended on 31 December 19-6. Show the ledger accounts for the following items including the balance transferred to the necessary part of the final accounts, also the balances carried down to 19-7:

(*a*) Motor Expenses: Paid in 19-6 £744; Owing at 31 December 19-6 £28.

(*b*) Insurance: Paid in 19-6 £420; Prepaid as at 31 December 19-6 £35.

(*c*) Stationery: Paid during 19-6 £1,800; Owing as at 31 December 19-5 £250; Owing as at 31 December 19-6 £490.

(*d*) Rent: Paid during 19-6 £950; Prepaid as at 31 December 19-5 £220; Prepaid as at 31 December 19-6 £290.

(*e*) Saunders sub-lets part of the premises. Receives £550 during the year ended 31 December 19-6. Tenant owed Saunders £180 on 31 December 19-5 and £210 on 31 December 19-6.

23.2A J Owen's year ended on 30 June 19-4. Write up the ledger accounts, showing the transfers to the final accounts and the balances carried down to the next year for the following:

(*a*) Stationery: Paid for the year on 30 June 19-4 £855; Stocks of stationery at 30 June 19-3 £290; at 30 June 19-4 £345.

(*b*) General expenses: Paid for the year to 30 June 19-4 £590; Owing at 30 June 19-3 £64; Owing at 30 June 19-4 £90.

(*c*) Rent and Rates (combined account): Paid in the year to 30 June 19-4 £3,890; Rent owing at 30 June 19-3 £160; Rent paid in advance at 30 June 19-4 £250; Rates owing 30 June 19-3 £205; Rates owing 30 June 19-4 £360.

(*d*) Motor Expenses: paid in the year to 30 June 19-4 £4,750; Owing as at 30 June 19-3 £180; Owing as at 30 June 19-4 £375.

(*e*) Owen earns commission from the sales of one item. Recieved for the year to 30 June 19-4 £850; Owing at 30 June 19-3 £80; Owing at 30 June 19-4 £145.

23.3 The balances on certain accounts of Foster Hardware Co as at 1 April 19-1 were:

		£
Rent and rates payable	– accruals	2,200
	– prepayments	1,940
Rent receivable	– prepayments	625
Vehicles (at cost)		10,540
Provision for depreciation of vehicles		4,720
During the financial year the business		
paid rent by cheque		5,200
paid rates by cheque		3,050
received cheque for rent of sub-let premises		960
traded in a vehicle	– original cost	4,710
	– accumulated depreciation	3,080
	– part exchange allowance	1,100
paid balance of price of new vehicle by cheque		5,280
Closing balances as at 31 March 19-2 were:		
Rent and rates payable	– accruals	2,370
	– prepayments	1,880
Rents receivable	– prepayments	680
Vehicles (at cost)		(to be derived)
Provision for depreciation of vehicles		3,890

Required

Post and balance the appropriate accounts for the year ended 31 March 19-2, deriving the transfer entries to profit and loss account where applicable.

(Chartered Association of Certified Accountants)

23.4A The ledger of RBD & Co included the following account balances

	At 1 June 19-4	At 31 May 19-5
	£	£
Rents receivable: prepayments	463	517
Rent and rates payable		
prepayments	1,246	1,509
accruals	315	382
Creditors	5,258	4,720
Provision for discounts on creditors	106	94

During the year ended 31 May 19-5, the following transactions had arisen:

	£
Rents received by cheque	4,058
Rent paid by cheque	7,491
Rates paid by cheque	2,805
Creditors paid by cheque	75,181
Discounts received from creditors	1,043
Purchases on credit	to be derived

Required

Post and balance the appropriate accounts for the year ended 31 May 19-5, deriving the transfer entries to profit and loss account, where applicable.

(Chartered Association of Certified Accountants)

23.5A The owner of a small business selling and repairing cars, which you patronise has just received a copy of his accounts for the current year.

He is rather baffled by some of the items and as he regards you as a financial expert, he has asked you to explain certain points of difficulty to him. This you have readily agreed to do.

His questions are as follows:

(*a*) 'What is meant by the term 'assets'? My mechanical knowledge and skill is an assset to the business but it does not seem to have been included.'

(*b*) 'The house I live in cost £30,000 five years ago and is now worth £60,000, but that is not included either.'

(*c*) 'What is the difference between 'fixed assets' and 'current assets'?'

(*d*) 'Why do amounts for 'vehicles' appear under both fixed asset and current asset headings?'

(*e*) 'Why is the 'bank and cash' figure in the balance sheet different from the profit for the year shown in the profit and loss account?'

(*f*) 'I see the profit and loss account has been charged with depreciation on equipment etc. I bought all these things several years ago and paid for them in cash. Does this mean that I am being charged for them again?'

Required

Answer each of his questions in terms which he will be able to understand.

(Chartered Association of Certified Accountants)

23.6 The following trial balance has been extracted from the ledger of Winston Elliot who trades as a general merchant.

Trial Balance as at 31 October 19-7

	Dr	Cr
	£	£
Sales		530,780
Purchases	388,650	
Discounts allowed	1,454	
Discounts received		1,973
Carriage outwards	5,328	
Carriage inwards	2,444	
Returns in	1,866	
Returns out		2,449
Rent, rates and insurance	15,769	
Heating and lighting	6,324	
Postage and stationery	7,660	
Advertising	13,765	
Salaries and wages	44,970	
Loan interest	1,650	
Bad debts	2,088	
Debtors	26,550	
Creditors		36,887
Cash on hand	515	
Bank overdraft		3,466
Stock (as at 1 November 19-6)	12,306	
Equipment – at cost	141,450	
– accumulated depreciation		55,320
Loan		13,500
Drawings	20,800	
Capital (as at 1 November 19-6)		49,214
	693,589	693,589

The following additional information as at 31 October 19-7 is available:

(*a*) Rent and rates have been prepaid by £750.

(*b*) Loan interest is accrued by £150.

(*c*) Equipment is to be depreciated at 10% per annum using the straight line method.

(*d*) Stock at the close of business was valued at £14,521.

Required

Prepare Winston Elliot's Trading and Profit and Loss Account for the year ended 31 October 19-7 and his Balance Sheet as at that date. *Note*: vertical style preferred.

(Association of Accounting Technicians)

23.7 The following is a list of balances taken from the ledger of Mr Banda, a sole trader, as at 31 July 19-6 – the end of his most recent financial year.

List of Balances as at 31 July 19-6

	£
Stock at 1 August 19-5	5,830
Plant and Machinery	
at cost	36,420
accumulated depreciation	14,568
Purchases	48,760
Sales	101,890
Discounts allowed	1,324
Discounts received	1,150
Returns to suppliers	531
Returns from customers	761
Wages and salaries	15,300
Other operating expenses	21,850
Trade Creditors	4,380
Trade Debtors	6,340
Cash on hand	199
Cash at bank	2,197
Drawings	8,465
Capital	24,927

The following additional information as at 31 July 19-6 is available:

(*a*) Stock at the close of business was valued at £6,140.

(*b*) Certain operating expenses have been prepaid by £172 and others have been accrued by £233.

(*c*) Plant and Machinery has still to be depreciated for 19-6 at 20% per annum on cost.

(*d*) Other operating expenses include the following:

	£
Carriage inwards	650
Carriage outwards	1,540

Required

Prepare for Mr Banda's business a Trading and Profit and Loss Account for the year ended 31 July 19-6 and a Balance Sheet as at that date. *Note*: vertical style preferred.

(Association of Accounting Technicians)

23.8 This question relates to worksheets, *see* page 171.

From the following Trial balance of John Brown, store owner, prepare a Trading Account and Profit and Loss Account for the year ended 31 December 19-7, and a Balance Sheet as at that date, taking into consideration the adjustments shown below:

Trial Balance as at 31 December 19-7

	Dr £	Cr £
Sales		400,000
Purchases	350,000	
Sales Returns	5,000	
Purchases Returns		6,200
Opening Stock at 1 January 19-7	100,000	
Provision for Bad Debts		800
Wages and salaries	30,000	
Rates	6,000	
Telephone	1,000	
Shop fittings at cost	40,000	
Van at cost	30,000	
Debtors and creditors	9,800	7,000
Bad Debts	200	
Capital		179,000
Bank balance	3,000	
Drawings	18,000	
	593,000	593,000

(*i*)   Closing stock at 31 December 19-7 £120,000.
(*ii*)   Accrued wages £5,000.
(*iii*)   Rates prepaid £500.
(*iv*)   The Provision for Bad Debts to be increased to 10 per cent of Debtors.
(*v*)   Telephone Account outstanding £220.
(*vi*)   Depreciate shop fittings at 10 per cent per annum, and van at 20 per cent per annum, on cost.

23.9A The following trial balance has been extracted from the ledger of Mr Yousef a sole trader.

Trial Balance as at 31 May 19-6

	Dr	Cr
	£	£
Sales		138,078
Purchases	82,350	
Carriage	5,144	
Drawings	7,800	
Rent, rates and insurance	6,622	
Postage and Stationery	3,001	
Advertising	1,330	
Salaries and wages	26,420	
Bad Debts	877	
Provision for bad debts		130
Debtors	12,120	
Creditors		6,471
Cash on hand	177	
Cash at bank	1,002	
Stock as at 1 June 19-5	11,927	
Equipment		
at cost	58,000	
accumulated depreciation		19,000
Capital		53,091
	216,770	216,770

The following additional information as at 31 May 19-6 is available:

(*a*) Rent is accrued by £210.

(*b*) Rates have been prepaid by £880.

(*c*) £2,211 of carriage represents carriage inwards on purchases.

(*d*) Equipment is to be depreciated at 15% per annum using the straight line method.

(*e*) The provision for bad debts to be increased by £40.

(*f*) Stock at the close of business has been valued at £13,551.

Required

Prepare a Trading and Profit and Loss Account for the year ended 31 May 19-6 and a Balance Sheet as at that date.

(*Association of Accounting Technicians*)

23.10A Mr Chai has been trading for some years as a wine merchant. The following list of balances has been extracted from his ledger as at 30 April 19-7, the end of his most recent financial year.

	£
Capital	83,887
Sales	259,870
Trade creditors	19,840
Returns out	13,407
Provision for bad debts	512
Discounts allowed	2,306
Discounts received	1,750
Purchases	135,680
Returns inwards	5,624
Carriage outwards	4,562
Drawings	18,440
Carriage inwards	11,830
Rent, rates and insurance	25,973
Heating and lighting	11,010
Postage, stationery and telephone	2,410
Advertising	5,980
Salaries and wages	38,521
Bad debts	2,008
Cash on hand	534
Cash at bank	4,440
Stock as at 1 May 19-6	15,654
Trade debtors	24,500
Fixtures and fittings – at cost	120,740
Provision for depreciation on fixtures and fittings – as at 30 April 19-7	63,020
Depreciation	12,074

The following additional information as at 30 April 19-7 is available:
   (*a*) Stock at the close of business was valued at £17,750.
   (*b*) Insurances have been prepaid by £1,120.
   (*c*) Heating and lighting is accrued by £1,360.
   (*d*) Rates have been prepaid by £5,435.
   (*e*) The provision for bad debts is to be adjusted so that it is 3% of trade debtors.

Required

Prepare Mr Chai's Trading and Profit and Loss Account for the year ended 30 April 19-7 and a Balance Sheet as at that date. *Note*: vertical style preferred.

(*Association of Accounting Technicians*)

24
Capital and revenue expenditure

When fixed assets are bought, or when a firm spends money to add to the value of an existing fixed asset, such expenditure is called 'Capital Expenditure'. This should include the costs of acquiring the fixed assets and bring them into the firm; this would include legal costs on buying buildings, carriage inwards on machinery bought and so on.

When there is expenditure which is not concerned with adding to the value of fixed assets, but represents the costs of running the business on a day-to-day basis, then this expenditure is known as 'Revenue Expenditure'.

This means that buying a motor van, which will be used in the business for the next few years, is Capital Expenditure. Paying for the petrol to run the motor van, such petrol to be used within a relatively short time, is Revenue Expenditure. Buying a machine is Capital Expenditure. Repairing the machine when it breaks down is not adding to the original value of the machine, and is therefore Revenue Expenditure. If, on the other hand, £900 was spent on the machine, £300 of which was to repair the machine and the other £600 was to make improvements to the machine in some way – for instance, to fit an extra attachment to it – then £300 would be Revenue Expenditure, while the £600 would be Capital Expenditure, as it represents an improvement.

It can be seen that Revenue Expenditure is that chargeable to the Trading or Profit and Loss Account, while Capital Expenditure will result in increased figures for Fixed Assets in the balance sheet.

The importance of ensuring that Capital Expenditure is not charged as Revenue Expenditure, and vice-versa, cannot be stressed often enough. Two cases can now be looked at where the different forms of expenditure have got mixed up.

Revenue expenditure overstated

Exhibit 24.1

The following trial balance of F Rankin has been extracted as on 31 December 19-8. In fact, two of the figures shown in it are incorrect. Included in purchases is £1,500 for the purchase of building materials which were for an addition to the premises. In error they have been charged to purchases, i.e. they have been charged as revenue expenditure instead of as capital expenditure. First will be shown the Trading and Profit and Loss Account for the year, and the Balance Sheet as at the year ended (a) as they were drawn up incorrectly, and (b) drawn up correctly, showing the £1,500 buildings materials as adding to the value of Premises.

Trial Balance as at 31 December 19-8

	Dr £	Cr £
General expenses	490	
Motor expenses	1,247	
Salaries	3,560	
Purchases	14,305	
Sales		26,815
Stock 1 January 19-8	4,080	
Motor vehicle	2,800	
Creditors		5,160
Debtors	4,090	
Premises	20,000	
Cash at bank	1,400	
Capital		24,347
Drawings	4,350	
	56,322	56,322

Stock at 31 December 19-8 was £4,960.

F Rankin

Trading and Profit and Loss Account for the year ended 31 December 19-8

	(a) Incorrect £	£	(b) Corrected £	£
Sales		26,815		26,815
less Cost of Goods Sold				
Opening Stock	4,080		4,080	
Add Purchases	14,305		12,805*	
	18,385		16,885	
less Closing Stock	4,960	13,425	4,960	11,925
Gross Profit		13,390		14,890*
Less Expenses				
Salaries	3,560		3,560	
Motor Expenses	1,247		1,247	
General Expenses	490	5,297	490	5,297
Net Profit		8,093		9,593*

		(a) Incorrect		(b) Corrected	
	£	£		£	£
Fixed Assets					
Premises		20,000		21,500*	
Motor Vehicle		2,800		2,800	
		22,800		24,300	
Current Assets					
Stock	4,960			4,960	
Debtors	4,090			4,090	
Bank	1,400			1,400	
	10,450			10,450	
less **Current Liabilities**					
Creditors	5,160			5,160	
Working Capital		5,290			5,290
		28,090			29,590
Financed by:					
Capital					
Balance as at 1.1.19-8		24,347			24,347
add Net Profit		8,093			9,593*
		32,440			33,940
less Drawings		4,350			4,350
		28,090			29,590

The items showing amendments are indicated by asterisks(*).

It can now be seen that, in this particular case, the overstatement of revenue expenditure has resulted in (i) gross profit was understated £1,500, (ii) net profit was understated £1,500, (iii) a fixed asset, Premises, was understated by £1,500.

Capital expenditure overstated

Exhibit 24.2

What happens when capital expenditure is overstated? Take the trial balance of F Rankin, as in Exhibit 24.1, but assume that a different error has been made. Suppose, instead of the error already shown, that one was made which resulted in an overstatement of capital expenditure. Assume that a replacement engine costing £420 has been fitted in the motor vehicle. Instead of charging the cost to Motor Expenses, it had instead been added in to the value of Motor Vehicle to give a total of £2,800. The final accounts can now be looked at (a) before correction, and (b) after correction.

	(a) Incorrect £	(a) Incorrect £	(b) Corrected £	(b) Corrected £
Sales		26,815		26,815
less Cost of Goods Sold				
Opening Stock	4,080		4,080	
Add Purchases	14,305		14,305	
	18,385		18,385	
less Closing Stock	4,960	13,425	4,960	13,425
Gross Profit		13,390		13,390
less Expenses				
Salaries	3,560		3,560	
Motor Expenses	1,247		1,667*	
General Expenses	490	5,297	490	5,717
Net Profit		8,093		7,673*

Balance Sheet as at 31 December 19-8

	(a) Incorrect £	(a) Incorrect £	(b) Corrected £	(b) Corrected £
Fixed Assets				
Premises		20,000		20,000
Motor Vehicles		2,800		2,380*
		22,800		22,380
Current Assets				
Stock	4,960		4,960	
Debtors	4,090		4,090	
Bank	1,400		1,400	
	10,450		10,450	
less Current Liabilities				
Creditors	5,160		5,160	
Working Capital		5,290		5,290
		28,090		27,670
Financed by:				
Capital				
Balance as at 1.1.19-8		24,347		24,347
add Net Profit		8,093		7,673*
		32,440		32,020
less Drawings		4,350		4,350
		28,090		27,670

The items showing amendment are indicated by asterisks(*).

It can now be seen in this particular case that overstatement of capital expenditure resulted in (i) overstatement of net profit, (ii) overstatement of value of fixed asset.

Capital expenditure: further analysis

Capital expenditure consists of not only the cost of purchasing the fixed asset, but also includes other costs necessary to get the fixed asset operational. Some of the possible additional costs are now given:

(*a*) Delivery cost;
(*b*) Installation costs;
(*c*) Inspection and testing the fixed asset before use;
(*d*) Legal costs in purchasing property and land;
(*e*) Architects fees for building plans and for supervising construction of buildings;
(*f*) Demolition costs to remove something before new building can begin.

At this stage of your studies it can be assumed that interest in money borrowed to finance the above costs should be treated as revenue expenditure. When your studies reach a later stage this aspect will need further investigation.

Apportioning expenditure

Sometimes one item of expenditure will need splitting between capital and revenue expenditure. A builder was engaged to tackle some work on your premises, the total bill being for £3,000. If one-third of this was for repair work and two-thirds for improvements, then £1,000 should be charged in the profit and loss account as revenue expenditure, and £2,000 added to the value of premises and shown as such in the balance sheet.

Capital and revenue receipts

As seen, 'Capital' items are long-term and have an enduring influence on the profit-making capacity of the business. 'Revenue' items are short-term and have only a temporary influence on the profit-making capacity of the business. The expenditure side of these items has been considered. There will also be a receipts side. 'Capital Receipts' will therefore consists of the sale of 'Capital' items, e.g. the sale of a vehicle used in the business, the sale of premises. 'Revenue Receipts' will be those receipts which cover revenue items received, such as Rent Receivable or Commissions Receivable.

Review questions

24.1 (a) What is meant by Capital Expenditure, and Revenue Expenditure?
(b) Some of the following items should be treated as Capital and some as Revenue. For each of them state which classification applies:
(i) The purchase of machinery for use in the business,
(ii) Carriage paid to bring the machinery in (i) above to the works,
(iii) Complete re-decoration of the premises at a cost of £1,500,
(iv) A quarterly account for heating,
(v) The purchase of a soft drinks vending machine for the canteen with a stock of soft drinks,
(vi) Wages paid by a building contractor to his own workmen for the erection of an office in the builder's stockyard.

(Joint Matriculation Board)

24.2A Indicate which of the following would be revenue items and which would be capital items in a wholesale bakery.

(*a*) Purchase of a new motor van
(*b*) Purchase of replacement engine for existing motor van
(*c*) Cost of altering interior of new van to increase carrying capacity
(*d*) Cost of motor taxation licence for new van
(*e*) Cost of motor taxation licence for existing van
(*f*) Cost of painting firm's name on new van
(*g*) Repair and maintenance of existing van

(Associated Examining Board)

24.3 For the business of J Charles, wholesale chemist, classify the following between 'Capital' and 'Revenue' expenditure:

(*a*) Purchase of an extra motor van.
(*b*) Cost of rebuilding warehouse wall which had fallen down.
(*c*) Building extension to the warehouse.
(*d*) Painting extension to warehouse when it is first built.
(*e*) Repainting extension to warehouse three years later than that done in (*d*).
(*f*) Carriage costs on bricks for new warehouse extension.
(*g*) Carriage costs on purchases.
(*h*) Carriage costs on sales.
(*i*) Legal costs of collecting debts.
(*j*) Legal charges on acquiring new premises for office.
(*k*) Fire insurance premium.
(*l*) Costs of erecting new machine.

24.4A For the business of H Ward, a food merchant, classify the following between 'Capital' and 'Revenue' expenditure:

(*a*) Repairs to meat slicer.
(*b*) New tyre for van.
(*c*) Additional shop counter.
(*d*) Renewing signwriting on shop.
(*e*) Fitting partitions in shop.
(*f*) Roof repairs.
(*g*) Installing thief detection equipment.
(*h*) Wages of shop assistant.
(*i*) Carriage on returns outwards.
(*j*) New cash register.
(*k*) Repairs to office safe.
(*l*) Installing extra toilet.

24.5 (*a*) Distinguish between Capital and Revenue expenditure.

(*b*) Napa Ltd took delivery of a microcomputer and printer on 1 July 19-6, the beginning of its financial year. The list price of the equipment was £4,999 but Napa Ltd was able to negotiate a price of £4,000 with the supplier. However, the supplier charged an additional £340 to install and test the equipment. The supplier offered a 5% discount if Napa Ltd paid for the equipment and the additional installation costs within seven days. Napa Ltd was able to take advantage of this additional discount. The installation of special electrical wiring for the computer cost £110. After initial testing certain modifictions costing £199 proved necessary. Staff were sent on special training courses to operate the microcomputer and this cost £990. Napa Ltd insured the machine against fire and theft at a cost of £49 per annum. A maintenance agreement was entered into with Sonoma plc. Under this agreement Sonoma plc promised to provide 24 hour breakdown cover for one year. The cost of the maintenance agreement was £350.

Required

Calculate the acquisition cost of the microcomputer to Napa Ltd.

(*c*) The following costs were also incurred by Napa Ltd during the financial year ended 30 June 19-7:

- (*1*) Interest on loan to purchase microcomputer
- (*2*) Cost of software for use with the microcomputer
- (*3*) Cost of customising the software for use in Napa Ltd's business
- (*4*) Cost of paper used by the computer printer
- (*5*) Wages of computer operators
- (*6*) Cost of ribbons used by the computer printer
- (*7*) Cost of adding extra memory to the microcomputer
- (*8*) Cost of floppy discs used during the year
- (*9*) Costs of adding a manufacturer's upgrade to the microcomputer equipment
- (*10*) Cost of adding air conditioning to the computer room

Required

Classify each of the above as capital expenditure or revenue expenditure
(*Association of Accounting Technicians*)

24.6 At the beginning of the financial year on 1 April 19-5, a company had a balance on plant account of £372,000 and on provision for depreciation of plant account of £205,400.

The company's policy is to provide depreciation using the reducing balance method applied to the fixed assets held at the end of the financial year at the rate of 20% per annum.

On 1 September 19-5 the company sold for £13,700 some plant which it had acquired on 31 October 19-1 at a cost of £36,000. Additionally, installation costs totalled £4,000. During 19-3 major repairs costing £6,300 had been carried out on this plant and, in order to increase the capacity of the plant, a new motor had been fitted in December 19-3 at a cost of £4,400. A further overhaul costing £2,700 had been carried out during 19-4.

The company acquired new replacement plant on 30 November 19-5 at a cost of £96,000, inclusive of installation charges of £7,000.

Required

Calculate:
- (*a*) the balance of plant at cost at 31 March 19-6
- (*b*) the provision for depreciation of plant at 31 March 29-6
- (*c*) the profit or loss on disposal of the plant.

(*Chartered Association of Certified Accountants*)

24.7A Sema plc, a company in the heavy engineering industry, carried out an expansion programme in the 19-6 financial year, in order to meet a permanent increase in contracts.

The company selected a suitable site and commissioned a survey and valuation report, for which the fee was £1,500. On the basis of the report the site was acquired for £90,000.

Solicitor's fees for drawing up the contract and conveyancing were £3,000.

Fees of £8,700 were paid to the architects for preparing the building plans and overseeing the building work. This was carried out partly by the company's own workforce (at a wages cost of £11,600), using company building materials (cost £76,800) and partly by sub-contractors who charged £69,400, of which £4,700 related to the demolition of an existing building on the same site.

The completed building housed two hydraulic presses.

The cost of press A was £97,000 (ex works), payable in a single lump sum two months after installation. Sema was given a trade discount of 10% and a cash discount for prompt payment of 2%. Hire of a transporter to collect the press and to convey it to the new building was £2,900. Installation costs were £2,310, including hire of lifting gear, £1,400.

Press B would have cost £105,800 (delivered) if it had been paid in one lump sum. However, Sema opted to pay three equal annual instalments of £40,000, starting on the date of acquisition. Installation costs were £2,550, including hire of lifting gear, £1,750.

The whole of the above expenditure was financed by the issue of £500,000 7% Debentures (on which the annual interest payable was £35,000).

Before the above acquisitions were taken into account, the balances (at cost) on the fixed asset accounts for premises and plant were £521,100 and £407,500 respectively.

Required

(a) Using such of the above information as is relevant, post and balance the premises and plant accounts for the 19-6 financial year.

(b) State, with reasons, which of the given information you have not used in your answer to (a) above.

(Chartered Association of Certified Accountants)

25

Bank reconciliation statements

Let us assume that we have just written up our cash book. We call at the bank on 30 June 19-5 and obtain from the bank manager a copy of our bank statement. On our return we tick off in our cash book and on the bank statement the items that are similar. A copy of our cash book (bank columns only) and of our bank statement are now shown as Exhibit 25.1.

Exhibit 25.1

Cash Book (bank columns only)

19-5			£	19-5			£
June 1 Balance b/fwd	√		80	June 27 I Gordon	√		35
,, 28 D Johnson	√		100	,, 29 B Tyrell			40
				,, 30 Balance c/d			105
			180				180
July 1 Balance b/d			105				

Bank Statement

19-5	Dr	Cr	Balance
	£	£	£
June 26 Balance b/fwd	√		80CR
,, 28 Banking	√	100	180CR
,, 30 I Gordon	√ 35		145CR

By comparing the cash book and the bank statement, it can be seen that the only item that was not in both of these was the cheque payment to B Tyrell £40 in the cash book.

The reason this was in the cash book, but not on the bank statement, is simply one of timing. The cheque had been posted to B Tyrell on 29 June, but there had not been time for it to be banked by Tyrell and pass through the banking system. Such a cheque is called an 'unpresented cheque' because it has not yet been presented at the drawer's bank.

To prove that, although they are different figures the balances are not different because of errors, a bank reconciliation statement is drawn up. This is as follows:

	£
Balance in hand as per Cash Book	105
add unpresented cheque: Tyrell	40
Balance in Hand as per Bank Statement	145

It would have been possible for the bank reconciliation statement to have started with the bank statement balance:

Bank Reconciliation Statement
as at 30 June 19-5

	£
Balance in Hand as per Bank Statement	145
less unpresented cheque: Tyrell	40
Balance in Hand as per Cash Book	105

You should notice that the bank account is shown as a debit balance in the firm's cash book because to the firm it is an asset. In the bank's books the bank account is shown as a credit balance because this is a liability of the bank to the firm.

We can now look at a more complicated example in Exhibit 25.2. Similar items in both cash book and bank statement are shown ticked.

Exhibit 25.2

Cash Book

19-5		£	19-5		£
Dec 27 Total b/fwd		2,000	Dec 27 Total b/fwd		1,600
,, 29 J Potter	√	60	,, 28 J Jacobs	√	105
,, 31 M Johnson (B)		220	,, 30 M Chatwood (A)		15
			,, 31 Balance c/d		560
		2,280			2,280
19-6					
Jan 1 Balance b/d		560			

Bank Statement

		Dr	Cr	Balance
19-5		£	£	£
Dec 27	Balance b/fwd			400 Cr
,, 29	Cheque √		60	460 Cr
,, 30	J Jacobs √	105		355 Cr
,, ,,	Credit transfers: L Shaw (C)		70	425 Cr
,, ,,	Bank charges (D)	20		405 Cr

The balance brought forward in the bank statement £400 is the same figure as that in the cash book, i.e., totals b/fwd £2,000 − £1,600 = £400. However, items (A) and (B) are in the cash book only, and (C) and (D) are on the bank statement only. We can now examine these in detail:

(A) This is a cheque sent by us yesterday to Mr Chatwood. It has not yet passed through the banking system and been presented to our bank, and is therefore an 'unpresented cheque'.

(B) This is a cheque banked by us on our visit to the bank when we collected the copy of our bank statement. As we handed this cheque over the counter at the same time as the bank clerk gave us our bank statement, naturally it has not yet been entered on the statement.

(C) A customer, L Shaw has paid his account by instructing his bank to pay us direct through the banking system, instead of paying by cheque. Such a transaction is usually called a **Bank Giro Transfer**. The term previously used was **Credit Transfer**.

(D) The bank has charged us for the services given in keeping a bank account for us. It did not send us a bill: it simply takes the money from our account by debiting it and reducing the amount of our balance.

We can show these differences in the form of a table. This is followed by bank reconciliation statements drawn up both ways. This is for illustration only; we do not have to draw up a table or prepare two bank reconciliation statments. All we need in practice is one bank reconciliation statement, drawn up whichever way we prefer.

Items not in both sets of books	Effect on Cash Book balance	Effect on Bank Statement	Adjustment required to one balance to reconcile it with the other	
			To Cash Book balance	To Bank Statement balance
1 Payment M Chatwood £15	reduced by £15	none – not yet entered	add £15	deduct £15
2 Banking M Johnson £220	increased by £220	none – not yet entered	deduct £220	add £220
3 Bank Commission £20	none – not yet entered	reduced by £20	deduct £20	add £20
4 Credit Transfers £70	none – not yet entered	increased by £70	add £70	deduct £70

Bank Reconciliation Statement as on 31 December 19-5

	£	£
Balance in hand as per Cash Book		560
add Unpresented cheque	15	
Credit transfers	70	
		85
		645
less Bank commission	20	
Bank lodgement not yet entered on bank statement	220	
		240
Balance in hand as per bank statement		405

191

	£	£
Balance in hand as per bank statement		405
add Bank commission	20	
Bank lodgement not yet entered on bank statement	220	
	———	240
		645
less Unpresented cheques	15	
Traders Credit Transfers	70	
	———	85
Balance in Hand as per Cash Book		560

Standing orders and direct debits

A firm can instruct its bank to make regular payments of fixed amounts at stated dates to certain persons or firms. These are standing orders. These payments would be automatically effected by the bank without the firm having to make out cheques or doing anything else once the instructions have been given to the bank. At a particular date such a payment might have been made by the bank, but the payments might not have been shown in the firm's cash book on that date. Such standing orders can only be altered by the paying firm.

There are also payments which have to be made, and where the authority to get the money is given to the firm to whom the money is to be paid, instead of giving one's bank the instructions to pay certain amounts. Instead of one's bank remembering to make the payment, the creditor can automatically charge one's bank account with the requisite amount. These are called 'direct debits'.

Writing up the cash book before attempting a reconciliation

It will soon become obvious that in fact the best procedure is to complete entering up the cash book before attempting the reconciliation, this being done by finding out the items that are on the bank statement but not in the cash book and making entries for them in the cash book. This is normally what would happen in practice. By this means the number of adjustments needed in the reconciliation statement are reduced. However, in examination the questions sometimes ask for the reconciliation to take place before completing the cash book entries.

If, in Exhibit 25.2 the cash book had been written up before the bank reconciliation statement had been drawn up, then the cash book and reconciliation statement would have appeared as follows in Exhibit 25.3.

Exhibit 25.3

Cash Book

19-5		£	19-5		£
Dec 27	Total b/fwd	2,000	Dec 27	Total b/fwd	1,600
,, 29	J Potter	60	,, 28	J Jacobs	105
,, 31	M Johnson	220	,, 30	M Chatwood	15
,, 31	Credit transfers		,, 31	Bank commission	20
	L Shaw	70	,, 31	Balance c/d	610
		2,350			2,350

19-6		
Jan 1	Balance b/d	610

Bank Reconciliation Statement as on 31 December 19-5

	£
Balance in hand as per cash book	610
add Unpresented cheque	15
	625
less Bank lodgement not yet entered on bank statement	220
Balance in hand as per bank statement	405

Bank overdrafts

The adjustments needed to reconcile the bank overdraft according to the firm's books with that shown in the bank's books are the complete opposite of that needed when the account is not overdrawn. It should be noticed that most banks show that an account has been overdrawn by putting the letters O/D after the amount of the balance; this is obviously the abbreviation for overdraft.

Exhibit 25.4 shows a cash book fully written up to date, and the bank reconciliation statement needed to reconcile the cash book and bank statement balances.

Exhibit 25.4

Cash Book

19-4		£	19-4		£
Dec 5	I Howe	308	Dec 1	Balance b/fwd	709
,, 24	L Mason	120	,, 9	P Davies	140
,, 29	K King	124	,, 27	J Kelly	63
,, 31	G Cumberbatch	106	,, 29	United Trust	77
,, ,,	Balance c/f	380	,, 31	Bank Charges	49
		1,038			1,038

Bank Statement

19-4		Dr £	Cr £	Balance £
Dec 1	Balance b/fwd			709 O/D
,, 5	Cheque		308	401 O/D
,, 14	P Davies	140		541 O/D
,, 24	Cheque		120	421 O/D
,, 29	K King: Credit Transfer		124	297 O/D
,, 29	United Trust: Standing order	77		374 O/D
,, 31	Bank Charges	49		423 O/D

Bank Reconciliation Statement as on 30 December 19-4

	£
Overdraft as per cash book	380
add Bank Lodgements not on bank statement	106
	486
less Unpresented cheque	63
Overdraft per bank statement	423

In examinations for the professional bodies the examiner may deliberately make the reconciliations more difficult. Review questions 25.4A and 25.6A in this book are examples of such questions.

Dishonoured cheques

When a cheque is received from a customer and paid into the bank, it is recorded on the debit side of the cash book. It is also shown on the bank statement as a banking by the bank. However, at a later date it may be found that the cheque has not gone through the account of the drawer, in other words his bank has failed to 'honour' the cheque, the cheque therefore is known as a 'dishonoured' cheque.

There are several possible reasons for this. Let us suppose that J Hewitson gave us a cheque for £5,000 on May 20 19-2. We bank it, but a few days later our bank returns the cheque to us. Typical reasons are:

(*a*) Hewitson had put £5,000 in figures on the cheque, but had written it in words as five thousand five hundred pounds. You will have to give the cheque back to Hewitson for amendment.

(*b*) Normally cheques are considered 'stale' six months after the date on the cheque, in other words the banks will not 'honour' cheques over six months old. If Hewitson had put the year 19-1 on the cheque instead of 19-2, then the cheque would be returned to us by our bank.

(*c*) Hewitson simply did not have sufficient funds in his bank account. Suppose he had previously got only a £2,000 balance, and his bank would not allow him an overdraft. In such a case the cheque would be dishonoured. The bank would write on the cheque 'refer to drawer', and we would have to get in touch with Hewitson to see what he was going to do to put matters right.

In all of these cases the bank would automatically show the original banking as being cancelled by showing the cheque paid out of our bank account. As soon as this happens they will notify us, and we will then also show the cheque as being cancelled by a credit in the cash book. We will then debit that amount to his account.

When Hewitson originally paid his account our records would appear as:

J Hewitson

19-2		£	19-2		£
May 1 Balance b/d		5,000	May 20 Bank		5,000

Bank Account

19-2		£
May 20 J Hewitson		5,000

After our recording the dishonour, the records will appear as:

J Hewitson

19-2		£	19-2		£
May 1 Balance b/d		5,000	May 20 Bank		5,000
May 25 Bank:					
cheque dishonoured		5,000			

Bank Account

19-2		£	19-2		£
May 20 J Hewitson		5,000	May 25 J Hewitson:		
			cheque dishonoured		5,000

In other words Hewitson is once again shown as owing us £5,000.

Reconciliation of our ledger accounts with supplier's statements

For reasons of differences in timing, the balance on a supplier's statement on a certain date can differ from the balance on that supplier's account in our Purchases Ledger. This is similar to the fact that a bank statement balance may differ from the cash book balance. In a similar fashion a reconciliation statement may also be necessary. This can now be illustrated, the capital letters in brackets being for illustration only.

Our Purchases Ledger
C Jackson

19-6			£	19-6		£
Jan 10 Bank			1,550	Jan 1 Balance b/d		1,550
,, 29 Returns	(A)		116	,, 6 Purchases		885
,, 31 Balance c/d			1,679	,, 18 Purchases		910
			3,345			3,345

Supplier's Statement
Frank Wood Ltd

	Dr £	Cr £	Balance £
19-6			
Jan 1 Balance b/f			1,550 Dr
,, 4 Sales	885		2,435 Dr
,, 13 Bank		1,550	885 Dr
,, 18 Sales	910		1,795
,, 31 Sales (B)	425		2,220

Comparing our Purchases Ledger Account with the Supplier's Statement, two differences can be seen.

(A) We sent returns £116 to C Jackson, but they had not received them and recorded them in their books by the end of January.

(B) Our supplier has sent goods to Frank Wood Ltd (our company), but we had not received them and entered the £425 in our books by the end of January.

A reconciliation statement can be drawn up by us, Frank Wood Ltd, as on 31 January 19-6.

Reconciliation of Suppliers' Statement
C Jackson as on 31 January 19-6

Balance per our Purchases Ledger			1,679
add Purchases not received by us	(B)	425	
Returns not received by supplier	(A)	116	541
Balance per Supplier's Statement			2,220

Review questions

25.1 From the following draw up a bank reconciliation statement from details as on 31 December 19-6:

	£
Cash at bank as per bank column of the Cash Book	678
Unpresented cheques	256
Cheques received and paid into the bank, but not yet entered on the bank statement	115
Credit transfers entered as banked on the bank statement but not entered in the Cash Book	56
Cash at bank as per bank statement	875

25.2A Draw up a bank reconciliation statement, after writing the cash book up-to-date, ascertaining the balance on the bank statement, from the following as on 31 March 19-9:

	£
Cash at bank as per bank column of the cash book (Dr)	3,896
Bankings made but not yet entered on bank statement	606
Bank charges on bank statement but not yet in cash book	28
Unpresented cheques C Clarke	117
Standing order to ABC Ltd entered on bank statement, but not in cash book	55
Credit transfer from A Wood entered on bank statement, but not yet in cash book	189

25.3 The summary of the bank column in the cash book of DVT Ltd for the year ending 30 November 19-0 is as follows:

		£
Opening balance		1,654
Receipts		332,478
		334,132
Payments		316,735
Closing balance		£17,397

Your investigation of the accounting records for this period reveals the following information:

(*a*) Cheques paid to suppliers of £1,435 have not yet been presented at the bank, and cheques paid into the bank of £1,620 on 30 November 19-0 have not yet been credited to the company's account.

(*b*) Standing orders entered in the bank statement have been omitted from the cash book in respect of lease payments on company car, 12 months at £96 per month, and annual insurance of £150.

(*c*) Bank charges of £452 shown in the bank statement have not been entered in the cash book.

(*d*) A cheque drawn for £127 has been entered in the cash book as £172, and a cash book page on the receipts side has been under added by £200.

(*e*) A cheque for £238 has been debited to the company's bank account in error by the bank.

(*f*) The bank statement shows a favourable balance as at 30 November 19-0 of £15,465.

Required:

Bank reconciliation statement as at 30th November 19-0 together with a corrected cash book position.

(Institute of Chartered Secretaries and Administrators)

25.4A The bank reconciliation statement as at 19 September 19-6 for the account number 0439567 of John Henry Limited with Industrious Bank Plc showed that the difference between the cash book and bank statement was due entirely to four unpresented cheques numbers 765417 to 765420 inclusive.

The cash book, bank columns, for the period from 19 September to 30 September 19-6, of John Henry Limited are as follows:

19-6		£	19-6		Cheque	£
23 Sept	B Main	692.30	19 Sept	Balance B/fwd		21.00
,, Sept	T Patrick	27.24	,, Sept	S Salter Ltd	765421	25.67
25 Sept	S Saunders	410.00	22 Sept	Sway District Council	765422	275.10
26 Sept	P King	400.00	23 Sept	North South Electricity	Direct	
26 Sept	K Plunket	39.60		Authority	debit	316.50
28 Sept	J Lim	324.92	,, Sept	John Peters Ltd	765423	18.34
30 Sept	S Balk	220.39	24 Sept	Furniture Trade Association	Standing	
					order	45.00
			,, Sept	K Patel	765424	19.04
			25 Sept	Cash (petty cash)	765425	50.00
			26 Sept	J Green Ltd	765426	45.00
			,, Sept	G Glinker	765427	174.00
			29 Sept	Deposit account		600.00
			,, Sept	Wages	Transfer	390.00
			30 Sept	Balance c/d		134.80
		£2,114.45				£2,114.45

1 Oct   Balance B/fwd   134.80

Early in October 19-6 John Henry Limited received the following statement from Industrious Bank Plc.

John Henry Ltd – *Statement of account with Industrious Bank Plc*
East Road, Streamly

Account number 0439567

Date 19-6	Particulars	Payments £	Receipts £	Balance £
19 Sept	Balance			453.26
22 Sept	765419	138.35		314.91
23 Sept	Sundry credits		719.54	1,034.45
,, Sept	Direct debit	316.50		717.95
24 Sept	765421	25.67		692.28
,, Sept	Standing order	45.00		647.28
25 Sept	765420	160.04		487.24
26 Sept	765422	275.10		212.14
,, Sept	Sundry credits		400.00	612.14
,, Sept	Bank Giro credit		410.00	1,022.14
29 Sept	Bank Giro credit		334.92	1,357.06
,, Sept	765418	21.69		1,355.37
,, Sept	765424	19.04		1,316.33
,, Sept	Transfer to Deposit account	600.00		716.33
,, Sept	Transfer	390.00		326.33
,, Sept	765425	50.00		276.33
,, Sept	As advised		65.00	341.33
,, Sept	Bank Giro credit		39.60	380.93
30 Sept	Loan account interest	41.25		339.68
,, Sept	Bank charges	16.70		322.98

The following additional information is given:

(*a*) The amount received from J Lim on 28 September 19-6 was £334.92 not £324.92:

(*b*) The amount credited in the bank statement on 29 September 19-6 and shown as 'As advised £65.00' concerned dividends received:

(c) John Henry Limited has written to the bank complaining concerning the bank charges of £16.70: the company's view is that no charges should arise for the month of September. The bank has a reputation for not cancelling bank charges.

Required

(a) Prepare a bank reconciliation statement as at 30 September 19-6;

Note: Indicate the amount which should be included in the balance sheet as at 30 September 19-6 of John Henry Limited for the company's account number 0439567 with Industrious Bank Plc.

(b) What are the major uses of a bank reconciliation statement?

(Association of Accounting Technicians)

25.5 The bank account for the month of September 19-3 for the firm of Rivers and Co was as follows:

Bank account

Receipts				Payments			
Sep		£		Sep		Cheque	£
1	Balance b/d	271.94		3	Derwent Ltd	052316	25.08
1	T Hames	53.40		4	Severn Bros	052317	31.72
1	Dove Enterprises	62.85		8	Clyde & Co	052318	121.86
13	Isis plc	1,793.48		9	Ribble Merchants	052319	1,374.29
20	Colne Electronics	2,404.37		13	Swale Assoc.	052320	10.35
				20	Don Eng.	052321	642.13
				24	Humber Water Authority	Direct Debit	32.00
				26	Arun Decorators	052322	90.44
				26	Tyne Borough Council	Standing order	123.57
				27	Salaries transfers		940.60
				28	Wyne & Sons	052323	4.30
				30	Balance c/d		1,189.70
		4,586.04					4,586.04
Oct							
1	Balance b/d	1,189.70					

In early October the firm's bank sent a statement for the month of September 19-3, as shown below:

Statement of account with Mersey Bank plc

Name: Rivers & Co Current Account. Date issued: 1 October 19-3

Sep	Description	Debit £	Credit £	Balance £
1	BCE			592.45
2	052315	85.16		507.29
5	052314	100.34		406.95
8	052316	25.08		381.87
12	DD (Medway Insurance)	26.26		355.61
13	CR		1,793.48	2,149.09
13	052318	121.86		2,027.23
15	052319	1,374.29		652.94
16	052317	31.72		621.22
20	CR		2,404.37	3,025.59
22	DD (Humber Water Authority)	32.00		2,993.59
23	052320	10.35		2,983.24
26	SO	123.57		2,859.67
28	TRFR	940.60		1,919.07
29	INT (Loan Account)	11.19		1,907.88
30	Bank charges	7.37		1,900.51
30	052321	642.13		1,258.38
30	BCE			1,258.38

BCE = Balance   SO = Standing order   CR = Credit   TRFR = Transfer
INT = Interest   DD = Direct debit (to current account)

Required
Prepare the firm's bank reconciliation statement as at 30 September 19-3.
(Chartered Association of Certified Accountants)

25.6A The bank account of Fuller Ltd, prepared by the company's book-keeper, was as shown below for the month of October 19-6.

Bank Account

19-6 Oct		£	19-6 Oct	Cheque No		£
1	Balance b/d	91.40	2	Petty cash 062313		36.15
3	McIntosh and Co	260.11	3	Freda's Fashions		
3	Malcolm Brothers	112.83		062314		141.17
3	Cash sales	407.54	6	Basford Ltd 062315		38.04
14	Rodney		8	Hansler Agencies		
	Photographic	361.02		062316		59.32
17	Puccini's Cold		9	Duncan's Storage		
	Store Ltd	72.54		062317		106.75
20	Eastern Divisional		9	Aubrey plc 062318		18.10
	Gas Board —		10	Secretarial Services		
	rebate (August			Ltd 062319		28.42
	direct credit)	63.40	14	Trevor's Auto		
22	Grainger's Garage	93.62		Repairs 062320		11.75
29	Cash sales	235.39	15	Wages cash 062321		115.52
31	Balance c/d	221.52	16	Towers Hotel		
				062322		44.09
			17	Bank Charges		
				(September) —		12.36
			20	Broxcliffe Borough		
				Council SO		504.22
			21	Eastern Area		
				Electricity Board		
				DD		196.83
			24	Eastern Divisional		
				Gas Board DD		108.64
			28	Petty cash 062323		41.20
			30	Wages cash 062324		119.07
			31	Salaries transfer —		337.74
		1,919.37				1,919.37
Nov						
1	Balance b/d	221.52				

In early November, the company's bank sent a statement of account which is reproduced below.

Statement of account with Lowland Bank plc

Account: Fuller Ltd Current Account No 10501191

Date of issue: 1 November 19-6

19-6 Oct	Description	Debit £	Credit £	Balance £
1	BCE			90.45
2	CR		175.02	265.47
,,	062310	111.34		154.13
3	062312	9.18		144.95
,,	062309	15.41		129.54
,,	CR		780.48	910.02
7	062313	36.15		873.87
10	ADJ		12.90	886.77
15	062315	38.04		848.73
16	062314	141.17		707.56
17	CR		443.56	1,151.12
20	SO	504.22		646.90
21	062317	106.75		540.15
,,	DD	196.83		343.32
,,	062320	11.75		331.57
22	141981	212.81		118.76
,,	ADJ	10.00		108.76
,,	062319	28.42		80.34
,,	062320	11.75		68.59
,,	CR		93.62	162.21
24	ADJ		212.81	375.02
27	INT (loan account)	26.35		348.67
,,	062321	115.52		233.15
28	062322	44.09		189.06
,,	DD	108.64		80.42
30	CGS	9.14		71.28
31	ADJ		11.75	83.03

Abbreviations:

BCE = Balance   SO = Standing order   CR = Credit   ADJ = Adjustment
INT = Interest   DD = Direct debit   CGS = Charges.

Required
Prepare the company's bank reconciliation statement as at 31 October 19-6.
(Chartered Association of Certified Accountants)

25.7 The bank statement for G Greene for the month of March 19-6 is:

19-6	Dr £	Cr £	Balance £
Mar 1 Balance			5,197 O/D
Mar 8 L Tulloch	122		5,319 O/D
Mar 16 Cheque		244	5,075 O/D
Mar 20 A Bennett	208		5,283 O/D
Mar 21 Cheque		333	4,950 O/D
Mar 31 M Turnbull: trader's credit		57	4,893 O/D
Mar 31 BKS: standing order	49		4,942 O/D
Mar 31 Bank Charges	28		4,970 O/D

The cash book for March 19-6 is:

19-6 Dr	£	19-6 Cr	£
Mar 16 N Marsh	244	Mar 1 Balance b/f	5,197
Mar 21 K Alexander	333	Mar 6 L Tulloch	122
Mar 31 U Sinclair	160	Mar 30 A Bennett	208
Mar 31 Balance c/d	5,280	Mar 30 J Shaw	490
	6,017		6,017

You are to:
    (a) Write the cash book up-to-date and
    (b) Draw up a bank reconciliation statement as on 31 March 19-6.

25.8 Included in the creditor's ledger of J Cross, a shop-keeper, is the following account which disclosed that the amount owing to one of his suppliers at 31 May 19-4 was £472.13.

Creditors Ledger
Nala Merchandising Company

19-4	£	19-4	£
May 18 Purchases returns	36.67	May 1 Balance b/d	862.07
27 Purchases returns	18.15	16 Purchases	439.85
,, Adjustment		25 Purchases	464.45
(overcharge)	5.80	,, Adjustment	
31 Discount received	24.94	(undercharge)	13.48
,, Bank	1,222.16		
,, Balance b/d	472.13		
	1,779.85		1,779.85
		June 1 Balance b/d	472.13

In the first week of June 19-4, J Cross received a statement (shown below) from the supplier which showed an amount owing of £2,424.53.

J Cross in account with
Nala Merchandising Company, Statement of Account

19-4		Debit £	Credit £	£
May 1	BCE			1,538.70 Dr
3	DISC		13.40	1,525.30 Dr
	CHQ		634.11	891.19 Dr
5	ALLCE		29.12	862.07 Dr
7	GDS	256.72		1.118.79 Dr
10	GDS	108.33		1,227.12 Dr
11	GDS	74.80		1,301.92 Dr
14	ADJ	13.48		1.315.40 Dr
18	GDS	162.55		1,477.95 Dr
23	GDS	301.90		1,779.85 Dr
25	ALLCE		36.67	1,743.18 Dr
28	GDS	134.07		1,877.25 Dr
29	GDS	251.12		2,128.37 Dr
30	GDS	204.80		2,333.17 Dr
31	GDS	91.36		2,424.53 Dr
31	BCE			2,424.53 Dr

Abbreviations:

BCE = Balance;   CHQ = Cheque;   GDS = Goods;   ALLCE = Allowance;
DISC = Discount;   ADJ = Adjustment.

Required
Prepare a statement reconciling the closing balance on the supplier's account in the creditor's ledger with the closing balance shown on the statement of account submitted by the supplier.
(Chartered Association of Certified Accountants)

26

The analytical petty cash book and the imprest system

With the growth of the firm it has been seen that it became necessary to have several books instead of just one ledger. As the firm further increased in size these books also were further sub-divided.

These ideas can be extended to the cash book. It is obvious that in almost any firm there will be a great deal of small cash payments to be made. It would be an advantage if the records of these payments could be kept separate from the main cash book. Where a separate book is kept it is known as a **Petty Cash Book**.

The advantages of such an action can be summarised as follows:
1   The task of handling and recording the small cash payments could be delegated by the cashier to a junior member of staff who would then be known as the **petty cashier**. Thus, the cashier, who is a relatively higher paid member of staff, would be saved from routine work easily performed by a junior and lower paid member of staff.
2   If small cash payments were entered into the main cash book these items would then need posting one by one to the ledgers. If travelling expenses were paid to staff on a daily basis this could involve over 250 postings to the Staff Travelling Expenses Account during the year. However, if a form of analytical petty cash book is kept it would only be the periodical totals that need posting to the general ledger. If this was done only 12 monthly entries would be needed in the staff travelling expenses account instead of over 250.

When the petty cashier makes a payment to someone, then that person will have to fill in a voucher showing exactly what the expense was. He may well have to attach bills obtained by him, e.g. bills for petrol, to the petty cash voucher. He would sign the voucher to certify that his expenses had been paid to him by the petty cashier.

The imprest system

The basic idea of this system is that the cashier gives the petty cashier an adequate amount of cash to meet his needs for the ensuing period. At the end of the period the cashier ascertains the amount spent by the petty cashier, and gives him an amount equal to that spent. The petty cash in hand should then be equal to the original amount with which the period was started.

Exhibit 26.1 shows an example of this procedure.

Of course, it may sometimes be necessary to increase the fixed sum, often called the **cash float**, to be held at the start of each period. In the following case if it had been desired to increase the 'float' at the end of the second period to £120, then the cashier would have given the petty cashier an extra £20, i.e. £84 + £20 = £104.

Exhibit 26.1

		£
Period 1	The cashier gives the petty cashier	100
	The petty cashier pays out in the period	78
	Petty cash now in hand	22
	The cashier now reimburses the petty cashier the amount spent	78
	Petty cash in hand end of period 1	100
Period 2	The petty cashier pays out in the period	84
	Petty cash now in hand	16
	The cashier now reimburses the petty cashier the amount spent	84
	Petty cash in hand end of period 2	100

Illustration of an analytical cash book

An analytical petty cash book is often used. One of these is shown as Exhibit 26.2.

The receipts column represents the debit side of the petty cash book. On giving £50 to the petty cashier on 1 September the credit entry is made in the cash book while the debit entry is made in the petty cash book. A similar entry is made on 30 September for the £44 reimbursement.

The entries on the credit side of the petty cash book are first of all made in the totals column, and then are extended into the relevant expense column. At the end of the period, in this case a month, the payments are totalled, it being made sure that the total of the totals column equals the sum of the other payments totals, in this case £44. The expense columns have been headed with the type of expense.

To complete double entry, the total of each expense column is debited to the relevant expense account in the general ledger, the folio number of the page in the general ledger then being shown under each column of the petty cash book.

The end column has been chosen as a ledger column. In this column items paid out of petty cash which need posting to a ledger other than the general ledger are shown. This would happen if a purchases ledger account was settled out of petty cash, or if a refund was made out of the petty cash to a customer who had overpaid his account.

The double entry for all the items in Exhibit 26.2 appears as Exhibit 26.3.

19-4

			£
Sep	1	The cashier gives £50 as float to the petty cashier	
		Payments out of petty cash during September:	
,,	2	Petrol	6
,,	3	J Green – travelling expenses	3
,,	3	Postages	2
,,	4	D Davies – travelling expenses	2
,,	7	Cleaning expenses	1
,,	9	Petrol	1
,,	12	K Jones – travelling expenses	3
,,	14	Petrol	3
,,	15	L Black – travelling expenses	5
,,	16	Cleaning expenses	1
,,	18	Petrol	2
,,	20	Postages	2
,,	22	Cleaning expenses	1
,,	24	G Wood – travelling expenses	7
,,	27	Settlement of C Brown's account in the Purchases Ledger	3
,,	29	Postages	2
,,	30	The cashier reimburses the petty cashier the amount spent in the month.	

Exhibit 26.2

Petty Cash Book (page 31)

Receipts	Folio	Date	Details	Voucher No	Total	Motor Expenses	Staff Travelling Expenses	Postages	Cleaning	Ledger Folio	Ledger Accounts
£					£	£	£	£	£		£
50	CB 19	Sep 1	Cash								
		,, 2	Petrol	1	6	6					
		,, 3	J Green	2	3		3				
		,, 3	Postages	3	2			2			
		,, 4	D Davies	4	2		2				
		,, 7	Cleaning	5	1				1		
		,, 9	Petrol	6	1	1					
		,, 12	K Jones	7	3		3				
		,, 14	Petrol	8	3	3					
		,, 15	L Black	9	5		5				
		,, 16	Cleaning	10	1				1		
		,, 18	Petrol	11	2	2					
		,, 20	Postages	12	2			2			
		,, 22	Cleaning	13	1				1		
		,, 24	G Wood	14	7		7				
		,, 27	C Brown	15	3					PL 18	3
		,, 29	Postages	16	2			2			
					44	12	20	6	3		3
44	CB 22	,, 30	Cash			GL 17	GL 29	GL 44	G 64		3
		,, 30	Balance	c/d	50						
94					94						
50		Oct 1	Balance	b/d							

Exhibit 26.3

Cash Book (Bank Column only)   Page 19

	19-4		£
	Sept 1 Petty Cash PCB 31		50
	,, 30 Petty Cash PCB 31		44

General Ledger
Motor Expenses   Page 17

19-4   £
Sept 30 Petty Cash PCB 31   12

Staff Travelling Expenses   Page 29

19-4   £
Sept 30 Petty Cash PCB 31   20

Postages   Page 44

19-4   £
Sept 30 Petty Cash PCB 31   6

Cleaning   Page 64

19-4   £
Sept 30 Petty Cash PCB 31   3

Purchases Ledger
C Brown   Page 18

19-4	£	19-4	£
Sept 30 Petty Cash PCB 31	3	Sept 1 Balance b/d	3

In a firm with both a cash book and a petty cash book, the cash book is often known as a **bank cash book**. This means that *all* cash payments are entered in the petty cash book, and the bank cash book will contain *only* bank columns and discount columns. In this type of firm any cash sales will be paid direct into the bank.

In such a cash book, as in fact could happen in an ordinary cash book, an extra column could be added. In this would be shown the details of the cheques banked, just the total of the banking being shown in the total column.

Exhibit 26.4 shows the receipts side of the Bank Cash Book. The totals of the bankings made on the three days were £192, £381 and £1,218. The details column shows what the bankings are made up of.

Exhibit 26.4

Bank Cash Book (Receipts side)

Date	Details	Discount	Items	Total banked
19-6		£	£	£
May 14	G Archer	5	95	
,, 14	P Watts	3	57	
,, 14	C King		40	192
,, 20	K Dooley	6	114	
,, 20	Cash Sales		55	
,, 20	R Jones		60	
,, 20	P Mackie	8	152	381
,, 31	J Young		19	
,, 31	T Broome	50	950	
,, 31	Cash Sales		116	
,, 31	H Tiller	7	133	1,218

Review questions

26.1 The following is a summary of the petty cash transactions of Jockfield Ltd for May 19-2.

May 1 Received from Cashier £300 as petty cash float

		£
,, 2	Postages	18
,, 3	Travelling	12
,, 4	Cleaning	15
,, 7	Petrol for delivery van	22
,, 8	Travelling	25
,, 9	Stationery	17
,, 11	Cleaning	18
,, 14	Postage	5
,, 15	Travelling	8
,, 18	Stationery	9
,, 18	Cleaning	23
,, 20	Postage	13
,, 24	Delivery van 5,000 mile service	43
,, 26	Petrol	18
,, 27	Cleaning	21
,, 29	Postage	5
,, 30	Petrol	14

You are required to:

(*a*) Rule up a suitable petty cash book with analysis columns for expenditure on cleaning, motor expenses, postage, stationery, travelling;

(*b*) Enter the month's transactions;

(*c*) Enter the receipt of the amount necessary to restore the imprest and carry down the balance for the commencement of the following month;

(*d*) State how the double entry for the expenditure is completed.

(Association of Accounting Technicians)

26.2A The Oakhill Printing Co Ltd operates its petty cash account on the imprest system. It is maintained at a figure of £80 on the first day of each month.

At 30 April 19-7 the petty cash box held £19.37 in cash.

During May 19-7, the following petty cash transactions arose:

Date			Amount
19-7			£
May	1	Cash received to restore imprest	to be derived
	1	Bus fares	0.41
,,	2	Stationery	2.35
,,	4	Bus fares	0.30
,,	7	Postage stamps	1.70
,,	7	Trade journal	0.95
,,	8	Bus fares	0.64
,,	11	Correcting fluid	1.29
,,	12	Typewriter ribbons	5.42
,,	14	Parcel postage	3.45
,,	15	Paper clips	0.42
,,	15	Newspapers	2.00
,,	16	Photocopier repair	16.80
,,	19	Postage stamps	1.50
,,	20	Drawing pins	0.38
,,	21	Train fare	5.40
,,	22	Photocopier paper	5.63
,,	23	Display decorations	3.07
,,	23	Correcting fluid	1.14
,,	25	Wrapping paper	0.78
,,	27	String	0.61
,,	27	Sellotape	0.75
,,	27	Biro pens	0.46
,,	28	Typewriter repair	13.66
,,	30	Bus fares	2.09
June	1	Cash received to restore imprest	to be derived

Required:

Open and post the company's petty cash account for the period 1 May to 1 June 19-7 inclusive and balance the account at 30 May 19-7.

In order to facilitate the subsequent double-entry postings, all items of expense appearing in the 'payments' column should then be analysed individually into suitably labelled expense columns.

(Chartered Association of Certified Accountants)

26.3A Rule up a petty cash book with analysis columns for office expenses, motor expenses, cleaning expenses, and casual labour. The cash float is £350 and the amount spent is reimbursed on 30 June.

19-7		£
June 1	H Sangster – casual labour	13
,, 2	Letterheadings	22
,, 2	Unique Motors – motor repairs	30
,, 3	Cleaning Materials	6
,, 6	Envelopes	14
,, 8	Petrol	8
,, 11	J Higgins – casual labour	15
,, 12	Mrs Body – cleaner	7
,, 12	Paper clips	2
,, 14	Petrol	11
,, 16	Typewriter repairs	1
,, 19	Petrol	9
,, 21	Motor Taxation	50
,, 22	T Sweet – casual labour	21
,, 23	Mrs Body – cleaner	10
,, 24	P Dennis – casual labour	19
,, 25	Copy paper	7
,, 26	Flat Cars – motor repairs	21
,, 29	Petrol	12
,, 30	J Young – casual labour	16

27

Errors not affecting trial balance agreement

In Chapter 6 it was seen that if someone followed these rules:
- every debit entry needs a corresponding credit entry
- every credit entry needs a corresponding debit entry

and entered up his books using these rules, then when he extracted the trial balance its totals would agree, i.e. it would 'balance'.

Suppose he correctly entered cash sales £70 to the debit of the cash book, but did not enter the £70 to the credit of the sales account. If this was the only error in the books, the trial balance totals would differ by £70. However, there are certain kinds of errors which would not affect the agreement of the trial balance totals, and we will now consider these:

1   **Errors of omission** – where a transaction is completely omitted from the books. If he sold £90 goods to J Brewer, but he did not enter it in either the sales or Brewer's personal account, the trial balance would still 'balance'.

2   **Errors of commission** – this type is where the correct amount is entered but in the wrong person's account, e.g. where a sale of £11 to C Green is entered in the account of K Green. It will be noted that the correct class of account was used, both the accounts concerned being personal accounts.

3   **Errors of principle** – where an item is entered in the wrong class of account, e.g. if a fixed asset such as a motor van is debited to an expenses account such as motor expenses account.

4   **Compensating errors** – where errors cancel out each other. If the sales account was added up to be £10 too much and the purchases account was also added up to be £10 too much, then these two errors would cancel out in the trial balance. This is because the totals both of the debit side of the trial balance and of the credit side will be £10 too much.

5   **Errors of original entry** – where the original figure is incorrect, yet double entry is still observed using this incorrect figure. An instance of this could be where there were sales of £150 goods but an error is made in calculating the sales invoice. If it was calculated as £130, and £130 was credited as sales and £130 was debited to the personal account of the customer, the trial balance would still 'balance'.

6   **Complete reversal of entries** – where the correct accounts are used but each item is shown on the wrong side of the account. Suppose we had paid a cheque to D Williams for £200, the double entry of which is Cr Bank £200, Dr D Williams £200. In error it is entered as Cr D Williams £200, Dr Bank £200. The trial balance totals will still agree.

Correction of errors

When these errors are found they have to be corrected. The entries have to be made in the double-entry accounts. In addition, an entry should be made in the journal, to explain the correction. We can now look at one of these for each type of error.

Error of omission

The sale of goods, £59 to E George, has been completely omitted from the books. We must correct this by entering the sale in the books.

The Journal

	Dr	Cr
	£	£
E George	59	
Sales account		59
Correction of omission of Sales Invoice No.......		
from sales journal		

Error of commission

A purchase of goods, £44 from C Simons, was entered in error in C Simpson's account. To correct this, it must be cancelled out of C Simpson's account, and then entered where it should be in C Simons' account. The double entry will be:

C Simpson

19-5	£	19-5	£
Sept 30 C Simons: Error corrected	44	Sept 30 Purchases	44

C Simons

		19-5	£
		Sept 30 Purchases:	
		Entered originally in C Simpson's	
		a/c	44

The Journal entry will be:

The Journal

	Dr	Cr
	£	£
C Simpson	44	
C Simons		44
Purchase Invoice No...... entered in wrong		
personal account, now corrected		

Error of principle

The purchase of a machine, £200, is debited to Purchases account instead of being debited to a Machinery account. We therefore cancel the item out of the Purchases account by crediting that account. It is then entered where it should be by debiting the Machinery account.

	Dr	Cr
	£	£
Machinery account	200	
Purchases account		200
Correction of error: purchase of fixed asset debited to purchases account.		

Compensating error

The sales account is overcast by £200, as also is the wages account. The trial balance therefore still 'balances'. This assumes that these are the only two errors found in the books.

The Journal

	Dr	Cr
	£	£
Sales account	200	
Wages account		200
Correction of overcasts of £200 each in the sales account and the wages account which compensated for each other.		

Error of original entry

A sale of £98 to A Smailes was entered in the books as £89. It needs another £9 of sales entering now.

The Journal

	Dr	Cr
	£	£
A Smailes	9	
Sales account		9
Correction of error whereby sales were understated by £9		

Complete reversal of entries

A payment of cash of £16 to M Dickson was entered on the receipts side of the cash book in error and credited to M Dickson's account. This is somewhat more difficult to adjust. First must come the amount needed to cancel the error, then comes the actual entry itself. Because of this, the correcting entry is double the actual amount first recorded. We can now look at why this is so:

What we should have had:

Cash

	£
M Dickson	16

M Dickson

	£
Cash	16

Was entered as:

Cash

	£	
M Dickson	16	

M Dickson

		£
	Cash	16

We can now see that we have to enter double the original amount to correct the error.

Cash

	£		£
M Dickson	16	M Dickson (error corrected)	32

M Dickson

	£		£
Cash (error corrected)	32	M Dickson	16

Overall, when corrected, the cash account showing £16 debit and £32 credit means a net credit of £16. Similarly, Dickson's account shows £32 debit and £16 credit, a net debit of £16. As the final (net) answer is the same as what should have been entered originally, the error is now corrected.

The Journal entry appears:

The Journal

	Dr	Cr
	£	£
M Dickson	32	
Cash		32

Payment of cash £16 debited to cash and credited to
M Dickson in error on .... Error now corrected.

Casting

You will often notice the use of the expression 'to cast', which means 'to add up'. **Overcasting** means incorrectly adding up a column of figures to give an answer which is greater than it should be. **Undercasting** means incorrectly adding up a column of figures to give an answer which is less than it should be.

Review questions

27.1 After preparing its draft Final Accounts for the year ended 31 March 19-6 and its draft Balance Sheet as at 31 March 19-6 a business discovered that the stock lists used to compute the value of stock as at the 31 March 19-6 contained the following entry:

Stock item	Number	Cost per unit	Total cost
Y 4003	100	£1.39	£1,390

Required
> (*a*) What is wrong with this particular entry?
> (*b*) What would the effect of the error have been on
>> (i) the value of stock as at 31 March 19-6?
>> (ii) the cost of goods sold for the year ended 31 March 19-6?
>> (iii) the net profit for the year ended 31 March 19-6?
>> (iv) the total for Current Assets as at 31 March 19-6?
>> (v) the Owner's Capital as at 31 March 19-6?

(*Association of Accounting Technicians*)

27.2 Show the journal entries necessary to correct the following errors:
> (*a*) A sale of goods £678 to J Harris had been entered in J Hart's account.
> (*b*) The purchase of a machine on credit from L Pyle for £4,390 had been completely omitted from our books.
> (*c*) The purchase of a motor van £3,800 had been entered in error in the Motor Expenses account.
> (*d*) A sale of £221 to E Fitzwilliam had been entered in the books, both debit and credit, as £212.
> (*e*) Commission received £257 had been entered in error in the Sales account.
> (*f*) A receipt of cash from T Heath £77 had been entered on the credit side of the cash book and the debit side of T Heath's account.
> (*g*) A purchase of goods £189 had been entered in error on the debit side of the drawings account.
> (*h*) Discounts Allowed £366 had been entered in error on the debit side of the Discounts Received account.

27.3A Show the journal entries needed to correct the following errors:
> (*a*) Purchases £699 on credit from K Ward had been entered in H Wood's account.
> (*b*) A cheque of £189 paid for advertisements had been entered in the cash column of the cash book instead of in the bank column.
> (*c*) Sale of goods £443 on credit to B Gorton had been entered in error in B Gorton's account.
> (*d*) Purchase of goods on credit K Isaacs £89 entered in two places in error as £99.
> (*e*) Cash paid to H Moore £89 entered on the debit side of the cash book and the credit side of H Moore's account.
> (*f*) A sale of fittings £500 had been entered in the Sales Account.
> (*g*) Cash withdrawn from bank £100, had been entered in the cash column on the credit side of the cash book, and in the bank column on the debit side.
> (*h*) Purchase of goods £428 has been entered in error in the Fittings Account.

27.4A Thomas Smith, a retail trader, has very limited accounting knowledge. In the absence of his accounting technician, he extracted the following trial balance as at 31 March 19-8 from his business's accounting records:

	£	£
Stock in trade at 1 April 19-7		10,700
Stock in trade at 31 March 19-8	7,800	
Discounts allowed		310
Discounts received	450	
Provision for doubtful debts	960	
Purchases	94,000	
Purchases returns	1,400	
Sales		132,100
Sales returns	1,100	
Freehold property: at cost	70,000	
provision for depreciation	3,500	
Motor vehicles: at cost	15,000	
provision for depreciation	4,500	
Capital – Thomas Smith		84,600
Balance at bank	7,100	
Trade debtors		11,300
Trade creditors	7,600	
Establishment and administrative expenditure	16,600	
Drawings	9,000	
	£ 239,010	£ 239,010

Required:

(*a*) Prepare a corrected trial balance as at 31 March 19-8.

After the preparation of the above trial balance, but before the completion of the final accounts for the year ended 31 March 19-8, the following discoveries were made:

(*i*) The correct valuation of the stock in trade at 1 April 19-7 is £12,000; apparently some stock lists had been mislaid.

(*ii*) A credit note for £210 has now been received from J Hardwell Limited; this relates to goods returned in December 19-7 by Thomas Smith. However, up to now J Hardwell Limited had not accepted that the goods were not of merchantable quality and Thomas Smith's accounting records did not record the return of the goods.

(*iii*) Trade sample goods were sent to John Grey in February 19-8. These were free samples, but were charged wrongly at £1,000 to John Grey. A credit note is now being prepared to rectify the error.

(*iv*) In March 19-8, Thomas Smith painted the inside walls of his stockroom using materials costing £150 which were included in the purchases figure in the above trial balance. Thomas Smith estimates that he saved £800 by doing all the painting himself.

(*b*) Prepare the journal entries necessary to amend the accounts for the above discoveries. *Note*: narratives are required.

(*Association of Accounting Technicians*)

28
Suspense accounts and errors

In Chapter 27 errors were looked at where the trial balance totals were not thrown out of agreement. However, there are many errors which will mean that the trial balance will not 'balance'.

We can now look at some of these. It is assumed that there are no compensating errors.

1 Incorrect additions, either totals too great or too small, in any account.

2 Entering an item on only one side of the books. For instance, if the debit entry is made but not the credit entry, or a credit entry but no debit entry.

3 Entering one figure on the debit side of the books but another figure on the credit side. For instance, if £80 for cash received from M Brown is entered in the cash book, but £280 is entered in respect of it in Brown's account.

Every effort should be made to find the errors immediately, but especially in examinations it is assumed that for one reason or another this is not possible. Making this assumption, the trial balance totals should be made to agree with each other by inserting the amount of the difference between the two sides in a Suspense Account. This occurs in Exhibit 28.1 where there is a £40 difference.

Exhibit 28.1

Trial Balance as on 31 December 19-5

	Dr	Cr
	£	£
Totals after all the accounts have been listed	100,000	99,960
Suspense Account		40
	100,000	100,000

Suspense Account

	£
19-5	
Dec 31 Difference per trial balance	40

If the errors are not found before the final accounts are prepared, the balance of £40, being a credit balance, will be shown on the capital and liabilities side of the balance sheet. This, however, should never occur if the figure is a large one: the error must always be found. If the item is small, however, it may be added to current liabilities if it is a credit balance, or to current assets if it is a debit balance.

When the error(s) are found they must be corrected. For each correction an entry must be made in the journal describing the correction.

Assume that the error of £40 as shown in Exhibit 28.1 is found in the following year on 31 March 19-6. The error was that the sales account was undercast by £40. The balance on the suspense account should now be cancelled. The sales account should be credited to increase the account that had been understated. The accounts will appear:

Suspense Account

19-6		£	19-5		£
Mar 31 Sales		40	Dec 31 Difference per trial balance		40

Sales

			19-6		£
			Mar 31 Suspense		40

This can be shown in journal form as:

The Journal

		Dr	Cr
19-6		£	£
Mar 31 Suspense		40	
Sales			40

Correction of undercasting of sales by £40 in last year's accounts.

We can now look at Exhibit 28.2 where the suspense account difference was caused by more than one error.

Exhibit 28.2

The trial balance at 31 December 19-7 showed a difference of £77, being a shortage on the debit side. A suspense account is opened, and the difference of £77 is entered on the debit side of the account.

On 28 February 19-8 all the errors from the previous year were found.

(*a*) A cheque of £150 paid to L Bond had been correctly entered in the cash book, but had not been entered in Bond's account.

(*b*) The purchases account had been undercast by £20.

(*c*) A cheque of £93 received from K Smith had been correctly entered in the cash book, but had not been entered in Smith's account.

These are corrected as follows:

Suspense Account

19-8		£	19-8		£
Jan 1 Balance b/fwd		77	Feb 28 L Bond		150
Feb 28 K Smith		93	,, 28 Purchases		20
		170			170

L Bond

19-8		£
Feb 28 Suspense		150

19-8	£
Feb 28 Suspense	20

K Smith

	19-8	£
	Feb 28 Suspense	93

The Journal

	Dr	Cr
19-8	£	£
Feb 28 L Bond	150	
Suspense		150
Cheque paid omitted from Bond's account		
Feb 28 Purchases	20	
Suspense		20
Undercasting of purchases by £20 in last year's accounts		
Feb 28 Suspense	93	
K Smith		93
Cheque received omitted from Smith's account		

Only those errors which do throw the trial balance totals out of balance have to be corrected via the Suspense Account.

The effect of errors on reported profits

When errors are not discovered until a later period, it will often be found that the gross and/or net profits will have been incorrectly stated for the earlier period when the errors were made but had not been found.

Exhibit 28.3 shows a set of accounts in which errors have been made.

Exhibit 28.3

K Black

Trading & Profit & Loss Account for the year ended 31 December 19-5

	£	£
Sales		8,000
less Cost of Goods Sold:		
Opening Stock	500	
add Purchases	6,100	
	6,600	
less Closing Stock	700	5,900
Gross Profit		2,100
add Discounts Received		250
		2,350
less Expenses:		
Rent	200	
Insurance	120	
Lighting and Heating	180	
Depreciation	250	750
		1,600

Balance Sheet as at 31 December 19-5

	£	£
Fixed Assets		
Fixtures at cost	2,200	
less Depreciation to date	800	1,400
Current Assets		
Stock	700	
Debtors	600	
Bank	340	
	1,640	
less Current Liabilities		
Creditors	600	
Working Capital		1,040
Suspense Account		60
		2,500
Financed by:		
Capital		
Balance as at 1.1.19-5	1,800	
add Net Profit	1,600	
	3,400	
less Drawings	900	2,500
		2,500

Now suppose that there had only been one error found on 31 March 19-6, and that was that sales had been overcast £60. The correction appears as:

Suspense

19-6		£	19-6		£
Jan	1 Balance b/d	60	Mar 31 Sales		60

Sales

19-6		£
Mar 31 Sales		60

The Journal

		Dr	Cr
		£	£
19-6			
Mar 31 Sales		60	
Suspense			60
Overcasting of sales by £60 in last year's accounts.			

If a statement of corrected net profit for the year ended 31 December 19-5 is drawn up it will be as shown in Exhibit 28.4.

Exhibit 28.4

K Black

Statement of Corrected Net Profit for the year ended 31 December 19-5

	£
Net profit per the accounts	1,600
less Sales overcast	60
Corrected net profit for the year	1,540

If instead there had been 4 errors in the accounts of K Black, found on 31 March 19-6, their correction can now be seen. Assume that the net difference had also been £60.

  (*a*) Sales overcast by   £70

  (*b*) Rent undercast by   £40

  (*c*) Cash received from a debtor entered in the Cash Book only   £50

  (*d*) A purchase of £59 is entered in the books, debit and credit entries, as £95

The entries in the suspense account, and the journal entries will be as follows:

Suspense

19-6		£	19-6		£
Jan	1 Balance b/d	60	Mar 31 Sales		70
Mar 31 Debtor		50	,, 31 Rent		40
		110			110

The Journal	Dr	Cr
19-6	£	£
Mar 31 Sales	70	
Suspense		70
Sales overcast of £70 in 19-5		
Mar 31 Rent	40	
Suspense		40
Rent expense undercast by £40 in 19-5		
Mar 31 Suspense	50	
Debtor's account		50
Cash received omitted from debtor's account in 19-5		
Mar 31 Creditor's account	36	
Purchases		36
Credit purchase of £59 entered both as debit and credit as £95 in 19-5		

NB Note that (*d*), the correction of the understatement of purchases, does not pass through the suspense account.

    Exhibit 28.5 shows the statement of corrected net profit.

Exhibit 28.5

K Black

Statement of Corrected Net Profit for the year ended 31 December 19-5

	£	£
Net profit per the accounts		1,600
add Purchases overstated		36
		1,636
less Sales overcast	70	
Rent undercast	40	110
Corrected net profit for the year		1,526

Error (c), the cash not posted to a debtor's account, did not affect profit calculations.

Multiple-choice questions

Now attempt Set No. 4, to be found on page 496.

Review questions

28.1 Your book-keeper extracted a trial balance on 31 December 19-4 which failed to agree by £330, a shortage on the credit side of the trial balance. A Suspense Account was opened for the difference.

In January 19-5 the following errors made in 19-4 were found:

(*i*) Sales day book had been undercast by £100.

(*ii*) Sales of £250 to J Cantrell had been debited in error to J Cochrane's account.

(*iii*) Rent account had been undercast by £70.

(*iv*) Discounts Received account had been undercast by £300.

(*v*) The sale of a motor vehicle at book value had been credited in error to Sales Account £360.

You are required to:

(*a*) Show the journal entries necessary to correct the errors.

(*b*) Draw up the suspense account after the errors described have been corrected.

(*c*) If the net profit had previously been calculated at £7,900 for the year ended 31 December 19-4, show the calculations of the corrected net profit.

28.2A You have extracted a trial balance and drawn up accounts for the year ended 31 December 19-6. There was a shortage of £292 on the credit side of the trial balance, a suspense account being opened for that amount.

During 19-7 the following errors made in 19-6 were located:

(*i*) £55 received from sales of old Office Equipment has been entered in the sales account.

(*ii*) Purchases day book had been overcast by £60.

(*iii*) A private purchase of £115 had been included in the business purchases.

(*iv*) Bank charges £38 entered in the cash book have not been posted to the bank charges account.

(*v*) A sale of goods to B Cross £690 was correctly entered in the sales book but entered in the personal account as £960.

Required:

(*a*) Show the requisite journal entries to correct the errors.

(*b*) Write up the suspense account showing the correction of the errors.

(*c*) The net profit originally calculated for 19-6 was £11,370. Show your calculation of the correct figure.

28.3 The totals of the draft Trial Balance of Brenda Kimm as at 30 November 19-7 did not agree. The difference was posted to a Suspense Account pending investigation of the accounts. This revealed the following errors:

(*i*) The Sales Book has been undercast by £1,000.

(*ii*) The Purchases Book has been undercast by £585.

(*iii*) Discount received of £27 from Penn Supplies Ltd, a supplier, has been correctly entered in the Cash Book but has not yet been posted to Penn Supplies Ltd's personal account.

(*iv*) The Discount Allowed column in the Cash Book has been undercast by £90.

(*v*) Value Added Tax (at 15%) amounting to £45 collected on Cash Sales of £300 has not been entered in the VAT column in the Cash Book. Instead the sales have been recorded in the cash column as £345.

(*vi*) Some goods returned to Farid Attar, a supplier, have been recorded at a value of £59 in the Returns Inwards Book. The value of the goods returned was, in fact, £95.

Required:

(*a*) Prepare journal entries to show how the above errors would be corrected. (*NB*: dates and narratives are not required.)

(*b*) Before discovering the above errors Brenda Kimm's draft final accounts for the financial year ended 30 November 19-7 showed a profit of £103,356.

What is profit for the year after correcting the above errors?

(*Association of Accounting Technicians*)

28.4A The trial balance as at 30 April 19-7 of Timber Products Limited was balanced by the inclusion of the following debit balance:

Difference on trial balance suspense account £2,513.

Subsequent investigations revealed the following errors:

(*i*) Discounts received of £324 in January 19-7 have been posted to the debit of the discounts allowed account.

(*ii*) Wages of £2,963 paid in February 19-7 have not been posted from the cash book.

(*iii*) A remittance of £940 received from K Mitcham in November 19-6 has been posted to the credit of B Mansell Limited.

(*iv*) In December 19-6, the company took advantage of an opportunity to purchase a large quantity of stationery at a bargain price of £2,000. No adjustments have been made in the accounts for the fact that three quarters, in value, of this stationery was in stock on 30 April 19-7.

(*v*) A payment of £341 to J Winters in January 19-7 has been posted in the personal account as £143.

(*vi*) A remittance of £3,000 received from D North, a credit customer, in April 19-7 has been credited to sales.

The draft accounts for the year ended 30 April 19-7 of Timber Products Limited show a net profit of £24,760.

Timber Products Limited has very few personal accounts and therefore does not maintain either a purchases ledger control account or a sales ledger control account.

Required:

(*a*) Prepare the difference on trial balance suspense account showing, where appropriate, the entries necessary to correct the accounting errors.

(*b*) Prepare a computation of the corrected net profit for the year ended 30 April 19-7 following corrections for the above accounting errors.

(*c*) Outline the principal uses of trial balances.

(*Association of Accounting Technicians*)

28.5 Chi Knitwear Ltd is an old-fashioned firm with a handwritten set of books. A trial balance is extracted at the end of each month, and a profit and loss account and balance sheet are computed. This month however the trial balance will not balance, the credits exceeding debits by £1,536.

You are asked to help and after inspection of the ledgers discover the following errors.

(*i*) A balance of £87 on a debtors account has been omitted from the schedule of debtors, the total of which was entered as debtors in the trial balance.

(*ii*) A small piece of machinery purchased for £1,200 had been written off to repairs.

(*iii*) The receipts side of the cash book had been undercast by £720.

(*iv*) The total of one page of the sales day book had been carried forward as £8,154, whereas the correct amount was £8,514.

(*v*) A credit note for £179 received from a supplier had been posted to the wrong side of his account.

(*vi*) An electricity bill in the sum of £152, not yet accrued for, is discovered in a filing tray.

(*vii*) Mr Smith whose past debts to the company had been the subject of a provision, at last paid £731 to clear his account. His personal account has been credited but the cheque has not yet passed through the cash book.

Required:

(*a*) Write up the Suspense Account to clear the difference, and

(*b*) State the effect on the accounts of correcting each error.

(*Chartered Association of Certified Accountants*)

28.6A Allan Smith, an inexperienced accounts clerk, extracted the following trial balance, as at 31 March 19-6, from the books of John Bold, a small trader:

	£	£
Purchases	75,950	
Sales		94,650
Trade debtors	7,170	
Trade creditors		4,730
Salaries	9,310	
Light and heat	760	
Printing and stationery	376	
Stock at 1 April 19-5	5,100	
Stock at 31 March 19-6		9,500
Provision for doubtful debts	110	
Balance at bank	2,300	
Cash in hand	360	
Freehold premises:		
At cost	22,000	
Provision for depreciation	8,800	
Motor vehicles:		
At cost	16,000	
Provision for depreciation	12,000	
Capital at 1 April 19-5		23,096
Drawings		6,500
Suspense		21,760
	£160,236	£160,236

In the course of preparing the final accounts for the year ended 31 March 19-6, the following discoveries were made:

(*i*) No entries have been made in the books for the following entries in the bank statements of John Bold:

19-6	Payments	£
March 26	Bank charges	16
March 31	Cheque dishonoured	25

Note: The cheque dishonoured had been received earlier in March from Peter Good, debtor.

(*ii*) In arriving at the figure of £7,170 for trade debtors in the above trial balance, a trade creditor (Lionel White £70) was included as a debtor.

(*iii*) No entries have been made in the books for a credit sale to Mary Black on 29 March 19-6 of goods of £160.

(*iv*) No entries have been made in the books for goods costing £800 withdrawn from the business by John Bold for his own use.

(*v*) Cash sales of £700 in June 19-5 have been posted to the credit of trade debtors' accounts.

(*vi*) Discounts received of £400 during the year under review have not been posted to the appropriate nominal ledger account.

(*vii*) The remaining balance of the suspense account is due to cash sales for January and February 19-6 being posted from the cash book to the debit of the purchases account.

Required:

(*a*) The journal entry necessary to correct for item (*vii*) above.

Note: A narrative should be included.

(*b*) Prepare a corrected trial balance as at 31 March 19-6.

(*Association of Accounting Technicians*)

28.7 The draft final accounts of RST Ltd for the year ended 30 April 19-5 showed a net profit for the year after tax of £78,263.

During the subsequent audit, the following errors and omissions were discovered. At the draft stage a Suspense account had been opened to record the net difference.

(*a*) Trade debtors were shown as £55,210. However,

   (*i*) bad debts of £610 had not been written off,

   (*ii*) the existing provision for doubtful debtors, £1,300, should have been adjusted to 2% of debtors,

   (*iii*) a provision of 2% for discounts on debtors should have been raised.

(*b*) Rates of £491 which had been prepaid at 30 April 19-4 had not been brought down on the rates account as an opening balance.

(*c*) A vehicle held as a fixed asset, which had originally cost £8,100 and for which £5,280 had been provided as depreciation, had been sold for £1,350. The proceeds had been correctly debited to Bank but had been credited to Sales. No transfers had been made to Disposals account.

(*d*) Credit purchases of £1,762 had been correctly debited to Purchases account but had been credited to the supplier's account as £1,672.

(*e*) A piece of equipment costing £9,800 and acquired on 1 May 19-4 for use in the business had been debited to Purchases account. (The company depreciates equipment at 20% per annum on cost.)

(*f*) Items valued at £2,171 had been completely omitted from the closing stock figure.

(*g*) At 30 April 19-5 an accrual of £543 for electricity charges and an insurance prepayment of £162 had been omitted.

(*h*) The credit side of the wages account had been under-added by £100 before the balance on the account had been determined.

Required:

Using relevant information from that given above

(*a*) Prepare a statement correcting the draft net profit after tax

(*b*) Post and balance the Suspense account. (*Note*: The opening balance of this account has not been given and must be derived.)

(*Chartered Association of Certified Accountants*)

28.8A The draft final accounts for the year ended 31 March 19-9 of Blackheath Limited, car dealers, show a gross profit of £36,000 and net profit of £9,000.

After subsequent investigations the following discoveries were made:

(*i*) Discounts received in August 19-8 of £210 have been credited, in error, to purchases.

(*ii*) A debt of £300 due from P Black to the company was written off as irrecoverable in the company's books in December 19-8. Since preparing the draft accounts, P Black has settled the debt in full.

(*iii*) The company's main warehouse was burgled in June 19-8, when goods costing £20,000 were stolen. This amount has been shown in the draft accounts as an overhead item 'Loss due to burglary'. Although the insurance company denied liability originally, in the past day or two that decision has been changed and Blackheath Limited have been advised that £14,000 will be paid in settlement.

(*iv*) On 2 January 19-9, a car which had cost the company £1,800 was taken from the showrooms for the use of one of the company's sales representatives whilst on company business. In the showrooms, this car had had a £2,400 price label. Effect has not been given to this transfer in the books of the company, although the car was not included in the trading stock valuation at 31 March 19-9. The company provides for depreciation on motor vehicles at the rate of 25% of the cost of vehicles held at the end of each financial year.

(*v*) Goods bought and received from L Ring on 30 March 19-9 at a cost of £1,200 were not recorded in the company's books of account until early April 19-9. Although they were unsold on 31 March 19-9, the goods in question were not included in the stock valuation at that date.

(*vi*) The company is hoping to market a new car accessory product in July 19-9. The new venture is to be launched with an advertising campaign commencing in April 19-9. The cost of this campaign is £5,000 and this has been debited in the company's profit and loss account for the year ended 31 March 19-9 and is included in current liabilities as a provision, notwithstanding the confident expectation that the new product will be a success.

(*vii*) On 31 March 19-9 the company paid an insurance premium of £600, the renewal being for the year commencing 1 April 19-9. This premium was included in the insurances of £1,100 debited in the draft profit and loss account.

Required:

(*a*) The journal entries necessary to adjust for items (*iii*), (*iv*) and (*vi*) above.
Note: Narratives are required.

(*b*) A computation of the corrected gross profit and net profit for the year ended 31 March 19-9.

(*Chartered Association of Certified Accountants*)

29
Control accounts

When all the accounts were kept in one ledger a trial balance could be extracted as a test of the arithmetic accuracy of the account. It must be remembered that certain errors were not revealed by such a trial balance. If the trial balance totals disagreed, the number of entries for such a small business being relatively few, the books could easily and quickly be checked so as to locate the errors. However, when the firm has grown and the accounting work has been so subdivided that there are several or many ledgers, a trial balance the totals of which did not agree could result in a great deal of unnecessary checking before the errors were found. What is required in fact is a type of trial balance for each ledger, and this requirement is met by the **Control Account**. Thus it is only the ledgers whose control accounts do not balance that need detailed checking to find errors.

The principle on which the control account is based is simple, and is as follows. If the opening balance of an account is known, together with information of the additions and deductions entered in the account, the closing balance can be calculated. Applying this to a complete ledger, the total of opening balances together with the additions and deductions during the period should give the total of closing balances. This can be illustrated by reference to a sales ledger:

	£
Total of Opening Balances, 1 January 19-6	3,000
add Total of entries which have increased the balances	9,500
	12,500
less Total of entries which have reduced the balances	8,000
Total of closing balances should be	4,500

Because totals are used the accounts are often known as Total Accounts. Thus a control account for a sales ledger could be known either as a **Sales Ledger Control Account** or as a **Total Debtors Account**. Similarly, a control account for a purchases ledger could be known either as a **Purchases Ledger Control Account** or as a **Total Creditors Account**.

It must be emphasised that in small organisations control accounts are not necessarily a part of the double-entry system. They are then merely arithmetical proofs performing the same function as a trial balance to a particular ledger. Larger organisations would however incorporate them as part of the double-entry record.

It is usual to find them in the same form as an account, with the totals of the debit entries in the ledger on the left-hand side of the control account, and the totals of the various credit entries in the ledger on the right-hand side of the control account.

Exhibit 29.1 shows an example of a sales ledger control account for a ledger in which all the entries are arithmetically correct.

Exhibit 29.1

	£
Sales Ledger No 3	
Debit balances on 1 January 19-6	1,894
Total credit sales for the month	10,290
Cheques received from customers in the month	7,284
Cash received from customers in the month	1,236
Returns Inwards from customers during the month	296
Debit balances on 31 January as extracted from the sales ledger	3,368

Sales Ledger Control

19-6		£	9-6		£
Jan	1 Balances b/f	1,894	Jan 31	Bank	7,284
,,	31 Sales	10,290	,,	,, Cash	1,236
			,,	,, Returns Inwards	296
			,,	,, Balances c/d	3,368
		12,184			12,184

On the other hand Exhibit 29.2 shows an example where an error is found to exist in a purchases ledger. The ledger will have to be checked in detail, the error found, and the control account then corrected.

Exhibit 29.2

	£
Purchases Ledger No 2	
Credit balances on 1 January 19-6	3,890
Cheques paid to suppliers during the month	3,620
Returns outwards to suppliers in the month	95
Bought from suppliers in the month	4,936
Credit balances on 31 January as extracted from the purchases ledger	5,151

Purchases Ledger Control

19-6		£	19-6		£
Jan 31	Bank	3,620	Jan	1 Balances b/f	3,890
,,	,, Returns Outwards	95	,,	31 Purchases	4,936
,,	,, Balances c/d	5,151			
		8,866*			8,826*

*There is a £40 error in the purchases ledger.

Other advantages of control accounts

Control accounts have merits other than that of locating errors. Normally the control accounts are under the charge of a responsible official, and fraud is made more difficult because transfers made (in an effort) to disguise frauds will have to pass the scrutiny of this person.

For management purposes the balances on the control account can always be taken to equal debtors and creditors without waiting for an extraction of individual balances. Management control is thereby aided, for the speed at which information is obtained is one of the prerequisites of efficient control.

The sources of information for control accounts

To obtain the totals of entries made in the various ledgers, analytical journals and cash books are often used. Thus a firm with sales ledgers split on an alphabetical basis might have a sales book as per Exhibit 29.3.

The totals of the A – F column will be the total sales figures for the sales ledger A – F control account, the total of the G – O column for the G – O control account and so on.

Exhibit 29.3

Sales Book

Date	Details	Total	A – F	G – O	P – Z
		Ledgers			
19-6		£	£	£	£
Feb 1	J Archer	58	58		
,, 3	G Gaunt	103		103	
,, 4	T Brown	116	116		
,, 8	C Dunn	205	205		
,, 10	A Smith	16			16
,, 12	P Smith	114			114
,, 15	D Owen	88		88	
,, 18	B Blake	17	17		
,, 22	T Green	1,396		1,396	
,, 27	C Males	48		48	
		2,161	396	1,635	130

A similar form of analysis can be used in the Purchases Book, Returns Inwards Book, Returns Outwards Book and the Cash Book. The *totals* necessary for each of the control accounts can be obtained from the appropriate columns in these books.

Other items, such as bad debts written off or transfers from one ledger to another will be found in The Journal where such items are recorded.

Other transfers

Transfers to bad debts accounts will have to be recorded in the sales ledger control account as they involve entries in the sales ledgers.

Similarly, a contra account whereby the same firm is both a supplier and a customer, and inter-indebtedness is set off, will also need entering in the control accounts. An example of this follows: G Carter has supplied the firm with £880 goods, and the firm has sold him £600 goods. In the firm's books the £600 owing by him is set off against the amount owing to him, leaving a net amount owing to Carter of £280.

Sales Ledger
G Carter

	£
Sales	600

Purchases Ledger
G Carter

	£
Purchases	880

The set-off now takes place.

Sales Ledger
G Carter

	£		£
Sales	600	Set-off: Purchases Ledger	600

Purchases Ledger
G Carter

	£		£
Set-off: Sales Ledger	600	Purchases	880
Balance c/d	280		
	880		880
		Balance b/d	280

The transfer of the £600 will therefore appear on the credit side of the sales ledger control account and on the debit side of the purchases ledger control account.

Exhibit 29.4 shows a worked example of a more complicated control account.

Exhibit 29.4

19-6		£
Aug 1	Sales ledger – debit balances	3,816
,, 1	Sales ledger – credit balances	22
,, 31	Transactions for the month:	
	Cash received	104
	Cheques received	6,239
	Sales	7,090
	Bad Debts written off	306
	Discounts allowed	298
	Returns inwards	164
	Cash refunded to a customer who had overpaid his account	37
	Dishonoured cheques	29
	At the end of the month:	
	Sales ledger – debit balances	3,879
	Sales ledger – credit balances	40

19-6		£	19-6		£
Aug	1 Balances b/d	3,816	Aug	1 Balances b/d	22
,,	31 Sales	7,090	,,	31 Cash	104
,,	,, Cash refunded	37	,,	,, Bank	6,239
,,	,, Cash; dishonoured		,,	,, Bad debts	306
	cheques	29	,,	,, Discounts allowed	298
,,	,, Balances c/d	40	,,	,, Returns inwards	164
			,,	,, Balances c/d	3,879
		———			———
		11,012			11,012

Control accounts as part of double entry

In larger organisations it would be normal to find that control accounts are an integral part of the double-entry system, the balances of the control accounts being taken for the purpose of extracting a trial balance. In this case the personal accounts are being used as subsidiary records.

Self-balancing ledgers and adjustment accounts

Because ledgers which have a control account system are proved to be correct as far as the double-entry is concerned they used to be called **self-balancing ledgers.** The control accounts where such terminology were in use were then often called **Adjustment Accounts**. These terms are very rarely used nowadays.

Review questions

29.1 You are required to prepare a sales ledger control account from the following for the month of May:

19-6		£
May	1 Sales Ledger Balances	4,936
	Totals for May:	
	Sales Journal	49,916
	Returns Inwards Journal	1,139
	Cheques and Cash received from customers	46,490
	Discounts allowed	1,455
May	31 Sales Ledger Balances	5,768

29.2A You are required to prepare a purchases ledger control account from the following for the month of June. The balance of the account is to be taken as the amount of creditors as on 30 June.

19-6		£
June	1 Purchases Ledger Balances	3,676
	Totals for June:	
	Purchases Journal	42,257
	Returns Outwards Journal	1,098
	Cheques paid to suppliers	38,765
	Discounts received from suppliers	887
June	30 Purchases Ledger Balances	?

233

29.3 The financial year of The Better Trading Company ended on 30 November 19-7. You have been asked to prepare a Total Debtors Account and a Total Creditors Account in order to produce end-of-year figures for Debtors and Creditors for the draft final accounts.

You are able to obtain the following information for the financial year from the books of original entry:

	£
Sales – cash	344,890
– credit	268,187
Purchases – cash	14,440
– credit	496,600
Total receipts from customers	600,570
Total payments to suppliers	503,970
Discounts allowed (all to credit customers)	5,520
Discounts received (all from credit suppliers)	3,510
Refunds given to cash customers	5,070
Balance in the sales ledger set off against	
balance in the purchases ledger	70
Bad debts written off	780
Increase in the provision for bad debts	90
Credit notes issued to credit customers	4,140
Credit notes received from credit suppliers	1,480

According to the audited financial statements for the previous year debtors and creditors as at 1 December 19-6 were £26,555 and £43,450 respectively.

Required:
Draw up the relevant Total Accounts entering end-of-year totals for debtors and creditors.

(*Association of Accounting Technicians*)

29.4A A sales ledger control account and a purchases ledger control account are maintained as integral parts of the accounting records of James Swift Limited.

The following information is relevant to the business of James Swift Limited for the year ended 30 November 19-7.

(*i*) Balances at 1 December 19-6:

	£	
Sales ledger	10,687	debit
	452	credit
Purchases ledger	1,630	debit
	9,536	credit

(*ii*) Sales totalled £130,382 whilst sales returns amounted to £1,810.

(*iii*) £127,900 was received from debtors in settlement of accounts totalling £130,650. In addition, £1,200 was received for a debt which had been written off as irrecoverable in the year ended 30 November 19-6.

(*iv*) A debt of £350 due from J Hancock was transferred to the purchases ledger and set of against a debt of £1,100 due to J Hancock.

(*v*) An amount of £560 due to James Swift Limited for goods supplied to T Dick was written off as bad in November 19-7.

(*vi*) Purchases amounted to £99,000 at list prices and purchases returns totalled £600 at list prices. All purchases and purchases returns were subject to a trade discount of 10%.

(*vii*) £83,500 was paid to suppliers in settlement of debts due of £85,000.

(*viii*) Balances at 30 November 19-7 *included*:

	£	
Sales ledger	1,008	credit
Purchases ledger	760	debit

Required

Prepare the following accounts for the year ended 30 November 19-7 in the books of James Swift Limited:

(*a*) Sales Ledger Control

(*b*) Purchases Ledger Control

(*Association of Accounting Technicians*)

29.5 The Sales Ledger Control Account of a trading business for the month of November 19-3 was prepared by the accountant, as shown below:

Sales Ledger Control

	£		£
Opening debit balance b/d	27,684.07	Opening credit balance b/d	210.74
Credit Sales	31,220.86	Allowances to customers	1,984.18
Purchase ledger contras	763.70	Cash received	1,030.62
		Cheques received	28,456.07
Discounts allowed	1,414.28	Cash received (on an account previously	
Closing credit balance c/d	171.08	written off as a bad debt)	161.20
		Closing debit balance c/d (balancing figure)	30,416.18
	£61,253.99		£61,258.99
Opening debit balance b/d	30,416.18	Opening credit balance b/d	171.08

The book-keeper balanced the individual customers' accounts and prepared a Debtors' Schedule of the closing balances which totalled £25,586.83 (net of credit balances).

Unfortunately, both the accountant and the book-keeper had been careless, and in addition to the errors which the accountant had made in the control account above, it was subsequently discovered that:

(*i*) in an individual debtor's account, a debt previously written off but now recovered (£161.20) had been correctly credited and redebited but the corresponding debit had not been posted in the control account;

(*ii*) discounts allowed had been correctly posted to individual debtors' accounts but had been under-added by £100 in the memorandum column in the combined bank and cash book;

(*iii*) allowances to customers shown in the control account included sums totalling £341.27 which had not been posted to individual debtors' accounts;

(*iv*) a cheque for £2,567.10 received from a customer had been posted to his account as £2,576.10;

(*v*) the credit side of one debtor's account had been over-added by £10 prior to the derivation of the closing balance;

(*vi*) a closing credit balance of £63.27 on one debtor's account had been included in the Debtors' Schedule among the debit balances;

(*vii*) the purchase ledger contras, representing the settlement by contra transfer of amounts owed to credit suppliers, had not been posted to individual debtors' accounts at all;

(viii) the balance on one debtor's account, £571.02, had been completely omitted from the Debtors' Schedule.

Required

Identify and effect the adjustments to the Sales Ledger Control Account and Debtors' Schedule, as appropriate, so that the net balances agree at 30 November 19-3.
(*Chartered Association of Certified Accountants*)

29.6A The trial balance of Happy Book-keeper Ltd, as produced by its book-keeper includes the following items:

Sales ledger control account	£110,172
Purchase ledger control account	£78,266
Suspense account (debit balance)	£2,315

You have been given the following information:

(*i*) The sales ledger debit balances total £111,111 and the credit balances total £1,234.

(*ii*) The purchase ledger credit balances total £77,777 and the debit balances total £1,111.

(*iii*) The sales ledger includes a debit balance of £700 for business X, and the purchase ledger includes a credit balance of £800 relating to the same business X. Only the net amount will eventually be paid.

(*iv*) Included in the credit balance on the sales ledger is a balance of £600 in the name of H Smith. This arose because a sales invoice for £600 had earlier been posted in error from the sales day book to the debit of the account of M Smith in the purchase ledger.

(*v*) An allowance of £300 against some damaged goods had been omitted from the appropriate account in the sales ledger. This allowance had been included in the control account.

(*vi*) An invoice for £456 had been entered in the purchase day book as £654.

(*vii*) A cash receipt from a credit customer for £345 had been entered in the cash book as £245.

(*viii*) The purchase day book had been overcast by £1,000.

(*ix*) The bank balance of £1,200 had been included in the trial balance, in error, as an overdraft.

(*x*) The book-keeper had been instructed to write off £500 from customer Y's account as a bad debt, and to reduce the provision for doubtful debts by £700. By mistake, however, he had written off £700 from customer Y's account and *increased* the provision for doubtful debts by £500.

(*xi*) The debit balance on the insurance account in the nominal ledger of £3,456 had been included in the trial balance as £3,546.

Required

Record corrections in the control and suspense accounts. Attempt to reconcile the sales ledger control account with the sales ledger balances, and the purchase ledger control account with the purchase ledger balances. What further action do you recommend?
(*Chartered Association of Certified Accountants*)

30
Introduction to accounting ratios

Mark-up and margin

The purchase and sale of a good may be shown as

Cost Price + Profit = Selling Price.

The profit when expressed as a fraction, or percentage, of the cost price is known as the **mark-up**.

The profit when expressed as a fraction, or percentage, of the selling price is known as the **margin**.

$$\begin{array}{lcccl}
\text{Cost Price} & + & \text{Profit} & = & \text{Selling Price} \\
£4 & + & £1 & = & £5.
\end{array}$$

Mark-up $= \dfrac{\text{Profit}}{\text{Cost Price}}$ as a fraction, or if required as a percentage

multiply by $\dfrac{100}{1}$

$= \dfrac{£1}{£4} = \dfrac{1}{4}$, or $\dfrac{1}{4} \times \dfrac{100}{1} = 25$ per cent.

Margin $= \dfrac{\text{Profit}}{\text{Selling Price}}$ as a fraction, or if required as a

percentage multiply by $\dfrac{100}{1}$

$= \dfrac{£1}{£5} = \dfrac{1}{5}$, or $\dfrac{1}{5} \times \dfrac{100}{1} = 20$ per cent.

The following illustrations[1] of the deduction of missing information assume that the rate of mark-ups and margins are constant, in other words the goods dealt in by the firm have uniform margins and mark-ups and they do not vary between one good and another. It also ignores wastages and pilferages of goods, also the fact that the market value of some goods may be below cost and therefore need to be taken into stock at the lower figure. These items will need to be the subject of separate adjustments

Example 1

The following figures are for the year 19-5:

	£
Stock 1.1.19-5	400
Stock 31.12.19-5	600
Purchases	5,200

---

[1] The horizontal style of accounts will be used in this chapter, simply because it is less confusing when showing illustrations of missing figures.

A uniform rate of mark-up of 20 per cent is applied.

Find the gross profit and the sales figure.

Trading Account

	£		£
Stock 1.1.19-5	400	Sales	?
add Purchases	5,200		
	5,600		
less Stock 31.12.19-5	600		
Cost of goods sold	5,000		
Gross profit	?		

Answer:

It is known that: Cost of goods sold + Profit = Sales.

and also that: Cost of goods sold + Percentage Mark-up = Sales

The following figures are also known:

£5,000 + 20 per cent = Sales

After doing the arithmetic:

£5,000 + £1,000 = £6,000

The trading account can be completed by inserting the gross profit £1,000 and £6,000 for Sales.

Example 2

Another firm has the following figures for 19-6:

	£
Stock 1.1.19-6	500
Stock 31.12.19-6	800
Sales	6,400

A uniform rate of margin of 25 per cent is in use.

Find the gross profit and the figure of purchases.

Trading Account

	£		£
Stock 1.1.19-6	500	Sales	6,400
add Purchases	?		
less Stock 31.12.19-6	800		
Cost of goods sold	?		
Gross Profit	?		
	6,400		6,400

238

Answer:	Cost of goods sold	+ Gross Profit	= Sales
Therefore	Sales	− Gross Profit	= Cost of Goods sold
	Sales	− 25 per cent Margin	= Cost of Goods Sold
	£6,400	− £1,600	= £4,800

Now the following figures are known:

	£
Stock 1.1.19-6	500
add Purchases (1)	?
	___
(2)	?
less Stock 31.12.19-6	800
	___
Cost of goods sold	4,800

The two missing figures are found by normal arithmetical deduction:

No (2) less £800	=	£4,800
Therefore No (2)	=	£5,600
So that: £500 opening stock + No (1)	=	£5,600
Therefore No (1)	=	£5,100

The completed trading account can now be shown:

Trading Account

	£		£
Stock 1.1.19-6	500	Sales	6,400
add Purchases	5,100		
	5,600		
less Stock 31.12.19-6	800		
Cost of goods sold	4,800		
Gross Profit	1,600		
	6,400		6,400

This technique is found very useful by retail stores when estimating the amount to be bought if a certain sales target is to be achieved. Alternatively, stock levels or sales figures can be estimated given information as to purchases and opening stock figures.

The relationship between mark-up and margin

As both of these figures refer to the same profit, but expressed as a fraction or a percentage of different figures, there is bound to be a relationship. If one is known as a fraction, the other can soon be found.

If the mark-up is known, to find the margin take the same numerator to be numerator of the margin, then for the denominator of the margin take the total of the mark-up's denominator plus the numerator. An example can now be shown:

Mark-up	Margin
$\dfrac{1}{4}$	$\dfrac{1}{4+1} = \dfrac{1}{5}$
$\dfrac{2}{11}$	$\dfrac{2}{11+2} = \dfrac{2}{13}$

If the margin is known, to find the mark-up take the same numerator to be the numerator of the mark-up, then for the denominator of the mark-up take the figure of the margin's denominator less the numerator:

MARGIN   MARK UP

Mark-up	Margin
$\dfrac{1}{6}$	$\dfrac{1}{6-1} = \dfrac{1}{5}$
$\dfrac{3}{13}$	$\dfrac{3}{13-3} = \dfrac{3}{10}$

Manager's commission

Managers of businesses are very often remunerated by a basic salary plus a percentage of profits. It is quite common to find the percentage expressed not as a percentage of profits before such commission has been deducted, but as a percentage of the amount remaining after deduction of the commission.

For example, assume that profits before the manager's commission was deducted amounted to £8,400, and that the manager was entitled to 5 per cent of the profits remaining after such commission was deducted. If 5 per cent of £8,400 was taken, this amounts to £420, and the profits remaining would amount to £7,980. However, 5 per cent of £7,980 amounts to £399 so that the answer of £420 is wrong.

The formula to be used to arrive at the correct answer is:

$$\frac{\text{Percentage commission}}{100 + \text{Percentage commission}} \times \text{Profits before commission.}$$

In the above problem this would be used as follows:

$$\frac{5}{100 + 5} \times £8,400 = £400 \text{ manager's commission.}$$

The profits remaining are £8,000 and as £400 represents 5 per cent of it the answer is verified.

Commonly used accounting ratios

There are some ratios that are in common use for the purpose of comparing one period's results against those of a previous period. Two of those most in use are the ratio of gross profit to sales, and the rate of turnover or stockturn.

Gross profit as percentage of sales

The basic formula is:

$$\frac{\text{Gross Profit}}{\text{Sales}} \times \frac{100}{1} = \text{Gross profit as percentage of sales.}$$

Put another way, this represents the amount of gross profit for every £100 of sales. If the answer turned out to be 15 per cent, this would mean that for every £100 of sales £15 gross profit was made before any expenses were paid.

This ratio is used as a test of the profitability of the sales. Just because the sales are increased does not of itself mean that the gross profit will increase. The trading accounts in Exhibit 30.1 illustrates this.

Exhibit 30.1

Trading Accounts for the year ended 31 December

	19-6	19-7		19-6	19-7
	£	£		£	£
Stock	500	900	Sales	7,000	8,000
Purchases	6,000	7,200			
	6,500	8,100			
less Stock	900	1,100			
Cost of goods sold	5,600	7,000			
Gross Profit	1,400	1,000			
	7,000	8,000		7,000	8,000

In the year 19-6 the gross profit as a percentage of sales was:

$$\frac{1,400}{7,000} \times \frac{100}{1} = 20 \text{ per cent}$$

In the year 19-7 it became:

$$\frac{1,000}{8,000} \times \frac{100}{1} = 12\frac{1}{2} \text{ per cent}$$

Thus sales had increased, but as the gross profit percentage had fallen by a relatively greater amount the actual gross profit has fallen.

There can be many reasons for such a fall in the gross profit percentage. Perhaps the goods being sold have cost more but the selling price of the goods has not risen to the same extent. Maybe, in order to boost sales, reductions have been made in the selling price of goods. There could be a difference in the composition of types of goods sold, called the **sales mix**, between this year and last, with different product lines carrying different rates of gross profit per £100 of sales. Alternatively there may have been a greater wastage or pilferage of goods. These are only some of the possible reasons for the decrease. The idea of calculating the ratio is to highlight the fact that the profitability per £100 of sales has changed, and so promote an inquiry as to why and how such a change is taking place.

As the figure of sales less returns inwards is also known as **turnover**, the ratio is also known as the **gross profit percentage on turnover**.

Stockturn or rate of turnover

This is another commonly used ratio, and is expressed in the formula:

$$\frac{\text{Cost of goods sold}}{\text{Average stock}} = \text{Number of times stock is turned over within the period}$$

Ideally, the average stock held should be calculated by taking a large number of readings of stock over the accounting year, then dividing the totals of the figures obtained by the number of readings. For instance, monthly stock figures added up then divided by twelve. It is a well-known statistical law that the greater the sample of figures taken the smaller will be the error contained in the answer.

However, it is quite common, expecially in examinations or in cases where no other information is available, to calculate the average stock as the opening stock plus the closing stock and the answer divided by two. The statistical limitations of taking only two figures when calculating an average must be clearly borne in mind.

Using the figures in Exhibit 30.1:

$$19\text{-}6 \quad \frac{5,600}{(500 + 900) \div 2} = \frac{5,600}{700} = 8 \text{ times per annum.}$$

$$19\text{-}7 \quad \frac{7,000}{(900 + 1,100) \div 2} = \frac{7,000}{1,000} = 7 \text{ times per annum.}$$

In terms of periods of time, in the year 19-6 a rate of 8 times per annum means that goods on average are held 12 months $\div$ 8 = 1.5 months before they are sold.

For 19-7 goods are held on average for 12 months $\div$ 7 = 1.7 months approximately before they are sold.

When the rate of stockturn is falling it can be due to such causes as a slowing down of sales activity, or to keeping a higher figure of stock than is really necessary. The ratio does not prove anything by itself, it merely prompts inquiries as to why it should be changing.

This chapter has only looked at ratios so as to help with the content of the next chapter. Later on in the book, in Chapter 44, we turn again to ratios, this time a more advanced and detailed survey.

Review questions

30.1 R Stubbs is a trader who sells all of his goods at 25 per cent above cost. His books give the following information at 31 December 19-5:

	£
Stock 1 January 19-5	9,872
Stock 31 December 19-5	12,620
Sales for year	60,000

You are required to:
(a) Ascertain cost of goods sold.
(b) Show the value of purchases during the year.
(c) Calculate the profit made by Stubbs.
Show your answer in the form of a trading account.

30.2A C White gives you the following information as at 30 June 19-7:

	£
Stock 1 July 19-6	6,000
Purchases	54,000

White's mark-up is 50 per cent on 'cost of goods sold'. His average stock during the year was £12,000.

Draw up a trading and profit and loss account for the year ended 30 June 19- 7.
(a) Calculate the closing stock as at 30 June 19-7.
(b) State the total amount of profit and loss expenditure White must not exceed if he is to maintain a *net* profit on sales of 10 per cent.

30.3 J Green's business has a rate of turnover of 7 times. Average stock is £12,600. Trade discount (i.e. margin allowed) is 33⅓ per cent off all selling prices.

Expenses are 66⅔ per cent of gross profit.

You are to calculate:
(a) Cost of goods sold,
(b) Gross Profit Margin
(c) Turnover
(d) Total Expenses
(e) Net Profit.

30.4A The following figures relate to the retail business of J Clarke for the month of May 19-9. Goods which are on sale fall into two categories, A and B.

	Category A	Category B
Sales to the public at manufacturer's recommended list price	£6,000	£14,000
Trade discount allowed to retailers	20%	25%
Total expenses as a percentage of sales	10%	10%
Annual rate of stock turnover	12	20

Calculate for each category:
(a) Cost of Goods sold
(b) Gross Profit
(c) Total expenses
(d) Net Profit
(e) Average stock at cost, assuming that sales are distributed evenly over the year, and that there are twelve equal months in the year.

30.5 The following information was available on Unisales Ltd.

	19-6	19-7	19-8
	£	£	£
Opening Stock			
Purchases	85,000		
Closing Stock	5,000		
Sales		140,000	
Gross Profit	25,000		
Variable expenses			18,900
Fixed expenses	5,500	5,000	
Net profit			9,100

For 19-6:
(a) Gross profit was 20% of sales.
(b) Variable expenses were 10% of sales.
(c) All purchases cost £1 per unit and stocks were valued at £1 per unit.

For 19-7:
(a) The purchase price of units increased by 10%, but the volume bought increased by 20% compared with 19-6.
(b) The closing stock of 8,000 units were bought in 19-7.
(c) Variable expenses amount to 13% of sales.

For 19-8:
(a) The net profit/sales ratio was 1% greater than the 19-7 figure.

(b) Fixed expenses increased by £1,000 on the 19-7 figure.

(c) The number of units purchased was 90,000 at the 19-7 purchase price.

Required

Draw a table the same as the one above. Use the information given to make the necessary calculations and complete the table.

(Associated Examining Board)

30.6A Trading Accounts for the year ended 31 December 19-1.

	£		£
Stock 1 January 19-1	3,000	Sales	60,000
Purchases	47,000		
	50,000		
Stock 31 December 19-1	4,500		
Cost of sales	45,500		
Gross Profit	14,500		
	60,000		60,000

R Sheldon presents you with the trading account set out above. He always calculates his selling price by adding $33\frac{1}{3}$% of cost on to the cost price.

(a) If he has adhered strictly to the statement above, what should be the percentage of gross profit to sales?

(b) Calculate his actual percentage of gross profit to sales.

(c) Give two reasons for the difference between the figures you have calculated above.

(d) His suppliers are proposing to increase their prices by 5%, but R Sheldon considers that he would be unwise to increase his selling price. To obtain some impression of the effect on gross profit if his costs should be increased by 5% he asks you to reconstruct his trading account to show the gross profit if the increase had applied from 1 January 19-1.

(e) Using the figures given in the trading account at the beginning of the question, calculate R Sheldon's rate of stock turnover.

(f) R Sheldon's expenses amount to 10% of his sales. Calculate his net profit for the year ended 31 December 19-1.

(g) If all expenses remained unchanged, but suppliers of stock increased their prices by 5% as in (d) above, calculate the percentage reduction in the amount of net profit which R Sheldon's accounts would have shown.

(University of London)

31

Single entry and incomplete records

For every small shopkeeper, market stall or other small business to keep its books using a full double-entry system would be ridiculous. First of all, a large number of the owners of such firms would not know how to write up double-entry records, even if they wanted to.

It is far more likely that they would enter down details of a transaction once only, that is why we could call it single entry. Also many of them would have failed to record every transaction, and these therefore would be incomplete – the reason why we would call these **incomplete** records.

It is perhaps only fair to remember that accounting is after all supposed to be an aid to management, it is not something to be done as an end in itself. Therefore, many small firms, especially retail stores, can have all the information they want by merely keeping a cash book and having some form of record, not necessarily in double-entry form, of their debtors and creditors.

Probably the way to start is to recall that, barring an introduction of extra cash or resources into the firm, the only way that capital can be increased is by making profits. Therefore, the most elementary way of calculating profits is by comparing capital at the end of last period with that at the end of this period. If it is known that the capital at the end of 19-4 was £2,000 and that at the end of 19-5 it has grown to £3,000, and that there have been no drawings during the period, nor has there been any fresh introduction of capital, the net profit must therefore be £3,000 − £2,000 = £1,000. If on the other hand the drawings had been £700, the profits must have been £1,700 calculated thus:

Last year's Capital + Profits − Drawings = this year's Capital
£2,000　　　　　 + 　?　 − £700　　　= £3,000

Filling in the missing figure by normal arithmetical deduction:

£2,000 + £1,700 − £700 = £3,000.

Exhibit 31.1 shows the calculation of profit where insufficient information is available to draft a trading and profit and loss account, only information of assets and liabilities being known.

Exhibit 31.1

H Taylor provides information as to his assets and liabilities at certain dates.
At 31 December 19-5. *Assets:* Motor van £1,000; Fixtures £700; Stock £850; Debtors £950; Bank £1,100; Cash £100. *Liabilities:* Creditors £200; Loan from J Ogden £600.
At 31 December 19-6. *Assets:* Motor van (after depreciation) £800; Fixtures (after depreciation) £630; Stock £990; Debtors £1,240; Bank £1,700; Cash £200. *Liabilities:* Creditors £300; Loan from J Ogden £400; Drawings were £900.

First of all a **Statement of Affairs** is drawn up as at 31 December 19- 5. This is the name given to what would have been called a balance sheet if it had been drawn up from a set of records. The capital is the difference between the assets and liabilities.

Statement of Affairs as at 31 December 19-5

	£	£
Fixed Assets		
Motor Van		1,000
Fixtures		700
		1,700
Current Assets		
Stock	850	
Debtors	950	
Bank	1,100	
Cash	100	
	3,000	
less Current Liabilities		
Creditors	200	
Working Capital		2,800
		4,500
Financed by		
Capital (difference)		3,900
Long-term liability		
Loan from J Ogden		600
		4,500

A statement of affairs is now drafted up at the end of 19-6. The formula of Opening Capital + Profit − Drawings = Closing Capital is then used to deduce the figure of profit.

	£	£
Fixed Assets		
Motor Van		800
Fixtures		630
		1,430
Current Assets		
Stock	990	
Debtors	1,240	
Bank	1,700	
Cash	200	
	4,130	
less Current Liabilities		
Creditors	300	3,830
		5,260

Financed by:		
Capital		
Balance at 1.1.19-6	3,900	
add Net Profit (C)	?	
(B)	?	
less Drawings	900 (A)	?
Long-term Loan		
Loan from J Ogden		400

Deduction of Net Profit:
Opening Capital + Net Profit − Drawings = Closing Capital. Finding the missing figures (A) (B) and (C) by deduction,
(A) is the figure needed to make the balance sheet totals equal, i.e. £4,860.
(B) is therefore £4,860 + £900 = £5,760
(C) is therefore £5,760 − £3,900 = £1,860.
To check:

Capital	3,900	
add Net Profit (C)	1,860	
(B)	5,760	
less Drawings	900 (A)	4,860

Obviously, this method of calculating profit is very unsatisfactory as it is much more informative when a trading and profit and loss account can be drawn up. Therefore, whenever possible the comparisons of capital method of ascertaining profit should be avoided and a full set of final accounts drawn up from the available records. When doing this it must be remembered that the principles of calculating profit are still those as described in the compilation of a double-entry trading and profit and loss account. Assume that there are two businesses identical in every way as to sales, purchases, expenses, assets and liabilities, the only difference being that one proprietor keeps a full double-entry set of books while the other keeps his on a single-entry basis. Yet, when each of them draws up his final accounts they should be identical in every way. Exhibit 31.2 shows the method for drawing up final accounts from single-entry records.

Exhibit 31.2

The accountant discerns the following details of transactions for J Frank's retail store for the year ended 31 December 19-5.

(a) The sales are mostly on a credit basis. No record of sales have been made, but £10,000 has been received, £9,500 by cheque and £500 by cash, from persons to whom goods have been sold.

(b) Amount paid by cheque to suppliers during the year = £7,200.

(c) Expenses paid during the year: by cheque, Rent £200, General Expenses £180; by cash, Rent £50.

(d) J Frank took £10 cash per week (for 52 weeks) as drawings.

(e) Other information is available:

	At 31.12.19-4	At 31.12.19-5
	£	£
Debtors	1,100	1,320
Creditors for goods	400	650
Rent Owing	–	50
Bank Balance	1,130	3,050
Cash Balance	80	10
Stock	1,590	1,700

(f) The only fixed asset consists of fixtures which were valued at 31 December 19-4 at £800. These are to be depreciated at 10 per cent per annum.

The first step is to draw up a statement of affairs as at 31 December 19-4.

Statement of Affairs as at 31 December 19-4

	£	£
Fixed Assets		
Fixtures		800
Current Assets		
Stock	1,590	
Debtors	1,100	
Bank	1,130	
Cash	80	
	3,900	
less Current Liabilities		
Creditors	400	
Working Capital		3,500
		4,300
Financed by:		
Capital (difference)		4,300
		4,300

All of these opening figures are then taken into account when drawing up the final accounts for 19-5.

Next a cash and bank summary is drawn up, followed by the final accounts.

	Cash	*Bank*		*Cash*	*Bank*
	£	£		£	£
Balances 31.12.19-4	80	1,130	Suppliers		7,200
Receipts from debtors	500	9,500	Rent	50	200
			General Expenses		180
			Drawings	520	
			Balances 31.12.19-5	10	3,050
	580	10,630		580	10,630

J Franks
Trading and Profit and Loss Account for the year ended 31 December 19-5

	£	£
Sales (note 2)		10,220
less Cost of Goods Sold:		
Stock at 1.1.19-5	1,590	
add Purchases (note 1)	7,450	
	9,040	
less Stock at 31.12.19-5	1,700	7,340
Gross Profit		2,880
less Expenses:		
Rent (note 3)	300	
General Expenses	180	
Depreciation: Fixtures	80	560
Net Profit		2,320

Note 1 In double entry, purchases means the goods that have been bought in the period irrespective of whether they have been paid for or not during the period. The figure of payments to suppliers must therefore be adjusted to find the figures of purchases.

	£
Paid during the year	7,200
less payments made, but which were for goods which were purchased in a previous year (creditors 31.12.19-4)	400
	6,800
add purchases made in this year, but for which payment has not yet been made (creditors 31.12.19-5)	650
Goods bought in this year, i.e. purchases	7,450

The same answer could have been obtained if the information had been shown in the form of a total creditors account, the figure of purchases being the amount required to make the account totals agree.

Total Creditors

	£		£
Cash paid to suppliers	7,200	Balances b/f	400
Balances c/d	650	Purchases (missing figures)	7,450
	7,850		7,850

Note 2 The sales figure will only equal receipts where all the sales are for cash. Therefore, the receipts figures need adjusting to find sales. This can only be done by constructing a total debtors account, the sales figures being the one needed to make the totals agree.

Total Debtors

	£		£
Balances b/f	1,100	Receipts: Cash	500
		Cheque	9,500
Sales (missing figures)	10,220	Balances c/d	1,320
	11,320		11,320

Note 3 Expenses are those consumed during the year irrespective of when payment is made. A rent account can be drawn up, the missing figure being that of rent for the year.

Rent Account

	£		£
Cheques	200	Rent (missing figure)	300
Cash	50		
Accrued c/d	50		
	300		300

The balance sheet can now be drawn up as in Exhibit 31.3.

Exhibit 31.3

Balance Sheet as at 31 December 19-5

	£	£	£
Fixed Assets			
Fixtures at 1.1.19-5		800	
less Depreciation		80	720
Current Assets			
Stock		1,700	
Debtors		1,320	
Bank		3,050	
Cash		10	
		6,080	
less Current Liabilities			
Creditors	650		
Rent Owing	50	700	
Working Capital			5,380
Financed by:			6,100
Capital			
Balance 1.1.19-5 (per Opening Statement of Affairs)			4,300
add Net Profit			2,320
			6,620
less Drawings			520
			6,100

Incomplete records and missing figures

In practice, part of the information relating to cash receipts or payments is often missing. If the missing information is in respect of one type of payment, then it is normal to assume that the missing figure is the amount required to make both totals agree in the cash column of the cash and bank summary. This does not happen with bank items owing to the fact that another copy of the bank statement can always be obtained from the bank. Exhibit 31.4 shows an example when the drawings figure is unknown, Exhibit 31.5 is an example where the receipts from debtors had not been recorded.

Exhibit 31.4

The following information of cash and bank receipts and payments is available:

	Cash	Bank
	£	£
Cash paid into the bank during the year	5,500	
Receipts from debtors	7,250	800
Paid to suppliers	320	4,930
Drawings during the year	?	–
Expenses paid	150	900
Balances at 1.1.19-5	35	1,200
Balances at 31.12.19-5	50	1,670

	Cash	Bank			Cash	Bank
	£	£			£	£
Balances 1.1.19-5	35	1,200	Bankings C		5,500	
Received from debtors	7,250	800	Suppliers		320	4,930
Bankings C		5,500	Expenses		150	900
			Drawings		?	
			Balances 31.12.19-5		50	1,670
	7,285	7,500			7,285	7,500

The amount needed to make the two sides of the cash columns agree is £1,265. Therefore, this is taken as the figure of drawings.

Exhibit 31.5

Information of cash and bank transactions is available as follows:

	Cash	Bank
	£	£
Receipts from debtors	?	6,080
Cash withdrawn from the bank for business use (this is the amount which is used besides cash receipts from debtors to pay drawings and expenses		920
Paid to suppliers		5,800
Expenses paid	640	230
Drawings	1,180	315
Balances at 1.1.19-5	40	1,560
Balance at 31.12.19-5	70	375

	Cash	Bank			Cash	Bank
	£	£			£	£
Balances 1.1.19-5	40	1,560	Suppliers			5,800
Received from debtors	?	6,080	Expenses		640	230
Withdrawn from Bank C	920		Withdrawn from Bank C			920
			Drawings		1,180	315
			Balances 31.12.19-5		70	375
	1,890	7,640			1,890	7,640

Receipts from debtors is, therefore, the amount needed to make each side of the cash column agree, £930.

It must be emphasised that balancing figures are acceptable only when all the other figures have been verified. Should for instance a cash expense be omitted when cash received from debtors is being calculated, then this would result in an understatement not only of expenses but also ultimately of sales.

Where there are two missing pieces of information

If both cash drawings and cash receipts from debtors were not known it would not be possible to deduce both of these figures. The only source lying open would be to estimate whichever figure was more capable of being accurately assessed, use this as a known figure, then deduce the other figure. However, this is a most unsatisfactory position as both of the figures are no more than pure estimates, the accuracy of each one relying entirely upon the accuracy of the other.

Goods stolen or lost by fire etc.

When goods are stolen, destroyed by fire, or lost in some other way, then the value of them will have to be calculated. This could be needed to substantiate an insurance claim or to settle problems concerning taxation etc.

If the stock had been properly valued immediately before the fire, burglary, etc, then the stock loss would obviously be known. Also if a full and detailed system of stock records were kept, then the value would also be known. However, as the occurrence of fires or burglaries cannot be foreseen, and not many businesses keep full and proper stock records, the stock loss will have to be calculated in some other way.

The methods described in this chapter and Chapter 30 are used instead. The only difference is that instead of computing closing stock at a year end, for example, the closing stock will be that as at immediately before the fire consumed it or it was stolen.

Exhibits 31.6 and 31.7 will now be looked at. The first exhibit will be a very simple case, where figures of purchases and sales are known and all goods are sold at a uniform profit ratio. The second exhibit is rather more complicated. Horizontal style accounts will be used for the sake of simplicity of illustration.

Exhibit 31.6

J Collins lost the whole of his stock by fire on 17th March 19-9. The last time that a stocktaking had been done was on 31 December 19-8, the last balance sheet date, when it was £1,950 at cost. Purchases from then to 17th March 19-9 amounted to £6,870 and Sales for the period were £9,600. All sales were made at a uniform profit margin of 20 per cent.

First, the Trading Account can be drawn up with the known figures included. Then the missing figures can be deduced afterwards.

J Collins
Trading Account for the period 1 January 19-9 to 17 March 19-9

		£		£
Opening Stock		1,950	Sales	9,600
add Purchases		6,870		
		8,820		
less Closing Stock	(C)	?		
Cost of Goods Sold	(B)	?		
Gross Profit	(A)	?		
		9,600		9,600

Now the missing figures can be deduced.

It is known that the gross profit margin is 20 per cent, therefore Gross Profit (A) is 20% of £9,600 = £1,920.

Now (B) ? + (A) £1,920 = £9,600, so that (B) is difference, i.e. £7,680.

Now that (B) is known (C) can be deduced, £8,820 − (C) ? = £7,680, so (C) is difference, i.e. £1,140.

The figure for goods destroyed by fire, at cost, is therefore £1,140.

Exhibit 31.7

T Scott had the whole of his stock stolen from his warehouse on the night of 20 August 19-6. Also destroyed were his sales and purchases journals, but the sales and purchases ledgers were salvaged. The following facts are known:

(*a*) Stock was known at the last balance sheet date, 31 March 19-6, to be £6,480 at cost.

(*b*) Receipts from debtors during the period 1 April to 20 August 19-6 amounted to £31,745. Debtors were: at 31 March 19-6 £14,278, at 20 August 19-6 £12,333.

(*c*) Payments to creditors during the period 1 April to 20 August 19-6 amounted to £17,720. Creditors were: at 31 March 19-6 £7,633, at 20 August 19-6 £6,289.

(*d*) The margin on sales has been constant at 25 per cent. Before we can start to construct a Trading Account for the period, we need to find out the figures of Sales and of Purchases. These can be found by drawing up Total Debtors' and Total Creditors' Accounts, sales and purchases figures being the difference on the accounts.

Total Creditors

		£			£
Cash and Bank		17,270	Balances	b/fwd	7,633
Balances	c/d	6,289	Purchases (difference)		15,926
		23,559			23,559

Total Debtors

		£			£
Balances	b/fwd	14,278	Cash and Bank		31,745
Sales (difference)		29,800	Balances	c/d	12,333
		44,078			44,078

The Trading Account can now show the figures already known.

Trading Account for the period 1 April to 20 August 19-6

		£		£
Opening Stock		12,480	Sales	29,800
add Purchases		15,926		
		28,406		
less Closing Stock	(C)	?		
Cost of Goods Sold	(B)	?		
Gross Profit	(A)	?		
		29,800		29,800

254

Gross Profit can be found, as the margin on sales is known to be 25%, therefore (A) = 25% of £29,800 = £7,450.

Cost of Goods Sold (B) ? + Gross Profit £7,450 = £29,800 therefore (B) is £22,350.

£28,406 − (C) ? = (B) £22,350, therefore (C) is £6,056.

The figure for cost of goods stolen is therefore £6,056.

Review questions

31.1 B Arkwright started in business on 1 January 19-5 with £10,000 in a bank account. Unfortunately he did not keep proper books of account.

He is forced to submit a calculation of profit for the year ended 31 December 19-5 to the Inspector of Taxes. He ascertains that at 31 December 19-5 he had stock valued at cost £3,950, a motor van which had cost £2,800 during the year and which had depreciated by £550, debtors of £4,970, expenses prepaid of £170, bank balance £2,564, cash balance £55, trade creditors £1,030, and expenses owing £470.

His drawings were: cash £100 per week for 50 weeks, cheque payments £673.

Draw up statements to show the profit or loss for the year.

31.2A J Kirkwood is a dealer who has not kept proper books of account. At 31 August 19-6 his state of affairs was as follows:

	£
Cash	115
Bank Balance	2,209
Fixtures	4,000
Stock	16,740
Debtors	11,890
Creditors	9,052
Motor Van (at valuation)	3,000

During the year to 31 August 19-7 his drawings amounted to £7,560. Winnings from a football pool £2,800 were put into the business. Extra fixtures were bought for £2,000.

At 31 August 19-7 his assets and liabilities were: Cash £84, Bank Overdraft £165, Stock £21,491, Creditors for goods £6,002, Creditors for expenses £236, Fixtures to be depreciated £600, Motor Van to be valued at £2,500, Debtors £15,821, Pre-paid expenses £72.

Draw up a statement showing the profit and loss made by Kirkwood for the year ended 31 August 19-7.

31.3 Following is a summary of Kelly's bank account for the year ended 31 December 19-7.

	£		£
Balance 1.1.19-7	405	Payments to creditors	
Receipts from debtors	37,936	for goods	29,487
Balance 31.12.19-7	602	Rent	1,650
		Rates	890
		Sundry Expenses	375
		Drawings	6,541
	38,943		38,943

All of the business takings have been paid into the bank with the exception of £9,630. Out of this, Kelly has paid wages of £5,472, drawings of £1,164 and purchase of goods £2,994.

The following additional information is available:

	31.12.19-6	31.12.19-7
Stock	13,862	15,144
Creditors for goods	5,624	7,389
Debtors for goods	9,031	8,624
Rates Prepaid	210	225
Rent Owing	150	–
Fixtures at valuation	2,500	2,250

You are to draw up a set of final accounts for the year ended 31 December 19-7. Show all of your workings.

31.4A The balance sheet as at 29 February 19-8 of Mark Bean, retailer, is as follows:

	£	£	£
Fixed Assets			
Fixtures and fittings:			
At cost		76,000	
less Provision for depreciation		18,000	
			58,000
Current Assets			
Stock	16,000		
Trade debtors	13,000		
Balance at bank	10,000		
		39,000	
less Current Liabilities			
Trade creditors		11,000	
			28,000
			£86,000
Mark Bean: Capital account			£86,000

The unexpected opportunity to acquire new business premises has necessitated 'final accounts' being required for the three months ended 31 May 19-8. Accordingly, the following information has been prepared from the business's bank account:

	19-8		
	March	April	May
	£	£	£
Receipts:			
Sales – Cash	6,000	9,000	8,000
Credit	15,500	11,500	13,000
Sale of surplus display cabinet		500	
Payments:			
Purchases	11,000	11,900	10,900
General expenses	4,600	3,700	2,700
Drawings	1,200	1,400	1,500

Additional information:

(*i*) All receipts and payments are passed through the business bank account.

(*ii*) A half of credit sales are paid for in the month sales take place and the balance of the cash due is received in the following month.

(*iii*) Purchases are paid for in the month following the receipt of goods; all general expenses are paid on a cash basis. Purchase creditors at 31 May 19-8 amounted to £9,600.

(*iv*) A gross profit of 30% is obtained on all sales.

(*v*) During March, April and May 19-8, Mark Bean withdrew from the business, goods for his own use of £600 at cost price.

(*vi*) The display cabinet sold in April 19-8 cost £2,000 when bought in 19-5 and had a written down book value in fixtures and fittings at 29 February 19-8 of £1,400.

(*vii*) The depreciation charge for fixtures and fittings for the three months to 31 May 19-8 is £1,850.

Required:

(*a*) Prepare a computation of the business bank account balance at 31 May 19-8 of Mark Bean.

(*b*) Prepare Mark Bean's trading and profit and loss account for the three months ended 31 May 19-8.

(*c*) Prepare Mark Bean's balance sheet as at 31 May 19-8.

31.5 The Carnaby Wholesale Clothing Company was burgled on the night of 14 December 19-2.

The raider stole all that day's cash takings together with the petty cash and a selection of the most expensive clothing.

On 30 November 19-2, the owner had taken a physical stock count for which the cost was evaluated as £32,540. The stock of clothing left after the burglary amounted to £11,300 at cost.

Deliveries from suppliers, of further stock items, between 1 and 14 December 19-2, were invoiced at £5,784 after deduction of trade discounts of £732.

Sales to retail customers (at selling prices) had been:

	Cash	Credit
	£	£
1 to 6 December	1,429.71	6,250.29
7 to 13 December	1,644.50	8,079.50
14 December	259.32	1,200.68

The cash and bank accounts showed that during the period 1 to 14 December 19-2:

(*a*) the cash takings for the 1 to 13 December, inclusive, had been banked intact;

(*b*) cheques for £168.92 and £192.67 had been drawn to pay staff wages;

(*c*) credit customers had paid cheques amounting to £15,867.11 (all of which had been banked) in full settlement of account totalling £16,102.83;

(*d*) the company had paid credit suppliers a total of £17,118.36 by cheque after deducting cash discounts of £940.45.

(*e*) the petty cash imprest account had been restored to its established level of £25.00 on 1 December by a withdrawal from the bank of £9.74. Subsequent disbursements to 14 December had amounted to £13.69.

Account balances in the firm's books on 30 November 19-2 had been:

	£	
Bank	6,625.08	(debit)
Cash	129.60	
Petty cash	15.26	

Gross profit on sales had been at the rate of 30% throughout 19-2 but on 7 December, as part of a sales campaign, this was reduced to 25% for the remainder of the month.

You are required to:
Calculate using such of the above information as is relevant:
  (*a*) the amount of cash and the value of stock at cost, which had been stolen;
  (*b*) the balance on the bank account at close of business on 14 December 19-2.
(Chartered Association of Certified Accountants)

31.6A The following is the Trading Account of William Martin, a sole trader.

Trading Account for the year ended 31 December 19-1

	Dr		Cr
	£		£
To Stock 1 January 19-1	3,200	By Sales	24,000
Purchases	17,700		
	20,900		
less Stock 31 December 19-1	2,900		
Cost of Goods Sold	18,000		
Gross Profit	6,000		
	24,000		24,000

During the night of 4 June 19-2 Martin's warehouse was broken into and his entire stock in trade was stolen except for a small quantity of goods in an office. The value – at cost price – of the goods which were not stolen was £190.

The following information is available from Martin's records.

Purchases	1 January 19-2 to 4 June 19-2 £6,400
	Of this total goods costing £240 had *not* been delivered by 4 June 19-2.
Sales	1 January 19-2 to 4 June 19-2 £8,280
	All the goods sold had been delivered from the warehouse by the close of business on 4 June 19-2.

Required
Calculate the value, at *cost price*, of the goods actually stolen. Calculations *must be shown*.
Note: Assume that the percentage of gross profit to Sales is the same for 19-2 as it was for 19-1.
(London Chamber of Commerce)

31.7 Philip Gold is a retailer in motor car accessories. Despite professional advice he does not maintain a full accounting system. He argues that if all cash transactions are dealt with through his bank account, and the bank does its job properly, then his annual accounts and particularly the reported profit figure for tax assessment are relatively easy to effect. You have been asked to prepare certain accounts from his bank statements and other business transactions in order to ascertain his profit performance and financial status in respect of the year ended 31 July 19-1. The following information is obtained.

(*i*) His current assets as at 31 July 19-0 and 31 July 19-1 were as follows:

	19-0 £	19-1 £
Trading stock at or below cost	4,230	3,560
Trade debtors	3,760	2,310
Advance payments – rates	75	90
Bank balance	–	1,190

(*ii*) His current liabilities as at 31 July 19-0 and 31 July 19-1 were as follows:

	19-0 £	19-1 £
Trade creditors	3,390	3,920
Accrued payments – electricity	50	70
Bank overdraft	2,100	–

(*iii*) Business transactions for the year ended 31 July 19-1 all effected through his bank account:

	£
Shop assistant's wages	3,400
Suppliers of accessories	25,140
Rent, rates and electricity	1,010
Other operating overheads	746
Interest-free loan from relative	2,500

(*iv*) Accessories costing £600 were withdrawn from the business by Gold for his own usage.

(*v*) Mark-up on accessories is 40 per cent on cost.

(*vi*) Shop fixtures and fittings at cost as at 31 July 19-0 were £2,900 and one year later £4,100. No fixed assets were sold during the year.

Accumulated depreciation as at 31 July 19-0 was £870. The annual depreciation expense is at the rate of 10 per cent based on the cost of the assets at the year end and still held in the business.

(*vii*) The source of all cash received was from trade debtors, except for the loan from the relative, and all cash received has been banked in the business, except for withdrawals of £5,200 by Gold.

Required:

(*a*) A summary of the business bank account for the year ended 31 July 19- 1.

(*b*) A business trading and profit and loss account for the year ended 31 July 19-1 and balance sheet as at that date.

(Institute of Chartered Secretaries and Administrators)

31.8A Jean Smith, who retails wooden ornaments, has been so busy since she commenced business on 1 April 19-5 that she has neglected to keep adequate accounting records. Jean's opening capital consisted of her life savings of £15,000 which she used to open a business bank account. The transactions in this bank account during the year ended 31 March 19-6 have been summarised from the bank account as follows:

	£
Receipts:	
Loan from John Peacock, uncle	10,000
Takings	42,000
Payments:	
Purchases of goods for resale	26,400
Electricity for period to 31 December 19-5	760
Rent of premises for 15 months to 30 June 19-6	3,500
Rates of premises for the year ended 31 March 19-6	1,200
Wages of assistants	14,700
Purchase of van, 1 October 19-5	7,600
Purchase of holiday caravan for Jean Smith's private use	8,500
Van licence and insurance, payments covering a year	250

According to the bank account, the balance in hand on 31 March 19-6 was £4,090 in Jean Smith's favour.

While the intention was to bank all takings intact, it now transpires that, in addition to cash drawings, the following payments were made out of takings before bankings:

	£
Van running expenses	890
Postages, stationery and other sundry expenses	355

On 31 March 19-6, takings of £640 awaited banking; this was done on 1 April 19-6. It has been discovered that amounts paid into the bank of £340 on 29 March 19-6 were not credited to Jean's bank account until 2 April 19-6 and a cheque of £120, drawn on 28 March 19-6 for purchases was not paid until 10 April 19-6. The normal rate of gross profit on the goods sold by Jean Smith is 50% on sales. However, during the year a purchase of ornamental gold fish costing £600 proved to be unpopular with customers and therefore the entire stock bought had to be sold at cost price.

Interest at the rate of 5% per annum is payable on each anniversary of the loan from John Peacock on 1 January 19-6.

Depreciation is to be provided on the van on the straight line basis; it is estimated that the van will be disposed of after five years' use for £100.

The stock of goods for resale at 31 March 19-6 has been valued at cost at £1,900.

Creditors for purchases at 31 March 19-6 amounted to £880 and electricity charges accrued due at that date were £180.

Trade debtors at 31 March 19-6 totalled £2,300.

Required:

Prepare a trading and profit and loss account for the year ended 31 March 19-6 and a balance sheet as at that date.

(Association of Accounting Technicians)

31.9 David Denton set up in business as a plumber a year ago, and he has asked you to act as his accountant. His instructions to you are in the form of the following letter.

Dear Henry,

I was pleased when you agreed to act as my accountant and look forward to your first visit to check my records. The proposed fee of £250 p.a. is acceptable. I regret that the paperwork for the work done during the year is incomplete. I started my business on 1 January last, and put £6,500 into a business bank account on that date. I brought my van into the firm at that time, and reckon that it was worth £3,600 then. I think it will last another three years after the end of the first year of business use.

I have drawn £90 per week from the business bank account during the year. In my trade it is difficult to take a holiday, but my wife managed to get away for a while. The travel agent's bill for £280 was paid out of the business account. I bought the lease of the yard and office for £6,500. The lease has ten years to run, and the rent is only £300 a year payable in advance on the anniversary of the date of purchase, which was 1 April. I borrowed £4,000 on that day from Aunt Jane to help pay for the lease. I have agreed to pay her 10% interest per annum, but have been too busy to do anything about this yet.

I was lucky enough to meet Miss Prism shortly before I set up on my own, and she has worked for me as an office organiser right from the start. She is paid a salary of £3,000 p.a. All the bills for the year have been carefully preserved in a tool box, and we analysed them last week. The materials I have bought cost me £9,600, but I reckon there was £580 worth left in the yard on 31 December. I have not yet paid for them all yet, I think we owed £714 to the suppliers on 31 December. I was surprised to see that I had spent £4,800 on plumbing equipment, but it should last me five years or so. Electricity bills received up to 30 September came to £1,122; but motor expenses were £912, and general expenses £1,349 for the year. The insurance premium for the year to 31 March next was £800. All these have been paid by cheque but Miss Prism has lost the rate demand. I expect the Local Authority will send a reminder soon since I have not yet paid. I seem to remember that rates came to £180 for the year to 31 March next.

Miss Prism sent out bills to my customers for work done, but some of them are very slow to pay. Altogether the charges made were £29,863, but only £25,613 had been received by 31 December. Miss Prism thinks that 10% of the remaining bills are not likely to be paid. Other customers for jobs too small to bill have paid £3,418 in cash for work done, but I only managed to bank £2,600 of this money. I used £400 of the difference to pay the family's grocery bills, and Miss Prism used the rest for general expenses, except for £123 which was left over in a drawer in the office on 31 December.

Kind regards,

Yours sincerely,

David.

You are required to draw up a Profit and Loss Account for the year ended 31 December, and a Balance Sheet as at that date.
(Chartered Association of Certified Accountants)

31.10 John Snow is the sole distribution agent in the Branton area for Diamond floor tiles. Under an agreement with the manufacturers, John Snow purchases the Diamond floor tiles at a trade discount of 20% off list price and annually in May receives an agency commission of 1% of his purchases for the year ended on the previous 31 March.

For several years, John Snow has obtained a gross profit of 40% on all sales. In a burglary in January 19-1 John Snow lost stock costing £4,000 as well as many of his accounting records. However, after careful investigations, the following information has been obtained covering the year ended 31 March 19-1:

(*i*) Assets and liabilities at 31 March 19-0, were as follows:

	£
Buildings: at cost	10,000
provision for depreciation	6,000
Motor vehicles: at cost	5,000
provision for depreciation	2,000
Stock: at cost	3,200
Trade debtors (for sales)	6,300
Agency commission due	300
Prepayments (trade expenses)	120
Balance at bank in hand	4,310
Trade creditors	4,200
Accrued expenses (vehicle expenses)	230

(*ii*)   John Snow has been notified that he will receive an agency commission of £440 on 1 May 19-1.

(*iii*)   Stock, at cost, at 31 March 19-1 was valued at £3,000 more than a year previously.

(*iv*)   In October 19-0 stock costing £1,000 was damaged by dampness and had to be scrapped as worthless.

(*v*)   Trade creditors at 31 March 19-1 related entirely to goods received whose list prices totalled £9,500.

(*vi*)   Discounts allowed amounted to £1,620 while discounts received were £1,200.

(*vii*)   Trade expenses prepaid at 31 March 19-1 totalled £80.

(*viii*)   Vehicle expenses for the year ended 31 March 19-1 amount to £7,020.

(*ix*)   Trade debtors (for sales) at 31 March 19-1 were £6,700.

(*x*)   All receipts are passed through the bank account.

(*xi*)   Depreciation is provided annually at the following rates:
        Buildings 5% on cost;
        Motor vehicles 20% on cost.

(*xii*)   Commissions received are paid direct to the bank account.

(*xiii*)   In addition to the payments for purchases, the bank payments were:

	£
Vehicle expenses	6,720
Drawings	4,300
Trade expenses	7,360

(*xiv*)   John Snow is not insured against loss of stock owing to burglary or damage to stock caused by dampness.

Required:

John Snow's trading and profit and loss account for the year ended 31 March 19-1 and a balance sheet at that date.

(Chartered Association of Certified Accountants)

31.11A Since commencing business several years ago as a cloth dealer, Tom Smith has relied on annual receipts and payments accounts for assessing progress. These accounts have been prepared from his business bank account through which all business receipts and payments are passed.

Tom Smith's receipts and payments account for the year ended 31 March 19-0 is as follows:

	£		£
Opening balance	1,680	Drawings	6,300
Sales receipts	42,310	Purchases payments	37,700
Proceeds of sale of		Motor van expenses	2,900
grandfather clock	870	Workshop: rent	700
Loan from John Scott	5,000	rates	570
Closing balance	1,510	Wages – John Jones	3,200
	———		———
	£51,370		£51,370

Additional information:

(*a*) The grandfather clock sold during the year ended 31 March 19-0 was a legacy received by Tom Smith from the estate of his late father.

(*b*) The loan from John Scott was received on 1 January 19-0; interest is payable on the loan at the rate of 10% per annum.

(*c*) In May 19-0 Tom Smith received from his suppliers a special commission of 5% of the cost of purchases during the year ended 31 March 19-0.

(*d*) On 1 October 19-9, Tom Smith engaged John Jones as a salesman. In addition to his wages, Jones receives a bonus of 2% of the business's sales during the period of his employment; the bonus is payable on 1 April and 1 October in respect of the immediately preceding six months' period.

Note: It can be assumed that sales have been at a uniform level throughout the year ended 31 March 19-0.

(*e*) In addition to the items mentioned above, the assets and liabilities of Tom Smith were as follows:

At 31 March	19-9	19-0
	£	£
Motor van, at cost	4,000	4,000
Stock in trade, at cost	5,000	8,000
Trade debtors	4,600	12,290
Motor vehicle expenses prepaid	–	100
Workshop rent accrued due	–	200
Trade creditors	2,900	2,200

(*f*) It can be assumed that the opening and closing balances in the above receipts and payments account require no adjustment for the purpose of Tom Smith's accounts.

(*g*) As from 1 April 19-9, it has been decided to provide for depreciation on the motor van annually at the rate of 20% of the cost.

Required:

The trading and profit and loss account for the year ended 31 March 19-0, and a balance sheet at that date of Tom Smith.

(*Chartered Association of Certified Accountants*)

Receipts and payments accounts and income and expenditure accounts

Clubs, associations and other non-profit-making organisations do not have trading and profit and loss accounts drawn up for them, as their principal function is not trading or profit making. They are run to further the promotion of an activity or group of activities, such as playing football or engaging in cultural or charitable activities. The kind of final accounts prepared by these organisations are either **Receipts and payments accounts** or **income and expenditure accounts**.

Receipts and payments accounts are merely a summary of the cash book for the period. Exhibit 32.1 is an example.

Exhibit 32.1

The Homers Running Club
Receipts and Payments Account for the year ended 31 December 19-5

Receipts	£	Payments	£
Bank Balance 1.1.19-5	236	Groundsman's wages	728
Subscriptions received for		Upkeep of sports stadium	296
19-5	1,148	Committee expenses	58
Rent from sub-letting ground	116	Printing and stationery	33
		Bank Balance 31.12.19-5	385
	1,500		1,500

However, when the organisation owns assets and has liabilities, the receipts and payments account is an unsatisfactory way of drawing up accounts as it merely shows the cash position. What is required is a balance sheet, and an account showing whether or not the association's capital is being increased. In a commercial firm the latter information would be obtained from a profit and loss account. In a non-profit-making organisation it is calculated in an account called the income and expenditure account. In fact the income and expenditure account follows all the basic rules of profit and loss accounts. Thus expenditure consists of those costs consumed during the period and income is the revenue earned in the period. Where income exceeds expenditure the difference is called **surplus of income over expenditure**. Where expenditure exceeds income the difference is called **excess of expenditure over income**.

There is, however, one qualification to the fact that normally such an organisation would not have a trading or profit and loss account. This is where the organisation has carried out an activity deliberately so as to make a profit to help finance the main activities. Running a bar so as to make a profit would be an example of this, or having dances. For this profit-aimed activity a trading or profit and loss account may be drawn up, the profit or loss being transferred to the income and expenditure account.

If the books had been kept on a double-entry basis, the income and expenditure account and balance sheet would be prepared in the same manner as the profit and loss account and the balance sheet of a commercial firm, only the titles of the accounts and terms like 'surplus' or 'excess' being different. It is perhaps more usual to find that the records have been kept in a single entry form. In this case the starting point is that as described in the last chapter, namely the drafting of an opening statement of affairs followed by a Cash Book Summary. If a receipts and payments accounts exists then this is in fact a cash book summary. The preparation of the income and expenditure account and the balance sheet then follows the normal single entry fashion. Exhibit 32.2 shows the preparation on such a basis.

Exhibit 32.2

Long Lane Football Club

Receipts and Payments Account for the year ended 31 December 19-6

Receipts		£	Payments	£
Bank Balance 1.1.19-6		524	Payment for bar supplies	3,962
Subscriptions received for			Wages:	
	19-5 (arrears)	55	Groundsman and assistant	939
	19-6	1,236	Barman	624
	19-7 (in advance)	40	Bar expenses	234
Bar Sales		5,628	Repairs to stands	119
Donations Received		120	Ground upkeep	229
			Secretary's expenses	138
			Transport Costs	305
			Bank Balance 31.12.19-6	1,053
		7,603		7,603

The treasurer of the Long Lane Football Club has prepared a receipts and payments account, but members have complained about the inadequacy of such an account. He therefore asks an accountant to prepare a trading account for the bar, and an income and expenditure account and a balance sheet. The treasurer gives the accountant a copy of the receipts and payments account together with information of assets and liabilities at the beginning and end of the year:

Notes:

1.

	31.12.19-5	31.12.19-6
	£	£
Stocks in the bar — at cost	496	558
Owing for bar supplies	294	340
Bar expenses owing	25	36
Transport costs	—	65

2. The land and football stands were valued at 31 December 19-5 at: land £4,000; football stands £2,000; the stands are to be depreciated by 10 per cent per annum.

3. The equipment at 31 December 19-5 was valued at £550, and is to be depreciated at 20 per cent per annum.

4. Subscriptions owing by members amounted to £55 on 31 December 19-5, and £66 on 31 December 19-6.

From this information the accountant drew up the accounts and statements that follow.

Working of purchases and bar expenses figures:

Purchases Control

	£		£
Cash	3,962	Balances (creditors) b/f	294
Balances c/d	340	Trading Account (difference)	4,008
	4,302		4,302

Bar Expenses

	£		£
Cash	234	Balance b/f	25
Balance c/d	36	Trading Account (difference)	245
	270		270

Statement of Affairs as at 31 December 19-5

	£	£	£
Fixed Assets			
Land			4,000
Stands			2,000
Equipment			550
			6,550
Current Assets			
Stock in bar		496	
Debtors for Subscriptions		55	
Cash at Bank		524	
		1,075	
less Current Liabilities			
Creditors	294		
Bar Expenses Owing	25	319	
Working Capital			756
			7,306
Financed by:			
Accumulated Fund (difference)			7,306
			7,306

Long Lane Football Club
Bar Trading Account for the year ended 31 December 19-6

	£	£
Sales		5,628
less Cost of Goods Sold:		
Stock 1.1.19-6	496	
add Purchases	4,008	
	4,504	
less Stock 31.12.19-6	558	3,946
Gross Profit		1,682
less Bar Expenses	245	
Barman's Wages	624	869
Net Profit to Income & Expenditure Account		813

Income & Expenditure Account for the year ended 31 December 19-6

	£	£	£
Income			
Subscriptions for 19-6			1,302
Profit from the bar			813
Donations Received			120
			2,235
less Expenditure			
Wages – Groundsman and Assistant		939	
Repairs to Stands		119	
Ground Upkeep		229	
Secretary's Expenses		138	
Transport Costs		370	
Depreciation			
Stands	200		
Equipment	110	310	2,105
Surplus of Income over Expenditure			130

Working on transport costs and subscriptions received figures:

Transport Costs

	£		£
Cash	305	Income and Expenditure	
Accrued c/d	65	Account	370
	370		370

	£		£
Balance (debtors) b/f	55	Cash 19-5	55
Income and Expenditure		19-6	1,236
Account (difference)	1,302	19-7	40
Balance (in advance) c/d	40	Balance (owing) c/d	66
	1,397		1,397

It will be noted that subscriptions received in advance are carried down as a credit balance to the following period.

The Long Lane Football Club
Balance Sheet as at 31 December 19-6

	£	£	£
Fixed Assets			
Land at valuation			4,000
Pavilion at valuation		2,000	
less Depreciation		200	1,800
Equipment at valuation		550	
less Depreciation		110	440
Current Assets			6,240
Stock of Bar Supplies		558	
Debtors for Subscriptions		66	
Cash at Bank		1,053	
		1,677	
less Current Liabilities			
Creditors for Bar Supplies	340		
Bar Expenses Owing	36		
Transport Costs Owing	65		
Subscriptions Received in Advance	40	481	
Working Capital			1,196
			7,436
Financed by:			
Accumulated Fund			
Balance as at 1.1.19-6			7,306
add Surplus of Income over Expenditure			130
			7,436

Life membership

In some clubs and societies members can make a payment for life membership. This means that by paying a fairly substantial amount now the member can enjoy the facilities of the club for the rest of his life.

Such a receipt should not be treated as income in the Income and Expenditure

Account solely in the year in which the member paid the money. It should be credited to a Life Membership Account, and transfers should be made from that account to the credit of the Income and Expenditure Account of an appropriate amount annually.

Exactly what is meant by an appropriate amount is decided by the committee of the club or society. The usual basis is to establish, on average, how long members will continue to use the benefits of the club. To take an extreme case, if a club was in existence which could not be joined until one achieved the age of 70, then the expected number of years' use of the club on average per member would be relatively few. Another club, such as a golf club, where a fair proportion of the members joined when reasonably young, and where the game is capable of being played by members until and during old age, would expect a much higher average of years of use per member. The simple matter is that the club should decide for itself.

In an examination the candidate has to follow the instructions set for him by the examiner. The credit balance remaining on the account, after the transfer of the agreed amount has been made to the credit of the Income and Expenditure Account, should be shown on the Balance Sheet as a liability. It is, after all, the liability of the club to provide amenities for the member without any further payment by him.

Entrance fees

In quite a lot of clubs, one has to pay certain fees on application for membership. Such fees are called entrance fees. They are paid quite apart from the usual monthly or quarterly subscription.

Such a receipt should not be treated as Income in the Income and Expenditure Account solely in the year in which the member is admitted. It should be credited to Entrance Fees Account and transfers should be made from that account to the Income and Expenditure Account by an appropriate amount annually, such amounts being decided by the committee of the club or society.

Outstanding subscriptions and the prudence concept

The treatment of subscriptions owing has so far followed the normal procedures as applied to debtors in a commercial firm. However, as most treasurers of associations are fully aware, many members who owe subscriptions leave the association and never pay the amounts owing. This is far more prevalent than with debtors of a commercial firm. It can perhaps be partly explained by the fact that a commercial firm would normally sue for unpaid debts, whereas associations rarely sue for unpaid subscriptions. To bring in unpaid subscriptions as assets therefore contravenes the prudence concept, which tends to understate assets rather than overstate them. With many clubs therefore, unpaid subscriptions are ignored in the income and expenditure account and balance sheet. If they are eventually paid they are then brought in as income in the year of receipt irrespective of the period covered by the subscriptions.

In the examinations, the student should bring debtors for subscriptions into account unless he is given instructions to the contrary. Exhibit 32.3 illustrates this point.

Exhibit 32.3

An amateur theatre organisation charges its members an annual subscription of £20 per member. It accrues for subscriptions owing at the end of each year and also adjusts for subscriptions received in advance.

(*i*)   On 1 January 19-2, 18 members owed £360 for the year 19-1.
(*ii*)   In December 19-1, 4 members paid £80 for the year 19-2.
(*iii*)   During the year 19-2 we received cash for subscriptions £7,420.

For 19-1	£360
For 19-2	£6,920
For 19-3	£140

(*iv*) At close of 31 December 19-2, 11 members had not paid their 19-2 subscriptions.

Subscriptions

19-2		£	19-2		£
Jan 1 Owing b/d		360	Jan 1 Prepaid b/d		80
Dec 31 Income & Expenditure		* 7,220	Dec 31 Bank		7,420
Dec 31 Prepaid c/d		140	Dec 31 Owing c/d		220
		7,720			7,720
19-3			19-3		
Jan 1 Owing b/d		220	Jan 1 Prepaid b/d		140

* Difference between two sides of the account.

Review questions

32.1 The following is a summary of the receipts and payments of the Praetorius Club during the year ended 30 September 19-7:

Praetorius Club
Receipts and Payments Account
for the year ended 30 September 19-7

	£		£
Cash and Bank balances b/f	1,247	Secretary's expenses	224
Sales of annual dinner tickets	990	Rent	1,300
Members' subscriptions	4,388	Purchase of office equipment	870
Donations	150	Donations to charities	87
		Meeting expenses	559
		Expenses of annual dinner	1,213
		Heating and lighting	446
		Stationery and printing	320
		Cash and Bank balances c/f	1,756
	6,775		6,775

The following valuations are also available:

as at 30 September	19-6	19-7
Subscriptions in arrears	150	90
Subscriptions in advance	75	35
Stocks of stationery	67	83
Meeting expenses prepaid	150	0
Heating and lighting accrued	110	83

On 1 October 19-6 the Praetorius Club owned office equipment costing £2,500 which had been depreciated by £500. The policy of the club is to depreciate office equipment at 10% per annum using the straight line method applied on a full year basis. The club did not sell any office equipment during the year ended 30 September 19-7.

Required:
Prepare an Income and Expenditure Account for the Praetorius Club for the year ended 30 September 19-7 and a Balance Sheet as at that date.
(*Association of Accounting Technicians*)

32.2A The following is a summary of the receipts and payments of the Miniville Rotary Club during the year ended 31 July 19-6.

Miniville Rotary Club
Receipts and Payments Account for the year ended 31 July 19-6

	£		£
Cash and Bank balances b/f	210	Secretarial expenses	163
Sales of competition tickets	437	Rent	1,402
Members' subscriptions	1,987	Visiting speakers' expenses	1,275
Donations	177	Donations to charities	35
Refund of rent	500	Prizes for competitions	270
Balance c/f	13	Stationery and printing	179
	£3,324		£3,324

The following valuations are also available:

as at 31 July	19-5	19-6
	£	£
Equipment	975	780
(original cost £1,420)		
Subscriptions in arrears	65	85
Subscriptions in advance	10	37
Owing to suppliers of competition prizes	58	68
Stocks of competition prizes	38	46

Required:
(*a*) Calculate the value of the Accumulated Fund of the Miniville Rotary Club as at the 1 August 19-5.
(*b*) Reconstruct the following accounts for the year ended 31 July 19- 6.
　(*i*) the Subscriptions Account,
　(*ii*) the Competition Prizes Account.
(*c*) Prepare an Income and Expenditure Account for the Miniville Rotary Club for the year ended 31 July 19-6 and a Balance Sheet as at that date.
(*Association of Accounting Technicians*)

32.3 The following receipts and payments account for the year ended 31 December 19-6 for the Springtime Gardeners' Club has been prepared by the club's treasurer:

	£		£
Opening bank balance	876	National Gardening Show:	
Seed sales	1,684	purchase of tickets and	
National Gardening Show:		brochures	3,600
ticket sales to		Seed purchases	1,900
non members	400	Lawn mower purchases	5,400
Lawn mower sales	3,800	Coaches to National	
Subscriptions received	7,190	Gardening Show	490
Closing bank overdraft	270	Club premises – rent	500
		Gardening magazines	
		for members' use	390
		Secretarial expenses	940
		Proposed new club	
		building plans –	
		architect's fees	1,000
	14,220		14,220

The club's executive committee has now decided that members should receive an income and expenditure account for the year ended 31 December 19-6 and a balance sheet as at that date.

Accordingly, the following additional information has been given:

(*i*) Club assets and liabilities, other than bank balances or overdrafts:

As at	1 January 19-6	31 December 19-6
	£	£
Plot of land for proposed new club building, bought 1 January 19-0 for £2,000; current market value	5,000	5,500
Stocks of seeds, at cost	250	560
Debtors — lawn mower sales	400	1,370
Membership subscriptions received in advance	240	390
Creditors — lawn mower supplier	800	170
seed growers	110	340

(*ii*) The club sells lawn mowers at cost price to members; however the club never holds any stock of unsold lawn mowers.

(*iii*) Membership benefits include a ticket and transport to the National Gardening Show.

Required:
(*a*) Prepare the club's accumulated fund as at 1 January 19-6.
(*b*) Prepare the club's income and expenditure account for the year ended 31 December 19-6.
(*c*) Prepare the club's balance sheet as at 31 December 19-6.
(*Association of Accounting Technicians*)

32.4 The following receipts and payments account for the year ended 31 March 19-1 for the Green Bank Sports Club has been prepared by the treasurer, Andrew Swann:

Receipts	£	Payments	£
Balances brought forward		Painting of Clubhouse	580
1 April 19-0:		Maintenance of grounds	1,310
Cash in hand	196	Bar steward's salary	5,800
Bank current account	5,250	Insurances	240
Members subscriptions:		General expenses	1,100
Ordinary	1,575	Building society investment	
Life	800	account	1,500
Annual dinner — ticket sales	560	Secretary's honorarium	200
Bar takings	21,790	Annual dinner - expenses	610
		New furniture and fittings	1,870
		Bar purchases	13,100
		Rent of clubhouse	520
		Balances carried forward	
		31 March 19-1:	
		Bank current account	3,102
		Cash in hand	239
	£30,171		£30,171

The following additional information has been given:

	£
(*i*) Ordinary membership subscriptions.	
Received in advance at 31 March 19-0	200

The subscriptions received during the year ended 31 March 19-1 included £150 in advance for the following year.

(*ii*) A life membership scheme was introduced on 1 April 19-9; under the scheme life membership subscriptions are £100 and are allocated to revenue over a ten year period.

Life membership subscriptions totalling £1,100 were received during the first year of the scheme.

(*iii*) The club's building society investment account balance at 31 March 19-0 was £2,676; during the year ended 31 March 19-1 interest of £278 was credited to the account.

(*iv*) All the furniture and fittings in the club's accounts at 31 March 19-0 were bought in January 19-8 at a total cost of £8,000; it is the club's policy to provide depreciation annually on fixed assets at 10% of the cost of such assets held at the relevant year end.

(*v*) Other assets and liabilities of the club were:

At 31 March	19-0	19-1
	£	£
Bar stocks	1,860	2,110
Insurance prepaid	70	40
Rent accrued due	130	140
Bar purchases creditors	370	460

Required:

(*a*) The bar trading and profit and loss account for the year ended 31 March 19-1.

(*b*) The club's income and expenditure account for the year ended 31 March 19-1 and a balance sheet at that date.

(*c*) Outline the advantages and disadvantages of receipts and payments accounts for organisations such as the Green Bank Sports Club.

(*Chartered Association of Certified Accountants*)

32.5A The following receipts and payments account for the year ended 31 October 19-0 has been prepared from the current account bank statements of the Country Cousins Sports Club:

19-9		£	19-0		£
Nov 1	Balance b/fwd	1,700	Oct 31	Clubhouse:	
19-0				Rates and insurance	380
Oct 31	Subscriptions	8,600		Decoration and	
	Bar takings	13,800		repairs	910
	Donations	1,168		Annual dinner —	
	Annual dinner —			Catering	650
	Sale of tickets	470		Bar purchases	9,200
				Stationery and	
				printing	248
				New Sports equipment	2,463
				Hire of films	89
				Warden's salary	4,700
				Petty cash	94
				Balance c/fwd	7,004
		£25,738			£25,738

The following additional information has been given:

At 31 October	19-9	19-0
	£	£
Clubhouse, at cost	15,000	15,000
Bar stocks, at cost	1,840	2,360
Petty cash float	30	10
Bank deposit account	600	730
Subscriptions received in advance	210	360
Creditors for bar supplies	2,400	1,900

It has been decided to provide for depreciation annually on the clubhouse at the rate of 10% of cost and on the new sports equipment at the rate of 33⅓% of cost.

The petty cash float is used exclusively for postages.

The only entry in the bank deposit account during the year ended 31 October 19-0 concerns interest.

One-quarter of the warden's salary and one-half of the clubhouse costs, including depreciation, are to be apportioned to the bar.

The donations received during the year ended 31 October 19-0 are for the new coaching bursary fund which will be utilised for the provision of training facilities for promising young sportsmen and sportswomen. It is expected to make the first award during 19-1.

Required:

(a) An account showing the profit or loss for the year ended 31 October 19-0 on the operation of the bar.

(b) An Income and Expenditure Account for the year ended 31 October 19-0 and a Balance Sheet at that date for the Country Cousins Sports Club.

(*Chartered Association of Certified Accountants*)

32.6A On 2 November 19-3, the treasurer of the Olympiad Athletics Club died. The financial year of the club, which had been formed to provide training facilities for both field and track event athletics, had ended two days previously on 31 October 19-3. An extraordinary general meeting was convened for the purpose of appointing a new treasurer whose task it would be to prepare the annual accounts for that financial year.

An enthusiastic club member, Guy Rowppe, was duly appointed but, having only an elementary knowledge of book-keeping, soon found himself in difficulty.

He sought your assistance which you agreed to give. During your conversation he said, 'The previous treasurer maintained a Cash and Bank Account. I have summarised the detailed entries into what I think you call a receipts and payments account, and have rounded the figures to the nearest £.'

At this point he supplied you with a copy of the following document:

Olympiad Athletics Club

Receipts and Payment account for 12 months ended 31 October 19-3

Note No	Receipts	Cash £	Bank £	Note No	Payments	Cash £	Bank £
	Balance b/d	73	—		Balance b/d	—	105
	Membership fees:			(4)	Insurance premiums		
(1)	entrance	80	170		paid to brokers		580
(1)	annual subs	215	4,465	(7)	Payments to suppliers of		
(2)	life membership		530		sporting requisites		5,270
(3)	Training ground fees	454	7,206	(5)	Wages of groundsman		3,600
	Insurance:			(8)	Postage and telephones		692
(4)	premiums		638	(9)	Stationery		629
(4)	commissions		53		Worldwide Athletics		
(11)	Interest received				Club affiliation fee		50
	from investments		626	(10)	Rates of training ground		846
(12)	Sale of office furniture		370		Upkeep of training		
(6)	Sale of sporting requisites		8,774		ground		1,200
					Transfers to bank	700	
	Advertising revenue		603	(11)	Purchases of investments		5,600
	Transfers from cash		700	(11)	Short term deposits		3,000
					Balances c/d	122	2,563
		822	24,135			822	24,135
	Balances c/d	122	2,563				

After you had perused the above account, Guy Rowppe explained the numbered items as follows:

(1)   On admittance to membersip of the club, new members pay an initial entrance fee together with their annual subscription. At 31 October 19-2, annual subscriptions of £70 had been paid in advance and £180 was owing but unpaid; of this latter amount, £40 related to members who left during the current year and is now no longer recoverable. The figures at 31 October 19-3 are £100 subscriptions in advance and £230

275

subscriptions in arrear. The policy of the club is to take credit for subscriptions when due and write off irrecoverable amounts as they arise.

(2) As an alternative to paying annual subscriptions, members at any time can opt to pay a lump sum which gives them membership for life without further payment. Amounts so received are held in suspense in a Life Membership Fund account and then credited to income and expenditure account in equal instalments over 10 years; the first such transfer takes place in the year in which the lump sum is received. On 31 October 19-2 the credit balance on the life membership fund account was £4,720 of which £850 was credited as income for year ended 31 October 19-3.

(3) The club has a permanent training ground. Non-members can use the facilities on payment of a fee. In order to guarantee a particular facility, advance booking is allowed. Advance booking fees received before 31 October 19-3 in respect of 19-4 total £470. The corresponding amount paid up to 31 October 19-2 in advance of 19-3 was £325. Members can use the facilities free of charge.

(4) Club members can take out insurances through the club at advantageous rates. Initially, premiums are paid by members to the club. Subsequently, the club pays the premium to an insurance broker and receives commission. At 31 October 19-2 premiums received but not yet paid over to the broker amounted to £102 and commissions due but not yet received were £11. The corresponding amounts at 31 October 19-3 are £160 and £13 respectively.

(5) The groundsman is employed for the six months, April to September, only. He is then paid a retaining fee to secure his services the following year. At 31 October 19-2 the groundsman had been paid a retainer (£250) for 19-3. Included in the wages figure (£3,600) is the retainer (£300) for 19-4.

(6) Sporting requisites are sold only on cash terms. There are therefore no debtors for these items.

(7) On 31 October 19-2 sums owed to suppliers of sporting requisites totalled £163; the corresponding figure on 31 October 19-3 was £202.

Stock of unsold sporting requisites on 31 October 19-2 was £811 and on 31 October 19-3 was £927. In arriving at this latter figure the sum of £137, representing damaged and unsaleable stock at cost price, had been excluded.

(8) Postage stamps unused at 31 October 19-3, totalled £4.

(9) Stock of stationery on 31 October 19-2 and 19-3 was £55 and £36 respectively.

(10) Rates are payable to the District Council in two instalments (in advance) each year. £360 had been paid on 1 October 19-2, £390 on 1 April 19-3 and £456 on 1 October 19-3.

(11) The club receives interest on investments bought a number of years ago at a cost of £7,400 (current valuation £7,550). At the end of October 19-3, the club had acquired further investments which cost £5,600 (current valuation £5,600) and at the same time placed £3,000 in a short term deposit account.

(12) The written down value of the furniture which had been sold during the year was £350; it had originally cost £800.

Other matters:

Initially, the training ground had been acquired freehold from a farmer at an inclusive cost of £4,000. Subsequently, the club had some timber buildings erected to provide various facilities for members. The total cost of these buildings was £35,000; depreciation is calculated at the rate of 10% per annum on a straight line basis. At 31 October 19-2, the provision for depreciation account had a balance of £9,400.

At 31 October 19-2, the furniture and equipment etc was recorded in the club's books as £7,900 (cost) against which there was a provision for depreciation of £4,150 (calculated on the same basis as for buildings). Apart from the disposal referred to in note (12) (above) there had been no other disposals or acquisitions during the year.

You are required to:

Prepare the club's income and expenditure account for year ended 31 October 19-3 and the balance sheet at that date.

All workings must be shown.

(*Chartered Association of Certified Accountants*)

33

Manufacturing accounts

The final accounts prepared so far have all been for firms whose function is limited to that of merchandising, i.e. the buying and selling of goods. Obviously there are many firms whose main activity is in the manufacture of goods for sale. For these firms a **Manufacturing Account** is prepared in addition to the trading and profit and loss accounts.

Because the costs in the manufacturing account are involved with production there is an obvious link with the costing records, and the concepts of the manufacturing account are in fact really costing concepts. It will therefore be necessary to first of all examine the main elements and divisions of cost as used in costing. These may be summarised in chart form as follows:

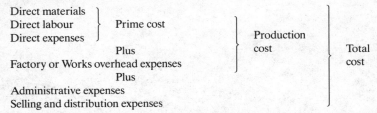

By 'direct' is meant that the materials, labour and expenses involved are traceable to the particular unit of goods being made, and that the trouble and labour involved in doing this are worthwhile. Labour such as that of a lathe operator will be direct labour, whereas that of a foreman who supervises many jobs cannot easily be traced down to each particular unit being produced and will accordingly be classified as indirect labour, forming part of the factory overhead expenses. The cost of direct materials will include the cost of carriage inwards on raw materials. Examples of direct expenses are the hire of special plant for a particular job, and royalties payable to inventors for use of a patent where a charge is levied on each unit produced.

Factory overhead expenses consist of all those expenses which occur in the factory where production is carried on, but which cannot easily be traced to the units being manufactured. Examples are wages of cleaners and crane drivers, rent and rates of the factory, depreciation of plant and machinery used in the factory, running of fork-lift trucks, factory power and lighting and heating.

Administration expenses consist of such items as managers' salaries, legal and accountancy charges, the depreciation of accounting machinery and secretarial salaries.

Selling and distribution expenses are items such as salesmen's salaries and commission, carriage outwards, depreciation of delivery vans, advertising and display expenses.

In the manufacturing account the production cost of goods completed during the accounting period is ascertained. This means that all the elements of production cost, i.e. direct materials, direct labour, direct expenses and factory overhead expenses, are charged to the manufacturing account. All administration and selling and distribution expenses are charged to the profit and loss account. Note that the manufacturing account is concerned with the production cost of goods completed in the year irrespective of when work started on them. For this reason goods partly finished, known as work in progress, must be taken into account.

The necessary details required to draw up a manufacturing account can now be looked at. In the first example, Exhibit 33.1, it has been assumed that there was no work in progress, either at the beginning or end of the accounting period.

Exhibit 33.1

Details of production cost for the year ended 31 December 19-7:

	£
1 January 19-7, stock of raw materials	500
31 December 19-7, stock of raw materials	700
Raw materials purchased	8,000
Manufacturing (direct) wages	21,000
Royalties	150
Indirect wages	9,000
Rent of Factory – excluding administration and selling and distribution blocks	440
Depreciation of plant and machinery in factory	400
General indirect expenses	310

The production cost of goods completed, when ascertained, is carried down to the trading account, taking the place where normally purchases are shown. As this is a manufacturing concern selling its own products there will not usually be a figure for the purchase of finished goods. Sometimes, however, if a firm has produced less than the customers have demanded, then the firm may well have bought an outside supply of finished goods. In this case, the trading account will have both a figure for purchases and for production cost of goods completed.

	£	£
Stock of raw materials 1.1.19-7		500
add Purchases		8,000
		8,500
less Stock of raw materials 31.12.19-7		700
Cost of raw materials consumed		7,800
Manufacturing wages		21,000
Royalties		150
Prime cost		28,950
Factory overhead expenses		
Rent	440	
Indirect wages	9,000	
General expenses	310	
Depreciation of plant and machinery	400	10,150
Production cost of goods completed c/d		39,100

When there is work in progress, i.e. goods only part completed at the beginning and end of an accounting period an adjustment is needed. To find the production cost of goods completed in the period the value of work in progress at the beginning must be brought into account as it will be work (provided it is not a job such as building a ship which will take more than a year) which is completed within the accounting period. On the other hand, work in progress at the end of the period must be carried forward to the next period, as it is completed within the next period. To do this, the value of work in progress at the beginning is added to the total production cost for the period, and the closing work in progress is deducted. An example is shown in Exhibit 33.2.

Exhibit 33.2

	£
1 January 19-7, Stock of raw materials	800
31 December 19-7, Stock of raw materials	1,050
1 January 19-7, Work in progress	350
31 December 19-7, Work in progress	420
Year to 31 December 19-7:	
Wages: Direct	3,960
Indirect	2,550
Purchase of raw materials	8,700
Fuel and power	990
Direct expenses	140
Lubricants	300
Carriage inwards on raw materials	200
Rent of factory	720
Depreciation of factory plant and machinery	420
Internal transport expenses	180
Insurance of factory buildings and plant	150
General factory expenses	330

	£	£
Stock of raw materials 1.1.19-7		800
add Purchases		8,700
,, Carriage inwards		200
		9,700
less Stock of raw materials 31.12.19-7		1,050
Cost of raw materials consumed		8,650
Direct wages		3,960
Direct expenses		140
Prime cost		12,750
Factory overhead expenses:		
Fuel and power	990	
Indirect wages	2,550	
Lubricants	300	
Rent	720	
Depreciation of plant	420	
Internal transport expenses	180	
Insurance	150	
General factory expenses	330	5,640
		18,390
add Work in progress 1.1.19-7		350
		18,740
less Work in progress 31.12.19-7		420
Production cost of goods completed c/d		18,320

The trading account is concerned with finished goods. If in the foregoing exhibit there had been £3,500 stock of finished goods at 1 January 19-7 and £4,400 at 31 December 19-7, and the sales of finished goods amounted to £25,000, then the trading account would appear:

Trading Account for the year 31 December 19-7

	£	£
Sales		25,000
less Cost of Goods Sold:		
Stock of finished goods 1.1.19-7	3,500	
add Production cost of goods completed b/d	18,320	
	21,820	
less Stock of finished goods 31.12.19-7	4,400	17,420
Gross Profit c/d		7,580

The profit and loss account is then constructed in the normal way.

A complete worked example is now given. Note that in the profit and loss account the expenses have been separated so as to show whether they are administration expenses, selling and distribution expenses, or financial charges.

The trial balance Exhibit 33.3 has been extracted from the books of J Jarvis, Toy Manufacturer, as on 31 December 19-7:

Exhibit 33.3

J Jarvis
Trial balance as on 31 December 19-7

	Dr	Cr
	£	£
Stock of raw materials 1.1.19-7	2,100	
Stock of finished goods 1.1.19-7	3,890	
Work in progress 1.1.19-7	1,350	
Wages (direct £18,000; Factory indirect £14,500)	32,500	
Royalties	700	
Carriage inwards (on raw materials)	350	
Purchases of raw materials	37,000	
Productive machinery (cost £28,000)	23,000	
Accounting machinery (cost £2,000)	1,200	
General factory expenses	3,100	
Lighting	750	
Factory power	1,370	
Administrative salaries	4,400	
Salesmen's salaries	3,000	
Commission on sales	1,150	
Rent	1,200	
Insurance	420	
General administration expenses	1,340	
Bank charges	230	
Discounts allowed	480	
Carriage outwards	590	
Sales		100,000
Debtors and creditors	14,230	12,500
Bank	5,680	
Cash	150	
Drawings	2,000	
Capital as at 1.1.19-7		29,680
	142,180	142,180

Notes at 31.13.19-7:

1 Stock of raw materials 2,400, stock of finished goods £4,000, work in progress £1,500.

2 Lighting, and rent and insurance are to be apportioned: factory 5/6ths, administration 1/6th.

3 Depreciation on productive and accounting machinery at 10 per cent per annum on cost.

**Manufacturing, Trading and Profit and Loss Account for the year ended
31 December 19-7**

	£	£	£
Stock of raw materials 1.1.19-7			2,100
add Purchases			37,000
,, Carriage inwards			350
			39,450
less Stock raw materials 31.12.19-7			2,400
Cost of raw materials consumed			37,050
Direct labour			18,000
Royalties			700
Prime cost			55,750
Factory Overhead Expenses:			
General factory expenses		3,100	
Lighting 5/6ths		625	
Power		1,370	
Rent 5/6ths		1,000	
Insurance 5/6ths		350	
Depreciation of plant		2,800	
Indirect labour		14,500	23,745
			79,495
add Work in progress 1.1.19-7			1,350
			80,845
less Work in progress 31.12.19-7			1,500
Production cost of goods completed c/d			79,345
Sales			100,000
less Cost of goods sold:			
Stock of finished goods 1.1.19-7		3,890	
add Production cost of goods completed		79,345	
		83,235	
less Stock of finished goods 31.12.19-7		4,000	79,235
Gross Profit			20,765
Administration Expenses			
Administrative salaries	4,400		
Rent 1/6th	200		
Insurance 1/6th	70		
General expenses	1,340		
Lighting 1/6th	125		
Depreciation of accounting machinery	200	6,335	
Selling and Distribution Expenses			
Salesmen's salaries	3,000		
Commission on sales	1,150		
Carriage outwards	590	4,740	
Financial Charges			
Bank charges	230		
Discounts allowed	480	710	11,785
Net Profit			8,980

J Jarvis
Balance Sheet as at 31 December 19-7

	£	£
Fixed Assets		
Productive Machinery at cost	28,000	
less Depreciation to date	7,800	20,200
Accounting Machinery at cost	2,000	
less Depreciation to date	1,000	1,000
		21,200
Current Assets		
Stock		
Raw Materials	2,400	
Finished Goods	4,000	
Work in Progress	1,500	
Debtors	14,230	
Bank	5,680	
Cash	150	
	27,960	
less Current Liabilities		
Creditors	12,500	
Working Capital		15,460
		36,660
Financed by		
Capital		
Balance as at 1.1.19-7		29,680
add Net Profit		8,980
		38,660
less Drawings		2,000
		36,660

Market value of goods manufactured

The accounts of Jarvis, just illustrated, are subject to the limitation that the respective amounts of the gross profit which are attributable to the manufacturing side or to the selling side of the firm are not known. A technique is sometimes used to bring out this additional information. By this method the cost which would have been involved if the goods had been bought in their finished state instead of being manufactured by the firm is brought into account. This is credited to the manufacturing account and debited to the trading account so as to throw up two figures of gross profit instead of one. It should be pointed out that the net profit will remain unaffected. All that will have happened will be that the figure of £20,765 gross profit will be shown as two figures instead of one.

The accounts in summarised form will appear:

Manufacturing, Trading and Profit and Loss Account for the year ended
31 December 19-7

	£	£
Market value of goods completed c/d		95,000
less Production cost of goods completed (as before)		79,345
Gross profit on manufacture c/d		15,655
Sales		100,000
Stock of finished goods 1.1.19-7	3,890	
add Market value of goods completed b/d	95,000	
	98,890	
less Stock of finished goods 31.12.19-7	4,000	94,890
Gross profit on trading c/d		5,110
Gross profit		
On manufacturing	15,655	
On trading	5,110	20,765

Further methods of providing for depreciation

Earlier in this volume the straight-line and reducing balance methods of making provisions for depreciation were discussed in detail. This chapter is concerned with some further methods of making provisions for depreciation. It must not be thought that this chapter will complete an examination of all the different methods in use. It is quite possible to devise one's own method of providing for depreciation. If it stands up to the test of common sense and does not distort the reported trading results of the firm, then the specially devised method will often be more applicable than those commonly used. There is therefore no limit to the number of different depreciation provision methods.

This chapter deals in some detail with the revaluation method. Some other methods are discussed in outline only. There is no information easily available of the number of firms using particular depreciation methods.

The revaluation method

There are some fixed assets for which it is inappropriate, or not worthwhile, to calculate depreciation provisions in a formal way, whereby each asset has to be identifiable and accurate records kept of its location and adjusting entries made when the asset is put out of use by the firm. Examples of these assets are loose tools such as spanners, screwdrivers, small drills, etc., in an engineering works, or barrels, bottles and crates in a brewery. A fixed asset such as a spanner or a barrel may be capable of a long life but its use may well be short-lived. Some will be lost, others stolen, some broken or damaged through ill-use, and all of these facts will not be reported to management. Even if an accounting system could be devised to throw up such wastage of assets the operation of the system could well, except in a few instances, cost more than the saving to be gained from it. A spanner costing less than £1 and which is used infrequently, could well last for seven years. If the straight-line or reducing balance methods were in use, then theoretically a calculation would have to be made of the over-depreciation or under-depreciation provided on the asset when it is put out of use and an adjusting entry made to correct the accounts. With such an asset it is clearly not worthwhile to make accounting entries in such a fashion. In addition some firms may well make their own tools, etc., and it might be difficult and costly to keep elaborate records for each small tool made.

To provide a solution at a reasonable cost the revaluation method of calculating depreciation provisions is used. The method used is simply that the assets are valued at the start of the period, the additions increase the value and then the assets are revalued at the end of the period. The amount of the decrease in value shows the amount by which the asset is deemed to have depreciated. This is now illustrated in Exhibit 33.4 by reference to a firm which uses metal crates.

Exhibit 33.4

The firm starts in business on 1 January 19-6.

	£
In its first year it buys crates costing	800
Their estimated value at 31 December 19-6	540
Crates bought in the year ended 31 December 19-7	320
Estimated value of all crates in hand on 31 December 19-7	530
Crates bought in the year ended 31 December 19-8	590
Estimated value of all crates in hand on 31 December 19-8	700

Crates

19-6		£	19-6		£
Dec 31	Cash (during the year)	800	Dec 31	Profit and Loss	260
			,, 31	Stock c/d	540
		800			800
19-7		£	19-7		£
Jan 1	Stock b/d	540	Dec 31	Profit and Loss	330
Dec 31	Cash (during the year)	320	,, 31	Stock c/d	530
		860			860
19-8			19-8		
Jan 1	Stock b/d	530	Dec 31	Profit and Loss	420
Dec 31	Cash (during the year)	590	,, 31	Stock c/d	700
		1,120			1,120
19-9					
Jan 1	Stock b/d	700			

Profit and Loss Account for the year ended 31 December

		£
19-6	Use of crates	260
19-7	Use of crates	330
19-8	Use of crates	420

The balance of the Crates Account at the end of each year is shown as a fixed asset in the Balance Sheet.

In an engineering firm the cost of wages and materials used in making loose tools may or may not be known. If it is known, the cost should be charged to the Loose Tools Account. If not known, the Loose Tools Account cannot be charged with the cost of such additions, and may well appear to reveal an appreciation in the value of tools rather than depreciation. The appreciation would be transferred to the credit of the Manufacturing Account (or shown as a deduction on the debit side). The different treatment makes no difference to the calculated profit as can now be shown in Exhibit 33.5.

Exhibit 33.5

	£
At 1 January 19-7 loose tools valued at	800
During the year the cost of all raw materials used in the factory amounted to	10,000
The cost of all wages in the factory was	20,000
At 31 December 19-7 the loose tools are valued at	1,000

However, in the Loose Tools Account and Manufacturing Account shown as (A) it is known that materials £300 and wages £400 have been used in making loose tools, while in the accounts lettered (B) this information is not known.

Loose Tools (A)

19-7		£	19-7		£
Jan 1	Stock b/d	800	Dec 31 Manufacturing Account		500
Dec 31	Transfer from wages	400	Dec 31 Stock c/d		1,000
,, 31	Transfer from Materials	300			
		1,500			1,500
19-8					
Jan 1	Stock b/d	1,000			

Manufacturing Account (A) for the year ended 31 December 19-7

	£
Materials (i.e. *less* transfer £300)	9,700
Wages (i.e. *less* transfer £400)	19,600
Use of Loose Tools	500

The total effective debits are therefore £19,600 + £9,000 + £500 = £29,800

Loose Tools (B)

19-7		£	19-7		£
Jan 1	Stock b/d	800	Dec 31 Stock c/d		1,000
Dec 31	Manufacturing Account	200			
		1,000			1,000
19-8					
Jan 1	Stock b/d	1,000			

Manufacturing Account (B) for the year ended 31 December 19-7

	£		£
Materials	10,000	Increase in the value of loose tools	200
Wages	20,000		

The total of effective debits is £10,000 + £20,000 − £200 = £29,800.

In both cases (A) and (B) the Balance Sheet on 31 December 19-7, will show a fixed asset of Loose Tools £1,000.

Some firms show the stock of such assets in the same way as the stock of goods or raw materials. Given the information in Exhibit 33.5 it would appear as Manufacturing Account (C) which now follows.

Manufacturing Account (C) for the year ended 31 December 19-7

	£
Materials	10,000
Wages	20,000
add Stock of Loose Tools on 1 January 19-7	800
	30,800
less Stock of Loose Tools on 31 December 19-7	1,000
	29,800

Here again the total effective debits amount to £29,800.

Manufacturing Account (A) gives the most useful information as it shows the cost of using tools during 19-7. In the other Manufacturing Accounts all that is known is that the estimated value of loose tools has risen by £200. This by itself is a relatively meaningless piece of information. Suppose that it was possible to hire loose tools instead of owning them, and that this could be done at a cost of £300 per year. Manufacturing Account (A) would show that tool hire would be the cheaper method, assuming that the experience in 19-7 was typical. The other Manufacturing Accounts would not reveal this figure for comparison. However, like most accounting statements it is only one measure to be taken into account when making a business decision. Other factors may well be:

(*a*) What will the reactions of the firm's own toolmakers and of their trade unions?

(*b*) Could our own tools cost less if our methods were changed?

(*c*) How long will it take to renew any tool when required?

(*d*) What provision are made for normal replacements?

(*e*) Would it make the firm too dependent on the firm of tool hirers?

The **value** to be carried forward is in fact the reappraised figure of the costs which should be carried forward to the following period. The 'value' is thus the **unapportioned cost value**. Expediency and custom will play a large part in any such valuation. It would be quite ludicrous for a firm with several thousand barrels of the same size to have any sort of scientific appraisal of every barrel at the end of each financial period with the object of placing a valuation on it. It would more likely be found that the number of barrels would be counted in some way and then multiplied by the amount which the management considered reflected the average value of all the barrels.

The cattle belonging to a farmer is one of his fixed assets. Like all other fixed assets depreciation should be provided for, but during the early life of an animal it will probably be appreciating in value only to depreciate later. The task of calculating the cost of an animal becomes almost impossible if it has been born on the farm, reared on the farm by grazing on the pasture land and from other foodstuffs, some grown by the farmer and others bought by him. Expediency therefore takes over and the revaluation method is used, the livestock being brought into account in the same way as stocks of goods. The cost factor being such an elusive one for many animals has led to the general practice being observed of valuing livestock at the price that the animals would fetch if sold at market. This therefore is an exception to the general rule regarding assets being shown at cost price.

Depletion unit method

With fixed assets such as mines or quarries the depreciation is often based on the quantity of raw materials extracted compared with the estimated total quantity available. For instance, if a firm bought for £5,000 a small mine which had an expected capacity of 1,000 tons of ore, then for each ton extracted during the accounting period the firm would provide for depreciation of the asset by £5 (expected average depreciation cost per ton).

Machine hour method

With a machine the depreciation provision may be based on the number of hours that the machine was operated during the period compared with the total expected running hours during the machine's life with the firm. A firm which bought a machine costing £2,000 having an expected running life of 1,000 hours, and no scrap value, could provide for depreciation of the machine at the rate of £2 for every hour it was operated during a particular accounting period.

Sum of the years' digits

This method is popular in the USA but not common in the UK. It provides for higher depreciation to be charged early in the life of an asset with lower depreciation in later years.

Given an asset costing £3,000 which will be in use for 5 years, the calculations will be:

From purchase the asset will last for	5 years
From the second year the asset will last for	4 years
From the third year the asset will last for	3 years
From the fourth year the asset will last for	2 years
From the fifth year the asset will last for	1 year
Sum of these digits	15

	£
1st Year of 5/15ths of £3,000 is charged =	1,000
2nd Year of 4/15ths of £3,000 is charged =	800
3rd Year of 3/15ths of £3,000 is charged =	600
4th Year of 2/15ths of £3,000 is charged =	400
5th Year of 1/15th of £3,000 is charged =	200
	3,000

Review questions

33.1 A firm both buys loose tools and also make some itself. The following data is available concerning the years ended 31 December 19-4, 19-5, and 19-6.

		£
19-4		
Jan 1	Stock of Loose Tools	1,250
	During the year:	
	Bought loose tools from suppliers	2,000
	Made own loose tools: the cost of wages of employees being £275 and the materials cost £169	
Dec 31	Loose Tools valued at	2,700
19-5		
	During the year	
	Loose tools bought from suppliers	1,450
	Made own loose tools: the cost of wages of employees being £495 and the materials cost £390	
Dec 31	Loose Tools valued at	3,340
19-6		
	During the year:	
	Loose tools bought from suppliers	1,890
	Made own loose tools: the cost of wages of employees being £145 and the	88
	materials cost £290. Received refund from a supplier for faulty tools returned to him	
Dec 31	Loose Tools valued at	3,680

You are to draw up the Loose Tools Account for the three years, showing the amount transfered as an expense in each year to the Manufacturing Account.

33.2A A firm both buys tools and makes them for itself. The following information is available to you for the year ended 31 December 19-5, 19-6 and 19- 7.

		£
19-5		
Jan 1	Stock of Tools	3,890
	Bought during the year 19-5	1,570
	Own Tools made: Cost of wages	705
	Cost of materials	500
Dec 31	Tools valued at	5,020
19-6		
	During the year:	
	Bought during 19-6	1,990
	Own Tools made: Cost of Wages	908
	Cost of materials	486
Dec 31	Tools valued at	4,950
19-7		
	During the year:	
	Bought during 19-7	3,665
	Own Tools made: Cost of wages	1,290
	Cost of materials	880
Dec 31	Tools valued at	6,868

Write up the Tools Account for the three years, showing the figure transferred each year to the Manufacturing Account.

33.3 On 1 April 19-6 a business purchased a machine costing £112,000. The machine can be used for a total of 20,000 hours over an estimated life of 48 months. At the end of that time the machine is expected to have a trade-in value of £12,000.

The financial year of the business ends on the 31 December each year. It is expected that the machine will be used for:

4,000 hours during the financial year ending 31 December 19-6
5,000 hours during the financial year ending 31 December 19-7
5,000 hours during the financial year ending 31 December 19-8
5,000 hours during the financial year ending 31 December 19-9
1,000 hours during the financial year ending 31 December 19-0

Required

(*a*) Calculate the annual depreciation charges on the machine on each of the following bases for each of the financial years ending on the 31 December 19-6, 19-7, 19-8, 19-9 and 19-0:

(*i*) the straight-line method applied on a month for month basis,

(*ii*) the diminishing balance method at 40% per annum applied on a full year basis, and

(*iii*) the units of output method.

(*b*) Suppose that during the financial year ended 31 December 19-7 the machine was used for only 1,500 hours before being sold for £80,000 on the 30 June.

Assuming that the business has chosen to apply the straight-line method on a month for month basis show the following accounts for 19-7 only:

(*i*) the Machine Account,

(*ii*) the Provision for Depreciation – Machine Account, and

(*iii*) the Assets Disposals Account.

(*Association of Accounting Technicians*)

33.4A On 1 January 19-1 a business purchased a laser printer costing £1,800. The printer has an estimated life of 4 years after which it will have no residual value.

It is expected that the output from the printer will be:

Year	Sheets printed
19-1	35,000
19-2	45,000
19-3	45,000
19-4	55,000
	180,000

Required:

(*a*) Calculate the annual depreciation charges for 19-1, 19-2, 19-3 and 19-4 on the laser printer on the following bases:

(*i*) the straight-line basis,

(*ii*) the diminishing balance method at 60% per annum, and

(*iii*) the units of output method.

Note: Your workings should be to the nearest £.

(*b*) Suppose that in 19-4 the laser printer were to be sold on 1 July for £200 and that the business had chosen to depreciate it at 60% per annum using the diminishing balance method applied on a month for month basis.

Reconstruct the following accounts for 19-4 only:

(*i*) the Laser Printer account,

(*ii*) the Provision for Depreciation – Laser Printer account, and

(*iii*) the Assets Disposals account.

(*Association of Accounting Technicians*)

33.5 Prepare Manufacturing, Trading and Profit and Loss Accounts from the following balances of T Jackson for the year ended 31 December 19-7.

	£
Stocks at 1 January 19-7:	
Raw Materials	18,450
Work in Progress	23,600
Finished Goods	17,470
Purchases: Raw Materials	64,300
Carriage on Raw Materials	1,605
Direct Labour	65,810
Office Salaries	16,920
Rent	2,700
Office Lighting and Heating	5,760
Depreciation: Works Machinery	8,300
Office Equipment	1,950
Sales	200,600
Factory Fuel & Power	5,920

Rent is to be apportioned: Factory ⅔rds; Office ⅓. Stocks at 31 December 19-7 were: Raw Materials £20,210, Work in Progress £17,390, Finished Goods £21,485.

33.6 D Saunders is a manufacturer. His trial balance at 31 December 19-6 is as follows.

	£	£
Delivery Van Expenses	2,500	
Lighting and Heating: Factory	2,859	
Office	1,110	
Manufacturing Wages	45,470	
General Expenses: Office	3,816	
Factory	5,640	
Salesmen: Commission	7,860	
Purchase of Raw Materials	39,054	
Rent: Factory	4,800	
Office	2,200	
Machinery (cost £50,000)	32,500	
Office Equipment (cost £15,000)	11,000	
Office Salaries	6,285	
Debtors	28,370	
Creditors		19,450
Bank	13,337	
Sales		136,500
Premises (Cost £50,000)	40,000	
Stocks at 31 December 19-5:		
Raw Materials	8,565	
Finished Goods	29,480	
Drawings	8,560	
Capital		137,456
	293,406	293,406

Prepare the Manufacturing, Trading and Profit and Loss Account for the year ended 31 December 19-6 and a Balance Sheet as at that date. Give effect to the following adjustments:

(a) Stocks at 31 December 19-6, Raw Materials £9,050, Finished Goods £31,200. There is no Work in Progress.

(b) Depreciate Machinery £2,000, Office Equipment £1,500, Premises £1,000.

(c) Manufacturing Wages due but unpaid at 31 December 19-6 £305, Office Rent prepaid £108.

33.7A The following list of balances as at 31 July 19-6 has been extracted from the books of Jane Seymour who commenced business on 1 August 19-5 as a designer and manufacturer of kitchen furniture:

	£
Plant and machinery, at cost on 1 August 19-5	60,000
Motor vehicles, at cost on 1 August 19-5	30,000
Loose tools, at cost	9,000
Sales	170,000
Raw materials purchased	43,000
Direct factory wages	39,000
Light and power	5,000
Indirect factory wages	8,000
Machinery repairs	1,600
Motor vehicle running expenses	12,000
Rent and insurances	11,600
Administrative staff salaries	31,000
Administrative expenses	9,000
Sales and distribution staff salaries	13,000
Capital at 1 August 19-5	122,000
Sundry debtors	16,500
Sundry creditors	11,200
Balance at bank	8,500
Drawings	6,000

Additional information for the year ended 31 July 19-6:

(i) It is estimated that the plant and machinery will be used in the business for 10 years and the motor vehicles used for 4 years: in both cases it is estimated that the residual value will be nil. The straight-line method of providing for depreciation is to be used.

(ii) Light and power charges accrued due at 31 July 19-6 amounted to £1,000 and insurances prepaid at 31 July 19-6 totalled £800.

(iii) Stocks were valued at cost at 31 July 19-6 as follows:

Raw materials	£7,000
Finished goods	£10,000

(iv) The valuation of work in progress at 31 July 19-6 included variable and fixed factory overheads and amounted to £12,300.

(v) Two thirds of the light and power and rent and insurances costs are to be allocated to the factory costs and one third to general administration costs.

(vi) Motor vehicle costs are to be allocated equally to factory costs and general administration costs.

(vii) Goods manufactured during the year are to be transferred to the trading account at £95,000.

(viii) Loose tools in hand on 31 July 19-6 were valued at £5,000.

Required

(a) Prepare a manufacturing, trading and profit and loss account for the year ended 31 July 19-6 of Jane Seymour.

(b) An explanation of how each of the following accounting concepts have affected the preparation of the above accounts:

- conservatism,
- matching,
- going concern.

(*Association of Accounting Technicians*)

33.8A The following balances as at 31 December 19-5 have been extracted from the books of William Speed, a small manufacturer:

	£
Stocks at 1 January 19-5: Raw Materials	7,000
Work in progress	5,000
Finished goods	6,900
Purchases of raw materials	38,000
Direct labour	28,000
Factory overheads: Variable	16,000
Fixed	9,000
Administrative expenses: Rent and rates	19,000
Heat and light	6,000
Stationery and postages	2,000
Staff Salaries	19,380
Sales	192,000
Plant and machinery: At cost	30,000
Provision for depreciation	12,000
Motor vehicles (for sales deliveries):	
At cost	16,000
Provision for depreciation	4,000
Creditors	5,500
Debtors	28,000
Drawings	11,500
Balance at Bank	16,600
Capital at 1 January 19-5	48,000
Provision for unrealised profit at 1 January 19-5	1,380
Motor vehicle running costs	4,500

Additional information:

(*i*) Stocks at 31 December 19-5 were as follows:

	£
Raw materials	9,000
Work in progress	8,000
Finished goods	10,350

(*ii*) The factory output is transferred to the trading account at factory cost plus 25% for factory profit. The finished goods stock is valued on the basis of amounts transferred to the debit of the trading account.

(*iii*) Depreciation is provided annually at the following percentages of the original cost of fixed assets held at the end of each financial year:

Plant and machinery	10%
Motor vehicles	25%

(*iv*) Amounts accrued due at 31 December 19-5 for direct labour amounted to £3,000 and rent and rates prepaid at 31 December 19-5 amounted to £2,000.

Required

Prepare a manufacturing, trading and profit and loss account for the year ended 31 December 19-5 and a balance sheet as at that date.

Note: The prime cost and total factory cost should be clearly shown.

(*Association of Accounting Technicians*)

34

Departmental accounts

Accounting information varies in its usefulness. For a retail store with five departments, it is obviously better to know that the store has made £10,000 gross profit than to be completely ignorant of this fact. The figure of £10,000 gross profit unfortunately does not give the owners the insight into the business necessary to control it much more effectively. What would be far more meaningful would be the knowledge of the amount of gross profit or loss for each department. Assume that the gross profits and losses for the department were as follows:

Department	Gross profit	Gross loss
	£	£
A	4,000	
B	3,000	
C	5,000	
D		8,000
E	6,000	
	18,000	8,000

Gross profit of the firm, £10,000

Ignoring the overhead expenses for the sake of simplicity, although in practice they should never be ignored, can any conclusions be drawn from the above? It may well appear that if department D was closed down then the store would make £18,000 gross profit instead of £10,000. This could equally well be true or false depending on circumstances. Department D may be deliberately run at a loss so that its cheap selling prices may attract customers who, when they come to the store, also buy goods in addition from departments A, B, C and E. If department D were closed down perhaps most of the customers would not come to the store at all. In this case all the other departments would only have small gross profits because of the falls in sales and if this happened the gross profits might well be – departments: A £1,000, B £500, C £2,500 and E £2,000, a total of £6,000. Therefore department D operating at a loss because of cheap prices would have increased the gross profit of the firm.

The converse could, however, hold true. If department D were closed down the sales in the other departments might rise. Department D could be a wine and spirits department at the entrance to the store through which all customers have to walk to the other departments. Teetotallers may therefore avoid the store because they would not like to be seen going into a department where alcohol was being sold. To close down the department, leaving it merely as an access route to the other departments, may result in higher sales in these other departments because the teetotallers who had previously shunned the store might now become customers. The effect on the existing non-teetotal customers could also be considered as well as the possibility of the relocation of the wine and spirits department.

Accounting information therefore seldom tells all the story. It serves as one measure, but there are other non-accounting factors to be considered before a relevant decision for action can be made.

The various pros and cons of the actions to be taken to increase the overall profitability of the business cannot therefore be efficiently considered until the departmental gross profits or losses are known. It must not be thought that departmental accounts refer only to departmental stores. They refer to the various facets of a business. Consider the simple case of a barber who does shaving and haircutting. He may find that the profit from shaving is very small, and that if he discontinues shaving he will earn more from extra haircutting because he does not have to turn customers away because of lack of time. The principle of departmental accounts is concerned just as much with the small barber's shop as with a large department store. The reputation of many a successful businessman has been built up on his ability to utilise the departmental account principle to guide his actions to increase the profitability of a firm. The lesson still has to be learned by many medium-sized and small firms. It is one of accounting's greatest, and simplest, aids to business efficiency.

Expenses

The expenses of the firm are often split between the various departments, and the net profit for each department then calculated. Each expense is divided between the departments on what is considered to be the most logical basis. This will differ considerably between businesses. An example of a Trading and Profit and Loss Account drawn up in such a manner is shown in Exhibit 34.1.

Exhibit 34.1

Northern Stores have three departments in their store:

	(a) Jewellery	(b) Ladies hairdressing	(c) Clothing
	£	£	£
Stock of goods or materials, 1 January 19-8	2,000	1,500	3,000
Purchases	11,000	3,000	15,000
Stock of goods or materials, 31 December 19-8	3,000	2,500	4,000
Sales and work done	18,000	9,000	27,000
Wages of assistants in each department	2,800	5,000	6,000

The following expenses cannot be traced to any particular department:

	£
Rent	3,500
Administration expenses	4,800
Air conditioning and lighting	2,000
General expenses	1,200

It is decided to apportion rent together with air conditioning and lighting in accordance with the floor space occupied by each department. These were taken up in the ratios of (*a*) one-fifth, (*b*) half, (*c*) three-tenths. Administration expenses and general expenses are to be split in the ratio of sales and work done.

The Northern Stores
Trading and Profit and Loss Account for the year ended 31 December 19-8

	(*a*) Jewellery £	(*a*) Jewellery £	(*b*) Hairdressing £	(*b*) Hairdressing £	(*c*) Clothing £	(*c*) Clothing £
Sales and Work Done		18,000		9,000		27,000
Cost of Goods or Materials:						
Stock 1.1.19-8	2,000		1,500		3,000	
add Purchases	11,000		3,000		15,000	
	13,000		4,500		18,000	
less Stock 31.12.19-8	3,000	10,000	2,500	2,000	4,000	14,000
Gross Profit		8,000		7,000		13,000
less Expenses:						
Wages	2,800		5,000		6,000	
Rent	700		1,750		1,050	
Administration expenses	1,600		800		2,400	
Air conditioning and lighting	400		1,000		600	
General expenses	400	5,900	200	8,750	600	10,650
Net Profit/Loss		2,100		(1,750)		2,350

This way of calculating net profits and losses seems to imply a precision that is lacking in fact, and would often lead to an interpretation that the hairdressing department has lost £1,750 this year, and that this amount would be saved if the department was closed down. It has already been stated that different departments are very often dependent on one another, therefore it will be realised that this would not necessarily be the case. The calculation of net profits and losses are also dependent on arbitrary division of overhead expenses. It is by no means obvious that the overheads of department (*b*) would be avoided if it were closed down. Assuming that the sales staff of the department could be discharged without compensation, then £5,000 would be saved in wages. The other overhead expenses shown under department (*b*) would not, however, necessarily disappear. The rent may still be payable in full even though the department were closed down. The administration expenses may turn out to be only slightly down, say from £4,800 to £4,600, a saving of £200; air conditioning and lighting down to £1,500, a saving of £500; general expenses down to £1,100, a saving of £100. Therefore the department, when open, costs an additional £5,800 compared with when the department is closed. This is made up as follows:

	£
Administration expenses	200
Air conditioning and lighting	500
General expenses	100
Wages	5,000
	5,800

But when open, assuming this year is typical, the department makes £7,000 gross profit. The firm is therefore £1,200 a year better off when the department is open than when it is closed, subject to certain assumptions. These are:

(*a*)That the remaining departments would not be profitably expanded into the space vacated to give greater proportionate benefits than the hairdressing department.

(*b*) That a new type of department which would be more profitable than hairdressing could not be set up.

(*c*) That the department could not be leased to another firm at a more profitable figure than that shown by hairdressing.

There are also other factors which, though not easily seen in an accounting context, are still extremely pertinent. They are concerned with the possible loss of confidence in the firm by customers generally; what appears to be an ailing business does not usually attract good customers. Also the effect on the remaining staff should not be ignored. The fear that the dismissal of the hairdressing staff may mirror what is also going to happen to themselves may result in the loss of staff, especially the most competent members who could easily find work elsewhere, and so the general quality of the staff may decline with serious consequences for the firm.

A far less misleading method of drafting departmental accounts is by showing costs which are in the nature of direct costs allocated entirely to the department, and which would not be payable if the department was closed down, in the first section of the Trading and Profit and Loss Account. The second section is left to cover those expenses which need arbitrary apportionment or which would still be payable on the closing of the department. The surpluses brought down from the first section represent the 'contribution' that each department makes to cover the expenses and profit. The contributions can thus be seen to be the results of activities which are under a person's control, in this case the departmental managers concerned. The sales revenue has been generated by the workforce, etc., all under their control, and the costs charged have been under their control, so that the surpluses earned (or deficits incurred) are affected by the degree of their control. The other costs in the second section are not, however, under their control. The departmental managers cannot directly affect to any great extent the costs of rent or of air conditioning and lighting, so that the contributions from the sections of the business must more than cover all these expenses if the business is to earn a profit. From the figures given in Exhibit 34.1 the accounts would appear as shown in Exhibit 34.2.

Exhibit 34.2

The Northern Stores

Trading and Profit and Loss Account for the year ended 31 December 19-8

	(a) Jewellery		(b) Hairdressing		(c) Clothing	
	£	£	£	£	£	£
Sales and Work Done		18,000		9,000		27,000
less Cost of Goods or Materials:						
Stock 1.1.19-8	2,000		1,500		3,000	
add Purchases	11,000		3,000		15,000	
	13,000		4,500		18,000	
less Stock 31.12.19-8	3,000		2,500		4,000	
	10,000		2,000		14,000	
Wages	2,800	12,800	5,000	7,000	6,000	20,000
Surpluses c/d		5,200		2,000		7,000

All Departments

		£
Surpluses b/d:		
Jewellery	5,200	
Hairdressing	2,000	
Clothing	7,000	14,200
less		
Rent	3,500	
Administration expenses	4,800	
Air conditioning and lighting	2,000	
General expenses	1,200	11,500
Net Profit		2,700

Nonetheless, frustrating though it may be, in examinations students must answer the questions as set, and not give their own interpretations of what the question should be. Therefore if an examiner gives details of the methods of apportionment of expenses, then he is really looking for an answer in the same style as Exhibit 34.1.

The balance sheet

The balance sheet does not usually show assets and liabilities split between different departments.

Inter-departmental transfers

Purchases made for one department may be subsequently sold in another department. In such a case the items should be deducted from the figure for Purchases of the original purchasing department, and added to the figure for Purchases for the subsequent selling department.

Review questions

34.1 From the following you are to draw up the Trading Account for Charnley's Department Store for the year ended 31 December 19-8.

Stocks:	1.1.19-8		31.12.19-8
	£		£
Electrical Department	6,080		7,920
Furniture Department	17,298		16,150
Leisure Goods Department	14,370		22,395
Sales for the Year:		£	
Electrical Department		29,840	
Furniture Department		73,060	
Leisure Goods Department		39,581	
Purchases for the year:			
Electrical Department		18,195	
Furniture Department		54,632	
Leisure Goods Department		27,388	

34.2 J Spratt is the producer of a shop selling books, periodicals, newspapers and children's games and toys. For the purposes of his accounts he wishes the business to be divided into two departments:

Department A   Books, periodicals and newspapers.
Department B   Games, toys and fancy goods.

The following balances have been extracted from his nominal ledger at 31 March 19-6:

	Dr	Cr
	£	£
Sales Department A		15,000
Sales Department B		10,000
Stocks Department A, 1 April 19-5	250	
Stocks Department B, 1 April 19-5	200	
Purchases Department A	11,800	
Purchases Department B	8,200	
Wages of sales assistants Department A	1,000	
Wages of sales assistants Department B	750	
Newspaper delivery wages	150	
General office salaries	750	
Rates	130	
Fire insurance — buildings	50	
Lighting and air conditioning	120	
Repairs to premises	25	
Internal telephone	25	
Cleaning	30	
Accountancy and audit charges	120	
General office expenses	60	

Stocks at 31 March 19-6 were valued at:
Department A £300
Department B £150

301

The proportion of the total floor area occupied by each department was:

Department A One-fifth

Department B Four-fifths

Prepare J Spratt's Trading and Profit and Loss Account for the year ended 31 March 19-6, apportioning the overhead expenses, where necessary, to show the Department profit or loss. The apportionment should be made by using the methods as shown:

Area — Rates, Fire Insurance, Lighting and Air Conditioning, Repairs, Telephone, Cleaning; Turnover — General Office Salaries, Accountancy, General Office Expenses.

34.3A From the following list of balances you are required to prepare a departmental trading and profit and loss account in columnar form for the year ended 31 March 19-0, in respect of the business carried on under the name of Ivor's Superstores:

		£	£
Rent and rates			4,200
Delivery expenses			2,400
Commission			3,840
Insurance			900
Purchases:	Dept. A	52,800	
	B	43,600	
	C	34,800	131,200
Discounts received			1,968
Salaries and wages			31,500
Advertising			1,944
Sales:	Dept. A	80,000	
	B	64,000	
	C	48,000	192,000
Depreciation			2,940
Opening Stock:	Dept. A	14,600	
	B	11,240	
	C	9,120	34,960
Administration and general expenses			7,890
Closing Stock:	Dept. A	12,400	
	B	8,654	
	C	9,746	30,800

Except as follows, expenses are to be apportioned equally between the departments.

Delivery expenses – proportionate to sales.

Commission – two per cent of sales.

Salaries and wages; Insurance – in the proportion of 6:5:4.

Discounts received – 1.5 per cent of purchases.

34.4A In 19-3, Keith Maltby had bought a café which he re-opened under the name of 'Keith's Kaff'. In February 19-5 he rented a grocery shop which he renamed 'Keith's Larder'.

Notes on the operations of the businesses:

(*a*) The annual rental of the grocery shop is £3,200 payable quarterly in advance on the last day of March, June, September and December.

(b) The shop buys food in bulk both for resale to the public and for supply to the café. Food is transferred to the café at cost.

(c) Each establishment is under the control of a manageress who is paid a basic salary plus a commission of 10% (calculated to the nearest £1) of the net profit of her establishment *before* charging the commission (*see* (i)) but after crediting the Enterprise Grant instalment (*See* (k)).

(d) The office work for both establishments is carried out by the shop manageress who receives an annual payment of £600 for the extra responsibilty. Two-thirds of this sum is charged to the café (*see* (i)).

(e) Maltby's accounting year runs from 1 April to 31 March and he accounts for the café and the shop as separate departments.

(f) The shop manageress lives above the shop in self-contained accommodation for which she pays an inclusive rental of £60 per month, payable one month in arrears (*see* (i)).

(g) Depreciation of fixed assets is provided on the reducing balance method at the following rates:

	%
Premises	2
Fixtures, etc.	10
Vehicles	20

(h)   Closing stocks at 31 March 19-7, at cost.

	£
Food – café	3,513
– shop	1,774
Cleaning materials — café	30
— shop	24
Wrapping materials — café	10
— shop	12

(i)   At 31 March 19-7

	£
Electricity accrued — café	131
— shop	78
General expenses accrued — café	46
— shop	68
Shop manageress' office allowance due	600
Shop manageress' accommodation rent receivable	60
Commission — café manageress	to be calculated
— shop manageress	to be calculated
Rent payable prepaid — shop	800

(j) On 31 March 19-6, Maltby had obtained a Business Development Loan for the café, to be repaid in one lump sum in 19-1, at a concessionary rate of interest (10% per annum), payable half yearly on 29 August and 31 March.

(k) Maltby has also been awarded an Enterprise Grant of £5,000 for the café, with effect from 1 April 19-6. He has decided to hold this sum in suspense and to credit it to the café profit and loss account in five equal instalments in the years ended 31 March 19-7 to 19-1 inclusive. However, at 31 March 19-7 the £5,000 had not yet been received.

(l) The sales of both the shop and the café are for cash, except that the café has a contract to supply meals to a local factory which is then invoiced with the cost, for which seven days credit is allowed.

(*m*) The overdraft finances Maltby's operations in general but is accounted for as a liability of the shop.

At 31 March 19-7, the following balances were extracted from the ledger.

	Café £	Shop £
Premises (at cost)	25,000	—
Fixtures, fittings (at cost)	7,500	—
Vehicles (at cost)	—	6,000
Provisions for depreciation at 1 April 19-6:		
Premises	6,000	—
Fixtures, fittings	1,600	—
Vehicles	—	1,000
Rent paid (*see* (*a*))	—	4,000
Manageress' salaries and related charges (*see* (*c*) and (*i*))	4,200	3,900
Assistants' wages and related charges	2,100	900
Electricity charges	1,874	851
Telephone charges	209	411
Stationery (*see* (*d*))	—	126
Turnover	36,791	27,430
Food transferred from shop to café	19,427	19,427
(*see* (*b*))	(debit)	(credit)
Stocks at 1 April 19-6:		
Food	1,272	303
Cleaning materials	44	32
Wrapping materials	27	28
Purchases:		
Food (*see* (*b*))	—	30,432
Cleaning materials	71	68
Wrapping materials	45	53
Loan interest paid (*see* (*j*))	700	—
Business development loan (*see* (*j*))	7,000	—
Bank overdraft (*see* (*m*))	—	2,209
Bank overdraft interest (*see* (*m*))	—	37
Creditors:		
Food	—	4,582
Other items	15	6
Rates (general and water)	2,943	1,864
General expenses	605	756
Cash	109	155
Rent receivable (*see* (*f*))	—	660
Debtors:		
Trade (*see* (*l*))	1,312	—

The only other balances are the personal accounts of the proprietor and are not allocated to departments:

	£	
K Maltby:		
Capital	9,000	
Current account	1,634	(credit)

Required

Prepare a departmental trading and profit and loss account for year ended 31 March 19-7 and a departmental balance sheet at that date, in each case using separate columns for the café, the shop and the total business.

(*Chartered Association of Certified Accountants*)

35
Columnar day books

Purchases analysis books

Provided firms finish up with the items needed for display in their final accounts, the actual manner in which they do it is completely up to them. Some firms use one book to record all items got on credit. These consist not only of the Purchases, but also of items such as Motor Expenses, Stationery, Fixed Assets, Carriage Inwards and so on. The idea is that all invoices for items which will not be paid for on the day that the item is received will be entered in this book. However, all of the various types of items are not simply lumped together, as the firm needs to know how much of the items were for Purchases, how much for Stationery, how much for Motor Expenses, etc., so that the relevant expense accounts can have the correct amount of expenses entered in them. This is achieved by having a set of analysis columns in the book, all of the items are entered in a Total Column, but then they are analysed as between the different sorts of expenses, etc.

Exhibit 35.1 shows such a Purchases Analysis book drawn up for a month from the following list of items got on credit:

19-5		£
May 1	Bought goods from D Watson Ltd on credit	296
,, 3	Bought goods on credit from W Donachie & Son	76
,, 5	Motor van repaired, received invoice from Barnes Motors Ltd	112
,, 6	Bought stationery from J Corrigan	65
,, 8	Bought goods on credit from C Bell Ltd	212
,, 10	Motor lorry serviced, received invoice from Barnes Motors Ltd	39
,, 13	Bought stationery on credit from A Hartford & Co	35
,, 16	Bought goods on credit from M Doyle Ltd	243
,, 20	Received invoice for carriage inwards on goods from G Owen	58
,, 21	Bought goods on credit from B Kidd & Son	135
,, 24	Bought goods on credit from K Clements	122
,, 24	Received invoice for carriage inwards from Channon Haulage	37
,, 26	Bought goods on credit from C Bell Ltd	111
,, 28	Bought stationery on credit from A Hartford & Co	49
,, 29	Bought goods on credit from B Kidd & Son	249
,, 31	Received invoice for petrol for the month, to be paid for in June, from Barnes Motors Ltd	280

Exhibit 35.1

Purchases Analysis Book

page 105

Date		Name of firm	PL Folio	Total	Purchases	Stationery	Motor expenses	Carriage inwards
19-5				£	£	£	£	£
May	1	D Watson Ltd	129	296	296			
,,	3	W Donachie & Son	27	76	76			
,,	5	Barnes Motors Ltd	55	112			112	
,,	6	J Corrigan & Co	88	65		65		
,,	8	C Bell Ltd	99	212	212			
,,	10	Barnes Motors Ltd	55	39			39	
,,	13	A Hartford & Co	298	35		35		
,,	16	M Doyle Ltd	187	243	243			
,,	20	G Owen	222	58				58
,,	21	B Kidd & Son	188	135	135			
,,	24	K Clements	211	122	122			
,,	24	Channon Haulage	305	37				37
,,	26	C Bell Ltd	99	111	111			
,,	28	A Hartford & Co	298	49		49		
,,	29	B Kidd & Son	188	249	249			
,,	31	Barnes Motors Ltd	55	280			280	
				2,119	1,444	149	431	95
					GL77	GL97	GL156	GL198

Exhibit 35.1 shows that the figure for each item is entered in the Total column, and is then also entered in the column for the particular type of expense. At the end of the month the arithmetical accuracy of the additions can be checked by comparing the total of the Total column with the sum of totals of all of the other columns. These two grand totals figures should equal each other. In this case $1,444 + 149 + 431 + 95 = 2,119$. The total column will also be useful for Control Accounts; examined in Chapter 29.

It can be seen that the total of Purchases for the month of May was £1,444 and therefore this can be debited to the Purchases Account in the General Ledger; similarly the total of Stationery bought on credit in the month can be debited to the Stationery Account in the General Ledger and so on. The folio number of the page to which the relevant total has been debited is shown immediately under the total figure for each column, e.g. under the column for Purchases is GL77, meaning that the item has been entered in the General Ledger page 77.

The entries can now be shown:

General Ledger
Purchases Account   Page 77

		£
19-5		
May 31	Purchases Analysis 105	1,444

19-5		£
May 31 Purchases Analysis		
105		149

19-5		£
May 31 Purchases Analysis		
105		431

19-5		£
May 31 Purchases Analysis		
105		95

The individual accounts of the creditors, whether they be for goods or for expenses such as Stationery or Motor Expenses, can be kept together in a single Purchases Ledger. There is no need for the Purchases Ledger simply to have accounts only for creditors for Purchases. Perhaps there is a slight misuse of the name Purchases Ledger where this happens, but it is common practice amongst a lot of firms. Many firms will give it the more correct title of Bought Ledger.

To carry through the double entry involved with Exhibit 35.1 the Purchases Ledger is now shown.

Purchases Ledger

W Donachie & Son Page 27

19-5			£
May 3 Purchases		PB105	76

Barnes Motors Ltd Page 55

19-5			£
May 5 Purchases		PB105	112
,, 10 ,,		PB105	39
,, 31 ,,		PB105	280

J Corrigan & Co Page 88

19-5			£
May 6 Purchases		PB105	65

C Bell Ltd Page 99

19-5			£
May 8 Purchases		PB105	212
,, 26 ,,		PB105	111

D Watson Ltd Page 129

19-5			£
May 1 Purchases		PB105	296

M Doyle Ltd Page 187

19-5			£
May 16 Purchases		PB105	243

19-5			£
May 21 Purchases		PB105	135
,, 29 ,,		PB105	249

19-5			£
May 24 Purchases		PB105	122

19-5			£
May 20 Purchases		PB105	58

19-5			£
May 13 Purchases		PB105	35
,, 28 ,,		PB105	49

19-5			£
May 24 Purchases		PB105	37

The reader has just been shown how to draw up Purchases Analysis Books. The basic idea of having a total column, and analysing the items under various headings, can be carried one stage further. This could be the case where it was desired to ascertain the profits of a firm on a departmental basis.

In such a case the Purchases Analysis Books already described could have additional columns so that the purchases of goods for each department could be easily ascertained. Taking the Purchases Analysis Book per Exhibit 35.1, assume that the firm had three departments, Sports Department, Household Department and Electrical Department. Instead of one column for Purchases there could be three columns, each one headed with the title of a Department. When the invoices for purchases were being entered in the enlarged Purchases Analysis Book, the amount of each invoice could be split as between each department, and the relevant figures entered in each column. The total figure of all the three columns would represent the total of Purchases, but it would also be known how much of the Purchases were for each department. This would help when the final accounts were being drafted in a departmental fashion. The Purchases Analysis Book per Exhibit 35.1 might appear instead as Exhibit 35.2.

Exhibit 35.2

Page 105

Date 19- 5	Name of firm	PL Folio	Total	Sports Dept	House-hold Dept	Elec-trical Dept	Station-ery	Motor Exps	Carriage Inwards
			£	£	£	£	£	£	£
May 1	D Watson Ltd	129	296	80	216				
,, 3	W Donachie & Son	27	76	76					
,, 5	Barnes Motors Ltd	55	112					112	
,, 6	J Corrigan & Co	88	65				65		
,, 8	C Bell Ltd	99	212	92		120			
,, 10	Barnes Motors Ltd	55	39					39	
,, 13	A Hartford & Co	298	35				35		
,, 16	M Doyle Ltd	187	243			243			
,, 20	G Owen	222	58						58
,, 21	B Kidd & Son	188	135	135					
,, 24	K Clements	211	122	70		52			
,, 24	Channon Haulage	305	37						37
,, 26	C Bell Ltd	99	111		111				
,, 28	A Hartford & Co	298	49					49	
,, 29	B Kidd & Son	188	249	60	103	86			
,, 31	Barnes Motors Ltd	55	280					280	
			2,119	513	430	501	149	431	95
				GL77	GL77	GL77	GL97	GL156	GL198

The Purchases Account in the General Ledger could also have three columns, so that the purchases for each department could be entered in separate columns. Then, when the Trading Account is drawn up the respective totals of each department could be transferred to it.

Of course, a Purchases Day Book could be kept, strictly for Purchases only, without the other expenses, such as Stationery, Motor Expenses and Carriage Inwards. In this case there would simply be the total column with an analysis column for each separate department's purchase.

With Purchases, the use of an analysis book with columns for other expenses is very useful. When looking at Sales, however, the need to split Sales between departments is not usually accompanied by the need to show analysis columns for other items of income. Involved in the expenditure of a firm are many items of expense besides Purchases. With income, the main part of income is represented by the Sales. The amount of transactions in such items as the selling of a fixed asset are relatively few. The Sales Analysis Book, or Columnar Sales Book as it might be called, therefore usually consists of the sales of goods only.

A columnar Sales Book for the same firm as in Exhibit 35.2 might appear as in Exhibit 35.3.

310

Exhibit 35.3

Columnar Sales Day Book

Date	Name of firm	Sl Folio	Total	Sports Dept	Household Dept	Electrical Dept
19-5		£	£	£	£	£
May 1	N Coward Ltd	87	190		190	
,, 5	L Oliver	76	200	200		
,, 8	R Colman & Co	157	307	102		205
,, 16	Aubrey Smith Ltd	209	480			480
,, 27	H Marshall	123	222	110	45	67
,, 31	W Pratt	66	1,800		800	1,000
			3,199	412	1,035	1,752
				GL 88	GL 88	GL 88

The Sales Account, and the Purchases Account, in the General Ledger could be in columnar form. From Exhibits 35.4 and 35.5 the Purchases and Sales Accounts would appear as:

General Ledger

Sales

Page 88

	19-5		Sports Dept	Household Dept	Electrical Dept
			£	£	£
	May 31 Credit Sales for the month		412	1,035	1,752

Page 77   *Purchases*

19-5	Sports Dept	Household Dept	Electrical Dept
	£	£	£
May 31 Credit Purchases for the month	513	430	501

The Purchases and Sales Accounts would then accumulate the figures for these items, so that when the final accounts were being drawn up the total figures for each department could be transferred to the Trading Account. There is, of course, nothing to stop a firm having one account for Purchases (Sports Dept), another for Purchases (Household Dept) and so on. The Stock Account could be kept in a columnar fashion as well, to aid the transfer of stock values to the respective departmental columns in the Trading Account.

The personal accounts in the Sales and Purchases Ledgers would not be in columnar form. As an instance of this, the personal account of W Pratt in the Sales ledger would simply be debited with £1,800 in respect of the goods sold to him, there being no need to show the analysis between Household and Electrical Departments in his account. If the firm wanted to have columnar personal accounts then there is nothing to stop them keeping them, but this would not normally be the case.

Sales analysis books and VAT

All that would be needed would be an extra column for VAT. In Exhibit 35.4 that follows the debtors would be charged up with the gross amount, whilst the VAT £276 would be credited to the VAT Account, and the Sales figures of £1,040, £410 and £390 credited to the Sales Account. (Assumed VAT rate of 15 per cent).

Date	Name of firm	Sl Folio	Total	VAT	Furniture Dept	Hardware Dept	General Dept
			Columnar Sales Day Book				
19-4			£	£	£	£	£
May 1	H Smedley	133	230	30	200		
,, 6	T Sarson	297	552	72	210	100	170
,, 16	H Hartley Ltd	444	299	39		110	150
,, 31	H Walls	399	1,035	135	630	200	70
			2,116	276	1,040	410	390
				GL 65	GL 177	GL 177	GL 177

Purchases analysis books and VAT

Here also an extra column is needed for VAT. Remember that VAT is not payable on some items, e.g. Rent, Electricity.

Books at collection points

We can see that the various Sales and Purchases Journals, and the ones for returns, are simply collection points for the data to be entered in the accounts of the double-entry system. There is nothing by law that says that, for instance, a Sales Journal has to be written up. What we could do is to look at the Sales Invoices and enter the debits in the customers' personal accounts from them. Then we could keep all the Sales Invoices together in a file. At the end of the month we could use an adding machine to add up the amounts of the Sales Invoices, and then enter that total to the credit of the Sales Account in the General Ledger.

That means that we would have done without the Sales Journal. As the debits in the customers' accounts are made, not by looking at the Sales Journal, but by looking at the Sales Invoices (we could say that these are 'slips' or paper), the system would be known as a 'slip' system. Such a system could lead to more errors being made and not being detected. It could also mean that book-keepers could more easily commit fraud as it would be more difficult for proprietors to see what was going on. The 'slip' system could also be used for Purchases and for Returns.

Exhibit 35.5

Columnar Purchases Day Book

Date	Name of firm	PL folio	Total £	VAT £	Purchases £	Rent £	Motor Expenses £	Electricity £	Repairs £	General Expenses £
19-7										
Jul 1	D Brown Ltd	77	1,610	210	1,400					
Jul 3	Kent C C	216	1,250			1,250				
Jul 6	A B C plc	69	1,150	150	1,000					
Jul 10	Rogers Garage	115	161	21			140			
Jul 13	K Brown Ltd	307	414	54	360					
Jul 18	Southern Electricity	218	307					307		
Jul 21	K J Builders	399	253	33					220	
Jul 28	B Jones Ltd	16	460	60	400					
Jul 30	P Smith	164	92	12						80
			5,697	540	3,160	1,250	140	307	220	80
				GL177	GL44	GL69	GL111	GL142	GL77	GL90

Post as follows:

Debits:
(to general ledger)

£540 to VAT account on GL177
£3,160 to Purchases account on GL44
£1,250 to Rent account on GL69
£140 to Motor Expenses account on GL111
£307 to Electricity account on GL142
£220 to Repairs account on GL77
£88 to General Expenses account on GL90

Credits: Gross amounts (per total column) to credit of each individual supplier, e.g. Cr K Brown Ltd £1,610 on page 77 of Purchases Ledger.

Review questions

35.1 C Taylor, a wholesale dealer in electrical goods, has three departments: (*a*) Hi Fi, (*b*) TV, and (*c*) Sundries. The following is a summary of Taylor's Sales Invoices during the period 1 to 7 February 19-7:

	Customer	Invoice No	Department	List price less trade discount	VAT	Total invoice price
				£	£	£
Feb 1	P Small	586	TV	2,600	260	2,860
2	L Goode	587	Hi Fi	1,800	180	1,980
3	R Daye	588	TV	1,600	160	1,760
5	B May	589	Sundries	320	Nil	320
7	L Goode	590	TV	900	90	990
7	P Small	591	Hi Fi	3,400	340	3,740

(*a*) Record the above transactions in a columnar book of original entry and post to the General Ledger in columnar form.

(*b*) Write up the Personal Accounts in the appropriate ledger.

NB Do not balance off any of your ledger accounts.

VAT was 10% rate.

35.2 Enter up a Purchases Analysis Book with columns for the various expenses for M Barber for the month from the following information on credit items.

19-6			£
July	1	Bought goods from L Ogden	220
,,	3	Bought goods from E Evans	390
,,	4	Received electricity bill (lighting & heating from North Electricity Board)	88
,,	5	Bought goods from H Noone	110
,,	6	Motor lorry repaired, received bill from Kirk Motors	136
,,	8	Bought stationery from Avon Enterprises	77
,,	10	Motor van serviced, bill from Kirk Motors	55
,,	12	Gas bill received from North Gas Board (lighting & heating)	134
,,	15	Bought goods from A Dodds	200
,,	17	Bought light bulbs (lighting & heating) from O Aspinall	24
,,	18	Goods bought from J Kelly	310
,,	19	Invoice for carriage inwards from D Adams	85
,,	21	Bought stationery from J Moore	60
,,	23	Goods bought from H Noone	116
,,	27	Received invoice for carriage inwards from D Flynn	62
,,	31	Invoice for motor spares supplied during the month received from Kirk Motors	185

35.3 Enter up the relevant accounts in the Purchases and General Ledgers from the Purchases Analysis Book you have completed for question 35.2.

35.4A During the quarter ended 31 May 19-6, the raw materials purchased by John Henry Limited manufacturers of furniture, amounted to £181,590 before VAT at the standard rate of 15% and, in addition, the following items of expenditure occurred:

March 12	*Highway Garage Limited*		
	Motor van C478 TBR	9,500.00	
	VAT @ 15%	1,425.00	
		10,925.00	
	Vehicle excise duty	100.00	11,025.00
March 19	*Smith Motors Limited*		
	Motor car C379 KTA	8,000.00	
	VAT @ 15%	1,200.00	
		9,200.00	
	Vehicle excise duty	100.00	9,300.00
April 23	*Super Machines Limited*		
	Used drilling machine Number KXY54	8,200.00	
	VAT @ 15%	1,230.00	9,430.00
May 7	*Highway Garage Limited*		
	Car repairs	210.00	
	VAT @ 15%	31.50	241.50
May 20	*Machine Repairs Limited*		
	Renovation drilling machine Number KXY54	500.00	
	VAT @ 15%	75.00	575.00

Note: This renovation was necessary before the drilling machine could be used in the factory.

The VAT due to the Customs and Excise Department on 28 February 19-6 amounting to £84,000 was paid on 20 March 19-6.

During the quarter ended 31 May 19-6, the company's turnover, before VAT, amounted to £800,000 and analysed for VAT purposes was as follows:

	Turnover
	£
Taxable: – Standard rate	620,000
– Zero rate	120,000
Non-taxable – exempt	60,000
	£800,000

The company maintains an analytical purchase day book.

Required

(a) Prepare the analytical purchases day book for the three months ended 31 May 19-6 of John Henry Limited.

(*Note*): Raw material purchases for the three months ended 31 May 19-6 should be shown as one entry in the purchases day book.

(b) Prepare the account for H M Customs and Excise – VAT for the three months ended 31 May 19-6 in the accounts of John Henry Limited.

(Association of Accounting Technicians)

36

Partnership accounts: an introduction

The final accounts so far described have, with the exception of income and expenditure accounts, been concerned with businesses each owned by one person. There must obviously come a time when it is desirable for more than one person to participate in the ownership of the business. It may be due to the fact that the amount of capital required cannot be provided by one person, or else that the experience and ability required to run the business cannot be found in any one person alone. Alternatively, many people just prefer to share the cares of ownership rather than bear all the burden themselves. Very often too there is a family relationship between the owners.

The form of business organisation necessary to provide for more than one owner of a business formed with a view of profit is either that of a limited company or of a partnership. This chapter deals with partnerships, the governing act being the Partnership Act 1890. A partnership may be defined as an association of from two to twenty persons (except that there is no maximum limit for firms of accountants, solicitors, Stock Exchange members or other professional bodies which receive the approval of the Board of Trade for this purpose) carrying on business in common with a view of profit. A limited company would have to be formed if it was desired to have more than twenty owners.

With the exception of one special type of partner, known as a limited partner, each partner is liable to the full extent of his personal possessions for the whole of the debts of the partnership firm should the firm be unable to meet them. Barring limited partners, each partner would have to pay his share of any such deficiency. A **limited partner** is one who is registered under the provisions of the Limited Partnership Act 1907, and whose liability is limited to the amount of capital invested by him; he can lose that but his personal possessions cannot be taken to pay any debts of the firm. A limited partner may not however take part in the management of the partnership business. There must be at least one general partner in a limited partnership.

Persons can enter into partnership with one another without any form of written agreement. It is, however, wiser to have an agreement drawn up by a lawyer, as this will tend to lead to fewer possibilities of misunderstandings and disagreements between partners. Such a partnership deed or articles of partnership can contain as much, or as little, as the partners desire. It does not cover every eventuality. The usual accounting requirements covered can be listed:

(a) The capital to be contributed by each partner.
(b) The ratio in which profits (or losses) are to be shared.
(c) The rate of interest, if any, to be given on capital before the profits are shared.
(d) The rate of interest, if any, to be charged on partners' drawings.
(e) Salaries to be paid to partners.
Some comments on the above are necessary.

Ratio in which profits are to be shared

It is often thought by students that profits should be shared in the same ratio as that in which capital is contributed. For example, suppose the capitals were Allen £2,000 and Beet £1,000, many people would share the profits in the ratio of two-thirds to one-third, even though the work to be done by each partner is similar. A look at the division of the first few years' profits on such a basis would be:

Years	1	2	3	4	5	Total
	£	£	£	£	£	£
Net profits	1,800	2,400	3,000	3,000	3,600	
Shared:						
Allen ⅔	1,200	1,600	2,000	2,000	2,400	9,200
Beet ⅓	600	800	1,000	1,000	1,200	4,600

It can now be seen that Allen would receive £9,200, or £4,600 more than Beet. Equitably the difference between the two shares of profit in this case, as the duties of the partners are the same, should be adequate to compensate Allen for putting extra capital into the firm. It is obvious that £4,600 extra profits is far more than adequate for this purpose.

Consider too the position of capital ratio sharing of profits if one partner put in £99 and the other put in £1 as capital.

To overcome the difficulty of compensating for the investment of extra capital, the concept of interest on capital was devised.

Interest on capital

If the work to be done by each partner is of equal value but the capital contributed is unequal, it is equitable to grant interest on the partners' capitals. This interest is treated as a deduction prior to the calculation of profits and their distribution according to the profit-sharing ratio.

The rate of interest is a matter of agreement between the partners, but it should theoretically equal the return which they would have received if they had invested the capital elsewhere.

Taking Allen and Beet's firm again, but sharing the profits equally after charging 5 per cent per annum interest on capital, the division of profits would become:

Years	1	2	3	4	5	Total
	£	£	£	£	£	£
Net Profit	1,800	2,400	3,000	3,000	3,600	
Interest on Capitals						
Allen	100	100	100	100	100 =	500
Beet	50	50	50	50	50 =	250
Remainder shared:						
Allen ½	825	1,125	1,425	1,425	1,725 =	6,525
Beet ½	825	1,125	1,425	1,425	1,725 =	6,525

Summary	Allen	Beet
	£	£
Interest of Capital	500	250
Balance of Profits	6,525	6,525
	7,025	6,775

Allen has thus received £250 more than Beet, this being adequate return (in the partners' estimation) for having invested an extra £1,000 in the firm for five years.

Interest on drawings

It is obviously in the best interests of the firm if cash is withdrawn from the firm by the partners in accordance with the two basic principles of: (*a*) as little as possible, and (*b*) as late as possible. The more cash that is left in the firm the more expansion can be financed, the greater the economies of having ample cash to take advantage of bargains and of not missing cash discounts because cash is not available and so on.

To deter the partners from taking out cash unnecessarily the concept can be used of charging the partners interest on each withdrawal, calculated from the date of withdrawal to the end of the financial year. The amount charged to them helps to swell the profits divisible between the partners.

The rate of interest should be sufficient to achieve this end without being unduly penal.

Suppose that Allen and Beet have decided to charge interest on drawings at 5 per cent per annum, and that their year end was 31 December. The following drawings are made:

Allen

Drawings		Interest	
			£
1 January	£100	£100 × 5% × 12 months =	5
1 March	£240	£240 × 5% × 10 months =	10
1 May	£120	£120 × 5% × 8 months =	4
1 July	£240	£240 × 5% × 6 months =	6
1 October	£80	£80 × 5% × 3 months =	1
		Interest charged to Allen =	26

Beet

Drawings		Interest	
			£
1 January	£60	£60 × 5% × 12 months =	3
1 August	£480	£480 × 5% × 5 months =	10
1 December	£240	£240 × 5% × 1 months =	1
		Interest charged to Beet =	14

Salaries

A partner may have some particular responsibility or extra task that the others have not got. It may in fact be of a temporary nature. To compensate him for this, it is best not to disturb the profit- and loss-sharing ratio. It is better to let him have a salary sufficient to compensate him for the extra tasks performed. This salary is deductible before arriving at the balance of profits to be shared in the profit-sharing ratio. A change in the profit- and loss-sharing ratio to compensate him would have meant bearing a larger share of any loss, hardly a fair means of compensation; or if there was only a small profit the extra amount received by him would be insufficient compensation, while if there was a large profit he may well be more than adequately compensated.

An example of the distribution of profits

Taylor and Clarke are in partnership sharing profits and losses in the ratio of Taylor 3/5ths, Clarke 2/5ths. They are entitled to 5 per cent per annum interest on capitals, Taylor having £2,000 capital and Clarke £6,000. Clarke is to have a salary of £500. They charge interest on drawings, Taylor being charged £50 and Clarke £100. The net profit, before any distributions to the partners, amounted to £5,000 for the year ended 31 December 19-7.

	£	£	£
Net Profit			5,000
add Charged for interest on drawings:			
Taylor		50	
Clarke		100	
			150
			5,150
less Salary: Clarke		500	
Interest on Capital:			
Taylor	100		
Clarke	300		
		400	
			900
			4,250
Balance of profits			
Shared:			
Taylor 3/5ths		2,550	
Clarke 2/5ths		1,700	
			4,250

The £5,000 net profits have therefore been shared:

	Taylor	Clarke
	£	£
Balance of profits	2,550	1,700
Interest on Capital	100	300
Salary	—	500
	2,650	2,500
less Interest on drawings	50	100
	2,600	2,400

£5,000

The final accounts

If the sales, stock and expenses of partnership were exactly the same as that of a sole trader then the trading and profit and loss account would be identical with that as prepared for the sole trader. However, a partnership would have an extra section shown under the profit and loss account. This section is called the profit and loss appropriation account, and it is in this account that the distribution of profits is shown. The heading to the trading and profit and loss account does not include the words 'appropriation account'. It is purely an accounting custom not to include it in the heading.

The trading and profit and loss account of Taylor and Clarke from the details given would appear:

Taylor and Clarke

Trading and Profit and Loss Account for the year ended 31 December 19-7

Trading Account – same as for sole trader

			£

Profit and Loss Account – same as for sole trader

	£	£	£
Net Profit			5,000
Interest on drawings:			
Taylor		50	
Clarke		100	150
			5,150
less:			
Interest on capitals			
Taylor	100		
Clarke	300	400	
Salary: Clarke		500	900
			4,250
Balance of profits shared:			
Taylor ⅗ths		2,550	
Clarke ⅖ths		1,700	4,250

Fixed and fluctuating capital accounts

There is a choice open in partnership accounts of:

Fixed capital accounts plus current accounts

The capital account for each partner remains year by year at the figure of capital put into the firm by the partners. The profits, interest on capital and the salaries to which the partner may be entitled are then credited to a separate current account for the partner, and the drawings and the interests on drawings are debited to it. The balance of the current account at the end of each financial year will then represent the amount of undrawn (or withdrawn) profits. A credit balance will be undrawn profits, while a debit balance will be drawings in excess of the profits to which the partner was entitled.

For Taylor and Clarke, capital and current accounts, assuming drawings of £2,000 each, will appear:

Taylor – Capital

	19-7		£
	Jan 1	Balance b/d	2,000

Clarke – Capital

	19-7		£
	Jan 1	Balance b/d	6,000

19-7		£	19-7		£
Dec 31 Cash: Drawings		2,000	Dec 31 Profit and Loss		
,, Profit and Loss			Appropriation		
Appropriation:			Account:		
Interest on			Interest on Capital		100
Drawings		50	Share of Profits		2,550
,, 31 Balance c/d		600			
		2,650			2,650
			Jan 1 Balance b/d		600

Clarke – Current Account

19-7		£	19-7		£
Dec 31 Cash: Drawings		2,000	Dec 31 Profit and Loss		
,, 31 Profit and Loss			Appropriation		
Appropriation:			Account:		
Interest on			Interest on Capital		300
Drawings		100	Share of Profits		1,700
,, 31 Balance c/d		400	Salary		500
		2,500			2,500
			Jan 1 Balance b/d		400

Notice that the salary of Clarke was not paid to him, it was merely credited to his account. If in fact it was paid in addition to his drawings, the £500 cash paid would have been debited to the current account changing the £400 credit balance into a £100 debit balance.

Examiners often ask for the capital accounts and current accounts to be shown in columnar form. For the previous accounts of Taylor & Clarke these would appear as follows:

Capitals

	Taylor	Clarke		Taylor	Clarke
	£	£	19-7	£	£
			Jan 1 Balances b/d	2,000	6,000

Current Accounts

	Taylor	Clarke		Taylor	Clarke
19-7	£	£	19-7	£	£
Dec 31 Cash: Drawings	2,000	2,000	Dec 31 Interest on Capital	100	300
,, 31 Interest on Drawings	50	100	,, 31 Share of Profits	2,250	1,700
,, 31 Balances c/d	600	400	,, 31 Salary		500
	2,650	2,500		2,650	2,500
			19-8		
			Jan 1 Balances b/d	600	400

Fluctuating capital accounts

The distribution of profits would be credited to the capital account, and the drawings and interest on drawings debited. Therefore the balance on the capital account will change each year, i.e. it will fluctuate.

If Fluctuating Capital Accounts had been kept for Taylor and Clarke they would have appeared:

Taylor – Capital

19-7		£	19-7		£
Dec 31	Cash: Drawings	2,000	Jan 1	Balance b/d	2,000
,, 31	Profit and Loss		Dec 31	Profit and Loss	
	Appropriation Account:			Appropriation Account:	
	Interest on			Interest on Capital	100
	Drawings	50		Share of Profits	2,550
,, 31	Balance c/d	2,600			
		4,650			4,650
			Jan 1	Balance b/d	2,600

Clarke – Capital

19-7		£	19-7		£
Dec 31	Cash: Drawings	2,000	Jan 1	Balance b/d	6,000
,, 31	Profit and Loss		Dec 31	Profit and Loss	
	Appropriation Account:			Appropriation Account:	
	Interest on			Interest on Capital	300
	Drawings	100		Salary	500
,, 31	Balance c/d	6,400		Share of Profit	1,700
		8,500			8,500
			Jan 1	Balance b/d	6,400

Fixed capital accounts preferred

The keeping of fixed capital accounts plus Current Accounts is considered preferable to fluctuating capital accounts. When partners are taking out greater amounts than the share of the profits that they are entitled to, this is shown up by a debit balance on the current account and so acts as a warning.

Where no partnership agreement exists

Where no agreement exists, express or implied, Section 24 of the Partnership Act 1890 governs the situation. The accounting contents of this section states:

(*a*) Profits and losses are to be shared equally.

(*b*) There is to be no interest allowed on capital.

(*c*) No interest is to be charged on drawings.

(*d*) Salaries are not allowed.

(*e*) If a partner puts a sum of money into a firm in excess of the capital he has agreed to subscribe, he is entitled to interest at the rate of 5 per cent per annum on such an advance.

This section applies where there is no agreement. There may be an agreement not by a partnership deed but in a letter, or it may be implied by conduct, for instance when a partner signs a balance sheet which shows profits shared in some other ratio than equally.

In some cases of disagreement as to whether agreement existed or not only the courts would be competent to decide.

The balance sheet

The capital part side of the balance sheet will appear:

Balance Sheet as at 31 December 19-7

			£	£
Capitals:	Taylor		2,000	
	Clarke		6,000	
				8,000

Current Accounts	*Taylor*	*Clarke*
	£	£
Interest on Capital	100	300
Share of profits	2,550	1,700
Salary	—	500
	2,650	2,500
less Drawings	2,000	2,000
Interest on drawings	50	100
	600	400

(totals column: 1,000)

If one of the current accounts had finished in debit, for instance if the current account of Clarke had finished up as £400 debit, the abbreviation Dr would appear and the balances would appear net in the totals column:

	Taylor	*Clarke*	
	£	£	£
Closing balance	600	400 *Dr*	200

If the net figure turned out to be a debit figure then this would be deducted from the total of the capital accounts.

Review questions

36.1 Graham, Harvey, Rutherford and Miles are in partnership. The capitals they have invested are £75,000, £70,000, £60,000 and £60,000 respectively.

The partners have agreed the following appropriation scheme:

(*a*) interest is to be allowed on capital at 10% per annum,

(*b*) Graham, Harvey, Rutherford and Miles are to receive salaries of £10,000, £10,000, £8,000 and £8,000 respectively.

(*c*) profits are to be shared as follows:

Graham	35%
Harvey	35%
Rutherford	20%
Miles	10%

(*d*) interest to be charged on drawings at 10% per annum. The amounts chargeable to each partner for the year ended 31 December 19-6 are:

	£
Graham	1,729
Harvey	1,100
Rutherford	832
Miles	789
	£4,450

During the year ended 31 December 19-6 the partners withdrew the following amounts from the partnership:

	£
Graham	23,050
Harvey	21,980
Rutherford	16,640
Miles	17,300
	£78,970

The partners had the following balances on their Current Accounts as at 1 January 19-6:

	£	
Graham	2,100	(credit)
Harvey	3,370	(credit)
Rutherford	1,240	(debit)
Miles	980	(credit)
	£5,210	

During the financial year ended 31 December 19-6 the partnership earned a net profit of £85,550.

Required:

(*a*) Draw up the Appropriation Account for the partnership for the year ended 31 December 19-6.

(*b*) Prepare the partners' Current Accounts for the year ended 31 December 19-6.

(*Association of Accounting Technicians*)

36.2A Grahame, Margo and Raj set up in partnership together some years ago with capitals of £50,000, £30,000 and £15,000 respectively. The following are summaries of the partners' Current Accounts for the year ended 31 December 19-5. Study these carefully and then answer the questions which follow.

Grahame – Current Account

19-5		£	19-5		£
	Drawings	13,031	Jan 1	Balance b/f	366
Dec 31	Share of Balance	200	Dec 31	Interest on Capital	6,000
Dec 31	Balance c/f	135	Dec 31	Salary	7,000
		13,366			13,366

Margo – Current Account

19-5		£	19-5		£
	Drawings	10,640	Jan 1	Balance b/f	264
Dec 31	Share of Balance	120	Dec 31	Interest on Capital	3,600
			Dec 31	Salary	6,500
			Dec 31	Balance c/f	396
		10,760			10,760

Raj – Current Account

19-5		£	19-5		£
Jan 1	Balance b/f	133	Dec 31	Interest on Capital	1,800
	Drawings	7,598	Dec 31	Salary	5,500
Dec 31	Share of Balance	80	Dec 31	Balance c/f	511
		7,811			7,811

Required:

(*a*) Reconstruct the appropriation scheme Grahame, Margo and Raj have agreed for the division of profits and losses.

(*b*) Calculate the Net Profit of the partnership for the year ended 31 December 19-5.

(*c*) How would the partners have shared this profit had they made no formal agreement as to the division of profits?

(*d*) What would the partners' shares in profit have been had the net profit for the year ended 31 December 19-5 been £60,000.

(*Association of Accounting Technicians*)

36.3 Bee, Cee and Dee have been holding preliminary discussions with a view to forming a partnership to buy and sell antiques.

The position has now been reached where the prospective partners have agreed the basic arrangements under which the partnership will operate.

Bee will contribute £40,000 as capital and, up to £10,000 as a long-term loan to the partnership, if needed. He has extensive other business interests and will not therefore be taking an active part in the running of the business.

Cee is unable to bring in more than £2,000 as capital initially, but, because he has an expert knowledge of the antique trade, will act as the manager of the business on a full-time basis.

Dee is willing to contribute £10,000 as capital. He will also assist in running the business as the need arises. In particular, he is prepared to attend auctions anywhere within the United Kingdom in order to acquire trading stock which he will transport back to the firm's premises in his van. On occasions he may also help Cee to restore the articles prior to sale to the public.

At the meeting, the three prospective partners intend to decide upon the financial arrangements for sharing out the profits (or losses) made by the firm and have approached you for advice.

You are required to prepare a set of explanatory notes, under suitable headings, of the considerations which the prospective partners should take into account in arriving at their decisions at the next meeting.

(*Chartered Association of Certified Accountants*)

36.4A The following list of balances as at 30 September 19-6 has been extracted from the books of Peter James and Angus Victor who are trading in partnership:

	£
Freehold property: at cost at 30 September 19-5	30,000
provision for depreciation at 30 September 19-5	6,000
Fixtures and fittings: at cost at 30 September 19-5	18,000
provision for depreciation at 30 September 19-5	9,600
Stock at 30 September 19-6	11,000
Debtors	4,600
Creditors	5,800
Balance at bank	2,700
Gross profit	39,000
Establishment and administrative expenses	9,100
Sales and distribution expenses	13,000
Capital accounts at 30 September 19-5: Peter James	25,000
Angus Victor	15,000
Current accounts at 30 September 19-5: Peter James	6,000 credit
Angus Victor	2,300 debit
Loan from Peter James	10,000
Drawings: Peter James	15,700
Angus Victor	10,000

Additional information for the year ended 30 September 19-6:

(*a*) Interest at the rate of 10% per annum is payable annually in arrears on the loan from Peter James; the loan was received on 1 April 19-6.

(*b*) All sales produce a uniform rate of gross profit.

(*c*) Provision is to be made for depreciation as follows:

Freehold property	5% per annum on cost
Fixtures and fittings	10% per annum on cost

(*d*) Electricity charges accrued due at 30 September 19-6 amounted to £360.
Note: The electricity charges are included in establishment and administrative expenses.

(*e*) 2/3rds of sales took place in the second half of the year.

(*f*) No provision has been made in the accounts for a sales commission of 2% of gross profit payable to sales staff as from 1 April 19-6.

(*g*) Provision is to be made for a salary of £10,000 per annum to be credited to Angus Victor as from 1 April 19-6.

(*h*) Partners are to be credited with interest on the balances of their capital accounts at the rate of 5% per annum.

Required:

(*a*) Prepare the profit and loss account and profit and loss appropriation partnership account for the year ended 30 September 19-6.

(*b*) Prepare the partnership balance sheet as at 30 September 19-6.

(*c*) Indicate one significant matter revealed in the accounting statements prepared which should be brought to the attention of the partners.

(*Association of Accounting Technicians*)

36.5 Mendez and Marshall are in partnership sharing profits and losses equally. The following is their trial balance as at 30 June 19-6.

	Dr £	Cr £
Buildings (cost £75,000)	50,000	
Fixtures at cost	11,000	
Provision for Depreciation: Fixtures		3,300
Debtors	16,243	
Creditors		11,150
Cash at Bank	677	
Stock at 30 June 19-5	41,979	
Sales		123,650
Purchases	85,416	
Carriage Outwards	1,288	
Discounts Allowed	115	
Loan Interest: King	4,000	
Office Expenses	2,416	
Salaries and Wages	18,917	
Bad Debts	503	
Provision for Bad Debts		400
Loan from J King		40,000
Capitals: Mendez		35,000
Marshall		29,500
Current Accounts: Mendez		1,306
Marshall		298
Drawings: Mendez	6,400	
Marshall	5,650	
	244,604	244,604

Required:

Prepare a trading and profit and loss appropriation account for the year ended 30 June 19-6, and a balance sheet as at that date.

(*a*) Stock, 30 June 19-6 £56,340.

(*b*) Expenses to be accrued: Office Expenses £96; Wages £200.

(*c*) Depreciate fixtures 10 per cent on reducing balance basis, buildings £1,000.

(*d*) Reduce provision for bad debts to £320.

(*e*) Partnership salary: £800 to Mendez. Not yet entered.

(*f*) Interest on drawings: Mendez £180; Marshall £120.

(*g*) Interest on capital account balances at 10 per cent.

36.6A Oscar and Felix are in partnership. They share profits in the ratio: Oscar 60 per cent; Felix 40 per cent. The following trial balance was extracted as at 31 March 19-6.

	Dr £	Cr £
Office Equipment at cost	6,500	
Motor Vehicles at cost	9,200	
Provision for depreciation at 31.3.19-5:		
Motor Vehicles		3,680
Office Equipment		1,950
Stock at 31 March 19-5	24,970	
Debtors and Creditors	20,960	16,275
Cash at Bank	615	
Cash in Hand	140	
Sales		90,370
Purchases	71,630	
Salaries	8,417	
Office Expenses	1,370	
Discounts Allowed	563	
Current Accounts at 31.3.19-5		
Oscar		1,379
Felix		1,211
Capital Accounts: Oscar		27,000
Felix		12,000
Drawings: Oscar	5,500	
Felix	4,000	
	153,865	153,865

Required:

Draw up a set of final accounts for the year ended 31 March 19-6 for the partnership. The following notes are applicable at 31 March 19-6.

(*a*) Stock 31 March 19-6 £27,340

(*b*) Office Expenses owing £110.

(*c*) Provide for depreciation: Motor 20 per cent of cost, Office Equipment 10 per cent of cost.

(*d*) Charge Interest on capitals at 10 per cent.

(*e*) Charge Interest on drawings: Oscar £180; Felix £210.

36.7A Duke and Earl are in partnership operating a garage business named Aristocratic Autos.

In addition to selling petrol and oil, the garage has a workshop where car repairs and maintenance are carried out and also a small showroom from which new and second hand cars are sold.

For accounting purposes, each of these three activities is treated as a separate department.

At 30 September 19-6, balances extracted from the ledgers of Aristocratic Autos comprised:

	£
Cash Sales	
Workshop (repair charges)	32,125
Petrol and oil	32,964
Showroom (car sales)	8,500
Credit sales:	
Workshop (repair charges)	65,892
Petrol and oil	41,252
Showroom (car sales)	81,914
Stocks (at 1 October 19-5):	
Workshop (repair materials)	1,932
Petrol and oil	3,018
Showroom (cars)	20,720
Credit purchases:	
Workshop (repair materials)	23,860
Petrol and oil	41,805
Showroom (cars)	52,100
Fixed assets (at 1 October 19-5) (at cost):	
* Freehold buildings (i.e. held in perpetuity):	
Workshop	12,600
Petrol and oil	14,200
Showroom	38,000
Plant, equipment and vehicles:	
Workshop	65,180
Petrol and oil	22,900
Showroom	17,450
Provisions for depreciation (at 1 October 19-5):	
Freehold buildings:	
Workshop	5,060
Petrol and oil	7,100
Showroom	19,390
Plant, equipment and vehicles:	
Workshop	48,254
Petrol and oil	17,077
Showroom	9,451
Fixed asset acquisitions during year (at cost):	
Plant and equipment:	
Workshop	26,210
Petrol and oil	4,520
Showroom	1,060

Fixed asset disposal proceeds during year (*see* (*c*)):
Plant and equipment:

Workshop	5,200
Salaries:	
Showroom	10,200
Rates	26,738
Electricity	9,453
General expenses	10,692
Wages:	
direct:	
Workshop	34,050
Petrol and oil	5,602
indirect:	
Workshop	6,810
Showroom	4,160
Creditors:	
Workshop	4,225
Petrol and oil	5,602
Showroom	15,250
Bank/cash:	
Workshop	316
Petrol and oil	1,605
Showroom	30,470
Debtors:	
Workshop	1,365
Petrol and oil	537
Drawings:	
Duke	12,190
Earl	9,740
Current accounts (at 1 October 19-5)(credit balances):	
Duke	9,750
Earl	10,477
Capital accounts:	
Duke	50,000
Earl	40,000

Notes at 30 September 19-6
(*a*) Stocks at 30 September 19-6:

	£
Workshop	2,752
Petrol and oil	2,976
Showroom	25,310

(*b*) Depreciation is calculated using the straight line method (assuming no residual value) – and is applied to the original cost of the asset at the end of the financial year, using the following rates:

	%
Freehold buildings	20
Plant, equipment and vehicles	20

The depreciation charges for the current year have not yet been posted to the accounts.

The freehold buildings are temporary structures with a five year life.

(*c*) No entries have yet been made to transfer the cost (£19,500) and accumulated depreciation (£15,633) of the workshop plant sold during the year.

(*d*) Accruals at 30 September 19-6

	£
Wages:	
direct:	
Workshop	113
Petrol and oil	83
indirect:	
Workshop	214
Showroom	231
Electricity	517
General expenses	1,304

(*e*) Prepayments at 30 September 19-6

	£
Rates	13,300

(*f*) Rates and electricity are apportioned over departments on the basis of the original cost of freehold buildings at the end of the current financial year.

(*g*) General expenses are apportioned over departments on the basis of turnover for the current year.

(*h*) Duke and Earl are credited with interest on their respective capital account balances at the rate of 5% per annum.

Required:

Prepare, using separate columns for each department and the business as a whole;

(*a*) a departmental trading and profit and loss account for Aristocratic Autos for the year ended 30 September 19-6

(*b*) a departmental balance sheet for Aristocratic Autos as at 30 September 19-6.

NB

(*a*) Marks will be awarded for workings which are an essential part of the answer.

(*b*) All calculations should be correct to the nearest whole £1.

(Chartered Association of Certified Accountants)

37

Goodwill

When a firm has been in existence for some time, then if the owner(s) wanted to sell the business, they may well be able to obtain more for the business as a going concern than they would if the assets shown on the Balance Sheet were sold separately. To simplify matters, imagine that a man has a small engineering works, of which he was the originator, and that the business was started by him some twenty years ago. He now wishes to sell the business. If sold separately, the assets on the balance sheet would fetch a total of £40,000, being £12,000 for machinery, £25,000 for premises and the stock £3,000. As a complete going concern a purchaser may be willing to pay a total of £50,000 for it. The extra £10,000 that the purchaser will pay over and above the total saleable values of the identifiable assets is known in accounting as goodwill. This is a technical term used in accounting, it must not be confused with the meaning of goodwill in ordinary language usage.

The reasons why the purchaser would be willing to pay £10,000 for goodwill are not always capable of being identified with precision, nor is it often possible to place any particular value on any of the reasons which have induced him to make this offer. One fact only is obvious, and that is that no rational person would be willing to pay a higher figure for the entire going concern than he would pay for buying the identifiable assets separately, unless the expected rate of return on the purchase money spent was greater in the case of the entire going concern. While it is not possible to list all of the factors which induce purchasers to pay for goodwill, it may be useful to examine some possible motives.

(a) The business may have enjoyed some form of monopoly, either nationally or locally. There may not be sufficient trade for two such engineering firms to be carried on profitably. If the purchaser buys this firm then no one may set up in competition with him. On the other hand, if he buys the other assets separately and sets up his own firm, then the original business will still be for sale and the owner may well fix a price that will induce someone to buy it. Many prospective entrants would therefore be prepared to pay an extra amount in the hope of preserving the monopoly position. The monopoly may possibly be due to some form of governmental licence not otherwise easily available.

(b) The purchaser could continue to trade under the same name as that of the original firm. The fact that the firm was well-known could mean that new customers would be attracted for this reason alone. The seller would probably introduce the purchaser to his customers. The establishment of a nucleus of customers is something that many new firms would be willing pay for, as full profits could be earned from the very start of the business instead of waiting until a large enough body of customers is built up. There could be profitable contracts that were capable of being taken over only by the purchaser of the firm.

(c) The value of the labour force, including management skills other than that of the retiring proprietor. The possession of a skilled labour force, including that of management, is an asset that Balance Sheets do not disclose. To recruit and train a suitable labour force is often costly in money and effort, and the purchaser of a going concern would obviously normally be in a position to take over most of the labour force.

(d) The possession of trade marks and patents. These may have cost the original owner little or nothing, not be shown on the Balance Sheet, and could be unsaleable unless the business is sold as a going concern.

(e) The location of the business premises may be more valuable if a particular type of business is carried on rather than if the premises were sold to any other kind of business firm.

(f) The costs of research and development which have brought about cheaper manufacturing methods or a better product may not have been capitalised, but may have been charged as revenue expenditure in the periods when the expenditure was incurred. For any new firm starting up it could well cost a considerable amount of money to achieve the same results.

The amount which someone is prepared to pay for goodwill therefore depends on their view of the future profits which will accrue to the business due to the factors mentioned, or similar assets difficult to identify. The seller of the business will want to show these additional assets to their best advantage, while the buyer will discount those that he feels are inappropriate or over-stressed. The figure actually paid for goodwill will therefore often be a compromise.

The economic state of the country, and whether or not a boom or a recession is in the offing, together with the effects of a credit squeeze or of reflation, plus the relative position of the particular industry, trade or profession, will all affect people's judgements of future profits. In addition the shortage of funds or relatively easy access to finance for such a purchase will, together with the factors already mentioned, lead to marked differences of money paid for goodwill of similar firms at different points in time.

There are also instances where the amount that could be obtained for an entire going concern is less than if all the assets were sold separately. This, contrary to many a person's guess is not 'badwill', as this is just not an accounting term, but would in fact be negative goodwill. The owner would, if he was a rational man, sell all the assets separately, but it does not always hold true. The owner may well have a pride in his work, or a sense of duty to the community, and may elect to sell only to those who would carry on in the same tradition despite the fact that higher offers for the assets had been made. Someone who has to sell his business quickly may also be forced to accept less than he would wish. In accounting it is well to remember that figures themselves only tell part of the story.

Methods of valuing goodwill

Custom plays a large part in the valuation of goodwill in many sorts of businesses. Goodwill exists sometimes only because of custom, because if a somewhat more scientific approach was used in certain cases it would be seen that there was no justification for a figure being paid for goodwill. However, justification or not, goodwill exists where the purchaser is willing to pay for it.

The mere calculation of a figure for goodwill does not mean that someone will be willing to pay this amount for it. As with the striking of any bargain there is no certainty until the price is agreed.

A very important factor to take into account in the valuation of goodwill is based on the 'momentum' theory of goodwill. This can be stated to be that the profits accruing to a firm from the possession of the goodwill at a point in time will lose momentum, and will be gradually replaced by profits accruing from new goodwill created later on. Thus the old goodwill fades away or loses momentum, it does not last for ever, and new goodwill is gradually created. Therefore in a business goodwill may always exist, but it will very rarely be either of the same value or composed of the same factors.

Some of the methods used in goodwill valuation can now be looked at. The rule of thumb approach can be seen in particular in methods (a), (b) and (c) which follow. However, the accountant's role has often been not necessarily to find any 'true' figure which could be validated in some way, but has instead been to find an 'acceptable' figure, one which the parties to a transaction would accept as the basis for settlement. In particular trades, industries and professions, these methods while not necessarily 'true' have certainly been acceptable as the basis for negotiations.

(a) In more than one type of retail business it has been the custom to value goodwill at the average weekly sales for the past year multiplied by a given figure. The given figure will, of course, differ as between different types of businesses, and often changes gradually in the same types of businesses in the long term.

(b) With many professional firms, such as accountants in public practice, it is the custom to value goodwill as being the gross annual fees times a given number. For instance, what is termed a two years' purchase of a firm with gross fees of £6,000 means goodwill = 2 × £6,000 = £12,000.

(c) The average net annual profit for a specified past number of years multiplied by an agreed number. This is often said to be x years purchase of the net profits.

(d) The super-profits basis.

The traditional view

The net profits are taken as not representing a realistic view of the 'true' profits of the firm. For a sole trader, no charge has been made for his services when calculating net profit, yet obviously he is working in the business just as is any other employee. If the net profit is shown as £5,000, can he say that he is better off by £5,000 than he would otherwise have been? The answer must be negative, since if he had not owned a business he could have been earning money from some other employment. Also, if he had not invested his money in the business he could have invested it somewhere else. If these two factors are taken into account, the amount by which he would have been better off is given the name of 'super-profit'.

Exhibit 37.1

Hawks, a chemist, has a shop from which he makes annual net profits of £4,300. The amount of his capital invested in the business was £10,000. If he had invested it elsewhere in something where the element of risk was identical he would have expected a 5 per cent return per annum. If, instead of working for himself, he had in fact taken a post as a chemist he would have earned a salary of £1,800 per annum.

	£	£
Annual net profits		4,300
less Remuneration for similar work	1,800	
" Interest on capital invested £10,000 at 5 per cent	500	2,300
Annual Super-profits		2,000

If it is expected that super-profits can be earned for each of the next five years, then the value of the goodwill is the value of receiving £2,000 extra for each of the next five years.

Sometimes the goodwill is calculated as x years purchase of the super-profits. If this were an eight-year purchase of super-profits of £5,000, then the goodwill would be stated to be worth £40,000.

The discounted momentum value method

The momentum theory of goodwill has already been discussed briefly. The benefits to be gained from goodwill purchased fall as that goodwill gradually ceases to esist, while other benefits are gained from new goodwill created by the new firm. The principle may be further illustrated by reference to the fact that old customers die or may leave the firm, and new ones coming along to replace them are likely to be due to the efforts of the new proprietors. Therefore when buying a business the goodwill should be assesses as follows:

(*a*) Estimate the profits that will accrue from the firm if the existing business is taken over.

(*b*) Estimate the profits that would be made if, instead of buying the existing business, identical assets are bought (other than the goodwill) and the firm starts from scratch.

The difference in the profits to be earned will therfore be as a result of the incidence of the goodwill.

Exhibit 37.2

Years	Estimated profits if existing business taken over	Estimated profits if new business set up	Excess profits caused by goodwill taken over
	£	£	£
1	10,000	4,000	6,000
2	11,000	6,000	5,000
3	11,500	8,500	3,000
4	12,000	11,000	1,000
5	12,000	12,000	–
(and later years will show no difference in profits)			15,000

Sole trader's books

It would not be normal for goodwill to be entered in a sole trader's books unless he had actually bought it. Therefore the very existence of goodwill in the Balance Sheet would result in the assumption that the sole trader had bought the business from someone previously and was not himself the founder of the business.

Partnership books

The partners may make any specific agreement between themselves concerning goodwill. There is no limit as to the ways that they may devise to value it or to enter it in the books, or to make adjusting entries in the books without opening a Goodwill Account. Whatever they agree will therefore take precedence over anything written in this chapter.

However, failing any agreement to the contrary, it is possible to state that a partner in a firm will own a share in the goodwill in the same ratio which he shares profits. Thus if A takes one-quarter of the profits, then he will be the owner of one-quarter of the goodwill. This will hold true whether or not a Goodwill Account is in existence. Should a new partner be introduced who will take a share of one-third of the profits, he will, subject to there being any contrary agreement, be the owner of one-third of the goodwill. It is therefore essential that he should either pay something for goodwill when he enters the firm, or else an amount should be charged to his Capital Account.

This can probably be seen more clearly if a simple example is taken. A and B are in partnership sharing profits one-half each. A new partner, C, is admitted and A, B and C will now take one-third share of the profits, and therefore each will now own one-third of the goodwill. As A and B used to own one-half of the goodwill each they have therefore given part of the asset to C. A few months later the business is sold to a large company and £30,000 is obtained for goodwill. A, B and C will thus receive £10,000 each for their respective shares of the goodwill. If C had not been charged for goodwill, or had paid nothing for it, then A and B would have surrendered part of their ownership of the firm to C and received nothing in return.

Any change in profit sharing will, unless specifically agreed to the contrary, mean that the ownership of the goodwill will also change. As some partners give up their share, or part of their share, of an asset while other partners gain, it is therefore essential that some payment or adjustment be made whenever profit sharing is altered. This will take place whenever any of the following events occur:

(a) There is a change in the profit-sharing ratios of existing partners.

(b) A new partner is introduced.

(c) A partner dies or retires.

In all these cases the whole of the goodwill is not sold. Only in (b) is part of the goodwill sold or charged to an outsider. In (c) the goodwill may be bought by the remaining partners, this is not necessarily the same figure that could be obtained by sale to an outsider. In the case of (b) it is usually assumed that if a new partner is to pay £1,000 to the old partners in satisfaction for a one-quarter share of the goodwill, then the entire goodwill is worth £4,000. The reasoning behind this is that if one-quarter could be sold for £1,000 then the total price would be in the same ratio, i.e. 25 per cent equals £1,000, therefore 100 per cent equals £4,000. This is very often just not true. A relatively higher price may be obtainable from someone who was to be a senior partner than from someone who was to be a junior partner. Thus a one-quarter share of the goodwill might fetch £1,000, but a three-quarters' share of the goodwill might fetch, say, £5,000 because of the factors of prestige and control that a senior partnership would give to the purchaser.

Similarly, with the retirement or death of a partner the amount payable to him or his representatives may not be directly proportional to the total value of goodwill. Circumstances vary widely, but personal relationships and other factors will affect the sum paid.

The question of the value to be placed on goodwill in all of these cases is therefore one of agreement between the partners, and is not necessarily equal to the total saleable value.

Goodwill accounts and partnerships

Unlike a sole trader, a partnership may therefore have a Goodwill Account opened in its books even though the goodwill has never been purchased from an outside source. For instance, a Goodwill Account may be opened just because the partners have changed profit-sharing ratios even though they were the partners that were the founders of the firm, and had not therefore ever paid anything to an outsider for goodwill

With some of the methods used a Goodwill Account is opened, whereas in others adjustments are made without the use of a Goodwill Account. It is not always advantageous to open a Goodwill Account. The mere existence of a Goodwill Account in the Balance Sheet may influence some prospective purchaser of the business, or of part of the business, in a way that was not intended when the Goodwill Account was opened. If a Goodwill Account showed a balance of £10,000 and the partners wanted to sell goodwill for £30,000, the purchaser's decision may be affected. He may have been quite content to pay £30,000 if a Goodwill Account had never existed, but he is now in the position of being asked to pay £30,000 for something which had been valued at £10,000 x years ago. On the other hand, suppose that the Goodwill Account was shown at £10,000 but that the price asked for it was only £4,000. Both of these cases may well put doubts into the mind of the purchaser that would never have existed if a Goodwill Account had never been shown. On the other hand, a lender of money may be happy to see the firm's belief in its goodwill valuation stated as an asset in the Balance Sheet. Business decisions can never be divorced from behavioural patterns. A feeling of 'he gave X £1,000 for it a year ago, why should I give £2,000 for it now?' is very often totally irrational, and would not exist if in fact the buyer never knew that the seller had bought it for that amount.

Where there is a change in the profit-sharing ratios of existing partners

This will normally occur when the effective contributions made by the partners in terms of skill or effort have changed in some way. A partner's contribution may be reduced because of ill-health or old age, or because he is now engaged in some other activity outside the partnership firm. A partner's contribution may have increased because of greater effort or skill compared with when he first joined the firm. The partners will then have to mutually agree to the new profit-sharing ratios. Lack of agreement could mean that the firm would have to be dissolved.

Taking the same basic data, the two methods used whereby (*a*) a Goodwill Account is opened, and (*b*) adjustments are made without the use of a Goodwill Account, can now be illustrated.

Exhibit 37.3

E, F and G have been in business for ten years. They have always shared profits equally. No Goodwill Account has ever existed in the books. On 31 December 19-6 they agree that G will take only a one-fifth share of the profits as from 1 January 19-7, this being due to the fact that he will be devoting less of his time to the business in future. E and F will then each take two-fifths of the profits. The summarised Balance Sheet of the business on 31 December 19-6 appears as follows:

Capitals:		£			£
	E	3,000			
	F	1,800	Net Assets		7,000
	G	2,200			
		7,000			7,000

The partners agree that the goodwill should be valued at £3,000.

(a) **Goodwill account opened**. A Goodwill Account is opened and the total value of goodwill is debited to it. The credit entries are made in the partner's Capital Accounts, being the total value of goodwill divided between the partners in their old profit-sharing ratio.

The Balance Sheet items before and after the adjustments will appear as:

		Before	*After*		*Before*	*After*
		£	£		£	£
Capitals:	E	3,000	4,000	Goodwill	–	3,000
	F	1,800	2,800			
	G	2,200	3,200	Other Assets	7,000	7,000
		7,000	10,000		7,000	10,000

(b) **Goodwill account not opened**. The effect of the change of ownership of goodwill may be shown in the following form:

	Before		*After*		*Loss or Gain*	*Action Required*
		£		£		
E One-third		1,000	Two-fifths	1,200	Gain £200	Debit E's Capital Account £200
F One-third		1,000	Two-fifths	1,200	Gain £200	Debit F's Capital Account £200
G One-third		1,000	One-fifth	600	Loss £400	Credit G's Capital Account £400
		3,000		3,000		

The column headed 'Action Required' shows that a partner who has gained goodwill because of the change must be charged for it by having his Capital Account debited with the value of the gain. A partner who has lost goodwill must be compensated for it by having his capital Account credited.

The Balance Sheet items before and after the adjustments will therefore appear as:

		Before	*After*		*Before*	*After*
		£	£		£	£
Capitals:	E	3,000	2,800	Net Assets	7,000	7,000
	F	1,800	1,600			
	G	2,200	2,600			
		7,000	7,000		7,000	7,000

It would appear at first sight that there is some disparity between the use of methods (*a*) and (*b*). Suppose however that very shortly after the above adjustments the business is sold, the time element being so short that there has been no change in the value of goodwill. If the other assets are sold for £7,000 and the goodwill for £3,000, then in method (*a*) the £10,000 would be exactly sufficient to pay the amounts due to the partners according to their Capital Accounts. In the method (*b*) the Capital Accounts total £7,000 and so the cash received from the sale of the other assets would be exactly enough to pay for those amounts due to the partners. In addition the goodwill has been sold for £3,000, and this sum can now be paid to the partners in the ratio which they owned goodwill, i.e. E two-fifths, £1,200, F two-fifths, £1,200 and G one-fifth, £600. This means that in total each would receive: E £2,800 + £1.200 = £4,000; F £1,600 + £1,200 = £2,800; and G £2,600 + £600 = £3,200. These can be seen to be the same amounts as those paid under method (*a*). The two methods therefore bring about the same end result, the only difference being that one method utilises a Goodwill Account whereas the other method avoids it.

A new partner is introduced

On the introduction of a new partner, unless he takes over the share of a retiring or deceased partner, then obviously the share of the profits taken by each of the partners must change. If A is taking two-thirds of the profits and B one-third, then with the introduction of C, the old partners must give up a share of the profits to him. They can do this by either (*a*) giving up the same proportion of their share of the profits so that the comparative ratios in which they share profits remain the same as before, or else (*b*) the sharing of profits becomes such that the relative profit-sharing ratios of the old partners change as between the new firm and the old firm.

If, (*a*) applies, then with the advent of C the profits shared could become any of the following:

Some possible solutions

	A	*B*	*C*
1	$\frac{1}{2}$	$\frac{1}{4}$	$\frac{1}{4}$
2	$\frac{2}{5}$	$\frac{1}{5}$	$\frac{2}{5}$
3	$\frac{4}{7}$	$\frac{2}{7}$	$\frac{1}{7}$
4	$\frac{4}{9}$	$\frac{2}{9}$	$\frac{3}{9}$

A used to have two-thirds of the profit and B one-third of the profit. A therefore always had a share of the profits which was twice as great as that of B. In all of the above solutions A still takes twice as much as B, irrespective of whatever C takes.

On the other hand, if the ratios became A one-third, B one-third and C one-third, then A would have ceased taking twice as much profits as B. This has been referred to as (*b*).

Where (*a*) applies the only adjustments needed are those between C and the old partnership to compensate for C taking over part of the goodwill. If (*b*) applies, then there will still be adjustments necessary for the goodwill taken over by C, but there will also be adjustments necessary for the change in the relative shares of goodwill held by the old partners.

No change in the old partners' relative shares of profits. The three basic methods in use have been designed to meet the particular wishes of the partners. Each one is used to meet a particular situation. Thus method (*a*) is suitable where the old partners want to be paid in cash privately, and (*b*) applies where the cash is to be retained in the business, whereas (*c*) will be used where an adjustment only is required, in all probability because the incoming partner has insufficient cash to pay separately for goodwill.

(*a*) The new partner pays a sum to the old partners privately which they share in their old profit-sharing ratios. Sometimes the money is paid into the business, only to be drawn out immediately, this is merely being a contra in the Cash Book.

(*b*) The new partner pays cash into the business. This is debited to the Cash Book, then credited to the old partners' Capital Accounts in their old profit-sharing ratios.

(*c*) A Goodwill Account is opened in which the total estimated value of goodwill is debited, and the credits are made in the old partner's Capital Accounts in their old profit-sharing ratios. No cash is paid in by the new partner specifically for goodwill. Any cash he does pay in, is in respect of capital and will therefore be credited to this Capital Account.

Where the old partners' relative shares of profits change with the introduction of a new partner. The introduction of a new partner often takes place because of some fundamental change in the business, and it is often found that the relative shares of profits taken by the old partners need adjusting to preserve an equitable division of the profits to be made in the future. Either the partner will pay a premium for his share of the goodwill, or else an adjustment will be made to charge his Capital Account without any cash being paid by him.

(*a*) **The new partner pays a premium for a share of goodwill.** Unless otherwise agreed, the assumption is that the total value of goodwill is directly proportionate to the amount paid by the new partner for the share taken by him. If a new partner pays £1,200 for a one-fifth share of the profits, then goodwill is taken to be £6,000. A sum of £800 for a one-quarter share of the profits would therefore be taken to imply a total value of £3,200 for goodwill.

It must be stressed tht where a Goodwill Account had been in existence in the old partnership showing the full value of goodwill then the old partners will have been credited with their respective shares, and the following adjustments would not be applicable. These two methods are therefore dependent on adjustments for goodwill rather than the opening of a Goodwill Account.

Exhibit 37.4

Partners, J, K, L and M share profits in the ratio 2:3:4:1 respectively. (In other words, there are 2 + 3 + 4 + 1 parts = 10 parts in all, so that J takes two-tenths, K three-tenths, L four-tenths and M one-tenth of the profits.) A new partner N is to be introduced, to pay £1,000 as a premium for his share of the goodwill. The profits will now be shared between J, K, L, M an N in the rations 2:1:2:2:1 respectively (8 parts in all). The effect of the changes in the ownership of goodwill is now shown in the form of a table. As £1,000 has been paid for one-eighth of the goodwill, the total goodwill is taken as £8,000.

Before		£	After		£	Loss or gain	Action Required
J	Two-tenths	1,600	Two-eighths	2,000	Gain £400	Debit J's Capital Account £400
K	Three-tenths	2,400	One-eighth	1,000	Loss £1,400	Credit K's Capital Account £1,400
L	Four-tenths	3,200	Two-eighths	2,000	Loss £1,200	Credit L's Capital Account £1,200
M	One-tenth	800	Two-eighths	2,000	Gain £1,200	Debit M's Capital Account £1,200
N	–	–	One-eighth	1,000	Gain £1,000	Debit N's Capital Account £1,000
		8,000		8,000		

K and L are the partners who have given up part of their ownership of goodwill. They are therefore compensated by having their Capital Accounts increased, while the partners who have gained are charged, i.e. debited, with the goodwill taken over. The debit in N's Capital Account will be cancelled by the credit entry made when he actually pays in the premium of £1,000 as arranged. Thus the new partner will have paid for his share of the goodwill, while the others will have had their claims against the assets of the firm, i.e. their Capital Accounts, adjusted accordingly.

(b) **The new partner does not pay a premium for goodwill.** Assuming that the facts were the same as in Exhibit 37.2, but that the new partner N was not to actually pay an amount specifically for goodwill yet the total value of goodwill was taken as £8,000, then the entries would be exactly the same as already shown. The only difference would be that the debit entry in N's Capital Account would not be cancelled out by an equal credit by an amount paid in specifically for the purpose. If N paid in £3,000 into the business, then the £1,000 debit for goodwill would reduce his capital to £2,000. Likewise if he only paid in £400 his Capital Account would show a debit balance of £600 until his share of the profits became sufficient to transform this into a normal credit balance.

A partner retires or dies

When a partner leaves the firm then he, or his personal representatives, will agree with the old partners as to how this shall be arranged. Perhaps the partnership deed will contain provisions for such an event, and if so this will normally be observed. Otherwise a new agreement will be arrived at. It would of course, be normal for any agreement to take the course that the retiring partner was entitled to have his share of the goodwill credited to his Capital Account in his profit-sharing ratio. He could leave the amount due to him as a loan to the partnership, or else all or part of it be repaid to him either immediately or be repaid by instalments.

It could well be the case that a new partner takes over the retiring partner's share, all transactions being between him and the retiring partner, the other partners not interfering in any way. The only point that can be made with any certainty is that if the partners cannot agree as to the manner in which any settlement is to be made, then the partnership will have to be dissolved. In this case the procedures are outlined in Volume 2.

Many students are needlessly upset in examinations, because sometimes the examiner sets a question involving partnership goodwill in which the procedures to be carried out are quite unlike anything the student has ever seen before. It must be borne in mind that the partners can agree to payments or adjustments for goodwill in a manner decided by themselves. It does not have to bear any relationship to normal practice; it is purely a matter for agreement. Therefore the examiner is imagining such a situation, and the instructions the examination candidates are given are in accordance with such imaginary agreement. If the student complies with the instructions he is therefore answering the question in the way required by the examiner.

Depreciation of goodwill

Opinion has always been split between two main schools of thought. One school considered that purchased goodwill should be written off directly and should not be maintained as an asset. The other school took the view that goodwill should be depreciated through the profit and loss account year by year over its useful life.

A company's books

In January 1985 Statement of Standard Account Practice No 22 (SSAP 22) 'Accounting for Goodwill' was issued. This relates to companies and groups of companies.

A brief summary of SSAP 22 is as follows:

(a) Purchased goodwill should normally be eliminated immediately as an asset from the books on acquisition.

(b) In some companies, where special needs are appropriate, the purchased goodwill can be 'amortised' (i.e. depreciated) year by year over its useful economic life.

(c) Goodwill which has not been bought, but has been created within the company (inherent goodwill) should never be brought into the books at all.

(d) Where there is 'negative goodwill' this should be added to the reserves in the balance sheet of the company.

Review questions

37.1. The partners have always shared their profits in the ratios of X 4: Y 3: Y 1. They are to alter their profit ratios to X 3: Y 5: Z 2. The last balance sheet before the change was:

Balance Sheet as at 31 December 19-7

	£
Net Assets (not including goodwill)	14,000
	14,000
Capitals:	
X	6,000
Y	4,800
Z	3.200
	14,000

The partners agree to bring in goodwill, being valued at £12,000 on the change.

Show the balance sheets on 1 January 19-8 after goodwill has been taken into account if:

(a) Goodwill account was opened.

(b) Goodwill account was not opened.

37.2A The partners are to change their profit ratios as shown:

	Old ratio	New ratio
A	2	3
B	3	4
C	4	3
D	1	2

They decide to bring in a goodwill amount of £18,000 on the change. The last balance sheet before any element of goodwill has been introduced was:

Balance Sheet as at 30 June 19-8

	£
Net Assets (not including Goodwill)	18,800
	18,000

Capitals:	
A	7,000
B	3,200
C	5,000
D	3,600
	18,800

Show the balance sheets on 1 July 19-8 after necessary adjustments have been made if;

(a) Goodwill account was opened.

(b) Goodwill account was not opened.

37.3 X and Y are in partnership, sharing profits and losses equally. They decide to admit Z. By agreement, goodwill valued at £6,000 is to be introduced into the business books. Z is required to provide capital equal to that of Y after he has been credited with his share of goodwill. The new profit sharing ratios is to be 4:3:3 respectively for X, Y and Z.

The Balance Sheet before admission of Z showed:

	£
Fixed and Current Assets	15,000
Cash	2,000
	17,000

	£
Capital X	8,000
Capital Y	4,000
Current Liabilities	5,000
	17,000

Show:

(a) Journal Entries for admission of Z.

(b) Opening Balance Sheet of new business.

(c) Journal entries for writing off the goodwill which the new partners decided to do soon after the start of the new business.

37.4 A, B and C are in partnership sharing profits and losses in the ratios of 5:4:1 respectively. Their Capital Accounts show credit balances of A £3,000, B £5,000 and C £4,000.

Two new partners are introduced, D and E. The profits are now to be shared: A 3; B 4; C 2; D 2; E 1. D is to pay in £3,000 for his share of the goodwill but E has insufficient cash to pay immediately.

No Goodwill Account is to be opened. Show the Capital Accounts for all of the partners after D has paid for his share of the goodwill.

37.5A L, M and S are in partnership. They shared profits in the ration 2:5:3. It is decided to admit R. It is agreed that goodwill was worth £10,000, but that this is not to be brought into the business records. R will bring £4,000 cash into the business for capital. The new profit sharing ratio is to be L 3: M 4: S 2: R 1.

The Balance Sheet before R was introduced was as follows:

		£
Assets (other than cash)		11,000
Cash		2,500
		13,500
Capitals:	L	3,000
	M	5,000
	S	4,000
Creditors		1,500
		13,500

Show:

(a) The entries in the Capital Accounts of L, M, S and R, the accounts to be in columnar form.

(b) The Balance Sheet after R has been introduced.

38

Partnership accounts continued: revaluation of assets

Revaluation of assets

It has been shown in Chapter 37 that adjustments or payments are required for goodwill in a partnership when a new partner is introduced, the partners change their relative profit-sharing ratios, or a partner retires or dies. Similarly, on each of those occasions the other assets may need to be revalued. Unless there is some agreement to the contrary, if the business is sold and the sale price of the assets exceeds their book values, then the resultant profit is shared between the partners in their profit- and loss-sharing ratios. Similarly, a loss would be borne by them in the same ratios. It is therefore essential that the assets on the Balance Sheet are not markedly out of touch with reality when any changes in partnership occur. Exhibit 38.1 illustrates the necessity for the revaluation of assets.

Exhibit 38.1

The summarised Balance Sheet of a partnership business is as follows:

Balance Sheet as at 31 December 19-6

	£
Property (at cost)	2,000
Machinery (at cost *less* depreciation)	3,500
Stock	1,500
Debtors	3,000
Bank	2,000
	12,000
Capitals: J	4,000
K	3,000
L	5,000
	12,000

J, K and L started the business thirty years perviously. They had always shared profits equally, but from 1 January 19-7 it was to change to J three-sevenths, K three-sevenths and L one-seventh. No revaluation of the assets took place. Six months later the business was sold because of friction between J and K. Because of the nature of the business the assets have to be realised separately and there is no goodwill. The firm had been extremely fortunate in the choice of its premises thirty years ago, they were sold for £23,000, a profit of £21,000. With the machinery the firm had been negligent in not realising that obsolescence had greatly reduced its value and the sale realised only £350 – a loss of £3,150. The stock was sold for £1,500. The debtors included a debt of £2,100 from Long Ltd which had to be written of as a bad debt, all the other debts being realised in full. In fact it was L who had strongly recommended that Long Ltd was acceptable as a customer. None of the realised prices had been affected to any marked extent by events of the previous six months.

The profit on the premises £21,000 is divided as to J three-sevenths, £9,000, K three-sevenths, £9,000 and L one-seventh, £3,000. L's chagrin can be understood when it can be stated that if the partnership assets had been sold more than six months previously, then his share would have been one-third, £7,000 instead of £3,000.

The loss on the machinery is £3,150, shared J three-sevenths, £1,350, K three-sevenths, £1,350, and L one-seventh, £450. As the obsolescence factor is traceable back to more than six months ago, then L's advantage is not an equitable one.

The loss on debtors of £2,100 can be largely traceable to L's action in recommending an uncreditworthy customer. Yet the loss is shared: J three-sevenths, £900, K three-sevenths, £900 and L one-seventh, only £300.

The need for the assets to be revalued upon some change in the basis of partnership is therefore obvious. The revised agreed values are amended quite simply. A Revaluation Account is opened, any increase is asset values being credited to it and the corresponding debits being in the asset accounts, while any reductions in asset values are debited to the Revaluation Account and credited to the asset accounts. If the increases exceed the reductions, then there is said to be a profit on revaluation, such a profit being shared by the old partners in their old profit-sharing ratio, the credit entries being made in the partners' Capital Accounts. The converse applies for a loss on revaluation. An illustration is now given in Exhibit 38.2.

Exhibit 38.2

The following is the summarised Balance Sheet of R, S and T who shared profits and losses in the ratios 3:2:1 respectively.

Balance Sheet as at 31 December 19-7

	£
Property (at cost)	4,500
Motor Vehicles (at cost *less* depreciation)	1,500
Fixtures (at cost *less* depreciation)	2,000
Stock	1,800
Debtors	1,600
Bank	600
	12,000
Capitals: R	4,000
S	5,000
T	3,000
	12,000

From 1 January 19-8 the profit-sharing ratios are to be altered to R 2:S 4:T 1. The following assets are to be revalued in the following amounts – Premises £7,000, Fixtures £1,800, Motor vehicles £1,300 and Stock to £1,500. The accounts needed to show the revaluation are as follows:

Revaluation

	£	£		£
Assets reduced in value:			Assets increased in value:	
Fixtures		200	Premises	2,500
Motor Vehicles		200		
Stock		300		
Profit on Revaluation carried to Capital Accounts				
	£			
R three-sixths	900			
S two-sixths	600			
T one-sixth	300	1,800		
		2,500		2,500

Premises

	£		£
Balance b/fwd	4,500		
Revaluation: Increase	2,500	Balance c/d	7,000
	7,000		7,000
Balance b/d	7,000		

Fixtures

	£		£
Balance b/fwd	2,000	Revaluation: Reduction	200
		Balance c/d	1,800
	2,000		2,000
Balance b/d	1,800		

Motor Vehicles

	£		£
Balance b/fwd	1,500	Revaluation: Reduction	200
		Balance c/d	1,300
	1,500		1,500
Balance b/d	1,300		

Stock

	£		£
Balance b/fwd	1,800	Revaluation: Reduction	300
		Balance c/d	1,500
	1,800		1,800
Balance b/d	1,500		

Capital: R

	£		£
		Balance b/fwd	4,000
Balance c/d	4,900	Revaluation: Share of profit	900
	4,900		4,900
		Balance b/d	4,900

Capital: S

	£		£
		Balance b/fwd	5,000
Balance c/d	5,600	Revaluation: Share of profit	600
	5,600		5,600
		Balance b/d	5,600

Capital: T

	£		£
		Balance b/fwd	3,000
Balance c/d	3,300	Revaluation: Share of profit	300
	3,300		3,300
		Balance b/d	3,300

The balances brought down are those used to start the recording of transactions for the following period.

Review questions

38.1

Hughes, Allen and Elliott

Balance Sheet as at 31 December 19-5

	£
Buildings at cost	8,000
Motor Vehicles (at cost *less* depreciation)	3,550
Office Fittings (at cost *less* depreciation)	1,310
Stock	2,040
Debtors	4,530
Bank	1,390
	20,820
Capitals:	£
Hughes	9,560
Allen	6,420
Elliott	4,840
	20,820

The above partners have always shared profits and losses in the ratio: Hughes 5: Allen 3: Elliott 2.

From 1 January the assets were to be revalued as the profit sharing ratios are to be altered soon. The following assets are to be revalued to the figures shown: Building £17,500, Motor Vehicles £2,600, Stock £1,890, Office Fittings £1,090.

(*a*) You are required to show all the ledger accounts necessary to record the revaluation.

(*b*) Draw up a balance sheet as at 1 January 19-6.

38.2A The following trial balance as at 30 September 19-7 has been extracted from the books of River, Stream and Pool who are trading in partnership:

	£	£
Freehold land and buildings – net book value	42,000	
Fixtures and fittings – net book value	16,000	
Stock	9,000	
Debtors	6,000	
Balance at bank	2,000	
Creditors		7,000
Capital accounts as at 1 October 19-6:		
River		30,000
Stream		20,000
Pool		15,000
Current accounts as at 1 October 19-6:		
River		1,000
Stream		700
Pool		–
Drawings:		
River	21,000	
Stream	13,000	
Pool	11,000	
Net profit for the year ended 30 September 19-7 per draft accounts		46,300
	£120,000	£120,000

Pool joined River and Stream in partnership on 1 October 19-6 under an agreement which included the following terms:

(*a*) Pool to introduce £15,000 cash to be credited to his capital account.

(*b*) The goodwill of the business of River and Stream as at 1 October 19-6 to be valued at £28,000, but a goodwill account is not to be opened.

(*c*) The value of the stock of River and Stream as at 1 October 19-6 to be reduced from £9,000 to £7,000.

(*d*) £10,000 is to be transferred on 1 October 19-6 from River's capital account to be credit of a loan account: River to be credited with interest at the rate of 10% per annum on his loan account balance.

(*e*) Pool to be credited with a partner's salary of £11,000 per annum.

(*f*) Interest at the rate of 5% per annum to be credited to partners in respect of their adjusted capital account balances at 1 October 19-6.

(*g*) The balances of profits and losses to be shared between River, Stream and Pool in the ratio 5:3:2 respectively.

It now transpires that effect has not yet been given to the above terms (b) to (g) inclusive in the partnership books.

Up to 30 September 19-6, River and Stream had no formal partnership agreement.

Required:

(*a*) Prepare the partnership profit and loss appropriation account for the year ended 30 September 19-7.

(*b*) Prepare the partners' capital and current accounts for the year ended 30 September 19-7.

(*Association of Accounting Technicians*)

38.3 Avon and Brown have been in partnership for many years sharing profits and losses in the ratio 3:2 respectively. The following was their Balance Sheet as at 31 December 19-6.

	£
Goodwill	2,000
Plant & Machinery	1,800
Stock	1,960
Debtors	2,130
Cash at Bank	90
	7,980

	£
Capital: Avon	4,000
Brown	3,000
	7,000
Sundry Creditors	980
	£7,980

On 1 January 19-7, they decided to admit Charles as a partner on the condition that he contributed £2,000 as his Capital but that the plant and machinery and stock should be revalued at £2,000 and £1,900 respectively, the other assets, excepting goodwill, remaining at their present book values. The goodwill was agreed to be valueless.

You are required to show:
(*a*) The ledger entries dealing with the above in the following accounts:
(*i*) Goodwill Account,
(*ii*) Revaluation Accounts,
(*iii*) Capital Accounts;
(*b*) The Balance Sheet of the partnership immediately after the admission of Charles.

38.4A The following trial balance as at 31 March 19-6 has been extracted from the books of John Brown, trading as Strongcolour Fabrics:

	£	£
John Brown: Capital account, at 1 April 19-5		61,000
John Brown: Drawings	22,600	
Freehold property:		
At cost	40,000	
Provision for depreciation		6,000
Fixtures and fittings:		
At cost	30,000	
Provision for depreciation		5,400
Motor vehicles:		
At cost	12,000	
Provision for depreciation		5,000
Debtors	14,000	
Creditors		9,000
Balance at bank	5,700	
Sales		240,000
Cost of sales	168,000	
Stock at 31 March 19-6	5,100	
Establishment and distribution expenses	29,000	
	£326,400	£326,400

On 1 January 19-6, Peter Grey, a senior employee, joined John Brown in partnership trading as Allcolour Cloths.

The goodwill of Strongcolour Fabrics was valued at 31 December 19-5 at £12,000, but it has been agreed that a goodwill account will not be opened. A John Brown Loan Account is to be opened as from 1 January 19-6 with a transfer of £20,000 from John Brown's Capital Account. A capital account and a current account are to be maintained for each partner.

Peter Grey has not been paid his salary of £12,000 per annum as administrative manager since 1 April 19-5 and no adjustment has been made yet in the books for such salary in view of the impending partnership. However, it has now been agreed that the amount due to Peter Grey as an employee will form the basis of his capital as a partner of Allcolour Cloths.

It has been agreed that all assets and liabilities recorded in the books of Strongcolour Fabrics will be carried forward to Allcolour Cloths at their book values with the exception of freehold property which has been revalued at 1 January 19-6 at £50,000.

The following additional information has been given for the year ended 31 March 19-6:

(a) All sales have produced a uniform rate of gross profit;

(b) One eighth of the turnover took place in the last quarter of the year;

(c) Establishment and distribution expenses accrued due at 31 March 19-6 amounted to £1,000;

(d) Establishment and distribution expenses are to be apportioned uniformly throughout the year;

(e) Depreciation, apportioned uniformly throughout the year, is to be provided at the following rates on the original cost of fixed assets held at the year end:

Fixtures and fittings	12%
Motor vehicles	25%

No depreciation is to be provided on the freehold property for the year.

Required:

(*a*) Prepare a trading and profit and loss account for the nine months ended 31 December 19-5 for Strongcolour Fabrics.

(*b*) Prepare a trading and profit and loss account for the three months ended 31 March 19-6 for Allcolour Cloths.

(*c*) Prepare a balance sheet as at 31 March 19-6 for Allcolour Cloths.

(*Association of Accounting Technicians*)

38.5 Alan, Bob and Charles are in partnership sharing profits and losses in the ratio 3:2:1 respectively.

The Balance Sheet for the partnership as at 30 June 19-2 is as follows:

	£	£
Fixed Assets		
Premises		90,000
Plant		37,000
Vehicles		15,000
Fixtures		2,000
		144,000
Current Assets		
Stock	62,379	
Debtors	34,980	
Cash	760	98,119
		£242,119

	£	£
Capital		
Alan		85,000
Bob		65,000
Charles		35,000
		185,000
Current Account		
Alan	3,714	
Bob	(2,509)	
Charles	4,678	5,883
Loan - Charles		28,000
Current Liabilities		
Creditors		19,036
Bank Overdraft		4,200
		£242,119

Charles decides to retire from the business on 30 June 19-2, and Don is admitted as a partner on that date. The following matters are agreed:

(*a*) Certain assets were revalued — Premises £120,000
                              — Plant £35,000
                              — Stock £54,179

(b) Provision is to be made for doubtful debts in the sum of £3,000.

(c) Goodwill is to be recorded in the books on the day Charles retires in the sum of £42,000. The partners in the new firm do not wish to maintain a goodwill account so that amount is to be written back against the new partners' capital accounts.

(d) Alan and Bob are to share profits in the same ratio as before, and Don is to have the same share of profits as Bob.

(e) Charles is to take his car at its book value of £3,900 in part payment, and the balance of all he is owed by the firm in cash except £20,000 which he is willing to leave as a loan account.

(f) The partners in the new firm are to start on an equal footing so far as capital and current accounts are concerned. Don is to contribute cash to bring his capital and current accounts to the same amount as the original partner from the old firm who has the lower investment in the business.

The original partner in the old firm who has the higher investment will draw out cash so that his capital and current account balances equal those of his new partners.

Required:

(a) Account for the above transactions, including Goodwill and retiring Partners Accounts.

(b) Draft a Balance Sheet for the partnership of Alan, Bob and Don as at 30 June 19-2.

(*Association of Accounting Technicians*)

39

An introduction to the final accounts of limited liability companies

The two main disadvantages of a partnership are that the number of owners cannot normally exceed twenty, and that their liability, barring limited partners, is not limited to the amount invested in the partnership but extends to the individual partners' private possessions. This means that the failure of the business could result in a partner losing both his share of the business assets and also part or all of his private assets as well.

The form of organisation to which these two limitations do not apply are known as **limited liability companies**. There are companies which have unlimited liability, but these are not dealt with in this volume. From this point any reference to a company in this textbook means a limited liability company. The law governing these companies in the United Kingdom is the Companies Act 1985.

The capital of a limited company is divided into **shares**. These can be of any denomination, such as £5 shares or £1 shares. To become a member of a limited company, alternatively called a **shareholder**, a person must buy one or more shares. He may either pay in full for the shares that he takes up, or else the shares may be partly paid for, the balance to be paid as and when the company may arrange. The liability of a member is limited to the shares that he holds, or where a share is only partly paid he is also liable to have to pay the amount owing by him on the shares. Thus, even if a company loses all its assets, a member's private possessions cannot be touched to pay the company's debts, other than in respect of the amount owing on partly paid shares.

Companies thus fulfil the need for the capitalisation of a firm where the capital required is greater than that which twenty people can contribute, or where limited liability for all members is desired.

Private and public companies

There are two classes of company, the **private company** and the **public company**. In fact, private companies outnumber public companies by a considerable number. In Section 1 of the Companies Act 1985 a public company is defined as one whose memorandum states that the company is a public company, and has registered as such. A public company must normally have an authorised capital of at least £50,000. Minimum membership is two, there is no maximum.

The name of a public company must either end with the words 'public limited company' or the abbreviation 'plc', or the Welsh equivalent if the registered office is situated in Wales.

Private companies are usually (but not always) smaller businesses, and may be formed by two or more persons. A private company is defined by the Act as a company which is not a public company. In fact the main difference, other than a private company can have authorised capitals less than £50,000, is that public companies are allowed to offer their shares for subscription by the public at large, whereas private companies cannot do this. Therefore if you were to walk into a bank, or similar public place, and see a prospectus offering anyone the chance to take up shares in a company, then that company would be a **public** company.

The day-to-day business of a company is not carried out by the shareholders. The possession of a share normally confers voting rights on the holder, who is then able to attend general meetings of the company. At one of these the shareholders will meet and will vote for **directors**, these being the people who will be entrusted with the running of the business. At each **Annual General Meeting** the directors will have to report on their stewardship, and this report is accompanied by a set of Final Accounts for the year.

Share capital

A shareholder of a limited company obtains his reward in the form of a share of the profits, known as a **dividend**. The directors consider the amount of profits and decide on the amount of profits which are placed to reserves. Out of the profits remaining the directors then propose the payment of a certain amount of dividend to be paid. It is important to note that the shareholders cannot propose a higher dividend for themselves than that already proposed by the directors. They can however propose that a lesser dividend should be paid, although this action is very rare indeed. If the directors propose that no dividend be paid then the shareholders are powerless to alter the decision.

The decision by the directors as to the amount proposed as dividends is a very complex one and cannot be fully discussed here. Such points as government directives to reduce dividends, the effect of taxation, the availability of bank balances to pay the dividends, the possibility of take-over bids and so on will all be taken into account.

The dividend is usually expressed as a percentage. Ignoring income tax, a dividend of 10 per cent in Firm A on 500,000 Ordinary Shares of £1 each will amount to £50,000, or a dividend of 6 per cent in Firm B on 200,000 Ordinary Shares of £2 each will amount to £24,000. A shareholder having 100 shares in each firm would receive £10 from Firm A and £12 from Firm B.

There are two main types of share, **preference shares** and **ordinary shares**. A preference share is one whose main characteristic is that it is entitled to a specified percentage rate of dividend before the ordinary shareholders receive anything. On the other hand the ordinary shares would be entitled to the remainder of the profits which have been appropriated for dividends.

For example, if a company had 10,000 5 per cent preference shares of £1 each and 20,000 ordinary shares of £1 each, then the dividends would be payable as in Exhibit 39.1.

Exhibit 39.1

Years	1	2	3	4	5
	£	£	£	£	£
Profits appropriated for Dividends	900	1,300	1,600	3,100	2,000
Preference Dividends (5%)	500	500	500	500	500
Ordinary Dividends	(2%) 400	(4%) 800	(5½%) 1,100	(13%) 2,600	(7½%) 1,500

There are two main types of preference share, these being **non-cumulative preference shares** and **cumulative preference shares**. A non-cumulative preference share is one which is entitled to a yearly percentage rate of dividend, and should the available profits be insufficient to cover the percentage dividend then the deficiency cannot be made good out of future years' profits. On the other hand, any deficiency on the part of cumulative preference shares can be carried forward as arrears, and such arrears are payable before the ordinary shares receive anything.

Illustrations of the two types of share should make this clearer:

Exhibit 39.2: A company has 5,000 £1 ordinary shares and 2,000 5 per cent non-cumulative preference shares of £1 each. The profits available for dividends are: year 1 £150, year 2 £80, year 3 £250, year 4 £60, year 5 £500.

Exhibit 39.2

Year	1	2	3	4	5
	£	£	£	£	£
Profits	150	80	250	60	500
Preference Dividend (limited in years 2 and 4)	100	80	100	60	100
Dividends on Ordinary Shares	50	—	150	—	400

Exhibit 39.3: Assume that the preference shares in Exhibit 41.2 had been cumulative, the dividends would have been:

Exhibit 39.3

Year	1	2	3	4	5
	£	£	£	£	£
Profits	150	80	250	60	500
Preference Dividend	100	80	120*	60	140*
Dividends on Ordinary Shares	50	—	130	—	360

*including arrears.

The total of the **share capital** which the company would be allowed to issue is known as the **authorised share capital**, or alternatively as the **nominal capital**. The share capital actually issued to shareholders is known as the **issued capital**. Obviously, if the whole of the share capital which the company is allowed to issue has in fact been issued, then the authorised and the issued share capital will be the same figure.

Where only part of the amount payable on each share has been asked for, then the total amount asked for on all shares is known as the **called-up capital**. The **uncalled capital** is therefore that part of the amount payable on all the shares for which payment has not been requested. Calls in arrear relate to amounts requests (called for) but not yet received, while calls in advance relate to moneys received prior to payment being requested. **Paid-up capital** will be that part of the capital which has actually been paid by shareholders.

An illustration should make this clearer. This is shown as Exhibit 39.4.

Exhibit 39.4

(i) Better Enterprises Ltd was formed with the legal right to be able to issue 100,000 shares of £1 each.

(ii) The company has actually issued 75,000 shares.

(iii) None of the shares have yet been fully paid up. So far the company has made calls of 80p (£0.80) per share.

(iv) All the calls have been paid by shareholders except for £200 owing from one shareholder.

(*a*) Authorised or Nominal Share Capital is (i) £100,000.

(*b*) Issued Share Capital is (ii) £75,000.

(*c*) Called up Capital is (iii) 75,000 × £0.80 = £60,000.

(*d*) Calls in arrear amounted to (iv) £200.

(*e*) Paid-up Capital is (c) £60,000 less (d) £200 = £59,800.

Debentures

The term **debenture** is used when a limited company receives money on loan and written acknowledgement is given, usually under the company. The debenture certificates thus issued, stating the rate of interest to be paid on the amount borrowed are known by the alternative names of debentures, **loan stock**, or **loan capital**.

A debenture may be **redeemable**, i.e. repayable at or by a specified date. Conversely they may be **irredeemable**, redemption only taking place when the company is eventually liquidated, or in a case such as when the debenture interest is not paid within a given time limit. If a date is shown behind a debenture, e.g. 2001/2008, it means that the company can redeem it in any of the years 2001 to 2008 inclusive.

People lending money to companies in the form of debentures will obviously be interested in how safe their investment will be. Some debentures are given the legal right that on certain happenings the debenture holders will be able to take control of specific assets, or of the whole of the assets. They can then sell the assets and recoup the amount due under their debentures, or deal with the assets in ways specified in the deed under which the debentures were issued. Such debentures are known as being secured against the assets, the term 'mortgage' debenture often being used. Other debentures have no prior right to control the assets under any circumstances. These are known as **simple** or **naked** debentures.

Trading and profit and loss accounts

From the viewpoint of the preparation of trading and profit and loss accounts, there are no differences as between public and private limited companies. The accounts now described are those purely for internal use by the company. Obviously, if a full copy of the trading and profit and loss accounts were given to each shareholder, the company's rivals could easily obtain a copy, and would then be in a position to learn about details of the company's trading which the company would prefer to keep secret. The Companies Act therefore states that only certain details of the trading and profit and loss account must be shown. Companies can, if they so wish, disclose more than the minimum information required by law, but it is simply a matter for the directors to decide whether or not it would be in the company's interest. A disussion of the minimum information required is contained in Volume 2.

The trading account of a limited company is no different from that of a sole trader or of a partnership. The profit and loss account also follows the same pattern as those of partnerships or sole traders except for some types of expense which are peculiar to limited companies. The two main expenses under this heading are:

(*a*) **Directors' remuneration**. This is obvious, since only in companies are directors found.

(*b*) **Debenture interest**. The interest payable for the use of the money is an expense of the company, and is payable whether profits are made or not. This means that debenture interest is charged as an expense in the Profit and Loss Account itself. Contrast this with dividends which are dependent on profits having been made.

When a company is being formed there are expenses concerned with its incorporation such as stamp duties, legal expenses etc. Collectively these are known as **preliminary expenses**. Before 1981 these could be shown as an asset in the balance sheet, but they should now be written off as an expense immediately.

The appropriation account

Next under the profit and loss account is a section called, as it would also be in a partnership, the profit and loss appropriation account. The net profit is brought down from the profit and loss account, and in the appropriation account is shown the manner in which the profits are to be appropriated, i.e. how the profits are to be used.

First of all, if any of the profits are to be put to reserve then the transfer is shown. To transfer to a reserve means that the directors wish to indicate that that amount of profits is not to be considered as available for dividends in that year. The reserve may be specific, such as a Fixed Asset Replacement Reserve or it may be a General Reserve.

Out of the remainder of profits the dividends are proposed and the unused balance of profits is carried forward to the following year, where it goes to swell the profits then available for appropriation. It is very rare, assuming the firm has not been incurring losses, for there not to be any unappropriated balance of profits carried forward even if it is the policy of the firm to declare the greatest possible dividends, because dividends are normally proposed either as a whole percentage or to a one-half or one-quarter per cent. Arithmetically it is uncommon for the profits remaining after transfers to reserves to exactly equal such a figure.

A set of appropriation accounts demonstrating these points is illustrated in Exhibit 39.5, but first the importance of Corporation Tax has to be explained.

Taxation

At this point in your studies you do not need to know very much about taxation. However, it does affect the preparation of accounts, and so we will tell you here as much as you need to know now. Sole traders and partnerships pay income tax based on their profits. Such income tax, when paid, is simply charged as drawings – it is not an expense.

In the case of companies, the taxation levied upon them is called **corporation tax**. It is also based on the amount of profits made. In the later stages of your examinations you will learn how to calculate it. At this point you will be told how much it is, or be given a simple arithmetical way of ascertaining the amount.

Corporation tax is *not* an expense, it is an appropriation of profits. This was established by two legal cases many years ago. However, for the sake of presentation and to make the accounts more understandable to the general reader, it is not shown with the other appropriations. Instead, as in Exhibit 39.5 it is shown as a deduction from profit for the year before taxation (i.e. this is the net profit figure) to show the net result, i.e. profit for the year after taxation.

A worked example

IDO Ltd has an Ordinary Share Capital of 40,000 ordinary shares of £1 each and 20,000 5 per cent preference shares of £1 each.

The net profits for the first three years of business ended 31 December are: 19-4, £10,967; 19-5, £14,864; and 19-6, £15,822.

Transfers to reserves are made as follows: 19-4 nil; 19-5, general reserve, £1,000, and 19-6, fixed assets replacement reserve, £2,250.

Dividends were proposed for each year on the preference shares and on the ordinary shares at: 19-4, 10 per cent; 19-5, 12.5 per cent; 19-6, 15 per cent.

Corporation Tax, based on the net profits of each year is 19-4 £4,100; 19-5 £5,250; 19-6 £6,300.

Exhibit 39.5

IDC Ltd
Profit and Loss Appropriation Accounts
(1) For the year ended 31 December 19-4

	£	£
Profit for the year before taxation		10,967
less Corporation Tax		4,100
Profit for the year after taxation		6,867
less Proposed Dividends:		
Preference Dividend of 5%	1,000	
Ordinary Dividend of 10%	4,000	5,000
Retained profits carried forward to next year		1,867

(2) For the year ended 31 December 19-5

	£	£
Profit for the year before taxation		14,864
less Corporation Tax		5,250
Profit for the year after taxation		9,614
add Retained profits from last year		1,867
		11,481
less Transfer to General Reserve	1,000	
Proposed Dividends:		
Preference Dividend of 5%	1,000	
Ordinary Dividend of 12½%	5,000	7,000
Retained profits carried forward to next year		4,481

(3) For the year ended 31 December 19-6

	£	£
Profit for the year before taxation		15,822
less Corporation Tax		6,300
Profit for the year after taxation		9,522
add Retained profits from last year		4,481
		14,003
less Transfer to Fixed Assets		
Replacement Reserve	2,250	
Proposed Dividends:		
Preference Dividend of 5%	1,000	
Ordinary Dividend of 15%	6,000	9,250
Retained profits carried forward to next year		4,753

In a balance sheet, Corporation Tax owing can normally be found as a current liability.

The balance sheet

Prior to the UK Companies Act 1981, a company could, provided it disclosed the necessary information, draw up its Balance Sheet and Profit and Loss Account for publication in any way that it wished. The 1981 Act, however, stopped such freedom of display, and laid down the precise details to be shown. These have been repeated in the current Companies Act dated 1985.

As many of the readers of this book will not be sitting UK examinations they will not have to comply with the UK Companies Act. We are therefore showing two specimen balance sheets containing the same facts:

(*a*) Exhibit 39.6 for students sitting examinations based on UK laws. The specimen shown does not contain all the possible items which could be shown, as this chapter is an introduction to the topic only. Volume 2 of this book gives a greater insight into company accounts.

(*b*) Exhibit 39.7 is for students sitting local overseas examinations not based on UK legislation.

Exhibit 39.6 (for students sitting examinations based on UK company legislation)

Letters in brackets (A) to (G): refer to notes following the balance sheet.

Balance Sheet as at 31 December 19-7

	£	£	£
Fixed Assets			
Intangible Assets (A)			
Goodwill		10,000	
Tangible Assets (B)			
Buildings	9,000		
Machinery	5,600		
Motor Vehicles	2,400	17,000	27,000
Current Assets			
Stock	6,000		
Debtors	3,000		
Bank	4,000	13,000	
Creditors: Amounts falling due within one year (C)			
Proposed Dividend	1,000		
Creditors	3,000		
Corporation Tax owing	2,000	6,000	
Net Current Assets (D)			7,000
Total Assets less Current Liabilities			34,000
Creditors: amounts falling due after more than one year (E)			
Debenture Loans			8,000
			26,000
Capital and Reserves			
Called-up share capital (F)			20,000
Share Premium account (G)			1,200
Other Reserves			
General Reserve			3,800
Profit and loss account			1,000
			26,000

Notes:

(A) Intangible Assets are those not having a 'physical' existence, for instance you can see and touch tangible assets under (B), i.e. buildings, machinery etc, but you cannot see and touch goodwill.

(B) Tangible fixed assets under a separate heading. Notice that figures shown net after depreciation. In a note accompanying the accounts the cost and depreciation on these assets would be given.

(C) Only items payable within one year go under this heading.

(D) The term 'net current assets' replaces the more familiar term of 'working capital'.

(E) These particular debentures are repayable several years hence. If they had been payable within one year they would have been shown under (D).

(F) An analysis of share capital will be given in supplementary notes to the balance sheet.

(G) One reserve that is in fact not labelled with the word 'reserve' in its title is the Share Premium account. For various reasons (discussed fully in Volume 2) shares can be issued for more than their face or nominal value. The excess of the price at which they are issued over the nominal value of the shares is credited to a Share Premium account.

Exhibit 39.7 (for local overseas examinations)

Balance Sheet as at 31 December 19-7

	Cost	Depreciation to date	Net
Fixed Assets	£	£	£
Goodwill	15,000	5,000	10,000
Buildings	15,000	6,000	9,000
Machinery	8,000	2,400	5,600
Motor Vehicles	4,000	1,600	2,400
	42,000	15,000	27,000
Current Assets			
Stock		6,000	
Debtors		3,000	
Bank		4,000	
		13,000	
less Current Liabilities			
Proposed Dividend	1,000		
Creditors	3,000		
Corporation Tax owing	2,000	6,000	
Working Capital			7,000
			34,000

Financed by:		
Share Capital	£	£
Authorised 30,000 shares of £1 each		30,000
Issued 20,000 Ordinary shares of £1 each, fully paid		20,000
Reserves		
Share premium	1,200	
General reserve	3,800	
Profit and Loss Account	1,000	
		6,000
		26,000
Debentures		
Six per cent Debentures: repayable 19-3		8,000
		34,000

Notes:

(*a*) Fixed assets should normally be shown either at cost or alternatively at some other valuation. In either case, the method chosen should be clearly stated.

(*b*) The total depreciation from date of purchase to the date of the balance sheet should be shown.

(*c*) The authorised share capital, where it is different from the issued share capital, is shown as a note.

(*d*) Reserves consist either of those unused profits remaining in the appropriation account, or transferred to a reserve account appropriately titled, e.g. General Reserve, Fixed Assets Replacement Reserve. At this juncture all that needs to be said is that any account labelled as a reserve has originated by being charged as a debit in the appropriation account and credited to a reserve account with an appropriate title. These reserves are shown in the balance sheet after share capital under the heading of 'Reserves'.

One reserve that is in fact not labelled with the word 'reserve' in its title is the Share Premium Account. For various reasons shares can be issued for more than their face or nominal value. The excess of the price at which they are issued over the nominal value of the shares is credited to a Share Premium Account. This is then shown with the other reserves in the Balance Sheet.

(*e*) Where shares are only partly called up, then it is the amount actually called up that appears in the balance sheet and not the full amount.

(*f*) The share capital and reserves should be totalled so as to show the book value of all the shares in the company. Either the terms 'Shareholders Funds' or 'Members Equity' are often given to the total of Share Capital plus Reserves.

A term which sometimes appears in examinations is that of 'Fungible Assets'. Fungible assets are assets which are substantially indistinguishable one from another.

A fully worked example

Exhibit 39.8

The following trial balance is extracted from the books of FW Ltd as on 31 December 19-5:

Trial balance as on 31 December 19-5

	Dr	Cr
10% Preference Share Capital		20,000
Ordinary Share Capital		70,000
10% Debentures (repayable 19-9)		30,000
Goodwill at cost	15,500	
Buildings at cost	95,000	
Equipment at cost	8,000	
Motor Vehicles at cost	17,200	
Provision for Depreciation: Equipment 1.1.19-5		2,400
Provision for Depreciation: Motors 1.1.19-5		5,160
Stock 1.1.19-5	22,690	
Sales		98,200
Purchases	53,910	
Carriage Inwards	1,620	
Salaries & Wages	9,240	
Directors' Remuneration	6,300	
Motor Expenses	8,120	
Rates & Insurances	2,930	
General Expenses	560	
Debenture Interest	1,500	
Debtors	18,610	
Creditors		11,370
Bank	8,390	
General Reserve		5,000
Share Premium Account		14,000
Interim Ordinary Dividend paid	3,500	
Profit & Loss Account 31.12.19-4		16,940
	273,070	273,070

The following adjustments are needed:

(i) Stock at 31.12.19-5 was £27,220.

(ii) Depreciate Motors £3,000, Equipment £1,200.

(iii) Accrue Debenture Interest £1,500.

(iv) Provide for Preference Dividend £2,000 and Final Ordinary Dividend of 10 per cent.

(v) Transfer £2,000 to General Reserve.

(vi) Write off Goodwill £3,000.

(vii) Authorised Share Capital is £20,000 in Preference Shares and £100,000 in Ordinary Shares.

(viii) Provide for Corporation Tax £5,000.

The final accounts will now be shown using a vertical form. The Profit and Loss

Account will be suitable both for those sitting UK examinations, and those sitting local overseas examinations. The balance sheets will be shown using separate balance sheets for both kinds of students.

Note that the profit and loss account is not restricted to that which must be published by companies.

(i) Trading & Profit and Loss Accounts suitable both for UK and overseas examinations. For internal use only, not for publication.

F W Ltd

Trading & Profit & Loss Account for the year ended 31 December 19-5

	£	£	£
Sales			98,200
less Cost of Goods Sold:			
Opening Stock		22,690	
add Purchases	53,910		
add Carriage Inwards	1,620	55,530	
		78,220	
less Closing Stock		27,220	51,000
Gross Profit			47,200
less Expenses:			
Salaries & Wages		9,240	
Motor Expenses		8,120	
Rates & Insurances		2,930	
General Expenses		560	
Directors' Remuneration (*A*)		6,300	
Debenture Interest (*B*)		3,000	
Depreciation: Motors		3,000	
Equipment		1,200	34,350
Profit for the year before taxation			12,850
less Corporation Tax			5,000
Profit for the year after taxation			7,850
add Retained profits from last year			16,940
			24,790
less Appropriations:			
Transfer to General Reserve		2,000	
Goodwill part written off		3,000	
Preference Share Dividend		2,000	
Ordinary Share Dividends:			
Interim	3,500		
Final (*C*)	7,000	10,500	17,500
Retained Profits carried forward to next year (*C*)			7,290

Notes:

(*A*) As stated earlier directors' remuneration is shown as an expense in the profit and loss account itself.

(*B*) As stated earlier, debenture interest is an expense to be shown in the profit & loss account itself.

(*C*) The final dividend of 10 per cent is based on the Issued Ordinary Share Capital and *not* on the Authorised Ordinary Share Capital.

(ii) Balance Sheet based on UK legislation

F W Ltd
Balance Sheet as at 31 December 19-7

	£	£	£
Fixed Assets			
Intangible Assets			
Goodwill		12,500	
Tangible Assets (*A*)			
Buildings	95,000		
Equipment	4,400		
Motors	9,040	108,440	120,940
Current Assets			
Stock	27,220		
Debtors	18,610		
Bank	8,390	54,220	
Creditors: amounts falling due within one year			
Creditors	11,370		
Proposed Dividend	9,000		
Debenture Interest Accrued	1,500		
Taxation	5,000	26,870	
Net Current Assets			27,350
Total Assets less Current Liabilities			148,290
Creditors: amounts falling due after more than one year			
Debentures			30,000
			118,290
Capital and Reserves (B)			
Called-up share capital (*C*)			90,000
Share Premium account			14,000
Other Reserves			
General Reserve			7,000
Profit and Loss Account			7,290
			118,290

(*A*) Notes to be given in an appendix as to cost, acquistions and sales in the year and depreciation.

(*B*) Reserves consist either of those unused profits remaining in the appropriation account, or transferred to a reserve account appropriately titled, e.g. General Reserve, Fixed Assets Replacement Reserve, etc.

At this juncture all that needs to be said is that any account labelled as a reserve has originated by being charged as a debit in the appropriation title. These reserves are shown in the balance sheet after share capital under the heading of 'Reserves'.

One reserve that is in fact not labelled with the word 'reserve' in its title is the Share Premium Account. This is shown with the other reserves in the Balance Sheet.

The closing balance on the Profit & Loss Appropriation Account is shown under Reserves. These are profits not already appropriated, and therefore 'reserved' for future use.

(*C*) The authorised share capital, where it is different from the issued share capital, is shown as a note. Notice that the total figure of £120,000 for Authorised Capital is not included when adding up the balance sheet sides. Only the Issued Capital figures are included in balance sheet totals.

(iii) Balance sheet for students sitting local overseas examinations.

Balance Sheet as at 31 December 19-5

Fixed Assets	Costs	Depreciation to date	Net
	£	£	£
Goodwill	15,500	3,000	12,500
Buildings	95,000	—	95,000
Equipment	8,000	3,600	4,400
Motors	17,200	8,160	9,040
	135,700	14,760	120,940

Current Assets			
Stock		27,220	
Debtors		18,610	
Bank		8,390	
		54,220	
less Current Liabilities			
Creditors	11,370		
Dividends Owing	9,000		
Debenture Interest Owing	1,500		
Taxation	5,000	26,870	
Working Capital			27,350
			148,290

Financed by:

Share Capital	*Authorised*	*Issued*	
	£	£	£
Preference Shares	20,000	20,000	
Ordinary Shares	100,000	70,000	90,000
	120,000		

Reserves		
Share Premium	14,000	
General Reserve	7,000	
Profit & Loss	7,290	28,290
		118,290
Loan capital		
10% Debentures		30,000
		148,290

Bonus shares

The issue of bonus shares would appear to be outside the scope of syllabuses at this level. However, some examinations have included a minor part of a question concerned with bonus shares. All that is needed here is a very brief explanation only, leaving further explanations at a later stage.

Bonus shares are 'free' shares issued to shareholders without any cash being paid for them. The Reserves are utilised for the purpose. Thus if before the bonus issue there was £20,000 share capital and £12,000 reserves, and then a bonus issue of 1 for 4 was made (i.e. 1 bonus share for every 4 shares already held) the bonus issue would amount to £5,000. The share capital then becomes £25,000 and the reserves become £7,000.

A proper and fuller explanation appears in Volume 2 of this book. A bonus issue is often known as a 'scrip' issue.

Other statutory books

Besides the normal accounting records as described already in this text, there are other books which the law says must be kept, i.e. they are **statutory** books. A list of them, what they should contain, and the need for them is now shown.

	Contains	*Purpose*
Register of members	Details of shareholders, giving names, addresses, amounts of shareholdings.	To enable anyone to find identities of shareholders.
Register of debenture holders	Details of debenture holders, giving names, addresses, amounts of debentures held.	To enable anyone to find identities of debenture holders.
Register of charges	Full details of each charge.	To enable anyone to discover amounts of charges, what they have been secured on and parties involved.
Register of directors & secretaries	Particulars of each person concerned.	To enable anyone to discover their identities.

Register of directors' interests	Full details shares & debentures held by directors or their close relatives.	To enable anyone to ascertain exact involvement of director with the company.
Minute book: general meetings	Proper account of items discussed, resolutions & voting.	To enable anyone to discover details of business concerned.
Minute book: directors' meetings	Proper account of items discussed and decisions taken.	Not open generally to examination. Serves as a record of business undertaken.
Register of shareholders' interests (where 5% or more shareholding is kept)	Full details of shareholders involved, amounts of shareholdings etc.	To enable anyone to find out who may be able to exert influence on company because of size of shareholding held.

Multiple-choice questions.

Now attempt Set No 5 of multiple-choice questions on p.499.

Review questions

39.1 After the preparation of the trading and profit and loss account the following balances remained in the books of A Co Ltd, at 31 December 19-6.

	£		£
Creditors	16,900	Depreciation on plant and	
Debenture interest owing	175	machinery	16,000
£1 ordinary shares fully paid	100,000	£1 5 per cent preference	
Trade expenses owing	3,075	shares fully paid	5,000
Cash	7,500	Debtors	18,900
Stock	25,000	Freehold premises	71,000
Profit and loss account	30,000	7 per cent debentures	5,000
		Plant and machinery	41,000
		Bank	12,750

The company had issued all its authorised ordinary share capital, but £5,000 of £1 5 per cent preference shares still remained unissued. The debentures are repayable in 5 years' time.

39.2A A balance sheet is to be drawn up from the following as at 30 June 19-6.

	£
Issued Share Capital: Ordinary Shares £1 each	100,000
Authorised Share Capital: Ordinary Shares of £1 each	200,000
10 per cent Debentures	40,000
Buildings at cost	105,000
Motor Vehicles at cost	62,500
Fixtures at cost	11,500
Profit and Loss Account	5,163
Fixed Assets Replacement Reserve	8,000
Stock	16,210
Debtors	14,715
General Reserve	6,000
Creditors	9,120
Proposed Dividend	5,000
Depreciation to date: Motor Vehicles	15,350
Premises	22,000
Fixtures	3,750
Bank (balancing figure for you to ascertain)	?

39.3 The following information was available on Z Ltd for the year ended 31 March 19-7.

Authorised Capital
1,000,000 £1 ordinary shares
250,000 9 per cent £1 preference shares

Issued Capital
800,000 £1 ordinary shares fully paid

Revenue profits earned for the year
£252,000

Dividends paid
Interim of 6 per cent of the nominal share value
Final of 9 per cent of the nominal share value
Profit and loss appropriation account
Credit balance 1 April 19-6 £340,000

1   From the above information calculate:
 (*a*) The total dividend paid by the company
 (*b*) The dividend paid per share (in pence).
 (*c*) The profits earned during the year per share (in pence).

2   Prepare the company's profit and loss appropriation account for the year ended 31 March 19-7, given that the directors had decided to transfer £100,000 to general reserve.
(Associated Examining Board)

39.4A (*a*) The following terms usually appear in the final accounts of a limited company:
 (*i*)   interim dividend,
 (*ii*) authorised capital,
 (*iii*) general reserve,
 (*iv*) share premium account.
Required:
An explanation of the meaning of each of the above terms.

 (*b*) The following information has been obtained from the books of Drayfuss Ltd:

Authorised capital	100,000 8% £1 preference shares
	400,000 50p ordinary shares
Profit and loss account balance	
1 April 19-8	*Cr* £355,000
General Reserve	£105,000
Issued capital	80,000 8% £1 preference shares (fully paid)
	250,000 50p ordinary shares (fully paid)
Net trading profit for the year to 31 March 19-9	£95,000.

The preference share interim dividend of 4% had been paid and the final dividend of 4% had been proposed by the directors.

No ordinary share interim dividend had been declared, but the directors proposed a final dividend of 15p per share.

The directors agreed to transfer to general reserve £150,000.

Required:
The profit and loss appropriation account for the year ended 31 March 19-9.
Ignore taxation.
(Associated Examining Board)

39.5 The following information was available on P Co Ltd, for the year ended 31 August 19-9, after the trading and profit and loss account had been prepared.

	£		£
Issued		*Authorised Capital*	
250,000 10p Ordinary shares	25,000	500,000 10p Ordinary shares	50,000
100,000 £1 10% Preference		100,000 £1 10% Preference	
shares	100,000	shares	100,000
Trade creditors	9,700	Cash	2,575
Profit and loss account cr.		Bank	10,000
balance	41,200	Stock	61,350
Freehold premises (at cost)	73,000	Trade expenses owing	
Plant and machinery (at cost)	49,000	31 August 19-9	350
Share premium account	15,000	8% Debentures - issued by	
Provision for depreciation		P Co Ltd (repayable 19-6)	10,000
on plant and machinery	11,370	Fixtures and fittings (at cost)	8,800
		Trade debtors	10,895
		Provision for depreciation on fixtures	
		and fittings	3,000

(*a*) The stock valuation at 31 August 19-9 included £7,350 of obsolete stock. The obsolete stock should now be written off.

(*b*) Insurance of £250 had been paid in advance, but no adjustment had been made in the profit and loss account for this item.

(*c*) A 10% preference dividend had been proposed, but no entry had been made.

Required:
A balance sheet as at 31 August 19-9 incorporating the necesssary adjustments to correct the errors made. It is important that the balance sheet should be presented in good form including appropriate sub-headings and sub-totals.
(Associated Examining Board)

39.6A The following balances were extracted from the books of H Lindas Ltd on 31 March 19-1, after the completion of the trading and profit and loss accounts:

	£
Stock at 31 March 19-1	7,000
Debtors	3,000
Bank overdraft	2,000
Creditors	9,000
Cash	100
Premises (at cost)	17,000
Machinery (at cost) 1 April 19-8	7,000
Motor Vans (at cost) 1 April 19-8	5,000
Goodwill	10,000

You are required to prepare a balance sheet as at 31 March 19-1 using the above balances and the following information:

(*a*) The company was formed and commenced business 3 years previously on 1 April 19-8, with an authorised share capital of 50,000 ordinary shares of £1 each.

(*b*) 20,000 shares each fully paid were issued at a premium of 10p per share.

(*c*) The company made the following net profits during its three years of trading:

March 19-9	£2,000
March 19-0	£3,000
March 19-1	£6,000

No dividends had been declared or paid and all but £2,000 of the profits had been transferred to a general reserve account.

(*d*) Depreciation had been provided each year on the original cost at the rate of 10% per annum on machinery and 20% per annum on motor vans.

(Joint Matriculation Board)

39.7 The following trial balance as at 31 March 19-7 has been extracted from the books of the Skymaster Manufacturing Company Limited:

	£	£
Market value of goods manufactured	80,000	
Profit on goods manufactured		14,000
Provision for unrealised profit on goods manufactured at 31 March 19-6		1,365
Stock of raw materials at 31 March 19-7	5,000	
Stock of finished goods at 31 March 19-6	7,800	
Work in progress at 31 March 19-7	9,100	
Plant and machinery: at cost	29,000	
provision for depreciation at 31 March 19-7		16,400
Shop fixtures and fittings: at cost	49,000	
provision for depreciation at 31 March 19-6		9,800
Sales		130,000
Debtors/Creditors	12,700	8,000
Shop rent and rates	3,900	
Shop light and heat	7,600	
Shop salaries	11,700	
Balance at bank	4,300	
Share Capital: Ordinary shares of 50p each, fully paid		30,000
Retained earnings		10,535
	£220,100	£220,100

Additional information:

(*a*) The stock of finished goods at 31 March 19-7 has been valued, at market value, at £6,600.

Note: The company only sells goods it manufactures.

(*b*) The provisions for unrealised profit on goods manufactured at 31 March 19-7 is to be £1,155.

(*c*) Depreciation is to be provided on shop fixtures and fittings at the rate of 10% of the cost of assets held at the accounting year end.

(*d*) Provision is to be made for a proposed dividend of 10p per ordinary share.

Required:

(*a*) Prepare a trading and profit and loss account for the year ended 31 March 19-7 of the Skymaster Manufacturing Company Limited.

(*b*) A balance sheet as at 31 March 19-7 of the Skymaster Manufacturing Company Limited.

(Association of Accounting Technicians)

39.8A Alan Smith is a director of Broadbent Limited, for which he receives an annual salary of £15,000, and owns half the share capital of the company. Alan's brother Norman is trading in partnership with Joseph Pain; under the partnership agreement Norman receives a partner's salary of £15,000 per annum and 50% of the balance of the net profit or net loss. The partners withdraw from the partnership all partners' salaries and all shares of profits immediately these are computed on the last day of the relevant financial period. It is generally agreed that Norman Smith's services to the partnership business are worth £16,000 per annum. The summarised balance sheets as at 31 October 19-7 of the company and partnership are as follows:

Broadbent Limited

	£
Net assets	160,000
Capital – Ordinary Shares of 50p each fully paid	100,000
Retained Profits	60,000
	160,000

Notes:

(*a*) Provision has been made in the accounts for the year ended 31 October 19-7 for a proposed final dividend of 10p per share.

Note: The company does not pay interim dividends.

(*b*) The company's net profit, after tax, for the year ended 31 October 19-7 is £26,000.

(*c*) Broadbent Limited did not issue any shares during the year ended 31 October 19-7.

Norman Smith and Joseph Pain Trading in partnership

	£
Net assets	160,000
Capital Accounts	
Norman Smith	80,000
Joseph Pain	80,000
	160,000

Note:
The net profit for the year ended 31 October 19-7 of the partnership is £36,000.

Required:

(*a*) Prepare the summarised balance sheet as at 31 October 19-6 of Broadbent Limited.

Note: Use a similar layout to that given above in the question.

(*b*) Prepare statements of the financial benefits which each of Alan and Norman Smith received from their respective businesses for the year ended 31 October 19-7.

(*c*) Assuming that the partnership had been a limited company during the year ended 31 October 19-7, paying market salary rates for all its staff, prepare a statement of its net profit for that year.

(*d*) Alan Smith has the opportunity to convert his shareholding in Broadbent Limited into £50,000 10% Loan Stock in the company.

Using appropriate computations as necessary, advise Alan Smith of the advantages and disadvantages to him of converting his shareholding to loan stock.

(Association of Accounting Technicians)

39.9 You are given the following trial balance of Grace Ltd as at 31 December 19-7, as prepared by the firm's book-keeper. All figures are in £000s:

	Dr	Cr
Share capital (200,000 50p shares)		100
Share premium		50
Profit and loss balance 1 January 19-7		100
Debentures (10% interest p.a.) issued in 1974		100
Stock	200	
Motor vehicles	100	
Motor vehicles depreciation 1 January 19-7		60
Machinery	120	
Machinery depreciation 1 January 19-7		50
Buildings at cost 1 January 19-7	230	
Sales		750
Purchases	350	
Discounts	2	
Returns	2	
Carriage	2	
General expenses	200	
Advertising	10	
Creditors		200
Debtors	200	
Provision for doubtful debts		6
Debenture interest	5	
Bank balance		5
	1,421	1,421

You are also given the following information:

(*a*) The book-keeper, in an attempt at simplification, has posted both discounts received and discounts allowed to the discounts account. He has also posted both returns inwards and returns outwards to the returns account, and both carriage inwards and carriage outwards to the carriage account.

Discounts received were actually	£1,000
Returns outwards were actually	£1,000
Carriage outwards was actually	£1,000

(*b*) The following items are already included in general expenses:

(i) Rates for the 12 months to 31 March 19-8, £4,000;

(ii) Insurance for the 12 months to 31 December 19-8, £2,000. Half of this amount relates to the managing director's private yacht.

(*c*) Your own charges of £1,000 for accountancy services need to be included.

(*d*) A debtor of £20,000 has gone bankrupt. The provision for doubtful debts is required to be 5% of debtors.

(*e*) A dividend of 5p per share is proposed.

(*f*) Closing stock is £180,000.

(*g*) Depreciation of £20,000 is to be provided on the motor vehicles and of £10,000 on the machinery. The buildings are to be revalued by £30,000.

Required:

Prepare a profit and loss account and balance sheet for Grace Ltd for the year (for internal purposes).

(Chartered Association of Certified Accountants)

39.10 The chairman of a public limited company has written his annual report to the shareholders, extracts of which are quoted below.

Extract 1

'In May 19-6, in order to provide a basis for more efficient operations, we acquired PAG Warehousing and Transport Ltd. The agreed valuation of the net tangible assets acquired was £1.4 million. The purchase consideration, £1.7 million, was satisfied by an issue of 6.4 million equity shares, of £0.25 per share, to PAG's shareholders. These shares do not rank for dividend until 19-7.'

Extract 2

'As a measure of confidence in our ability to expand operations in 19-7 and 19-8, and to provide the necessary financial base, we issued £0.5 million 8% Redeemable Debenture Stock, 2000/2007, 20 million 6% £1 Redeemable Preference Shares and 4 million £1 equity shares. The opportunity was also taken to redeem the whole of the 5 million 11% £1 Redeemable Preference Shares.'

Required:

Answer the following questions on the above extracts.
Extract 1

(a) What does the difference of £0.3 million between the purchase consideration (£1.7m) and the net tangible assets value (£1.4m) represent?

(b) What does the difference of £0.1 million between the purchase consideration (£1.7m) and the nominal value of the equity shares (£1.6m) represent?

(c) What is the meaning of the term 'equity shares'?

(d) What is the meaning of the phrase 'do not rank for dividend'?

Extract 2

(e) In the description of the debenture stock issue, what is the significance of
    (i) 8%?
    (ii) 2000/2007?

(f) In the description of the preference share issue, what is the significance of
    (i) 6%?
    (ii) Redeemable?

(g) What is the most likely explanation for the company to have redeemed existing preference shares but at the same time to have issued others?

(h) What effect will these structural changes have had on the gearing of the company?

(j) Contrast the accounting treatment, in the company's profit and loss accounts, of the interest due on the debentures with dividends proposed on the equity shares.

(k) Explain the reasons for the different treatments you have outlined in your answer to (j) above.

(Chartered Association of Certified Accountants)

39.11 The directors of the company by which you are employed as an accountant have received the forecast profit and loss account for 19-3 which disclosed a net profit for the year of £36,000.

This is considered to be an unacceptably low figure and a working party has been set up to investigate ways and means of improving the forecast profit.

The following suggestions have been put forward by various members of the working party:

(*a*) 'Every six months we deduct income tax of £10,000 from the debenture interest and pay it over to the Inland Revenue. If we withhold these payments, the company's profit will be increased considerably.'

(*b*) 'I see that in the three months August to October 19-3 we have forecast a total amount of £40,000 for repainting the exterior of the company's premises. If, instead, we charge this amount as capital expenditure, the company's profit will be increased by £40,000.'

(*c*) 'In November 19-3, the replacement of a machine is forecast. The proceeds from the sale of the old machinery should be credited to profit and loss account.'

(*d*) 'There is a credit balance of £86,000 on General Reserve account. We can transfer some of this to profit and loss account to increase the 19-3 profit.'

(*e*) 'The company's £1 ordinary shares, which were originally issued at £1 per share, currently have a market value of £1.60 per share and this price is likely to be maintained. We can credit the surplus £0.60 per share to the 19-3 profit and loss account.'

(*f*) 'The company's premises were bought many years ago for £68,000, but following the rise in property values, they are now worth at least £300,000. This enhancement in value can be utilised to increase the 19-3 profit.'

You are required as the accounting member of the working party, to comment on the feasibility of each of the above suggestions for increasing the 19-3 forecast profit.
(Chartered Association of Certified Accountants)

39.12 Soon after he had started to prepare the final accounts of Toncliffe Ltd for the year ended 31 March 19-2, the accountant was seriously injured in an accident.

The wife of one of the directors volunteered to finish the task. Her offer was eagerly accepted because the accounts had already been posted and balanced, the trading account had been prepared, and it was not thought that she could make any mistakes.

However, the final accounts which she produced (shown below) contained a varied assortment of compilation errors.

Toncliffe Limited

Profit and Loss Account as at 31 March 19-2

	£	£		£	£
Rates & insurance	11,450		Debtors	42,400	
Add prepayment	150		Less provision		
		11,600	for bad debts	2,120	
					44,520
Wages & salaries		32,398	Carriage out		2,172
Discounts received		2,195	Depreciation		
Gross profit		146,595	– premises	2,000	
Provision for doubtful			– vehicles	25,000	
debts, decrease		400	– fixtures	5,000	
Debenture interest					32,000
paid		1,800	Rent received		500
Carriage out		2,172	Loss on sale		
General expenses		7,423	of vehicle		762
Power, heat & light		5,571	Obsolete stock		
Ordinary dividend			written off		934
proposed		8,000	Carriage out		2,172
			Debenture		
			interest paid		1,800
			Unappropriated		
			profit b/f from		
			previous year		14,650
			Preference		
			dividend paid		15,200
			Unappropriated		
			balance c/f		57,804
		£218,154			£182,514

Toncliffe Limited

Balance Sheet for year ended 31 March 19-2

	£		£ Cost	£ Depreciation	£ Net
Share capital		Fixed Assets			
authorised 200,000		Premises	220,000	20,000	240,000
8% Preference shares		Fixtures	34,002	14,000	38,002
of £1 per share	200,000	Motor vehicles	260,008	107,000	153,008
800,000 Ord shares					
of £0.50 per share	400,000				
– issued and fully			514,010	141,000	431,010
paid 190,000 8%					
Preference shares		Current Assets			
of £1 per share	190,000	Stock		73,216	
540,000 Ord shares		Balance at bank		94,070	
of £0.50 per share	270,000	Proposed dividends		8,000	
6% Debentures					
19-4/19-9	30,000			165,286	
Reserves					
Profit and loss		*add*			
account	(57,804)	Current Liabilities			
		Creditors		41,340	
		Prepayments		150	
		Cash in hand		5,394	
				36,884	
		Working capital			202,170
	£1,042,204				£633,180

The director's wife attached a note which stated 'I think I may have made a slight mistake somewhere because it does not quite balance'.

You are required to:

Rewrite the final accounts of Toncliffe Ltd in vertical format correcting the errors as you do so. Assume that all the figures she has picked up from the trial balance are correct.

(Chartered Association of Certified Accountants)

39.13A Artic Haulage plc is a general transport company. As an extra service to its customers, it provides storage facilities which can be hired on a semi permanent basis under contract or casually as required.

At 31 December 19-5, the company's ledger included the following list of balances:

	£
Assets	
Premises (*see* note (5))	675,300
Vehicles	1,141,700
Plant and equipment	203,200
Stock (closing) of repair materials, fuel oil, etc	154,031
Trade debtors – storage	15,503
– haulage	131,480
Bank	42,356
Cash	7,063
Liabilities	
Provisions for depreciation at 1 January 19-5	
– premises	117,800
– vehicles	472,400
– plant and equipment	51,100
Trade creditors (*see* note (1))	125,607
9% Debentures 2001/2007	50,000
Ordinary share capital (*see* notes (3) and (4))	800,000
6% preference share capital (*see* note (4))	50,000
General reserve	40,000
Profit and loss account at 1 January 19-5	46,823
Share premium	5,000
Revenues	
Storage rentals – Long term contracts	151,260
– casual	29,752
Haulage charges	1,734,611
Expenses	
Wages, salaries and related charges (see note (5))	581,826
Rates	62,500
Power, heat and light	86,330
Repairs – vehicles	91,413
– other (see note (5))	156,494
Diesel oil, etc	179,809
Postages, stationery, telephones	25,605
Insurance	21,480
Debenture interest	4,500
Sundry expenses	11,273
Other	
Suspense account (debit balance)	
(*see* notes (1), (2) and (3))	82,490

Notes at 31 December 19-5

(1) In September 19-5, a consignment of perishable goods was delayed in transit due to the negligence of the transport manager. As a result, the entire consignment deteriorated to such an extent that it had to be destroyed on arrival at its destination. The total cost of this loss, which has been assessed at £84,680, has been claimed from the company by the consignor and has been debited to suspense account and temporarily credited to Trade Creditors prior to being settled *in contra* at 31 December 19-5. The claim is not covered by the company's insurance policy.

(2) In October 19-5, one of the vehicles was seriously damaged in an accident. Repairs costing £37,810 were carried out in the company's own vehicle workshops. The cost has been held in suspense account pending the outcome of the claim under the insurance policy. This has now been agreed in full.

(3) On 1 September 19-5, the company had declared a 1 for 20 bonus issue of ordinary shares (which do not rank for dividend until 19-6). The amount involved has been appropriated out of general reserve and credited to suspense account.

(4) The issued share capital consists of 6% preference shares of £1.00 per share and ordinary shares of £0.50 per share. The directors have recommended payment of the preference dividend and an ordinary dividend of £0.075 per share.

(5) During 19-5, the company had extended one of its warehouses and used its own labour and materials in the construction. The amounts expended are included in the above list under wages (£52,000) and repairs - other (£148,000).

(6) Depreciation is provided on a straight line basis on the cost of fixed assets held at the end of each financial year and assuming no residual value. Assumed asset lives are:

Premises	50 years
Vehicles	5 years
Plant	8 years

(7) The company's liability for corporation tax (Hong Kong: Taxation) for the year 19-5 has been estimated at £90,000.

(8) Adjustments, not yet posted to the accounts, should be made for:

	£
Storage rentals (long term contracts) prepaid	13,644
Power charges accrued	5,005
Telephone rentals prepaid	207
Telephone calls accrued	548
Rates prepaid	16,730
Wages accrued	10,834
Insurance prepaid	1,747

Required:

(*a*) Open the suspense account and post the entries needed to eliminate the opening debit balance.

(*b*) Prepare, for internal circulation purposes, the profit and loss account for Artic Haulage plc for year ended 31 December 19-5 and a balance sheet at that date.

(Chartered Association of Certified Accountants)

39.14A Qwik-Freez (East Anglia) plc is a company which provides refrigerated storage facilities to local farmers.

Services offered include the collection of produce, the use of rapid freezing equipment, storage of the frozen produce and transport from frozen storage in refrigerated vehicles to any point within the country. Orders for these services are secured by the company's sales staff.

The company's revenue consists of charges for transport and freezing, and of storage rentals. Customers may hire storage space either on a long-term contract basis at advantageous charges (payable in advance) or on a casual basis (invoiced monthly).

A considerable amount of electricity from the public supply is used by the company in the freezing and storage operations. In the event of a sudden failure in this supply, the company is able to generate its own emergency supplies from standby generators kept for this purpose. An insurance policy has been taken out to protect the company against the claims which would arise should any of the frozen produce deteriorate as the result of power or equipment failure.

At the end of the company's financial year ended 30 September 19-2, the assistant accountant extracted the following balances from the ledgers.

	£
Asset Accounts	
Land and buildings (at cost)	390,000
Plant (at cost)	271,900
Vehicles (at cost)	82,600
Provision for depreciation (at 1 October 19-1):	
Land and buildings	39,600
Plant	144,800
Vehicles	27,050
Stock of consumable stores (at 30 September 19-2):	23,449
Debtors – for rentals	18,204
Debtors – for charges	2,332
Bank	30,710
Cash	1,103
Liability Accounts	
Trade creditors	7,390
7% debentures 2004/2012	80,000
Ordinary share capital (*see* note 7)	200,000
General reserve	25,000
Unappropriated profit (at 1 October 19-1)	108,284
Share premium	15,000
Revenue Accounts	
Storage rentals – Long-term contracts	302,090
– casual	85,063
Freezing charges	112,810
Transport charges	90,107
Expense Accounts	
Wages, salaries and related expenses	128,004
Rates	79,112
Electricity	76,860
Transport costs	43,271
Repairs	30,319
Consumable stores	29,800
Postages, stationery, telephones	15,604
Insurance premiums	7,800
Debenture interest	5,600
Sundries	9,176
Other Accounts	
Suspense (credit balance)	8,650

Notes at 30 September 19-2:

(*a*) At the beginning of the 19-1/2 financial year, the company had sold refrigeration plant (which had originally cost £26,000 and on which £20,800 had been provided as depreciation to date of disposal) for £4,000. The only accounting entries relative to this disposal which have been made so far, are a debit to bank and a credit to suspense of the amount of the sale proceeds.

(*b*) In April 19-2, the compressor unit in No 7 storage unit failed and as a consequence the contents deteriorated to such an extent that they had to be disposed of by incineration. Compensation of £1,350 was paid to the farmer by Qwik-Freez by cheque and debited to suspense. The insurance company has admitted liability under the policy but no further ledger entries have as yet been made.

(*c*) During the 19-1/2 financial year, the company replaced one of its refrigerated vehicles, which had originally cost £16,400 and on which £13,120 had been provided as depreciation to date of disposal. A trade-in (part exchange) allowance of £6,000 was granted in respect of this vehicle. A replacement vehicle was acquired at a list price of £27,000. The entries relating to the disposal of the old vehicle have not yet been made, except that the trade-in allowance has been debited to vehicles and credited to suspense. The balance of the price of the new vehicle has been paid by cheque and debited to vehicles account.

(*d*) It is the company's policy to provide for depreciation on a straight line basis calculated on the cost of fixed assets held at the end of each financial year and assuming no residual value. Annual depreciation rates are:

	%
Buildings	2
Plant	10
Vehicles	25

The buildings content of the item 'land and buildings' included in asset account balances is £120,000.

(*e*) Adjustments, not yet posted to the accounts, should be made for the following items:

	£
Storage rentals received in advance	25,631
Insurance premium prepaid	600
Wages and salaries accrued	1,920
Rates prepaid	28,820
Electricity accrued	5,757

(*f*) Consumable stores include £4,131 and repairs include £9,972 relating to vehicles.

(*g*) The authorised and issued capital of the company consists of 400,000 ordinary shares of £0.50 per share. The directors have recommended a dividend for the year of £0.12 per share.

Required:

(*a*) Prepare for internal circulation purposes, a profit and loss account for Qwik-Freez for the year ended 30 September 19-2 and a balance sheet at that date. All workings must be shown.

(*b*) Open the suspense account and post the entries needed to eliminate the opening credit balance.

(Chartered Association of Certified Accountants)

382

40

Purchase of existing partnership and sole traders' businesses

Quite frequently an existing partnership or sole trader's business is taken over as a going concern. At this juncture several methods of how this is done can be considered:

(a) An individual purchases the business of a sole trader.

(b) A partnership acquires the business of a sole trader.

(c) Existing businesses of sole traders join together to form a partnership.

(d) A limited company takes over the business of a sole trader or partnership.

It must not be thought that because the assets bought are shown in the selling firm's books at one value, that the purchaser(s) must record the assets taken over in its own books at the same value. The values shown in the books of the purchaser(s) are those values at which they are buying the assets, such values being frequently quite different than those shown in the selling firm's books. As an instance of this, the selling firm may have bought premises many years ago for £10,000, but they may now be worth £50,000. The purchaser buying the premises will obviously have to pay £50,000, and it is therefore this value that is recorded in the books of the purchaser(s). Alternatively, the value at which it is recorded in the books of the purhaser(s) may be less than that shown in the selling firm's books. Where the total purchase consideration exceeds the total value of the indentifiable assets then such excess is the goodwill. Should the total purchase consideration be less than the values of the identifiable assets, then the difference would be entered in a Capital Reserve Account.

It is easier to start with the takeover of the simplest sort of business unit, that of a sole trader. Some of the Balance Sheets shown will be deliberately simplified so that the principles involved are not hidden behind a mass of complicated calculations.

To illustrate the takeover of a business, given varying circumstances, the same business will be assumed to be taken over in different ways. The balance sheet of this business is that of A Brown, Exhibit 40.1.

Exhibit 40.1

A Brown
Balance Sheet as at 31 December 19-6

	£
Fixtures	30,000
Stock	8,000
Debtors	7,000
Bank	1,000
	46,000

	£
Capital	43,000
Creditors	3,000
	46,000

An individual purchases business of sole trader

(*a*) Assume that the assets and liabilities of A Brown, with the exception of the bank balance are taken over by D Towers. He is to take over the assets and liabilities at the valuations as shown. The price to be paid is £52,000. The opening balance sheet of Towers will be as in Exhibit 40.2.

Exhibit 40.2

D Towers
Balance Sheet as at 1 January 19-7

	£
Goodwill	10,000
Fixtures	30,000
Stock	8,000
Debtors	7,000
	55,000

	£
Capital	52,000
Creditors	3,000
	55,000

As £52,000 has been paid for net assets (assets less liabilities) valued at £30,000 + £8,000 + £7,000 − £3,000 = £42,000, the excess £10,000 represents the amount paid for goodwill.

(*b*) Suppose that, instead of the information just given, the same amount has been paid by Towers, but the assets were taken over at a value of Fixtures £37,000; Stock

£7,500; Debtors £6,500; the opening balance sheet of D Towers would have been as in Exhibit 40.3.

Exhibit 40.3

D Towers
Balance Sheet as at 1 January 19-7

	£
Goodwill	4,000
Fixtures	37,000
Stock	7,500
Debtors	6,500
	55,000

	£
Capital	52,000
Creditors	3,000
	55,000

As £52,000 had been paid for net assets valued at £37,000 + £7,500 + £6,500 − £3,000 = £48,000, the excess £4,000 represents the amount paid for goodwill. The other assets are shown at their value to the purchaser, Towers.

Partnership acquires business of a sole trader

Assume instead that the business of Brown had been taken over by M Ukridge and D Allen. The partners are to introduce £30,000 each as capital. The price to be paid for the net assets, other than the bank balance, is £52,000. The purchasers placed the following values on the assets taken over: Fixtures £40,000: Stock £7,000: Debtors £6,000.

The opening balance sheet of Ukridge and Allen will be as in Exhibit 40.4.

Exhibit 40.4

M Ukridge & D Allen
Balance Sheet as at 1 January 19-7

	£
Goodwill	2,000
Fixtures	40,000
Stock	7,000
Debtors	6,000
Bank	8,000
	63,000

Capitals:	£
M Ukridge	30,000
D Allen	30,000
	60,000
Creditors	3,000
	63,000

The sum of £52,000 has been paid for net assets of £40,000 + £7,000 + £6,000 − £3,000 = £50,000. This makes goodwill be the excess of £2,000.

The bank balance is made up of £30,000 + £30,000 introduced by the partners, less £52,000 paid to Brown = £8,000.

Amalgamation of existing sole traders

Now assume that Brown was to enter into partnership with T Owens whose last balance sheet was shown in Exhibit 40.5.

Exhibit 40.5

T Owens
Balance Sheet as at 1 January 19-6

	£
Premises	20,000
Fixtures	5,000
Stock	6,000
Debtors	9,000
Bank	2,000
	42,000
	£
Capital	37,000
Creditors	5,000
	42,000

(*a*) If the two traders were to amalgamate all their business assets and liabilities, at the values as shown, the opening balance sheet of the partnership would be as in Exhibit 40.6.

Exhibit 40.6

A Brown & T Owens
Balance Sheet as at 1 January 19-7

	£
Premises	20,000
Fixtures	35,000
Stock	14,000
Debtors	16,000
Bank	3,000
	88,000
Capitals:	£
Brown	43,000
Owens	37,000
Creditors	8,000
	88,000

(*b*) Suppose that instead of both parties agreeing to amalgamation at the asset values as shown, the following values had been agreed to:

Owen's premises to be valued at £25,000, and his stock at £5,500. Other items as per last balance sheet, Brown's fixtures to be valued at £33,000, his stock at £7,200 and debtors at £6,400. It is also to be taken that Brown has goodwill, value £7,000, whereas Owen's goodwill was considered valueless. Other items as per last balance sheet.

The opening balance sheet will be at the revised figures, and is shown as Exhibit 40.7.

Exhibit 40.7

A Brown & T Owen

Balance Sheet as at 1 January 19-7

	£
Goodwill	7,000
Premises	25,000
Fixtures	38,000
Stock	12,700
Debtors	15,400
Bank	3,000
	101,100

	£
Capitals:	
Brown	51,600
Owen	41,500
Creditors	8,000
	101,100

Brown's capital can be seen to be £43,000 + £3,000 (fixtures) − £800 (stock) − £600 (debtors) + £7,000 (goodwill) = £51,600.

Owen's capital is £37,000 + £5,000 (premises) − £500 (stock) = £41,500.

Limited company acquires business of sole trader

More complicated examples will be examined in Volume two. In this volume only an elementary treatment will be considered.

Before the acquisition the balance sheet of D Lucas Ltd was as shown in Exhibit 40.8.

Exhibit 40.8

D Lucas Ltd
Balance Sheet as at 1 January 19-7

	£
Fixtures	36,000
Stock	23,000
Debtors	14,000
Bank	6,000
	79,000

	£
Share Capital:	
Preference Shares	20,000
Ordinary Shares	40,000
Profit and Loss	8,000
Creditors	11,000
	79,000

(*a*) Assume that Brown's business had been acquired, except for the bank balance, goodwill being valued at £8,000 and the other assets and liabilities at balance sheet values. Lucas Ltd is to issue an extra £32,000 £1 ordinary shares at par and 18,000 £1 preference shares at par – to Brown, in full settlement of the £50,000 net assets taken over.

Exhibit 40.9 show the balance sheet of the company before and after the acquisition.

Exhibit 40.9

Lucas Ltd
Balance Sheets

	Before £	+or−	After £
Goodwill	–	+8,000	8,000
Fixtures	36,000	+30,000	66,000
Stock	23,000	+8,000	31,000
Debtors	14,000	+7,000	21,000
Bank	6,000		6,000
	79,000		132,000

	Before £	+or−	After £
Share Capital:			
Preference	20,000	+18,000	38,000
Ordinary	40,000	+32,000	72,000
Profit & Loss	8,000		8,000
Creditors	11,000	+3,000	14,000
	79,000		132,000

(*b*) If instead we assume that the business of Brown was acquired as follows:

The purchase price to be satisfied by Brown being given £5,000 cash and to issue to him an extra 50,000 ordinary shares at par and £10,000 debentures at par. The assets taken over to be valued at Fixtures £28,000; Stock £7,500; Debtors £6,500. The bank balance is not taken over.

Exhibit 40.10 shows the balance sheet of the company after the acquisition.

Exhibit 40.10

Lucas Ltd
Balance Sheets

	Before £	+or−	After £
Goodwill	–	+26,000	26,000
Fixtures	36,000	+28,000	64,000
Stock	23,000	+7,500	30,500
Debtors	14,000	+6,500	20,500
Bank	6,000	− 5,000	1,000
	79,000		142,000

	Before £	+or−	After £
Share Capital:			
Preference	20,000		20,000
Ordinary	40,000	+50,000	90,000
Debentures		+10,000	10,000
Profit & Loss	8,000		8,000
Creditors	11,000	+3,000	14,000
	79,000		142,000

Goodwill is calculated: Purchase consideration is made up of ordinary shares £50,000 + debentures £10,000 + bank £5,000 = £65,000.

Net assets bought are: Fixtures £28,000 + Stock £7,500 + Debtors £6,500 − Creditors £3,000 = £39,000.

Therefore Goodwill is £65,000 − £39,000 = £26,000.

Business purchase account

In this chapter, to economise on space and descriptions, only the balance sheets have been shown. However, in the books of the purchaser the purchase of a business should pass through a 'Business Purchase Account'.

This would be as follows:

Business Purchase Account

Debit	Credit
Each liability taken over.	Each asset taken over at
Vendor: net amount of	values placed on it,
purchase price.	including Goodwill.

Vendor's Account (Name of seller/s)

Debit	Credit
Bank (or Share capital)	Amount to be paid
Amount paid	for business

Various Asset Accounts

Debit
Business Purchase (value placed on asset
taken over).

Various Liability Accounts

Credit
Amount of liability taken over

Bank (or Share Capital)

Credit
Amount paid to vendor.

Review questions
40.1

C Allen
Balance Sheet as at 31 December 19-4

	£
Premises	21,000
Stock	9,600
Debtors	6,300
Bank	1,700
	38,600

	£
Capital	31,800
Creditors	6,800
	38,600

(a) The business of Allen is taken over by S Walters in its entirety. The assets are deemed to be worth the balance sheet values as shown. The price paid by Walters is £40,000. Show the opening balance sheet of Walters.

(b) Suppose instead that R Jones had taken over Allen's business. He does not take over the bank balance, and values premises at £28,000 and stock at £9,200. The price paid by him is £46,000. Show the opening balance sheet of Jones.

40.2A I Dodgem's balance sheet on 31 December 19-8 was as follows:

	£
Premises	55,000
Plant and machinery at cost	
less depreciation	21,000
Fixtures and fittings at cost *less* depreciation	4,000
Stock	17,000
Trade debtors	9,500
Cash	4,500
	£111,000

	£
Capital	87,000
Trade creditors	8,000
Bank overdraft	15,800
Expenses owing	200
	£111,000

An opportunity had arisen for Dodgem to acquire the business of A Swing who is retiring.

A Swing
Balance Sheet as at 1 January 19-8

	£
Premises	25,000
Plant	9,000
Motor Vehicle	3,500
Stock	11,000
Trade debtors	6,000
Bank	8,000
Cash	500
	£63,000

	£
Capital	54,000
Trade Creditors	9,000
	63,000

Dodgem agreed to take over Swing's premises, plant, stock, trade debtors and trade creditors.

For the purpose of his own records Dodgem valued the premises at £35,000, plant at £6,000 and stock at £8,000.

The agreed purchase price was £50,000 and in order to finance the purchase Dodgem had obtained a fixed loan for 5 years from his bank, for one half of the purchase price on the condition that he contributed the same amount from his own private resources in cash. The purchase price was paid on 1 January 19-9.

Dodgem also decided to scrap some of his oldest plant and machinery which cost £9,000 with depreciation to date £8,000. This was sold for scrap for £300 cash on 1 January 19-9. On the same date he bought one new plant for £4,000, paying in cash.

Required:

(*a*) The purchase of business account in I Dodgem's books.

(*b*) I Dodgem's balance sheet as at 1 January 19-9 after all the above transactions have been completed.

(Associated Examining Board)

40.3 (*a*) On 31 May 19-2 T Roberts' Balance Sheet was as follows:

	£
Premises	80,000
Stock	5,000
Debtors	4,000
Cash and bank	2,450
	£91,450,

	£
Capital	90,000
Creditors	1,450
	£91,450

On 1 June 19-2 W Deakins, who had £120,000 in his business account, bought the business as a going concern for £110,000, taking over all liabilities and assets except cash and bank, at T Roberts' valuation.

Set out W Deakins' Balance Sheet on 1 June 19-2.

(*b*) Smith and Williams were in partnership sharing profit and loss equally.

Their Balance Sheet on 31 May 19-2 was as follows:

	£
Premises	80,000
Stock	14,000
Debtors	4,000
Bank	2,000
	£100,000

		£
Capital:	Smith	50,000
	Williams	50,000
		£100,000

Vernon was admitted as a partner from 1 June 19-2, bringing in £50,000 in cash. £40,000 of this cash was used immediately to purchase additional fixtures and fittings. However, before admitting Vernon the original partners agreed that the business was worth £140,000 as a going concern. The partners also agreed that for the time being the accounts should represent the full value of the business as a going concern.

Set out the opening Balance Sheet of the new partnership.

(c) Outline one method of dealing with the goodwill of the business when the proprietors decide to eliminate it from the accounts.

(University of London)

40.4A T Smith, R Wilkins and R Yarrow were three small haulage contractors.

Their assets and liabilities on 31 May 19-1 were as follows:

	Smith £	Wilkins £	Yarrow £
Premises	13,000	15,000	8,000
Vehicles	10,000	18,000	6,000
Equipment	4,000	8,000	3,000
Debtors	1,300	1,800	600
Balance in bank	1,400	2,700	800
	29,700	45,500	18,400
Creditors	400	1,250	180
Capital	29,300	44,250	18,220
	29,700	45,500	18,400

The three decided to amalgamate into one partnership, which took over all assets and liabilities.

An independent valuer agreed the book values of all fixed assets, but considered a provision for doubtful debts should be made in each case as follows:

Smith	1% of debtors
Wilkins	2% of debtors
Yarrow	£200

He valued the businesses as going concerns as follows:

	£
Smith	35,000
Wilkins	50,000
Yarrow	25,000

(a) The new partnership came into existence on 1 June 19-1. Set out the opening Balance Sheet on that date.

(b) On 2 June 19-1 it was agreed to seal the premises which had belonged to Yarrow and to operate from the other two depots. Yarrow insisted that as the property had belonged to him he should receive the proceeds of the sale for his private purposes. Explain whether or not Yarrow is justified in his claim.

(University of London)

40.5 A small private company is formed to take over the manufacturing business of John Crofton. The company will be known as John Crofton (Successor) Ltd.

The Company has an authorised capital of £100,000 divided into shares of 50p each. All the shares are issued and fully paid, including a premium of 10p per share. Fees and expenses paid in forming the new company amounted to £500.

The company took over all assets and liabilities with effect from 1 April 19- 9, paying immediately a purchase price of £90,000.

The tangible assets taken over were valued as follows:

	£
Premises	30,000
Machinery and plant	15,000
Vehicles	13,000
Stocks	3,170
Debtors	2,400 (book value £3,000)

The liabilities taken over amounted to £4,000.

The company immediately bought new machinery at a cost of £20,000.

One half of this price was paid immediately, the remainder will be paid during July 19-9.

Additional stocks were bought on credit for £5,400.

Set out (in long form) the opening Balance Sheet of John Crofton (Successor) Ltd as at 1 April 19-9.

(University of London)

40.6A Spectrum Ltd is a private company with an authorised capital of £700,000 divided into shares of £1 each. 500,000 shares have been issued and are fully paid. The company has been formed to acquire small retail shops and establish a chain of outlets.

The company made offers to three sole traders and puchased the businesses run by Red, Yellow and Blue.

The assets acquired, liabilities taken over, and prices paid are listed below:

	Red	Yellow	Blue
	£	£	£
Premises	75,000	80,000	90,000
Delivery vans	7,000	–	10,000
Furniture & Fittings	12,000	13,000	13,000
Stock	8,000	7,000	12,000
Creditors	6,000	8,000	7,000
Purchase price	120,000	130,000	150,000

The company also purchased a warehouse to be used as a central distribution store for £60,000. This has been paid.

Preliminary expenses (formation expenses) of £15,000 have also been paid.

The company took over the three shops outlined above and started trading on 1 January 19-2.

Approaches have also been made to Green for the purchase of his business for £100,000. Green has accepted the offer and the company will take over in the near future the following assets and liabilities:

	£
Premises	70,000
Stock	18.000
Creditors	3,000

The transaction had not been completed on 1 January 19-2 and Green was still running his own business.

(*a*) Prepare the opening Balance Sheet of Spectrum Ltd as at 1 January 19- 2.

(*b*) How would you advise Spectrum Ltd to finance the purchase of Green's business when the deal is completed?

(University of London)

41

Funds flow statements: an introduction

Profit and Loss accounts for each period are published by each company, as well as a balance sheet as at the period's closing date. These disclose the profit, or loss, made by the company for that period, and how the resources were being used at the end of the period.

However, when we want to try to assess whether or not the company has used its resources to good effect during the period, these two statements do not give us enough information. What we could also do with is something that shows the funds coming into the company or firm during the period, and what it has done with all the resources. The financial statement which gives us this information is usually called **a statement of source and application of funds**, or a **funds statement**.

Definition of funds

There are usually two meanings given to 'funds'. They are:

(*a*) Cash funds. This means both cash and bank balances.

(*b*) Working Capital Funds.

Financial statements concerned with cash funds are usually known as **cash flow statements**. Basically they are concerned with examining the reasons underlying the rise or fall in cash funds over a period.

The financial statements concerned with working capital funds are normally known as **statements of sources and application of funds**. In 1975 Statement of Standard Accounting Practice No 10 (SSAP10) was issued. In it was stated the fact that UK companies, with the exception of very small ones, have to prepare statements of sources and application of funds.

As accountants usually take 'funds statements' to be those concerned with working capital, then this would be what would be required in an examination, unless the examiner specifically asked for one concerned with 'cash'.

Movements of funds

A leading accountant once referred to all funds statements as 'where from: where to' statements. Before we start to construct funds statements of both types, let us look at where the funds can come from, and where they can go to.

Remember, we are looking at the following:

Balance sheet (figures end of previous period)		+	Changes – which must be because of flows of funds during intervening period	=	Balance sheet (figures end of following period)

Let us examine 'cash funds' first of all. We will show them in the form of a diagram, Exhibit 41.1, and then look at them in greater detail.

Exhibit 41.1

Funds come from (sources)	Cash funds		Funds go to (applications)
	In	Out	
1 Profits	—>	—>	1 Losses
2 Sales of Fixed Assets	—>	—>	2 Purchase Fixed Assets
3 Decrease in Stock	—>	—>	3 Increase in Stock
4 Decrease in Debtors	—>	—>	4 Increase in Debtors
5 Capital Introduced	—>	—>	5 Drawings/Dividends
6 Loans Received	—>	—>	6 Loans Repaid
7 Increase in Creditors	—>	—>	7 Decrease in Creditors

These can be explained as:

1 Profits bring a flow of cash into the firm. Losses take cash out of it.

2 The cash received from sales of fixed assets comes into the firm. A purchase of fixed assets takes it out.

3 Reducing stock means turning it into cash. An increase in stock ties up cash funds.

4 A reduction in debtors means that the extra amount paid comes into the firm as cash. Letting debtors increase stops that extra amount of cash coming in.

5 An increase in a sole proprietor's capital, or issues of shares in a company bring cash in. Drawings or dividends take it out.

6 Loans received bring in cash, while their repayment reduces cash.

7 An increase in creditors keeps the extra cash in the firm. A decrease in creditors means that the extra payments take cash out.

Exhibit 41.2 now shows the movement of working capital funds.

Exhibit 41.2

Sources of funds	Working Capital Funds		Application of funds
	Current Assets *less* Current Liabilities		
	+	−	
(A) Sales of Fixed Assets	—>	—>	(E) Purchase of Fixed Assets
(B) Capital Introduced	—>	—>	(F) Drawings/Dividends
(C) Profits	—>	—>	(G) Losses
(D) Loans Received	—>	—>	(H) Loans Repaid

Following double-entry principles, changes of two balance sheet items which are *both* in current assets or current liabilities will *not* affect working capital. That is why changes in stock, debtors, cash or creditors have been omitted from Exhibit 41.2.

Exhibit 41.3

The table shows how various transactions affect working capital. Items (i) to (iv) do *not* affect working capital, as they affect items which are themselves part of working capital. Items (A) to (H) are as per the diagram Exhibit 41.2.

Item no	Current Assets	Current Liabilities	Change in working capital
(i) Stock bought for £500 cash	+ £500 − £500		None
(ii) Stock bought on credit £320	+ 320	+ £320	None
(iii) Debtors pay in £190 cash	+ £190 − £190		None
(iv) Paid creditors £270 cash	− £270	− £270	None
(A) Fixed asset sold for £1,000 cash	+ £1,000		+ £1,000
(B) Proprietor puts in extra £5,000 capital	+ £5,000		+ £5,000
(C) Sold stock costing £800 for £960, i.e. £160 profit	+ £960 − £800		+ £160
(D) Loan received in cash £2,000	+ £2,000		+ £2,000
(E) Fixed Assets bought for cash £750	− £750		− £750
(F) Cash Drawings £400	− £400		− £400
(G) Sold stock costing £600 for £480 cash, i.e. £120 loss	+ £480 − £600		− £120
(H) We repaid loan £500 cash	− £500		− £500

Construction of funds statements

Now that we have seen how both cash funds and working capital funds are affected by transactions, we can turn to the construction of the funds statements themselves.

We will start from Exhibit 41.4 and construct both (a) Exhibit 41.5 a cash flow statement and (b) Exhibit 41.6 a statement of sources and application of funds.

Exhibit 41.4

The following are the balance sheets of T Holmes as at 31 December 19-6 and 31 December 19-7:

	31.12.19-6 £	£	31.12.19-7 £	£
Fixed Assets				
Premises at cost		25,000		28,800
Current Assets				
Stock	12,500		12,850	
Debtors	21,650		23,140	
Cash and Bank Balances	4,300		5,620	
	38,450		41,610	
less Current Liabilities				
Creditors	11,350		11,120	
Working Capital		27,100		30,490
		52,100		59,290
Financed by:				
Capital				
Opening Balances b/fwd		52,660		52,100
add Net Profit for year		16,550		25,440
		69,210		77,540
less Drawings		17,110		18,250
		52,100		59,290

Note: No depreciation has been charged in the accounts.

Exhibit 41.5

T Holmes

Cash Flow Statement for the year ended 31 December 19-7

		£	£
Source of Funds			
Net Profit			25,440
Application of Funds			
Drawings		18,250	
Extra premises bought		3,800	
Increase in stock		350	
Increase in debtors		1,490	
Decrease in creditors		230	24,120
Increase in cash funds			1,320
Cash and bank balances	31.12.19-6	4,300	
Cash and bank balances	31.12.19-7	5,620	1,320

Exhibit 41.6

T Holmes

Statement of Source and Application of Funds
for the year ended 31 December 19-7

	£	£
Source of Funds		
Net Profit		25,440
Application of Funds		
Drawings	18,250	
Extra premises bought	3,800	22,050
		3,390
Increase in working capital		
Increase in stock	350	
Increase in debtors	1,490	
Decrease in creditors	230	
Increase in cash and bank	1,320	3,390

If you compare Exhibit 41.5 with Exhibit 41.1, and Exhibit 41.6 with Exhibit 41.2 you will see that the sources and applications in the worked exhibits match up with the previous descriptions. At the bottom of each exhibit you will notice the reconciliation part, e.g. 41.5, the increase in cash funds £1,320 is demonstrated by then showing cash and bank balances with the resultant increase of £1,320. Similarly the £3,390 increase in working capital is demonstrated by changes in the items which make up working capital.

In accounting, it is customary to show a figure in brackets if it is a minus figure. This would be deducted from the other figures to arrive at the total of the column. These are seen very frequently in flow of funds statements.

For instance suppose that the increase in working capital in Exhibit 41.6 had been £1,630 instead of £3,390 and that there had been a decrease in debtors of £270 instead of an increase of £1,490. In this case the latter part of the statement would have been shown as:

	£	£
Increase in working capital		1,630
Increase in stock	350	
Decrease in debtors	(270)	
Decrease in creditors	230	
Increase in cash and bank	1,320	1,630

Adjustments needed to net profit

When net profit is included as a source of funds, we usually have to adjust the net profit figure to take account of items included which do not involve a movement of funds *in the period covered by the funds statement.*

Depreciation

For instance, suppose we bought equipment costing £3,000 in year ended 31 December 19-3. It is depreciated £1,000 per annum for 3 years and then scrapped, disposal value being nil. This would result in the following:

	Years to 31 December		
	19-3	*19-4*	*19-5*
	£	£	£
(i) Item involving flow of funds:			
Cost of equipment	3,000		
(ii) Items not involving flow of funds:			
Depreciation	1,000	1,000	1,000
(iii) Net Profit before depreciation	12,000	13,500	15,000
(iv) Net Profit after depreciation	11,000	12,000	14,000

Now the question arises as to which of figures (i) to (iv) are the ones to be used in funds statements. As funds statements are those involving flows (movements) of funds, let us examine items (i) to (iv) accordingly.

(*i*)   A payment of £3,000 is made to buy equipment. This *does* involve a flow of funds and should therefore be included in a funds statement for 19-3.

(*ii*)   Depreciation is represented by a book-keeping entry: Debit Profit and Loss: Credit Provision for Depreciation. This does not involve any flow of funds and cannot be shown as a source or application of funds.

(*iii*)   Net Profit before depreciation. This brings cash flowing into the firm and therefore should be shown in funds statements.

(*iv*)   Net Profit after depreciation. Depreciation does not involve flow of funds, and therefore (*iii*) is the net profit we need.

In most examination questions (*iii*) will not be shown. As we will show you, the figure for net profit before depreciation will be calculated in the funds flow statement itself.

Bad debts provisions

If a debt is written off as bad, then that involves a flow of funds. A debt would have become cash when paid. Now you are saying that this will not happen and have written it off to Profit and Loss Account.

On the other hand a provision for bad debts is similar in this respect to a provision for depreciation. The flow of funds occurs *when* a bad debt *is* written off, and not when provisions are made in case there may be bad debts in the future.

If an examination question gives you the net profits *after* bad debts provisions then the provision has to be added back to exclude it from the profit calculations.

Book profit/loss on sales of fixed assets

If a fixed asset with a book value (after depreciation) of £5,000 is sold for £6,400 cash, then the flow of funds is £6,400. The fact that there has been a book profit of £1,400 does not provide any more funds above the figure of £6,400. Similarly, the sale of an asset with a book value of £3,000 for £2,200 cash produces a flow of funds of £2,200. The £800 book loss does mean that there has been a further overflow.

As the net profit figure in accounts is:

(*i*)   *after* adjustments for depreciation
(*ii*)   *after* provisions for bad debts adjustments
(*iii*)   *after* book profits/losses on sales of fixed assets

the profits figures will need adjusting in flow of funds statements. Note that the adjustments needed are only for depreciation in *that period*, fixed asset book profits/losses for *that period*. No adjustments are needed with reference to previous periods.

This means that in the funds flow statements the profits will need adjusting. Examples of three firms are given in Exhibit 41.7.

Exhibit 41.7

	Firm A £	Firm B £	Firm C £
Depreciation for year	2,690	4,120	6,640
Increases in bad debts provision	540	360	
Decrease in bad debt provision			200
Book loss on sale of fixed assets	1,200		490
Book profit on sale of fixed assets		750	
Net profit after the above items included	16,270	21,390	32,410

	£	£	£
Source of funds			
Net Profit	16,270	21,390	32,410
Adjustment for items not involving the movement of funds:			
Depreciation	2,690	4,120	6,640
Book profit on sale of fixed assets		(750)	
Book loss on sale of fixed assets	1,200		490
Increase in bad debt provision	540	360	
Decrease in bad debt provision			(200)
Total generated from operations	20,700	25,120	39,340

You will notice that the items in brackets, i.e. (750) and (200) had been credits in the profit and loss accounts and need deducting, while the other items were debits and need adding back.

A comprehensive example

Exhibit 41.8

The balance sheets of R Lester are as follows:

	31.12.19-3			31.12.19-4		
	£	£	£	£	£	£
Fixed Assets						
Equipment at cost		28,500			26,100	
less Depreciation to date		11,450	17,050		13,010	13,090
Current Assets						
Stock		18,570			16,250	
Debtors	8,470			14,190		
less Bad Debts Provision	420	8,050		800	13,390	
Cash and Bank Balances		4,060			3,700	
		30,680			33,340	
less Current Liabilities						
Creditors		4,140			5,730	
Working Capital			26,540			27,610
			43,590			40,700
Financed by:						
Capital						
Opening Balances b/d			35,760			33,590
add Net Profit			10,240			11,070
add Cash Introduced			–			600
			46,000			45,260
less Drawings			12,410			8,560
			33,590			36,700
Loan from J Gorsey			10,000			4,000
			43,590			40,700

Notes: Equipment with a book value of £1,350 was sold for £900. Depreciation written off equipment during the year was £2,610.

The following are now drawn up:

(*a*) A cash flow statement.

(*b*) A statement of sources and application of funds.

R Lester

Cash Flow Statement for the year ended 31 December 19-4

	£	£
Source of funds		
Net profit		11,070
Adjustment for items not involving the movement of funds:		
Depreciation	2,610	
Loss on sale of fixed assets	450	
Increase in bad debts provision	380	3,440
Total generated from operations		14,510
Funds from other sources		
Sales of equipment	900	
Decrease in stock	2,320	
Increase in creditors	1,590	
Capital introduced	600	5,410
		19,920
Application of funds		
Loan repaid to J Gorsey	6,000	
Increase in debtors	5,720	
Drawings	8,560	20,280
Decrease in cash funds		(360)
Cash and bank balances 31.12.19-3	4,060	
Cash and bank balances 31.12.19-4	3,700	(360)

(b)

R Lester

Statement of Source and Application of Funds
for the year ended 31 December 19-4

	£	£
Sources of funds		
Net Profit		11,070
Adjustment for items not involving		
movement of funds:		
Depreciation	2,610	
Loss on sale of fixed assets	450	3,060
Total generated from operations		14,130
Funds from other sources		
Sales of equipment	900	
Capital introduced	600	1,500
		15,630
Application of funds		
Loan repaid to J Gorsey	6,000	
Drawings	8,560	14,560
		1,070
Increase in working capital		
Decrease in stock	(2,320)	
Increase in debtors	5,340	
Decrease in cash balances	(360)	
Increase in creditors	(1,590)	1,070

UK companies and SSAP10

We have already stated that UK companies, except the very smallest, have to publish a statement of source and application of funds for each accounting period. Students whose level of studies terminate with the conclusion of Volume 1 will not normally need to know more than has already been written in this chapter. However, some will need to know the basic layout proposed in SSAP10. For these students, the basic layout is shown as Exhibit 41.9.

Exhibit 41.9

A limited company
Statement of Source and Application of Funds
Year ended ...

	£	£
Source of funds		
Profit before tax		x
Adjustments for items not involving the movement of funds: Depreciation		x
Total generated from operations		x
Funds from other sources		
Issue of shares for cash	x	
Issue of loan capital	x	x
		x
Application of funds		
Dividends paid	x	
Tax paid	x	
Purchase of fixed assets	x	x
Increase/decrease in working capital		x
Increase/Decrease in stocks	x	
Increase/Decrease in debtors	x	
Decrease/Increase in creditors	x	
Movement in net liquid funds:		
Increase/Decrease in		
Cash Balances	x	
Short-term investments	x	x	x

The basic layout cannot be adhered to for all possible items. For instance, if there had been no purchase of fixed assets, but instead there had been a sale of fixed assets, then 'Sale of fixed assets' would appear under 'Funds from other sources'.

Some points must be stressed:

(*a*) It is taxation *paid*, not taxation charged, that is needed.

(*b*) It is dividends *paid*, not dividends proposed, that is needed.

Review questions

41.1 The following Balance Sheets relate to a business run by T Welldone:

Balance Sheet as at 31 December 19-6

	£		£
Fixed Assets	20,000	Capital	34,000
Current Assets:		Creditors	2,000
Stock	4,000		
Debtors	1,000		
Bank	11,000		
	16,000		
	36,000		36,000

Balance Sheet as at 31 December 19-7

	£		£
Fixed Assets	35,000	Capital	40,000
Current Assets:		Loan	5,000
Stock	13,000	Creditors	6,000
Debtors	2,000		
Bank	1,000		
	16,000		
	51,000		51,000

Mr Welldone considers that he has not done well, as his money in the bank has fallen from £11,000 to £1,000, in spite of the fact that he has borrowed £5,000 and left £6,000 of his profit in the business.

(*a*) Set out a statement to show Mr Welldone how the money has been spent.

(*b*) Comment on Mr Welldone's judgement of his success based upon the balance in the bank.

(*University of London*)

41.2A

Robert Taylor

Balance Sheet as at 31 December 19-6

	£		£
Premises	20,000	Capital 1 January 19-6	25,000
Fixtures	4,000	*add* Net profit	5,000
Stock	3,000		
Debtors	1,000		30,000
Cash in bank	1,000	*less* drawings	3,000
Cash in hand	300		
			27,000
		Trade creditors	2,300
	29,300		29,300

Balance Sheet as at 31 December 19-7

	£		£
Premises	20,000	Capital 1 January 19-7	27,000
Fixtures	3,000	*add* Net Profit	3,000
Stock	6,000		
Debtors	3,500		30,000
Cash in hand	100	*less* Drawings	4,000
			26,000
		Trade creditors	5,000
		Bank overdraft	1,600
	32,600		32,600

Study the Balance Sheets shown above.

(*a*) Calculate the working capital on 31 December 19-6 and on 31 December 19-7.

(*b*) Calculate the percentage of net profit on capital at the beginning of each year.

(*c*) Comment on the changes which have taken place in the figures for net profit and drawings.

(*d*) Explain why it has become necessary to raise an overdraft during 19-7 and, paying attention to and comparing the figures for debtors, creditors, stock and cash, comment briefly on the state of the business.

(*University of London*)

41.3 The Balance Sheets of a sole trader for two successive years are given below. You are required to calculate the variation in working capital and to explain how the variation has arisen.

Balance Sheets – as on 31 December

	19-3	19-4		19-3	19-4
	£	£		£	£
Land and Premises			Capital Account:		
(cost £3,000)	2,600	2,340	1 January	4,200	4,700
Plant and Machinery			*add* Net Profit for		
(cost £2,000)	1,500	–	the year	1,800	2,200
(cost £3,000)	–	2,300			
Stocks	660	630		6,000	6,900
Trade Debtors	1,780	1,260	Deduct Drawings	1,300	1,500
				4,700	5,400
Bank	–	710	Trade Creditors	1,200	840
			Bank Overdraft	640	–
			Loan (repayable		
			December 19-0)	–	1,000
	6,540	7,240		6,540	7,240

41.4A John Flynn

Balance Sheets – as on 31 December

	19-8	19-9		19-8	19-9
	£	£		£	£
Buildings	5,000	5,000	Capital at 1 January	15,500	16,100
Fixtures			*add* Cash Introduced	–	2,500
less Depreciation	1,800	2,000	,, Net Profit for year	6,800	7,900
Motor					
less Depreciation	2,890	5,470		22,300	26,500
Stock	3,000	8,410	*less* Drawings	6,200	7,800
Debtors	4,860	5,970		16,100	18,700
Bank	3,100	–	Creditors	2,900	2,040
Cash	350	150	Bank Overdraft	–	1,260
			Loan (repayable 19-5)	2,000	5,000
	21,000	27,000		21,000	27,000

From the balance sheets above draw up a statement showing how the variation in working capital has arisen. Fixtures bought during the year amounted to £400, and a motor was bought for £4,000.

41.5 A friend of yours who owns a newsagent's and confectionery business has asked for your help. He is very worried because he suspects that a shop assistant is stealing money from his till. He comments as follows:

'For the year 31 March 19-2 my shop made a profit of £8,600 and yet I have had to ask the bank for an overdraft,' then adds 'will you check the figures for me please?' You agree to help and he supplies the following information:

Nick's Newsmart

Balance Sheets as at 31 March

	19-1 £	19-1 £	19-2 £	19-2 £
Fixed Assets				
Premises, at cost	16,000		16,000	
less depreciation	3,600		3,900	
		12,400		12,100
Fixtures and fittings, at cost	3,000		8,200	
less depreciation	1,000		1,300	
		2,000		6,900
		14,400		19,000
Current Assets				
Stocks – magazines, periodicals	5,400		8,060	
– sweets, tobacco	1,480		3,240	
Debtors – trade	2,200		4,900	
– other	140		420	
Bank	6,400		–	
Cash	280		500	
	15,900		17,120	
Current Liabilities				
Creditors – trade	4,200		3,600	
– other	100		120	
Bank overdraft	–		4,000	
	4,300		7,720	
Working Capital		11,600		9,400
Net Assets Employed		£26,000		£28,400
Opening capital	24,600		26,000	
add net profit	6,800		8,600	
	31,400		34,600	
less drawings	5,400		6,200	
Closing capital		£26,000		£28,400

You confirm that he has not disposed of any fixed assets during the year.

You are required to prepare a statement of source and application of funds to show Nick where his profit has gone.

(*Chartered Association of Certified Accountants*)

41.6 The balance sheets of Antipodean Enterprises at the end of two consecutive financial years, were:

Balance Sheets as at

31 December 19-2			31 December 19-3	
£	£		£	£
		Fixed Assets at written down value		
38,000		Premises	37,000	
17,600		Equipment	45,800	
4,080		Cars	18,930	
	59,680			101,730
	17,000	*Investments (long-term)*		25,000
		Current Assets		
27,500		Stocks	19,670	
14,410		Debtors and prepayments	11,960	
3,600		Short-term investments	4,800	
1,800		Cash and bank balances	700	
47,310			37,130	
		Current Liabilities		
20,950		Creditors and accruals	32,050	
–		Bank overdraft	28,200	
20,950			60,250	
	26,360	*Working Capital*		(23,120)
	£103,040	*Net Assets Employed*		£103,610
		Financed by:		
67,940		Opening capital	75,040	
4,000		Capital introduced/(withdrawn)	(6,500)	
15,300		Profit/(loss) for year	25,200	
(12,200)		Drawings	(15,130)	
	75,040	*Closing Capital*		78,610
		Long-term liability		
	28,000	Business development loan		25,000
	£103,040			£103,610

Profit for year ended 31 December 19-3 (£25,200) is after accounting for:

	£
Depreciation – premises	1,000
– equipment	3,000
– cars	3,000
Profit on disposal of equipment	430
Loss on disposal of cars	740

The written down value of the assets at date of disposal was:

	£
Equipment	5,200
Cars	2,010

Required:

(*a*) Prepare a Statement of Sources and Applications of Funds for Antipodean Enterprises for the year ended 31 December 19-3.

(*b*) Comment on the financial position of the business as revealed by your answer to (*a*) and by the balance sheet as at 31 December 19-3.

(*Chartered Association of Certified Accountants*)

41.7A The balance sheets of SAF (1979) Ltd were as shown below. During the year ended 31 March 19-6 the company had

(*a*) sold plant with a written down value of £25,800 for £22,400

(*b*) made a profit before tax of £749,400 after charging depreciation of the following amounts:

	£
Buildings	4,000
Plant and machinery	110,200
Fixtures and equipment	28,100

SAF (1979) Ltd
Balance Sheets as at 31 March

19-5 £	19-5 £		19-6 £	19-6 £
		Fixed Assets		
		Tangible assets (at written down values)		
200,000		Land and buildings	196,000	
830,700		Plant and machinery	925,800	
182,400		Fixtures, fittings, tools and equipment	204,600	
	1,213,100			1,326,400
		Investments		
		Investments other than		
	10,800	loans		72,000
		Current Assets		
421,500		Stock	381,000	
134,600		Debtors	110,200	
89,200		Bank and cash	92,400	
645,300			583,600	
		Creditors amounts due in less than one year		
–		Bank loans and overdrafts	77,300	
120,900		Trade creditors	9,400	
16,000		Bills of exchange payable	51,900	
		Other creditors		
157,300		Taxation	163,200	
175,000		Proposed dividends	190,500	
469,200			492,300	
	176,100	*Net Current Assets*		91,300
	1,400,000	*Total Assets less Current Liabilities*		1,489,700

	19-5			19-6
£	£		£	£
		Creditors: amounts due in more than one		
		year		
	400,000	Debenture loans		150,000
		Provisions for liabilities and charges		
		Provision for legal damages		
	56,000	and costs		–
		Capital and Reserves		
	700,000	Called-up share capital		700,000
	5,000	Share premium		5,000
	239,000	Profit and loss		634,700
	1,400,000			1,489,700

Note:

The amounts shown in 19-5 for taxation, proposed dividends and legal damages and costs were paid in year ended 31 March 19-6 at the amounts stated.

Required:

(*a*) Prepare a Statement of Source and Application of Funds for SAF (1979) Ltd for the year ended 31 March 19-6.

(*b*) Comment briefly on the financial position of the company disclosed by your answer to (*a*).

(*Chartered Association of Certified Accountants*)

42

The calculation of wages and salaries payable to employees

In the UK wages are generally taken to be the earnings paid on a weekly basis to employees, while salaries are those paid on a monthly basis.

The earnings of employees, whether paid monthly or weekly, are subject to various deductions. These can consist of the following items.

1 Income Tax. In the UK the wages and salaries of all employees are liable to have income tax deducted from them. This does not mean that everyone will pay Income Tax, but that if Income Tax is found to be payable then the employer will deduct the tax from the employee's wages or salary.

Each person in the UK is allowed to set various personal reliefs against the amount earned to see if he/she is liable to pay Income Tax. The reliefs given for each person depend upon his or her personal circumstances. Extra relief is given to a man who is married, as compared to a single man; further extra relief will be given for factors such as having dependent relatives, and so on. The reliefs given are changed from time to time by Parliament. Most students will know of the **Budget** which is presented to Parliament by the Chancellor of the Exchequer, in which such changes are announced. After discussion by Parliament, and subject to possible changes there, the changes will be incorporated into a Finance Act. This means that, for instance, a single man earning a given amount might pay Income Tax, whereas a married man who is eligible for extra reliefs might earn the same amount and pay no Income Tax at all.

Once the reliefs have been deducted from the earnings, any excess of the earnings above that figure will have to suffer Income Tax being levied on it. As the rates of Income Tax change regularly, all that can be given here are the basic principles; the rates given are for purposes of illustration only. A further complication arises because the rate of tax increases in steps when the excess of the earnings exceeds certain figures.

For instance, assume that the rates of Income Tax are (on the amount actually exceeding the reliefs for each person):

On the first £1,000	Income Tax at 20 per cent
On the next £5,000	Income Tax at 30 per cent
On the remainder	Income Tax at 50 per cent

The Income Tax payable by each of four persons can now be looked at.

Miss Jones earns £1,500 per annum. Her personal reliefs amount to £1,700. Income Tax payable = Nil.

Mr Bland earns £4,000 per annum. His personal reliefs are £3,400. He therefore has £600 of his earnings on which he will have to pay Income Tax. As the rate on the first £1,000 taxable is 20 per cent, then he will pay £600 × 20 per cent = £120.

Mrs Hugo earns £6,500 per annum. She has personal reliefs amounting to £2,700. She will therefore pay Income Tax on the excess of £3,800. This will amount to:

On the first £1,000 tax at 20 per cent	=	200
On the remaining £2,800 tax at 30 per cent	=	840
Total Income Tax		£1,040

Mr Pleasance has a salary of £10,000 per annum. His personal reliefs amount to £3,560. He will therefore pay Income Tax on the excess of £6,440. This will amount to:

On the first £1,000 tax at 20 per cent	=	200
On the next £5,000 tax at 30 per cent	=	1,500
On the next £440 tax at 50 per cent	=	220
Total Income Tax		£1,920

The actual deduction of the Income Tax from the earnings of the employee is made by the employer. The tax is commonly called PAYE tax, which represents the initial letters for **Pay As You Earn**. The amount of reliefs to which each employee is entitled is communicated to the employer in the form of a **Notice of Coding**, on which a code number is stated. The code number is then used in conjunction with special tax tables to show the amount of the tax deductible from the employee's earnings.

So far the amount of tax payable by anyone has been looked at on an annual basis. However, PAYE means precisely that: it involves paying the tax as the earnings are calculated on each pay date, weekly or monthly, and not waiting until after the end of the year to pay the bill. The code numbers and the tax tables supplied to the employer by the Inland Revenue are so worked out that this is possible. It is outside the scope of this book to examine in detail how this is done. However, in the case of the three people already listed who will have to pay Income Tax, if we assume that Mrs Hugo is paid weekly, then from each week's wage she will have to pay one week's tax, in her case £1,040 ÷ 52 = £20. If Mr Bland and Mr Pleasance are paid on a monthly basis, then Mr Bland will have to pay £120 ÷ 12 = £10 per month, and Mr Pleasance £1,920 ÷ 12 = £160 per month.

It may well have crossed the reader's mind that, for many people, the year's earnings are not known in advance, and that the total amount payable, divided neatly into weekly or monthly figures, would not be known until the year was finished. The operation of the PAYE system automatically allows for this problem. A book on Income Tax should be studied if the reader would like to investigate further how this is carried out.

2 In the UK employees are also liable to pay **National Insurance** contributions. The deduction of these is carried out by the employer at the same time as the PAYE Income Tax deductions are effected. The payment of such National Insurance contributions is to ensure that the payer will be able to claim benefits from the State, if and when he is in a position to claim, such as unemployment benefit, sickness benefit, retirement pension and so on.

There is a lower limit for each employee below which no National Insurance is payable at all, and there is also a top limit, earnings above this amount being disregarded for National Insurance. These limits are changed by Parliament, usually annually. Any figures given in this book are by way of illustration only.

If it is assumed that the lower limit of earnings eligible for National Insurance contributions is £1,000 and that the top limit is £10,000, and that the rate of National Insurance payable by the employee is 5 per cent, then the following contributions would be made:

Mrs Jones: part-time cleaner, earns £900 per annum. National Insurance contributions nil.

Miss Hardcastle, earnings £3,000 per annum. National Insurance contribution £3,000 × 5 per cent = £150. The fact that there is a lower limit of £1,000 does not mean that the first £1,000 of the earnings are free of National Insurance contributions, but simply that anyone earning less than £1,000 will not pay any. Someone earning £1,100 would pay National Insurance of £1,100 × 5 per cent = £55.

Mr Evergreen earns £12,000 per annum. He would pay at the rate of 5 per cent on £10,000 only = £500.

As with the PAYE Income Tax, the National Insurance contribution is payable per week or per month.

It should be noted that in the UK part of the National Insurance contributions can be in respect of a supplement to the retirement pension. This supplement is based on the person's earnings during this working life, and is called **State Earnings Related Pensions Scheme** (abbreviated as SERPS). Anyone can opt out of paying this extra amount in National Insurance contributions.

3 Pension contributions. Many organisations have their own pension schemes. Employees receive a pension on retirement plus, usually, a lump sum payment in cash. They also usually include benefits which will be paid to an employee's spouse if the employee dies before reaching retirement age.

Some of these schemes are **non-contributory**. This means that the organisation pays for these benefits for its employees without deducting anything from the employee's earnings. The other schemes are contributory schemes whereby the employee will pay a part of the cost of the scheme by an agreed deduction from his earnings. In addition the organisation will pay part of the cost of the scheme without any cost to the employee.

Since July 1988 any employee has been allowed to opt out of his organisation's contributory scheme and buy his own private pension.

Normally, pensions contributions, whether to the organisation's pension scheme or to the employee's private pension scheme, are tax deductible items. This means that the part of their earnings taken as pension contributions, within agreed limits, will escape Income Tax. This is not the case with the State National Insurance contributions paid by employees.

Statutory Sick Pay (SSP)

In the UK employers are responsible for paying their employees statutory sick pay when they are absent from work. At the time of writing, employers pay this for up to 28 weeks of sickness.

SSP is treated in the same manner as other pay, in that tax and national insurance is deducted from it. Employers recover the gross amount of SSP by deducting it each month from the national insurance contributions they remit each month to the Collector of Taxes. They are also compensated for the national insurance contributions suffered by the employee on SSP.

Calculation of net wages/salary payable

Two illustrations of the calculation of the net pay to be made to various employees can now be looked at.

		£
(A) G Jarvis:	Gross Earning for the week ended 8 May 19-4	100
	Income Tax: found by consulting tax tables and employee's code number	12
	National Insurance 5%	

G Jarvis: Payslip Week ended 8 May 19-4

	£	£
Gross pay for the week		100
less Income Tax	12	
,, National Insurance	5	17
Net Pay		83

		£
(B) H Reddish:	Gross earnings for the month of May 19-4	800
	Income Tax (from tax tables)	150
	Superannuation: 6% of gross pay	
	National Insurance 5% of gross pay	

H Reddish: Payslip Month ended 31 May 19-4

	£	£
Gross pay for the month		800
less Income Tax	150	
,, Superannuation	48	
,, National Insurance	40	238
Net Pay		562

National insurance: employer's contribution

Besides the amount of the National Insurance which has to be suffered by the employee, the employer also has to pay a percentage based on the employee's pay as the firm's own contribution. This expense is suffered by the firm; it has no recourse against its employee. The percentage which the firm will have to pay varies as Parliament amend it to deal with the changing economic climate of the country. In this book it will be treated as though it is 10 per cent, but this figure is simply for illustration purposes. It does, however, at the time that this book is being written, equate to the approximate proportion which the employer pays as compared with that paid by the employee, the latter being about one-half of that suffered by the employer.

The entry of salaries and wages in the books of a firm can now be seen. A firm owned by H Offerton has one employee, whose name is F Edgeley. For one month of June 19-3 the payslip made out for Edgeley has appeared as:

	£	£
Gross Pay for the month		600
less Income Tax	90	
,, National Insurance 5%	30	120
Net Pay		480

Additional to this, the firm will also have to pay its own share of the National Insurance contribution for Edgeley. This will be 10 per cent of £600 = £60. Therefore to employ Edgeley in the firm for this month has cost the firm the amount of his gross pay £600, plus £60 National Insurance, a total of £660. This means that when the firm draws up its Profit and Loss Account, the charge for the employment of this person for the month should be £660.

The firm has however acted as a collector of taxes and National Insurance on behalf of the government, and it will have to pay over to the government's agent, which is the Inland Revenue, the amount collected on its behalf. If it is assumed that the £90 deducted from pay for Income Tax, and the £30 deducted for National Insurance, are paid to the Inland Revenue on 30 June 19-3, then the cash book will appear as:

Cash Book (bank columns)

Dr		*Cr*	
		19-3	£
		June 30 Wages (cheque to Edgeley)	480
		,, ,, Inland Revenue (see below)*	180
*Made up of: Income Tax PAYE	90		
National Insurance (employee's part)	30		
National Insurance (employer's part)	60		
	180		

In a firm as small as the one illustrated, both the figure of £480 and the £180 could be posted to a 'Wages and National Insurance Account', to give a total for the month of £660. In a larger firm such payments would be best posted to separate accounts for National Insurance and for PAYE Income Tax, transfers then being made when the final accounts are drawn up.

Review questions

42.1 H Smith is employed by a firm of carpenters at a rate of £1.50 per hour. During the week to 18 May 19-5 he worked his basic week of 40 hours. The Income Tax due on his wages was £8, and he is also liable to pay National Insurance contributions of 5 per cent. Calculate his net wages.

42.2 B Charles is employed as an undertaker's assistant. His basic working week consists of 40 hours, paid at the rate of £2 per hour. For hours worked in excess of this he is paid at the rate of 1½ times his basic earnings. In the week ended 12 March 19-6 he worked 60 hours. Up to £40 a week he pays no Income Tax, but he pays it at the rate of 30 per cent for all earnings above that figure. He is liable to pay National Insurance at the rate of 5 per cent. Calculate his net wages.

42.3 B Croft has a job as a car salesman. He is paid a basic salary of £200 per month, with a commission extra of 2 per cent on the value of his car sales. During the month of April 19-6 he sells £30,000 worth of cars. He pays Income Tax at the rate of 30 per cent on all earnings above £100 per month. He also pays National Insurance at the rate of 5 per cent on the first £500 of his monthly earnings, paying nothing on earnings above that figure. Calculate his net pay for the month.

42.4A T Penketh is an accountant with a firm of bookmakers. He has a salary of £500 per month, but he also has a bonus dependent on the firm's profits. The bonus for the month was £200. He pays National Insurance at the rate of 5 per cent on his gross earnings up to a maximum of £600 per month, there being no contribution for earnings above that figure. He pays Income Tax at the rate of 30 per cent on his earnings between £100 and £300 per month, and at the rate of 50 per cent on all earnings above that figure. However, before calculating earnings on which he has to pay Income Tax, he is allowed to deduct the amount of superannuation payable by him which is at the rate of 10 per cent on gross earnings. Calculate his net pay for the month.

42.5A R Kennedy is a security van driver. He has a wage of £100 per week, and danger money of £1 per hour in addition for every hour he spends in transporting gold bullion. During the week ended 16 June 19-3 he spends 20 hours taking gold bullion to London Airport. He pays Income Tax at the rate of 25 per cent on all his earnings above £80 per week. He pays National Insurance at the rate of 5 per cent on gross earnings. Calculate his net wage for the week.

42.6A V Mevagissey is a director of a company. She has a salary of £500 per month. She pays superannuation at the rate of 5 per cent. She also pays National Insurance at the rate of 5 per cent of gross earnings. Her Income Tax, due on gross salary less superannuation, is at the rate of 30 per cent after her personal reliefs for the month, other than superannuation, of £300 have been deducted. Calculate her net pay for the month.

43

The valuation of stock

To the general public accounting often seems to imply a precision down to the final pence. A firm will usually know the exact amount of debtors or creditors, or the exact amount spent on wages or other expenses, and this gives the appearance of precision in all matters connected with accounting. In fact this is only true of some parts of accounting. A re-examination of the chapter on depreciation will illustrate a part of accounting dealing with provisions for depreciation which are normally nothing more than sheer guesswork.

Precision is also lacking when stock is valued at the end of each financial year. This does not necessarily mean a lack of precision in actually counting the number of items in stock. In all but the very smallest businesses there will often be errors in checking the quantities in stock. There will be human errors unless everything is double-checked, and the cost of doing this is often not worth while for many items of small value. Then there will be defects in such aids to checking quantities as weighing machines or liquid measures, even though the margin of error may be very small. The real lack of precision exists in giving one indisputable value to the total quantity of stock.

It is possible to state that J Smith is a debtor for £155 and to be perfectly correct in this case there is only one correct figure. With stock valuation there is usually a whole spectrum of possible figures. The one chosen will depend on the attitudes and opinions of those whose responsibility it is to value stock.

Up to this point it has been assumed, for the sake of simplicity, that the stock of unsold goods at the end of each financial year is valued at cost. This might appear to be an easy task to be undertaken by the management of the firm. It is, however, far from the truth. Even if 'cost' was the only measure of the value of stock, it will be shown that 'cost' can have many different meanings attached to it.

Assume that a firm has just completed its first financial year and is about to value stock at cost price. It has dealt in only one type of goods. A record of the transaction is as follows:

Bought		£	*Sold*		£
January	10 at £30 each	300	May	8 for £50 each	400
April	10 at £34 each	340	November	24 for £60 each	1,440
October	20 at £40 each	800			
	40	1,440		32	1,840

Still in Stock at 31 December, 8 units.

The total figure of purchases is £1,440 and that of sales is £1,840. The trading account for the first year of trading can now be completed if the closing stock is brought into the calculations. This brings to light the question as to exactly which eight units of stock remain on hand. If each of the units bought had cost exactly the same, then the question would not matter from an accounting point of view. However, the three lots of purchases were bought at different prices. The cost of the goods unsold therefore rests on exactly which goods are taken for this calculation. They are most probably eight of the October purchases, but they could well be eight of the April or January purchases instead, or else be some of each of these purchases. If it is the type of goods which is subject to a fairly speedy deterioration because of age, then obviously a great deal of attention will be given to ensure that goods are issued or sold in chronological order. There are, however, many types of goods which do not suffer undue deterioration in the short term, and it will not matter vitally to the firms as to which items are sold first.

Therefore many firms will not know when the units in stock at the end of the financial year were purchased. Even if they could, many firms would not take the trouble of finding this out, nor would they want to incur the cost involved in obtaining the information. The valuation of stock therefore becomes one of an accounting custom rather than one based on any scientific facts. In accounting what matters is not which units were actually sold, but instead rests on the surmise of which units were 'deemed' to have been sold.

Three accounting methods of stating which goods were sold are now listed. It must not be thought that the list is comprehensive.

First In, First Out

This is abbreviated as FIFO, and this 'shorthand' term is often being used.

The first goods received are deemed to be the first to be issued. With this method, using the data already given, the stock figure at 31 December would be calculated as follows:

	Received	Issued	Stock after each transaction		
				£	£
January	10 at £30 each		10 at £30 each		300
				£	£
April	10 at £34 each		10 at £30 each	300	
			10 at £34 each	340	640
May		8 at £30 each	2 at £30 each	60	
			10 at £34 each	340	400
October	20 at £40 each		2 at £30 each	60	
			10 at £34 each	340	
			20 at £40 each	800	1,200
November		2 at £30 each			
		10 at £34 each			
		12 at £40 each			
		—			
		24	8 at £40 each		320
		=			

Last In, First Out (abbreviated as LIFO)

With this method, as each issue of goods is made they are deemed to be from the last lot of goods received prior to that date, and where the last lot received are insufficient to meet the issue then the balance is deemed to come from the next previous lot received still available. The stock figure at 31 December becomes £240.

	Received	Issued	Stock after each transaction	£	£
January	10 at £30 each		10 at £30 each		300
April	10 at £34 each		10 at £30 each	300	
			10 at £34 each	340	640
May		8 at £34 each	10 at £30 each	300	
			2 at £34 each	68	368
October	20 at £40 each		10 at £30 each	300	
			2 at £34 each	68	
			20 at £40 each	800	1,168
November		20 at £40 each			
		2 at £34 each			
		2 at £30 each	8 at £30 each		240
		——			
		24			
		==			

Average cost

With each receipt of goods the average cost of goods held in stock is recalculated. Any subsequent issue is then made at that price until a further receipt of goods necessitates the average cost of goods held being recalculated. This shows a stock at 31 December of £296.

	Received	Issued	Average cost per unit of stock held £	Number of units in stock	Total value of stock £
January	10 at £30		30	10	300
April	10 at £34		32	20	640
May		8 at £32	32	12	384
October	20 at £40		37	32	1,184
November		24 at £37	37	8	296

Stock valuation and the calculation of profits

Using each of the three methods already described, the Trading Accounts would appear:

Trading Account for the year ended 31 December 19–

		Methods				
		1		2		3
		£		£		£
Sales		1,840		1,840		1,840
Less Cost of Goods Sold:						
Purchases	1,440		1,440		1,440	
Less Closing Stock	320	1,120	240	1,200	296	1,144
Gross Profit		720		640		696

The amount of profits calculated is therefore always dependent on the basis on which the stock has been valued.

Profits as a periodic calculation

While it is true to say that the profits calculated for any year will differ if other bases were used for stock valuation purposes, it must be born in mind that the total profits over the whole life-span of the business will be the same irrespective of which basis is used at the end of each intervening year.

An illustration of this can now be shown. Assume that a business commences without any stock and terminates its activities four years later, the stock then in hand being taken over by the purchaser of the business for £2,000. A record of the sales and purchases, together with two possible stock valuations for each year, are as follows:

	Year 1	Year 2	Year 3	Year 4
	£	£	£	£
Sales (excluding the sale of the final stock)	5,000	7,000	8,000	9,000
Purchases	4,000	5,000	6,200	7,500
Stock valuations:				
Basis (a)	800	1,000	1,500	
Basis (b)	500	800	1,100	

Trading Account
Stock valuation basis (a)

		Years						
		1		2		3		4
		£		£		£		£
Sales		5,000		7,000		8,000		9,000
less Cost of Goods Sold:								
Opening Stock			800		1,000		1,500	
Add Purchases	4,000		5,000		6,200		7,500	
	4,000		5,800		7,200		9,000	
less Closing Stock	800	3,200	1,000	4,800	1,500	5,700	2,000	7,000
Gross Profit		1,800		2,200		2,300		2,000

Stock valuation basis (b)

	Years							
		1 £		2 £		3 £		4 £
Sales		5,000		7,000		8,000		9,000
less Cost of Goods Sold:								
Opening Stock			500		800		1,100	
Add Purchases	4,000		5,000		6,200		7,500	
	4,000		5,500		7,000		8,600	
less Closing Stock	500	3,500	800	4,700	1,100	5,900	2,000	6,600
Gross Profit		1,500		2,300		2,100		2,400

Adding the profits together basis (*a*) shows £1,800 + £2,200 + £2,300 + £2,000 = £8,300, while basis (*b*) shows £1,500 + £2,300 + £2,100 + £2,400 = £8,300.

Different meanings of 'cost'

Dealing in the first instance with a retailing business, the word 'cost' may well mean just the actual cash paid to the supplier. However, where the retailer has paid separately for carriage inwards on the items bought, then he should undoubtedly treat this as part of the cost. Some firms will in addition add an amount representing the cost of storing the goods prior to resale, other firms will ignore such expenses for stock valuation purposes. Even firms who do bring in an amount for storage expenses will differ in the ways that they calculate it. There is no way that is laid down and adhered to by all firms.

With a manufacturing firm the problem becomes even more complex. It is possible (but see summary of SSAP 9 at the end of the chapter) to value stock of goods manufactured by the firm either at prime cost or at production cost or at some point in between. The difference between the prime cost and production cost is made up of factory indirect expenses. Where these indirect expenses are small relative to the prime cost the difference in the profits calculated may also be small, but the greater the relative indirect expenses then the greater the difference in profit calculations. An example of this can be seen in Exhibits 43.1 and 43.2.

Exhibit 43.1

A firm manufactures its own goods for resale. In its first year of trading it has incurred £10,000 for prime cost of goods completed and £2,000 for factory indirect expenses. There was no work in progress at the end of the year. The number of units made was 1,000 and the number sold was 800 at £20 each.

The directors wish to know what the profit calculations would be (*a*) if prime cost was taken as the stock valuation basis, and (*b*) if production cost was taken.

Trading Account for the year ended ...

	(a)		(b)	
	£			£
Sales		16,000		16,000
Production Cost of Goods b/d from Manufacturing Account	12,000		12,000	
less Closing Stock (see following calculations	2,000	10,000	2,400	9,600
Gross Profit		6,000		6,400

$$\text{Closing Stock } (a) \ \frac{\text{Units in Stock}}{\text{Total Produced}} \times \text{Prime Cost} = \frac{200}{1,000} \times £10,000 = £2,000$$

$$(b) \ \frac{\text{Units in Stock}}{\text{Total Produced}} \times \text{Production Cost} = \frac{200}{1,000} \times £12,000 = £2,400$$

Exhibit 43.2

All the facts are the same as in Exhibit 43.1 except that in this case the prime cost is £2,000 and the factory indirect expenses are £10,000.

Trading Account for the year ended ...

	(a)		(b)	
	£			£
Sales		16,000		16,000
Production Cost of Goods b/d from Manufacturing Account	12,000		12,000	
less Closing Stock (see following calculations	400	11,600	2,400	9,600
Gross Profit		4,400		6,400

$$\text{Closing Stock } (a) \ \frac{\text{Units in Stock}}{\text{Total Produced}} \times \text{Prime Cost} = \frac{200}{1,000} \times £2,000 = £400$$

$$(b) \text{ Same as in Exhibit 43.1} = £2,400$$

Reduction to net realisable value

When the cost of the stock, using the applicable method, has been determined, it is necessary to ascertain whether any part of such costs will not be recouped when the goods are sold. To do this the cost is compared with the 'net realisable value', this term meaning the amount that would be received from the sale of stock after deducting all expenditure to be incurred on or before disposal. If the net realisable value is less than the cost, then the stock valuation is reduced to the net realisable value instead of cost.

This is obviously the application of the accounting concept of prudence, already discussed in Chapter 10. A somewhat exaggerated example will show the necessity for this action. Assume that an art dealer has bought only two paintings during the financial year ended 31 December 19-8. He starts off the year without any stock, and then buys a genuine masterpiece for £6,000, selling this later in the year for £11,500. The other is a fake, but he does not realise this when he buys it for £5,100, only to discover during the year that in fact he had made a terrible mistake and that the net realisable value is £100. The fake remains unsold at the end of the year. The trading accounts, Exhibit 43.3, would appear as (a) if stock is valued at cost, and (b) if stock is value at net realisable value.

Exhibit 43.3

Trading Account for the year ended 31 December 19-8

		(a) £		(b) £
Sales		11,500		11,500
Purchases	11,100		11,100	
Closing Stock	5,100	6,000	100	11,000
Gross Profit		5,500		500

Method (a) ignores the fact that the dealer had a bad trading year owing to his skill being found wanting in 19-8. If this method was used, then the loss on the fake would reveal itself in the following year's trading account. Method (b), however, realises that the loss really occurred at the date of purchase rather than at the date of sale. Following the concept of prudence accounting practice chooses method (b).

Stock groupings and valuation

It has already been seen that the valuation normally takes the lower or cost or net realisable value. This can be further interpreted in two different ways.

The article method

The cost and net realisable value are compared for each article and the lower figure taken. These lower figures are then added together to give the total valuation. It must be stressed that an article means a type of goods, so that if there are 50 units of an article in stock and that should the lower figure be £5 for one unit of an article, then the stock valuation for this item will be shown as £250.

The category method

Similar or interchangeable articles are put together into categories. Then the cost and net realisable values for each category is compared, and the lower of these two figures for each category is then taken. For one category it may well be the cost figure, while for another category it will be the net realisable figure. The figures chosen for each category are then added together to give the total valuation.

Exhibit 43.4

From the following data the different stock figures can be calculated.

Stock at 31 December 19-8

Article	Different categories	Cost	Net realisable value
		£	£
1	A	10	8
2	A	12	15
3	A	30	40
4	B	18	17
5	B	15	13
6	B	26	21
7	C	41	54
8	C	36	41
9	C	42	31
		230	240

Article method:

Taking the lower figure for each article.

£8+£12+£30+£17+£13+£21+£41+£36+£31=£209

Category method:

	Cost	Net realisable value
Category A	£10+£12+£30=£52	£8+£15+£40=£63
Category B	£18+£15+£26=£59	£17+£13+£21=£51
Category C	£41+£36+£42=£119	£54+£41+£31=£126

The valuation is therefore £52+£51+£119=£222

SSAP 9 states that the article method should be used, except where this is impractical, and in such a case the category method would be used. The idea of taking the lower of the total of cost or of the total of net realisable value, i.e. the lower of £230 or £240 in Exhibit 43.4, is specifically excluded.

Reduction to replacement cost

In other businesses it may well be important to pay attention to the cost at which stock could be replaced, if such a price is less than original cost. This will be particularly applicable where there is uncertainty as to net realisable value; where the selling prices are based on current replacement prices; or where there is a desire to recognise uneconomic buying or production.

The stock may therefore in this case be stated as the lowest of (*a*) cost, (*b*) net realisable value, or (*c*) replacement cost.

Some other bases in use

Retail businesses often estimate the cost of stock by calculating it in the first place at selling price, and then deducting the normal margin of gross profit on such stock. Adjustment is made for items which are to be sold at other than normal selling prices.

Where standard costing is in use the figure of standard cost is frequently used.

Factors affecting the stock valuation decision

Obviously the overriding consideration applicable in all circumstances when valuing stock is the need to give a 'true and fair view' of the state of the affairs of the undertaking as on the Balance Sheet date and of the trend of the firm's trading results. There is, however, no precise definition of 'true and fair view'; it obviously rests on the judgement of the persons concerned. It would be necessary to study the behavioural sciences to understand the factors that affect judgement. However, it should be possible to state that the judgement of any two persons will not always be the same in the differing circumstances of various firms.

If fact, the only certain thing about stock valuation is that the concept of consistency should be applied, i.e. that once adopted, the same basis should be used in the annual accounts until some good reason occurs to change it. A reference should then be made in the final accounts as to the effect of the change on the reported profits, if the amount involved is material.

It will perhaps be useful to look at some of the factors which cause a particular basis to be chosen. The list is intended to be indicative rather than comprehensive, and is merely intended as a first brief look at matters which will have to be studied in depth by those intending to make a career in accountancy.

Ignorance

The personalities involved may not appreciate the fact that there is more than one possible way of valuing stock.

Convenience

The basis chosen may not be the best for the purposes of profit calculation but it may be the easiest to calculate. It must always be borne in mind that the benefits which flow from possessing information should be greater than the costs of obtaining it. The only difficulty with this is actually establishing when the benefits do exceed the cost, but in some circumstances the decision not to adopt a given basis will be obvious.

Custom

It may be the particular method used in a certain trade or industry.

Taxation

The whole idea may be to defer the payment of tax for as long as possible. Because the stock figures affect the calculation of profits on which the tax is based the lowest possible stock figures may be taken to show the lowest profits up to the Balance Sheet date.

The capacity to borrow money or to sell the business at the highest possible price.

The higher the stock value shown, then the higher will be the profits calculated to date, and therefore at first sight the business looks more attractive to a buyer or lender. Either of these considerations may be more important to the proprietors than anything else. It may be thought that businessmen are not so gullible, but all businessmen are not necessarily well acquainted with accounting customs. In fact, many small businesses are bought, or money is lent to then, without the expert advice of someone well versed in accounting.

Remuneration purposes

Where someone managing a business is paid in whole or in part by reference to the profits earned, then one basis may suit him better than others. He may therefore strive to have that basis used to suit his own ends. The owner, however, may try to follow another course to minimise the remuneration that he will have to pay out.

Lack of information

If proper stock records have not been kept, then such bases as the average cost method or the LIFO method may not be calculable.

Advice of the auditors

Many firms use a particular basis because the auditors advised its use in the first instance. If a different auditor is appointed he may well advise that a different basis be used.

The conflict of aims

The list of some of the factors which affect decisions is certainly not exhaustive, but it does illustrate the fact that stock valuation is usually a compromise. There is not usually only one figure which is true and fair, there must be a variety of possibilities. Therefore the desire to borrow money, and in so doing to paint a good picture by being reasonably optimistic in valuing stock, will be tempered by the fact that this may increase the tax bill. Stock valuation is therefore a compromise between the various ends for which it is to be used.

Work in progress

The valuation of work in progress is subject to all the various criteria and methods used in valuing stock. Probably the cost element is more strongly pronounced than in stock valuation, as it is very often impossible or irrelevant to say what net realisable value or replacement price would be applicable to partly finished goods. Firms in industries such as those which have contracts covering several years have evolved their own methods.

Long term contract work in progress will be dealt with in Volume 2.

Goods on sale or return

Quite often goods are supplied by a manufacturer (or a wholesaler) to a retailer on the basis of 'sale or return'. This means that should the retailer sell the goods, then he will incur liability for them to the manufacturer. Failing his being able to sell the goods he will then return them to the manufacturer, having incurred no liability for the goods. This is true where part of the goods are sold by the retailer and part are returned, the only goods being payable for to the manufacturer being those which were sold.

There is no one way of accounting for such activities. All that can be said is that the goods are not effectively sold to the retailer until he in turn has sold them to someone else. It is only then that the manufacturer's sales figures should be increased. Such goods still unsold by the retailer at the financial years end are not part of the retailer's stock, they are part of the manufacturer's stock and should be treated as such. Sometimes the manufacturer's sales figures includes goods which are on sale or return, and which the retailer himself has not yet sold. Where this happens adjustments are needed for the Final Accounts.

Exhibit 43.5

A manufacturer's year end is 31 December 19-7. When he sends goods on sale or return to retailers he charges them out as ordinary sales. The following details are relevant to his end of year position:

	£
Stock (at factory) at cost 31 December 19-7	10,400
Sales (including goods on sale or return £15,000 of which £3,000 have not yet been sold by the retailer)	60,000
Debtors at 31 December 19-7 (including goods booked out on sale or return)	8,800

The goods sent on sale or return were at cost price plus 25 per cent for profit (mark-up).

The figures needed for the Final Accounts are:

	£	£
Sales		60,000
less Goods on sale or return still unsold		3,000
		57,000
Debtors		8,800
less Charges for goods on sale or return in respect of goods not sold		3,000
		5,800
Stocks		
At the factory (at cost)		10,400
add Goods in customers' hands on sale or return (selling price)	3,000	
less Profit content (20 per cent of selling price)	600	2,400
		12,800

From the retailer's point of view, goods on sale or return are not purchases until he actually incurs liability for them, i.e. he sells the goods. Neither do they constitute part of his stock, as they belong to the manufacturer.

Stocktaking and the balance sheet date

It is often thought by students that the actual physical counting of stock all takes place after the close of business on the last day of the financial period. This could well be done in some small businesses with only a fews items of a limited number of different types of stock. Other businesses will have hundreds, or even thousands, of different types of stock, and each type of stock may consist of thousands of items. Stocktaking in such a case will have to be spread over a period.

At one time it was very rare for the auditors to attend at stocktaking time as observers. The professional accounting bodies now encourage the auditors to be present if at all possible. Some financial year ends are so popular with firms that it would be impossible for a representative of the auditors to be present at all the stocktakings, or even a reasonable number of them, if they were all held at the same time. The practice has started to grow up of the stocktaking being held in large firms at some time before the financial years end, the stock records (not being part of the double entry system of financial accounts) from then to the end of the financial year being relied upon to show the stock at the Balance Sheet date. Naturally this would not be done where it was felt that the stock records could not be relied upon, and various sample checks would be carried out to try to ensure that all was in order. This technique has the advantage, other than that of the auditors attending the stocktaking, of enabling the Balance Sheet to be published at a date earlier than would be normal if all stocktaking was done at the Balance Sheet date.

In many firms stocktaking takes place after the financial year end, and calculations are needed to work out the stock at the Balance Sheet date. Exhibit 43.6 shows just such a calculation.

Exhibit 43.6

Bloom Ltd has a financial year which ends on 31 December 19-7. The stocktaking is not in fact done until 8 January 19-8. When the items in stock on that date are priced out, it is found that the stock value amounted to £28,850. The following information is available about transactions between 31 December 19-7 and 8 January 19-8.

(i) Purchases since 31 December 19-7 amounted to £2,370 at cost.
(ii) Returns inwards since 31 December 19-7 were £350 at selling price.
(iii) Sales since 31 December 19-7 amounted to £3,800 at selling price.
(iv) The selling price is always made up of cost price + 25 per cent = selling price.

Bloom Ltd
Computation of stock as on 31 December 19-7

	£	£	£
			£
Stock (at cost)			28,850
add Items which were in stock on 31 December 19-7 (at cost)			
		£	
Sales		3,800	
less Profit content (20 per cent of selling price)		760	3,040
			31,890
less Items which were not in stock on 31 December 19-7 (at cost)			
	£	£	
Returns Inwards	350		
less Profit content (20 per cent of selling price)	70	280	
Purchases (at cost)		2,370	2,650
Stock in Hand as on 31 December 19-7			29,240

Stock levels

One of the most common faults found in the running of businesses is that too high a level of stock in maintained. It is not the purpose of this book to deal with this in any detail, but merely to point out the dangers of carrying too much stock.

Generalisation is always dangerous, for the scope and variety of businesses is unlimited. For many firms the danger attached to running out of a particular item of stock can be very high indeed. Imagine a motor car manufacturer who ran out of stock of driving wheels. He would not be able to despatch any cars until new stock of this item was received.

The whole of the various items in stock should be scrutinised. In the case of a motor car manufacturer this consists of several thousand parts which go together in the assembly of a car, whereas for other firms the items will be very few indeed. For each item there should be established:

(a) A maximum stock level beyond which the stock should not be allowed to rise.

(b) A minimum stock level below which it would be highly undesirable for the stock to fall.

Looking at the problem simply, suppose that an item has a minimum stock level of 100 units. The firm uses 50 units per week, and it takes 6 weeks for the supplier to deliver an order. This means that 300 units will be used whilst waiting for the order to be delivered, i.e. 6 weeks × 50 units = 300. The order for 300 units must therefore be placed at the date when stock reaches 400 units, for by the time the delivery takes place 300 units will have been used, and stock will have fallen to 100 units. For each item of stock there should therefore be established:

(c) A re-order stock level. This is the level at which an order should be sent to the supplier, so that stock will be received before the stock in hand of the item falls below the minimum stock level.

Of course, this is looking at the problem very simply indeed. There are many factors to be considered besides those mentioned, such a quantity discounts, the cost of money tied up in stock, warehousing costs and so on. If you proceed further in your studies into a more detailed knowledge of Business Mathematics you will find that there are various mathematical techniques to assist in this field.

For a lot of firms in certain industries, it will be found on investigation that the bulk of the stock used consists of a relatively few items. Take a publisher as an instance who has 1,000 different titles which he publishes. Of these titles 50 may be best-sellers accounting for, say, a total of 2 million sales per annum, whilst the other 950 titles may sell only ½ million copies between them. It is obvious therefore that in this firm the highest priority be given to stocking the best- sellers. If a best-seller runs out of stock at a peak time, e.g. before Christmas in the case of novels bought as Christmas presents, the sales lost forever could be considerable. If a low-selling book ran out of stock the loss would normally be relatively small.

A considerable number of firms that have problems of the shortage of finance will find that they can help matters by having a sensible look at the amounts of stock they hold. It would be a very rare firm indeed which, if they had not investigated the matter previously could not manage to let parts of their stock run down. As this would save spending cash on items not really necessary, this cash could be better utilised elsewhere.

Conclusion

It is not possible in a book of this type to give the arguments for and against the use of different stock bases. Any 'potted' version would probably be more misleading than it would be useful. There is a danger of thinking that the arguments for and against can be summarised in a few words. Many experts have argued on behalf of or against the bases described in this chapter, and there is no universal agreement as to which is the best one. Economists and operational research teams are often astounded by the lack of any 'scientific' approach. All that can be said here is that firms would be well advised to rethink their stock valuation procedures in terms of obtaining information from which they can derive the greatest possible benefit, and wherever possible to use different stock figures to serve different purposes.

Review questions

43.1 At the end of a company's first financial year on 31 December 19-5, the directors of your firm ask you to ascertain the stock figure. The following information is presented to you.

	Purchases				Items sold		Net realisable value at 31 December 19-5	
Item 1	January	500 at	£5 each	July	200			
	September	300 ,,	£6 ,,	October	350	£5½	each
Item 2	March	100 ,,	£2 ,,	April	50			
	November	200 ,,	£3 ,,	December	100	£3⅓	,,
Item 3	June	600 ,,	£10 ,,	July	500			
	September	400 ,,	£12 ,,	October	100	£15	,,
Item 4	April	200 ,,	£16 ,,	June	150			
	October	200 ,,	£18 ,,	November	50	£14	,,
Item 5	October	1,000 ,,	£12 ,,					
	November	800 ,,	£10 ,,	December	1,200	£9	,,
Item 6	January	200 ,,	£4 ,,					
	July	400 ,,	£5 ,,	September	500	£7	,,

You are also told that there are three distinct groups or categories of items, Group A being items 1 and 2, Group B being items 3 and 4, and Group C being items 5 and 6.

You inform the directors that it is possible to arrive at more than one stock figure. The directors thereupon ask you to give them the various figures that are possible using the following bases:

(*a*) First In, First Out Method;
(*b*) Last In, First Out Method;
and applying the Category and Article methods to each of these bases.

Show all your workings clearly.

43.2A The following details are available to you concerning the activity of a manufacturing firm:

		Units
1st year	Opening Stock	500
	Sales	1,000
	Produced	800
	Closing Stock	300
2nd year	Opening Stock	300
	Sales	1,000
	Produced	1,400
	Closing Stock	700
3rd year	Opening Stock	700
	Sales	1,000
	Produced	800
	Closing Stock	500

There was no work in progress at the end of any of these years. For each of the years the prime cost of each unit produced was £1, while the production cost of each units was £2. The selling price of all units was £3 each. You are required to:

(a) Draw up the Trading Account for each year if the stock was valued at prime cost.

(b) Draw up the Trading Account for each year if the stock was valued at production cost.

(c) Which method would you advise if income tax was the main consideration and all profits under £800 per annum were free of tax, while profits above that figure were taxable at the rate of 40 per cent.

(d) What is the main factor contributing to different reported profits under (a) and (b) above.

43.3 The following is a copy of a Stores Ledger Card for Stock Item DH 900 showing receipts and issues during the month of November 19-6. There were no items of DH 900 in stock at the beginning of November. Study the Stores Ledger Card carefully then answer the questions which follow.

Stores Ledger Card - Stock Item: DH 900

Receipts				Issues					Balance	
Date 19-6	Qty	Price/ Unit	Amount £	Date 19-6	Qty		Price/ Unit	Amount £	Qty	Amount £
Nov 3	260	0.90	234.00						260	234.00
Nov 13	140	0.95	133.00						400	367.00
				Nov 14	300	{ 260	0.90	234.00	140	133.00
						40	0.95	38.00	100	95.00
Nov 17	140	0.98	137.20						240	232.20
				Nov 18	70	70	0.95	66.50	170	165.70
				Nov 19	70	{ 30	0.95	28.50	140	137.20
						40	0.98	39.20	100	98.00
Nov 20	140	1.00	140.00						240	238.00
				Nov 24	150	{ 100	0.98	98.00	140	140.00
						50	1.00	50.00	90	90.00

Required

(a) Calculate the value of purchases of DH 900 for November.

(b) What method of pricing issues has been used for this item of stock?

(c) Identify and describe a common alternative method of pricing issues from stock.

(d) Redraft the Store Ledger Card using the alternative method you have identified in (c) above.

(e) The draft account for November 19-6 show a profit for November of £267,890. What would the profit be had the alternative method of valuation been used?

(Association of Accounting Technicians)

43.4A Megalot Ltd made the following purchases and sales of Stock Item C4321 during May 19-6·

May 10 Purchased 3,000 units at £6.00 each
May 15 Sold 2,500 units at £9.00 each
May 16 Purchased 1,000 units at £6.60 each
May 23 Sold 900 units at £9.70 each

Assume there were no units of Stock Item C4321 in stock as at 1 May 19-6.

Required

(a) Compute the values for Sales and Purchases of Stock Item C4321 for May.

(b) How many units should there be in stock at the 31 May 19-6?

(c) Compute the value of closing stock on each of the following bases:

  (i) FIFO, and (ii) LIFO.

(d) Calculate the Gross Profit earned on this item during May if closing stock were to be valued under each of the two bases in (c) above.

(e) Suppose that a physical check of the number of items of C4321 in stock as at the end of May 19-6 revealed a number different to what you had calculated in (b) above. What factors might account for the difference?

(Association of Accounting Technicians)

43.5A The account of Fine Spindles Limited are prepared on a quarterly basis. Owing to very severe staff shortage at 31 March 19-7, the usual stock taking was not undertaken.

However, the following information has now been produced:

(a) The accounts for the quarter ended 31 December 19-6 showed stock in trade, at cost, at that date of £16,824.

(b) An error, only now discovered, in the stock sheets for 31 December 19-6 shows an overcast of £2,000.

(c) Goods invoiced to customers during the quarter ended 31 March 19-7 totalled £54,210; however this includes goods invoiced at £1,040 despatched to customers in December 19-6.

(d) Goods invoiced to customers at £3,900 in April 19-7 were despatched by Fine Spindles Limited in March 19-7.

(e) Goods purchased by the company during the quarter ended 31 March 19-7 amounted to £46,680, at invoice prices.

(f) A burglary at the company's stores in March 19-7 resulted in stock costing £8,000 being stolen.

(g) In March 19-7, it was decided that a quantity of stock, which would normally be sold for £1,950, will only realise half cost price. This stock was unsold at 31 March 19-7.

(h) Credit notes totalling £4,550 were issued to customers for returns inwards during the quarter ended 31 March 19-7.

(i) The company normally obtains a gross profit of 30% on cost price on all sales.

Required

(a) A computation of the stock valuation at 31 March 19-7.

(b) The trading account for the quarter ended 31 March 19-7.

(Association of Accounting Technicians)

43.6 An evaluation of a physical stock count on 30 April 19-2 in respect of the financial year ending on that date at Cranfleet Commodities has produced a figure of £187,033.

The firm's book-keeper has approached you, as the accountant, for assistance in dealing with the following matters to enable him to arrive at a final figure of closing stock for inclusion in the annual accounts:

(a) 320 components included at their original cost of £11 each can now be bought in for only £6 each due to over production by the manufacturer. This drop in price is expected to be only temporary and the purchase price is expected to exceed its original figure within 12 months. Cranfleet Commodities intends to continue selling the existing stock at the present price of £15 each.

(b) It has been discovered that certain items which had cost £5,657 have been damaged. It will cost £804 to repair them after which they can be sold for £6,321.

(c) On one stock sheet a sub-total of £9,105 has been carried forward as £1,095.

(d) 480 units which cost £1.50 each have been extended at £15.00 each.

(e) The firm has sent goods with a selling price of £1,500 (being cost plus 25%) to a customer on a sale or return basis. At 30 April 19-2, the customer had not signified acceptance, but the goods have not been returned, and consequently had not been included in the physical stock count.

(f) Included in stock were goods bought on credit for £4,679 from Byfleet Enterprises. At 30 April 19-2, Cranfleet Commodities had not paid this account.

(g) Byfleet Enterprises had also sent some free samples (for advertising purposes only). These have been included in stock at their catalogue price of £152.

You are required, taking account of such of the above facts as are relevant, to calculate a closing stock figure for inclusion in the 19-2 annual accounts of Cranfleet Commodities, giving reasons for the action you have taken in each individual case.

(Chartered Association of Certified Accountants)

43.7A After stocktaking for the year ended 31 May 19-5 had taken place, the closing stock of Cobden Ltd, was aggregated to a figure of £87,612.

During the course of the audit which followed, the undernoted facts were discovered:

(a) Some goods stored outside had been included at their normal cost price of £570. They had, however, deteriorated and would require an estimated £120 to be spent to restore them to their original condition, after which they could be sold for £800.

(b) Some goods had been damaged and were now unsaleable. They could, however, be sold for £110 as spares after repairs estimated at £40 had been carried out. They had originally cost £200.

(c) One stock sheet had been over-added by £126 and another under-added by £72.

(d) Cobden Ltd. had received goods costing £2,010 during the last week of May 19-5 but because the invoices did not arrive until June 19-5, they have not been included in stock.

(e) A stock sheet total of £1,234 had been transferred to the summary sheet as £1,243

(f) Invoices totalling £638 arrived during the last week of May 19-5 (and were included in purchases and in creditors) but, because of transport delays, the goods did not arrive until late June 19-5 and were not included in closing stock.

(g) Portable generators on hire from another company at a charge of £347 were included, at this figure, in stock.

(h) Free samples sent to Cobden Ltd by various suppliers had been included in stock at the catalogue price of £63.

(i) Goods costing £418 sent to customers on a sale or return basis had been included in stock by Cobden Ltd at their selling price, £602.

(j) Goods sent on a sale or return basis to Cobden Ltd. had been included in stock at the amount payable (£267) if retained. No decision to retain had been made.

Required:

Using such of the above information as is relevant, prepared a schedule amending the stock figure as at 31 May 19-5. State your reason for each amendment or for not making an amendment.

(Chartered Association of Certified Accountants)

44

An introduction to the analysis and interpretation of accounting statements

The need for ratios

Let us take the performance of four companies, all dealing in the same type of goods.

	Gross profit £	Sales £
Company A	10,000	84,800
Company B	15,000	125,200
Company C	25,000	192,750
Company D	17,500	146,840

Suppose you want to know which company gets the best profit margins. Simply inspecting these figures and trying to decide which performance was the best, and which was the worst, is virtually impossible. To bring the same basis of comparison to each company we need some form of common measure. As you have already seen earlier in this manual, the common measure used would be a ratio — the amount of gross profit on sales as a percentage. The comparison now becomes:

	%
Company A	11.79
Company B	11.98
Company C	12.97
Company D	11.91

Company C, with 12.97%, or in other words £12.97 gross profit per £100 sales, has performed better than the other companies.

How to use ratios

You can only sensibly compare like with like. There is not much point in comparing the gross profit percentage of a wholesale chemists with that of a restaurant, for example.

Similarly, figures are only comparable if they have been built up on a similar basis. The sales figures of Company X which treat items as sales only when cash is received cannot be properly compared with Company Z which treats items as sales as soon as they are invoiced.

Another instance of this could be that of stockturn, if Company K is compared with Company L. They are both toy shops so would seem to be comparable. However, although both companies have sales of £100,000 the average stock of K is £40,000 whilst that of L is £10,000. Cost of sales is £50,000, so stockturn ratios are:

$$\frac{\text{Cost of sales}}{\text{Average stock}} \qquad \overset{K}{\frac{50,000}{40,000}} = 1.25 \qquad \overset{L}{\frac{50,000}{10,000}} = 5$$

It looks as though L has managed to turn its stock over five times during the year compared with K, 1.25 times. Is it true? In fact you were not told that K had a financial year end of 31 October, just before Christmas, so toy stocks would be extremely high. On the other hand, L had a year end of 31 January, when after Christmas sales the stock had dropped to the year's lowest figures. In fact, if stock had been valued at 31 October in Company L, then the average stock would also have been £40,000.

Ratios therefore need very careful handling. They are extremely useful if used properly, and very misleading otherwise.

Types of ratio

Liquidity ratios

The return of profit on capital employed, as you will see, gives an overall picture of profitability. It cannot always be assumed, however, that profitability is everything that is desirable. Chapter 1 stresses that accounting is needed, not just to calculate profitability, but also to know whether or not the business will be able to meet its commitments as they fall due.

The two main measures of liquidity are the **current ratio** and the **acid test ratio**.

(a) *Current ratio*

$$\text{Current ratio} = \frac{\text{Current assets}}{\text{Current liabilities}}$$

This compares assets which will become liquid in approximately 12 months with liabilities which will be due for payment in the same period.

(b) *Acid test ratio*

$$\text{Acid test ratio} = \frac{\text{Current assets} - \text{Stock}}{\text{Current liabilities}}$$

This shows that provided creditors and debtors are paid at approximately the same time, a view might be made as to whether the business has sufficient liquid resources to meet its current liabilities.

Exhibit 44.1 shows how two businesses may have similar profitability, yet their liquidity positions may be quite different.

Exhibit 44.1

	£	E £	£	E £
Fixed assets		40,000		70,000
Current assets				
Stock	30,000		50,000	
Debtors	45,000		9,000	
Bank	15,000		1,000	
	90,000		60,000	
less Current Liabilities: creditors	30,000	60,000	30,000	30,000
		100,000		100,000
Capital				
Opening capital		80,000		80,000
add Net Profit		36,000		36,000
		116,000		116,000
less Drawings		16,000		16,000
		100,000		100,000

Notes: sales for both E and F amounted to £144,000. Gross Profits for E and F were identical at £48,000.

Profitability: this is the same for both businesses. However, there is a vast difference in the liquidity of the two businesses.

$$\text{Current ratios } E = \frac{90,000}{30,000} = 3: F = \frac{60,000}{30,000} = 2$$

this looks adequate on the face of it, but the acid test ratio reveals that F is in distress, as it will probably find it difficult to pay its current liabilities on time.

$$\text{Acid test ratio } E = \frac{60,000}{30,000} = 2: F = \frac{10,000}{30,000} = 0.33$$

Therefore, for a business to be profitable is not enough, it should also be adequately liquid as well.

(c) Stockturn

Stockturn has already been described in Chapter 30. A reduction in stockturn can mean that the business is slowing down. Stocks may be piling up and not being sold. This could lead to a liquidity crisis, as money may be being taken out of the bank simply to increase stocks which are not then sold quickly enough.

For Exhibit 44.1 the cost of sales for each company was £144,000 − £48,000 = £96,000. If opening stocks had been E £34,000 and F £46,000, then stockturns would have been:

	E	F
$\dfrac{\text{Cost of sales}}{\text{Average stock}}$	$\dfrac{96,000}{(34,000 + 30,000) \div 2}$	$\dfrac{96,000}{(46,000 + 50,000) \div 2}$
	$= \dfrac{96,000}{32,000} = 3$ times	$= \dfrac{96,000}{48,000} = 2$ times

It appears that F's stock is starting to pile up, because it is having difficulty selling it compared with E.

(d) Debtor/sales ratio

The resources tied up in debtors is an important ratio subject. Money tied up unnecessarily in stock is unproductive money.

In the example in Exhibit 44.1 this can be calculated for the two companies as:

	E	F
Debtor/sales	$45,000/144,000 = 1{:}3.2$	$9,000/144,000 = 1{:}16$

This relationship is often translated into the length of time a debtor takes to pay. This turns out to be:

E
$$365 \times \frac{1}{3.2} = 114 \text{ days}$$

F
$$365 = \frac{1}{16} = 22.8 \text{ Days}$$

Why Company E should have allowed so much time for its debtors to pay is a matter for investigation. Possibly the company was finding it harder to sell goods, and to sell at all, was eventually forced to sell to customers on long credit terms. It could well be that E has no proper credit control system, whereas F has an extremely efficient one.

(e) Creditor/purchases ratio

Assuming that purchases for E amounted to £92,000 and for F £100,000 then the ratios are:

	E	F
Creditor/Purchases	$30,000/92,000 = 1{:}3.07$	$30,000/100,000 = 1{:}3.3$

This also is often translated into the length of time we take to pay our creditors. This turns out to be:

E
$$365 \times \frac{1}{3.07} = 118.9 \text{ days}$$

F
$$365 \times \frac{1}{3.3} = 110.6 \text{ days}$$

Profitability ratios

Rate of return to net profit on capital employed

This is the most important of all profitability ratios, as it encompasses all the other ratios, and an adequate return on capital employed is why the person(s) invested their money in the first place.

(a) Sole traders

In an earlier chapter it was stated that the term 'capital employed' had not been standardised. In this chapter the average of the capital account will be used, i.e. (opening balance × closing balance) ÷ 2.

In businesses C and D in Exhibit 44.2 the same amount of net profits have been made, but capitals employed are different.

Exhibit 44.2

Balance Sheets

	C £	D £
Fixed + Current assets − Current liabilities	10,000	16,000
Current accounts		
Opening balance	8,000	14,000
add Net Profits	3,600	3,600
	11,600	17,600
less Drawings	1,600	1,600
	10,000	16,000

Return on capital employed is:

$$\frac{\text{Net profit}}{\text{Capital employed}} \times 100$$

$$C \quad \frac{3,600}{(8,000 + 10,000) \div 2} \times \frac{100}{1} = 40\%$$

$$D \quad \frac{3,600}{(14,000 + 16,000) \div 2} \times \frac{100}{1} = 24\%$$

The ratio illustrates that what is important is not simply how much profit has been made but how well the capital has been employed. Business C has made far better use of its capital, achieving a return of £40 net profit for every £100 invested, whereas D has received only a net profit of £24 per £100.

(b) Limited companies

Again, different meanings are attached to **capital employed**. The main ones are:

(*i*) return on capital employed by ordinary shareholders;

(*ii*) return on capital employed by all long term suppliers of capital.

Given the following balance sheets of two companies, P Ltd and Q Ltd, the calculation of (i) can be attempted:

	P Ltd		Q Ltd	
	£	£	£	£
	19-8	19-9	19-8	19-9
Fixed assets	5,200	5,600	8,400	9,300
Net current assets	2,800	3,400	1,600	2,700
	8,000	9,000	10,000	12,000
Share capital (ordinary)	3,000	3,000	5,000	5,000
Reserves	5,000	6,000	3,800	5,800
	8,000	9,000	8,800	10,800
10 per cent debentures			1,200	1,200
			10,000	12,000

Profit and Loss Accounts for years to 31 December

	P Ltd	Q Ltd
	£	£
Net profit	2,200	3,800
Dividends	1,200	1,800
	1,000	1,000

Return on Capital Employed by Ordinary Shareholders

P Ltd

$$\frac{2,200}{(8,000 + 9,000) \div 2} \times \frac{100}{1} = 25.9\%$$

Q Ltd

$$\frac{3,800}{(8,800 + 10,800) \div 2} \times \frac{100}{1} = 38.8\%$$

The return on capital employed by all long term suppliers of capital is not relevant in the case of P Ltd, as there are only ordinary shareholders in P Ltd.

$$Q \text{ Ltd} = \frac{3,800 + 120^*}{(1,000 + 12,000) \div 2} \times \frac{100}{1} = 35.6\%$$

*The debenture interest 10% of £1,200 = £120 must be added back here, as it was an expense in calculating the £3,800 net profit.

Gross profit as percentage of sales

The formula is: $\dfrac{\text{gross profit}}{\text{sales}} \times 100$

This was dealt with in Chapter 30.

Net profit as a percentage of sales

The formula is: $\dfrac{\text{NET gross profit}}{\text{sales}} \times 100$

Other ratios

There are a large number of other ratios which could be used, far more than can be mentioned in a textbook such as this. It will depend on the type of company exactly which ratios are the most important and it is difficult to generalise too much.

Different users of the accounts will want to use the ratio analysis which is of vital concern to them. If we can take a bank as an example, which lends money to a company, it will want to ensure two things:

(a) that the company will be able to pay interest on the loan as it falls due; *and*

(b) that it will be able to repay the loan on the agreed date.

The bank is therefore interested in:

(a) short term liquidity, concerning payment of loan interest; and

(b) long term solvency for eventual repayment of the loan. Possible ratios would be:

Short-term liquidity

This could include mainly the *acid test ratio* and the *current ratio*, already described.

Long-term solvency

This might include:

(a) **Operating profit/loan interest.** This indicates how much of the profits are taken up by paying loan interest. Too great a proportion would mean that the company was borrowing more than was sensible, as a small fall in profits could mean the company operating at a loss with the consequent effect upon long-term solvency.

(b) **Total external liabilities/shareholders' funds.** This ratio measures how much financing is done via share capital and retained profits, and how much is from external sources. Too high a proportion of external liabilities could bring about long-term solvency problems if the company's profit making capacity falls by a relatively small amount, as outside liabilities still have to be met.

(c) **Shareholders' funds/total assets (excluding intangibles).** This highlights the proportion of assets financed by the company's own funds. Large falls in this ratio will tend to show a difficulty with long-term solvency. Similarly, investors will want to see ratios suitable for their purposes, which are not the same as those for the bank. These will not only be used on a single company comparison, but probably with the average of the same type of ratios for other companies in the same industry.

These will include the following ratios. Note that **price** means the price of the shares on the stock exchange.

(i) **Price/earnings ratio** (P/E).

The formula is:

$$\text{Price/earnings ratio} = \frac{\text{Market price per share}}{\text{Earnings per share}}$$

This puts the price into context as a multiple of the earnings. The greater the P/E ratio, the greater the demand for the shares. A low P/E means there is little demand for shares.

(ii) **Earnings per share (EPS).**

The formula is:

$$\text{Earnings per share} = \frac{\text{Net profit after tax and preference dividends}}{\text{Number of ordinary shares issued}}$$

This gives the shareholder (or prospective shareholder) a chance to compare one year's earnings with another in terms easily understood.

(*iii*) **Dividend cover** (P/E).

This is found by the formula:

$$\text{Dividend cover} = \frac{\text{Net profit after tax and preference dividends}}{\text{Ordinary dividends paid and proposed}}$$

This gives the shareholder some idea as to the proportion that the ordinary dividends bear to the amount available for distribution to ordinary shareholders. Usually, the dividend is described as being so many times covered by profits made. If therefore the dividend is said to be *three times covered*, it means that one third of the available profits are being distributed as dividends.

Capital gearing ratio

There is more than one way of calculating this ratio. The most common method is:

$$\text{Capital gearing ratio} = \frac{\text{Preference shares} + \text{long term loans}}{\text{All shareholders' funds} + \text{long term loans}} \times 100$$

Let us look at the calculations for the three companies:

	R Ltd	S Ltd	T Ltd
	£	£	£
Ordinary shares of £1	6,000	4,000	2,000
Profit and loss	1,000	1,000	1,000
8% preference shares of £1	1,000	2,000	3,000
10% debentures	2,000	3,000	4,000
	10,000	10,000	10,000

$$\underset{R\ Ltd}{\frac{1,000 + 2,000}{10,000} \times 100 = 30\%} \quad \underset{S\ Ltd}{\frac{2,000 + 3,000}{10,000} \times 100 = 50\%} \quad \underset{T\ Ltd}{\frac{3,000 + 4,000}{10,000} \times 100 = 70\%}$$

A company financed by a high level of borrowing (whether long-term loans or preference shares) is called a **high-geared company**. A company is a **low-geared company** where it has a low level of borrowing.

With a highly-geared company a change in profits has a much greater proportionate effect upon profits available for ordinary shareholders than in a low-geared company. Exhibit 44.3 illustrates this.

Exhibit 44.3

For each of the three companies, *R*, *S* and *T*, the amounts payable in debenture interest and preference dividends are:

	R Ltd	S Ltd	T Ltd
	£	£	£
8% preference dividend	80	160	240
10% debenture interest	200	300	400
Prior charges	280	460	640

The profit, before debenture interest and preference dividends, was identical for each of the companies for the first three years of their existence. The profits were: *Year 1* £640; *Year 2* £1,000; *Year 3* £2,000. The profits were usable as follows:

	Low-geared R Ltd	S Ltd	High-geared T Ltd
Year 1			
Profits	640	640	640
less prior charges	280	460	640
Available for ordinary shares	360	180	–
Year 2			
Profits	1,000	1,000	1,000
less prior charges	280	460	640
Available for ordinary shares	720	540	360
Year 3			
Profits	2,000	2,000	2,000
less prior charges	280	460	640
Available for ordinary shares	1,720	1,540	1,360

Profit available per ordinary share, is found by dividing available profit by ordinary shares:

	R Ltd	S Ltd	T ltd
Year 1	6.0p	4.5p	–
Year 2	12.0p	13.5p	18.0p
Year 3	28.7p	38.5p	68.0p

Low-geared companies see a lesser change in ordinary dividends than high-geared companies.

Fixed and variable expenses

Some expense will remain constant whether activity increases or falls, at least within a given range of change of activity. These expenses are called **fixed expenses**. An example of this would be the rent of a shop which would remain at the same figure, whether sales increased ten per cent or fell ten per cent. The same would remain true of such things as rates, fire insurance and so on.

Wages of shop assistants could also remain constant in such a case. If, for instance, the shop employed two assistants then it would probably keep the same two assistants, on the same wages, whether sales increased or fell by ten per cent.

Of course, such 'fixed expenses' can only be viewed as fixed in the short term. If sales doubled then the business might well need a larger shop or more assistants. A larger shop would also certainly mean higher rates, higher fire insurance and so on, and with more assistants the total wage bill would be larger.

Variable expenses on the other hand will change with swings in activity. Suppose that wrapping materials are used in the shop, then it could well be that an increase in sales of ten per cent may see ten per cent more wrapping materials used. Similarly an increase of ten per cent of sales, if all sales are despatched by parcel post, could well see delivery charges increase by ten per cent.

Some expenses could be part fixed and part variable. Suppose that because of an increase in sales of ten per cent, telephone calls made increased by ten per cent. With telephone bills the cost falls into two parts, one for the rent of the phone and the second part corresponding to the actual number of calls made. The rent would not change in such a case, and therefore this part of telephone expense would be 'fixed' whereas the calls part of the expense could increase by 10 per cent.

This means that the effect of a percentage change in activity could have a more/or less percentage change in net profit, because the fixed expenses (within that range of activity) may not alter.

Exhibit 44.3 shows the change in net profit in business A which has a low proportion of its expenses as 'fixed' expenses, whereas in business B the 'fixed' expenses are a relatively high proportion of its expenses.

Exhibit 44.4

Business A			(a) If sales fell 10%		(b) If sales rose 10%	
	£	£		£		£
Sales		50,000		45,000		55,000
less Cost of goods sold		30,000		27,000		33,000
		20,000		18,000		22,000
Gross profit						
less Expenses:						
Fixed:	3,000		3,000		3,000	
Variable	13,000	16,000	11,700	14,700	14,300	17,300
Net profit		4,000		3,300		4,700

Business B			(a) If sales fell 10%		(b) If sales rose 10%	
	£	£		£		£
Sales		50,000		45,000		55,000
less Cost of goods sold		30,000		27,000		33,000
		20,000		18,000		22,000
Gross profit						
less Expenses:						
Fixed:	12,000		12,000		12,000	
Variable	4,000	16,000	3,600	15,600	4,400	16,400
Net profit		4,000		2,400		5,600

The comparison of percentage changes in net profit therefore works out as follows:

$$A \qquad\qquad\qquad B$$

Decrease of 10% sales

$$\frac{\text{Reduction in profit}}{\text{Original profit}} \times \frac{100}{1} \quad \frac{700}{4,000} \times \frac{100}{1} = 17.5\% \qquad \frac{1,600}{4,000} \times \frac{100}{1} = 40\%$$

Increase of 10% sales

$$\frac{\text{Increase in profit}}{\text{Original profit}} \times \frac{100}{1} \quad \frac{700}{4,000} \times \frac{100}{1} = 17.5\% \qquad \frac{1,600}{4,000} \times \frac{100}{1} = 40\%$$

It can be seen that a change in activity in business B which has a higher fixed expense content, will result in greater percentage changes in profit, 40% in B compared with 17.5% in A.

Trend figures

In examinations a student is often given just one year's accounting figures and asked to comment on them. Obviously, lack of space on an examination paper may preclude several years' figures being given, also the student lacks the time to prepare a comprehensive survey of several years' accounts.

In real life, however, it would be extremely stupid for anyone to base decisions on just one year's accounts, if more information was available. What is important for a business is not just what, say, accounting ratios are for one year, but what the trend has been.

Given two similar types of businesses G and H, both having existed for 5 years, if both of them had exactly the same ratios in year 5, are they both exactly desirable as investments? Given one year's accounts it may appear so, but if one had all the 5 years' figures it may not give the same picture, as Exhibit 44.5 illustrates.

Exhibit 44.5

		Years				
		1	2	3	4	5 (current)
Gross profit as % of sales	G	40	38	36	35	34
	H	30	32	33	33	34
Net profit as % of sales	G	15	13	12	12	11
	H	10	10	10	11	11
Net profit as % of capital employed	G	13	12	11	11	10
	H	8	8	9	9	10
Liquidity	G	3	2.8	2.6	2.3	2.0
	H	1.5	1.7	1.9	1.0	2.0

From these figures G appears to be the worst investment for the future, as the trend appears to be downwards. If the trend for G is continued it could be in a very dangerous financial situation in a year or two. Business H, on the other hand, is strengthening its position all the time.

Of course, it would be ridiculous to assert that H will continue on an upward trend. One would have to know more about the business to be able to judge whether or not that could be true.

However, given all other desirable information, trend figures would be an extra important indicator.

Limitations of accounting statements

Final accounts are only partial information. They show the reader of them, in financial terms, what has happened *in the past*. This is better than having no information at all, but one needs to know much more.

First, it is impossible to sensibly compare two businesses which are completely unlike one another. To compare a supermarket's figures with those of a chemical factory would be rather pointless. It would be like comparing a lion with a lizard.

Second, there are a whole lot of factors that the past accounts do not disclose. The desire to keep to the money measurement concept, and the desire to be objective, both dealt with in Chapter 10, exclude a great deal of desirable information. Some typical desirable information can be listed, beware, the list is indicative rather than exhaustive.

(*a*) What are the future plans of the business? Without this an investment in a business would be sheer guesswork.

(*b*) Has the firm got good quality staff?

(*c*) Is the business situated in a location desirable for such a business? A ship-building business situated a long way up a river which was becoming unnavigable, to use an extreme example, could soon be in trouble.

(*d*) What is its position as compared with it competitors? A business manufacturing a single product, which has a foreign competitor which has just invented a much improved product which will capture the whole market, is obviously in for a bad time.

(*e*) Will future government regulations affect it? Suppose that a business which is an importer of goods from Country *X*, which is outside the EEC, finds that the EEC is to ban all imports from Country *X*?

(*f*) Is its plant and machinery obsolete? If so, the business may not have sufficient funds to be able to replace it.

(*g*) Is the business of a high-risk type or in a relatively stable industry?

(*h*) Has the business got good customers? A business selling largely to Country *Y*, which is getting into trouble because of shortage of foreign exchange, could soon lose most of its trade. Also if one customer was responsible for, say, 60 per cent of sales, then the loss of that one customer would be calamitous.

(*i*) Has the business got good suppliers of its needs? A business in wholesaling could, for example, be forced to close down if manufacturers decided to sell direct to the general public.

(*j*) Problems concerned with the effects of distortion of accounting figures caused by inflation (or deflation).

The reader can now see that the list would have to be an extremely long one if it was intended to cover all possibilities.

Further thoughts on concepts and conventions

In Chapter 10 you were introduced to the concepts and conventions used in accounting. Since then further chapters have consolidated your knowledge on specific points.

In recent years there has been a considerable change in the style of examinations in accounting at all levels. At one time practically nearly every examination question was simply of a computational nature, requiring you to prepare final accounts, draft journal entries, extract a trial balance and so on. Now, *in addition* to all that (which is still important) there are quite a lot of questions asking such things as:

- Why do we do it?
- What does it mean?
- How does it relate to the concepts and conventions?

Such questions depend very much on the interests and ingenuity of examiners. They like to set questions worded to find out those who can understand and interpret financial information, and eliminate those who cannot and simply try to repeat information learned by rote.

The examiners will often draw on knowledge from any part of the syllabus. It is therefore impossible for a student (or an author) to guess exactly how an examiner will select a question and how he will word it.

Review questions 44.8 to 44.21 are typical examination questions which obviously relate to concepts and conventions, and to general understanding of the subject.

Review questions

44.1 You are to study the following financial statements for two similar types of retail store and then answer the questions which follow.

Summary of Financial Statements

	A £	£	B £	£
Sales		80,000		120,000
less Cost of goods sold				
Opening stock	25,000		22,500	
add Purchases	50,000		91,000	
	75,000		113,500	
less Closing stock	15,000	60,000	17,500	96,000
Gross profit		20,000		24,000
less Depreciation	1,000		3,000	
Other expenses	9,000	10,000	6,000	9,000
Net profit		10,000		15,000

Balance sheets		A		B
Fixed assets				
Equipment at cost	10,000		20,000	
less Depreciation to date	8,000	2,000	6,000	14,000
Current assets				
Stock	15,000		17,500	
Debtors	25,000		20,000	
Bank	5,000		2,500	
	45,000		40,000	
less Current liabilities				
Creditors	5,000	40,000	10,000	30,000
		42,000		44,000
Financed by:				
Capitals				
Balance at start of year		30,000		36,000
add Net profit		10,000		15,000
		48,000		51,000
less Drawings		6,000		7,000
		42,000		44,000

Required

   (*a*) Calculate the following ratios:

(*i*) gross profit as percentage of sales;
(*ii*) net profit as percentage of sales;
(*iii*) expenses as percentage of sales;
(*iv*) stockturn;
(*v*) rate of return of net profit on capital employed (use the average of the capital account for this purpose);

(*vi*) current ratio;
(*vii*) acid test ratio;
(*viii*) debtor/sales ratio;
(*ix*) creditor/purchases ratio.

   (*b*) Drawing upon all your knowledge of accounting, comment upon the differences, and similarities of the accounting ratios for A and B. Which business seems to be the most efficient? Give possible reasons.

44.2A Study the following accounts of two companies and then answer the questions which follow. Both companies are stores selling textile goods.

Trading and Profit and Loss Accounts

	£	R Ltd £	£	T Ltd £
Sales		250,000		160,000
less Cost of goods sold				
Opening stock	90,000		30,000	
add Purchases	210,000		120,000	
	300,000		150,000	
less Closing stock	110,000	190,000	50,000	100,000
Gross profit		60,000		60,000
less Expenses				
Wages and salaries	14,000		10,000	
Director's remuneration	10,000		10,000	
Other expenses	11,000	35,000	8,000	28,000
Net profit		25,000		32,000
add Balance from last year		15,000		8,000
		40,000		40,000
less Appropriations				
General reserve	2,000		2,000	
Dividend	25,000	27,000	20,000	22,000
Balance carried to next year		13,000		18,000
Balance sheets				
Fixed assets				
Equipment at cost	20,000		5,000	
less Depreciation to date	8,000	12,000	2,000	3,000
Motor lorries	30,000		20,000	
less Depreciation to date	12,000	18,000	7,000	13,000
		30,000		16,000
Current assets				
Stock	110,000		50,000	
Debtors	62,500		20,000	
Bank	7,500		10,000	
	180,000		80,000	
less Current liabilities				
Creditors	90,000		16,000	
		90,000		64,000
		120,000		80,000
Financed by:				
Issued share capital		100,000		50,000
Reserves				
General reserve	7,000		12,000	
Profit and loss	13,000	20,000	18,000	30,000
		12,000		80,000

    (*a*) Calculate the following ratios for each of *R Ltd* and *T Ltd*:

(*i*) gross profit as percentage of sales;	(*vi*) current ratio;
(*ii*) net profit as percentage of sales;	(*vii*) acid test ratio;
(*iii*) expenses as percentage of sales;	(*viii*) debtor/sales ratio;
(*iv*) stockturn;	(*ix*) creditor/purchases ratio.

(*v*) rate of return of net profit on capital employed (for the purpose of this question only, take capital as being total of share capitals + reserves at the balance sheet date);

    (*b*) Comment briefly on the comparison of each ratio as between the two companies. State which company appears to be the most efficient, giving what you consider to be possible reasons.

44.3 John Timpson, an established retail trader, who is very pleased with the expansion of his business during the past financial year, has been warned by his accountant that he must not simply concentrate his attention on profit growth. John Timpson recognises that a legacy from his late father has made an important contribution to the recent development of his business.

    The following summarised information relates to John Timpson's business during the year ended 30 September 19-6 and 19-7:

Summarised Balance Sheets

As at 30 September	19-6 £	£	19-7 £	£
Fixed Assets				
At cost		280,000		350,000
less Depreciation provision		80,000		50,000
		200,000		300,000
Current Assets				
Stock	40,000		147,000	
Debtors	45,000		58,000	
Balance at bank	35,000		5,000	
	120,000		210,000	
less Current Liabilities				
Creditors	50,000	70,000	84,000	126,000
		270,000		426,000
less Long term loan – 10% pa.		30,000		50,000
		240,000		376,000

Year ended 30 September	19-6	19-7
Sales	200,000	300,000
Gross profit	60,000	108,000
Net profit	30,000	37,600

Required

    (*a*) Brief notes in support of John Timpson's optimistic view of the progress of his business.

    (*b*) Brief notes in support of the accountant's warning concerning developments in John Timpson's business.

    Note: Answers should be supported by the use of appropriate financial ratios.

(*Association of Accounting Technicians*)

44.4 John Bright has provided his son, Thomas, with all the capital required in the setting up of a business on 1 April 19-5 and its subsequent development. Thomas has now produced the following summarised accounts as a basis for discussing the business's progress with his father:

Trading and profit and loss accounts

Year ended	31 March 19-6 £'000	31 March 19-7 £'000
Sales	100	140
Cost of sales	60	90
Gross profit	40	50
Overheads: Variable	20	35
Fixed	12	16
	32	51
Net profit/(net loss)	8	(1)

Balance sheets

As at	1 April 19-5 £'000	31 March 19-6 £'000	31 March 19-7 £'000
Fixed Assets	70	70	80
Net current assets			
Stock	5	7	8
Debtors	–	11	24
Bank balance/(overdraft)	13	2	(4)
(Creditors	(3)	(5)	(8)
	15	15	20
Net Capital employed	85	85	100

Thomas is keen for his father to increase the capital employed in the business and has drawn his father's attention to the following matters revealed in the accounts:

(a) £15,000 increase in net capital employed can be linked with a £40,000 increase in sales during the past year.

(b) The rate of stock turnover during the past year has been 12 as compared with 10 in the previous year.

(c) The increased fixed overheads last year is due to the renting of larger premises; however these new premises would be adequate for a turnover of £200,000.

John Bright is not pleased with the results of his son's business.

Thomas Bright can easily obtain employment offering a salary of £10,000 per annum and John Bright can obtain 10% per annum from a bank deposit account.

Required

(*a*) Calculate for each of the years ended 31 March 19-6 and 19-7, four financial ratios which draw attention to matters which could give John Bright cause for concern. *Note*: State clearly the formula or basis of each ratio used.

(*b*) Outline three reasons for closing the business and one reason in favour of its continuance.

(*c*) Outline the importance of distinguishing between fixed and variable overheads.

(*Association of Accounting Technicians*)

44.5 The trading stock of Joan Street, retailer, has been reduced during the year ended 31 March 19-8 by £6,000 from its commencing figure of £21,000.

A number of financial ratios and related statistics have been compiled relating to the business of Joan Street for the year ended 31 March 19-8; these are shown below alongside comparative figures for a number of retailers who are members of the trade association to which Joan Street belongs:

	Joan Street %	Trade association %
Net profit as % Net capital employed*	15	16
$\dfrac{\text{Net profit}}{\text{Sales}}$	9	8
$\dfrac{\text{Sales}}{\text{Net capital employed}}$	166⅔	200
$\dfrac{\text{Fixed assets}}{\text{Sales}}$	45	35
Working capital ratio: $\dfrac{\text{Current assets}}{\text{Current liabilities}}$	400	287½
Acid test ratio: $\dfrac{\text{Bank + Debtors}}{\text{Current liabilities}}$	275	187½
$\dfrac{\text{Gross profit}}{\text{Sales}}$	25	26
Debtors collection period: $\dfrac{\text{Debtors} \times 365}{\text{Sales}}$	36½ days	32¹⁷⁄₂₀ days
Stock turnover (based on average stock for the year)	10 times	8 times

Joan Street has supplied all the capital for her business and has had no drawings from the business during the year ended 31 March 19-8.

Required:

(*a*) Prepare the trading and profit and loss account for the year ended 31 March 19-8 and balance sheet as at that date of Joan Street in as much detail as possible.

(*b*) Identify two aspects of Joans Street's results for the year ended 31 March 19-8 which compare favourably with the trade association's figures and identify two aspects which compare unfavourably.

(*c*) Outline two drawbacks of the type of comparison used in this question.

(*Association of Accounting Technicians*)

Note from author: take closing figure at 31 March 19-8.

44.6A The following are the summarised trading and profit loss accounts for the years ended 31 December 19-3, 19-4 and 19-5 and balance sheets as at 31 December 19-2, 19-3, 19-4 and 19-5 of James Simpson, a retail trader.

Trading and profit and loss accounts years ended 31 December 19-3, 19-4 and 19-5.

	19-3	19-4	19-5
	£'000	£'000	£'000
Sales	100	120	140
Cost of sales	60	72	98
Gross profit	40	48	42
Expenses (including loan interest)	20	30	28
Net profit	20	18	14

Balance sheets as at 31 December 19-2, 19-3, 19-4 and 19-5

	19-2	19-3	19-4	19-5
	£'000	£'000	£'000	£'000
Fixed assets	38	48	68	90
Current assets				
Stocks	14	16	20	29
Trade debtors	10	18	40	52
Balance at bank	9	13	39	16
	71	95	167	187
Financed by:				
Capital at 1 January	51	67	87	105
add Net profit for the year	16	20	18	14
	67	87	105	119
Loan (received 31 December 19-4)	–	–	50	50
Current liabilities – Trade creditors	4	8	12	18
	71	95	167	187

Additional information:

(1) James Simpson, a man of modest tastes, is the beneficiary of a small income from his grandfather and therefore has taken no drawings from his retail business.

(2) Interest of 10% per annum has been paid on the loan from 1 January 19-5.

(3) It is estimated that £12,000 per annum would have to be paid for the services rendered to the business by James Simpson.

(4) All sales are on a 30 days credit basis.

(5) James Simpson is able to invest in a bank deposit account giving interest at the rate of 8 per cent per annum.

Required:

(*a*) Calculate for each of the years ended 31 December 19-3, 19-4 and 19-5 the following financial ratios – return on gross capital employed; acid or quick; stock turnover; net profit to sales.

(*b*) Use two financial ratios (not referred to in (*a*) above) to draw attention to two aspects of the business which would appear to give cause for concern.

(*c*) Advise James Simpson whether, on financial grounds, he should continue his retail business.

Note: answers should include appropriate computations.

(*d*) Advise James Simpson as to whether it was a financially sound decision to borrow £50,000 on 31 December 19-4.

(*Association of Accounting Technicians*)

44.7A Gordon Ray is currently reviewing his results for the year ended 31 December 19-5 and comparing them with those of Smooth Dealers Limited, a company engaged in the same trade.

The chairman of Smooth Dealers Limited receives an annual salary of £12,000 for performing duties very similar to those performed by Gordon Ray in his business. The summarised final accounts for 19-5 of Gordon Ray and Smooth Dealers Limited are as follows:

Trading and profit and loss accounts for the year ended 31 December 19-5

Gordon Ray £'000		Smooth Dealers Limited £'000
90	Turnover	150
48	*less* Cost of sales	80
42	Gross profit	70
12	Administrative expenses	37
15	Sales and distribution expenses	25
–	Debenture interest	3
27		65
15	Net profit	5

Balance sheets as at 31 December 19-5

Gordon Ray £'000		Smooth Dealers Limited £'000
60	Fixed assets	50
	Current assets	
28	Stock	56
22	Debtors	69
6	Balance at bank	10
56		135
	Current liabilities	
16	Creditors	25
40	Net current assets	110
100	Net capital employed	160
100	**Capital account**	
	Ordinary share capital	80
	Retained earnings	50
	10% Debenture stock	30
100		160

Required

(*a*) Calculate five appropriate ratios comparing the results of Gordon Ray with those of Smooth Dealers Limited and briefly comment on each ratio.

(*b*) Outline three distinct reasons why a comparison of the amount of profit earned by different businesses should be approached with great care.

(*Association of Accounting Technicians*)

44.8 Bradwich plc is a medium-sized engineering company whose shares are listed on a major Stock Exchange.

It has recently applied to its bankers for a 7 year loan of £500,000 to finance a modernisation and expansion programme.

Mr Whitehall, a recently retired civil servant, is contemplating investing £10,000 of his lump sum pension in the company's ordinary shares in order to provide both an income during his retirement and a legacy to his grandchildren after his death.

The bank and Mr Whitehall have each acquired copies of the company's most recent annual report and accounts.

Required:

(*a*) State, separately for each of the two parties, those aspects of the company's performance and financial position which would be of particular interest and relevance to their respective interests.

(*b*) State, separately for each of the two parties, the formula of four ratios which would assist in measuring or assessing the matters raised in your answer to (*a*).

(*Chartered Association of Certified Accountants*)

453

44.9 An acquaintance of yours, H Gee has recently set up in business for the first time as a general dealer.

The majority of his sales will be on credit to trade buyers but he will sell some goods to the public for cash.

He is not sure at which point of the business cycle he can regard his cash and credit sales to have taken place.

After seeking guidance on this matter from his friends, he is thoroughly confused by the conflicting advice he has received. Samples of the advice he has been given include:

'The sale takes place when:
    (*a*) 'you have bought goods which you know you should be able to sell easily';
    (*b*) 'the customer places the order';
    (*c*) 'you deliver the goods to the customer';
    (*d*) 'you invoice the goods to the customer';
    (*e*) 'the customer pays for the goods';
    (*f*) 'the customer's cheque has been cleared by the bank'.

He now asks you to clarify the position for him.

Required:

(*a*) Write notes for Gee, setting out, in as easily understood a manner as possible, the accounting conventions and principles which should generally be followed when recognising sales revenue.

(*b*) Examine each of the statements (*a*) to (*f*) above and advise Gee (stating your reasons) whether the method advocated is appropriate to the particular circumstances of his business.

(*Chartered Association of Certified Accountants*)

44.10 The annual final accounts of businesses are normally prepared on the assumption that the business is a going concern.

Required:

Explain and give a simple illustration of

(*a*) the effect of this convention on the figures which appear in those final accounts.

(*b*) the implications for the final accounts figures if this convention were deemed to be inoperative.

(*Chartered Association of Certified Accountants*)

44.11 One of the well known accounting concepts is that of materiality.

Required:

(*a*) Explain what is meant by this concept.

(*b*) State and explain three types of situation to which this concept might be applicable.

(*c*) State and explain two specific difficulties in applying this concept.

(*Chartered Association of Certified Accountants*)

44.12 State three classes of people, other than managers and owners, who are likely to need to use financial accounting information. Discuss whether you think their requirements are compatible.

(*Chartered Association of Certified Accountants*)

44.13 In preparing the annual accounts of the medium-sized business by which you are employed as assistant accountant, the following items require to be dealt with at the financial year end, 31 March 19-7.

(*a*) There is a stock of unused postage stamps which had cost £3.

(*b*) A customer had paid his outstanding account by cheque, £35. Your company's bank has now returned this cheuqe marked 'Refer to drawer – insufficient funds'.

(*c*) The company's office block has been extended to house a computer installation. The company's own workmen carried out the building work at a wages cost of £764 and used materials which had cost £2,681.

(*d*) The computer equipment is rented at an annual rental of £19,200, paid quarterly in arrears on the last day of January, April, July and November.

(*e*) A contract has been signed for the removal of the existing heating system from the company's premises and its replacement by a new one, at a total cost of £22,700. Work is not scheduled to start until July 19-7.

Required:

State the accounting treatment, including available alternative treatments, you could apply to each of the above items.

(*Chartered Association of Certified Accountants*)

44.14A (*a*) In accounting practice a distinction is drawn between the terms 'reserves' and 'provisions' and between 'accrued expenses' and 'creditors'.

Required:

Briefly define each of the four terms quoted and explain the effect of each on the preparation of accounts

(*b*) While preparing the final accounts for year ended 30 September 19-3, the accountant of Lanep Lighting Ltd had to deal with the following matters:

(*i*) the exterior of the company's premises were being repaired. The contractors had started work in August but were unlikely to finish before the end of November 19-3. The total cost would not be known until after completion. Cost of work carried out to 30 September 19-3 was estimated at £21,000;

(*ii*) the company rented a sales showroom from Commercial Properties plc at a rental of £6,000 per annum payable half yearly in arrear on 1 August and 1 February;

(*iii*) on 3 October 19-3 an invoice was received for £2,500, less a trade discount of 30 per cent, from Lucifer Ltd for goods for resale supplied during September 19-3;

(*iv*) the directors of Lanep Lighting Ltd have decided that an annual amount of £5,000 should be set aside, starting with year ended 30 Sept 19-3, for the purpose of plant replacement.

Required:

State the accounting treatment which should be accorded to each of the above matters in the Lanep Lighting Ltd profit and loss account for year ended 30 September 19-3 and balance sheet at that date.

(*Chartered Association of Certified Accountants*)

44.15A (*a*) It is widely recognised that in order to succeed, a business must pay regard not only to its profitability but also to its financial stability.

Required:

     (*i*) State briefly what you understand to be the meaning of the terms 'profitability' and 'financial stability';

     (*ii*) Name three ratios which can be used for measuring profitability and three ratios for measuring financial stability.

     (*b*) The figures shown below relate to a medium sized company.

	£
For year ended 31 October 19-3;	
Gross profit	797,000
Net profit	255,000
Turnover (Sales)	2,743,000
As at 31 October 19-3;	
Shareholders funds	1,335,000
Total tangible assets	2,008,000
Current assets	32,000
Current liabilities	25,000
Long-term loans	648,000
Non-liquid current assets	19,000

Required:

Using such of the above figures and their derivatives as are relevant, calculate each of the ratios which you have named in your answer to (*a*) (*ii*) above.

(*Chartered Association of Certified Accountants*)

44.16A You are interested in acquiring some shares in Varac plc and have acquired the most recent set of the company's accounts for appraisal purposes.

     The accounts are supported by explanatory notes, extracts of which are reproduced below:

'*Turnover*

The figure includes only the cash actually received for cash and credit sales less actual and estimated amounts of bad debts'.

'*Cost of Sales*

Stocks

Opening stock is at FIFO* cost. Following a policy review the directors have decided that a more accurate valuation would be obtained by a percentage addition for overheads; accordingly closing stock has been valued on this new basis (*See* also Purchases below.)

Purchases

Purchases have been accounted for at their gross (catalogue) prices. Trade discounts received on purchases have been included in discounts received and have been credited to profit and loss account.

     It is the company's policy to account only for those goods for which it has paid. Goods which the company has received before the year-end, but for which it has not paid, are excluded from purchases, from closing stocks and from creditors.'

'*Depreciation*

During the current year the level of business activity has been much lower than had been anticipated resulting in a greatly reduced amount of net profit. It has been decided, therefore, that it would be inadvisable to charge any depreciation to profit and loss account as to do so would convert the small net profit into a net loss.

Should this situation recur in the next financial year, the directors propose to transfer a suitable amount from the accumulated provision for depreciation to the credit of profit and loss account in order to maintain the ordinary dividend.'

Required:

Comment on the extent to which Varac plc's accounts adhere to, or conflict with, recognised accounting principles and practices, so far as can be elicited from the above extracts.

(*Chartered Association of Certified Accountants*)

Note from author: FIFO and LIFO are not now part of new ACCA syllabus.

44.17 For a number of years Martin Smith has been employed as the works' manager of a company which manufactures cardboard cartons.

He has now decided to leave the company and to set up a similar business of his own on 1 January 19-6 but, before taking this step he wants to see what his financial results are likely to be for his first year of operations.

In order to do this, he has obtained certain 'average industry' ratios from his trade association, the Cardboard Carton Manufacturers' Association (CCMA), which he wants to use as his norm for predicting the first year's results.

At this stage he consults you, asks for your professional assistance and supplies the following information.

	CCMA statistics 19-4 (based on year-end figures)
Sales/Net assets employed	2.8 times
Gross profit/Sales	28.0%
Net profit/Sales	10.0%
Fixed assets/Working capital	1.5:1
Current assets/Current liabilities	2.25:1
Debtors collection period	36.5 days
Creditors payment period	58.4 days

He informs you that he is able to contribute £40,000 as capital and has been promised a long term loan of £6,000 from a relative.

Initially, he intends to acquire a stock of materials at a cost of £20,000 but his (simple) average stock for the first year will be £18,500. Purchases of materials for the year, excluding the initial purchase of stock, £20,000, will be £97,800. All purchases and sales will be on credit.

Sundry accruals at 31 December 19-6 are estimated at £350 and bank and cash balances at £5,000.

He proposes to withdraw £10,000 during the year for living expenses.

Required:

Prepare, in as much detail as can be elicited from the information supplied, a forecast trading and profit and loss account for Martin Smith's proposed business for the year ended 31 December 19-6, and a forecast balance sheet at that date.

All figures should be stated to the nearest £10. Workings must be shown.

(*Chartered Association of Certified Accountants*)

44.18 The outline balance sheets of the Nantred Trading Co Ltd were as shown below:

Balance Sheets as at 30 September

19-5			19-6	
£	£		£	£
		Fixed assets (at written down values)		
40,000		Premises	98,000	
65,000		Plant and equipment	162,000	
	105,000			260,000
		Current assets		
31,200		Stock	95,300	
19,700		Trade debtors	30,700	
15,600		Bank and cash	26,500	
66,500			152,500	
		Current liabilities		
23,900		Trade creditors	55,800	
11,400		*Corporation tax	13,100	
17,000		Proposed dividends	17,000	
52,300			85,900	
	14,200	Working capital		66,600
	119,200	Net assets employed		326,600
		Financed by		
100,000		Ordinary share capital	200,000	
19,200		Reserves	26,600	
	119,200	Shareholders' funds		226,600
	–	7% Debentures		100,000
	119,200			326,600

The only other information available is that the turnover for the years ended 30 September 19-5 and 19-6 was £202,900 and £490,700, respectively, and that on 30 September 19-4 Reserves were £26,100.

*Hong Kong and Singapore candidates read taxation.

Required:

(*a*) Calculate, for each of the two years, six suitable ratios to highlight the financial stability, liquidity and profitability of the company.

(*b*) Comment on the situation revealed by the figures you have calculated in your answer to (*a*) above.

(*Chartered Association of Certified Accountants*)

44.19A The summarised balance sheet of Ritt Ltd at the end of two consecutive financial years were as shown below.

Summarised Balance Sheets as at 31 March

19-6 £'000	£'000		£'000	19-7 £'000
		Fixed assets (at written down values)		
50		Premises	48	
115		Plant and equipment	196	
42		Vehicles	81	
	207			325
		Current assets		
86		Stock	177	
49		Debtors and prepayments	62	
53		Bank and cash	30	
188			269	
		Current liabilities		
72		Creditors and accruals	132	
20		Proposed dividends	30	
92			162	
	96	*Working capital*		107
	303	*Net assets employed*		432
		Financed by		
250		Ordinary share capital	250	
53		Reserves	82	
	303	*Shareholders' funds*		332
	–	Loan capital: 7% Debentures		100
	303			432

Turnover was £541,000 and £675,000 for the years ended 31 March 19-6 and 19-7 respectively. Corresponding figures for cost of sales were £369,000 and £481,000, respectively.

At 31 March 19-5, reserves had totalled £21,000. Ordinary share capital was the same at the end of 19-5 as at the end of 19-6.

Required:

(*a*) Calculate, for each of the two years, the ratios listed below:
- Gross profit/Turnover percentage.
- Net profit/Turnover percentage.
- Turnover/Net assets employed.
- Net profit/Net assets employed percentage.
- Current assets/Current liabilities.
- Quick assets/Current liabilities.

Calculations should be correct to one decimal place.

(*b*) Comment on each of the figures you have calculated in (*a*) above, giving probable reasons for the differences between the two years.

(*Chartered Association of Certified Accountants*)

44.20A The net assets of three unconnected companies are financed as follows, as at 31 December 19-4:

	X plc		Y plc		Z plc	
	£'000	£'000	£'000	£'000	£'000	£'000
Share capital authorised						
Ordinary shares of £1.00 per share		12,000		–		–
Ordinary shares of £0.25 per share		–		6,000		6,000
8% preference shares of £1.00 per share		–		4,000		4,000
		12,000		10,000		10,000
Called up and issued						
Ordinary shares of £1.00 per share £0.75 paid		6,000	–		–	
Ordinary shares of £0.25 per share fully paid		–	4,000		1,000	
80 preference shares of £1.00 per share, fully paid		–	4,000		2,000	
		6,000		8,000		3,000
Reserves						
Share premium account (raised on issue of ordinary shares)			500		200	
General reserve	1,000		–		1,300	
Fixed asset revaluation reserve	2,000		–		–	
Fixed asset replacement reserve	–		1,000		–	
Profit and loss account	1,000		500		1,500	
		4,000		2,000		3,000
Shareholders' funds		10,000		10,000		6,000
10% Debenture stock		–		–		4,000
		10,000		10,000		10,000

For all three companies, the profit before interest and tax is estimated at £5,000,000 for the next 12 months ended 31 December 19-5. The capital structure of each company will remain unaltered.

Taxation on profits after interest is an effective rate of 40 per cent. Assume that an ordinary dividend of 12 per cent of the paid up share capital will be paid.

Required:

For each of the three companies,

(a) prepare the estimated profit and loss accounts for the year ended 31 Dec 19-5.

(b) calculate

(i) basic earnings per share for the year ended 31 December 19-5,

(ii) gearing ratio as at 31 December 19-4.

(c) briefly explain, in relation to gearing, the effects on earnings of substantial changes in profit after tax. Workings must be shown.

(*Chartered Association of Certified Accountants*)

44.21A The Gravelea Haulage Company plc is an established company which intends to expand its activities from 19-2 onwards.

In the opinion of the directors, the only feasible means of financing the expansion programme is by obtaining funds from outside sources.

Over a period of weeks, the directors have been considering alternative ways of raising the £500,000 needed.

They have now narrowed down the choice to one of three possibilities:

Scheme:

(A) an issue of £500,000 7 per cent redeemable debentures 2001/2007 at par;

(B) an issue of 500,000 10 per cent redeemable preference shares of £1.00 per share, at par;

(C) an issue of 400,000 ordinary shares of £1.00 per share, at a premium of £0.25 per share, on which it is hoped to pay an annual dividend of 15 per cent currently paid on existing ordinary shares.

Currently, the company's issued share capital consists of 3,000,000 ordinary shares of £1.00 per share, fully paid.

The chief accountant has estimated that the company's profit before interest and tax (without taking account of the additional profit from the expansion programme) is likely to remain static at £574,000 for the next five years. Interest payable on bank overdraft for each of these years has been estimated at £4,000.

It has also been estimated that, after it has been implemented, the programme will produce an annual amount of £130,000 profit before interest and tax, additional to the figure shown above.

Corporation tax has been estimated at an effective rate of 40 per cent on the company's total profit after interest and before tax.

Without taking the expansion programme into account, the company's earnings per share is estimated to be 1.4p, arrived at as follows:

	£
Profit before interest and tax	574,000
less interest	4,000
Profit after interest before tax	570,000
less corporation tax (40% × £570,000)	228,000
Profit after tax	342,000
less preference dividends	Nil
Earnings (attributable to ordinary shareholders)	342,000
Number of ordinary shares in issue and ranking for dividend	3,000,000
Earnings per share (EPS) (342,000 × 100) (3,000,000)	11.4p

You are required to:

(*a*) In schemes (A) and (B) what is the significance of the term 'redeemable'?

(*b*) For what reasons might the company wish to redeem its shares or debentures?

(*c*) What is the significance of the data 2001/2007 in Scheme (A)?

(*d*) In scheme (C) will the dividend of 15 per cent be calculated on the nominal value (£400,000) of the additional ordinary shares or on the issued value (£500,000)? What is an alternative way in which the dividend could be expressed?

(*e*) What will be the company's annual earning per share on the basis that:

(*i*) Scheme A is adopted?

(*ii*) Scheme B is adopted?

(*iii*) Scheme C is adopted?

(Earnings per share (EPS) is defined as the profit in pence attributable to each ordinary share after tax and before taking extraordinary items into account. No extraordinary items have been forecast for the next five years.)

(*f*) What will be the company's capital gearing in a full year after implementation separately for each of the schemes?

(*Chartered Association of Certified Accountants*)

45
Accounting theory

Part I: an introduction

To many students it will seem strange that a discussion of accounting theory has been left until this late stage of the book. Logically you could argue that it should have preceded all the practical work.

The reason for not dealing with theory at the beginning is simple. From a practical standpoint of teaching, it could easily have confused you then, and make it more difficult to assimilate the basic rules of accounting. The terms used in theory, such as what is meant in accounting by capital, liabilities, assets, net profit and so on, would not then have been understood. Leaving it until now, if theory points out what is wrong with accounting methods, at least you know those methods. Theory taught in a vacuum is counter-productive for most students.

In the discussion which follows, we want you to remember that this is your first proper look at accounting theory. We do not intend it to be an exhaustive examination, but simply an introduction to give you an overall appreciation. If you carry your studies to a higher level you will have to study accounting theory in much greater depth. At this level all you will need is an appreciation aspect only.

An overall accepted theory?

It would not be surprising if you were expecting to read now exactly what the overall accepted theory of accounting is, and then proceed to examine the details later. We are afraid there is no such 'accepted' theory. This is much regretted by those accountants who have chosen an academic life. Many 'practical' accountants, and you will meet quite a few of them, are quite pleased that no such theory exists. To them, accounting is what accountants do, and they feel theory has little place in that. Such a narrow view is to be deprecated. Accounting theory provides a general frame of reference by which accounting practices can be judged, and it also guides the way to the development of new practices and procedures.

The lack of an accepted theory of accounting does not mean that it has not been attempted; there have been numerous attempts. At first they consisted of an **inductive** approach. This involved observing and analysing the practices of accountants to see if any consistent behaviour could be detected. Should a general principle be observed, anyone deviating from it could be criticised accordingly. Such attempts failed. First, it was impossible to find consistent patterns of behaviour amongst the mass of practices which had developed over the years. Second, such an approach would not have brought about any important improvements in accounting practices, as it looked at 'what accountants do' rather than 'what accountants *should* be doing'.

A different approach emerged, as recently as the 1950s. It was a **normative** approach, in that it was aimed at the improvement of accounting practice. It also included elements of the inductive approach in attempting to derive rules based on logical reasoning when given a set of objectives. The combination of these approaches has been a valuable and productive one, albeit still in its infancy. For instance, it had an important effect upon current value accounting which we will examine later. The main problem has been that of a general agreement as to the objectives of accounting.

As you might expect, general attention has more recently tended to switch away to a less ambitious approach. This is based, first, on identifying the users of accounts, and then finding out what kind of information they require. Such an approach was used in *The Corporate Report*, produced under the auspices of the Accounting Standards Committee (ASC), and published in 1975. We will look later at the user groups which were identified. The other important report using this approach was that of the Sandilands Committee in 1975. This will also be considered more fully later.

There is still a major problem here. Should accountants give the user groups the information they are asking for, or the information for which they should be asking? With management accounts this is not such a great problem, as management and accountants get together to agree on what should be produced. The financial accounts present greater problems. First, there is not such a close relationship between the accountant and the user groups. Second, there are the legal and other regulations governing financial accounts which the accountant must observe. Another point which will be considered later is whether only one report should be issued for all user groups, or whether each group should have its own report.

Having had an overall look at how theory construction is proceeding, we can now turn to look at theory in more detail.

Measurement of income

The syllabus uses the word 'income', but the words 'net profit' mean exactly the same. In this book the calculation of net profit is done within fairly strict guidelines. Chapter 10 gave you guidance on the overall concepts ruling such calculations. However, just because the business world and the accounting profession use this basic approach does not mean it is the only one available. We will now consider possible alternatives to the basic method.

Let us start by looking at the simplest possible example of the calculation of profit, where everyone would agree with the way it is calculated. John is starting in business, his only asset being cash £1,000. He rents a stall in the market for the day, costing him £40. He then buys fruit for cash £90, and sells it all during the day for cash £160. At the end of the day John's only asset is still cash: £1,000 − £40 − £90 + 160 = £1,030. Everyone would agree that his profit for that day was £30, i.e. £160 sales − £90 purchases − £40 expenses = £30. In this case his profit equals the increase in his cash.

Suppose that John now changes his style of trading. He buys the market stall, and he also starts selling nuts and dried fruit, of which he can keep a stock from one day to another. If we now want to calculate profit we cannot do it simply in terms of cash, we will also have to place a value both on the stock of fruit and nuts and on his stall, both at the beginning and end of each day.

The argument just put forward assumes that we can all agree that profit represents an increase in wealth or 'well-offness'. It assumes that John will make a profit for a period if either:

(a) he is better off at the end of it than he was at the beginning; or

(b) he would have been better off at the end than the beginning had he not consumed some of the profits by taking drawings.

Sir John Hicks, the economist, expressed this view by saying that the profit was the maximum value which a person could consume during a period and still be as well off at the end of the period as at the beginning.

In terms of a limited company, the Sandilands Committee, which will be mentioned in greater detail later, said that a company's profit for the year is the maximum value which the company can distribute as dividends during the year, and still be as well off at the end of the year as it was at the beginning.

There are some important questions here which need answering. They are:

(*a*) how can we measure wealth at the beginning and end of a period?

(*b*) how do we measure the change in wealth over a period?

(*c*) having measured wealth over a period, how much can be available for consumption and how much should not be consumed?

There are basically two approaches to the measurement of wealth of a business.

(*a*) Measuring the wealth by finding the values of the individual assets of a business.

(*b*) Measuring the expectation of future benefits.

In Volume 2 of this book you will learn the technique of discounting. We will use it here to calculate the present value of the expected future net flow of cash into the firm.

We will first look at the different methods of valuation on an individual asset basis.

Asset valuation alternatives

Historical cost

This method is the one you have used so far in the financial accounting in this book. Even in that case there is not always one single figure to represent it. Let us look at a few examples.

(*a*) **Depreciation**. How do we 'precisely' charge the cost of using an asset to a particular period? As you have already seen, there is no one 'true' answer; the choice of method, expected length of use of the asset, etc, is quite arbitrary.

(*b*) Stocks to be used during the period can be charged out at FIFO, LIFO, AVCO, NIFO, and so on. There is no one 'true' figure.

(*c*) Suppose we buy a block of assets, e.g. we take over the net assets of another organisation. How do we allocate the cost exactly? There is no precise way, we simply use a 'fair value' for each asset. Any excess of cost over the total of fair values we call goodwill.

Adjusted historical cost

Because of the changes in the value or purchasing of money, the normal historical cost approach can be very unsatisfactory. Take the case of a buildings account; in it we find that two items have been debited. One was a warehouse bought in 1950 for £100,000 and the other an almost identical warehouse bought in 1985 for £400,000. These two figures are added together to show cost of warehouses £500,000, quite clearly a value which has little significance.

To remedy this defect, the original historical cost of an asset is adjusted for the changes in the value or purchasing power of money over the period from acquisition to the present balance sheet date. The calculations are effected by using a price index.

This method does not mean that the asset itself is revalued. What is revalued is the money for which the asset was originally bought. This method forms the basis of what is known at **current purchasing power** accounting, abbreviated as CPP.

It does not remove the original problems of historical accounting which we have already described (*see* above). All this does is to take the original historical cost as accurate and then adjust it.

To illustrate this method, let us take an instance which works out precisely, just as the proponents of CPP would wish.

A machine which will last for five years, depreciated using the straight line method, was bought on 1 January 19-4 for £5,000. On 1 January 19-6 exactly the same kind of machine (there have been no technological improvements) is bought for £6,000. The price index was 100 at 1 January 19-4, 120 at 1 January 19-6 and 130 at 31 December 19-6. The machines would appear in the balance sheet at 31 December 19-6 as follows, the workings being shown in the box alongside.

	Historial cost £	Conversion factor £		Balance sheet CPP at 31 Dec 19-6 £
Machine 1	5,000	130/100	6,500	
Machine 2	6,000	130/120	6,500	13,000
less Depreciation				
Machine 1	3,000	130/100	3,900	
Machine 2	1,200	130/120	1,300	5,200
				7,800

You can see that the CPP balance sheet shows two exactly similar machines at the same cost, and each has been depreciated £1,300 for each year of use. In this particular case CPP has achieved exactly what it sets out to do, namely put similar things on a similar basis.

Underlying this method are the problems inherent in the price index used to adjust the historical cost figures. Any drawbacks in the index will result in a distortion of the adjusted historical cost figures.

Replacement cost

Replacement cost, abbreviated as RC, is the estimated amount that would have to be paid to replace the asset at the date of valuation. You will often see it referred to as an 'entry value' as it is the cost of an asset entering the business.

How do we 'estimate' the replacement cost? As we are not in fact replacing the asset we will have to look at the state of the market at the date of valuation. If the asset is exactly the same as those currently being traded, perhaps we can look at suppliers' price lists.

Even with exactly the same item, there are still problems. Until you have actually negotiated a purchase it is impossible to say how much discount you could get – you might guess but you could not be certain. Also, if the asset consists of, say, ten drilling machines, how much discount could you get for buying ten machines instead of one only?

If we have those difficulties looking at identical assets, what happens when we are trying to find out these figures for assets which cannot still be matched on the market? Technological change has greatly speeded up in recent years. If there is a second-hand market, it may be quite possible to get a valuation. However, in second-hand markets the price is often even more subject to negotiation. It becomes even more complicated when the original asset was specially made and there is no exactly comparable item, new or second-hand.

The difficulties outlined above mean that solutions to valuation can be sought under three headings:

(*a*) **Market prices.** As already mentioned, there will often be a market, new or second-hand, for the assets. For instance, this is particularly true for motor vehicles. If our asset differs in some way an adjustment may be necessary, thus cutting into the desirable degree of objectivity.

(*b*) **Units of service.** Where a market price is unobtainable, this being especially so with obsolete assets, a value is placed on the units of service which the asset can provide, rather than trying to value the asset itself.

For instance, assume that a machine has an estimated future production capacity of 1,000 units. A new machine producing the same type of product might have a total future capacity of 5,000 units. If the running costs of the machines are the same, the value of the old machine can be said to be one-fifth of the cost of the new one, as that is the proportion its future capacity bears to the new one. If the running costs were different an adjustment would be made.

(*c*) **Cost of inputs.** If the asset was made or constructed by the owner, it may be possible to calculate the cost of replacing it at the balance sheet date. Present rates of labour and materials costs could be worked out to give the replacement cost.

Net realisable value

Net realisable value means the estimated amount that would be received from the sale of the asset less the estimated costs on its disposal. The term **'exit value'** is often used as it is the amount receivable when an asset leaves the business.

A very important factor affecting such a valuation is the conditions under which the assets are to be sold. To realise in a hurry would often mean accepting a very low price. Look at the sale prices received from stock from bankruptcies – usually very low figures. The standard way of approaching this problem is to value as though the realisation were 'in the normal course of business'. This is not capable of an absolutely precise meaning, as economic conditions change and the firm might never sell such an asset 'in the normal course of business'.

The difficulties of establishing an asset's net realisable value are similar to those of the replacement value method when similar assets are not being bought and sold in the market-place. However, the problems are more severe as the units of service approach cannot be used, since that takes the seller's rather than buyer's viewpoint.

Economic value (present value)

As any economist would be delighted to tell you, he/she would value an asset as the sum of the future expected net cash flows associated with the asset, discounted to its present value. The technicalities of discounting are discussed in Volume 2 of this book.

Certainly, if you really did know (not guess) the future net cash flows associated with the asset and you had the correct discount rate, your valuation would be absolutely correct. The trouble is that it is impossible to forecast future net cash flows with certainty, neither will we necessarily have chosen the correct discount rate. It is also very difficult to relate cash flows to a particular asset, since a business's assets combine together to generate revenue.

Deprival value

The final concept of value is based on ideas propounded in the USA by Professor Bonbright in the 1930s, and later developed in the UK for profit measurement by Professor W T Baxter.

Deprival value is based on the concept of the value of an asset being the amount of money the owner would have to receive to compensate him or her exactly for being deprived of it. We had better point out immediately that the owner does not have to be deprived of the asset to ascertain this value, it is a hypothetical exercise.

This leads to a number of consequences.

(*a*) Deprival value cannot exceed replacement cost, since if the owner were deprived of the asset he/she could replace it for a lesser amount. Here we will ignore any costs concerned with a delay in replacement.

(*b*) If the owner feels that the asset is not worth replacing, its replacement cost would be more than its deprival value. He/she simply would not pay the replacement cost, so the value to the owner is less than that figure.

(*c*) If the asset's deprival value is to be taken as its net relisable value, that value must be less than its replacement cost. It would otherwise make sense for someone to sell the asset at net realisable value and buy a replacement at a lower cost. Again, delays in replacement are ignored.

(*d*) Take the case where an owner would not replace the asset, but neither would he/she sell it. It is possible to envisage a fixed asset which has become obsolete but might possibly be used, for example, when other machines break down. It is not worth buying a new machine, as the replacement cost is more than the value of the machine to the business. Such a machine may well have a very low net realisable value.

The benefit to the business of keeping such a machine can be said to be its 'value in use'. This value must be less than its replacement cost, as pointed out above, but more than its net realisable value for otherwise the owner would sell it.

It is probably easier to summarise how to find 'deprival value' by means of the diagram in Exhibit 45.1.

Exhibit 45.1 Deprival value

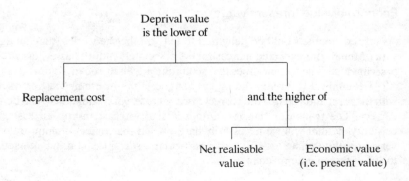

This can be illustrated by a few examples, using assets A, B and C.

	Asset A	Asset B	Asset C
	£	£	£
Replacement cost (RC)	1,000	800	600
Net realisable value (NRV)	900	500	400
Economic value (EV)	2,000	700	300

The deprival values can be explained as follows; check them against Exhibit 45.1.

(a) Asset A. If the firm were deprived of asset A, what would it do? As economic value is greater than replacement cost it would buy another asset A. The deprival value to the business is therefore £1,000, i.e. replacement cost.

(b) Asset B. If deprived of asset B, what would the firm do? It would not replace it, as RC £800 is greater than its value to the business – its economic value £700. If deprived, the firm would therefore lose the present value of future cash flows, i.e. economic value £700. This then is the deprival value for asset B.

(c) Asset C. With this asset there would be no point in keeping it, as its economic value to the firm is less than the firm could sell it for. Selling it is the logical way, so the deprival value is net realisable value £400.

Capital maintenance

Let us go back to Sir John Hicks's definition of income (profit): 'A man's income is the maximum value which he can consume during a week, and still expect to be as well off at the end of the week as he was at the beginning.'

We have looked at the different ways we could value assets as a preliminary to totalling them to find the wealth or 'well-offness' at a particular date. Before going any further we must examine the problems of measuring the maintenance of wealth (or 'well-offness') over a period. We could call this **capital maintenance.**

The basic method used in accounting, and described earlier throughout this book, is that of **money capital maintenance**. Using this approach, if a firm has £1,000 in capital or net assets on 1 January 19-1 it must have £1,000 in capital or net assets at 31 December 19-1 to be as well off at the end of the period. This means that, provided no new share capital has been issued and no dividends paid or share capital withdrawn, a company starting with capital of £1,000 on 1 January 19-2 and finishing with capital of £1,600 on 31 December 19-2 must have made a profit of £600, using this approach to capital maintenance.

Such a method would be acceptable to everyone in a period when there is no change in prices. However, most people would agree that the approach is not satisfactory when either prices in general, or specific prices affecting the firm, are changing. In these two cases, to state that £600 profit has been made for 19-2 completely ignores the fact that the £1,000 at 1 January 19-2 and the £1,000 at 31 December 19-2 do not have the same value. From this we can see the possibilities of three different concepts.

(a) **Money capital maintenance.** The traditional system of accounting as already described.

(b) **Real capital maintenance.** This concept is concerned with maintaining the general purchasing power of the equity shareholders. This takes into account changes in the purchasing power of money as measured by the retail price index.

(c) **Maintenance of specific purchasing power of the capital of the equity.** This uses a price index which is related to the specific price changes of the goods in which the firm deals.

From these we can look at the following example, which illustrates three different figures of profit being thrown up for a firm.

A worked example

A company has only equity share capital. Its net assets on 1 January 19-5 are £1,000, and on 31 December 19-5 £1,400. There have been no issues or withdrawal of share capital during the year. The general rate of inflation, as measured by the retail price index is ten per cent, whereas the specific rate of price increase for the type of goods in which the company deals, is 15 per cent. The profits for the three measures are as follows:

	(a) Money maintenance of capital	(b) Real capital maintenance	(c) Maintenance of specific purchasing power
	£	£	£
Nett assets 31 Dec 19-5	1,400	1,400	1,400
less What net assets would have to be at 31 Dec 19-5 to be as well off on 1 Jan 19-5			
(a) Money maintenance	1,000		
(b) Real capital 1,000 + 10%		1,100	
(c) Specific purchasing power maintenance 1,000 + 15%			1,150
Profit	400	300	250

Note that under the three methods:

(a) here the normal accounting method gives £400 profit;

(b) this case recognises that there has been a fall in the purchasing power of money;

(c) this takes into account that it would cost £1,150 for goods whose value at the start of the year was £1,000.

Combinations of different values and capital maintenance concepts

We have just looked at three ways of calculating profits based on historical cost allied with three capital maintenance concepts. This can be extended by using replacement cost or net realisable value instead. Each of these, when adjusted by each capital maintenance concept, will give three separate figures for profit. Together the three different means of valuation, multiplied by three different concepts of capital maintenance, will give us nine different profit figures.

At this stage in your studies it will be difficult to understand how such different profit measures could be useful for different purposes. We can leave this until your studies progress to more advanced examinations. However, we can use one simple example to illustrate how using only the traditional way of calculating profits can have dire consequences. The next example shows how this can happen.

A worked example

A company has net assets on 1 January 19-7 of £100,000 financed purely by equity share capital. During 19-7 there has been no injection or withdrawal of capital. At 31 December 19-7 net assets have risen to £115,000. Both the retail price index and the specific price index for the goods dealt in have risen by 25 per cent. Taxation, based on traditional historical cost calculations (maintenance of money capital), is at the rate of 40 per cent. The profit may be calculated as follows.

	Maintenance of money capital	Maintenance of real capital and of specific purchasing power
	£	£
Net assets on 31 Dec 19-7	115,000	115,000
Less net assets needed to be as well off at 31 Dec 19-7 as with £100,000 on 1 Jan 19-7		
(a) Money capital	100,000	
(b) Both real capital and specific purchasing power £100,000 + 25%		125,000
Profit/Loss	15,000	(10,000)

Tax payable is £15,000 × 40% = £6,000. Yet the real capital or that of specific purchasing power has fallen by £10,000. When tax is paid that would leave us with net assets of £115,000 − £6,000 = £109,000. Because of price changes £109,000 could not finance the amount of activity financed by £100,000 one year before. The operating capacity of the company would therefore be reduced.

Obviously it is not equitable for a company to have to pay tax on what is in fact a loss. It is only the traditional way of measuring profits that has thrown up a profit figure.

Operating capital maintenance concept

This approach looks at the output which could be generated by the initial holding of assets. A profit will only be made if the assets held at the end of the period are able to maintain the same level of output.

A very simple example of this is that of a trader who sells only one product, a particular kind of watch. The only costs the trader incurs are those of buying the watches. He/she has no assets apart from watches. In this case the operating capital consists solely of watches.

Using the historical cost concept the trader will recognise a profit if the revenue from the sale of a watch exceeded the historic cost of it. However, using the operating capital maintenance concept he will recognise a profit only if the revenue from the sale is greater than the cost of buying another watch to replace the watch sold.

Part II: accounting for changing price levels

As you have seen already in this chapter, changes in price levels can lead to both profit and asset valuation figures being far from reality if simple historical cost figure are used. This is not a recently observed phenomenon. As far back as 1938, Sir Ronald Edwards wrote several classic articles which were published in *The Accountant*. You can find these in the book, *Studies in Accounting Theory*, edited by W T Baxter and S Davidson and published by the Institute of Chartered Accountants, London, 1977.

The greater the rate of change in price levels, the greater the distortion. The clamour for changes to simple historical cost accounting is noticeably greater when the inflation rate is high – at such times the deficiencies of historical cost accounts are most obvious. If there were a period of deflation, however, the historical cost accounts would be still misleading.

In certain countries in the world the annual rate of inflation in recent years has been several hundred per cent. Historical cost accounts in those countries would certainly be at odds with accounts adjusted for inflation. In the UK the highest rate in recent years, based on the RPI was 17.8 per cent for 1979, falling to as low as 3.7 per cent for 1986.

We can now look, in outline only, at suggestions made in the UK since 1968 as to methods which could be used to adjust accounts for changing price levels.

Current purchasing power (CPP)

This proposal is something you have already read about. It is the adjustment of historical cost accounting figures by a price index figure to give figures showing what we called real capital maintenance. It will convey more of the problems and uncertainties facing the accounting profession in this regard, if we look at the history of the various proposals.

First came *Accounting for stewardship in a period of inflation*, published in 1968 by the Research Foundation of the Institute of Chartered Accountants in England and Wales (ICAEW). Stemming from this came Exposure Draft No 8 (ED 8), published in 1973. ED 8 contained the proposal that companies should be required to publish, in addition to their conventional accounts, supplementary statements which would be, in effect, their final accounts amended to conform to CPP principles. In May 1974 a Provisional Statement of Standard Accounting Practice No. 7 (PSSAP 7) was published. Notice the sign of uncertainty, it was a **provisional** standard – the only one yet published. Compared with ED 8 which said that a company should be *required* to publish CPP acounts, PSSAP 7 simply *requested* them to publish such accounts. Many companies would not accede to such a request.

PSSAP 7 stipulated that the price index to be used in the conversion of accounts from historical cost should be the retail price index (RPI). As the actual price index relating to the goods dealt in by the firm might be quite different from RPI, the CPP accounts could well be distant from the current values of the firm itself.

The exact nature of the calculations needed for CPP accounts is not part of your syllabus, and we will not repeat them here.

Many people, including the government, were completely dissatisfied with the CPP approach. After ED 8 was issued the government set up its own committee of inquiry into inflation accounting. The chairman of the committee was Mr (now Sir) Francis Sandilands. The report, often known as the Sandilands Report, was published in September 1975.

Current cost accounting (CCA)

The Sandilands Committee's approach was quite different from ED 8 and PSSAP 7. The committee recommended a system called **current cost accounting** (CCA). This basically approved the concept of capital maintenance as the maintenance of operating capacity.

After the Sandilands Report appeared, the accounting bodies, as represented by their own Accounting Standards Committee (ASC), abandoned their proposals in PSSAP 7. A working party, the Inflation Accounting Steering Group (IASG), was set up to prepare a Statement of Standard Accounting Practice based on the Sandilands Report.

This group published ED 18, 'Current cost accounting', in November 1976. It was attacked by many members of the ICAEW, whose members passed, in July 1977, a resolution rejecting compulsory use of CCA. However, the government continued its support, and in November 1977 the accounting profession issued a set of interim recommendations called the Hyde guidelines (named after the chairman of the committee). The second exposure draft, ED 24, was issued in April 1979, followed by SSAP 16 in March 1980. SSAP 16 was to last three years to permit the evaluation of the introduction of CCA. After this, ED 35 was published in July 1984.

In November 1986 the CCAB Accounting Standards Committee published its handbook, *Accounting for the effects of changing prices*. At the same time presidents of five of the leading accountancy bodies issued the following statement:

'The presidents of five of the leading accountancy bodies welcome the publication by the CCAB Accounting Standards Committee of its Handbook on *Accounting for the effects of changing prices*.

The presidents endorse the CCAB Accounting Standards Committee's view that, where a company's results and financial position are materially affected by changing prices, historical cost accounts alone are insufficient and that information on the effects of changing prices is important for an appreciation of the company's results and financial position. The presidents join the Accounting Standards Committee in encouraging companies to appraise and, where material, report the effects of changing prices.

The five bodies have proposed that SSAP 16, 'Current cost accounting', which was made non-mandatory by all the CCAB bodies in June 1985, should now be formally withdrawn. They take the view, however, that the subject of accounting for the effects of changing prices is one of great importance. Accordingly, they support the Accounting Standards Committee in its continuing work on the subject and agree that an acceptable accounting standard should be developed'.

The Institute of Chartered Accountants in England and Wales; The Institute of Chartered Accountants of Scotland; The Institute of Chartered Accountants in Ireland; The Chartered Institute of Management Accountants; The Chartered Institute of Public Finance and Accountancy.

So once again the idea of forcing companies to produce accounts adjusted for changing prices has been rejected. The emphasis is now on encouragement, rather than trying to force companies to do it.

The reason why, at this early stage in your studies, we have given you some of the history behind the efforts to compel companies to produce CCA accounts is to illustrate the conflicts that have taken place inside and outside the accountancy profession. Opinions on the merits of CCA accounts are widely divided. You will study this in greater detail in the later stages of more advanced examinations, but we feel we should make clear at the outset that it is a controversial topic.

Handbook on *Accounting for the effects of changing price levels*

We can now look at the main outlines of this handbook. The ASC is now trying to encourage companies to co-operate in an attempt to produce accounts suitable for the effects of changing price levels. In doing this it does not try to recommend any one method, or even recommend one way only of publishing the results. The handbook says that the information may be presented:

(*a*) as the main accounts; or
(*b*) in the notes to the accounts; or
(*c*) as information supplemental to the financial statements.

The handbook first examines the problems.

Problems during a period of changing price levels

Obviously, the greater the rate of change, the greater will be the problems. We can now list some of them.

(*a*) **Fixing selling prices.** If you can change your prices very quickly, an extreme case being a market trader, this problem hardly exists. For a company setting prices which it is expected to maintain for a reasonably long period, the problems are severe. It dare not price too highly, as early demand may be reduced by an excessive price; on the other hand, the company has to guess how prices are going to change over a period so that sufficient profit is made.

(*b*) **Financial planning.** As it is so difficult to guess how prices are going to change over a period, planning the firm's finances becomes particularly trying. Obviously, it would be better if the plans were revised frequently as conditions changed.

(*c*) **Paying taxation and replacing assets.** We have seen earlier how, during a period of inflation, traditional historic accounting will tend to overstate profits. Such artificial 'profits' are then taxed. Unless various supplementary tax allowances are given, the taxation paid is both excessive and more than true profits, adjusted for inflation, can bear easily. This tends to lead to companies being short of cash, too much having been taken in tax. Therefore, when assets which have risen in price have to be replaced, adequate finance may not be available.

(*d*) **Monetary assets.** If stocks of goods are held, they will tend to rise in money terms during a period of inflation. On the other hand, holding monetary assets, e.g. cash, bank and debtors, will be counter-productive. A bank balance of £1,000 held for six months, during which the purchasing power of money has fallen ten per cent, will in real terms be worth only 90 per cent of its value six months before. Similarly, in real terms debt of £5,000 owed continually over that same period will have seen its real value fall by ten per cent.

(*e*) **Dividend distribution.** Just as it is difficult to calculate profits, so is it equally difficult to decide how much to pay as dividends without impairing the efficiency and operating capability of the company. At the same time the shareholders will be looking to payment of adequate dividends.

Solutions to the problems

The handbook recommends the use of one of two concepts. These will now be examined fairly briefly, in as much detail as is needed at this stage of your examinations.

Profit under the operating capital maintenance concept

This has been mentioned previously, with a simple example given of a trader buying and selling watches. Under this concept several adjustments are needed to the profit calculated on the historical cost basis. Each adjustment is now considered.

Adjustment 1: holding gains and operating gains

Nearly all companies hold fixed assets and stocks. For each of these assets the opportunity cost will bear little relationship to its historic cost. Instead it is the asset's value to the business at date of consumption, and this is usually the replacement cost of the asset.

Accordingly the historic cost profit, which was based on money capital maintenance, can be divided into two parts.

(*a*) Current cost profit, or operating gains. This is the difference between sales revenue and the replacement cost of the assets.

(*b*) Holding gains. This is the replacement cost of the assets less historical cost of those assets.

For example, a company buys an asset for £1,000 on 1 January 19-4. It holds it for one year and sells it for £1,600 when the replacement cost is £1,200. There has been a historical cost profit of £600. This can be analysed as in Exhibit 45.2.

Exhibit 45.2

Profit for 19-4

	£
Historical cost profit (£1,600−£1,000)	600
less Holding gain (£1,200−£1,000)	200
Current cost profit (or operating gain)	400

To put it another way, the company makes £200 historical profit by simply holding the asset from when its replacement cost (i.e. original cost) was £1,000, until the date of sale when its replacement cost was £1,200. The actual current cost profit at point of sale must reflect conditions at date of sale, i.e. the company has sold for £1,600 something which would currently cost £1,200 to replace. The current cost profit is therefore £400.

The holding gains are often described as a cost of sales adjustment (COSA).

Adjustment 2: depreciation

Depreciation is to be adjusted to current replacement cost values. Without going into complicated examples, this means that if the historical cost of depreciation is £4,000 and the current cost of depreciation, based on current replacement cost values, is £7,000, the adjustment should be £3,000 as follows:

	£
Depreciation based on historical cost	4,000
Adjustment needed to bring depreciation charge to CCA basis	3,000
CCA depreciation	7,000

Adjustment 3: monetary working capital adjustment

The monetary working capital needed to support the operating capability of the business will be affected by inflation. An adjustment will be needed to the historic profits in respect of this.

Adjustment 4: gearing adjustment

If we borrow £1,000 now, and have to pay back exactly £1,000 in five years, we will gain during a period of inflation. We will be able to put the £1,000 to use at current purchasing power. In five years' time, if £1 now is worth only 60p then, we will have gained because we will only be giving up £600 of current purchasing power now. The gearing adjustment is an attempt to adjust current cost operating profits for this factor.

Profit and loss account based on the operating capital maintenance concept

A general idea how such a profit and loss account could appear can now be given.

RST Ltd
Profit and Loss Account incorporating Operating Capital Maintenance Concept adjustments

	£	£
Profit on the historical cost basis, before interest and taxation		100,000
less Current cost operating adjustments:		
(1) Holding gains (COSA)	15,000	
(2) Depreciation	10,000	
(3) Monetary working capital	5,000	30,000
Current cost operating profit		70,000
(4) Gearing adjustment	(2,000)	
Interest payable less receivable	6,000	4,000
Current cost profit before taxation		66,000
Taxation		25,000
Current cost profit attributable to shareholders		41,000
Dividends		30,000
Retained current cost profit for the year		11,000

Profit under the financial capital maintenance concept

According to the handbook this method is sometimes known as the 'real terms' system of accounting. The steps by which the profit is calculated can be summarised as:

(*a*) calculate shareholders' funds at the beginning of the period, based on current cost asset values; then

(*b*) restate that opening amount in terms of pounds at the end of the period, by adjusting (*a*) by the relevant change in a general price index (e.g. RPI); then

(*c*) calculate shareholders' funds at the end of the period, based on current cost values.

Assuming that there have been no introductions or withdrawals of capital, including dividends, if (*c*) is greater than (*b*) a 'real terms' profit will have been made. Otherwise a loss will have been incurred.

Allowance will have to be made in steps (*a*) to (*c*) above where there have been introductions or withdrawals of capital, or where there have been dividends.

The calculation of 'real terms' profit, as described, has been by way of comparing opening and closing balance sheets. Suppose that the 'real terms' profit figure had been £10,000, it could if fact have been calculated in the following manner:

	£	£
Historical cost profit		7,800
Add holding gains: the amount by which the current costs of the assets have increased over the period	3,400	
less Inflation adjustment: the amount by which general inflation has eroded shareholders' funds	1,200	
Real holding gains		2,200
Total real gains		10,000

The balance sheet approach was described first, as it is probably the easier to understand in the first instance. Obviously the link between opening and closing balance sheets can be traced to total real gains, which can also be explained using the profit and loss account concept.

Current cost balance sheet

The two main differences between a current cost balance sheet and a historical cost balance sheet are as follows:

(*a*) assets are shown at value to the business on the balance sheet date, rather than at any figure based on historical cost or at any previous revaluation;

(*b*) obviously the balance sheet would not balance if asset values were altered without an amendment somewhere else. A current cost reserve account is opened, additions to historical cost account values are debited to each asset account, whilst a credit will be made in the current cost reserve account. Entries are also made here to complete the double entry in respect of the four adjustments in the current cost profit and loss account. As a result, all double entry adjustments are made in this account and so the balance sheet will now balance.

Part III: objectives of financial statements

Earlier in this chapter we pointed out that a recent development in accounting theory had been towards identifying the users of accounts, and then finding out the type of information they require. Both *The Corporate Report 1975* and the 1975 *Sandilands Report* were directed in this fashion.

Users of accounts

The main users of published accounts of large companies are now identified with the main reasons they require the accounts.

(*a*) **Shareholders of the company**, both existing and potential, will want to know how effectively the directors are performing their stewardship function. They will use the accounts as a base for decisions to dispose of some or all of their shares, or to buy some.

(*b*) **The loan-creditor group.** This consists of existing and potential debenture and loan stock holders, and providers of short-term secured funds. They will want to ensure that interest payments will be made promptly and capital repayments will be made as agreed. Debenture and loan stock holders, whether redeemable or irredeemable, will also want to be able to assess how easily they may dispose of their debentures or loan stocks, should they so wish.

(*c*) **Employee groups**, including existing, potential and past employees. These can include trade unions whose members are employees. Past employees will be mainly concerned with ensuring that any pensions, etc, paid by the company are maintained.

Present employees will be interested in ensuring that the company is able to keep on operating, so maintaining their jobs and paying them acceptable wages, and that any pension contributions are maintained. In addition, they may want to ensure that the company is being fair to them, so that they get a reasonable share of the profits accruing to the firm from their efforts. Trade unions will be upholding the interests of their members, and will possibly use the accounts in wage and pension negotiations. Potential employees will be interested in assessing whether or not it would be worth seeking employment with the company.

(*d*) **Bankers.** Where the bank has not given a loan or granted an overdraft, there will be no great need to see the accounts. Where money is owed to the banks, they will want to ensure that payments of interest will be made when due, and that the firm will be able to repay the loan or overdraft at the correct time.

(*e*) **The business contact group.** This includes trade creditors and suppliers, who will want to know whether or not they will continue to be paid, and the prospects for a profitable future association. Customers are included, since they will want to know whether or not the company is a secure source of supply. Business rivals in this group will be trying to assess their own position compared with the firm. Potential takeover bidders, or those interested in a merger will want to assess the desirability of any such move.

(*f*) **The analyst/adviser group.** These will need information for their clients or their readers. Financial journalists need information for their readers. Stockbrokers need it to advise investors. Credit agencies want it to be able to advise present and possible suppliers of goods and services to the company as to its creditworthiness.

(*g*) **The Inland Revenue** will need the accounts to assess the tax payable by the company.

(*h*) **Other official agencies.** Various organisations concerned with the supervision of industry and commerce may want the accounts for their purposes.

(*i*) **Management.** In addition to the internally produced management accounts the management is also vitally concerned with any published accounts. It has to consider the effect of such published accounts on the world at large.

(*j*) **The public.** This consists of groups such as ratepayers, taxpayers, political parties, pressure groups and consumers. The needs of these parties will vary accordingly.

Characteristics of useful information

From the various reports which have appeared since 1975 the following characteristics have been noted.

(*a*) **Relevance.** This is regarded as one of the two main qualities. The information supplied should be that which will satisfy the needs of its users.

(*b*) **Reliability.** This is regarded as the other main quality. Obviously, if such information is also subject to an independent check, such as that of the auditor, this will considerably enhance the reliance people can place on the information.

(*c*) **Objectivity.** Information which is free from bias will increase the reliance people place on it. It is, therefore, essential that the information is prepared as objectively as possible. Management may often tend to give a better picture of its own performance that is warranted, and is therefore subjective. It is the auditor's task to counter this view, and to ensure objectivity in the accounts.

(*d*) **Ability to be understood.** Information is not much use to a recipient if it is presented in such a manner that no one can understand it. This is not necessarily the same as simplicity.

(*e*) **Comparability.** Recipients of accounts will want to compare them both with previous accounts of that company and with the results of other companies; without comparability the accounts would be of little use.

(*f*) **Realism.** This can be largely covered by the fact that accounts should show a 'true and fair' view. It has also been contended that accounts should not give a sense of absolute precision when such precision cannot exist.

(*g*) **Consistency.** This is one of the basic concepts, but it is not to be followed slavishly if new and improved accounting techniques indicate a change in methods.

(*h*) **Timeliness.** Up-to-date information is of more use to recipients than outdated news.

(*i*) **Economy of presentation.** Too much detail can obscure the important factors in accounts and cause difficulties in understanding them.

(*j*) **Completeness.** A rounded picture of the company's activities is needed.

Problems of information production in accounting

You have seen that a company's profit and loss account and balance sheet produced for general publication is a multi-purpose document. The present state of the art of accounting is such that we have not yet arrived at producing specific financial reports for each group of users, tailored to their special needs.

At times, companies do produce special reports for certain groups of users. A bank, for instance, will almost certainly want to see a forecast of future cash flows before granting a loan or overdraft. The Inland Revenue will often require various analyses in order to agree the tax position. Some companies produce special reports for the use of their employees. In total, such extra reports are a very small part of the reports which could be issued.

Of course, producing reports is not costless. To produce special reports, exactly tailored to every possible group of users, would be extremely costly and time-consuming. It is hardly likely that any existing company would wish to do so. There is, however, no doubt that this is the way things are moving and will continue to move.

For the present, however, most companies produce one set of accounts for all the possible users, with the exception that management will have produced its own management accounts for its own internal purposes. Obviously such a multi-purpose document cannot satisfy all the users. In fact, it will almost certainly not fully satisfy the needs of any one user group – save that it must satisfy the legal requirements of the Companies Act.

Published accounts are, therefore, a compromise between the requirements of users and the maintenance of accounting concepts, subject to the overriding scrutiny of the auditor. Judgment forms so much a part of presenting information, that it can be said that if it were possible to have two large companies with identical share capitals, numbers of employees, fixed assets, turnover, costs, etc, the published accounts of the two companies would not be identical. Just a few straightforward items will suffice to show why there would be differences. Depreciation methods and policies may vary, as may stock valuation assessments, bad debt provisions, figures for revaluation of properties, and so on. There will probably be rather more subtle distinctions, many of which you will come across in the later stages of your studies.

Appendix I
Review questions: the best approach

At the ends of chapters we have set review questions for you to attempt. If you simply read the text without attempting the questions then we can tell you now that you will not pass your examinations. You should first of all attempt the question, and then check it fully against the answers at the back of the book.

What you should not do is perform a 'ticking' exercise. By this we mean that you should not simply compare the question with the answer and tick off the bits of the answer which compare with the question. No one ever learned to do accounting properly that way. It is tempting to save time in so doing, but believe us you will regret it eventually. We have deliberately had the answers printed using a different page layout to try to stop you indulging in a 'ticking' exercise.

Need for practice

You should also try to find the time to answer as many exercises as possible. Our reasons for saying this are as follows:

(*a*) Even though you may think you understand the text, when you come to answer the questions you may often find your understanding incomplete. The true test of understanding is whether or not you can tackle the questions competently.

(*b*) It is often said that practice makes perfect, a sentiment we don't fully agree with. There is enough sense in it, however, in that if you don't do quite a lot of accounting questions you will almost certainly not become good at accounting.

(*c*) You simply have got to get up to a good speed in answering questions: you will always fail accounting examinations if you are a very slow worker.

The history of accountancy examinations so far has always been that a ridiculously large amount of work has been expected from a student during a short time. However, examining boards maintain that the examination could be completed in the time by an adequately prepared student. You can take it for granted that *adequately prepared students* are those who not only have the knowledge, but have also been trained to work quickly and at the same time maintain accuracy and neatness.

(*d*) Speed itself is not enough; you also have to be neat and tidy, and follow all the proper practices and procedures while working at speed. Fast but really scruffy work can also mean failing the exam. Why is this so? At this level the examiner is very much concerned with your practical ability in the subject. Accounting is a practical subject, and your practical competence is about to be tested. The examiner will therefore expect the answers to be neat and well set out. Untidy work with figures spread over the sheet in a haphazard way, badly written figures, and columns of figures in which the vertical columns are not set down in straight lines, will incur the examiner's displeasure.

Need for headings

The next thing is that work should not only be neat and well laid out. Headings should always be given, and any dates needed should be inserted. The test you should apply is to imagine that you are a partner in a firm of professional accountants and you are away on holiday for a few weeks. During that time your assistants have completed all sorts of work including reports, drafting final accounts, various forms of other computations and so on. All of this work is deposited on your desk while you are away. When you return you look at each item in the pile awaiting your attention. Suppose the first item is a Balance Sheet as at 31 December 19-5 in respect of J King, one of your clients. When you looked at it you could see that it was a Balance Sheet, but you didn't know for which client, neither did you know which year it was for. Would you be annoyed with your staff? Of course you would. So therefore in an examination why should the examiner accept as a piece of your work a Balance Sheet answer without either the date or the name of the business or the fact that it is a Balance Sheet written clearly across the top? If proper headings are not given you will lose a lot of marks. Always therefore put in the headings properly; don't wait until your examination to start this correct practice. Similar attention should be paid to sub-totals which need showing, e.g. for Fixed Assets, Current Assets.

We will be looking at examination techniques later on in Appendix II. There is no point in dealing with that important topic at this juncture.

The examiner's attitude

Really, what you should say to yourself is: 'Suppose I was in charge of an office, doing this type of accounting work, what would I say if one of my assistants put on my desk a sheet of paper with accounting entries on it written in the same manner as my own efforts in attempting this examination question?' Just look at some of the work you have done in the past. Would you have told your assistant to go back and do the work again because it is untidy? If you say that about your own work why should the examiner think any differently?

Anyone who works in accounting knows well that untidy work leads to completely unnecessary errors. Therefore the examiner's insistence on clear, tidy, well laid-out work is not an outdated approach; he/she wants to ensure that you are not going to mess up the work of an accounting department. Imagine going to the savings bank and the manager says to you 'We don't know whether you've got £5 in the account or £5,000. You see the work of our clerks is so untidy that we can never sort out exactly how much is in anybody's account'. We would guess that you would not want to put a lot of money into an account at that bank. How would you feel if someone took you to court for not paying a debt of £100 when in fact you owed them nothing? This sort of thing would happen all the time if we simply allowed people to keep untidy accounts. The examiner is there to ensure that the person to whom he/she gives a certificate will be worthy of it, and will not continually mess up the work of any firm at which he/she may work in the future.

We can imagine quite a few of you groaning at all this, and if you do not want to pass the examination please give up reading here. If you do want to pass, and your work is untidy, what can you do about it? Well, the answer is simple enough: start right now to be neat and orderly in your work. Quite a lot of students have said to me over the years 'I may be giving you untidy work now, but when I actually get in the exam room I will then do my work neatly enough'. This is as near impossible as anything can be. You cannot suddenly become able to do accounting work neatly, and certainly not when you are under the stress and strain of an examination. Even the neatest worker may well find in an examination that his/her work may not be of its usual standard as nervousness will cause them to make mistakes. If this is true, then if you are an untidy worker now your work in an examination is likely to be even more untidy. Have we convinced you yet?

The structure of the questions

Finally, the review questions have been written to build up in a structured way to the examination itself. We would like to have avoided unnecessarily complicated questions. They only waste your time, sap your confidence, and generally lead to a lot of students losing their interest in the subject.

On the other hand, we are fully aware that you are going to have to sit an examination eventually. Questions do tend to get more complicated as you work through the book, as and when you should be able to tackle them.

Now tackle the review questions.

Appendix II
Examination techniques

As an author I can change my writing style here into that of the first person singular, as I want to put across to you a message about examinations, and I want you to feel that I am writing this for you as an individual rather than simply as one of the considerable number of people who have read the technical part of the book.

When you think about it, you have spent a lot of hours trying to master such things as double entry, balance sheets, suspense accounts and goodness knows what else. Learning accounting/book-keeping does demand a lot of discipline and practice. Compared with the many hours learning the subject, most students spend very little time actually considering in detail how to tackle the examination. You are probably one of them, and I would like you to take some time away from your revision of the various topics in the syllabus, and instead I want you to think about the examination.

Understanding examiners

Let me start by saying that if you want to understand anything about examinations then you have got to understand examiners, so let us look together at what these peculiar creatures get up to in an examination. The first thing is that when they set an examination they are looking at it on the basis that they want good students to get a pass mark. Obviously anyone who doesn't achieve the pass mark will fail, but the object of the exercise is to find those who will pass rather than to find the failures. This means that if you have done your work properly, and if you are not sitting for an examination well above your intellectual capabilities, then you should manage to get a pass mark. It is important to stress that before I could get down to the details of setting about the task.

There are, however, quite a large number of students who will fail, not because they haven't put in enough hours on their studies, not because they are unintelligent, but simply because they throw away marks unnecessarily by poor examination technique. If you can read the rest of this piece, and then say honestly that you wouldn't have committed at least one of the mistakes that I am going to mention, then you are certainly well outside the ordinary range of students.

Punctuality

Before thinking about the examination paper itself, let us think about how you are going to get to the examination room. If it is at your own college then you have no problems as to how you will get there. On the other hand it may be at external centre. Do you know exactly where the place is? If not, you had better have a trip there if possible. How are you going to get there? If you are going by bus or train do you know which bus or train to catch? Will it be the rush hour when it may well take you much longer than mid-day? Quite a large proportion of students lose their way to the examination room, or else arrive, breathless and flustered, at the very last minute.

They then start off the attempt at the examination in a somewhat nervous state, a recipe for disaster for a lot of students. So plan how you are going to get there and give yourself enough time.

Last minute learning for your examination will be of little use to you. The last few days before the examination should not be spent cramming. You can look at past examination papers and rework some of them. This is totally different from trying to cram new facts into your head. On the way to exam don't read textbooks, try reading the newspaper or something similar.

Time planning

We must now look at the way in which you should tackle the examination paper when the time comes. One of the troubles about book-keeping/accounting examinations is that the student is expected to do a lot of work in a relatively short time. I have personally campaigned against this attitude, but the tradition is of long-standing and I am therefore afraid that you are stuck with it. It will be the same for every other student taking your examination, so it is not unfair as far as any one student is concerned. Working at speed does bring about various disadvantages, and makes the way you tackle the examination of even greater importance than for examinations where the pace is more leisurely.

Time per question

The marks allotted to each question will indicate how long you should take in tackling the question. Most examinations are of 3 hours' duration, i.e. 180 minutes. This means that in a normal examination, with 100 marks in total, a 20-mark question should be allocated 20 per cent of the time, i.e. $20\% \times 180 = 36$ minutes. Similarly, a question worth 30 marks should take up 30 per cent of the time, i.e. $30\% \times 180 = 54$ minutes, and so on.

Do the easiest questions first

Always tackle the easiest question first, then the next easiest question and so on, leave the most difficult question as the last one to be attempted. Why is this good advice? The fact is that most examiners usually set what might be called 'warm up' questions. These are usually fairly short, and not very difficult questions, and the examiner will expect you to tackle these first of all. You may be able to do the easiest question in less than the time allocated. The examiner is trying to be kind to you. He knows that there is a certain amount of nervousness on the part of a student taking an examination, and he wants to give you the chance to calm down by letting you tackle these short, relatively easy questions, first of all, and generally settle down to your work.

Even where all the questions are worth equal marks, you are bound to find some easier than the others. It is impossible for an examiner to set questions which are equally as difficult as each other. So, remember, start with the easiest question. This will give you a feeling of confidence, it is very desirable to start off in this way.

Do not expect that these 'warm up' questions will be numbered 1 and 2 on your examination paper. Most accounting examinations start off with a rather long question, worth quite a lot of marks, as question number 1 on the paper. Over the years I have advised students not to tackle these questions first. A lot of students are fascinated by the fact that such a question is number 1, that it is worth a lot of marks, and their thinking runs: 'If I do this question first, and make a good job of it, then I am well on the way to passing the examination.' I do not deny that a speedy and successful attempt at such a question would probably lead to a pass. The trouble is that this doesn't usually happen, and many students have told me afterwards that their failure could be put down to simply ignoring this advice. What happens very often, is that the student starts off on such a question, things don't go very well, a few mistakes are made, the student then looks at the clock and see that he/she is not 'beating the clock' in terms of possible marks, and then panic descends on him/her. Leaving that question very hastily the student then proceeds to the next question, which normally might have been well attempted, but because of the state of mind a mess is made of that one as well, and so you may fail an examination which you had every right to think you could pass.

Attempt every question

The last point concerning time allocation which I want to get through to you is that you should attempt each and every question. On each question the first few marks are the easiest to get. For instance, on an essay question it is reasonably easy to get, say, the first 5 marks in a 20 mark question. Managing to produce a perfect answer to get the last 5 marks, from 15 to 20, is extremely difficult. This applies also to computational questions.

This means that, in an examination of, say, 5 questions with 20 marks possible for each question, there is not much point in tackling 3 questions only and trying to make good job of them. The total possible marks would be 60 marks, and if you had not achieved full marks for each question, in itself extremely unlikely, you could easily fall below the pass mark of, say, 50 marks. It is better to leave questions unfinished when your allotted time, calculated as shown earlier, has expired, and to then go on immediately to the other questions. It is so easy, especially in an accounting examination, to find that one has exceeded the time allowed for a question by a considerable margin. So, although you may find it difficult to persuade yourself to do so, move on the next question when your time for a question has expired.

Computations

One golden rule which should always be observed is 'show all of your workings'. Suppose for instance you have been asked to work out the Cost of Goods Sold, not simply as part of a Trading Account but for some other reason. On a scrap of paper you work out the answers below.

	£
Opening Stock	4,000
add Purchases	11,500
	15,500
less Closing Stock	3,800
	12,700

You put down the answer as £12,700. The scrap of paper with your workings on it is then crumpled up by you and thrown in the wastepaper basket as you leave the room. You may have noticed in reading this that in fact the answer should have been 11,700 and not 12,700, as the arithmetic was incorrect. The examiner may well have allocated say, 4 marks for this bit of the question. What will he do when he simply sees your answer as £12,700? Will he say: 'I should imagine that the candidate mis-added to the extent of £1,000, and as I am not unduly penalising for arithmetic, I will give the candidate 3½ marks.' I'm afraid the examiner cannot do this; the candidate has got the answer wrong, there is no supporting evidence, and so the examiner gives marks as nil.

If you had only attached the workings to your answer, then I have no doubt that you would have got 3½ marks at least.

Do balance sheets have to balance?

Many students over the years, have asked me 'What happens if my balance sheet doesn't balance?'. The answer is to leave the question, not to look for error(s) at that juncture, and to tackle the next question. One of the reasons for this is contained in the next paragraph which is concerned with making certain you attempt every question. You might spend 20 minutes to find the error, which might save you 1 mark. In that time you might have gained, say, 10 marks, if instead you had tackled the next question, for which you would not have had time if you had wasted it by searching for the error(s). That assumes that you actually find the error(s). Suppose you don't, you have spent 20 minutes looking for it, have not found it, so how do you feel now? The answer is, of course, quite terrible. You may make an even bigger mess of the rest of the paper than you would have done if you had simply ignored the fact that the balance sheet did not balance. In any case, it is quite possible to get, say, 29 marks out of 30 even though the balance sheet does not balance. The error may be a very minor case for which the examiner deducts one mark only. Of course, if you have finished all of the questions, then by all means spend the rest of your time tracing the error and correcting it. Be certain, however, that your corrections are carried out neatly, as untidy crossings-out can result in the loss of marks. So, sometimes, an error found can get back one mark, which is then lost again because the corrections make untidy mess of your paper, and examiners usually do deduct marks, quite rightly so, for untidy work.

Essay questions

In the past there were not many essay questions in accounting examinations at this level. This is going to change in the future, and you therefore need to know the approach to use in answering such questions.

(i) Typical questions

Before I discuss these I want you to look at two questions set recently at this stage. Having done that visualise carefully what you would write in answer to them. Here they are:

(a) You are employed as a book-keeper by G Jones, a trader. State briefly what use you would make of the following documents in relation to your book-keeping records.

(i) A bank statement.
(ii) A credit note received to correct an overcharge on an invoice.
(iii) A paying-in slip
(iv) Petty cash voucher.

(b) Explain the term 'depreciation'. Name and describe briefly two methods of providing for depreciation of fixed assets.

Now we can test whether or not you would have made a reasonably good attempt at the questions. With question (a) a lot of students would have written down what a bank statement is, what a paying-in slip is, what a petty cash voucher is and so on. Marks gained by you for an answer like that would be . . . nil. Why is this? Well you simply have not read the question properly. The question asked what use you would make of the documents, and not instead to describe what documents were. The bank statement would be used to check against the bank column in the cash book or cash records to see that the bank's entries and your own are in accordance with one another, with a bank reconciliation statement being drawn up to reconcile the two sets of records. The petty cash voucher would be used as a basis for entering up the payments columns in the petty cash book. Therefore the *use* of the items was asked for, not the *descriptions* of the items.

Let us see if you have done better on question (*b*). Would you have written down how to calculate two methods of depreciation, probably the reducing balance method and the straight-line method? But have you remembered that the question also asked you to *explain the term depreciation*? In other words, what is depreciation generally. A fair number of students will have omitted that part of the question. My own guess is that far more students would have made a rather poor attempt at question (*a*) rather than question (*b*).

(ii) Underline the key words

I have already illustrated that a large percentage of students fail to answer the question as set, instead answer the question they imagine it to be. Too many students write down everything they know about a topic, rather than what the examiner has asked for.

To remedy this defect, *underline the key words* in a question. This brings out the meaning so that it is difficult to misunderstand the question. For instance, let us look at the following question:

'Discuss the usefulness of departmental accounts to a business.'

Many students will write down all they know about departmental accounts, how to draw them up, how to appportion overheads between departments, how to keep columnar sales purchases journals to find the information etc.

Number of marks gained . . . nil.

Now underline the key words. They will be

<u>Discuss</u>   <u>usefulness</u>   <u>departmental accounts</u>

The question is now seen to be concerned not with *describing* departmental accounts, but instead discussing the *usefulness* of departmental accounts.

Lastly, if the question says 'Draft a report on . . . ' then the answer should be in the firm of a *report*, if it says 'List the . . .' then the answer should consist of a *list*. Similarly 'Discuss . . .' asks for a *discussion*. 'Describe . . . wants you to *describe* something, and so on.

You should therefore ensure that you are going to give the examiner:

(*a*) What he is asking for   plus   (*b*) In the way that he wants it.

If you do not comply with (*a*) you may lose all the marks. If you manage to fulfil (*a*) but do not satisfy the examiner on (*b*) you will still lose a lot of marks.

Summary

Remember:

(*a*) Tackle the easiest questions first.

(*b*) Finish off answering each question when your time allocation for the question is up.

(*c*) Hand in all your workings.

(*d*) Do remember to be neat, also include all proper headings, dates, sub-totals, etc. A lot of marks can be lost here.

(*e*) Only answer as many questions as you are asked to tackle by the examiner. Extra answers will not be marked.

(*f*) Underline the *key* words in each question to ensure that you answer the question set, and not the question you wrongly take it to be.

Best of luck with your examination. I hope you get the rewards you deserve!

Multiple-choice questions

Each multiple-choice question has four suggested answers letter (A), (B), (C) or (D). You should read each question and then decide which choice is best, either (A) or (B) or (C) or (D). On a separate piece of paper you should then write down your choice. Unless the textbook you are reading belongs to you, you should not make a mark against your choice in the textbook.

Answers to multiple choice questions are given on page 558 of this book.

Set No 1: 20 questions

MC1 Which of the following statements is incorrect?
(A)   Assets — Capital = Liabilities
(B)   Liabilities + Capital = Assets
(C)   Liabilites + Assets = Capital
(D)   Assets — Liabilities = Capital.

MC2 Which of the following is not an asset?
(A)   Buildings
(B)   Cash balance
(C)   Debtors
(D)   Loan from K Harris.

MC3 Which of the following is a liability?
(A)   Machinery
(B)   Creditors for goods
(C)   Motor Vehicles
(D)   Cash at Bank.

MC4 Which of the following is incorrect?

	Assets	Liabilities	Capital
	£	£	£
(A)	7,850	1,250	6,600
(B)	8,200	2,800	5,400
(C)	9,550	1,150	8,200
(D)	6,540	1,120	5,420

MC5 Which of the following statements is correct?

		Effect upon	
		Assets	*Liabilities*
(A)	We paid a creditor by cheque	−Bank	−Creditors
(B)	A debtor paid us £90 in cash	+Cash	+Debtors
(C)	J Hall lends us £500 by cheque	+Bank	−Loan from Hall
(D)	Bought goods on credit	+Stock	+Capital

MC6 Which of the following are correct?

	Accounts	*To record*	*Entry in the account*
(i)	Assets	an increase	Debit
		a decrease	Credit
(ii)	Capital	an increase	Debit
		a decrease	Credit
(iii)	Liabilities	an increase	Credit
		a decrease	Debit

(A) (i) and (ii)
(B) (ii) and (iii)
(C) (i) and (iii)
(D) None of them.

MC7 Which of the following are correct?

		Account to be debited	*Account to be credited*
(i)	Bought office furniture for cash	Office furniture	Cash
(ii)	A debtor, P Sangster, pays us by cheque	Bank	P Sangster
(iii)	Introduced capital by cheque	Capital	Bank
(iv)	Paid a creditor, B Lee, by cash	B Lee	Cash

(A) (i), (ii) and (iii) only
(B) (ii), (iii) and (iv) only
(C) (i), (ii) and (iv) only
(D) (i) and (iv) only.

MC8 Which of the following are incorrect?

		Account to be debited	*Account to be credited*
(i)	Sold motor van for cash	Cash	Motor van
(ii)	Returned some of Office Equipment to Suppliers Ltd	Office Equipment	Suppliers Ltd
(iii)	Repaid part of Loan from C Charles by cheque	Loan from C Charles	Bank
(iv)	Bought Machinery on credit from Betterways Ltd	Betterways Ltd	Machinery

(A) (ii) and (iv) only
(B) (iii) and (iv) only
(C) (ii) and (iii) only
(D) (i) and (iii) only.

MC9 Which of the following best describes the meaning of 'Purchases'?
(A) Items bought
(B) Goods bought on credit
(C) Goods bought for resale
(D) Goods paid for.

MC10 Which of the following should not be called 'Sales'?
(A)   Office Fixtures sold
(B)   Goods sold on credit
(C)   Goods sold for cash
(D)   Sale of item previously included in 'Purchases'.

MC11 Of the following, which are correct?

	Account to be debited	Account to be credited
(i) Goods sold on credit to R Williams	R Williams	Sales
(ii) S Johnson returns goods to us	Returns Inwards	S Johnson
(iii) Goods bought for cash	Cash	Purchases
(iv) We returned goods to A Henry	A Henry	Returns Inwards

(A)   (i) and (iii) only
(B)   (i) and (ii) only
(C)   (ii) and (iv) only
(D)   (iii) and (iv) only.

MC12 Which of the following are incorrect?

	Account to be debited	Account to be credited
(i) Goods sold for cash	Cash	Sales
(ii) Goods bought on credit from T Carter	Purchases	T Carter
(iii) Goods returned by us to C Barry	C Barry	Returns Outwards
(iv) Motor Van bought for cash	Purchases	Cash

(A)   (i) and (iii) only
(B)   (iii) only
(C)   (ii) and (iv) only
(D)   (iv) only.

MC13 Given the following, what is the amount of Capital? Assets: Premises £20,000, Stock £8,500, Cash £100. Liabilities: Creditors £3,000, Loan from A. Adams £4,000
(A)   £21,100
(B)   £21,600
(C)   £32,400
(D)   None of the above.

MC14 Which of the following is correct?
(A)   Profit does not alter Capital
(B)   Profit reduces Capital
(C)   Capital can only come from profit
(D)   Profit increases Capital

MC15 Which of the following are correct?

	Account to be debited	Account to be credited
(i) Received commission by cheque	Bank	Commission Received
(ii) Paid rates by cash	Rates	Cash
(iii) Paid motor expenses by cheque	Motor Expenses	Bank
(iv) Received refund of insurance by cheque	Insurance	Bank

(A)   (i) and (ii) only
(B)   (i), (ii) and (iii) only
(C)   (ii), (iii) and (iv) only
(D)   (i), (ii) and (iv) only.

MC16 Of the following, which are incorrect?

		Account to be debited	Account to be credited
(i)	Sold Motor Van for Cash	Cash	Sales
(ii)	Bought stationery by cheque	Stationery	Bank
(iii)	Took cash out of business for private use	Cash	Drawings
(iv)	Paid General Expenses by cheque	General Expenses	Bank

(A) (ii) and (iv) only
(B) (i) and (ii) only
(C) (i) and (iii) only
(D) (ii) and (iii) only.

MC17 What is the balance on the following account on 31 May 19-5?

C De Freitas

19-5		£	19-5		£
May 1	Sales	205	May 17	Cash	300
,, 14	Sales	360	,, 28	Returns	50
,, 30	Sales	180			

(A) A credit balance of £395
(B) A debit balance of £380
(C) A debit balance of £395
(D) There is a nil balance on the account.

MC18 What would have been the balance on the account of C De Freitas in MC17 on 19 May 19-5?
(A) A debit balance of £265
(B) A credit balance of £95
(C) A credit balance of £445
(D) A credit balance of £265.

MC19 Which of the following best describes a Trial Balance?
(A) Shows the financial position of a business
(B) It is a special account
(C) Shows all the entries in the books
(D) It is a list of balances on the books.

MC20 It is true that the trial balance totals should agree?
(A) No, there are sometimes good reasons why they differ
(B) Yes, except where the trial balance is extracted at the year end
(C) Yes, always
(D) No, because it is not a balance sheet.

Set No 2: 20 questions

Answers on page 558

MC21 Gross Profit is:
(A) Excess of sales over cost of goods sold
(B) Sales less Purchases
(C) Cost of Goods Sold + Opening Stock
(D) Net Profit less expenses of the period.

MC22 Net Profit is calculated in the
(A) Trading Account
(B) Profit and Loss Account
(C) Trial Balance
(D) Balance Sheet.

MC23 To find the value of closing stock at the end of a period we
(A) Do this by stocktaking
(B) Look in the stock account
(C) Deduct opening stock from cost of goods sold
(D) Deduct cost of goods sold from sales.

MC24 The credit entry for Net Profit is on the credit side of
(A) The Trading Account
(B) The Profit and Loss Account
(C) The Drawings Account
(D) The Capital Account.

MC25 Which is the best definition of a balance sheet?
(A) An account proving the books balance
(B) A record of closing entries
(C) A listing of balances
(D) A statement of assets.

MC26 The descending order in which current assets should be shown in the balance sheet are:
(A) Stock, Debtors, Bank, Cash
(B) Cash, Bank, Debtors, Stock
(C) Debtors, Stock, Bank, Cash
(D) Stock, Debtors, Cash, Bank.

MC27 Which is the best description of Fixed Assets?
(A) Are bought to be used in the business
(B) Are items which will not wear out quickly
(C) Are expensive items bought for the business
(D) Are of long-life and are not bought specifically for resale.

MC28 Carriage Inwards is charged to the Trading Account because:
(A) It is an expense connected with buying goods
(B) It should not go in the Balance Sheet
(C) It is not part of motor expenses
(D) Carriage outwards goes in the Profit and Loss Account.

MC29 Given figures showing: Sales £8,200; Opening Stock £1,300; Closing Stock £900; Purchases £6,400; Carriage Inwards £200, the cost of goods sold figure is
(A) £6,800
(B) £6,200
(C) £7,000
(D) Another figure.

MC30 The costs of putting goods into a saleable condition should be charged to:
(A) Trading Account
(B) Profit and Loss Account
(C) Balance Sheet
(D) None of these.

MC31 Suppliers' personal accounts are found in
(A)   Nominal Ledger
(B)   General Ledger
(C)   Purchases Ledger
(D)   Sales Ledger.

MC32 The Sales Journal is best described as
(A)   Part of the double entry system
(B)   Containing customers' accounts
(C)   Containing real accounts
(D)   A list of credit sales.

MC33 Of the following which are Personal Accounts?
(i)   Buildings
(ii)   Wages
(iii)   Debtors
(iv)   Creditors.
(A)   (i) and (iv) only
(B)   (ii) and (iii) only
(C)   (iii) and (iv) only
(D)   (ii) and (iv) only.

MC34 When Lee makes out a cheque for £50 amd sends it to Young, then Lee is known as
(A)   The payee
(B)   The banker
(C)   The drawer
(D)   The creditor.

MC35 If you want to make sure that your money will be safe if cheques sent are lost in the post, you should
(A)   Not use the Postal Service in future
(B)   Always pay by cash
(C)   Always take the money in person
(D)   Cross your cheques 'Account Payee only, Not Negotiable'.

MC36 When banking money in to your current account you should always use
(A)   A cheque book
(B)   A paying-in slip
(C)   A cash book
(D)   A general ledger.

MC37 A debit balance of £100 in a cash account shows that:
(A)   There was £100 cash in hand
(B)   Cash has been overspent by £100
(C)   £100 was the total of cash paid out
(D)   The total of cash received was less than £100.

MC38 £50 cash taken from the cash till and banked is entered:
(A)   Debit cash column £50: Credit bank column £50
(B)   Debit bank column £50: Credit cash column £50
(C)   Debit cash column £50: Credit cash column £50
(D)   Debit bank colunm £50: Credit bank column £50.

MC39 A credit balance of £200 on the cash columns of the cash book would mean
(A)   We have spent £200 more than we have received
(B)   We have £200 cash in hand
(C)   The book-keeper has made a mistake
(D)   Someone has stolen £200 cash.

MC40 'Posting' the transactions in book-keeping means
(A)   Making the first entry of a double-entry transaction
(B)   Entering items in a cash book
(C)   Making the second entry of a double-entry transaction
(D)   Something other than the above.

Set No 3: 20 questions

Answers on page 558

MC41 A cash discount is best described as a reduction in the sum to be paid
(A)   If payment is made within a previously agreed period
(B)   If payment is made by cash, not cheque
(C)   If payment is made either by cash or cheque
(D)   If purchases are made for cash, not on credit.

MC42 Discounts Received are
(A)   Deducted when we receive cash
(B)   Given by us when we sell goods on credit
(C)   Deducted by us when we pay our accounts
(D)   None of these.

MC43 The total of the Discounts Allowed column in the Cash Book is posted to
(A)   the debit of the Discount Allowed Account
(B)   the debit of the Discounts Received Account
(C)   the credit of the Discounts Allowed Account
(D)   the credit of the Discounts Received Account.

MC44 Sales Invoices are first entered in
(A)   The Cash Book
(B)   The Purchases Journal
(C)   The Sales Account
(D)   The Sales Journal.

MC45 The total of the Sales Journal is entered on
(A)   The credit side of the Sales Account in the General Ledger
(B)   The credit side of the General Account in the Sales Ledger
(C)   The debit side of the Sales Account in the General Ledger
(D)   The debit side of the Sales Day Book.

MC46 Given a purchases invoice showing 5 items of £80, each less trade discount of 25 per cent and cash discount of 5 per cent, if paid within the credit period, your cheque would be made out for
(A)   £285
(B)   £280
(C)   £260
(D)   None of these.

MC47 An alternative name for a Sales Journal is
(A)   Sales Invoice
(B)   Sales Day Book
(C)   Daily Sales
(D)   Sales Ledger.

MC48 Entered in the Purchases Journal are
(A)   Payments to Suppliers
(B)   Trade Discounts
(C)   Purchases Invoices
(D)   Discounts Received.

494

MC49 The total of the Purchases Journal is transferred to the
(A) Credit side of the Purchases Account
(B) Debit side of the Purchases Day Book
(C) Credit side of the Purchases Book
(D) Debit side of the Purchases Account.

MC50 Credit notes issued by us will be entered in our
(A) Sales Account
(B) Returns Inwards Account
(C) Returns Inwards Journal
(D) Returns Outwards Journal.

MC51 The total of the Returns Outwards Journal is transferred to
(A) The credit side of the Returns Outwards Account
(B) The debit side of the Returns Outwards Account
(C) The credit side of the Returns Outwards Book
(D) The debit side of the Purchases Returns Book.

MC52 We originally sold 25 items at £12 each, less 33⅓ per cent trade discount. Our customer now returns 4 of them to us. What is the amount of credit note to be issued?
(A) £48
(B) £36
(C) £30
(D) £32.

MC53 Depreciation is
(A) The amount spent to buy a fixed asset
(B) The salvage value of a fixed asset
(C) The part of the cost of the fixed asset consumed during its period of use by the firm
(D) The amount of money spent in replacing assets.

MC54 A firm bought a machine for £3,200. It is to be depreciated at a rate of 25 per cent using the Reducing Balance Method. What would be the remaining book value after 2 years?
(A) £1,600
(B) £2,400
(C) £1,800
(D) Some other figure.

MC55 A firm bought a machine for £16,000. It is expected to be used for 5 years then sold for £1,000. What is the annual amount of depreciation if the straight line method is used?
(A) £3,200
(B) £3,100
(C) £3,750
(D) £3,000.

MC56 At the balance sheet date the balance on the Provision for Depreciation Account is
(A) transferred to Depreciation Account
(B) transferred to Profit and Loss Account
(C) simply deducted from the asset in the Balance Sheet
(D) transferred to the Asset Account.

MC57 In the trial balance the balance on the Provision for Depreciation Account is
(A) shown as a credit item
(B) not shown, as it is part of depreciation
(C) shown as a debit item
(D) . something shown as a credit, sometimes as a debit.

MC58 If a provision for depreciation account is in use then the entries for the year's depreciation would be
(A)   credit Provision for Depreciation account, debit Profit and Loss Account
(B)   debit Asset Account, credit Profit and Loss Account
(C)   credit Asset Account, debit Provision for Depreciation Account
(D)   credit Profit and Loss Account, debit Provision for Depreciation Account.

MC59 When the final accounts are prepared the Bad Debts Account is closed by a transfer to the
(A)   Balance Sheet
(B)   Profit and Loss Account
(C)   Trading Account
(D)   Provision for Bad Debts Account.

MC60 A Provision for Bad Debts is created
(A)   When debtors become bankrupt
(B)   When debtors cease to be in business
(C)   To provide for possible bad debts
(D)   To write off bad debts.

Set No 4: 20 questions

Answers on page 558

MC61 Working Capital is a term meaning
(A)   The amount of capital invested by the proprietor
(B)   The excess of the current assets over the current liabilities
(C)   The capital less drawings
(D)   The total of Fixed Assets + Current Assets.

MC62 A credit balance brought down on a Rent Account means
(A)   We owe that rent at that date
(B)   We have paid that rent in advance at that date
(C)   We have paid too much rent
(D)   We have paid too little in rent.

MC63 A debit balance brought down on a Packing Materials Account means
(A)   We owe for packing materials
(B)   We are owed for packing materials
(C)   We have lost money on packing materials
(D)   We have a stock of packing materials unused.

MC64 If we take goods for own use we should
(A)   Debit Drawings Account: Credit Purchases Account
(B)   Debit Purchases Account: Credit Drawings Account
(C)   Debit Drawings Account: Credit Stock Account
(D)   Debit Sales Account: Credit Stock Account.

MC65 Capital Expenditure is
(A)   The extra capital paid in by the proprietor
(B)   The costs of running the business on a day-to-day basis
(C)   Money spent on buying fixed assets or adding value to them
(D)   Money spent on selling fixed assets.

MC66 In the business of C Sangster, who owns a clothing store, which of the following are Capital Expenditure?
(i)   Shop fixtures bought
(ii)   Wages of assistants
(iii) New motor van bought
(iv)   Petrol for motor van
(A)   (i) and (iii)
(B)   (i) and (ii)
(C)   (ii) and (iii)
(D)   (ii) and (iv).

MC67 If £500 was shown added to Purchases instead of being added to a fixed asset
(A)   Net Profit only would be understated
(B)   Net Profit only would be overstated
(C)   It would not affect net profit
(D)   Both Gross and Net Profits would be understated.

MC68 A cheque paid by you, but not yet passed through the banking system is
(A)   A standing order
(B)   A dishonoured cheque
(C)   A credit transfer
(D)   An unpresented cheque.

MC69 A Bank Reconciliation Statement is a statement
(A)   Sent by the bank when the account is overdrawn
(B)   Drawn up by us to verify our cash book balance with the bank statement balance
(C)   Drawn up by the bank to verify the cash book
(D)   Sent by the bank when we have made an error.

MC70 Which of the following are not true? A Bank Reconciliation Statement is
(i)   Part of the double entry system
(ii)   Not part of the double entry system
(iii) Sent by the firm to the bank
(iv)   Posted to the ledger accounts
(A)   (i), (iii) and (iv)
(B)   (i) and (ii)
(C)   (i), (ii) and (iv)
(D)   (ii), (iii) and (iv)

MC71 Which of the following should be entered in the Journal?
(i)   Payment for cash purchases
(ii)   Fixtures bought on credit
(iii) Credit sale of goods
(iv)   Sale of surplus machinery.
(A)   (i) and (iv)
(B)   (ii) and (iii)
(C)   (iii) and (iv)
(D)   (ii) and (iv)

MC72 The Journal is
(A)   Part of the double-entry system
(B)   A supplement to the Cash Book
(C)   Not part of the double entry system
(D)   Used when other journals have been mislaid.

MC73 Given a desired cash float of £200, if £146 is spent in the period, how much will be reimbursed at the end of the period?

(A) £200

(B) £54

(C) £254

(D) £146

MC74 When a petty cash book is kept there will be

(A) More entries made in the general ledger

(B) Fewer entries made in the general ledger

(C) The same number of entries in the general ledger

(D) No entries made at all in the general ledger for items paid by petty cash.

MC75 Which of the following do *not* affect trial balance agreement?

(i) Sales £105 to A Henry entered in P Henry's account

(ii) Cheque payment of £134 for Motor Expenses entered only in Cash Book

(iii) Purchases £440 from C Browne entered in both accounts as £404

(iv) Wages account added up incorrectly, being totalled £10 too much.

(A) (i) and (iv)

(B) (i) and (iii)

(C) (ii) and (iii)

(D) (iii) and (iv).

MC76 Which of the following are *not* errors of principle?

(i) Motor expenses entered in Motor Vehicles account

(ii) Purchases of machinery entered in Purchases account

(iii) Sale of £250 to C Phillips completely omitted from books

(iv) Sale to A Henriques entered in A Henry's account.

(A) (ii) and (iii)

(B) (i) and (ii)

(C) (iii) and (iv)

(D) (i) and (iv).

MC77 Errors are corrected via The Journal because

(A) It saves the book-keeper's time

(B) It saves entering them in the ledger

(C) It is much easier to do

(D) It provides a good record explaining the double-entry entries.

MC78 Which of these errors would be disclosed by the Trial Balance?

(A) Cheque £95 from C Smith entered in Smith's account as £59

(B) Selling expenses had been debited to Sales Account

(C) Credit sales of £300 entered in double entry accounts as £30

(D) A purchase of £250 was omitted entirely from the books.

MC79 If a trial balance totals do *not* agree, the difference must be entered in

(A) The Profit and Loss Account

(B) A Suspense Account

(C) A Nominal Account

(D) The Capital Account.

MC80 What should happen if the balance on Suspense Account is of a material amount?

(A) Should be written off to the balance sheet

(B) Carry forward the balance to the next period

(C) Find the error(s) before publishing the final accounts

(D) Write it off to Profit and Loss Account.

Set No 5: 20 questions

Answers on page 558

MC81 Given opening debtors of £11,500, Sales £48,000 and receipts from debtors £45,000, the closing debtors should total
(A) £8,500
(B) £14,500
(C) £83,500
(D) £18,500.

MC82 In a Sales ledger Control Account the Bad Debts written off should be shown in the account
(A) As a debit
(B) As a credit
(C) Both as a debit and as a credit
(D) As a balance carried down.

MC83 If cost price is £90 and selling price is £120, then
(i) Mark-up is 25 per cent
(ii) Margin is 33⅓ per cent
(iii) Margin is 25 per cent
(iv) Mark-up is 33⅓ per cent
(A) (i) and (ii)
(B) (i) and (iii)
(C) (iii) and (iv)
(D) (ii) and (iv).

MC84 Given cost of goods sold £16,000 and margin of 20 per cent, then sales figure is
(A) £20,160
(B) £13,600
(C) £21,000
(D) None of these.

MC85 If opening stock is £3,000, closing stock £5,000, Sales £40,000 and margin 20 per cent, then stockturn is
(A) 8 times
(B) 7½ times
(C) 5 times
(D) 6 times.

MC86 If creditors at 1 January 19-3 were £2,500 creditors at 31 December 19-3 £4,200 and payments to creditors £32,000, then purchases for 19-3 are
(A) £30,300
(B) £33,700
(C) £31,600
(D) None of these.

MC87 Given opening capital of £16,500, closing capital as £11,350 and drawings were £3,300, then
(A) Loss for the year was £1,850
(B) Profit for the year was £1,850
(C) Loss for the year was £8,450
(D) Profit for the year was £8,450.

MC88 A Receipts and Payments Accounts is one

(A) Which is accompanied by a balance sheet
(B) In which the profit is calculated
(C) In which the opening and closing cash balances are shown
(D) In which the surplus of income over expenditure is calculated.

MC89 Prime cost includes

(i) Direct Labour
(ii) Factory overhead expenses
(iii) Direct Labour
(iv) Direct Expenses.
(A) (i), (ii) and (iii)
(B) (ii), (iii) and (iv)
(C) (i), (iii) and (iv)
(D) (i), (ii) and (iv).

MC90 Which of the following should be charged in the Profit and Loss Account?

(A) Office Rent
(B) Work in Progress
(C) Direct Materials
(D) Carriage on Raw Materials.

MC91 In the Manufacturing Account is calculated

(A) The Production Costs paid in the year
(B) The Total Cost of Goods Produced
(C) The Production Cost of Goods Completed in the period
(D) The Gross Profit on goods sold.

MC92 The best method of departmental accounts is

(A) To allocate expenses in proportion to sales
(B) To charge against each department its controllable costs
(C) To charge all each expenses between the departments.

MC93 Where there is no partnership agreement then profits and losses

(A) Must be shared in same proportion as capitals
(B) Must be shared equally
(C) Must be shared equally after adjusting for interest on capital
(D) None of these.

MC94 If it is required to maintain fixed capitals then the partners' shares of profits must be

(A) Debited to Capital Accounts
(B) Credited to Capital Accounts
(C) Debited to partners' Current Accounts
(D) Credited to partners' Current Accounts.

MC95 You are to buy an existing business which has assets valued at buildings £50,000, motor vehicles £15,000, fixtures £5,000 and stock £40,000. You are to pay £140,000 for the business. This means that

(A) You are paying £40,000 for Goodwill
(B) Buildings are costing you £30,000 more than their value
(C) You are paying £30,000 for Goodwill
(D) You have made an arithmetical mistake.

MC96 Assets can be revalued in a partnership change because

(A) The law insists upon it
(B) It helps prevent injustice to some partners
(C) Inflation affects all values

MC97 Any loss on revaluation is
(A)   Credited to old partners in old profit sharing ratios
(B)   Credited to new partners in new profit sharing ratios
(C)   Debited to old partners in old profit sharing ratios
(D)   Debited to new partners in new profit sharing ratios

MC98 In a limited company which of the following are shown in the Appropriation Account?
(i)   Debenture Interest
(ii)   Proposed Dividend
(iii)   Transfers to Reserves
(iv)   Directors' Remuneration.
(A)   (i) and (ii)
(B)   (ii) and (iii)
(C)   (i) and (iv)
(D)   (ii) and (iv).

MC99 The Issued Capital of a company is
(A)   Always the same as the Authorised Capital
(B)   The same as Preference Share Capital
(C)   Equal to the reserves of the company
(D)   None of the above.

MC100 A company wishes to pay out all available profits as dividends. Net Profit is £26,600. There are 20,000 8% Preference Shares of £1 each, and 50,000 Ordinary Shares of £1 each. £5,000 is to be transferred to General Reserve. What Ordinary dividends are to be paid, in percentage terms?
(A)   20 per cent
(B)   40 per cent
(C)   10 per cent
(D)   60 per cent.

Answers to review questions

1.1 (a) 10,700 (b) 23,100 (c) 4,300 (d) 3,150
(e) 25,500 (f) 51,400

1.3 (a) Asset (b) Liability (c) Asset
(d) Asset (e) Liabilities (f) Asset

1.5 Wrong: Assets: Loan from C. Smith; Creditors; Liabilities: Stock of Goods; Debtors.

1.7 Assets: Motor 2,000; Premises 5,000; Stock 1,000; Bank 700; Cash 100 = total 8,800:
Liabilities: Loan from Bevan 3,000; Creditors 400 = total 3,400. Capital 8,800 − 3,400 = 5,400.

1.9

A Foster
Balance Sheet as at 31 December 19-4

Fixtures	23,750	Capital	5,500
Motor Vehicles	2,450	Creditors	5,700
Stock of Goods			8,800
Debtors			4,950
Cash at Bank			1,250
	26,200		26,200

1.11

	Assets	Liabilities	Capital
(a)	− Cash	− Creditors	
(b)	− Bank		
(c)	+ Stock	+ Creditors	
(d)	+ Cash		
(e)	+ Bank	+ Loan from J. Walker	
(f)	+ Bank − Debtors		
(g)	− Stock	− Creditors	
(h)	+ Premises − Bank		

1.13

C Sangster
Balance Sheet as at 7 May 19-4

Assets		Capital and Liabilities	
Fixtures	4,500	Capital	18,900
Motor Vehicle	4,200	Loan from T Sharples	2,000
Stock	5,720	Creditors	2,370
Debtors	3,000		
Bank	5,450		
Cash	400		
	23,270		23,270

2.1

	Debited	Credited
(a)	Office Machinery	D Isaacs Ltd
(c)	Cash	N Fox
(e)	D Isaacs Ltd	Office Machinery
(g)	Motor Van	Cash
(b)	C Jones	Capital
(d)	Loan: P Exeter	Bank
(f)	Bank	N Lyn

2.3

Bank
(1) Capital	2,500	(2) Office F	150
		(5) Motor Van	600
		(15) Planners	750
		(31) Machinery	280

Capital
		(1) Bank	2,500

Office Furniture
(2) Bank	150	(8) J Walker	60

Machinery
(3) Planers Ltd	750		
(31) Bank	280		

Cash
(23) J Walker	60		

Planers Ltd
(15) Bank	750	(3) Machinery	750

Motor Van
(5) Bank	600		

J Walker & Sons
(8) Office F	60	(23) Cash	60

2.4

Bank
(1) Capital	1,800	(8) M Van	950
(25) W Machinery	75	(26) Betta-Built	58
(28) Bank	100	(28) Cash	100

Capital
		(1) Cash	1,800

Cash
(1) Capital	2,000	(2) Bank	2,000
(30) J Smith	100		

Office Furniture
(18) Office Furn	2,000	(5) Office F	120
(1) Cash			

Betta-Built Ltd
(26) Bank	58	(5) Office F	62

Evans & Sons
(26) Bank	62	(12) W Machy	560

Works Machinery
(8) Bank	950	(25) Cash	75
(12) Evans & Sons	560		

Motor Van
(5) Betta-Built	120		
(8) Bank	950		

J Smith (Loan)
(30) Bank	500		

3.1

	Debited	Credited
(a)	Purchases	J Reid
(c)	Motor Van	H Thomas
(e)	Cash	Sales
(g)	Cash	Machinery
(i)	Purchases	D Simpson
(b)	B Perkins	Sales
(d)	Bank	Sales
(f)	H Hardy	Returns Outwards
(h)	Returns Inwards	J Nelson
(j)	H Forbes	Returns Outwards

3.3

Cash

Dr		Cr	
(1) Capital	500	(3) Purchases	85
(10) Sales	42	(25) E Morgan	55
(31) A Knight	55		

A Knight

Dr		Cr	
(24) Sales	55	(31) Cash	55

Purchases

Dr	
(3) Cash	85
(7) E Morgan	116

E Morgan

Dr		Cr	
(14) Returns	28	(7) Purchases	116
(25) Cash	55		

A Moses

Dr		Cr	
(21) Returns	19	(18) Purchases	98

Sales

Cr	
(10) Cash	42
(24) A Knight	55

Capital

Cr	
(1) Cash	500

Returns Outwards

Cr	
(14) E Morgan	28
(21) A Moses	19

3.4

Cash

Dr		Cr	
(1) Capital	1,000	(2) Bank	900
(19) Sales	78	(7) Purchases	28

Bank

Dr		Cr	
(2) Cash	900	(5) Motor Van	500
(24) D Watson (Loan)	55	(29) S Holmes	60
		(31) Kingston Eqt	100

Purchases

Dr	
(7) Cash	28
(4) S Holmes	78

S Holmes

Dr		Cr	
(12) Returns	18	(4) Purchases	78
(29) Bank	60		

Returns Outwards

Cr	
(12) S Holmes	18

D Moore

Dr	
(10)	98

Sales

Cr	
(10) D Moore	98
(19) Cash	78

Fixtures

Dr	
(22) Kingston Eqt	150

Motor Van

Dr	
(5) Bank	500

D Watson (Loan)

Cr	
(24) Bank	55

Kingston Equipment

Dr		Cr	
(31) Bank	100	(22) Fixtures	150

Capital

Cr	
(1) Cash	1,000

3.5

Bank

Dr		Cr	
(1) Capital	10,000	(25) F Jones	1,070
(6) Cash	250	(29) Manchester M	2,600

Cash

Dr		Cr	
(2) T Cooper (Loan)	400	(6) Bank	250
(4) Sales	200	(20) Purchases	220
(24) Sales	500	(31) Office Furn	100
(28) Capital	500		

Sales

Cr	
(4) Cash	200
(8) C Moody	180
(10) J Newman	220
(14) H Morgan	190
(14) J Peat	320
(24) Cash	70

Purchases

Dr	
(3) F Jones	840
(3) S Charles	3,600
(11) F Jones	370
(20) Cash	220

Returns Inwards

Dr	
(12) C Moody	40
(26) H Morgan	30

Motor Van

Dr		Cr	
(17) Manchester M	2,600	(29) Bank	2,600

Office Furniture

Dr		Cr	
(18) Faster S	600	(27) Office Furn	160
(31) Cash	100		

Capital

Cr	
(1) Bank	10,000
(28) Cash	500

J Newman

Dr	
(10) Sales	220

H Morgan

Dr		Cr	
(14) Sales	190	(26) Returns	30

C Moody

Dr		Cr	
(8) Sales	180	(12) Returns	40

J Peat

Dr	
(14) Sales	320

Returns Outwards

Cr	
(15) F Jones	140
(19) S Charles	110

Manchester Motors

Dr		Cr	
(29) Bank	2,600	(17) Motor Van	2,600

Faster Supplies Ltd

Dr		Cr	
(27) Office Furn	160	(18) Office Furn	600

F Jones

Dr		Cr	
(15) Returns	140	(3) Purchases	840
(25) Bank	1,070	(11) Purchases	370

S Charles

Dr		Cr	
(19) Returns	110	(3) Purchases	3,600

T Cooper (Loan)

Cr	
(2) Cash	400

4.1

(A) Bought motor vehicle £5,000, paying by bank.
(B) Paid off £4,000 creditors in cash.
(C) Lee lent us £150,000, this being paid into the bank.
(D) Bought land & buildings £125,000, paying by bank.
(E) Debtors paid cheques £80,000, being paid into bank.
(F) Land & buildings sold for £300,000, the proceeds being paid into the bank.
(G) Loan from Lee repaid out of the bank.
(H) Creditors £8,000 paid in cash.
(I) Stock costing £17,000 sold for £12,000 on credit. Loss of £5,000 shown deducted from Capital.

4.3

Account to be debited	Account to be credited
(a) Insurance	Bank
(c) Cash	Rent Received
(e) Bank	Rates
(g) Wages	Cash
(i) Bank	Sales Commission

Account to be debited	Account to be credited
(b) Motor Expenses	Cash
(d) Rates	Bank
(f) Stationery	Cash
(h) Bank	Stationery
(j) Motor Van	Bank

4.4

Capital
Cr: (1) Bank 2,000

Bank
Dr: (1) Capital 2,000; (21) Rent 5
Cr: (3) Fixtures 150; (24) Motor Van 300

M Mills
Dr: (18) Returns Out 23
Cr: (2) Purchases 175

Cash
Dr: (5) Sales 275
Cr: (10) Rent 15; (12) Stationery 27; (30) Wages 117; (31) Drawings 44

S Waites
Cr: (6) Purchases 114

U Henry
Dr: (23) Sales 77

Purchases
Dr: (2) M Mills 175; (6) S Waites 114

Rent Received
Cr: (21) Bank 5

Stationery
Dr: (12) Cash 27

Returns Out
Cr: (18) M Mills 23

Sales
Cr: (5) Cash 275; (23) U Henry 77

Motor Van
Dr: (24) Bank 300

Fixtures
Dr: (3) Bank 150

Wages
Dr: (30) Cash 117

Rent
Dr: (10) Cash 15

Drawings
Dr: (31) Cash 44

4.5

Capital
Cr: (1) Cash 1,500

Cash
Dr: (1) Capital 1,500; (11) Sales 49
Cr: (3) Rent 28; (4) Bank 1,000; (20) B Repairs 18; (28) Purchases 125; (30) Motor Exps 15

Bank
Dr: (4) Cash 1,000
Cr: (7) Stationery 15; (27) A Hanson 279; (29) M Van 395

Purchases
Dr: (2) A Hanson 296; (28) Cash 125

Sales
Cr: (5) E Linton 54; (11) Cash 49; (17) S Morgan 29

A Hanson
Dr: (14) Returns Out 17; (27) Bank 279
Cr: (2) Purchases 296

E Linton
Dr: (5) Sales 54
Cr: (22) Returns In 14

S Morgan
Dr: (17) Sales 29

Rent
Dr: (3) Cash 28

Building Repairs
Dr: (20) Cash 18

Motor Expenses
Dr: (30) Cash 15

Motor Van
Dr: (29) Bank 395

Stationery 15
Dr: (7) Bank 15

Returns Inwards 15
Dr: (22) E Linton 14

Returns Outwards 15
Cr: (14) A Hanson 17

A Webster
Dr: (31) Fixtures 120

Fixtures 120
Dr: (7) Bank 17
Cr: (31) A Webster 120

N Morgan
Dr: (1) Sales 153
Cr: (18) Bank 153

5.1

H Harvey
Dr: (1) Sales 690; (4) Sales 66
Cr: (10) Returns 40; (24) Cash 300; (31) Balance c/d 416
756 = 756
Dr: (1) Balance b/d 416

J. Lindo
Dr: (1) Sales 420
Cr: (10) Returns 20; (20) Bank 400
420 = 420

L Masters
Dr: (4) Sales 418; (31) Sales 203
Cr: (31) Balance c/d 621
621 = 621
Dr: (1) Balance b/d 621

5.2

J Young
Dr: (10) Returns 55; (28) Cash 250; (30) Balance c/d 233
Cr: (1) Purchases 458; (15) Purchases 80
538 = 538
Cr: (1) Balance b/d 233

L Williams
Dr: (30) Returns 17; (30) Balance c/d 180
Cr: (1) Purchases 120; (3) Purchases 77
197 = 197
Cr: (1) Balance b/d 180

G Norman
Dr: (10) Returns 22; (30) Balance c/d 686
Cr: (1) Purchases 708
708 = 708
Cr: (1) Balance b/d 686

T Harris
Dr: (19) Bank 880
Cr: (3) Purchases 880

5.3A

H Harvey

19-6		Dr	Cr	Balance	
May 1	Sales	690		690	Dr
May 4	Sales	66		756	Dr
May 10	Returns		40	716	Dr
May 24	Cash		300	416	Dr

N Morgan

19-6		Dr	Cr	Balance	
May 1	Sales	153		153	Dr
May 18	Bank		153	0	

J Lindo

19-6		Dr	Cr	Balance	
May 1	Sales	420		420	Dr
May 10	Returns		20	400	Dr
May 20	Bank		400	0	

L Masters

19-6		Dr	Cr	Balance	
May 4	Sales	418		418	Dr
May 31	Sales	203		621	Dr

5.4A

J Young

19-8		Dr	Cr	Balance	
Jun 1	Purchases		458	458	Cr
Jun 10	Returns	55		403	Cr
Jun 15	Purchases		80	483	Cr
Jun 28	Cash	250		233	Cr

L Williams

19-8		Dr	Cr	Balance	
Jun 1	Purchases		120	120	Cr
Jun 3	Purchases		77	197	Cr
Jun 30	Returns	17		180	Cr

G Norman

19-8		Dr	Cr	Balance	
Jun 1	Purchases		708	708	Cr
Jun 10	Returns	22		686	Cr

T Harris

19-8		Dr	Cr	Balance	
Jun 3	Purchases		880	880	Cr
Jun 19	Bank	880		0	

5.5

D Williams

(1) Sales	458	(24) Bank	300
		(28) Cash	100
		(30) Balance c/d	58
	458		458
(1) Balance b/d	58		

J Moore

(1) Sales	235	(12) Returns	26
(8) Sales	444	(20) Balance c/d	653
	679		679
(1) Balance b/d	653		

G Grant

(1) Sales	98	(12) Returns	9
		(30) Balance c/d	89
	98		98
(1) Balance b/d	89		

F. Franklin

(8) Sales	249	(30) Bank	249

A White

		(2) Purchases	77

H Samuels

(17) Returns	24	(2) Purchases	219
(30) Balance c/d	219	(10) Purchases	12
	243		243
		(1) Balance b/d	219

P Owen

		(2) Purchases	65

O Oliver

(17) Returns	12	(10) Purchases	222
(26) Cash	210		
	222		222

6.1

Cash

(1) Capital	250	(6) Rent	12
		(15) Carriage	23
		(31) Balance c/d	215
	250		250

Bank

(9) C Bailey	43	(12) K Gibson	25
(10) H Spencer	150	(12) D Ellis	54
		(31) Rent	18
		(31) Balance c/d	96
	193		193

Capital

		(1) Cash	250

Rent

(6) Cash	12		
(31) Bank	18		

Carriage

(15) Cash	23		

D Ellis

(12) Bank	54	(2) Purchases	54

C Mendez

		(2) Purchases	87
		(18) Purchases	43

K Gibson

(12) Bank	25	(2) Purchases	25

D Booth

		(2) Purchases	76
		(18) Purchases	110

L Lowe

		(2) Purchases	64

C Bailey

(4) Sales	43	(9) Bank	43

B Hughes

(4) Sales	62		
(21) Sales	67		

H Spencer

(4) Sales	176	(10) Bank	150

Purchases

(2) D Ellis	54
(2) C Mendez	87
(2) K Gibson	25
(2) D Booth	76
(2) L Lowe	64
(18) C Mendez	43
(18) D Booth	110

Sales

(4) C Bailey	43
(4) B Hughes	62
(4) H Spencer	176
(21) B Hughes	67

Trial Balance as at 31 May 19-8

	Dr	Cr
Cash	215	
Bank	96	
Capital		250
Rent	30	
Carriage	23	
C Mendez		130
D Booth		186
L Lowe		64
B Hughes	129	
H Spencer	26	
Purchases	459	
Sales		348
	978	978

6.2

Bank

(1) Capital	800	(17) M Hyatt	84
(24) J Carlton	95	(21) Betta Ltd	50
		(31) Motor Van	400
		(31) Balance c/d	361
	895		895

Cash

(5) Sales	87	(6) Wages	14
(30) J King (Loan)	60	(9) Purchases	46
		(12) Wages	14
		(31) Balance c/d	73
	147		147

Capital

		(1) Bank	800

Motor Van

(31) Bank	400		

Wages

(6) Cash	14		
(12) Cash	14		

Shop Fixtures

(15) Betta Ltd	50		

J King (Loan)

		(30) Cash	60

H Elliott

(7) Sales	35		

L Lane

(7) Sales	42		
(13) Sales	32		

J Carlton

(7) Sales	72	(24) Bank	72
(13) Sales	23		

K Henriques

(27) Returns	24	(2) Purchases	76

M Hyatt

(17) Bank	84	(2) Purchases	27
		(10) Purchases	57

T Braham

(18) Returns	20	(2) Purchases	56
		(10) Purchases	98

Betta Ltd

(21) Bank	50	(15) S. Fixtures	50

Purchases

(2) K Henriques	76
(2) M Hyatt	27
(2) T Braham	56
(9) Cash	46
(10) M Hyatt	57
(10) T Braham	98

Sales

(5) Cash	87
(7) H Elliott	35
(7) L Lane	42
(7) J Carlton	72
(13) L Lane	32
(13) J Carlton	23

Returns Outwards

(18) T Braham	20
(27) K Henriques	24

Trial Balance as on 31 March 19-6

	Dr	Cr
Bank	361	
Cash	73	
Capital		800
Motor Van	400	
Wages	28	
Shop Fixtures	50	
J King (Loan)		60
H Elliott	35	
L Lindo	74	
K Henriques		52
T Braham		134
Sales		291
Purchases	360	
Returns Outwards		44
	1.381	1.381

7.1

B Webb
Trading & Profit & Loss Account for the year ended 31 December 19-6

Purchases	14,629		Sales	18,462
less Closing Stock	2,548			
	12,081			
Cost of Goods Sold				
Gross Profit c/d	6,381			
		18,462		18,462
Salaries	2,150		Gross Profit b/d	6,381
Motor Expenses	520			
Rent & Rates	670			
Insurance	111			
General Expenses	105			
Net Profit	2,825			
		6,381		6,381

7.2

C Worth
Trading & Profit & Loss Account for the year ended 30 June 19-4

Purchases	23,803		Sales	28,794
less Closing Stock	4,166			
	19,637			
Cost of Goods Sold				
Gross Profit c/d	9,157			
		28,794		28,794
Salaries	3,164		Gross Profit b/d	9,157
Rent	854			
Lighting	422			
Insurance	105			
Motor Expenses	1,133			
Trade Expenses	506			
Net Profit	2,973			
		9,157		9,157

8.1

B Webb
Balance Sheet as at 31 December 19-6

Fixed Assets			Capital			
Premises		1,500	Balance at 1.1.19-6		5,424	
Motors		1,200	add Net Profit		2,825	
		2,700			8,249	
Current Assets			less Drawings		895	7,354
Stock	2,548					
Debtors	1,950		Current Liabilities			
Bank	1,654		Creditors			1,538
Cash	40	6,192				
		8,892				8,892

8.2

C Worth
Balance Sheet as at 30 June 19-4

Fixed Assets			Capital			
Buildings		50,000	Balance at 1.7.19-3		65,900	
Fixtures		1,000	add Net Profit		2,973	
Motors		5,500			68,873	
		56,500	less Drawings		2,400	66,473
Current Assets						
Stock	4,166		Current Liabilities			
Debtors	3,166		Creditors			1,206
Bank	3,847	11,179				
		67,679				67,679

9.1

Trading Account for the year ended 31 December 19-3

Purchases	33,333		Sales	38,742	
less Returns Out	495		less Returns In	890	
	32,838				37,852
Carriage Inwards	670				
	33,508				
less Closing Stock	7,489				
Cost of Goods Sold	26,019				
Gross Profit	11,833				
		37,852			37,852

9.3

R Graham
Trading & Profit & Loss Account for the year ended 30 September 19-6

Opening Stock		2,368	Sales	18,600	
add Purchases	11,874		less Returns In	205	18,395
less Returns Out	322	11,552			
Carriage Inwards		310			
		14,230			
less Closing Stock		2,946			
Cost of Goods Sold		11,284			
Gross Profit c/d		7,111			
		18,395			18,395
Salaries & Wages		3,862	Gross Profit b/d		7,111
Rent & Rates		304			
Carriage Out		200			
Insurance		78			
Motor Expenses		664			
Office Expenses		216			
Lighting & Heating		166			
General Expenses		314			
Net Profit		1,307			
		7,111			7,111

Balance Sheet as at 30 September 19-6

Capital		
Balance at 1.10.19-5		12,636
add Net Profit		1,307
		13,943
− Drawings		1,200
		12,743
Current Liabilities		
Creditors		1,731
		14,474
Fixed Assets		
Premises		5,000
Fixtures		350
Motor Vehicles		1,800
		7,150
Current Assets		
Stock	2,946	
Debtors	3,896	
Bank	482	7,324
		14,474

9.4

B Jackson
Trading & Profit & Loss Account for the year ended 30 April 19-7

Opening Stock		3,776	Sales	18,600	
add Purchases	11,556		less Returns Inn	440	18,160
less Returns Out	355	11,201			
Carriage Inwards		234			
		15,211			
less Closing Stock		4,998			
		10,213			
Gross Profit c/d		7,947			
		18,160			18,160
Salaries & Wages		2,447	Gross Profit b/d		7,947
Motor Expenses		664			
Rent		576			
Carriage Out		326			
Sundry Expenses		1,202			
Net Profit		2,732			
		7,947			7,947

Balance Sheet as at 30 April 19-7

Capital		
Balance as at 1.5.19-6		12,844
add Net Profit		2,732
		15,576
less Drawings		2,050
		13,526
Current Liabilities		
Creditors		3,045
		16,571
Fixed assets		
Fixtures		600
Motors		2,400
		3,000
Current Assets		
Stock	4,998	
Debtors	4,577	
Bank	3,876	
Cash	120	13,571
		16,571

13.1

Cash Book

		Cash	Bank			Cash	Bank
(1)	Capital	100		(2)	Rent	10	
(3)	F Lake (Loan)		500	(4)	B McKenzie		65
(5)	Sales	98		(9)	B Burton	22	
(7)	N Miller	62		(16)	Bank C	50	
(11)	Sales	53		(19)	F Lake (Loan)		100
(15)	G Moores		65	(26)	Motor Expenses		12
(16)	Cash C	50		(30)	Cash C		100
(22)	Sales		66	(31)	Wages	97	
(30)	Bank C		100	(31)	Balances c/d	184	454
		363	731			363	731

508

13.2

Cash Book

		Cash	Bank				Cash	Bank
(1)	Balances b/d	56	2,356	(2)	Rates		156
(5)	Sales		74	(3)	Postages	5	
(7)	Cash C	60		(7)	Bank C		60
(12)	J Moores	50	100	(8)	T Lee		75
(20)	P Jones	79		(10)	C Brooks	2	
(22)	Bank C	200		(17)	Drawings	20	
(31)	Sales		105	(22)	Cash C		200
				(24)	Motor Van		40
				(28)	Rent	195	
				(31)	Balance c/d	98	2,229
		380	2,700			380	2,700

14.1

Cash Book

		Disct	Cash	Bank			Disct	Cash	Bank
(1)	Capital			6,000	(1)	Fixtures			950
(3)	Sales		407		(2)	Purchases			1,240
(5)	N Morgan	10		210	(4)	Rent		200	
(9)	S Cooper	20		380	(7)	S Thompson & Co	4		76
(14)	L Curtis		115		(12)	Rates			410
(20)	P Exeter	2	78		(16)	M Monroe	6	114	
(31)	Sales			88	(31)	Balance c/d		93	4,195
		32	407	6,871			10	407	6,871

In General Ledger:
Debit Discounts Allowed 32: Credit Discounts Received 10.

14.2

Cash Book

		Disct	Cash	Bank			Disct	Cash	Bank
(1)	Balance b/d		230	4,756	(4)	Rent			120
(2)	R Burton	7	133		(8)	N Black	9		351
(2)	E Taylor	11	209		(8)	P Towers	12		468
(2)	R Harris	15	285		(8)	C Rowse	20		780
(6)	J Cotton: loan			1,000	(10)	Motor Expenses		44	
(12)	H Hankins	3	74		(15)	Wages'		160	
(18)	C Winston	13	247		(21)	Cash		120	350
(18)	R Wilson & Son	17	323		(24)	Drawings		120	
(18)	H Winter	23	437		(25)	T Briers	7	133	
(21)	Bank		350		(29)	Fixtures			650
(31)	Commission			88	(31)	Balances c/d		123	4,833
		89	580	7,552			48	580	7,552

Discounts Received
(31) Total for month 48

Discounts Allowed
(31) Total for month 89

15.1

Sales Journal

(1)	J Gordon	187
(3)	G Abrahams	166
(6)	V White	12
(10)	J Gordon	55
(17)	F Williams	289
(19)	U Richards	66
(27)	V Wood	28
(31)	L Simes	78
(31)	Total for month	881

Sales Ledger

J Gordon		
(1)	Sales	187
(10)	Sales	55

G Abrahams		
(3)	Sales	166

V White		
(6)	Sales	12

F Williams		
(17)	Sales	289

U Richards		
(19)	Sales	66

V Wood		
(27)	Sales	28

L Simes		
(31)	Sales	78

General Ledger
Sales Account

(31)	Total for month	881

15.3 Workings of invoices:

(1) F Gray
- 3 rolls white tape × 10 = 30
- 5 sheets blue cotton × 6 = 30
- 1 dress length × 20 = 20
- 80
- less Trade Discount 25% 20
- 60

(4) A Gray
- 6 rolls white tape × 10 = 60
- 30 metres green baize × 4 = 120
- 180
- less Trade Discount 33⅓% 60
- 120

(8) E Hines / (20) M Allen
- 1 dress length black silk × 20 = 100
- 10 rolls white tape × 10 = 36
- 6 sheets blue cotton × 6 = 60
- 3 dress lengths black silk × 20 = 44
- 11 metres green baize × 4 = 240
- less Trade Discount 25% 60
- 180 20

(31) B Cooper
- 12 rolls white tape × 10 = 120
- 14 sheets blue cotton × 6 = 84
- 9 metres green baize × 4 = 36
- 240
- less Trade Discount 33⅓% 80
- 160

Sales Journal

(1) F Gray	(1) Sales	60
(4) A Gray	(4) Sales	120
(8) E Hines	(8) Sales	20
(20) M Allen	(20) Sales	180
(31) B Cooper	(31) Sales	160
		540

Sales Ledger

F Gray	60
A Gray	120
E Hines	20
M Allen	180
B Cooper	160

General Ledger
Sales Account

(31) Total for month 540

16.1 Workings of purchases invoices

(1) K King
- 4 radios × 30 = 120
- 3 music centres × 160 = 480
- 600
- less Trade Discount 25% 150
- 450

(3) A Bell
- 2 washing machines × 200 = 400
- 5 vacuum cleaners × 60 = 300
- 2 dish dryers × 150 = 300
- 1,000
- less Trade Discount 20% 200
- 800

(15) J Kelly
- 1 music centre × 300 = 300
- 2 washing machines × 250 = 500
- 800
- less Trade Discount 25% 200
- 600

(20) B Powell
- 6 radios × 70 = 420
- less Trade Discount 33⅓% 140
- 280

(30) B Lewis
- 4 dish dryers × 200 = 800
- less Trade Discount 20% 160
- 640

Purchases

(1) K King		450
(3) A Bell		800
(15) J Kelly		600
(20) B Powell		280
(30) B Lewis		640
		2,770

General Ledger
Purchases Account

(31) Total for month 2,770

Purchases Ledger

K King	(1) Purchases	450
A Bell	(3) Purchases	800
J Kelly	(15) Purchases	600
B Powell	(20) Purchases	280
B Lewis	(30) Purchases	640

16.3

Purchases Journal

(1)	Smith Stores	90
(23)	C Kelly	105
(31)	J Hamilton	180
		375

Sales Journal

(8)	A Grantley	72
(15)	A Henry	240
(24)	D Sangster	81
		393

Purchases Ledger

Smith Stores — (1) Purchases 90

C Kelly — (23) Purchases 105

J Hamilton — (31) Purchases 180

Sales Ledger

A Grantley — (8) Sales 72

A Henry — (15) Sales 240

D Sangster — (24) Sales 81

General Ledger

Sales Account — (31) Sales 393

Purchases Account — (31) Total for month 375

17.1

Purchases Journal

(4)	H Lloyd	119
(4)	D Scott	98
(4)	A Williams	114
(4)	S Wood	56
(10)	A Simpson	59
(18)	M White	89
(18)	J Wong	67
(18)	H Miller	196
(18)	H Lewis	119
(31)	A Williams	56
(31)	C Cooper	98
(31)	Total for month	1,096

Purchases Ledger

H Lloyd — (7) Returns 16 (1) | (1) Purchases 119

D Scott — (7) Returns 14 (4) | (4) Purchases 98

A Williams — (31) Purchases 114 (4) | (4) Purchases 56

A Simpson — (25) Returns 11 (4) | (10) Purchases 59

S Wood — (4) Purchases 89

M White — (18) Purchases 67

J Wong — (25) Returns 5 (18) | (18) Purchases 196

H Miller — (18) Purchases 119

H Lewis — (18) Purchases 56

C Cooper — (31) Purchases 98

Returns Outwards Journal

(7)	H Lloyd	16 (25)
(7)	D Scott	14
(25)	J Wong	5
(25)	A Simpson	11
		46

General Ledger

Purchases Account — (31) Total for month 1,096

Returns Outwards Account — (31) Total for month 46

17.3

Purchases Journal

(3)	P Potter	144
(3)	H Harris	25
(3)	B Spencer	76
(9)	B Perkins	24
(9)	H Harris	58
(9)	H Miles	123
(17)	H Harris	54
(17)	B Perkins	65
(17)	L Nixon	75
		644

Returns Outwards Journal

(11)	P Potter	12
(11)	B Spencer	22
(20)	B Spencer	14
		48

Sales Journal

(1)	T Thompson	56
(1)	L Rodriguez	148
(1)	K Barton	145
(7)	K Kelly	89
(7)	N Mendes	78
(7)	N Lee	257
(24)	K Mohammed	57
(24)	K Kelly	65
(24)	O Green	112
(31)	N Lee	55
		1,062

Returns Inwards Journal

(14)	T Thompson	5
(14)	K Barton	11
(14)	K Kelly	14
(28)	N Mendes	24
		54

Purchases Ledger

P Potter — (11) Returns 12 | (3) Purchases 144

H Harris — (3) Purchases 25; (9) Purchases 58; (17) Purchases 54

B Spencer — (11) Returns 22; (20) Returns 14 | (3) Purchases 76

B Perkins — (9) Purchases 24; (17) Purchases 65

H Miles — (9) Purchases 123

L Nixon — (17) Purchases 75

Sales Ledger

T Thompson — (1) Sales 56 | (14) Returns 5

L Rodriguez — (1) Sales 148

K Barton — (1) Sales 145 | (14) Returns 11

K Kelly — (7) Sales 89; (24) Sales 65 | (14) Returns 14

N Mendes — (7) Sales 78 | (28) Returns 24

N Lee — (7) Sales 257; (31) Sales 55

K Mohammed — (24) Sales 57

O Green — (24) Sales 112

18.1

The Journal

(1)	Premises	2,000	
	Motor Van	450	
	Fixtures	600	
	Stock	1,289	
	Debtors: N Hardy	40	
	M Nelson	180	
	Bank	1,254	
	Cash	45	
	Creditors: B Blake		60
	V Reagan		200
	Capital		5,598
		5,858	5,858
(14)	Motor Van	300	
	Better Motors		300

Returns Inwards Journal

(11)	K O'Connor		16
(11)	L Staines		18
			34

Returns Outwards Journal

(19)	N Lee		9

Purchases Journal

(2)	B Blake	20
(2)	C Harris	56
(2)	H Gordon	38
(2)	N Lee	69
(22)	J Johnson	89
(22)	T Best	72
		344

Sales Journal

(3)	K O'Connor	56
(3)	M Benjamin	78
(3)	L Staines	98
(3)	N Duffy	48
(3)	B Green	118
(9)	M Nelson	40
(9)	M Benjamin	22
(9)	L Pearson	67
		527

Trial Balance as at 31 May 19-6

	Dr	Cr
C Harris		56
H Gordon		38
J Johnson		89
T Best		72
M Benjamin	100	
N Duffy	48	
B Green	118	
L Pearson	67	
Capital		5,598
Rent	15	
Motor Expenses	13	
Drawings	20	
Salaries	56	
Rates	66	
Sales		527
Purchases	344	
Returns Inwards	34	
Returns Outwards		9
Premises	2,000	
Motor Vans	750	
Fixtures	600	
Stock	1,289	
Discounts Allowed	19	
Discounts Received		17
Bank	855	
Cash	12	
	6,406	6,406

T Best

	(22) Purchases	72

N Hardy

	(16) Bank & Disct	40

M Nelson

(1)	Balance	40	(16) Bank & Disct	180
(3)	Sales	40		
		220		220

K O'Connor

(3)	Sales	56	(11) Returns	16
			(16) Bank & Disct	40
		56		56

J Johnson

	(22) Purchases	89

Cash Book

		Disct	Cash	Bank			Disct	Cash	Bank
(1)	Balances		45	1,254	(1)	Rent			15
(16)	N Hardy	2		38	(4)	Motor Expenses		13	
(16)	M Nelson	11		209	(7)	Drawings		20	
(16)	K O'Connor	2		38	(24)	B Blake	4		76
(16)	L Staines	4		76	(24)	V Reagan	10		190
					(24)	N Lee	3		57
					(24)	Salaries			56
					(30)	Rates			66
					(31)	Better Motors			300
					(31)	Balance c/d		12	855
		19	45	1,615			17	45	1,615

512

Discounts Allowed

(31) Total for month 19

Discounts Received

(31) Total for month 17

Kingston	Cr	6,790
H Newman	Cr	34
Office Furniture	Cr	490
W Charles	Cr	39
W Charles	Cr	111
Purchases	Cr	45
Insurance	Cr	76
Systems Accelerated	Cr	980

18.2

(i)	Motor Vehicles	Dr.	6,790
(ii)	Bad Debts	Dr.	34
(iii)	Unique Offices	Dr.	490
(iv)	Bank	Dr.	39
(a)	Bad Debts	Dr.	111
(b)			
(v)	Purchases	Dr.	45
(vi)	Drawings	Dr.	76
(vii)	Machinery	Dr.	980

19.1

(i) Style of invoice will vary

Calculations:

	£
3 sets of Boy Michael Golf Clubs × £270	810
150 Watson golf balls at £8 per 10 balls	120
4 Faldo golf bags at £30	120
	1,050
less Trade Discount 33⅓%	350
	700
Add VAT 10%	70
	770

(ii)

D Wilson Ltd Ledger

G Christie & Son

	£
19-7	
May 1 Sales	770

G Christie & Son Ledger

D Wilson Ltd

	£
19-7	
May 1 Purchases	770

19.2

Sales Book

	Net	VAT	£
(1) B Davies & Co	150	15	
(4) C Grant Ltd	220	22	
(16) C Grant Ltd	140	14	
(31) B Karloff	80	8	
	590	59	

General Ledger

Capital
(1) Balance 5,598

Rent
15

Motor Expenses
13

Drawings
20

Salaries
56

Rates
66

Sales
(31) Total for month 527

Purchases
(31) Total for month 344

Returns Inwards
(31) Total for month 34

Returns Outwards
(31) Total for month 9

Premises
(1) Balance 2,000

Motor Vans
(1) Balance 450
(14) Better Motors 300

Fixtures
(1) Balance 600

Stock
(1) Balance 1,289

B Blake
(24) Bank 76 — (1) Balance 60
(24) Discount 4 — (2) Purchases 20
80 — 80
(1) Bank 80

V Reagan
(24) Bank & Disct. 200 — (1) Balance b/d 200
(4) Cash 200
(7) Cash

C Harris
(2) Purchases 56 — (27) Bank 56

H Gordon
(2) Purchases 38 — (30) Bank 38

N Lee
(2) Purchases 69 — (19) Returns 9
— (24) Bank & Disct 60
69 — 69

M Benjamin
78
22

L Staines
(16) Bank & Disct 98 — (11) Returns 18
— (16) Bank & Disct 80
98 — 98

N Duffy
(3) Sales 48

B Green
(1) Balance 118
(3) Sales

L Pearson
(9) Sales 67

Better Motors
(14) Motor Van 300 — (1) Balance 300
(31) Bank

Purchases Book

	Net	VAT
(10) G Cooper & Son	400	40
(10) J Wayne Ltd	190	19
(14) B Lugosi	50	5
(23) S Hayward	60	6
	700	70

Sales Ledger

B Davies & Co
(1) Sales 165

C Grant Ltd
(4) Sales 242

B Karloff
(16) Sales 154
88

Purchases Ledger

G Cooper & Son
(10) Purchases 440

J Wayne Ltd
(10) Purchases 209

B Lugosi
(14) Purchases 55

S Hayward
(23) Purchases 66

General Ledger

Sales
(31) Credit Sales for month 590

Purchases
(31) Credit Purchases for month 700

Value Added Tax
(31) VAT Content in Purchases Book 70   (31) VAT Content in Sales Book 59
   (31) Balance c/d 11
70   70

19.3 (a)

Sales Book

19-7		Invoice No	Net	VAT	Gross
May 25	Laira Brand	3045	1,060.00	159.00	1,219.00
May 27	Brown Bros	3046	2,200.00	330.00	2,530.00
May 28	Penfold's	3047	170.00	25.50	195.50
May 29	T Tyrell	3048	460.00	69.00	529.00
May 30	Laira Brand	3049	1,450.00	217.50	1,667.50
			5,340.00	801.00	6,141.00

(b)

Personal accounts in Sales Ledger: debit gross amounts
Sales account in General Ledger: credit net total for period
VAT account in General Ledger: credit total of VAT column for period

(c)

Laira Brand

£

19-7					
May 1	Balances b/f	2,100.47	May 21	Bank	2,500.00
May 15	Sales	680.23	May 29	Returns In	609.50
May 25	Sales	1,219.00	May 31	Balance c/d	2,557.70
May 30	Sales	1,667.50			
		5,667.20			5,667.20

20.1

Straight-line		Reducing Balance	
Cost	4,000	Cost	4,000
Yr 1 Depreciation	700	Yr 1 Depn 40% of 4.000	1,600
	3,300		2,400
Yr 2 Depreciation	700	Yr 2 Depn 40% of 2.400	960
	2,600		1,440
Yr 3 Depreciation	700	Yr 3 Depn 40% of 1.440	576
	1,900		864
Yr 4 Depreciation	700	Yr 4 Depn 40% of 864	346
	1,200		518
Yr 5 Depreciation	700	Yr 5 Depn 40% of 518	207
	500		311

$4.000 - 500 = 3,500 \div 5 = 700$

20.2

(a) Straight-line

Cost	12,500
Yr 1 Depreciation	1,845
	10,655
Yr 2 Depreciation	1,845
	8,810
Yr 3 Depreciation	1,845
	6,965
Yr 4 Depreciation	1,845
	5,120

$$\frac{12,500 - 5,120}{4} = 1,845$$

(b) Reducing Balance

Cost	12,500
Yr 1 Depn 20% of 12,500	2,500
	10,000
Yr 2 Depn 20% of 10,000	2,000
	8,000
Yr 3 Depn 20% of 8,000	1,600
	6,400
Yr 4 Depn 20% of 6,400	1,280
	5,120

20.3

(a) Reducing Balance

Cost	6,400
Yr 1 Depn 50% of 6,400	3,200
	3,200
Yr 2 Depn 50% of 3,200	1,600
	1,600
Yr 3 Depn 50% of 1,600	800
	800
Yr 4 Depn 50% of 800	400
	400
Yr 5 Deprn 50% of 400	200
	200

(b) Straight-line

Cost	6,400
Yr 1 Depreciation	1,240
	5,160
Yr 2 Depreciation	1,240
	3,920
Yr 3 Depreciation	1,240
	2,680
Yr 4 Depreciation	1,240
	1,440
Yr 5 Depreciation	1,240
	200

$$\frac{6,400 - 200}{5} = 1,240$$

20.7

			Machines	
		A	B	C
Bought 1.1.19-4		3,000		
19-4 Depreciation 10% for 12 months		300		
		2,700		
Bought 1.4.19-5			2,000	
19-5 Depreciation 10% × 2,700		270		
" 10% for 9 months			150	
		2,430	1,850	
Bought 1.7.19-6				1,000
19-6 Depreciation 10% × 2,430		243		
" 10% × 1,850			185	
" 10% for 6 months				50
		2,187	1,665	950

19-6 Total Depreciation 243 + 185 + 50 = 478

21.1

Motor Vans

19-1					
Jan 1	Bank	2,400	19-1		
Jul 1	Bank	1,400	Dec 31	Balance c/d	3,800
		3,800			3,800

Provision for Depreciation: Motor Vans

19-1			19-1		
Dec 31	Balance c/d	620	Dec 31	Profit & Loss	620

21.2

Machinery

19-3			19-3		
Jan 1	Bank	800	Dec 31	Balance c/d	800
19-4			19-4		
Jan 1	Balance b/d	800	Dec 31	Balance c/d	2,400
Jul 1	Bank	1,000			
Oct 1	Bank	600			
		2,400			2,400
19-5			19-6		
Jan 1	Balance b/d	2,400	Dec 31	Balance c/d	2,600
19-6					
Apl 1	Bank	200			
		2,600			2,600

515

Provision for Depreciation: Machinery

Date	Details	£	Date	Details	£
19-3 Dec 31	Balance c/d	80	19-3 Dec 31	Profit & Loss	80
19-4 Dec 31	Balance c/d	225	19-4 Jan 1	Balance b/d	80
			Dec 31	Profit & Loss	145
		225			225
19-5 Dec 31	Balance c/d	465	19-5 Jan 1	Balance b/d	225
			Dec 31	Profit & Loss	240
		465			465
19-6 Dec 31	Balance c/d	720	19-6 Jan 1	Balance b/d	465
			Dec 31	Profit & Loss	255
		720			720

Balance Sheet Extracts

31 December 19-3
Machinery at cost   800
less Depreciation   80   720

31 December 19-4
Machinery at cost   2,400
less Depreciation to date   225   2,175

31 December 19-5
Machinery at cost   2,400
less Depreciation to date   465   1,935

31 December 19-6
Machinery at cost   2,600
less Depreciation to date   720   1,880

21.3

(a) Machinery

Date	Details	£	Date	Details	£
19-5 Jan 1	Bank	640			
19-6 Oct 1	Bank	720	19-6 Dec 31	Balance b/d	1,360
		1,360			1,360

(b) Fixtures

Date	Details	£	Date	Details	£
19-5 Jan 1	Bank	100			
Jul 1	Bank	200	19-5 Dec 31	Balance c/d	300
		300			300
19-6 Jan 1	Balance b/d	300	19-6 Dec 31	Balance c/d	350
Dec 1	Bank	50			
		350			350

(c)

Provision for Depreciation: Machinery

Date	Details	£	Date	Details	£
19-6 Dec 31	Balance c/d	240	19-5 Dec 31	Profit & Loss	80
			19-6 Dec 31	Profit & Loss	160
		240			240

Provision for Depreciation: Fixtures

Date	Details	£	Date	Details	£
19-6 Dec 31	Balance c/d	62	19-5 Dec 31	Profit & Loss	30
			19-6 Dec 31	Profit & Loss	32
		62			62

(d) Balance Sheets (extracts)

31 December 19-5
Machinery at cost   640
less Depreciation   80   560
Fixtures at cost   300
less Depreciation   30   270

31 December 19-6
Machinery at cost   1,360
less Depreciation to date   240   1,120
Fixtures at cost   350
less Depreciation to date   62   288

21.4 Workings:
AAT 101

Cost   8,500
less Estimated residual value   2,500
Estimated total depreciation   6,000
Estimated life 5 years
Depreciation charge per year   1,200

Accumulated depreciation at 1.4.19-6
2 years 6 months × 1,200   3,000
Depreciation 1.4.-6 – 30.6.-6
3 months × 1,200 p.a.   300
Depreciation to 30.6.19-6   3,300
Cost was   8,500
Written down value on disposal   5,200
Trade-in allowance   5,000
Loss on disposal   200

DJH 202

Cost	12,000
less Estimated residual value	2,000
Estimated total depreciation	10,000
Estimated life 8 years	
Depreciation charge per year	1,250
Accumulated depreciation at 1.4.19-6	
2 years × 1,250	2,500
	7,500
Remainder of estimated depreciation	
Adjust to cover 4 years in future:	
i.e. 7,500 ÷ 4 now yearly charge	1,875

Depreciation for year to 31 March 19-7

AAT 101	As above	300
DJH 202	As above	1,875
KGC 303	Cost 15,000 – residual value 4,000	
	= 11,000 ÷ 5 years = 2,200 p.a.	
	For 9 months 30.6.19-6 to 31.3.19-7	
	2,200 × 9/12	1,650
		3,825

(i) (dates omitted) Journal

	Dr	Cr
Motor Vehicles	15,000	
Motor Vehicle Disposals		
Pinot Finance		5,000
Bank		6,000
Purchase of KGC 303		4,000
Motor Vehicle disposals	8,500	
Motor Vehicles		8,500
Cost of vehicle disposed AAT 101		
Provision for depreciation: Motors	3,300	
Motor Vehicle Disposals		3,300
Depreciation on date on disposal of AAT 101		
Profit and Loss	200	
Motor Vehicle Disposals		200
Loss on Vehicle disposed AAT 101		

(ii)

	Dr	Cr
Profit and Loss	3,825	
Provision for Depreciation: Motors		3,825
Depreciation on motor vehicles for year to 31 March 19-7		

(iii) (dates omitted) Motor Vehicles

Balance b/f	20,500	M Vehicle Disposals	8,500
Purchase of KGC 303	15,000	Balance c/f	27,000
	35,500		35,500

Provision for Depreciation: Motor Vehicles

Assets Disposals	3,300	Balance b/f	5,500
Balance c/f	6,025	Profit and Loss	3,825
	9,325		9,325

21.7 (a) (i) Straight line depreciation method

Fixed asset

Year 1 Bank	10,000	Year 3 Asset disposals	10,000

Provision for depreciation

		Year 1 Profit & loss	2,000
Year 2 Balance c/d	4,000	Year 2 Profit & loss	2,000
	4,000		4,000
Year 3 Asset disposals	4,000	Year 3 Balance b/d	4,000

Asset disposals

Year 3 Fixed asset	10,000	Year 5 Bank	5,000
		" 5 Provision for depreciation	4,000
		" 5 Profit & loss	1,000
	10,000		10,000

(ii) Reducing balance method

Fixed asset

Year 1 Bank	10,000	Year 3 Asset disposals	10,000

Provision for depreciation

		Year 1 Profit & loss	4,000
Year 2 Balance c/d	6,400	" 1 Profit & Loss	2,400
	6,400		6,400
Year 3 Asset disposals	6,400	Year 3 Balance b/d	6,400

Asset disposals

Year 3 Fixed asset	10,000	Year 3 Bank	5,000
" 3 Profit & loss	1,400	" 3 Provision for depreciation	6,400
	11,400		11,400

(b) (i) The purpose of depreciation provisions is to apportion the cost of a fixed asset over the useful years of its life to the organisation.

The matching concept concerns the matching of costs against the revenues which those costs generate. If the benefit to be gained is equal in each year then the straight-line method is to be preferred. If the benefits are greatest in year 1 and then falling year by year, then the reducing balance method would be preferred. The impact of maintenance costs of the fixed asset, if heavier in later years, may also give credence to the reducing balance method.

(ii) The net figure at the end of year 2 is the amount of original cost not yet expensed against revenue.

(c) The charge in year 1 should be nil in this case. The matching concept concerns matching costs against revenues. There have been no revenues in year 1, therefore there should be no costs.

21.8 (a) Depreciation method

There have been no additions or disposals over first two years. We can therefore rework depreciation easily.

Plant at cost	80,000
less: 19-4 Depreciation (i.e., it is 20%)	16,000
	64,000
less: 19-5 Depreciation (i.e., 20% of 64,000)	12,800
	51,200

As this fits in with the figures given the method used is reducing balance at 20%.

(b) *Accumulated depreciation: schedule*

19-4	Charge 20% × 80,000		16,000
	Balance 31 March 19-4		16,000
19-5	Charge 20% × 64,000		12,800
	Balance 31 March 19-5		28,800
19-6	less: Depreciation on plant sold	(A)	5,400
			23,400
	add: Charge (D) 20% × 66,600	(C)	13,320
	Balance 31 March 19-6	(B)	36,720
19-7	less: Depreciation on plant sold	(E)	14,640
			22,080
	add: Charge	(F)	17,584
			39,664

(A) is 15,000 × 20% reducing balance for 2 years, i.e. 3,000 + 2,400 = 5,400.

(B) is given as 36,720 and can be inserted.

(C) is missing figure = 13,320.

(D) can therefore be deduced. If 13,320 is 20%, therefore amount on which it is calculated is 13,320 × 100/20 = 66,600.

(E) is reducing balance on 30,000 for 3 years, i.e. 6,000 + 4,800 + 3,840.

(F) Plant WDV 31 March 19-4 (D) – (C)

66,600 (WDV b/f) (30,000 – 6,000 – 4,800 – 3,840) – (C) 13,320 =

less: Disposal at WDV (30,000 – 6,000 – 4,800 – 3,840) =		53,280
		15,360
		37,920
add: Purchase		50,000
		87,920
Depreciation 20% × 87,920	=	17,584

(c)

Plant at cost 19-4		80,000
less: sale at cost 19-6		15,000
		65,000
Addition at cost 19-6	(G)	25,000
		90,000
Plant at cost 19-6		30,000
less: sale at cost 19-7		60,000
Addition at cost 19-7		50,000
		110,000

(G) is missing figure and is therefore deduced as 25,000.

Trend Statement missing figures are therefore:

		31 March 19-7
(A)	Plant at cost (see part c)	110,000
(B)	Accumulated depreciation (see part b)	39,664
(C)	Net (written down value)	70,336

(d)

	19-6	19-7
Disposals		
Cost	15,000	30,000
Depreciation (see note b)	5,400	
(see note b)		14,640
	9,600	15,360
Sold for	8,000	21,000
Profit/(loss)	(1,600)	5,640

22.1

Bad Debts

19-4				19-4		
Apr 30	H Gordon		110	Dec 31	Profit & Loss	186
Aug 31	D Bellamy		64			
Oct 31	J Alderton		12			
			186			186

Provision for Bad Debts

			19-4		
			Dec 31	Profit & Loss	220

Profit & Loss

Bad Debts	186
Provision for Bad Debts	220

Balance Sheet as at 31 December 19-4

Debtors	6,850	
less Provision for Bad Debts	220	6,630

22.2

Bad Debts

19-6			19-6		
Aug 31	W Beet	85	Dec 31	Profit & Loss	225
Sep 30	S Avon	140			
		225			225
19-7			19-7		
Feb 28	L J Friend	180	Dec 31	Profit & Loss	490
Aug 31	N Kelly	60			
Nov 30	A Oliver	250			
		490			490

Provision for Bad Debts

19-7			19-6		
Dec 31	Balance c/d	550	Dec 31	Profit & Loss	550
			19-7		
			Dec 31	Profit & Loss	50
		600			600

(iii)

Balance Sheet (extracts)

	19-6		
Debtors	40,500		
less Provision for Bad Debts	550	39,950	
	19-7	47,300	
		600	46,700

22.4

Provision for Doubtful Debts

19-6			19-6		
Dec 30	Debtors Ledger:		Jan 1	Balance b/d (w1)	2,640
	J Sinder	600		Debtors Ledger:	
	K Lambert	2,000		K Dodds	3,000
Dec 31	Profit & Loss	592			
Dec 31	Balance c/d (w2)	2,448			
		5,640			5,640

Debtors' Ledger

19-6			19-6		
Jan 1	Balance b/d	88,000	Dec 31	Bank	510,150
Dec 31	Sales (w3)	511,200	Dec 31	Discounts Allowed	4,850
Dec 31	Provision for Doubtful Debts:			Bank (K Dodds)	3,000
	K Dodds	3,000		Written off to Provision:	
			Dec 31	J Sinder	600
				K Lambert	2,000
			Dec 31	Balance c/d (w4)	81,600
		602,200			602,200

(w1) Debtors (net) brought forward 85,360. As provision was 3% then 85,360 = 97% of gross debtors. Therefore gross debtors b/f = 85,360 x $^{100}/_{97}$ = 88,000

(w2) 3% of (w4) below = 81,600 × 3% = 2,448

(w3) 568,000 × 90% = 511,200

(w4) This is missing figure and is therefore total of balance.

23.1

Motor Expenses

19-6			19-6		
Dec 31	Cash & Bank	744	Dec 31	Profit & Loss	772
.. 31	Owing c/d	28			
		772			772

Insurance

19-6			19-6		
Dec 31	Cash & Bank	420	Dec 31	Prepaid c/d	35
			.. 31	Profit & Loss	385
		420			420

Stationery

19-6			19-6		
Dec 31	Cash & Bank	1,800	Jan 1	Owing b/f	250
.. 31	Owing c/d	490	Dec 31	Profit & Loss	2,040
		2,290			2,290

Rates

19-6			19-6		
Jan 1	Prepaid b/f	220	Dec 31	Prepaid c/d	290
Dec 31	Cash & Bank	950	.. 31	Profit & Loss	880
		1,170			1,170

23.3

Rent Received

19-6			19-6		
Jan 1	Owing b/f	180	Dec 31	Cash & Bank	550
Dec 31	Profit & Loss	580	" 31	Owing c/d	210
		760			760

(Dates omitted)

Rent and rates payable

Prepayment b/f		1,940	Accruals b/f		2,200
Bank (rent)		5,200	Profit and loss		8,480
Bank (rates)		3,050	Prepayments c/d		1,880
Accruals c/d		2,370			
		12,560			12,560

Rent receivable

			19-6		
Prepayments b/d		1,889	Accruals b/d		2,370
19-6					
Profit and loss		905	Prepayments b/f		625
Prepayment c/d		680	Bank		960
					1,585
		1,585			

Prepayments b/d 680

Vehicles (at cost)

Balance b/f		10,540	Vehicle disposal		4,710
Bank	5,280	*6,380	Balance c/d		12,210
Trade-in (see disposal a/c)	1,100				
		16,920			16,920

Balance b/d 12,210

*Would be recorded as journal entry.

Provision for depreciation: vehicles

Vehicle disposal		3,080	Balance b/f		4,720
Balance c/d		3,890	Profit and loss		*2,250
		6,970			6,970

*Charge deducted as difference in the account

Vehicles disposal

Vehicles	4,710	Provision for depreciation		3,080
		Trade-in allowance (Journal)		1,100
		Profit and loss: book		530
		loss on sale		
	4,710			4,710

23.6

Winston Elliot

Trading and Profit & Loss Account for the year ended 31 October 19-7

Sales (530,780 – 1,866)			528,914
less Cost of Goods Sold			
Opening Stock		12,306	
add Purchases (388,650 – 2,449)		386,201	
Carriage Inwards		2,444	
		400,951	
less Closing Stock		14,521	386,430
Gross Profit			142,484
add Discounts Received			1,973
			144,457
less Expenses:			
Rent, Rates & Insurance (15,769 – 750)		15,019	
Heating & Lighting		6,324	
Advertising		13,765	
Salaries & Wages		44,970	
Postage & Stationery		7,660	
Carriage Outwards		5,328	
Discounts Allowed		1,454	
Loan Interest		1,800	
Bad Debts		2,088	
Depreciation		14,145	112,553
Net Profit			31,904

Winston Elliot

Balance Sheet as at 31 October 19-7

Fixed Assets			
Equipment at cost		141,450	
less Depreciation to date		69,465	71,985
Current Assets			
Stock		14,521	
Debtors		26,550	
Prepayments		750	
Cash		515	
		42,336	
less Current Liabilities			
Creditors	36,887		
Bank Overdraft	3,466		
Expenses Accrued	150	40,503	
Working Capital			1,833
			73,818

Financed by:

Capital		
Balance as at 1 November 19-7	49,214	
Add Net Profit	31,904	
	81,118	
less Drawings	20,800	
	60,318	
Loan	13,500	
	73,818	

Balance Sheet as at 31 July 19-6

Fixed Assets			
Plant and machinery at cost		36,420	
Less Depreciation		21,852	14,568
Current Assets			
Stock		6,140	
Trade Debtors		6,340	
Prepayments		172	
Bank		2,197	
Cash		199	
		15,048	
Less Current Liabilities			
Trade Creditors	4,380		
Expenses Accrued	233	4,613	
Working Capital			10,435
			25,003
Financed by:			
Capital			
Balance at 1.8.19-5			24,927
add Net Profit for year			8,541
			33,468
less Drawings			8,465
			25,003

23.7

Mr Banda

Trading and Profit & Loss Account for the year ended 31 July 19-6

Sales			101,890
less Returns In			761
			101,129
less: Cost of Goods Sold			
Stock at 1.8.19-5		5,830	
add Purchases	48,760		
less Returns Out	531	48,229	
Carriage In		650	
		54,709	
less Stock at 31.7.19-6		6,140	48,569
Gross Profit			52,560
add Discounts Received			1,150
			53,710
less Salaries & Wages		15,300	
Other Operating Expenses (w1)		21,261	
Discounts Allowed		1,324	
Depreciation		7,284	45,169
Net profit			8,541

521

23.8

John Brown

Trading and Profit & Loss Account for the year ended 31 December 19-7

Sales		400,000	395,000
less Returns In		5,000	
less: Cost of Goods Sold			
Stock at 1.1.19-7		100,000	
add Purchases	350,000	343,800	
less Returns Out	6,200		
		443,800	
less Stock at 31.12.19-		120,000	323,800
Gross Profit			71,200
less Wages		35,000	
Rates		5,500	
Telephone		1,220	
Bad Debts		200	
Provision for Bad Debts		180	
Depreciation: Shop fittings		4,000	
Van		6,000	52,100
Net Profit			19,100

Balance Sheet as at 31 December 19-7

Fixed Assets

Shop Fittings at cost		40,000	
less Depreciation		4,000	36,000
Van at cost		30,000	
less Depreciation		6,000	24,000
			60,000
Current Assets			
Stock		120,000	
Debtors	9,800		
less Provision	980	8,820	
Prepayments		500	
Bank		3,000	132,320
less Current Liabilities			
Creditors	7,000		
Expenses Accrued	5,220	12,220	
Working Capital			120,100
			180,100

Financed by:

Capital	
Balance as at 1.1.19-7	179,000
add Net Profit	19,100
	198,100
less Drawings	18,000
	180,100

24.1 (b) Capital: (i) (ii) Machine part of (v) (vi)
Revenue: (iii) (iv) Drinks part of (v)

24.3 Capital (a) (c) (d) (f) (j) (l): Revenue (b) (e) (g) (h) (i) (k)

24.5 (a) Per text
(b) Microcomputer – acquisition cost

Basic cost	4,000
Installation and testing	340
	4,340
less 5% discount	217
	4,123
Special wiring	110
Modifications	199
Staff training	990
Total cost	5,422

(c) 1. Revenue. 2. Capital. 3. Capital. 4. Revenue. 5. Revenue. 6. Revenue. 7. Capital. 8. Revenue. 9. Capital. 10. Capital.

24.6

(a) *Plant at cost*

Balance 1 April 19-5	372,000
add Acquisitions during year	96,000
	468,000
less Disposals (36,000 + 4,000 + 4,400)	44,400
Balance 31 March 19-6	423,600

(b) *Provision for depreciation of plant*

Balance 1 April 19-5	205,400
less Depreciation on disposals (W1)	25,200
	180,200
add Provision for year 20% × (423,600 − 180,200)	48,680
Balance 31 March 19-6	228,880

Plant sold

Cost: year to 31 March 19-2		40,000
Depreciation: year to 31 March 19-2	20%	8,000
		32,000
Depreciation: year to 31 March 19-3	20%	6,400
		25,600
Addition		4,400
		30,000
Depreciation: year to 31 March 19-4	20%	6,000
		24,000
Depreciation: year to 31 March 19-5	20%	4,800
		19,200

Depreciation accumulated: 8,000 + 6,400 + 4,000 + 4,800 = 25,200.

(c) *Sale of plant*

		13,700
less Cost (40,000 + 4,400)	44,400	
Depreciation	25,200	
Book value at date of sale		19,200
Loss on disposal		5,500

25.1

Bank Reconciliation as on 31 December 19-6

Cash at bank as per cash book		678
add Unpresented cheques	256	
Credit transfers	56	312
		990
less Bank Lodgements		115
Cash at bank as per bank statement		875

> **Note for students**
> Both in theory and in practice you can start with the cash book balance working to the bank statement balance, or you can reverse this method. Many teachers have their preferences, but this is a personal matter only. Examiners sometimes ask for them using one way, sometimes the other. Students should therefore be able to tackle them both ways.

25.3

DVT Ltd

Corrected cash book position as on 30 November 19-0

Uncorrected balance		17,397
add overstated cheque (172 − 27)		45
" undercast total		200
		17,642
less standing orders: on cash 12 × £96 =	1,152	
: insurance	150	
" bank charges	452	1,754
Corrected cash book balance		15,888 (Dr)

Bank Reconciliation Statement as on 30 November 19-0

Balance per cash book (as corrected)		15,888
add unpresented cheques		1,435
		17,323
less bankings not credited on bank statement	1,620	
" cheque debited in error by bank	238	1,858
Balance per bank statement		15,465 (Cr)

25.5 A quick check will reveal that opening balances do not agree, as there is a missing figure. You should therefore also show (as workings) an opening bank reconciliation.

Workings

Balance per cash book Sept 1		271.94
add unpresented cheques Sept 1	85.16	
	100.34	
		185.50
add Lodgements in bank but not recorded in cash book until September	53.40	
		301.75
		573.69
	62.85	
	116.25	

Difference: impossible to say with accuracy what it is. Assumed to be old cheque not presented at either Sept 1 or Sept 30 18.76

Balance per bank statement Sept 1 592.45

Answer

Rivers & Co.
Bank Reconciliation Statement as at 30 September 19 × 3

Balance per cash book		1,189.70
add September's unpresented cheques		
052322	90.44	
052323	4.30	
Old unpresented cheque (see workings)	18.76	
		113.50
		1,303.20
less Items not debited		
DD (MedWay Insurance)	26.26	
Interest on Loan	11.19	
Bank charges	7.37	
		44.82
Balance per bank statement		1,258.38

Note The question does not ask that the cash book be written up before attempting the bank reconciliation statement.

25.7

Cash Book

19-6 (Totals so far)		19-6 (Totals so far)	
	737		6,017
Mar 31 M Turnbull	57	Mar 31 BKS	49
,, 31 Balance c/d	5,300	,, 31 Bank Charges	28
	6,094		6,094

Bank Reconciliation Statement as at 31 March 19-6

Overdraft per Cash Book		5,300
add Bankings not yet in bank statement		160
		5,460
less Unpresented cheques		490
Overdraft per Bank Statement		4,970

26.1

Petty Cash Book

Receipts		Total	Cleaning	Motor Expenses	Postages	Stationery	Travelling
300	(1)						
	(2) Postages	18			18		
	(3) Travelling	12					12
	(4) Cleaning	15	15				
	(7) Petrol	22		22			
	(8) Travelling	25					25
	(9) Stationery	17				17	
	(11) Cleaning	18	18				
	(14) Postages	5			5		
	(15) Travelling	8					8
	(18) Stationery	9				9	
	(18) Cleaning	23	23				
	(20) Postages	13			13		
	(24) Motor Service	43		43			
	(26) Petrol	18		18			
	(27) Cleaning	21	21				
	(29) Postages	5			5		
	(30) Petrol	14		14			
		286	77	97	41	26	45
286	(31) Cash						
	(31) Balance c/d	300					
586		586					

27.1

(a) 100 units × £1.39 = £139 *not* £1,390.

(b)
(i) Stock overstated by £1,251 (i.e. 1,390 − 139).
(ii) Cost of Goods sold understated by £1,251.
(iii) Net profit overstated by £1,251.
(iv) Current Assets overstated by £1,251.
(v) Owner's Capital overstated by £1,251.

To economise on space, all narratives for journal entries are omitted.

27.2

(a)	J Harris	Dr.	678	: L Hart	Cr. 678
(b)	Machinery	Dr.	4,390	: L Pyle	Cr. 4,390
(c)	Motor Van	Dr.	3,800	: Motor Expenses	Cr. 3,800
(d)	E Fitzwilliam	Dr.	9	: Sales	Cr. 9
(e)	Sales	Dr.	257	: Commissions Rec'd	Cr. 257
(f)	Cash needs	Dr.	154	: T Heath	Cr. 154
	double the amount.				
(g)	Purchases	Dr.	189	: Drawings	Cr. 189
(h)	Discounts Allowed	Dr.	366	: Discounts Received	Cr. 366

28.1

(a) The Journal (narratives omitted)

	Dr	Cr
(i) Suspense	100	
Sales		100
(ii) J Cantrell	250	
J Cochrane		250
(iii) Rent	70	
Suspense		70
(iv) Suspense	300	
Discounts Received		300
(v) Sales	360	
Motor Disposals		360

(b) Suspense Account

	100	Balance b/f	330
	300	Rent	70
	400		400

(c)
Net Profit per accounts		7,900
Add (i) Sales undercast	100	
(iv) Discounts undercast	300	400
		8,300
Less (iii) Rent undercast	70	
(v) Reduction in sales	360	430
Corrected Net Profit		7,870

28.3

The Journal

		Dr	Cr
(a)			
(i)	Suspense	1,000	
	Sales		1,000
(ii)	Purchases	585	
	Suspense		585
(iii)	Suspense	27	
	Penn Supplies Ltd		27
(iv)	Suspense	90	
	Discount Allowed		90
(v)	Suspense	45	
	Sales		45
	Value Added Tax		
(vi)	Farid Attar	154	
	Returns Inwards		59
	Returns Outwards		95

(b) Profit for the year per draft accounts

Adjustments	+	−
Increase in Sales	1,000	
Increase in Purchases		585
Discount from Penn supplies	—	—
Increase in Discounts Allowed		90
Reduction in Sales		45
Increase in Returns Inwards	59	
Increase in Returns Outwards	95	
	1,154	720
Net adjustment		434

28.5

(a)

Suspense

Balance b/fwd	1,536	(i)	Debtor balance omitted	87
(iv) Sales undercast	360	(iii)	Undercast of cash book	720
		(v)	Supplier incorrectly credited for Returns Out (double the amount)	358
		(vii)	Cheque omitted: Mr. Smith	731
	1,896			1,896

Items (ii) and (vi) do not pass through Suspense account.

(b)
(i) Debtor increased in balance sheet.
(ii) Net profit will be increased by 1,200 but further depreciation needed. Machinery increased by 1,200 (subject to depreciation) in the balance sheet.
(iii) Cash in the balance sheet increased by 720.

(iv) Sales increased 360, so too is gross profit and net profit.
(v) Creditors reduced 358 in balance sheet.
(vi) Electricity increased 152, so net profit reduced 152. Also electricity owing 152 to be included as extra creditor in balance sheet.
(vii) Cash increased 731 in balance sheet. Can now be removed from bad debt provision, so net profit increased 731 and debtors (net) in balance sheet increased 731.

28.7 RST Ltd
Statement of corrected net profit

	Increase profit	Reduce profit
(a) (i) Bad debts now written off		610
(ii) Bad debts provision revised (55,210 − 610) 54,600 × 2% = 1,092	208	
(iii) Provision for discounts 54,600 − 1,092 = 53,508 × 2%		1,070
(b) Opening rates prepayment omitted		491
(c) Transfer vehicle disposal from sales		1,350
Now charge loss on disposal 8,100 − 5,280 = 2,820 − 1,350		1,470
(e) Transfer equipment from purchases	9,800	
Depreciation on it 9,800 × 20%		1,960
(f) Increase in stock	2,171	
(g) Electricity accrual now made		543
Insurance prepayment now made	162	
(h) Casting errors in wages	100	
	12,441	7,494

Net increase	4,947
Original incorrect figure	78,263
Amended net profit for the year	83,210

(d) Does not affect profit calculation

Suspense		Rates (b)	
Opening balance (difference)	301		491
Creditors (d)	90		
Wages (h)	100		
	491		491

29.1 Sales Ledger Control

Balances b/f	4,936	Returns Inwards	1,139
Sales Journal	49,916	Cheques and Cash	46,490
		Discounts Allowed	1,455
		Balances c/d	5,768
	54,852		54,852

29.3 Total Debtors Account

Balance b/f	26,555	Cash (600,570 − 344,890)	255,680
Credit Sales	268,187	Discounts Allowed	5,520
		Set-offs (Total Debtors)	70
		Bad Debts	780
		Returns Inwards	4,140
		Balances c/d	28,552
	294,742		294,742
Balances b/d	28,552		

Total Creditors Account

Cash (503,970 − 14,440)	489,530	Balances b/f	43,450
Discounts Received	3,510	Credit Purchases	496,600
Set-offs (Total Creditors)	70		
Returns Outwards	1,480		
Balances c/d	45,460		
	540,050		540,050
		Balances b/d	45,460

29.5

Adjustment of balances to both sales ledger control and debtors' schedule at 30 November 19-3

	Control a/c	Debtors' schedule
Net balances on 30 November 19-3 as shown (30,416.18 - 171.08)	30,245.10	25,586.83
(i) Bad debt recovered	161.20	
(ii) Discounts allowed: casting error	(100.00)	
(iii) Allowances to customers not entered		(341.27)
(iv) Posting error		9.00
(v) Casting error – debtor's account		10.00
(vi) Credit balance 63.27 in error shown as debit balance (must correct by 2 × 63.27)		(126.54)
(vii) Purchase ledger contras not posted		(763.70)
Purchase ledger contras entered wrong side of control. To correct 2 × 763.70	(1,527.40)	
(viii) Balance omitted		571.02
Discounts allowed shown on wrong side of control. To correct 2 × 1414.28	(2,828.56)	
Error in casting: credit side of control a/c Reduces balance	(1,000.00)	
Error in totals of control a/c	(5.00)	
Amended balances	24,945.34	24,945.34

30.1

R Stubbs

Trading Account for the year ended 31 December 19-5

Stock 1.1.19-5		9,872	Sales	60,000
Add Purchases	(D)	50,748		
		60,620		
	(C)	12,620		
Less Stock 31.12.19-5	(B)	48,000		
Cost of Goods Sold	(B)	48,000		
Gross Profit	(A)	12,000		
		60,000		60,000

Missing figures found in following order (A) to (D).
(A) Mark-up is 25%, therefore Margin is 20%. Sales are 60,000 so Margin is 20% × 60,000 = 12,000 Gross Profit.
(B) + (A) = 60,000. Therefore (B) + 12,000 = 60,000 and accordingly is 48,000.
(C) -12,620 = 48,000 therefore (C) is 60,620.
(D) + 9,872 = 60,620. Therefore (D) is 50,748.

30.3

(a) We know that
$$\frac{\text{Cost of Goods Sold}}{\text{Average Stock}} = \text{Rate of Turnover}$$
substituting $\frac{x}{12,600} = 7$

x = Cost of Goods Sold = 88,200.

(b) If margin is 33⅓% then mark-up will be 50% Gross Profit is therefore 50% of 88,200 = 44,100.

(c) Turnover is (a) + (b) = 88,200 + 44,100 = 132,300.

(d) 66⅔% × 44,100 = 29,400.

(e) Gross Profit - Expenses = Net Profit = 14,700.

30.5

	19-6	19-7	19-8
Opening Stock	20,000	5,000	8,800
Purchases	85,000	112,200	99,000
Closing Stock	5,000	8,800	11,800
Sales	125,000	140,000	130,000
Gross Profit	25,000	31,600	34,000
Variable Expenses	12,500	18,200	18,900
Fixed Expenses	5,500	5,000	6,000
Net Profit	7,000	8,400	9,100

Workings

19-6
(a) Gross Profit 20% of sales, therefore sales = 25,000 × 100/20 = 125,000.
(b) Variable expenses 10% of sales = 10% × 125,000 = 12,500 Sales - Gross Profit = Cost of Goods Sold so 125,000 - 25,000 = Cost of Goods Sold 100,000.
Opening Stock ? + Purchases 85,000 - Closing Stock 5,000 = Cost of Goods Sold 100,000. By deduction Opening Stock is 20,000.

19-7
(a) Purchases.
Same quantity as last year but at new price 85,000 + 10% = 93,500.
But increase in volume 20% so Purchases are 93,500 + 20% = 112,200.
Closing Stock 8,000 units at 1.10
Variable Expenses 140,000 × 13% = 18,200.

19-8
Purchases 90,000 × 1.10 = 99,000
Gross Profit = Net Profit 9,100 + Fixed Expenses 6,000 + Variable Expenses 18,900 = 34,000

Net Profit for 19-7 as % on Sales = $\frac{8,400}{140,000} \times \frac{100}{1} = 6\%$

So for 19-8 Net Profit for 19-8 as % on Sales = 6 + 1 = 7%

As Net Profit = 9,100 the Sales can be calculated = $\frac{9,100}{7} \times 100 = 130,000$.

Sales 130,000 - Gross Profit 34,000 = 96,000 Cost of Goods Sold. Opening Stock 8,800 + Purchases 99,000 - Closing Stock? = Cost of Goods Sold 96,000. so by deduction Closing Stock is 11,800.

31.1

B Arkwright
Statement of Affairs as at 31 December 19-5

Fixed Assets		
Motor Van at cost	2,800	
Less Depreciation	550	2,250
Current Assets		
Stock	3,950	
Debtors	4,970	
Prepaid Expenses	170	
Bank	2,564	
Cash	55	
	11,709	
Less Current Liabilities		
Trade Creditors	1,030	
Expenses Owing	470	1,500
Working Capital		10,209
Capital		12,459
Cash Introduced	(C)	10,000
Add Net Profit	(B)	
Less Drawings	(A)	5,673

Missing figures (A) (B) and (C) deduced in that order. (A) to balance is 12,459. thus (B) has to be 18,132 and (C) becomes 8,132.

31.3 *Workings:*

Purchases Bank	29,487	*Sales Banked*	37,936
Cash	2,994	Cash	9,630
	32,481		47,566
- Creditors 31.12.19-6	5,624	- Debtors 31.12.19-6	9,031
	26,857		38,535
+ Creditors 31.12.19-7	7,389	+ Debtors 31.12.19-7	8,624
Purchases for 19-7	34,246	Sales for 19-7	47,159

Opening Capital:

Bank	405	
Stock	13,862	
Debtors	9,031	
Rates Prepaid	210	
Fixtures	2,500	
	26,008	
Less Creditors	5,624	
Rent Owing	150	
	5,774	
	20,234	

Kelly
Trading & Profit & Loss Account for the year ended 31 December 19-7

Sales			47,159
Less Cost of Goods Sold:			
Opening Stock		13,862	
Add Purchases		34,246	
		48,108	
Less Closing Stock		15,144	32,964
Gross Profit			14,195
Less Expenses:			
Wages		5,472	
Rent (1,650 - 150)		1,500	
Rates (890 + 210 - 225)		875	
Sundry Expenses		375	
Depreciation: Fixtures		250	8,472
Net Profit			5,723

Balance Sheet as at 31 December 19-7

Fixed Assets			
Fixtures at Valuation		2,500	
Less Depreciation		250	2,250
Current Assets			
Stock		15,144	
Debtors		8,624	
Prepayments		225	
		23,993	
Less Current Liabilities			
Trade Creditors	7,389		
Bank Overdraft	602	7,991	
Working Capital			16,002
			18,252
Capital			
Balance at 1.1.19-7			20,234
Add Net Profit			5,723
			25,957
Less Drawings (1,164 + 6,541)			7,705
			18,252

31.5

(a)

Computation of cash stolen

Balance 30 November 19-2	129.60
Takings December 14	259.32
Petty Cash (25.00 – 13.69)	11.31
Total stolen	400.23

Computation of stock stolen

Stock 30 November 19-2 at cost		32,540
add Purchases at cost		5,784
		38,324
less Sales at cost (see W1)	13,764	
Stock unstolen	11,300	
		25,064
Stock stolen (at cost)		13,260

(W1) 1429.71 + 6,250.29 = 7,680 – 30% profit = 5,376

1,644.50 + 8,079.50 + 259.32 + 1,200.68 = 11,184 – profit 25% = 8,388

13,764

(b)

Computation of bank balance 14 December 19-2

Balance on 30 November 19-2		6,625.08
add Cash takings 1-13 December	3,074.21	
Receipts from debtors	15,867.11	18,941.32
		25,566.40
less Suppliers	17,118.36	
Petty cash imprest 1 December	9.74	
Wages	361.59	17,489.69
Bank balance 14 December 19-2		8,076.71

31.7

(a)

Bank Summary

Loan		2,500	Overdraft b/f	2,100
Trade Debtors*	37,486		Wages	3,400
Less Drawings	5,200	32,286	Rent, Rates & Electricity	1,010
			Suppliers	25,140
			Other Operating Overheads	746
			Shop Fittings bought	1,200
			Balance c/d	1,190
		34,786		34,786

*balancing figure

(b)

Philip Gold
Trading & Profit & Loss Account for the year ended 31 July 19-1

Sales		36,036
less Cost of Goods Sold:		
Opening Stock	4,230	
Add Purchases	25,070	
	29,300	
less Closing Stock	3,560	25,740
Gross Profit		10,296
less Expenses:		
Wages	3,400	
Rent, Rates & Electricity (1,010 + 75 + 70 – 90 – 50)	1,015	
Other Operating Overheads	746	
Depreciation	410	5,571
Net Profit		4,725

Balance Sheet as at 31 July 19-1

Fixed Assets			
Shop Fixtures & Fittings at cost		4,100	
Less Depreciation to date		1,280	2,820
Current Assets			
Stock		3,560	
Debtors		2,310	
Prepaid Expenses		90	
Bank		1,190	
		7,150	
less *Current Liabilities*			
Creditors	3,920		
Expenses Owing	70	3,990	
Working Capital			3,160
			5,980
Financed by:			
Capital			
Balance at 1.8.19-0		4,555	
add Net Profit		4,725	
		9,280	
less Drawings (600 + 5,200)		5,800	3,480
Loan from Relative			2,500
			5,980

Workings:

Sales: Cash received 37,486 – Opening debtors 3,760 +
Closing debtors 2,310 = 36,036

Purchases: Paid 25,140 – Opening Creditors 3,390 +
Closing creditors 3,920 – goods own use 600 = 25,070.

Capital 1.7.19-0 Fixtures 2,900
less Depreciation 870
2,030

Stock 4,230
Debtors 3,760
Rates prepaid 75
10,095

less Creditors Bank Overdraft 3,390
Electricity Owing 2,100
50
5,540
4,555

Balance Sheet as at 31 December 19-0

	Cost	Depreciation	
Fixed Assets			
Lease	6,500	487	6,013
Equipment	4,800	960	3,840
Vehicle	3,600	900	2,700
	14,900	2,347	12,553
Current Assets			
Stock		580	
Debtors	4,250		
less Provision for Bad Debts	425		
		3,825	
Prepaid Expenses (75 + 200)		275	
Bank (see workings)		6,084	
Cash		123	
		10,887	
less Current Liabilities			
Trade Creditors	714		
Interest Owing	300		
Accountancy Fee Owing	250		
Rates Owing	135		
Electricity Owing	374		
		1,773	
Working Capital			9,114
			21,667

Financed by:

Capital
Introduced (6,500 + 3,600) 10,100
add Net Profit 12,927
23,027
less Drawings (4,680 + 280 + 400) 5,360
17,667
Loan 4,000
21,667

31.9

David Denton

Profit & Loss Account for the year ended 31 December 19-0

Work Done: Credit Account 29,863
For Cash 3,418
33,281

less Expenses:
Materials (9,600 – 580) 9,020
Secretarial Salary 3,000
Rent 225
Rates (180 – 45) 135
Insurance (800 – 200) 600
Electricity (1,122 + 374 estimated) 1,496
Motor Expenses 912
General Expenses (1,349 + 295) 1,644
Loan Interest (4,000 × 10% × ¾) 300
Provision for Bad Debts 425
Accounting Fee 250
Amortisation of Lease (650 × ¾) 487
Depreciation: Equipment 960
Van 900
1,860
20,354

Net Profit 12,927

Workings:

Bank

Capital	6,500	Lease	6,500
Bills	25,613	Drawings 52 × 90	4,680
Loan	4,000	" Holiday	280
Cash Banked	2,600	Secretary	3,000
		Equipment	4,800
		Materials	8,886
		Electricity	1,122
		Motor Expenses	912
		Rent	300
		Insurance	800
		General Expenses	1,349
			32,629
		Balance	6,084
	38,713		38,713
	38,713		

31.10 John Snow

Trading & Profit & Loss Account for the year ended 31 March 19-1

Sales (note 5)			60,000
less Cost of Goods Sold:			
Opening Stock		3,200	
add Purchases (note 1)		44,000	
		47,200	
less Burglary Loss	4,000		
Damaged Stock	1,000	5,000	
		42,200	
less Closing Stock		6,200	36,000
Gross Profit (note 2)			24,000
add Discounts Received		1,200	
Agency Commission		440	1,640
			25,640
less Trade Expenses (7,360 + 120 – 80)		7,400	
Stock Losses: Burglary	4,000		
Damaged Stock	1,000	5,000	
Motor Expenses (6,720 – 230 + 530)		7,020	
Discounts Allowed		1,620	
Depreciation: Motor Vehicles	1,000		
Buildings	500	1,500	22,540
Net Profit			3,100

Balance Sheet as at 31 March 19-1

Fixed Assets			
Buildings at cost		10,000	
less Depreciation to date		6,500	3,500
Motor Vehicles at cost		5,000	
less Depreciation to date		3,000	2,000
			5,500
Current Assets			
Stock at cost		6,200	
Debtors (see note 3)		7,140	
Prepayments		80	
Bank (see note 4)		4,810	
		18,230	
less Current Liabilities			
Creditors	7,600		
Expenses	530	8,130	
Working Capital			10,100
			15,600

Financed by:			
Capital			
Balance at 1.4.19-0 (see note 6)			16,800
add Net Profit			3,100
			19,900
less Drawings			4,300
			15,600

Notes

1 **Purchases Control**

Discounts Received	1,200	Balance b/f	4,200
Bank (note 4)	39,400	Trading	44,000
Balance c/f (9,500 – 20%)	7,600		
	48,200		48,200

*Commission is 1% of Purchases = 440
Note 2 Gross Profit is 40% of Sales
3 Trade Debtors 6,700 + Commission 440 = 7,140.

32.1

Praetorius Club

Income & Expenditure Account for the year ended 30 September 19-7

Income			
Subscriptions (W1)		4,368	
Donations		150	
			4,518
Less Expenditure			
Rent		1,300	
Meeting Expenses (559 + 150)		709	
Heating & Lighting (446 - 110 + 83)		419	
Stationery & Printing (320 + 67 - 83)		304	
Donations to Charities		87	
Secretary's Expenses		224	
Expenses of Annual Dinner	1,213		
Less Sale of Tickets	990	223	
			3,603
Deficit			
Depreciation (10% × 2,500 + 870)		337	
Surplus of Income over Expenditure			915

Balance Sheet as at 30 September 19-7

Fixed Assets			
Office Equipment at cost		3,370	
Less Depreciation to date		837	
			2,533
Current Assets			
Stock of Stationery		83	
Subscriptions in Arrears		90	
Cash & Bank		1,756	
		1,929	
Less Current Liabilities			
Subscriptions in Advance	35		
Accrued Expenses	83	118	
Working Capital			1,811
			4,344
Financed by:			
Accumulated Fund (W2)			
Balance at 1 October 19-6			3,429
Add Surplus for the year			915
			4,344

4

Bank

Balance b/f	4,310	Motor Expenses	6,720
Commission	300	Purchases (note 1)	39,400
Sales (note 5)	57,980	Drawings	4,300
		Trade Expenses	7,360
		Balance c/fwd	4,810
	62,590		62,590

5

Sales

Balance b/f	6,300	Bank	57,980
Sales	60,000	Discounts Allowed	1,620
		Balance c/f	6,700
	66,300		66,300

6

Capital 31 March 19-0

Buildings	10,000		
less Depreciation	6,000		
		4,000	
Vehicles at cost	5,000		
less Depreciation	2,000		
		3,000	
Stock (cost)		3,200	
Debtors		6,300	
Commission owing		300	
Prepaid		120	
Bank		4,310	
		14,230	
less Creditors	4,200		
Expenses Owing	230	4,430	
		9,800	
		16,800	

Workings
(W1)

		Subscriptions	
Arrears b/f	150	In advance b/f	75
Income & Expenditure	4,368	Cash	4,388
In advance c/d	35	Arrears c/d	90
	4,553		4,553

(W2)

Opening Accumulated Fund		2,000
Office Equipment (2,500 - 500)		67
Stocks of Stationery		150
Subscriptions in Arrears		150
Prepaid Meeting Expenses		1,247
Cash & Bank		3,614
Subscriptions in advance	75	
Accrued Heating & Lighting	110	185
		3,429

32.3 (a) *Accumulated Fund 1 January 19-6*

Bank		876
Debtors – lawn mowers		400
Stocks of seeds		250
Land		2,000
		3,526
less Subs in advance	240	
Creditor: mower supplier	800	
seed growers	110	1,150
		2,376

(b)   **Springtime Gardeners' Club**

Income & Expenditure Accounts for the year ended 31 December 19-6

Subscriptions (see W1)		7,040
less: Loss on seed sales (W2)	136	
Costs of National Garden Show (W3)	3,690	
Garden magazines	390	
Secretarial expenses	940	
Rent of premises	500	5,656
Surplus of Income over Expenditure		1,384

(W1) Subscriptions: Received		7,190
add in advance b/f		240
		7,430
less in advance c/f		390
		7,040

(W2) Seeds: Paid		1,900
– Creditors b/f		110
		1,790
+ Creditors c/f		340
		2,130
- Stock increase (560 -250)		310
Cost of sales		1,820
Sales		1,684
Loss		136

(W3) Tickets & brochures		3,600
Coaches		490
		4,090
less sales to non-members		400
		3,690

Balance Sheet as at 31 December 19-6

Fixed Assets		
Land at cost	2,000	
Architect's fees	1,000	3,000
Current Assets		
Stocks of seeds	560	
Debtors	1,370	
	1,930	
less Current Liabilities		
Creditors (170 + 340)	510	
Subs received in advance	390	
Bank overdraft	270	1,170
Working Capital		760
		3,760
Financed by:		
Accumulated fund at 1.1.19-6		2,376
add Surplus for year		1,384
		3,760

32.4 (a)   Green Bank Sports Club

Bar Trading & Profit & Loss Account for the year ended 31 March 19-1

Sales		21,790
Less Cost of Sales:		
Opening Stock	1,860	
Purchases (13,100 + 460 − 370)	13,190	
	15,050	
Less Closing Stock	2,110	12,940
Gross Profit		8,850
Less Bar Steward's Salary		5,800
Net Profit		3,050

(b)   Income & Expenditure Account for the year ended 31 March 19-1

Income		
Subscriptions: Ordinary (1,575 + 200 − 150)	1,625	
Life Membership (10% of 800 + 1,100)	190	1,815
Net Profit on Bar		3,050
Building Society Interest		278
		5,143
Less Expenditure:		
Annual Dinner: net cost (610 − 560)	50	
Clubhouse Rent (520 − 130 + 140)	530	
Clubhouse Painting	580	
Insurance (240 + 70 − 40)	270	
Depreciation: Fixtures (10% of 9,870)	987	
General Expenses	1,100	
Maintenance of Grounds	1,310	
Secretary's Honorarium	200	5,027
Surplus of Income over Expenditure		116

32.4 (c)   *Balance Sheet as at 31 March 19-1*

Fixed Assets		
Fixtures & Fittings at cost (8,000 + 1,870)	9,870	
Less Depreciation to date	3,387	6,483
Investment		
Building Society Investment (2,676 + 1,500 + 278)		4,454
Current Assets		
Bar Stock	2,110	
Prepayments	40	
Bank	3,102	
Cash	239	5,491
Less Current Liabilities		
Creditors	460	
Accrued Expenses	140	
Subscriptions in Advance	150	750
Working Capital		4,741
		15,678

33.1

Loose Tools

			£					£
19-4					19-4			
Jan	1	Stock b/d	1,250		Dec	31	Manufacturing	994
Dec	31	Bank	2,000			31	Stock c/d	2,700
..	31	Wages	275					
..	31	Materials	169					
			3,694					3,694
19-5					19-5			
Jan	1	Stock b/d	2,700		Dec	31	Manufacturing	1,695
Dec	31	Bank	1,450			31	Stock c/d	3,340
..	31	Wages	495					
..	31	Materials	390					
			5,035					5,035
19-6					19-6			
Jan	1	Stock b/d	3,340		Dec	31	Bank: Refund	88
Dec	31	Bank	1,890			31	Manufacturing	1,897
..	31	Wages	145			31	Stock c/d	3,680
..	31	Materials	290					
			5,665					5,665

Financed by:

Accumulated Fund at 1.4.19-0 (see workings)			13,962
Add Surplus of Income over Expenditure			116
			14,078
Life Membership Fund (990 + 800 - 190)			1,600
			15,678

Workings:

	£	£
Accumulated fund at 31 March 19-0:		
Fixtures and fittings: at cost	8,000	
less Depreciation to date	2,400	
		5,600
Bar stocks		1,860
Amounts prepaid		70
Building society investment account		2,676
Balance at bank		5,250
Cash in hand		196
		15,652

	£	
Less Life membership fund: Received year ended 31 March 19-0	1,100	
Apportioned year ended 31 March 19-0	110	
	990	
Subscriptions received in advance	200	
Creditors	370	
Accrued expenses	130	
	1,690	
	£13,962	

(c) See text.

33.3 (a) (i) Straight line
Cost £112,000 – trade in £12,000 = £100,000
Per month £100,000 ÷ 48 = 2,083·33

19-6	9 months	=	18,750
19-7	12 months	=	25,000
19-8	12 months	=	25,000
19-9	12 months	=	25,000
19-0	3 months	=	6,250
			100,000

(ii) Diminishing (Reducing) Balance:

Cost	112,000
Depreciation 91-6 (40%)	44,800
	67,200
Depreciation 19-7	26,880
	40,320
Depreciation 19-8	16,128
	24,192
Depreciation 19-9	9,677
	14,515
Depreciation 19-0	5,806
	8,709

(iii) Units of output (Total £100,000)

19-6	4,000/20,000	=	20,000
19-7	5,000/20,000	=	25,000
19-8	5,000/20,000	=	25,000
19-9	5,000/20,000	=	25,000
19-0	1,000/20,000	=	5,000

(b) (i)
Machine

19-7 Jan 1	Balance b/d	112,000

(ii) **Provision for Depreciation**

19-7			19-7	
Dec 31	Balance c/d	43,750	Jan 1 Balance b/d	18,750
			Dec 31 Profit & Loss	25,000
		43,750		43,750

(iii) There would not be any entries in the Assets Disposals account.

33.5

Manufacturing, Trading & Profit & Loss Accounts
for the year ended 31 December 19-7

Stock Raw Materials 1.1.19-7			18,450
Add Purchase		64,300	
Add Carriage Inwards		1,605	
			84,355
Less Stock Raw Materials 31.12.19-7			20,210
Cost of Raw Materials Consumed			64,145
Direct Labour			65,810
Prime Cost			129,955
Factory Overhead Expenses			
Rent 2/3	1,800		
Fuel & Power	5,920		
Depreciation: Machinery	8,300		
			16,020
			145,975
Add Work-in-Progress 1.1.19-7			23,600
			169,575
Less Work-in-Progress 31.12.19-7			17,390
Production Cost Goods Completed c/d			152,185
Sales			200,600
Less Cost of Goods Sold			
Stock Finished Goods 1.1.19-7		17,470	
Add Production Cost Goods Completed b/d		152,185	
		169,655	
Less Stock Finished Goods 31.12.19-7		21,485	
			148,170
Gross Profit			52,430
Less Expenses:			
Office Salaries		16,920	
Rent 1/3		900	
Lighting & Heating		5,760	
Depreciation: Office Equipment		1,950	
			25,530
Net Profit			26,900

D Saunders
Manufacturing, Trading & Profit & Loss Account
for the year ended 31 December 19-6

Stock of Raw Materials 1.1.19-6		8,565	
Add Purchases		39,054	
		47,619	
Less Stock of Raw Materials 31.12.19-6		9,050	
Cost of Raw Materials Consumed		38,569	
Manufacturing Wages (45,370 + 305)		45,775	
Prime Cost		84,344	
Factory Overhead Expenses:			
Factory Lighting & Heating	2,859		
General Expenses: Factory	5,640		
Rent of Factory	4,800		
Depreciation: Machinery	2,000	15,299	
Production Cost of Goods Completed c/d		99,643	
Sales			136,500
Less Cost of Goods Sold:			
Stock Finished Goods 1.1.19-6		29,480	
Add Production Cost of Goods Completed b/d		99,643	
		129,123	
Less Stock Finished Goods 31.12.19-6		31,200	97,923
Gross Profit			38,577
Less Expenses			
Office Salaries		6,285	
General Expenses: Office		3,816	
Office Rent (2,200 - 108)		2,092	
Office Heating & Lighting		1,110	
Salesmens Commission		7,860	
Delivery Van Expenses		2,500	
Depreciation: Office Equipment		1,500	
Premises		1,000	26,163
Net Profit			12,414

Balance Sheet as at 31 December 19-6

	Cost	Depreciation	Net
Fixed Assets			
Premises	50,000	11,000	39,000
Machinery	50,000	19,500	30,500
Office Equipment	15,000	5,500	9,500
	115,000	36,000	79,000
Current Assets			
Stocks: Finished Goods		31,200	
Raw Materials		9,050	
Debtors		28,370	
Prepaid Expenses		108	
Bank		13,337	
		82,065	
Less Current Liabilities			
Creditors		19,450	
Expenses Owing		305	
		19,755	
Working Capital			62,310
			141,310
Capital			
Balance 1.1.19-6			137,456
Add Net Profit			12,414
			149,870
Less Drawings			8,560
			141,310

Charnley's Department Store
Trading Account for the year ended 31 December 19-8

	Electrical		Furniture		Leisure Goods	
Sales		29,840		73,060		39,581
less Cost of Goods Sold:						
Stock 1.1.19-8	6,080		17,298		14,370	
add Purchases	18,195		54,632		27,388	
	24,275		71,930		41,758	
less Stock 31.12.19-8	7,920	16,355	16,150	55,780	22,395	19,363
Gross Profit		13,485		17,280		20,218

34.2

J Spratt

Trading & Profit & Loss Account for the year ended 31 March 19-6

	A		B	
Sales		15,000		10,000
less Cost of Goods Sold:				
Stock 1.4.19-5	250		200	
add Purchases	11,800		8,200	
	12,050		8,400	
less Stock 31.3.19-6	300		150	
		11,750		8,250
Gross Profit		3,250		1,750
Less Expenses:				
Wages	1,000		750	
Newspapers: Delivery	150			
General Office Salaries	450		300	
Rates	26		104	
Fire Insurance	10		40	
Lighting & Air Conditioning	24		96	
Repairs to Premises	5		20	
Internal Telephone	5		20	
Cleaning	6		24	
Accounting & Audit	72		48	
General Office Expenses	36		24	
		1,784		1,426
Net Profits		1,466		324

35.1

Columnar Sales Day Book

19-7		Inv No	Total	VAT	Hi Fi Dept	TV Dept	Sundries Dept
Feb	1 P Small	586	2,860	260		2,600	
‟	2 L Goode	587	1,980	180	1,800		
‟	3 R Daye	588	1,760	160		1,600	
‟	5 B May	589	320	–			320
‟	7 L Goode	590	990	90		900	
‟	7 P Small	591	3,740	340	3,400		
			11,650	1,030	5,200	5,100	320

General Ledger

Sales

19-7		Hi Fi	TV	Sundries
Feb 28	Total for month	5,200	5,100	320

Value Added Tax

19-7		
Feb 28	Total for month	1,030

P Small

Feb 1	Sales	2,860
‟ 7	Sales	3,740

L Goode

Feb 2	Sales	1,980
‟ 7	Sales	990

R Daye

Feb 3	Sales	1,760

B May

Feb 5	Sales	320

35.2

M Barber

Purchases Analysis Book

19-6		Total Purchases	Purchases	Light & Heat	Motor Exps	Stationery	Carriage Inwards
Jul	1 L Ogden	220	220				
‟	3 E Evans	390	390				
‟	4 North Electricity	88		88			
‟	5 H Noone	110	110				
‟	6 Kirk Motors	136			136		
‟	8 Avon Enterprises	77				77	
‟	10 Kirk Motors	55			55		
‟	12 North Gas Board	134		134			
‟	15 A Dodds	200	200				
‟	17 O Aspinall	24		24			
‟	18 J Kelly	310	310				
‟	19 D Adams	85					85
‟	21 J Moore	60				60	
‟	23 H Noone	116	116				
‟	27 D Flynn	62					62
‟	31 Kirk Motors	185			185		
		2,252	1,346	246	376	137	147

35.3 General Ledger : Purchases Dr 1,346; Lighting & Cooling Dr 246; Motor Expenses Dr 376; Stationery Dr 137; Carriage Inwards Dr 147.

Purchases Ledger : Credits in Personal Accounts should be obvious

36.1 (i)

Graham, Harvey, Rutherford & Miles
Appropriation Account for the year ended 31 December 19-6

Net Profit b/d			85,550
add Interest on Drawings:			
Graham		1,729	
Harvey		1,100	
Rutherford		832	
Miles		789	4,450
			90,000
less Salaries:			
Graham	10,000		
Harvey	10,000		
Rutherford	8,000		
Miles	8,000		36,000
Interest on Capital:			
Graham	7,500		
Harvey	7,000		
Rutherford	6,000		
Miles	6,000		26,500
Share of Balance:			
Graham	35%	9,625	
Harvey	35%	9,625	
Rutherford	20%	5,500	
Miles	10%	2,750	27,500
			90,000

(ii)(Initials of partners used to save space. Dates omitted).

	G	H	R	M
Balance b/f			1,240	
Interest on Drawings	1,729	1,100	832	789
Drawings	23,050	21,980	16,640	17,300
Balances c/d	4,446	6,915	788	
	29,225	29,995	19,500	18,089

	G	H	R	M
Balance b/f	2,100	3,370	–	980
Interest on Capital	7,500	7,000	6,000	6,000
Salaries	10,000	10,000	8,000	8,000
Profit shared	9,625	9,625	5,500	2,750
Balance c/d				359
	29,225	29,995	19,500	18,089

36.3 Considerations

(a) *Legal position re Partnership Act 1890:* Partners can agree to anything. The main thing is that of mutual agreement. The agreement can either be very formal in a partnership deed drawn up by a lawyer or else it can be evidenced in other ways.

The Act lays down the provisions for profit sharing if agreement has not been reached, written or otherwise.

(b) As Bee is not taking active part in the running of the business he could be registered as a limited partner under the 1907 Limited Partnership Act. This has the advantage that his liability is limited to the amount of capital invested by him; he can lose that but his personal possessions cannot be taken to pay any debts of the firm.

As Bee is a 'sleeping partner' you will have to decide whether his reward should be in the form of a fixed amount, or should vary according to the profits made. In this context you should also bear in mind whether or not he would suffer a share of losses if they occurred.

If he was to have a fixed amount, irrespective as to whether profits had been made or not then the question arises as to the amount required. This is obviously a more risky investment than, say, government securities. He therefore would naturally expect to get a higher return.

Bee would probably feel aggrieved if the profits rose sharply, but he was still limited to the amounts already described. There could be an arrangement for extra payments if the profits exceeded a given figure.

Cee is the expert conducting the operations of the business. He will consequently expect a major share of the profits.

One possibility would be to give him a salary, similar to his current salary, before dividing whatever profits then remain.

(c) Dee is making himself available, as well as bringing in some capital. Because of this active involvement the will affect the profits made. It would seem appropriate to give him a salary commensurate with such work, plus a share of the profits.

(d) *Interest on capital:* Whatever is decided about profit-sharing, it would seem appropriate for each of the partners to be given interest on their capitals before sharing the balance of the profits.

36.5

Mendez & Marshall
Trading & Loss Account for the year ended 30 June 19-6

Sales			123,650
less Cost of Goods Sold:			
Opening Stock		41,979	
add Purchases		85,416	
		127,395	
Less Closing Stock		56,340	71,055
Gross Profit			52,595
add Reduction in Provision for Bad Debts			80
			52,675
less Salaries & Wages (18,917 + 200)		19,117	
Office Expenses (2,416 + 96)		2,512	
Carriage Outwards		1,288	
Discounts Allowed		115	
Bad Debts		503	
Loan Interest		4,000	
Depreciation: Fixtures	770		
Buildings	1,000	1,770	29,305
Net Profit			23,370
add Interest on Drawings: Mendez		180	
Marshall		120	300
			23,670
less Interest on Capitals: Mendez	3,500		
Marshall	2,950	6,450	
Salary: Mendez		800	7,250
			16,420
Balance of Profits Shared: Mendez		8,210	
Marshall		8,210	16,420

Balance Sheet as at 30 June 19-6

	Cost	Depc'n	
Fixed Assets			
Buildings	75,000	26,000	49,000
Fixtures	11,000	4,070	6,930
	86,000	30,070	55,930
Current Assets			
Stock			56,340
Debtors		16,243	
Less Provision for Bad Debts		320	15,923
Bank			677
			72,940
Less Current Liabilities			
Creditors		11,150	
Expenses Owing		296	11,446
Working Capital			61,494
			117,424
Financed by			
Capitals: Mendez		35,000	
Marshall		29,500	64,500

Current Accounts	Mendez	Marshall	
Balance 1.7.19-6	1,306	298	
add Interest on Capital	3,500	2,950	
add Salary	800		
add Balance of Profit	8,210	8,210	
	13,816	11,458	
less Drawings	6,400	5,650	
less Interest on Drawings	180	120	
	7,236	5,688	12,924
			77,424
Loan from J King			40,000
			117,424

37.1

(a)

Goodwill	12,000
Other Assets	14,000
	26,000
Capitals X (6,000 + 6,000)	12,000
Y (4,800 + 4,500)	9,300
Z (3,200 + 1,500)	4,700
	26,000

(b) Goodwill Workings

	Before		After		Loss or Gain	Action needed	
X	4/8	6,000	3/10	3,600	Loss 2,400	Credit X	2,400
Y	3/8	4,500	3/10	6,000	Gain 1,500	Debit Y	1,500
Z	1/8	1,500	3/10	2,400	Gain 900	Debit Z	900
		12,000		12,000			

Balance Sheet as at 1 January 19-8

Net Assets	14,000
	14,000
Capitals X (6,000 + 2,400)	8,400
Y (4,800 − 1,500)	3,300
Z (3,200 − 900)	2,300
	14,000

37.3 (a)

Goodwill	Dr	6,000	
Capitals X			3,000
Y			3,000
Cash	Dr	7,000	
Capital Z			7,000

Balance Sheet

(b)

Goodwill	6,000
Fixed & Current Assets	15,000
Cash	9,000
	30,000
Capitals X	11,000
Y	7,000
Z	7,000
	25,000
Current Liabilities	5,000
	30,000

(c)

Capitals X	Dr	2,400	
Y	Dr	1,800	
Z	Dr	1,800	
Goodwill			6,000

37.4

A

Balance c/d	7,500	Balance b/f	3,000
		Adjustment for Goodwill	4,500
	7,500		7,500

B

Balance c/d	6,200	Balance b/f	5,000
		Adjustment for Goodwill	1,200
	6,200		6,200

C

Adjustment for Goodwill	1,200	Balance b/f	4,000
Balance c/d	2,800		
	4,000		4,000

D

Adjustment for Goodwill	3,000	Cash	3,000

E

Adjustment for Goodwill	1,500	Balance c/d	1,500

Goodwill Workings

	Before		After		Loss or Gain		Action needed	
A	5/10	9,000	3/12	4,500	Loss	4,500	Credit A	4,500
B	4/10	7,200	4/12	6,000	Loss	1,200	Credit B	1,200
C	1/10	1,800	2/12	3,000	Gain	1,200	Debit C	1,200
D			2/12	3,000	Gain	3,000	Debit D	3,000
E			1/12	1,500	Gain	1,500	Debit E	1,500
				*18,000				18,000

* If D is to pay £3,000 for 2/12 share, therefore Goodwill (total) is worth

$$\frac{3,000}{2} \times 12 = 18,000$$

38.1

Buildings

Balance b/f	8,000	Balance c/d	17,500
Revaluation: Increase	9,500		
	17,500		17,500

Motor Vehicles

Balance b/f	3,550	Revaluation: Reduction	950
		Balance c/d	2,600
	3,550		3,550

Stock

Balance b/f	2,040	Revaluation: Reduction	150
		Balance c/d	1,890
	2,040		2,040

Office Fittings

Balance b/f	1,310	Revaluation: Reduction	220
		Balance c/d	1,090
	1,310		1,310

Revaluation

Motor Vehicles	950	Buildings	9,500
Stock	150		
Office Fittings	220		
Profit on Revaluation			
Hughes	4,090		
Allen	2,454		
Elliott	1,636		
	8,180		
	9,500		9,500

Capitals

	Hughes	Allen	Elliott		Hughes	Allen	Elliott
Balances c/d	13,650	8,874	6,476	Balances b/f	9,560	6,420	4,840
				Profit on Revaluation	4,090	2,454	1,636
	13,650	8,874	6,476		13,650	8,874	6,476

Balance Sheet as at 31 December 19-5

Fixed Assets		
Buildings at valuation		17,500
Motors at valuation		2,600
Office Fittings at valuation		1,090
		21,190
Current Assets		
Stock at valuation	1,890	
Debtors	4,530	
Bank	1,390	7,810
Capitals:		
Hughes	13,650	
Allen	8,874	
Elliott	6,476	29,000
		29,000

38.3

Goodwill

Revaluation	2,000	Balance b/f	2,000

Revaluation

Plant & Machinery	2,000	Goodwill	2,000
Loss on revaluation	60	Stock	200
Avon ⅔	1,116		
Brown ⅓	744		
	1,860		
	2,060		2,060

Capitals

	Avon	Brown	Charles		Avon	Brown	Charles
Loss on Revaluation	1,116	744		Balances b/f	4,000	3,000	2,000
Balances c/d	2,884	2,256	2,000	Cash			2,000
	4,000	3,000	2,000		4,000	3,000	2,000

Balance Sheet

Fixed Assets		
Plant & Machinery at valuation		2,000
Current Assets		
Stock	1,900	
Debtors	2,130	
Bank	2,090	
	6,120	
less Current Liabilities		
Creditors	980	
Working Capital		5,140
		7,140
Capitals		
Avon		2,884
Brown		2,256
Chike		2,000
		7,140

Capitals

	Alan	Bob	Charles	Don			Alan	Bob	Charles	Don
Goodwill			42,000		Balances b/d	85,000	65,000	35,000	–
Retirement				–12,000	Goodwill	21,000	14,000	7,000	–
Cash				67,000	Cash				79,000
Balances b/f	106,000	79,000	42,000	79,000		106,000	79,000	42,000	79,000

Current Accounts

	Alan	Bob	Charles	Don			Alan	Bob	Charles	Don
Balance b/f		2,509			Balance b/d	3,714		4,678	
Retirement			7,478		Profit on Revaluation	8,400	5,600	2,800	
Cash	9,023			3,091	Cash				3,091
Balances c/d	3,091	3,091								
	12,114	5,600	7,478	3,091		12,114	5,600	7,478	3,091

Charles: Retirement

Car	3,900	Capital	53,578
Cash	53,578	Current	7,478
Balance c/d	20,000	Loan	28,000
	77,478		77,478

Bank

Balance b/f	79,000	Don: Capital	4,200
Retirement – Charles	3,091	Don: Current	53,578
Repaid Alan – Capital	5,710	Balance c/d	21,000
		Current	9,023
	87,801		87,801

38.5

Revaluation*

Premises	90,000	Premises	120,000
Plant	37,000	Plant	35,000
Stock	62,379	Stock	54,179
Provision Doubtful Debts	3,000		
Profit on Revaluation			
Alan % 8,400			
Bob % 5,600			
Charles % 2,800	16,800		
	209,179		209,179

* Just the net increases/decreases could have been recorded. Either method acceptable.

Goodwill

Goodwill: Alan %	21,000	Goodwill cancelled	
Bob %	14,000	Capitals: Alan %	18,000
Charles %	7,000	Bob %	12,000
	42,000	Don %	12,000
			42,000

Balance Sheet as at 30 June 19-2

Fixed Assets			
Premises			120,000
Plant			35,000
Vehicles			11,100
Fittings			2,000
			168,100
Current Assets			
Stock		54,179	
Debtors less provision		31,980	
Cash		760	
		86,919	
less Current Liabilities			
Creditors	19,036		
Bank Overdraft	5,710		
		24,746	
Working Capital			62,173
			230,273
Financed by:			
Capitals:	Alan	67,000	
	Bob	67,000	
	Don	67,000	
			201,000
Current Accounts:	Alan	3,091	
	Bob	3,091	
	Don	3,091	
			9,273
Loan:	Charles		20,000
			230,273

39.1

A Co Ltd

Balance Sheet as at 31 December 19-6

Fixed Assets			
Tangible Assets			
Freehold Premises		71,000	
Machinery		25,000	
			96,000
Current Assets			
Stock	25,000		
Debtors	18,900		
Bank & Cash	20,250		
		64,150	
Creditors: amounts falling due within one year			
Creditors	16,900		
Expenses Owing	3,250		
		20,150	
Net Current Assets			44,000
Total Assets less Current Liabilities			140,000
Creditors amounts falling due after more than one year			
Debentures			5,000
			135,000
Capital and Reserves			
Called up Share Capital			105,000
Profit and Loss Account			30,000
			135,000

Notes: re fixed assets and depreciation re share capital.

39.3
(a) Total dividend 6% + 9% = 15% of 800,000 = 120,000
(b) 15% of £1 = 15 pence
(c) $\dfrac{252,000}{800,000}$ x 100 = 31.5 pence per share

Z Ltd

Appropriation Account for the year ended 31 March 19-7

Net Profit brought down		252,000
Balance forward from last year		340,000
		592,000
less Transfer to General Reserve	100,000	
Ordinary Dividends Paid	120,000	
		220,000
Balance carried forward to next year		372,000

39.5

P Co Ltd
Balance Sheet as at 31 August 19-9

Fixed Assets
Tangible Assets

Freehold Premises		73,000
Plant & Machinery		37,630
Fixtures & Fittings		5,800
		116,430

Current Assets

Stock (61,350 − 7,350)	54,000		
Debtors (10,895 + 250)	11,145		
Bank & Cash	12,575	77,720	

Creditors: amounts falling due within one year

Creditors	9,700		
Expenses Owing	350		
Preference Dividend	10,000	20,050	

Net Current Assets		57,670
Total Assets less Current Liabilities		174,100

Creditors: amounts falling due after more than one year

Debentures		10,000
		164,100

Capital and Reserves

Called-up Share Capital		125,000
Share Premium Account		15,000
Profit & Loss Account		24,100
		164,100

Notes: re fixed assets & depreciation
re share capital

39.7

Skymaster Manufacturing Company Ltd
Trading & Profit & Loss Account for the year ended 31 March 19-7

Sales			130,000
less Cost of Sales			
Opening stock finished goods	7,800		
Market value of manufactures	80,000		
		87,800	
less Closing stock of finished goods		6,600	81,200
Gross Profit			48,800
less Salaries	11,700		
Rent & Rates	3,900		
Light & Heat	7,600		
Depreciation	4,900		28,100
Net profit on sales			20,700
Profit on goods manufactured			14,000
Decrease in provision for unrealised profit on manufactured goods			210
			34,910
Retained profits from last year			10,535
			45,445
Proposed dividend			6,000
Retained profits to next year			39,445

39.9

Grace Ltd
Profit & loss account for the year ended 31 December 19-7

	£000	£000	£000
Sales		750	
less Returns inwards		3	
			747
less Cost of goods sold			
Opening stock		200	
Purchases	350		
less Returns outwards	1	349	
Carriage inwards		1	
		550	
less Closing stock		180	
			370
Gross profit			377
add Discounts received			1
			378
less Expenses:			
General expenses (200 – 2 – 1)		197	
Advertising		10	
Bad debts		20	
Provision for bad debts		3	
Discounts allowed		3	
Carriage outwards		1	
Accountancy charges		1	
Debenture interest		10	
Depreciation: motor vehicles		20	
machinery		10	
			275
Net profit			103
add Retained profits from last year			100
			203
less Proposed dividend			10
Retained profits carried forward			193

Balance Sheet as at 31 March 19-7

Fixed Assets			
Tangible Assets			
Plant & Machinery		12,600	
Shop Fixtures		34,300	
			46,900
Current Assets			
Stocks: Finished Goods (6,600–1,155)		5,445	
Raw Materials		5,000	
Work in Progress		9,100	
Debtors		12,700	
Bank		4,300	
		36,545	
Creditors: amounts falling due within one year			
Creditors	8,000		
Proposed Dividends	6,000		
		14,000	
Net Current Assets			22,545
			69,445
Capital and Reserves			
Called-up Share Capital			30,000
Profit and Loss Account			39,445
			69,445
Notes re fixed assets and depreciation			
re share capital			

Grace Ltd

Balance sheet as at 31 December 19-7

Fixed assets	Cost or valuation	Depreciation	Net
Buildings	260	–	260
Motor vehicles	100	80	20
Machinery	120	60	60
	480	140	340
Current assets			
Stock		180	
Debtors	180		
less Provision	9	171	
Prepayment		3	
		354	
less Current liabilities			
Creditors	200		
Debenture interest owing	5		
Proposed dividend	10		
Accountancy charges owing	1		
Bank overdraft	5	221	
Working capital			133
			473
Financed by:			
Share capital			100
Reserves			
Share premium		50	
Revaluation reserve		30	
Profit & loss account		193	273
Members' equity			373
10 per cent debentures			100
			473

39.10 Extract 1

(a) The amount paid for goodwill.
(b) The excess represents share premium.
(c) Equity shares generally means ordinary shares.
(d) That although issued in 19-6 a dividend will not be paid in that year. The first year that dividends *could* be paid is 19-7.

Extract 2

(e) (i) A rate of 8% per annum interest will be paid on them, irrespective of whether profits are made or not.
(ii) These are the years within which the debentures could be redeemed, if the company so wished.
(f) (i) This is the rate per annum at which preference dividends will be paid, subject to there being sufficient distributable profits.
(ii) That the shares could be bought back by the company.
(g) Probably because there was currently a lower interest rate prevailing at the time of redemption and the company took advantage of it.
(h) Large amounts of both fixed interest and fixed dividend funds have resulted in a raising of the gearing.
(i) Debenture interest gets charged before arriving at net profit. Dividends are an appropriation of profits.
(k) Shareholders are owners and help decide appropriations. Debenture holders are external lenders and interest expense has to be paid.

39.11 (a) This is incorrect. The tax portion has to be counted as part of the total cost, which is made up of debenture interest paid plus tax. Holding back payment will merely see legal action taken by the Inland Revenue to collect the tax.
(b) This cannot be done. The repainting of the exterior does not improve or enhance the original value of the premises. It cannot therefore be treated as capital expenditure.
(c) This is not feasible. Only the profit on the sale of the old machinery, found by deducting net book value from sales proceeds, can be so credited to the profit and loss account. The remainder is a capital receipt and should be treated as such.
(d) This is an incorrect view. Although some of the General Reserve could, if circumstances allowed it, be transferred back to the Profit and Loss Account, it could not be shown as affecting the operating profit for 1983. This is because the reserve was built up over the years before 1983.
(e) This is not feasible. The share capital has to be maintained at nominal value as per the Companies Act. A share premium cannot be created in this fashion, and even if it could, it would still have to be credited to *share premium account* and not the profit and loss account.
(f) Incorrect. Although the premises could be revalued the credit for the increase has to be to a Capital Reserve account. This cannot then be transferred to the credit of the profit and loss account.

39.12 *Notes:* First draw up the balance sheet. The missing figure needed to make the totals agree is the balance of retained profits carried to next year.

Toncliffe Ltd
Balance sheet as at 31 March 19-2

	Cost	Depn	Net
Fixed assets			
Premises	220.000	20.000	200.000
Fixtures	34.002	14.000	20.002
Motor vehicles	260.008	107.000	153.008
	514.010	141.000	373.010
Current assets			
Stock			73.216
Debtors		42.400	
less Provision for bad debts		2.120	40.280
Prepayments			150
Bank			94.070
Cash			5.394
			213.110
Creditors: amounts falling due within one year			
Trade creditors		41.340	
Proposed dividend		8.000	49.340
Net current assets			163.770
Total assets *less* current liabilities			536.780
Creditors: amounts falling due after more than one year			
6% debentures 19-4/-9			30.000
			506.780
Capital and reserves			
Called-up share capital			
190,000 8% preference shares £1		190.000	
540,000 ordinary shares 50p		270.000	460.000
Reserves			
Profit and loss account (*see note below*)			46.780
			506.780

46.780 is the figure needed to balance.

Toncliffe Ltd
Profit and loss account for the year ended 31 March 19-2

Gross profit on trading			146.595 (D)
add Rent received		500	
Discounts received		2.195	
Reduction in bad debts provision		400	3.095
			149.690 (C)
less Wages and salaries		32.398	
Rates and insurance (11,450 − 150)		11.300	
Power, heat and light		5.571	
General expenses		7.423	
Carriage out		2.172	
Obsolete stock written off		934	
Debenture interest		1.800	
Loss on sale of vehicle		762	
Depreciation: premises		2.000	
vehicles		25.000	
fixtures		5.000	94.360
Net profit			55.330 (B)
Dividends: preference dividend		15.200	
proposed ordinary dividend		8.000	23.200
			32.130 (A)
add Retained profits from last year			14.650
Retained profits carried to next year			46.780

40.1

Balance Sheet as at 31 December 19-4

	(i) S Walters	(ii) R Jones
Goodwill	8.200	9.300
Premises	21.000	28.000
Stock	9.600	9.200
Debtors	6.300	6.300
Bank	1.700	–
	46.800	52.800
Capital	40.000	46.000
Creditors	6.800	6.800
	46.800	52.800

Note: Fill in all known figures in the profit and loss account. Then put in final figure, from balance sheet (46.780) representing Unappropriated Profits carried forward. Consequently fill in all other figures (A) to (D) by deduction. working upwards.

548

40.3 (a)

W Deakins
Balance Sheet as at 1 June 19-2

Goodwill	22,450
Premises	80,000
Stock	5,000
Debtors	4,000
Bank	10,000
	121,450
Capital	120,000
Creditors	1,450
	121,450

(b)

Smith, Williams and Vernon
Balance Sheet as at 1 June 19-2

Goodwill	40,000
Premises	80,000
Fixtures & Fittings	40,000
Stock	14,000
Debtors	4,000
Bank (2,000 + 50,000 − 40,000)	12,000
	190,000
Capital: Smith (50,000 + 20,000 Goodwill)	70,000
Williams (50,000 + 20,000 Goodwill)	70,000
Vernon	50,000
	190,000

(c) See text.

40.5

John Crofton (Successor) Ltd
Balance Sheet as at 1 April 19-9

Fixed Assets			
Goodwill (see workings)			30,430
Premises			30,000
Machinery & Plant (15,000+20,000)			35,000
Vehicles			13,000
			108,430
Current Assets			
Stocks (3,170+5,400)		8,570	
Debtors	3,000		
less Provision	600	2,400	
Bank		14,100	
		25,070	
less Current Liabilities			
Creditors (4,000+10,000)		14,000	
Working Capital			11,070
			119,500
Financed by			
Share Capital			
Authorised & Issued: 200,000 shares 50p			100,000
Reserves			
Share Premium		20,000	
Profit & Loss		(500)	19,500
			119,500

Workings

Issues of Shares			90,000
200,000+60p			120,000

Bank

John Crofton	120,000	John Crofton	90,000
		Preliminary Expenses	500
		Machinery	10,000
		Purchases	5,400
		Balance	14,100
	120,000		120,000

Goodwill: Paid	90,000
Net Assets taken over	59,570
	30,430

Note: Profit & Loss – debit balance 500. Before the 1981 Companies Act the preliminary expenses could have been shown as an asset. They must now be written off to profit & loss immediately.

41.1 *(a)*

T Welldone

Statement of Source and Application of Funds for the year ended 31 December 19-7

Source of Funds		
Profits Retained		6,000
Increase in Creditors		4,000
Loan		5,000
		15,000
Application of Funds		
Increase in Stock	9,000	
Increase in Debtors	1,000	
Fixed Assets Purchased	15,000	25,000
		(10,000)
Reduction in Bank Funds		
Bank Balance 31.12.19-6	11,000	
Bank Balance 31.12.19-7	1,000	10,000

(b) Basically profit does not mean an increase in bank or cash.

41.3 *Statement of Source and Application of Funds for the year ended 31 December 19-4*

Source of Funds		
Net Profits	2,200	
add Depreciation: Land	260	
Plant	200	
Total Generated from Operations		2,660
Loan		1,000
		3,660
Application of Funds		
Drawings	1,500	
Plant Bought	1,000	2,500
		1,160
Increase in Working Capital		
Working Capital 31.12.19-3 (note 1)	600	
Working Capital 31.12.19-4 (note 2)	1,760	1,160

Notes (1) 660+1,780 − 1,200 − 640=600
(2) 630+1,260+710 − 840=1,760

41.5

Nick's Newsmart

Source and application of funds statement for the year ended 31 March 19-2

Source of Funds		
Net profit for the year		8,600
add non-cash item: Depreciation		600
Total generated from operations		9,200
Application of funds:		
Additional fittings	5,200	
Additional stocks	4,420	
Additional debtors	2,980	
Reduction in amounts owing to creditors	580	
Drawings	6,200	19,380
		10,180
Excess of applications over sources		
Financed as follows:		
Reduction in bank balance to nil	6,400	
Bank overdraft taken	4,000	
		10,400
less Cash increased		220
		10,180

41.6 Antipodean Enterprises

(a) Statement of source and application of funds for the year ended 31 December 19-3

Source of funds		
Profit before tax		25,200
Adjustment for items not involving movement of funds:		
Depreciation	7,000	
Net book losses on disposal of assets (740 − 430)	310	7,310
		32,510
Total generated from operations		
Funds from other sources		
Disposals of equipment (5,200 + 430)	5,630	
Disposals of cars (2,010 − 740)	1,270	6,900
		39,410
Application of funds		
Fixed assets bought:		
Equipment (W1)	36,400	
Cars (W2)	19,860	
Long-term investments	8,000	
Loan repayments	3,000	
Drawings	15,130	
Capital taken out	6,500	88,890
		(49,480)
Decrease in working capital		
Decrease in stocks		(7,830)
Decrease in debtors		(2,450)
Decrease in creditors		(11,100)
Increase in short-term investments		1,200
Decrease in cash		(1,100)
Increase in bank overdraft		(28,200)
		(49,480)

Workings (complete accounts from known information)

W1
Equipment			
Balance b/fwd	17,600	Sales: Cash (5,200 + 430)	5,630
Profit to P/L A/c	430	Depreciation	3,000
Bank: Equipment bought	36,400	Balance c/d	45,800
(Missing figure to balance)	54,430		54,430

W2
Cars			
Balance b/fwd	4,080	Loss to P/L A/c	740
Bank: Cars bought	19,860	Sales: Cash (2,010 − 740)	1,270
(Missing figure to balance)		Depreciation	3,000
		Balance c/d	18,930
	23,940		23,940

(b) No set answer.

42.1 *H Smith*

Gross Pay: 40 × £1.50		60
less Income Tax	8	
National Insurance (5%)	3	11
Net Pay		49

42.2 *B Charles*

Gross Pay: 40 × £2	80	
20 × £3	60	140
less Income Tax (140 − 40) 100 × 30%	30	
National Insurance 5%	7	37
Net Pay		103

42.3 *B Croft*

Gross Pay: Basic	200	
Commission 2% × £30.00	600	800
less Income Tax (800 − 100) 700 × 30%	210	
National Insurance 5% × 500	25	235
Net Pay		565

43.1

(a) FIFO

Item		Cost	Net Realisable Value	
1	250 × 6	1,500	250 × 5.5	1,375
2	150 × 3	450	150 × 3⅓	500
3	400 × 12	4,800	400 × 15	6,000
4	200 × 18	3,600	200 × 14	2,800
5	600 × 10	6,000	600 × 9	5,400
6	100 × 5	500	100 × 7	700
		16,850		16,775

Article Method 1,375 + 450 + 4,800 + 2,800 + 5,400 + 500 = 15,325
Category Method 1,875 + 8,400 + 6,100 = 16,375

(b) LIFO: Assuming perpetual inventory in use

Item			Cost	Net Realisable Value	
1	250 × 5		1,250	250 × 5.5	1,375
2	50 × 2	= 100	400	150 × 3⅓	500
	100 × 3	= 300			
3	100 × 10	= 1,000	4,600	400 × 15	6,000
	300 × 12	= 3,600			
4	50 × 16	= 800	3,500	200 × 14	2,800
	150 × 18	= 2,700			
5	600 × 12		7,200	600 × 9	5,400
6	100 × 4		400	100 × 7	700
			17,350		16,775

Article Method 1,250 + 400 + 4,600 + 2,800 + 5,400 + 400 = 14,850
Category Method 1,650 + 8,100 + 6,100 = 15,850

43.3

(a) Cost of the (450 + 340 + 100 + 170) 1,060 units.
541.45 + 419.70 + 123.44 + 205.02 = 1,289.61
(b) Average cost.
(c) First In, First Out (FIFO). Another possibility is LIFO.
(d) (FIFO method)

Stores Ledger Card – Stock Item AAT 25

Date 19-7	Purchases Qty	Cost	Amt	Sales Qty	Cost	Amt	Balance Qty	Cost	Amt
Nov 2	300	1.10	330.00				300	1.10	330.00
Nov 9	320	1.30	416.00				620		746.00
Nov 11				300					
				150	1.30	195.00	170	1.30	221.00
Nov 16	340	1.25	425.00				510		646.00
Nov 17				170	1.30	221.00			
				170	1.25	212.50	170	1.25	212.50
Nov 20	330	1.20	396.00				70	1.25	87.50
Nov 23							400		483.50
Nov 26				70	1.25	87.50			
				100	1.20	120.00	230	1.20	276.00
									55,750.00

(e) Profit using average cost method 277.38
Closing stock at average cost 276.00
Closing stock at FIFO 276.00

Amended profit 1.38
.... 55,748.62

Note: If LIFO had been used – Final Stock per (d) would have been 269.00.
Amended profit per (e) would have been 55,741.62.

43.6

Cranfleet Commodities
Stock valuation as on 30 April 19-2

	+	–	
Original valuation figure			187,033
Amendments (see details below)			
(a)		–	
(b)		–	140
(c)	8,010		
(d)			6,480
(e)	1,200		
(f)		–	
(g)		152	
	9,210	6,772	= 2,438
Amended valuation as on 30 April 19-2			189,471

Reasons

(1) As original cost is still below net realisable value, it does not need amending.

(2) The net realisable value is 6,321 – 804 = 5,517. This is 140 below cost, and so reduction is needed.

(3) Error made show stock under-valued by 9,105 – 1,095 = 8,010. Needs adjusting.

(4) Error over-valuing stock by (480 × 15) 7,200 – (480 × 1.50) 720 = 6,480. Adjustment needed.

(5) Goods sent on sale or return, and not sold, belong to Cranfleet and need including, but at cost to Cranfleet, i.e. 1,500 – profit element (20% of S.P.) 300 = 1,200.

(6) Cranfleet owns the goods legally, even though payment not made. No adjustment needed.

(7) Although these samples now belong to Cranfleet they have cost nothing, therefore should not be included.

44.1 (a)

(i) Gross profit as % of sales
$$\frac{20,000}{80,000} \times \frac{100}{1} = 25\% \qquad \frac{24,000}{120,000} \times \frac{100}{1} = 20\%$$

(ii) Net profit as % of sales
$$\frac{10,000}{80,000} \times \frac{100}{1} = 12.5\% \qquad \frac{15,000}{120,000} \times \frac{100}{1} = 12.5\%$$

(iii) Expenses as % of sales
$$\frac{10,000}{80,000} \times \frac{100}{1} = 12.5\% \qquad \frac{9,000}{120,000} \times \frac{100}{1} = 7.5\%$$

(iv) Stockturn
$$\frac{60,000}{(25,000+15,000)\div 2} = 3 \text{ times} \qquad \frac{96,000}{(22,500+17,500)\div 2} = 4.8 \text{ times}$$

(v) Rate of return on capital employed
$$\frac{10,000}{(38,000+42,000)\div 2} \times \frac{100}{1} = 25\% \qquad \frac{15,000}{(36,000+44,000)\div 2} \times \frac{100}{1} = 37.5\%$$

(vi) Current ratio
$$\frac{45,000}{5,000} = 9 \qquad \frac{40,000}{10,000} = 4$$

(vii) Acid test ratio
$$\frac{30,000}{5,000} = 6 \qquad \frac{22,500}{10,000} = 2.25$$

(viii) Debtor/sales ratio
$$\frac{25,000}{80,000} \times 12 = 3.75 \text{ months} \qquad \frac{20,000}{120,000} \times 12 = 2 \text{ months}$$

(ix) Creditor/purchases ratio
$$\frac{5,000}{50,000} \times 12 = 1.2 \text{ months} \qquad \frac{10,000}{91,000} \times 12 = 1.3 \text{ months approx.}$$

(b) Business B is the most profitable, both in terms of actual net profits £15,000 compared to £10,000, but also in terms of Capital Employed. B has managed to achieve a return of £37.50 for every £100 invested, i.e. 37.5% A has managed a lower return of 25%. Reasons – possibly only – as not until you know more about the business could you give a definite answer.

(i) Possibly managed to sell far more merchandise because of lower prices, i.e. took only 20% margin as compared with A's 25% margin.

(ii) Maybe more efficient use of mechanised means in the business. Note he has more equipment, and perhaps as a consequence kept other expenses down to 6,000 as compared with A's 9,000.

(iii) Did not have as much stock lying idle. Turned over stock 4.8 times in the year as compared with 3 for A.

(iv) A's current ratio of 9 far greater than normally needed. B kept it down to 4. A therefore had too much money lying idle and not doing anything.

(v) Following on from (iv) the Acid Test ratio for A also higher than necessary.

(vi) Part of the reasons for (iv) and (v) is that A waited (on average) 3.75 months to be paid by his customers. B managed to collect them on a 2 months' average. Money represented by debts is money lying idle.

(vii) A also paid his creditors quicker than did B, but not by much.
Put all these factors together, and it is obvious that B is running his business far more efficiently, and is more profitable as a consequence.

44.3 (Brief answers requested)

(a) Ratios supporting his optimism:

	19-5/6	19-6/7
(i) Gross Profit/Sales	30%	36%
(ii) Current ratio	2.4	2.5
(iii) Debtor's collection period	81 days	69.6 days
(iv) Debtors' turnover ratio	4.4	5.2
i.e. Credit sales/final debtors		

Therefore there is:
(i) Increases in sales, gross & net profits
(ii) Working capital improvement
(iii) Gross Profit as % sales increased.
(iv) Debtors' collection period reduced.

(b) Accountant's warnings:
Ratios supporting his views:

	19-5/6	19-6/7
(i) ROCE	12.5%	10%
(ii) Net capital capital employed Liquidity (quick ratio)		
(iii) Bank + Debtors/Creditors	160%	75%
(iv) Net Profit/Sales	15%	12.5%
(v) Sales/Net capital employed	83.3%	79.8%
Stock turnover (calculated on closing stock)	3.5	1.3

(vi) Large increase in creditors. Extended credit being taken?
So Accountant can say:
(i) Fall in ROCE.
(ii) Fall in liquidity.
(iii) Fall in net profit %.
(iv) Worse use of capital in trading.
(v) Large capital expenditure has not yet benefited firm.
(vi) Loan taken without due regard to eventual repayment.

44.4

(a) Thomas Bright: Any four from

	31.3.19-6			31.3-19-7	
(i) Net Profit % Sales	8/100	= 8%	(1)/100	=	−0.7%
(ii) Gross Profit as % Sales	40/100	= 40%	50/140	=	35.7%
(iii) Current Ratio	20/5	= 4:1	32/12	=	2.7:1
(iv) Ratio of Debtors/Sales	11/100	= 11%	24/140	=	17.1%
(v) Return on capital employed	8/85	= 9.4%	(1)/100	=	−1%

(b) Any three from
(i) Thomas Bright's income would be higher if he took up alternative employment at £10,000 p.a.
(ii) John Bright could obtain more for his investment in a secure investment with a bank.
(iii) The second year has produced worse results than the first year.
(iv) Son's business acumen does not seem to accord with possible future success.
(c)
(i) Need to understand this to ascertain breakeven point.
(ii) An understanding of how costs change with activity is necessary for proper operation of an organisation.
(iii) May be possible to accept orders covering variable costs and increase profitability.

44.5

Joan Street
Trading & Loss Account for the year ended 31 March 19-8

Sales			(W3)	240,000
Cost of Sales				
Opening Stock		21,000		
add Purchases	(W6)	174,000		
		195,000		
less Closing Stock	(W7)	15,000	(W1)	180,000
Gross Profit			(W2)	60,000
Sundry Expenses			(W5)	38,400
Net Profit			(W4)	21,600

Balance Sheet as at 31 March 19-8

Fixed Assets			(W9)	108,000
Current Assets				
Stock	(W8)	15,000		
Debtors	(W15)	24,000		
Bank		9,000		
	(W14)	48,000		
less Current Liabilities	(W14)	12,000		
Working Capital			(W13)	36,000
			(W12)	144,000
Financed by:				
Capital: Balance at 1.4. 19-7			(W11)	122,400
Add Net Profit			(W10)	21,600
				144,000

Workings (could possibly find alternatives)
(W1) As average stock 21,000 + 15,000 ÷ 2 = 18,000 and stock turnover is 10. this means that cost of sales = 18,000 × 10 = 180,000
(W2) As gross profit is 25% of sales, it must therefore be 33⅓% of cost of sales.
(W3) As (W1) is 180,000 & (W2) is 60,000 therefore sales = (W1) + (W2) = 240,000
(W4) Net profit = 9% of sales = 21,600
(W5) Missing figure, found by arithmetical deduction
(W6) & (W7) Missing figures – found by arithmetical deduction
(W8) Debtors (?) × 365 = 36½, i.e.
    $$\frac{\text{Sales}}{} $$
    $$\frac{? \times 365}{240,000} = 36\tfrac{1}{2}, \text{ by arithmetic}$$
    $$\frac{24,000 \times 365}{240,000} = 36\tfrac{1}{2}$$
    debtors = 24,000. Proof $\dfrac{24,000 \times 365}{240,000} = 36\tfrac{1}{2}$
(W9) 45% × 240,000 = 108,000
(W10) Knowing that Net Profit 21,600 is 15% of W10, so W10 = 21,600 × 100/15 = 144,000
(W11) Missing figure
(W12) & (W13) Put in after (W11)
(W14) If Working Capital Ratio is 4, it means a factor of current assets 4, current liabilities 1 = working capital 3. As (W13) is 36,000. current assets therefore 4/3 × 36,000 = 48,000 and current liabilities
1/3 × 36,000 = 12,000
(W15) Is new missing figure.

(b) Question limited to two favourable and two unfavourable aspects (four given here for reader's benefit)
Favourable: Stock turnover, liquidity, working capital, net profit on sales
Unfavourable: Gross profit to sales, debtors collection, return on capital employed.
turnover to net capital employed.

(c) Drawbacks (more than two listed for reader's benefit)
(i) No access to trends over recent years.
(ii) No future plans etc. given.
(iii) Each business is often somewhat different.
(iv) Size of businesses not known.

44.8

(a) *The bank*
The bank will be interested in two main aspects. The first is the ability to repay the loan as and when it falls due. The second is the ability to pay interest on the due dates.

Mr Whitehall
He will be interested in the expected return on his investment. This means that recent performance of the company and its plans will be important to him. In addition the possible capital growth of his investment would be desirable.

(b) *Note:* More than four ratios for bank are given, but you should give four only as your answer.

Bank
Long-term ability to repay loan

(i)
(ii)
(iii)
(iv)

Members equity/total assets
Loan capital/Members equity
Total liabilities/Members equity
Operating profit/Loan interest.

Short term liquidity

(i)
(ii)

Liquid assets/Current liabilities.
Current assets/Current liabilities.

Mr Whitehall
Return on investment

(i)

Price per share/Earnings per share.

(ii)
(iii)

Trends of (i) for past few years.
Net profit — preference dividend/ordinary dividend.

(iv)

Trends of (iii) for past few years.

44.9 (a) The basis on which accounts are prepared is that of an 'accruals basis'. By this it is meant that the recognition of revenue and expenditure takes place not at the point when cash is received or paid out, but instead is at the point when the revenue is earned or the expenditure is incurred.

To establish the point of recognition of a sale, several criteria are necessary:
(i) The product, or the service, must have been supplied to the customer.
(ii) The buyer must have indicated his willingness to pay for the product or services, and has accepted liability.
(iii) A monetary value of the goods or services must have been agreed to by the buyer.
(iv) Ownership of the goods must have passed to the buyer.

(b) (i) This cannot be recognised as a sale. It does not comply with any of the four criteria above.
(ii) This also cannot be recognised as a sale. Neither criteria (i) nor (iv) have been covered.
(iii) If this was a cash sale, all of the above criteria would probably be achieved on delivery, and therefore it could be appropriate to recognise the sale.
If it was a credit sale, if the invoice was sent with the goods, and a delivery note stating satisfaction by the customer is signed by him, then it would also probably be appropriate to recognise the sale.
(iv) Usually takes place after the four criteria have been satisfied. If so, the sales should be recognised.
(v) In the case of cash sales this would be the point of recognition.
In the case of credit sales it would depend on whether or not criteria (a) (i) and (iv) had also been satisfied.
(vi) This would only influence recognition of sales if there was serious doubt about the ability of the customer to pay his debts.

44.10 Obviously there is no set answer to this question. However, the following may well be typical.
(a) If the business is going to carry on operating, then the going concern concept comes into operation. Consequently, fixed assets are valued at cost, less depreciation to date. Stocks will be valued at lower of cost or net realisable value. The 'net realisable value' will be that based on the business realising stock through normal operations.

(b) Should the business be deemed as a case for cessation, then the going concern concept could not be used. The values on fixed assets and stocks will be their disposal values. This should be affected by whether or not the business could be sold as a whole or whether it would have to be broken up. Similarly, figures would be affected by whether or not assets had to be sold off very quickly at low prices, or sold only when reasonable prices could be achieved.
It is not only the balance sheet that would be affected, as the profit and loss account would reflect the changes in values.

44.11 (a) See Text, Chapter 10

(b) Various illustrations are possible, but the following are examples.

(i) Appointment of expenses between one period and another. For instance, very rarely would very small stocks of stationery be valued at the year end. This means that the stationery gets charged against one year's profits whereas in fact it may not all have been used up in that year.

(ii) Items expensed instead of being capitalised. Small items which are, in theory, capital expenditure will often be charged up to an expense account.

(iii) The value of assets approximated, instead of being measured with absolute precision.

(c) (i) An illustration could be made under (b) (iii). A stock of oil could well be estimated, the true figure, if known, might be one or two litres out. The cost of precise measurement would probably not be worth the benefit of having such information.

(ii) What is material in one company may not be material in another.

44.12 No set answer. Question is of a general nature rather than being specific. A variety of answers is therefore acceptable.

The examiner might expect to see the following covered. (This is not a model answer):

(a) Different reports needed by different outside parties, as they have to meet different requirements. Might find they therefore include;

(i) for bankers – accounts based on 'break-up' value of the assets if they have to be sold off to repay loans or overdrafts.

(ii) for investors – to include how business has fared against budgets set for that year to see how successful business is at meeting targets.

(iii) for employees – include details of number of employees, wages and salaries paid, effect on pensions funds.

(iv) for local community – to include reports showing amounts spent on pollution control, etc.

And any similar instances.

(b) The characteristics of useful information have been stated in the Corporate Report 1975, and the accounting reports should be measured against this.

(c) Presentation (additional) in form of pie charts, bar charts, etc., as these are often more easily understood by readers.

44.13 (a) Carry down as debit balance on stationery account, and show as current asset in balance sheet. Most firms would ignore as it is not a material item.

(b) Debt the customer's account and credit bank account with £35. Consider possibility of its inclusion in calculations for a bad debts provision account.

(c) To be capitalised: Dr Premises £3,445; Cr. Wages £764; Cr. Materials £2,681.

(d) Accrue computer rental for February and March 19-7: 2 months x £19,200 p.a. = £3,200. Carry forward as credit balance on computer hire account.

(e) No liability for the period has been incurred. If material, a note to the balance sheet should be given.

44.17

Martin Smith

Forecast trading profit and loss account for the year to 31 December 19-6

Sales (C)			140,000
less:	Cost of sales		
	Opening stock	20,000	
	Purchases	97,800	
		117,800	
less:	Closing stock (A)	17,000	
			100,800
Gross profit (B)			39,200
less expenses (E)			25,200
Net profit for the year (D)			14,000

Solved in order (A) then (B) then (C) and so on.

(A) We know that average stock is 18,500. Therefore if $(20,000 + ?) \div 2 = 18,500$ means that ? is 17,000.

(B) If Gross Profit is 28% of Sales (margin), therefore mark-up is $28 \div 72 \times$ Cost of Sales $= 28 \div 72 \times 100,800 = 39,200$.

(C) is Cost of Sales $100,800 +$ Gross Profit $39,200 = 140,000$.

(D) is 10% of (C).

(E) is (B) − (D).

Martin Smith

Forecast balance sheet as at 31 December 19-6

Fixed assets (J)			30,000
Current assets			
	Stock	17,000	
	Debtors (F)	14,000	
	Bank (I)	5,000	
(H)		36,000	
less	Current liabilities		
	Creditors (G)	15,650	
	Accruals	350	
		16,000	
Working capital			20,000
Net assets employed			50,000
Financed by:			
Capital: Opening			40,000
add net profit			14,000
			54,000
less drawings			10,000
			44,000
Long-term loan			6,000
			50,000

(F)　Debtors　= Sales × 36.5 ÷ 365
　　　　　　　= 140,000 × 36.5 ÷ 365 = 14,000.

(G)　Creditors　= Purchases × 58.4 ÷ 365
　　　　　　　= 97,800 × 58.4 ÷ 365 = 15,648
　　Creditors　= to nearest £10,　= 15,650

(H)　This is 2.25 × 16,000 = 36,000.
(I)　is (F) + (H) + (I) ? = 36,000
　　i.e. 17,000 + 14,000 + ? = 36,000
　　therefore (I) = 5,000
(J)　Is 1.5 × Working Capital
　　1.5 × 20,000 = 30,000.

44.18 (a)　Suitable ratios

	1985	1986
(i)	$\dfrac{\text{Net profit before tax}}{\text{Sales}}\quad \dfrac{21,500}{202,900} \times 100 = 10.6\%$	$\dfrac{37,500}{490,700} \times 100 = 7.6\%$
(ii)	$\dfrac{\text{Net profit before tax}}{\text{Net assets employed}}\quad \dfrac{21,500}{119,200} \times 100 = 18.04\%$	$\dfrac{37,500}{326,600} \times 100 = 11.48\%$
(iii)	$\dfrac{\text{Current assets}}{\text{Current liabilities}}\quad \dfrac{66,500}{52,300} = 1.27:1$	$\dfrac{152,500}{85,900} = 1.78:1$
(iv)	$\dfrac{\text{Quick assets}}{\text{Current liabilities}}\quad \dfrac{35,300}{52,300} = 0.67:1$	$\dfrac{57,200}{85,900} = 0.67:1$
(v)	$\dfrac{\text{External liabilities}}{\text{Shareholders' funds}}\quad \dfrac{52,300}{119,200} = 0.45$	$\dfrac{185,900}{226,600} = 0.82$
(vi)	$\dfrac{\text{Shareholders' funds}}{\text{Tangible assets}}\quad \dfrac{119,200}{171,500} = 0.70$	$\dfrac{226,600}{412,500} = 0.55$

(b) Ratios (v) and (vi) reveal that external finance has increased by a considerable proportion. This weakens financial stability.

Current radio (iii) shows an improvement as might be expected after issuing loan capital. However the acid test ratio (iv) is still not healthy.

Profitability (i) and (ii) has fallen dramatically. The reasons for this cannot be deduced here but need urgent investigation.

The asset base increased during the year by over 2 times. It may well be that such investment in assets has not yet borne fruit in the form of extra profits.

Answers to multiple-choice questions

Set No 1									
1	(C)	2	(D)	3	(B)	4	(C)	5	(A)
6	(C)	7	(C)	8	(A)	9	(C)	10	(A)
11	(B)	12	(D)	13	(B)	14	(D)	15	(B)
16	(C)	17	(C)	18	(A)	19	(D)	20	(C)

Set No 2									
21	(A)	22	(B)	23	(A)	24	(D)	25	(C)
26	(A)	27	(D)	28	(A)	29	(C)	30	(A)
31	(C)	32	(D)	33	(C)	34	(C)	35	(D)
36	(B)	37	(A)	38	(B)	39	(C)	40	(C)

Set No 3									
41	(A)	42	(C)	43	(A)	44	(D)	45	(A)
46	(A)	47	(B)	48	(C)	49	(D)	50	(C)
51	(A)	52	(D)	53	(C)	54	(C)	55	(D)
56	(C)	57	(A)	58	(A)	59	(B)	60	(C)

Set No 4									
61	(B)	62	(A)	63	(D)	64	(A)	65	(C)
66	(A)	67	(D)	68	(D)	69	(B)	70	(A)
71	(D)	72	(C)	73	(B)	74	(B)	75	(B)
76	(C)	77	(D)	78	(A)	79	(B)	80	(C)

Set No 5									
81	(B)	82	(B)	83	(C)	84	(C)	85	(A)
86	(B)	87	(A)	88	(C)	89	(C)	90	(A)
91	(C)	92	(B)	93	(B)	94	(D)	95	(C)
96	(B)	97	(C)	98	(B)	99	(D)	100	(B)

Index

Teachers' Manuals are available free of charge to lecturers using **Business Accounting** Volumes 1 and 2. The manuals include:

- Fully displayed answers to all questions not answered in the textbook.
- Guidelines on how to prepare students for examinations.
- Background to SSAPs.

These manuals are available from the local agents listed below. Apply for your copy on official letterheaded paper.

Longman Group (Far East) Ltd
PO Box 223
Cornwall House
18th Floor
Taikoo Trading Estate
Tong Chong Street
Quarry Bay
HONG KONG

Longman Jamaica Ltd
43 Second Street
Newport West
PO Box 489
Kingston 10
JAMAICA

Longman Kenya Ltd
PO Box 18033
Kjabe Street
PO Box 47540
Nairobi
KENYA

Longman Singapore Publishers (Pty) Ltd
25 First Lok Yang Road
Off International Road
Jurong Town
SINGAPORE 2262

RIK Service Ltd
104 High Street
San Fernando
TRINIDAD

Longman Zimbabwe (Pvt) Ltd
PO Box ST 125
Southerton
Harare
ZIMBABWE